# Give Me Five! English 5

## TEACHER'S BOOK

Donna Shaw • Rob Sved

macmillan education

Macmillan Education
4 Crinan Street
London N1 9XW
A division of Springer Nature Limited

Companies and representatives throughout the world

Teacher's Book ISBN 978-1-380-02509-8
Teacher's Book Pack ISBN 978-1-380-02508-1



This edition published 2018
First edition entitled *High Five! English* published 2014 by Springer Nature Limited



Teacher's Edition credits:
Original design by Amanda Easter and Sue Bushell
Page make-up by emc design ltd
Cover design by Bigtop Design Limited
Cover photograph by Getty Images/hadynyah, Springer Nature Ltd/Tom Dick and Debbie Productions

**Authors' acknowledgements**
The authors would like to thank everyone at Macmillan who has given help and advice throughout this project. Special thanks from Rob to Belén, Natalia, Xana and Pablo for all their inspiration. Special thanks from Donna to José, Elisa, Teresa and Marina for their encouragement and enthusiasm.

**The publishers would like to thank the following teachers for their contribution to the project:**
Ana Postigo, CEIP Vicálvaro, Madrid; Beatriz García Vaquero, CEIP Mariano José de Larra, Madrid; Damián Quiralte Fresneda, CEIP Claudio Moyano, Madrid; Eamonn Healy, Colegio SEK Santa Isabel, Madrid; Elvira Robledo Gandarias, Colegio Ayalde, Loiu, Vizcaya; Francisco Javier Navarro Pineda, Colegio Tajamar, Madrid; Guiomar Yagüe Martínez, CEIP Celso Emilio Ferreiro, Móstoles, Madrid; Henar Del Gallo Muñoz, CEIP Cantos Altos, Collado Villalba, Madrid; Ignacio de la Puente Rodríguez, CEIP El Cantizal, Las Rozas, Madrid; Inmaculada Romero Fanego, CEIP Príncipes de Asturias, Pozuelo de Alarcón, Madrid; Laura Tenorio, CEIP Esperanza, Madrid; María del Rosario García Leal, CEIP Rufino Blanco, Madrid; Patricia Sanz, CEIP Félix Rodríguez de la Fuente, Coslada, Madrid; Silvia San José Paul, CEIP El Cantizal, Las Rozas, Madrid; Víctor Molinero Cuartango, CEIP Ciudad de Roma, Madrid; Virginia Escalona Monreal, CEIP La Encina, Las Rozas, Madrid; Laura Zarzuelo, Colegio Virgen de la Almudena, Collado Villalba, Madrid; Eugenio Domínguez, Colegio Virgen de la Almudena, Collado Villalba, Madrid; Silvia Díez de Rivera, Colegio Orvalle, Las Rozas, Madrid; Maite Crespo, Colegio Jesús Nazareno, Madrid; Rocío González, Colegio Jesús Nazareno, Madrid; Silvia Valderrama, CEIP Benito Pérez Galdós, Arganda del Rey, Madrid; Lilian Villafuerte, CEIP Rosa Chacel, Collado Villalba, Madrid; Cristina Baeza, CEIP Rosa Chacel, Collado Villalba, Madrid; Carlota Padovani, CEIP Vicálvaro, Madrid; Leyre, Alcalde CEIP Cortes de Cádiz, Madrid; María Andrés, Colegio Matter Inmaculata, Madrid.

Full acknowledgements for illustrations and photographs in the facsimile pages can be found in the Pupil's Book ISBN 978-1-380-01360-6 and the Activity Book ISBN 978-1-380-01380-4.



Printed and bound in Spain
2022 2021 2020 2019 2018
10 9 8 7 6 5 4 3 2 1

# Give Me Five!

TEACHER'S BOOK 5

# Syllabus

| Unit | Key Competences and Key Learning Outcomes | Contents |
| --- | --- | --- |
| | | Lexis |
| **Starter Unit The school fair** | • Understand and act out a dialogue (Lesson 3)<br>• Listen and read information about a balloon race (Lesson 4)<br>• Review countries of the world (Lesson 4)<br>• Review vocabulary: school subjects, character adjectives, transport, fruit and verbs (Lessons 1 and 2)<br>• Review the use of relative pronouns (Lesson 2)<br>• Review superlative adjectives (Lesson 3)<br>• Review 'must' and 'mustn't' for obligation (Lesson 4)<br>• Read personal descriptions and write a personal profile (Lesson 1)<br>• Work in pairs or small groups to practise and reinforce learning (all lessons)<br>• Learn about school fairs and balloon races (Lessons 2 and 3) | **Core vocabulary**<br>• *balloon race, school fair*<br>• *borrow, cook, dance, drink, eat, sell tickets, sing, throw*<br>**Other vocabulary**<br>• *air, at the same time, coconut, shy, email address, heavy, helium, kilometres, latex, light, organic, paper, rules, winner*<br>• *burst, degrade, explode, float away, label, land, let go, release, rise, tie the balloons together*<br>**Recycled vocabulary**<br>• *brother, sister; bananas, chocolate, coconut, eggs, flour, pasta, pineapple, pizza, smoothies, sugar, tomatoes; Art, Geography, History, ICT, Maths, Science; active, confident, friendly, lazy, noisy, quiet, shy, tidy, unfriendly, untidy;* dates; *black / blonde / short / straight hair; guitar; Brazil, China, France, Germany, Italy, Mexico, Portugal, Russia* |
| **Unit 1 My clothes** | • Review and learn the names of clothes (Lesson 1)<br>• Review and contrast the present simple and the present continuous tenses (Lesson 2)<br>• Learn and practise using 'too' and 'not enough' (Lesson 4)<br>• Review and learn adjectives to describe clothing (Lesson 5)<br>• Learn about and use the linkers 'and', 'also' and 'too' (Lesson 7)<br>• Talk about your favourite item of clothing (Lesson 8)<br>• Watch and understand a video about making clothes (Video and 21st Century Skills)<br>• Learn about different types of materials (Lesson 6)<br>• Use the Pupil's App on Navio<br>• Identify and practise saying the stress in words (Lesson 4)<br>• Reflect on your own learning (Lesson 8)<br>• Practise activity types found in the Cambridge Exams: A2 Key for Schools<br>•Think about the importance of perseverance (Lesson 3)<br>• Work in pairs or small groups to practise and reinforce learning (all lessons)<br>• Do a communication task (Lesson 5)<br>• Design a sports kit (Video and 21st Century Skills)<br>• Read and understand a story (Lesson 3)<br>• Learn about Switzerland and a Swiss inventor (Lesson 3)<br>• Read and write a magazine article (Lessons 6 and 7)<br>• Sing a song (Lesson 8) | **Core vocabulary**<br>• *baseball boots, belt, cardigan, jeans, leggings, polo shirt, sweatshirt, tie, tights, top, tracksuit, waistcoat*<br>• *baggy, flowery, long-sleeved, patterned, plain, short-sleeved, striped, tight*<br>**Extension vocabulary**<br>• *blazer, blouse, pyjamas, suit, underwear, uniform*<br>• *dark blue, light green, gold, silver*<br>**Other vocabulary**<br>• *bright, casual, dark, fashionable, clear, comfortable, rough, smart, smooth, sticky, uncomfortable, unfair, unfashionable, weak*<br>• *chemical, cloak, engineer, equipment, hooks, nylon, pocket, seeds, sleeve, slime, stick, waterproof, zip; creative, fashion designer, interview, research, sew, sewing machine, sketch; smart, spotted*<br>**Recycled vocabulary**<br>• *clothes, dress, gloves, helmet, T-shirt; big, dirty, dry, happy, healthy, heavy, kind, light, long, noisy, quiet, short, small, soft, strong, tidy, unhappy, unhealthy, unkind, untidy; astronaut, autumn, flowers, fur, invention, inventor, material, natural, watch; cotton, wool* |

Competence in linguistic communication | Competence in mathematics, science and technology | Digital competence
Learning to learn | Social and civic competences | Sense of initiative and entrepreneurship | Cultural awareness and expression

| Contents | | | | | Cross-curricular links |
| --- | --- | --- | --- | --- | --- |
| **Structures** | **Phonics** | **Sociocultural aspects** | **Culture around the world and Literacy** | **21st Century Skills** | |
| **Core structures**<br>• *What's (Tom) like? He's (a bit untidy, quiet and shy).*<br>• *What does (Jess) look like? She's got (straight blonde hair and brown eyes). She's (tall).*<br>• *He's / She's the person who's (buying a smoothie and has got straight blonde hair).*<br>• *It's the place where (you can win a coconut).*<br>• *It's a food that's (made from flour, butter and sugar).*<br>• *It's something which (you use to take photos).*<br>• *You mustn't tie the balloons together.*<br>• *The balloons must be made of latex.*<br>**Other structures**<br>• *There's going to be a balloon race. What's your favourite item of clothing? What do you like doing in your free time? Where do you live? What interesting things can you see there? How often do you use a computer? Which wild animals can you see in your country? Do you like music, art, films and plays? How do you help others? How do you look after the environment? What are your favourite natural places?* | | **Cooperative learning Skills**<br>• Working together (Lessons 1–4)<br>• Collaborating (Lessons 1–4)<br>• Checking learning (Lessons 1–4)<br>• Participating (Lessons 1–4)<br>• Helping and encouraging (Lessons 1–4)<br>• Reflecting and setting goals (Lesson 1–4) | | **Thinking skills**<br>• Hypothesising (Lesson 1); Finding information (Lesson 1);<br>• Matching words and pictures (Lessons 1 and 2);<br>• Ordering information (Lesson 3); Analysing and applying rules (Lesson 4); Logical thinking (Lesson 4);<br>• Reflecting on learning (Lesson 4) | |
| **Core structures**<br>• *I / You / We / They wear (a helmet). He / She / It wears (a helmet). I / You / We / They don't wear (a helmet). He / She / It doesn't wear (a helmet).*<br>• *I am / am not wearing (a hat). He / She / It is / isn't wearing (a helmet). We / You / They are / aren't wearing (a helmet).*<br>• *Are we / you / they wearing (a helmet)? Is he / she / it wearing (a helmet)? Do you / we / they wear (a T-shirt)? Does he / she / it wear (a T-shirt)?*<br>• *The (sweatshirt is) too big. The (sweatshirt isn't) big enough.*<br>**Other structures**<br>• *What's (Sally) wearing?*<br>**Recycled structures**<br>• *What's your favourite item of clothing? (Wool) comes from (sheep). I agree with you. I disagree. Let's choose a T-shirt first. What about having some plain shorts?* | • Stressed syllables in words | **Cooperative learning Skills**<br>• Working together (Lessons 1–8)<br>• Collaborating (Lessons 1–8)<br>• Checking learning (Lessons 1–8)<br>• Peer evaluation and feedback (Lesson 7)<br>• Helping and encouraging (Lessons 1–8)<br>• Reflecting and setting goals (Lessons 1 and 8)<br>**Values**<br>• The importance of persevering | **Culture around the world**<br>• The invention of Velcro in Switzerland<br>**Literacy**<br>**Text type**<br>• A magazine article (information text; writing preparation)<br>**Reading skills**<br>• Scanning<br>**Writing skills**<br>• Adding new information | **21st Century Skills**<br>• **Ways of thinking:** developing your ideas<br>**Thinking skills**<br>• Categorising (Lesson 1); Problem solving (Lesson 1); Analysing and applying rules (Lessons 2 and 4); Hypothesising (Lesson 3); Logical thinking (Lesson 4); Defining and describing (Lesson 5); Finding information (Lesson 6); Planning, checking and correcting (Lesson 7); Seeing another's point of view (Lesson 8); Reflecting on learning (Lesson 8) | **Link to Science**<br>• Properties of materials<br>**Arts and Crafts**<br>• Exploring proportion in figure drawing and drawing a classmate with correct proportion |

# Syllabus

| Unit | Key Competences and Key Learning Outcomes | Contents: Lexis |
|---|---|---|
| **Unit 2 Adventure holiday** | • Review and learn the names of outdoor activities and equipment (Lesson 1)<br>• Identify and review the past simple (Lesson 2)<br>• Learn how to form 'Wh-' questions in the past simple (Lesson 4)<br>• Review and learn objects in a survival kit (Lesson 5)<br>• Learn about and practise using time connectives (Lesson 7)<br>• Talk about your favourite place to visit (Lesson 8)<br>• Watch and understand a video about adventurous sports (Video and 21st Century Skills)<br>• Learn about prehistoric art (Lesson 3)<br>• Use the Pupil's App on Navio<br>• Identify and practise intonation in questions (Lesson 4)<br>• Reflect on your own learning (Lesson 8)<br>• Practise activity types found in the Cambridge Exams: A2 Key for Schools<br>• Think about the importance of looking after old things (Lesson 3)<br>• Prepare and give a presentation to the class (Lesson 8)<br>• Learn about safety equipment when doing dangerous activities (Video and 21st Century Skills)<br>• Work in pairs or small groups to practise and reinforce learning (all lessons)<br>• Do a communication task (Lesson 5)<br>• Read and understand a story (Lesson 3)<br>• Learn about the Dordogne region of France and the history of cave paintings (Lesson 3)<br>• Read and write a travel blog (Lessons 6 and 7) | **Core vocabulary**<br>• *camping, compass, helmet, hiking, lifejacket, map, mountain biking, rock climbing, rucksack, torch, wetsuit, whitewater rafting*<br>• *binoculars, camping stove, insect repellent, matches, rope, saucepan, sleeping bag, sun cream, torch, walking boots, wildlife guidebooks*<br>**Extension vocabulary**<br>• *abseiling, bungee jumping, canoeing, canyoning, kite surfing, snorkelling*<br>• *alarm clock, water bottle, waterproof jacket, waterproof trousers*<br>**Other vocabulary**<br>• *bike rack, blog, campsite, caravan, canyoning, clouds, equipment, helicopter, hole, lightening, shower, thunder, treasure; goat, deer; climb, find, explore, get lost, put up a tent; lantern, meanwhile, paintings, secret, spectacular, timeline, tunnels; adventurous, icy; paragliding, race, rocks, scary, skiing, snowboarding, tightrope walking*<br>**Recycled vocabulary**<br>• *beach, cliff, cow, duck, horse riding, rain, river, rocks, wet, woods; cousins, family, parents; after an hour, at 11 o'clock, at first, finally, first of all, soon, suddenly, then; sunny, tired; had breakfast; cereal, cheese, fried eggs, hot dog, toast* |
| **Unit 3 I ♥ my city** | • Review and learn the names of places in a city (Lesson 1)<br>• Identify and practise the past continuous (Lesson 2)<br>• Identify and practise using the past continuous with the past simple (Lesson 4)<br>• Review and learn activities you do in a city (Lesson 5)<br>• Review and practise using adverbs of manner (Lesson 7)<br>• Talk about your favourite place in town (Lesson 8)<br>• Watch and understand a video about other people's favourite cities (Video and 21st Century Skills)<br>• Learn about volcanic activity (Lesson 3)<br>• Learn about Venn diagrams (Video and 21st Century Skills)<br>• Use the Pupil's App on Navio<br>• Identify and practise the weak and strong forms of 'was' (Lesson 4)<br>• Identify and use expressions to ask for repetition and clarification (Lesson 5)<br>• Reflect on your own learning (Lesson 8)<br>• Practise activity types found in the Cambridge Exams: A2 Key for Schools<br>• Think about things you must and mustn't do in an emergency (Lesson 3)<br>• Work in pairs or small groups to practise and reinforce learning (all lessons)<br>• Do a communication task (Lesson 5)<br>• Read and understand a story (Lesson 3)<br>• Learn about Italy and the ancient city of Pompeii (Lesson 3)<br>• Read and write a story opener (Lessons 6 and 7)<br>• Sing a song (Lesson 8)<br>• Learn about the city of Venice (Video and 21st Century Skills) | **Core vocabulary**<br>• *bridge, castle, crossroads, fountain, pavement, pedestrian crossing, square, statue, steps, tower, town hall, traffic lights*<br>• *catch a taxi, cross the road, get off the bus, get on the bus, go sightseeing, have a snack, meet a friend, wait for a bus*<br>**Extension vocabulary**<br>• *cycle path, post box, phone box, underpass, signpost, tunnel*<br>• *miss a bus, take the underground, wait at a crossing, wait in a queue*<br>**Other vocabulary**<br>• *adventure / fairy / mystery / science fiction / sports / spy story*<br>• *archaeologist, ash, Colosseum, emergency, erupt, fire alarm, gladiator, monuments, rescue, ruins, shield, sword, tragedy, volcano*<br>• *characters, genre, setting; exciting, floating, islands, gondola, guide book, relaxing, traditional, water bus, water taxi*<br>**Recycled vocabulary**<br>• *cooking, drinking, reading, running, sleeping, speaking, studying; cloud, coast, newspaper, planet, woollen hat; boat trip, costume, half past, o'clock, ride a horse, scary, scientists* |

Competence in linguistic communication · Competence in mathematics, science and technology · Digital competence · Learning to learn · Social and civic competences · Sense of initiative and entrepreneurship · Cultural awareness and expression

| Contents | | | | | Cross-curricular links |
|---|---|---|---|---|---|
| **Structures** | **Phonics** | **Sociocultural aspects** | **Culture around the world and Literacy** | **21st Century Skills** | |
| **Core structures**<br>• *I / He / She / It was / wasn't really loud. You / We / They were / weren't really loud.*<br>• *Was I / he / she / it cold? Were you / we / they cold?*<br>• *I / He / She / It / You / We / They jumped / didn't jump. Did I / you / he / she / it / we / they jump? Yes, I / you / he / she / it / we / they did.*<br>• *Where / When / Why did (you) go?*<br>• *What did (you) do?*<br>• *How did (you) get there?*<br>• *Who did (you) go with?*<br>• *How long did (you) go for?*<br>**Other structures**<br>• *The boys made the hole bigger. You have to wait your turn.*<br>**Recycled structures**<br>• *Do you want to go whitewater rafting? Yes, because I love water sports. We couldn't see very well. What do you want to take with you?* | • Intonation in 'Did ...?' and 'Wh-' questions in the past | **Cooperative learning Skills**<br>• Working together (Lessons 1–8)<br>• Collaborating (Lessons 1–8)<br>• Checking learning (Lessons 1–8)<br>• Peer evaluation and feedback (Lesson 7)<br>• Helping and encouraging (Lessons 1–8)<br>• Reflecting and setting goals (Lesson 8)<br>**Values**<br>• The importance of looking after old things | **Culture around the world**<br>• The discovery of ancient cave paintings in France<br>**Literacy**<br>**Text type**<br>• A travel blog (chronological account; writing preparation)<br>**Reading skills**<br>• Skimming<br>**Writing skills**<br>• Using time connectives | **21st Century Skills**<br>• **Digital skills:** researching a topic online<br>**Thinking skills**<br>• Matching words and pictures (Lesson 1); Analysing and applying rules (Lessons 2 and 4); Predicting (Lesson 2); Hypothesising (Lesson 3); Defining and describing (Lesson 5); Finding information (Lesson 6); Planning, checking and correcting (Lesson 7); Seeing another's point of view (Lesson 8); Reflecting on learning (Lesson 8) | **Link to Science**<br>• Prehistoric art<br>**Arts and Crafts**<br>• Identifying scale and proportion and constructing a scale model |
| **Core structures**<br>• *I / He / She / It was / wasn't eating at 2pm. You / We / They were / weren't eating at 2pm.*<br>• *Was I / he / she / it eating at 2pm? Were you / we / they eating at 2pm? Yes, I / he / she / it was. No, I / he / she / it wasn't. Yes, you / we / they were. No, you / we / they weren't.*<br>• *I / He / She / It was reading when it rang. You / We / They were reading when it rang. What was I / he / she / it doing when it rang? What were you / we / they doing when it rang?*<br>**Other structures**<br>• *Pardon. What did you say? I'm sorry. Could you say that again, please? Where shall we visit next? How long shall we stay there?*<br>**Recycled structures**<br>• *Where are they going to be at ten o'clock? They're going to be at the Trevi Fountain. What are they going to do there? They're going to throw a coin into the fountain. The setting is the place where the story happens.* | • Weak and strong forms of 'was' | **Cooperative learning Skills**<br>• Working together (Lessons 1–8)<br>• Collaborating (Lessons 1–8)<br>• Checking learning (Lessons 1–8)<br>• Peer evaluation and feedback (Lesson 7)<br>• Participating (Lessons 1–8)<br>• Helping and encouraging (Lessons 1–8)<br>• Reflecting and setting goals (Lessons 1 and 8)<br>**Values**<br>• The importance of knowing safety procedures at school | **Culture around the world**<br>• The tragedy of Pompeii in Italy<br>**Literacy**<br>**Text type**<br>• A story opener (text to entertain; writing preparation)<br>**Reading skills**<br>• Predicting content from pictures<br>**Writing skills**<br>• Using adverbs of manner | **21st Century Skills**<br>• **Ways of working:** making detailed comparisons<br>**Thinking skills**<br>• Categorising (Lesson 1); Analysing and applying rules (Lessons 2 and 4); Creating (Lesson 4); Defining and describing (Lesson 5); Finding and classifying information (Lesson 6); Planning, checking and correcting (Lesson 7); Seeing another's point of view (Lesson 8); Reflecting on learning (Lesson 8) | **Link to Science**<br>• Volcanic activity<br>**Arts and Crafts**<br>• Observing contour lines and using contour lines to show volume and mass |

# Syllabus

| Unit | Key Competences and Key Learning Outcomes | Contents: Lexis |
|---|---|---|
| **Project 1: A health life digital poster** | • Present your digital poster in a group (Lesson 2)<br>• Learn about healthy lives (Lesson 1)<br>• Investigate healthy living habits (Lesson 1)<br>• Listen for specific information and take notes (Lesson 1)<br>• Reflect on what you've learnt and how you've worked together (Lesson 2)<br>• Interview a partner about their lifestyle (Lesson 1)<br>• Make suggestions about how they can live more healthily (Lesson 1)<br>• Create your digital poster in a group (Lesson 2) | **Key vocabulary**<br>• *brush your teeth, campaign, doctor, do exercise, drink water, eat breakfast / fruit, fast food, feel tired, fizzy drinks, have a check-up, healthy, look after our teeth, nutritionist, questionnaire, sports coach, stay up late, sun cream, walk to school, watch TV* |
| **Unit 4 My technology** | • Review and learn words related to technology (Lesson 1)<br>• Learn the similarity between 'must' and 'have to' and the difference between 'mustn't' and 'don't have to' (Lesson 2)<br>• Learn and practise how to use 'if' and 'when' in zero conditional sentences (Lesson 4)<br>• Review and practise using the present simple and the past simple (Lesson 7)<br>• Talk about your favourite object (Lesson 8)<br>• Watch and understand a video about new technology (Video and 21st Century Skills)<br>• Learn about webcams (Lesson 3)<br>• Learn expressions for using touchscreen devices (Lesson 5)<br>• Learn about augmented reality glasses (Video and 21st Century Skills)<br>• Use the Pupil's App on Navio<br>• Read a message and a list of rules for specific information (Lesson 1)<br>• Identify and practise intonation in zero conditional sentences (Lesson 4)<br>• Reflect on your own learning (Lesson 8)<br>• Practise activity types found in the Cambridge Exams: A2 Key for Schools<br>• Think about the importance of acting quickly in an emergency (Lesson 3)<br>• Prepare and give a short presentation to the class (Lesson 8)<br>• Work in pairs or small groups to practise and reinforce learning (all lessons)<br>• Do a communication task (Lesson 5)<br>• Think about new ways in which technology can help us (Video and 21st Century Skills)<br>• Read and understand a story (Lesson 3)<br>• Learn about Germany (Lesson 3)<br>• Read and write reviews (Lessons 6 and 7)<br>• Sing a song (Lesson 8) | **Core vocabulary**<br>• *camera, CD player, computer game, interactive whiteboard, karaoke, laptop, MP3 player, mobile phone, tablet, video call, webcam, website*<br>• *move down, move left, move right, move up, pause the game, start the game, swipe the screen, tap the screen, tilt the screen*<br>**Extension vocabulary**<br>• *charger, download, share, the cloud, upload, USB*<br>• *download a game, get a high score, get a low score, read the instructions*<br>**Other vocabulary**<br>• *shore, sunset*<br>• *careful, lost, safe, useful*<br>• *car lights, flash, get dark*<br>• *article, brain, electric currents, entertainment, news, quizzes, sections, sport*<br>• *computer company / game / programmer / screen, description, experience, facts, introduction, rating, swipe; app, augmented reality, cardboard, e-reader, headset, robotic, virtual reality*<br>**Recycled vocabulary**<br>• *beach, foggy, future, ice, masks, police, help, science; play music / online, press the button, record a video, take a photo; after that, first, then; drawing, gallery, paintbrush, painting, sculptures* |

| | | | |
|---|---|---|---|
| Competence in linguistic communication | Competence in mathematics, science and technology | Digital competence | |
| Learning to learn | Social and civic competences | Sense of initiative and entrepreneurship | Cultural awareness and expression |

| Contents | | | | | Cross-curricular links |
|---|---|---|---|---|---|
| **Structures** | **Phonics** | **Sociocultural aspects** | **Culture around the world and Literacy** | **21st Century Skills** | |
| **Key structures**<br>• *How often do you (have a check-up at the dentist)? I have a check-up once a year.*<br>• *You should brush your teeth two or three times a day.*<br>• *You need (nine hours' sleep every night).*<br>• *Why don't we (make a poster)?*<br>• *What about (writing an article)?*<br>• *We need to (look for pictures).*<br>• *I can do that.* | | **Cooperative learning Skills**<br>• Sharing knowledge and information (Lessons 1 and 2)<br>• Working together (Lessons 1 and 2) | | | **Link to Science**<br>• Being healthy |
| **Core structures**<br>• *I / You / We / They have to (use the Internet). He / She / It has to (use the Internet).*<br>• *I / You / He / She / It / We / They had to (carry CDs). I / You / We / They don't have to (carry CDs). He / She / It don't have to (carry CDs).*<br>• *I / You / He / She / It / We / They didn't have to (leave).*<br>• *What happens if you heat ice? It changes to water.*<br>• *If you press here, you take a photo.*<br>• *When you turn it off, the screen goes black.*<br>**Other structures**<br>• *What website do you prefer? What does it look like? What do I do with it? What is it? Where did I get it from? Why do I like it so much?*<br>**Recycled structures**<br>• *I can use (the Internet for my homework).*<br>*I must (share my passwords with my parents). I mustn't (send photos).*<br>*A tourist was walking. Jennifer wants to work on games about football.* | • Intonation in zero conditional sentences | **Cooperative learning Skills**<br>• Working together (Lessons 1–8)<br>• Collaborating (Lessons 1–8)<br>• Checking learning (Lessons 1–8)<br>• Peer evaluation and feedback (Lessons 7 and 8)<br>• Participating (Lessons 1–8)<br>• Helping and encouraging (Lessons 1–8)<br>• Reflecting and setting goals (Lesson 8)<br>**Values**<br>• Acting quickly in an emergency | **Culture around the world**<br>• How a man's life was saved by a webcam in Germany<br>**Literacy**<br>**Text type**<br>• A review (information text; writing preparation)<br>**Reading skills**<br>• Identifying opinions<br>**Writing skills**<br>• Using the present and the past simple | **21st Century Skills**<br>• **Digital skills:** using technology to help us<br>**Thinking skills**<br>• Expanding on lexical sets (Lesson 1); Matching words and pictures (Lesson 1); Analysing and applying rules (Lessons 2, 4 and 7); Hypothesising and thinking laterally (Lesson 3); Logical thinking (Lesson 5); Finding information (Lesson 6); Planning, checking and correcting (Lesson 7); Seeing another's point of view (Lesson 8); Reflecting on learning (Lesson 8) | **Link to Science**<br>• Technology<br>**Arts and Crafts**<br>• Identifying tints and shades and making a pattern collage using tints and shades |

# Syllabus

| Unit | Key Competences and Key Learning Outcomes | Contents |
|---|---|---|
| | | Lexis |
| **Unit 5 Amazing animals** | • Learn the names of parts of an animal's body (Lesson 1)<br>• Learn and practise making deductions using modal verbs (Lesson 2)<br>• Learn and practise describing things with verbs of the senses (Lesson 4)<br>• Learn the names of new animals and adjectives to describe them (Lesson 5)<br>• Review and practise using direct speech (Lesson 7)<br>• Talk about pets (Lesson 8)<br>• Watch and understand a video about animals that are in danger (Video and 21st Century Skills)<br><br>• Review and categorise animals (Lesson 1)<br>• Compare and describe different animals (Lesson 5)<br>• Learn about the habitat of the koala (Video and 21st Century Skills)<br><br>• Use the Pupil's App on Navio<br><br>• Identify and practise rising and falling intonation in questions (Lesson 4)<br>• Reflect on your own learning (Lesson 8)<br>• Practise activity types found in the Cambridge Exams: A2 Key for Schools<br><br>• Think about how to deal with fears (Lesson 3)<br>• Work in a group to choose the best pets for people (Lesson 8)<br>• Think about the importance of helping to protect endangered species (Video and 21st Century Skills)<br><br>• Do a communication task (Lesson 5)<br><br>• Read and understand a story (Lesson 3)<br>• Learn about Australia and a mythical Australian animal (Lesson 3)<br>• Read and write a newspaper report (Lessons 6 and 7) | **Core vocabulary**<br>• *beak, claws, fangs, feathers, fins, fur, jaw, scales, spikes, tail, whiskers, wings*<br>• *bull, donkey, eagle, grasshopper, mole, praying mantis, silkworm, swan*<br>**Extension vocabulary**<br>• *gills, hoof, horn, paw, shell, tentacle*<br>• *deer, fox, wasp, wolf*<br>**Other vocabulary**<br>• *length, speed, weight*<br>• *budgie, creepy crawlies, eel, great white shark, hamster, kitten, mammals, platypus, puppy, reptiles, saltwater crocodile, Tasmanian devil, tropical fish, white-bellied sea eagle*<br>• *colourful, domestic, enormous, fierce, harmless, lucky, mysterious, poisonous, wild*<br>• *creature, flippers, headline, hero*<br>• *cut down, eucalyptus, forest, gas, habitat, joey, leaves, marsupial, power station*<br><br>**Recycled vocabulary**<br>• *birds, cat, dog, dolphin, fish, guinea pig, hippo, koala, lion, lizard, pony, seal, snake, spider, whale; scary, strange; bones, teeth; news, newspaper, noise, pet, skeleton; lake, river* |
| **Unit 6 Entertainment** | • Review and learn words about entertainment (Lesson 1)<br>• Talk about past experiences using the present perfect simple (Lesson 2)<br>• Use the present perfect and past simple together (Lesson 4)<br>• Learn expressions for making art and entertainment (Lesson 5)<br>• Learn about onomatopoeic words (Lesson 7)<br>• Talk about your favourite type of entertainment (Lesson 8)<br>• Watch and understand a video about art (Video and 21st Century Skills)<br><br>• Use the Internet to learn about Uganda (Lesson 3)<br>• Use the Pupil's App on Navio<br><br>• Identify and practise the weak sound 'e' in past participles (Lesson 4)<br>• Reflect on your own learning (Lesson 8)<br>• Practise activity types found in the Cambridge Exams: A2 Key for Schools<br>• Use a mind map to brainstorm ideas for a talent day (Video and 21st Century Skills)<br><br>• Talk about activities you prefer doing at a festival (Lesson 1)<br>• Think about the importance of music in bringing the world together (Lesson 3)<br>• Prepare and carry out a conversation about a topic (Lesson 8)<br><br>• Do a communication task (Lesson 5)<br>• Think about activities and products for a talent day (Video and 21st Century Skills)<br><br>• Read and understand a story (Lesson 3)<br>• Learn about Uganda and the African Children's Choir (Lesson 3)<br>• Read a poem (Lesson 6)<br>• Write two haiku poems (Lesson 7)<br>• Sing a song (Lesson 8) | **Core vocabulary**<br>• *3D film, art exhibition, ballet, circus, classical music concert, comedy show, dance show, magazines, play, poems, pop concert, sculpture*<br>• *act in a play, create a comic, compose music, juggle, make a film, make a sculpture, paint a portrait, play in an orchestra, sing in a choir, write a poem*<br>**Extension vocabulary**<br>• *audience, face painting, juggling, live music, performance*<br>• *dance in a dance troupe, direct a play, perform in a show, play in a band*<br>**Other vocabulary**<br>• *lines, onomatopoeic, rhyme, rhythm, sound, syllable, verse; bow, cello, clarinet, cymbals, double bass, drums, drumsticks, flute, French horn, orchestra, violin; arts festival, drumming, poetry competition, wall painting, walk the tightrope, workshop; art gallery, cartoon, chalk, colour in, playground, talent day*<br><br>**Recycled vocabulary**<br>• *been, bought, broken, decided, eaten, given, made, ridden, seen, sung, taken, went, written; bigger, deep, deeper, loudly, low, pretty, sad, slow, sweet; adventure / action / comedy films, cinema, environment, film director, nature, painting, restaurant, TV, zoo* |

Competence in linguistic communication · Competence in mathematics, science and technology · Digital competence
Learning to learn · Social and civic competences · Sense of initiative and entrepreneurship · Cultural awareness and expression

| Contents | | | | | Cross-curricular links |
|---|---|---|---|---|---|
| **Structures** | **Phonics** | **Sociocultural aspects** | **Culture around the world and Literacy** | **21st Century Skills** | |
| **Core structures**<br>• *It must / may / might / could / can't be a (koala).*<br>• *What does it look / smell / taste / feel / sound like?*<br>• *It (looks) like a snake.*<br>• *It (sounds) dangerous.*<br>• *Does it (look) scary?*<br>• *Does it (smell) like a dog? Yes, it does. No, it doesn't.*<br>**Other structures**<br>• *Emma's mum said 'Sandy isn't a big dog, but she's very brave.' Tropical fish are a good idea. I agree. I think he would like a budgie. I don't think that's a good idea. That could be a possibility.*<br>**Recycled structures**<br>• *The great white shark is the heaviest animal. The saltwater crocodile has got the most teeth. What happened? Why / When / Where did it happen? Who was there?* | • Rising and falling intonation in questions | **Cooperative learning Skills**<br>• Working together (Lessons 1–8)<br>• Collaborating (Lessons 1–8)<br>• Checking learning (Lessons 1–8)<br>• Peer evaluation and feedback (Lesson 7)<br>• Participating (Lessons 1–8)<br>• Helping and encouraging (Lessons 1–8)<br>• Reflecting and setting goals (Lessons 1 and 8)<br>**Values**<br>• Recognising and learning to deal with fears | **Culture around the world**<br>• The myth of the bunyip in Australia<br>**Literacy**<br>**Text type**<br>• A newspaper report (non-chronological report; writing preparation)<br>**Reading skills**<br>• Predicting content from headlines<br>**Writing skills**<br>• Direct speech | **21st Century Skills**<br>• **Living in the world:** protecting animals in danger<br>**Thinking skills**<br>• Categorising (Lesson 1); Comparing and contrasting (Lesson 1); Analysing and applying rules (Lessons 2 and 4); Logical thinking (Lessons 2 and 5); Finding and classifying information (Lesson 6); Planning, checking and correcting (Lesson 7); Seeing another's point of view (Lesson 8); Reflecting on learning (Lesson 8) | **Link to Science**<br>• The five classes of vertebrates<br>**Arts and Crafts**<br>• Identifying light and shadows and drawing shadows of figures |
| **Core structures**<br>• *I / You / We / They have / haven't been to a play. He / She / It has / hasn't been to a play.*<br>• *Have I / you / we / they (ever) been to a play? Has he / she / it (ever) been to a play? Yes, I / you / we / they have. No, I / you / we / they haven't. Yes, he / she / it has. No, he / she / it hasn't.*<br>• *I / You / We / They have / haven't listened to the song.*<br>• *He / She / It has / hasn't bought a concert ticket.*<br>• *Has he / she / it (ever) been to the circus? Yes, he / she / it has. No, he / she / it hasn't.*<br>**Other structures**<br>• *I prefer art to films. The sound booms around the room.*<br>**Recycled structures**<br>• *I like writing poetry. I've made films with my friend, Ben. Can you repeat the question, please? Let's (watch a 3D film).* | • The weak sound 'e' in past participles | **Cooperative learning Skills**<br>• Working together (Lessons 1–8)<br>• Collaborating (Lessons 1–8)<br>• Checking learning (Lessons 1–8)<br>• Peer evaluation and feedback (Lesson 7)<br>• Participating (Lessons 1–8)<br>• Helping and encouraging (Lessons 1–8)<br>• Reflecting and setting goals (Lesson 8)<br>**Values**<br>• How music helps people and how it makes you feel | **Culture around the world**<br>• The creation of the African Children's Choir in Uganda<br>**Literacy**<br>**Text type**<br>• A poem (text to express; writing preparation)<br>**Reading skills**<br>• Reading with rhythm<br>**Writing skills**<br>• Onomatopoeic words | **21st Century Skills**<br>• **Ways of thinking:** being creative and original<br>**Thinking skills**<br>• Categorising (Lesson 1); Analysing and applying rules (Lessons 2 and 4); Predicting (Lesson 2); Hypothesising (Lesson 3); Logical thinking (Lesson 5); Defining and describing (Lesson 5); Finding information (Lesson 6); Planning, checking and correcting (Lesson 7); Seeing another's point of view (Lesson 8); Reflecting on learning (Lesson 8) | **Link to Science**<br>• Urban and rural populations<br>**Arts and Crafts**<br>• Identifying shade and shadow and painting a still life |

# Syllabus

| Unit | Key Competences and Key Learning Outcomes | Contents: Lexis |
|---|---|---|
| **Project 2: A film script** | • Perform the script for the class (Lesson 2)<br>• Investigate how people lived in the Middle Ages (Lesson 1)<br>• Listen to and identify correct information (Lesson 1)<br>• Reflect on what you've learnt and how you've worked together (Lesson 2)<br>• Work in groups to plan and write a script (Lesson 2)<br>• Rehearse performing your script in groups (Lesson 2)<br>• Share information about films (Lesson 1)<br>• Learn about life in the Middle Ages (Lesson 1)<br>• Learn about scripts for films and TV shows (Lesson 2) | **Key vocabulary**<br>• *castle, characters, go hunting, have a banquet, have a tournament, historical film, jester, king, knight, medieval times, Middle Ages, noble, palace, peasant, queen, script, suit of armour, TV show, wooden hut*<br>• *angrily, desperately, hopefully, kindly, politely, worriedly*<br>• *children, directions, heavy, hungry, market, sack, script, sick, wife* |
| **Unit 7 A helping hand** | • Name different ways of preparing for a party (Lesson 1)<br>• Learn and practise the present perfect simple with 'yet' and 'already' (Lesson 2)<br>• Learn and practise the present perfect simple with 'just' (Lesson 4)<br>• Learn phrases related to accidents (Lesson 5)<br>• Identify the use of questions to create interest (Lesson 7)<br>• Talk about an activity to raise money (Lesson 8)<br>• Watch and understand a video about volunteering (Video and 21st Century Skills)<br>• Learn about the discovery of insulin (Lesson 3)<br>• Use the Pupil's App on Navio<br>• Identify and practise intonation of sentences in the present perfect simple (Lesson 4)<br>• Review and practise the present perfect simple for present evidence of a past action (Lesson 5)<br>• Review and practise the past continuous tense (Lesson 5)<br>• Practise using questions to make your writing more interesting (Lesson 7)<br>• Reflect on your own learning (Lesson 8)<br>• Practise activity types found in the Cambridge Exams: A2 Key for Schools<br>• Think about the importance of being optimistic (Lesson 3)<br>• Learn about volunteering and ways to help your community and environment (Video and 21st Century Skills)<br>• Think about the qualities of a leader (Video and 21st Century Skills)<br>• Work in pairs or small groups to practise and reinforce learning (all lessons)<br>• Do a communication task (Lesson 5)<br>• Read and understand a story (Lesson 3)<br>• Learn about Canada (Lesson 3)<br>• Read and write a publicity leaflet (Lessons 6 and 7)<br>• Sing a song (Lesson 8) | **Core vocabulary**<br>• *blow up balloons, choose the music, clean the furniture, decorate the room, go shopping, make a cake, make posters, put out the food, sell tickets, send invitations, serve drinks, sweep the floor*<br>• *break my arm, bruise my arm, burn my hand, cut my finger, hurt my knee, scratch my leg, twist my ankle*<br>**Extension vocabulary**<br>• *give directions, invite a band, put up banners, sell raffle tickets, set up stalls, write thank you letters*<br>• *bang my head, feel sick, have a fever, have a sore throat*<br>**Other vocabulary**<br>• *amount, blood, control, cure, diabetes, insulin, medicine, pancreas; fundraising event, volunteer; strapline, testimonials, title*<br>• *animal care home, community, rubbish, rugby, tyre, volunteering*<br>**Recycled vocabulary**<br>• *do my homework, feed (Charlie), have a party, tidy up my room, water the plants; been, bought, broken, eaten, finished, met, read* |

Competence in linguistic communication | Competence in mathematics, science and technology | Digital competence
Learning to learn | Social and civic competences | Sense of initiative and entrepreneurship | Cultural awareness and expression

| Contents | | | | | |
|---|---|---|---|---|---|
| **Structures** | **Phonics** | **Sociocultural aspects** | **Culture around the world and Literacy** | **21st Century Skills** | **Cross-curricular links** |
| **Key structures**<br>• *Will you help me?*<br>• *If I don't take it to market, my wife and children will be hungry.*<br>• *I am too important to help you.*<br>• *I can't sing and I can't tell jokes.* | | **Cooperative learning Skills**<br>• Sharing knowledge and information (Lessons 1 and 2)<br>• Working together (Lesson 2) | | | **Link to Science**<br>• Medieval civilisations |
| **Core structures**<br>• *I / You / We / They have already made a cake. He / She / It has already made a cake. I / You / We / They haven't made a cake yet. He / She / It hasn't made a cake yet.*<br>• *Have I / you / we / they made a cake yet? Has he / she / it made a cake yet?*<br>• *No, I / you / we / they haven't. Yes, he / she / it has. No, he / she / it hasn't.*<br>• *I / You / We / They have just eaten an apple. He / She / It has just eaten an apple.*<br>• *Have I / you / we / they just eaten an apple? Has he / she / it just eaten an apple? Yes, I / you / we / they have.*<br>**Other structures**<br>• *What shall we do a week before the party? We could make posters. What will we need? We'll need pens. When I was seven, I (broke my leg). Let's raise money for a new school sports field. What shall we do? How about a talent show? What help will we need?*<br>**Recycled structures**<br>• *Elizabeth was living with her family. If she eats very little food, she can live for longer. What's happened to you? I've twisted my ankle. What were you doing? I was playing basketball.* | • Intonation of sentences in the present perfect simple | **Cooperative learning Skills**<br>• Working together (Lessons 1–8)<br>• Collaborating (Lessons 1–8)<br>• Checking learning (Lessons 1–8)<br>• Peer evaluation and feedback (Lesson 7)<br>• Participating (Lessons 1–8)<br>• Helping and encouraging (Lessons 1–8)<br>• Reflecting and setting goals (Lessons 1 and 8)<br>**Values**<br>• The importance of being optimistic | **Culture around the world**<br>• The discovery of a cure for diabetes in Canada<br>**Literacy**<br>**Text type**<br>• A publicity leaflet (text to persuade; writing preparation)<br>**Reading skills**<br>• Predicting content from pictures<br>**Writing skills**<br>• Using questions to create interest | **21st Century Skills**<br>• **Ways of working:** being a leader<br>**Thinking skills**<br>• Categorising (Lesson 1); Analysing and applying rules (Lessons 2 and 4); Creating (Lesson 4); Defining and describing (Lesson 5); Finding and classifying information (Lesson 6); Planning, checking and correcting (Lesson 7); Seeing another's point of view (Lesson 8); Reflecting on learning (Lesson 8) | **Link to Science**<br>• The tertiary sector<br>**Arts and Crafts**<br>• Identifying placement of objects to create a sense of depth and creating a silhouette collage |

# Syllabus

| Unit | Key Competences and Key Learning Outcomes | Contents<br>Lexis |
|---|---|---|
| **Unit 8 Green technology** | • Name recyclable objects and materials (Lesson 1)<br>• Use the present passive (Lesson 2)<br>• Learn and practise asking questions using the present passive (Lesson 4)<br>• Learn to describe how different materials are recycled (Lesson 5)<br>• Talk about the environment (Lesson 8)<br>• Watch and understand a video about recycling (Video and 21st Century Skills)<br><br>• Learn about the technology of marine robots (Lesson 3)<br>• Describe a recycling process (Lesson 5)<br>• Read and write some instructions (Lessons 6 and 7)<br><br>• Use the Pupil's App on Navio<br><br>• Practise placing the stress correctly in countries' names (Lesson 4)<br>• Practise using the imperative to give instructions (Lesson 7)<br>• Reflect on your own learning (Lesson 8)<br>• Practise activity types found in the Cambridge Exams: A2 Key for Schools<br><br>• Think about the importance of protecting the oceans (Lesson 3)<br>• Think about why recycling is important (Video and 21st Century Skills)<br><br>• Work in pairs or small groups to practise and reinforce learning (all lessons)<br>• Do a communication task (Lesson 5)<br>• Use a digital poster to persuade (Video and 21st Century Skills)<br><br>• Read and understand a story (Lesson 3)<br>• Learn about Japan (Lesson 3)<br>• Design an object made of recycled materials (Lesson 7) | **Core vocabulary**<br>• *bottle top, button, can, cardboard box, cardboard tube, carton, elastic band, fabric, lolly stick, plastic bottle, straw, string*<br>• *add water, collect paper, cut paper, remove ink, roll paper, transport paper, use paper, wash paper*<br>**Extension vocabulary**<br>• *egg carton, jar, packet, paper bag, tin, tub*<br>• *recycling bin, recycling containers, recycling plant, recycling lorry*<br>**Other vocabulary**<br>• *absolutely (not), definitely, not at all, not really, of course*<br>• *battery, collect, container, environment, factories, felt-tip pens, recycling plant, screws, spray cans*<br>• *being green, plant a tree, switch off lights, throw away*<br>• *bury, melt, recycling container, recycling lorry, reduce*<br><br>**Recycled vocabulary**<br>• *rice, vegetables; Argentina, Brazil, Canada, Germany, Italy, Japan, Switzerland; cut out, draw, glue, stick; card, paper, scissors; bin, cameras, computers, glass, metal, plastic, printers, recycle, robot, rubbish, technology; after that, first, next* |
| **Unit 9 Amazing places** | • Name natural places in the world (Lesson 1)<br>• Using the present continuous for future plans (Lesson 2)<br>• Learn and use the first conditional (Lesson 4)<br>• Review and name items to take on a trip (Lesson 5)<br>• Review and use prepositions of time (Lesson 7)<br>• Talk about a trip to a place near where you live (Lesson 8)<br>• Watch and understand a video about different places where people live (Video and 21st Century Skills)<br><br>• Categorise natural and man-made things (Lesson 1)<br><br>• Use the Pupil's App on Navio<br><br>• Identify and practise correct pronunciation of contracted forms in first conditional sentences (Lesson 4)<br>• Reflect on your own learning (Lesson 8)<br>• Practise activity types found in the Cambridge Exams: A2 Key for Schools<br><br>• Think about stories and the importance of sharing stories (Lesson 3)<br>• Show curiosity about the lives of people who live in different places (Video and 21st Century Skills)<br><br>• Do a communication task (Lesson 5)<br><br>• Learn about Brazil and the legend of the Vitória Régia water lily (Lesson 3)<br>• Read a tourist website (Lesson 6)<br>• Write a travel itinerary (Lesson 7)<br>• Sing a song (Lesson 8)<br>• Learn about life in Alaska (Video and 21st Century Skills) | **Core vocabulary**<br>• *canyon, coast, desert, island, lake, ocean, plain, rainforest, reef, valley, volcano, waterfall*<br>• *anorak, dictionary, money, passport, suitcase, ticket, towel, umbrella, wallet*<br>**Extension vocabulary**<br>• *bay, cliff, creek, geyser, lagoon, oasis*<br>• *puzzle book, sun hat, toothbrush, washbag*<br>**Other vocabulary**<br>• *canoe trip, dive, equator, full moon, legend, reflection, search on the Internet, water lily*<br>• *variety of wildlife*<br>• *climate, glacier, fishing, moose, otter, snow storm, state*<br><br>**Recycled vocabulary**<br>• *binoculars, camera, celebration, climb, cousins, guidebook, MP3 player, pencils, sketchpad, stars, summer, swimming pool, touch, winter; Brazil, England, the UK; at 9.00, for two hours, in the morning, on Saturday* |

Competence in linguistic communication · Competence in mathematics, science and technology · Digital competence
Learning to learn · Social and civic competences · Sense of initiative and entrepreneurship · Cultural awareness and expression

| Contents | | | | | |
|---|---|---|---|---|---|
| **Structures** | **Phonics** | **Sociocultural aspects** | **Culture around the world and Literacy** | **21st Century Skills** | **Cross-curricular links** |
| **Core structures**<br>• *Rice is / isn't grown in (Japan). Robots are / aren't produced in (the UK).*<br>• *Is rice grown in (Japan)? Yes, it is. No, it isn't.*<br>• *Are cars produced in (Japan)? Yes, they are. No, they aren't.*<br>• *Where are robots produced? Where is rice grown?*<br>• *What is made / produced / grown in Japan?*<br>**Other structures**<br>• *What a shame. How is paper recycled?*<br>**Recycled structures**<br>• *What are the toys made of? Have you ever made something with recycled objects? Do you recycle batteries in your home? How do you recycle them? Be creative.* | • Stress in countries' names | **Cooperative learning Skills**<br>• Working together (Lessons 1–8)<br>• Collaborating (Lessons 1–8)<br>• Checking learning (Lessons 1–8)<br>• Peer evaluation and feedback (Lesson 7)<br>• Participating (Lessons 1–8)<br>• Helping and encouraging (Lessons 1–8)<br>• Reflecting and setting goals (Lessons 1 and 8)<br>**Values**<br>• Protecting our oceans and sea animals | **Culture around the world**<br>• Robotic fish made from recycled objects in Japan<br>**Literacy**<br>**Text type**<br>• Instructions (text to instruct; writing preparation)<br>**Reading skills**<br>• Inferring meaning<br>**Writing skills**<br>• Imperatives | **21st Century Skills**<br>• **Digital skills:** using a digital poster to persuade<br>**Thinking skills**<br>• Categorising (Lesson 1); Analysing and applying rules (Lessons 2 and 4); Questioning (Lesson 4); Forming conceptual links (Lesson 5); Making inferences (Lesson 6); Logical thinking (Lesson 7); Planning, checking and correcting (Lesson 7); Reflecting on learning (Lesson 8) | **Link to Science**<br>• Recycling<br>**Arts and Crafts**<br>• Identifying and drawing using linear perspective |
| **Core structures**<br>• *I am / am not camping this weekend. You / We / They are / aren't camping this weekend. He / She / It is / isn't camping this weekend.*<br>• *Are you / we / they camping this weekend? Is he / she / it camping this weekend?*<br>• *If we're late, they won't let us in.*<br>• *If you don't wear a coat, you'll be cold.*<br>**Other structures**<br>• *If we go on the trip to Legoland, when will we leave? Which place would you most like to visit?*<br>**Recycled structures**<br>• *Brazil has won the World Cup more times than any other country. Have you ever been to (an island)? Which (island) did you go to?* | • Contracted forms in first conditional sentences | **Cooperative learning Skills**<br>• Collaborating (Lessons 1–8)<br>• Checking learning (Lessons 1–8)<br>• Peer evaluation and feedback (Lesson 7)<br>• Helping and encouraging (Lessons 1–8)<br>• Reflecting and setting goals (Lessons 1 and 8)<br>**Values**<br>• The importance of sharing stories | **Culture around the world**<br>• The legend of Vitória Régia water lily in Brazil<br>**Literacy**<br>**Text type**<br>• A travel itinerary (text to inform; writing preparation)<br>**Reading skills**<br>• Scanning text for information<br>**Writing skills**<br>• Using prepositions of time | **21st Century Skills**<br>• **Ways of thinking:** thinking about how other people live<br>**Thinking skills**<br>• Categorising (Lesson 1); Analysing and applying rules (Lessons 2 and 4); Defining and describing (Lesson 5); Finding and classifying (Lesson 6); Planning, checking and correcting (Lesson 7); Seeing another's point of view (Lesson 8); Reflecting on learning (Lesson 8) Working together (Lessons 1–8) | **Link to Science**<br>• Life in medieval times<br>**Arts and Crafts**<br>• Identifying different points of view and drawing from distinct points of view |

# Syllabus

| Unit | Key Competences and Key Learning Outcomes | Contents: Lexis |
| --- | --- | --- |
| **Project 3: An eco tourist attraction** | • Present your poster to the rest of the class (Lesson 2)<br>• Share information about places and landscapes around the world (Lesson 1)<br>• Investigate different eco tourist attractions (Lesson 1)<br>• Listen for specific information and take notes (Lesson 1)<br>• Reflect on what you've learnt and how you've worked together (Lesson 2)<br>• Work in groups to plan an eco tourist attraction (Lesson 2)<br>• Share the information with your group (Lesson 1)<br>• Learn about a famous tourist attraction in the UK (Lesson 1)<br>• Design and draw a poster to advertise the eco tourist attraction (Lesson 2) | **Key vocabulary**<br>• *beach, cliff, hill, lake, marsh, mountain, plain, river, sand dune, stream, valley, waterfall*<br>• *arctic, alpine, desert, rainforest*<br>• *biologist*<br>• *climate, landscape, landforms*<br>• *activities, alpine, animals, cactuses, cave, hill, iceberg, ice skate, landforms, leaflet, penguin, plants, seal* |
| **Festivals: Happy New Year!** | • Make and discuss your New Year's resolutions<br>• Learn about New Year traditions in the UK and around the world<br>• Listen to and perform a poem about New Year's resolutions | **Key vocabulary**<br>• *celebrate, count down, dawdle, envelope, feast, ink, New Year's Day, New Year's Eve, New Year's resolutions, strike midnight*<br>• *curry, mangoes, noodles, pancakes, papaya* |
| **Festivals: World Environment Day** | • Learn about carbon footprints<br>• Listen to and do a quiz to find out about your carbon footprint<br>• Discuss what you should and shouldn't do to reduce your carbon footprint<br>• Learn about World Environment Day | **Key vocabulary**<br>• *absorb, burn, $CO_2$ carbon, carbon footprint, coal, energy, environment, gas, oxygen, standby, trap*<br>• *less, more, the least, the most*<br>• *always, every day, never, once or twice a (week), sometimes, usually*<br>• *by (car), on foot* |

Competence in linguistic communication
Competence in mathematics, science and technology
Digital competence
Learning to learn
Social and civic competences
Sense of initiative and entrepreneurship
Cultural awareness and expression

| Contents | | | | | Cross-curricular links |
|---|---|---|---|---|---|
| Structures | Phonics | Sociocultural aspects | Culture around the world and Literacy | 21st Century Skills | |
| **Key structures**<br>• *What's the (landscape) like in a tropical rainforest?*<br>• *Which environment shall we choose for our tourist attraction?*<br>• *Why don't we create (an alpine) environment?*<br>• *What about having (a river) in the attraction?*<br>• *We could grow (cactuses) in the environment.*<br>• *Visitors could (ice skate) in the attraction.*<br>• *We need to have (toilets) for visitors.* | | **Cooperative learning Skills**<br>• Sharing knowledge and information (Lessons 1 and 2)<br>• Working together (Lesson 2) | | | **Link to Science**<br>• Landscapes and landforms<br>• Flora<br>• Fauna |
| **Key structures**<br>• *I promise I will (watch less TV). I promise I won't (shout).* | | **Cooperative learning Skills**<br>• Working together (Lesson 1) | | | |
| **Key structures**<br>• *How often do you leave the TV on standby? How much TV do you watch every day?* | | **Cooperative learning Skills**<br>• Working together (Lesson 1) | | | |

# Introduction to *Give Me Five!*

***Give Me Five!*** is a six-level course for pupils who have an extended English timetable and are being taught at a faster pace. It is designed to develop pupils' communicative competences in a systematic and comprehensive manner.

## With *Give Me Five!* 5, pupils …

- **develop multi-cultural understanding** by investigating nine different countries from around the world.
- **use new technologies and multimedia** as tools for learning.
- **develop their social and civic competences** through a hands-on cooperative project each term and the integration of collaborative tasks and strategies.
- **link their learning to other areas in the curriculum** such as Science and Arts and Crafts.
- **develop literacy skills** through a range of enjoyable and motivating real-world texts and a focus on the key reading and writing skills.
- **identify and talk about language patterns** and use them to personalise and be creative with new language.
- **communicate confidently** through a wide variety of well supported speaking tasks.
- **develop their oral fluency** through integrated practice of connected speech, stress, rhythm and intonation.
- **participate fully** through a range of engaging activities such as stories, dialogues, games and problem solving tasks.
- **develop reading, writing, listening and speaking** in a balanced and integrative manner.
- **prepare for Cambridge Exams** through the systematic integration of exam practice material and a dedicated Exams Practice lesson in each unit.
- **become independent and reflective learners** through the integration of learning-to-learn strategies and activities.
- **develop their thinking skills and multiple intelligences** through a variety of stimulating and challenging activities.
- **develop their 21st century skills** through real-life videos and interesting tasks to practise and perfect the skills needed in the 21st century.

## Meet the characters in *Give Me Five! 5*

**Callum**, **Jess** and **Tom** are ten and eleven years old and they are friends and classmates. We first meet them at a traditional school fair where they release nine balloons as part of a balloon race. Each of the following units begins with news about where one of the balloons has landed and we are introduced to a child from that country. Callum, Jess and Tom are delighted to make nine new friends from around the world and to find out about life in the different countries.

## Cooperative learning

*Give Me Five! 5* incorporates a variety of **cooperative learning tasks and strategies** which require the pupils to work together in a structured way. Working in pairs and small groups has many benefits. The pupils are prepared to spend more time on the tasks, are motivated to produce more language and are more likely to use creative and logical thinking. Cooperative learning also helps develop a positive classroom environment as the pupils have a greater sense of belonging and learn to understand and value all the members of the group. Finally, cooperative tasks require the pupils to be active and more independent learners, building their self-confidence and their ability to cope with uncertainty and unpredictability.

*Give Me Five! 5* provides many opportunities to use common and well-researched cooperative learning activities and strategies. A bank of these can be found below. There is also a simple, clearly staged **cooperative project** at the end of each term which provides the pupils with the opportunity to learn and practise **interpersonal skills** such as agreeing, disagreeing and negotiating roles and responsibilities.

In order to support the pupils when they work in pairs and groups, the teacher is provided with a set of **Talk role cards** (available in the Teacher's Resource Bank on Navio). These cards can be used to introduce and practise specific group skills and functions, such as recording information, organising materials or checking noise levels. They also encourage the pupils to take more responsibility for their actions and behaviour in the classroom. The different roles should be introduced one at a time and modelled by the teacher. As children become familiar with the role cards, the teacher can allocate different roles to pupils in the same group.

## Cooperative learning activities and strategies bank

### 1 Three-step interview

The pupils work with a partner to ask and answer questions, e.g. about their preferences or their routines. Once they have completed the task, they turn to a new partner and report what their first partner has told them, e.g. *Peter loves skating.* This strategy can be used for personal questions, for example in some *Talk Partner* activities.

### 2 Think – write – pair – compare

Ask the pupils a question, e.g. **What water sports do you know?** Each pupil should think and write down their ideas. The pupils then share and compare their ideas with a partner or in a small group. Asking pupils to write down their ideas helps them to organise their thoughts and ensures full participation. This strategy can be used for brainstorming new vocabulary items.

### 3 Numbered heads

When the class is working in small groups, give each pupil a number (1–3). At the end of the task ask a question and say one of the numbers. The pupil with that number in each group should answer the question. Repeat the process with other questions, choosing a different number to answer each time. This strategy can be used when the pupils are planning and creating projects in small groups or when they are doing the review quiz in pairs at the end of the unit.

### 4 Round robin

Organise the class into small groups. Then ask an open-ended question. Each pupil should take turns to share their answer with their group. To prevent interruptions, give pupils a *talk token,* e.g. a rubber, to place on the table when they speak. Once they have done this, they cannot speak again until all their group's tokens are on the table. This strategy can be used, for example, when talking about values in Lesson 3 or in Lesson 8.

### 5 Board sharing

When pupils have discussed a question in small groups, ask them to choose their best answer. One pupil from each group should then write the information on the board. The class can then compare and discuss the different answers. This strategy can be used for brainstorming ideas or for making predictions, for example before reading the story in lesson 3.

### 6 Reading partners

Organise the class into pairs to read a text. The two pupils should take it in turns to read a section of the text, e.g. a paragraph, to each other. At the end of each section they should check each other's understanding. This strategy can be used, for example, after a class reading of the literacy texts in lessons 6 and 7.

# 21st century learning

## *Give Me Five! 5* and 21st Century learning

Today's learners are growing up in a complex, changing world where an enormous amount of information is available at the touch of a button and where social media allows them to communicate with people all around the world. Technology is transforming the way we live and the way we learn. A key objective of *Give Me Five! 5* is to support learners in developing the necessary skills for the digital age. Apart from using digital technology, skills such as communicating and collaborating with others, thinking creatively and critically, and working to become a caring global citizen are an essential part of this course.

*Give Me Five! 5* takes an integrated approach to the use of digital technology and the teaching of **digital skills**. In each unit there is a comprehensive set of digital practice material for the learner, helping them to become autonomous and digitally confident. Pupils are also supported in developing specific ICT skills. There are tips on how to use the Internet to find, select and present information, and there is a selection of projects with digital outcomes. Guided web quests also support pupils in using the Internet to explore new places around the world.

There are multiple opportunities for **communication** and **collaboration** in *Give Me Five! 5*. Learners are encouraged to work together to discover and build knowledge through quizzes and questionnaires, whole class discussions and a wide range of *Talk Partner* activities. Pupils also work with *Writing Partners* to plan, write and evaluate pieces of written work, and are encouraged to work cooperatively to review learning and reflect on progress at the end of each unit. Finally, there are structured cooperative projects which by providing opportunities for authentic communication, they encourage the development of interpersonal skills and enable learners to celebrate achievement.

Each unit of *Give Me Five! 5* provides a range of tasks to build the pupil's **critical and creative thinking skills.** These include problem-solving, evaluating information, and using imaginative thinking. The Video and 21st Century Skills lessons also focus on a selection of discrete thinking skills. They provide practical tips and thinking strategies.

The interconnectivity of the 21st Century and the increasing diversity of our communities mean that pupils need to learn how to respect and value other cultures. *Give Me Five! 5* provides learners with historical, geographical and cultural information about nine different places in the world. This rich content provides opportunities for **intercultural learning,** where learners identify cultural differences and similarities and build a positive attitude toward their own and other cultures. Finally, a dedicated *Values* section in each unit supports learners in developing their **social and civic competencies** and helps them to make a positive difference in the world.

## Video and 21st Century Skills lessons

Video generates interest and supports learners' listening skills by providing a clear visual context and model to practise speaking. It is also a flexible tool, allowing teachers to pause the recording or turn off the sound, and can be used as a stimulus for thinking, language practice and communication. Each unit in *Give Me Five! 5* concludes with a Video and 21st Century Skills lesson. These video lessons help to build key 21st Century Skills, develop visual literacy and provide a springboard for authentic communication.

The stars of the videos are Amy and Max, the two children presenters of *Channel 21*. The children begin each programme by introducing a new topic and then share a selection of related video clips and interviews they have made. These visually rich videos, bring images of the world into the classroom and offer insights into British culture. Amy and Max interview various people to find out about a diverse range of topics and proceed to show a video related to these topics. The children then discuss and highlight a 21st Century Skill in the material. This serves to contextualise the 21st Century Skill and show the learner how it is relevant in their learning and in their lives.

The 21st Century Skills selected for this level are the following:

**Ways of thinking**: these skills focus on critical and creative thinking and include developing your ideas (Unit 1), being creative and original (Unit 6) and thinking about how other people live (Unit 9).

**Ways of working**: these skills focus on collaboration and communication and include making detailed comparisons (Unit 3) and being a leader (Unit 7).

**Digital skills**: these skills focus on researching and evaluating information and include researching a topic online (Unit 2), using technology to help us (Unit 4) and using a digital poster to persuade (Unit 8).

**Living in the world**: these skills focus on values, responsibility and cultural awareness and focus on protecting animals in danger (Unit 5).

# Multiple Intelligences

According to the theory of **multiple intelligences**, each human being possesses a set of intelligences. As a consequence, learners have different needs, strengths and abilities in the classroom. In *Give Me Five! 5* seven key intelligences are highlighted:

### Logical-mathematical intelligence

Activities and tasks that require the pupils to use mathematical and logical **thinking skills** are integrated into the material. These include **higher-order thinking skills** such as **problem solving**, **hypothesising** and **inferring**.

### Musical intelligence

The pupils are exposed to **songs** and **poems** in *Give Me Five! 5*. These help them to appreciate and produce **natural-sounding sounds**, **rhythm**, **stress** and **intonation**.

### Bodily-kinaesthetic intelligence

**Physical expression** is an important part of communication. The pupils are given the opportunity to develop fine motor skills by doing different tasks.

### Intrapersonal intelligence

The pupils are encouraged to think about their **inner feelings**, **values** and **beliefs** through the values section in each unit. The use of discussion questions also help the pupils to develop and articulate their ideas.

### Interpersonal intelligence

A **values section** in each unit provides an opportunity for the pupils to reflect on their relationship with people around them and draws their attention to key **social and civic values and codes of conduct**.

### Visual-spatial intelligence

The dynamic design of *Give Me Five! 5* supports meaning and helps the pupils to **visualise contexts for language**. **Graphic organisers** help pupils form their own conceptual links and order new information.

### Linguistic intelligence

The pupils are supported on their journey to becoming confident **and accurate speakers**, listeners, readers and writers of the English language. The pupils are given opportunities to use this language in a range of contexts.

# Tips for teaching pupils with Special Educational Needs

### Setting up the class and Working together

- Change the groupings regularly to make sure the SEN pupils have an opportunity to work with all their classmates.
- Make instructions clear and on a step-by-step basis. Check understanding by giving an example.
- Use positive classroom language. Say what you want pupils to do, not what you don't want them to do. For example say ***Look at the board*** not ***Don't keep turning round***.
- Develop a peer mentoring system to encourage pupils help each other and share skills.

### Hearing Impaired (HI) pupils

- Write instructions on the board or highlight them on the IWB. Make sure you have your pupil's attention before you read out the instructions or speak.
- Seat your hearing impaired (HI) pupil facing and close to you to make lip reading and following instruction gestures easier.
- Assign or ask for a volunteer helper or note-taker to support the HI pupil.
- Give copies of the audioscripts for the pupil to follow.

### Visually Impaired (VI) learners

- Say every word you write on the board and use realia to teach vocabulary. Realia allows the visually impaired pupils to use all their senses.
- *Give Me Five! 5* offers plenty of songs, stories and dialogues with lesson tips. Use the audio script for reading texts, stories, and example dialogues.
- Encourage other pupils to describe experiences and create an active and engaging learning environment.

### Dyslexic learners

- For brainstorming activities, do the first few examples with the class. For writing activities at sentence level, provide the pupils with a model which can be done as a whole class first.
- Encourage the use of mind maps to illustrate, collate and organise vocabulary and ideas. Note-taking is a useful skill to help dyslexic pupils recognise keywords in listening and reading activities.
- Provide photocopies to allow pupils with dyslexia to mark the text or cut it and move it around. This allows for information to be processed in manageable chunks.

# Key Competences and Key Learning Outcomes

The **Key Competences and Key Learning Outcomes** outline the **knowledge**, **skills** and **behaviour** that the pupils need to develop in order to achieve their full personal potential, participate in an effective and constructive way in society and become responsible and autonomous life-long learners.

**Competence in linguistic communication:** the ability to use language as an instrument to express and interpret concepts, facts, feelings and ideas in an appropriate and creative way.

**Cultural awareness and expression:** the ability to understand and appreciate different art and cultural forms.

**Competence in mathematics, science and technology:** the ability to develop and apply mathematical thinking to solve everyday problems and to use scientific knowledge to explain the natural world and understand the consequences of human action.

**Sense of initiative and entrepreneurship:** the ability to apply qualities and skills such as creativity, critical thinking and perseverance, and to plan and manage projects.

**Digital competence:** the ability to use digital technology confidently, critically and responsibly.

**Social and civic competences:** the ability to understand and appreciate diversity in society and to develop personal and interpersonal competences.

**Learning to learn:** the ability to organise one's own learning and work efficiently and autonomously as an individual or in a group.

## How *Give Me Five! 5* develops the Key Competences and Key Learning Outcomes

### Competence in linguistic communication

*Give Me Five! 5* develops the pupils' linguistic skills in a systematic and integrative manner. The pupils learn to identify the meaning of words and phrases through working with **definitions, dialogues and stories.** The use of short **listening texts** helps them develop the ability to understand a range of communicative messages in everyday contexts.

The pupils have the opportunity to work intensively on key pronunciation features at sentence level, helping them **develop a clear and natural pronunciation**. The structured use of games, personalisation activities and problem-solving activities provide the pupils with frequent opportunities to communicate in the classroom and express their feelings and opinions in English. A **cooperative project** each term also helps the pupils develop social competences and introduces language and strategies for working successfully in small groups.

Each unit of *Give Me Five! 5* has a **double-page literacy spread** which introduces the pupils to a variety of engaging real-world texts. **Reading strategies** are systematically introduced to support readers in understanding, responding to and reflecting on these texts, whilst an analysis of features such as the writer's purpose, audience and the informational content of a text help prepare pupils for writing. Discrete **writing skills** such as the use of time connectives, paragraphs or punctuation are also highlighted in the literacy lessons.

## Competence in mathematics, science and technology

In *Give Me Five! 5* mathematical competence is developed in a number of ways. The pupils' understanding of **numbers, shapes, space and time** is reinforced and **language patterns** are identified and highlighted. The pupils also have the opportunity to work with **charts and diagrams**, and to do activities which require them to **solve problems**. Each unit of *Give Me Five! 5* is also **linked to an area of learning in the Science curriculum**, reinforcing key concepts and language across the curriculum.

## Digital competence

*Give Me Five! 5* uses **digital resources** as tools to support learning, familiarising the pupils with computer technology and showing them how technology can be used for learning purposes. The **Pupil's App on Navio** serves to consolidate class work and provide a **home-school link** by allowing the pupils to work independently outside the classroom. Within the classroom, the **Teacher's App on Navio** provide enhanced digital resources for presentation and practice, integrated audio and interactive activities.

## Learning to learn

*Give Me Five! 5* introduces a variety of **learning strategies** to help the pupils become more independent and reflective learners. Learning objectives are set at the beginning and are reviewed at the end of each lesson to check that the objectives have been met. The pupils are also encouraged to reflect on their learning and progress at the end of each unit through the use of a **self-evaluation task**. A Working with Words section in each unit introduces simple **strategies for recording, retrieving and extending vocabulary**. The use of writing criteria in the literacy lessons helps to develop pupils' **self-assessment skills**.

Finally, throughout *Give Me Five! 5* there is an emphasis on good learning habits and the importance of making an effort and being responsible for your work. Personal qualities such as self-confidence, initiative, curiosity, interest and creativity are also explicitly promoted, preparing pupils for life-long learning.

## Social and civic competences

Developing the ability to understand how somebody else is feeling and knowing how to respond appropriately is an important objective of *Give Me Five! 5* and emphasis is placed on **positive classroom behaviour**. **Cooperative projects** provide the pupils with the language needed to engage effectively with others, whilst the integration of **collaborative activities and strategies** reinforces the importance of active participation, cooperation and respect and support for others.

A **values section** in each unit also encourages the pupils to reflect on their natural, social and cultural environment, integrating real-world topics such as recycling, what to do in an emergency and the importance of respecting and protecting our heritage.

## Sense of initiative and entrepreneurship

*Give Me Five! 5* develops a sense of initiative and entrepreneurship through the inclusion of **cooperative group tasks and projects**. These require the pupils to work in groups to plan and complete a task, such as designing a tourist attraction or organising a sightseeing trip. Working together to complete a task helps the pupils to take responsibility for their work and gain confidence in their abilities. Initiative is also encouraged through personalisation activities, problem-solving tasks and creative activities.

## Cultural awareness and expression

In *Give Me Five! 5* the pupils are introduced to the real-world culture of nine different **countries around the world**. In addition to reading emails and text messages from children in these countries, there is an illustrated culture story in each unit which has been selected to be of **intrinsic interest** to the age group. Stories include the tragedy of Pompeii, the invention of Velcro and the history of a mythical beast.

*Give Me Five! 5* also provides the opportunity to experience and appreciate a **range of art forms** such as songs, poems, literature, drawing, mime and performance and encourages the pupils to express their ideas, experiences and emotions through these mediums.

# *Give Me Five! 5* Pupil's components

## Pupil's Book

This is a 128-page, full-colour book that contains a Starter Unit, nine thematic units, three cooperative projects and material for two festivals (New Year and World Environment Day). Each unit is divided into eight lessons and provides vocabulary input and practice, short dialogues to contextualise and practise language, grammar tables with guided questions to support inductive thinking. A Values task after the story encourages the pupils to discuss and reflect on personal, social or civic values. At the end of each unit there is a Video and 21st Century Skills lesson which supports the development of different skills. In addition, each unit contains opportunities for whole-class discussion, a selection of communicative activities, a pronunciation task to develop the pupils' fluency and an engaging two-page literacy spread. Material such as practice material for Cambridge English Young Learners exams, a grammar and vocabulary review section for each unit and a songs bank is provided at the back of the book.

## Activity Book

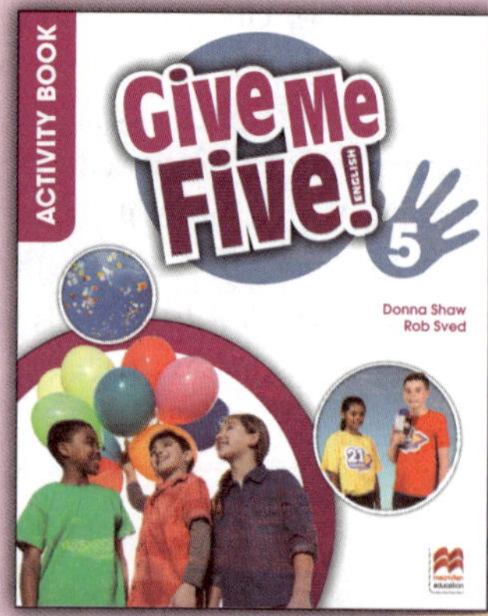


This 136-page, write-in book works in tandem with the Pupil's Book to reinforce and extend language learning, support and develop reading and writing and provide further practice of the listening and speaking skills. Each unit comprises a variety of activities which are devised to engage and challenge the pupils, activate different intelligences, encourage creativity and allow the pupils to use language in a personal and meaningful way. At the end of each unit there is a full-page unit review and a Video and 21st Century Skills lesson. At the back of the Activity Book there is an additional full grammar and vocabulary practice section for each unit. There is also material to support Study Skills lessons and extra Cambridge Exams Practice for each unit.

## Pupil's App on Navio

Powered By NAVIO

The Pupil's App on Navio is designed to accompany the course and provide extra practice in class or at home. Pupils can create avatars and then explore Navio's immersive worlds. Pupils complete game-based activities designed to practise and review the language and content learnt in class. As they do so, they earn rewards, points and badges. The app tracks pupils' progress so the teacher can see how they are doing and provide extra support where it is needed. The app also includes all the songs, stories and animations from the course so that pupils can review them at home and share them with their family. The access code for the Pupil's App can be found inside the front cover of the Pupil's Book.

## IDEAL WITH

BY ME

**ByME Social Science Primary 5**

**ByME Natural Science Primary 5**

**ByME Arts and Crafts Primary 5**

**Grammar Goals 5**

# *Give Me Five! 5* Teacher's components

## Teacher's Book

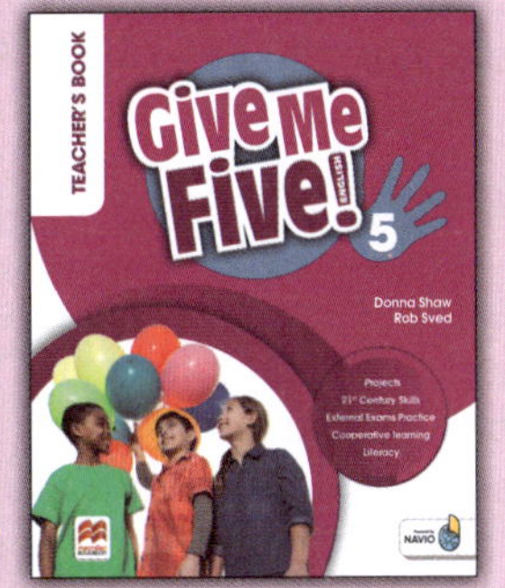


This user-friendly, spiral-bound book provides teachers with as much or as little support as they need. The At a Glance Lesson Plans, illustrated with images of the Pupil's Book and Activity Book, clearly highlight the learning aims, key language, materials required, learning routines, key activities and a range of optional extra activities, including cross-curricular links. These are accompanied by Detailed Lesson Plans which provide complete and concise teaching notes for each activity and answer keys. Full audioscripts can be found at the back of the book. In addition, there is a Reflective Teacher page after each unit for documenting learning, noting ideas and planning actions.

## Teacher's App on Navio

Powered By NAVIO

The Teacher's App on Navio offers one-stop access to all the many resources which accompany the course. **Tap and Teach Lessons** with **integrated audio and video** ensure that everything you need to teach each lesson is in one place. You can use the **Classroom Management tool** to award points for good behaviour or success in class, and track your pupils' marks and progress using the **Progress Tracker**. You'll find additional photocopiable resources in the **Teacher's Resource Bank** (see opposite) and **Test Generator**.

## Class CDs

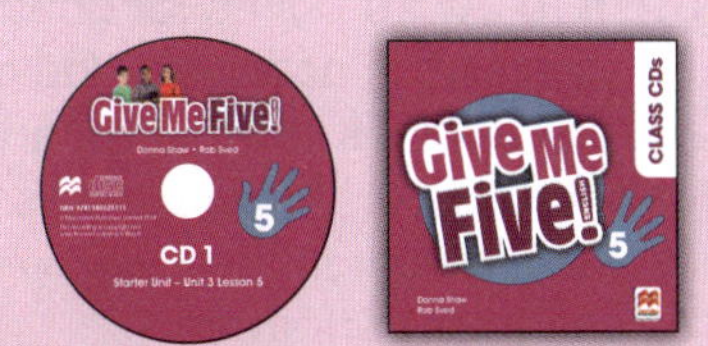


Four class CDs provide all the recorded material for the Pupil's Book and Activity Book. These include recordings of the key vocabulary, dialogues, pronunciation activities, stories, listening tasks, songs and Cambridge Exams Practice.

## Flashcards

A set of 118 full-colour flashcards with photographs of the key vocabulary from Lesson 1 of each unit. Suggestions for using them are given in the Detailed Lesson Plans and in the Games bank on page 27.

## Teacher's Resource Bank: Course resources

The **Teacher's Resource Bank** located within the teacher's app on Navio, contains a wealth of resources that complement *Give Me Five!* In addition to providing downloads for all class audio and video, the resource bank contains:

- **Letters to parents:** an introductory letter, followed by a letter to present each unit.
- **Talk role cards:** a set of role cards to help develop teamwork and to encourage pupils to take responsibility for their work.

- **Vocabulary and Grammar worksheets:** to reinforce and extend the vocabulary and grammar syllabus.
- **Evaluation Rubrics:** one grid per unit to evaluate pupils' level of achievement of the Unit Key Competences and Key Learning Outcomes, as well as their cooperative learning skills.

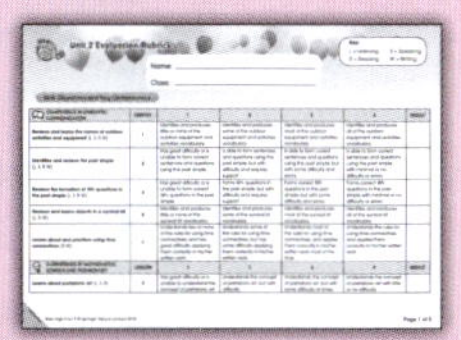

- **Tests:** a Diagnostic Test, Unit Tests, Term Tests and an End-of-Year Test with audio and Teacher's Notes including answer keys. Each test has a standard and a higher level version.

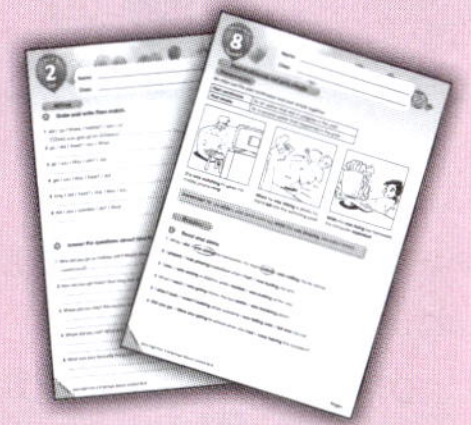

- **Word cards:** A set of 118 word cards. Suggestions for using them can be found in the Detailed Lesson Plans and in the Games bank on page 27.

## Teacher's Resource Bank: External Exams Resources

This section in the Teacher's Resource Bank supports teachers who are preparing their pupils for either one of the ***Trinity Graded Exams in Spoken English*** (Elementary Stage, Grade 6) or the ***Cambridge English Key for Schools (A2)***.

The external exams resources contain the following:

- **Videos** of children doing speaking practice.
- **Teacher's Notes** on how to exploit these videos in the classroom.
- Extra **Cambridge Exams practice material** and **practice tests** and **tips for teachers**.
- **Trinity Exams Practice Worksheets**
- Tips for preparing pupils for the exams and working with the Language Assistant.
- A set of **Trinity Exams Practice cards** for optional Trinity-type speaking practice at the start of each lesson.

# Teacher's and Pupil's Apps on Navio

The Navio app which accompanies this course offers one-stop access to the huge range of resources that come with *Give Me Five! 5*. **Tap and Teach Lessons** enable you to move seamlessly between the book and digital components, and you can track your pupils' marks and review their progress using the **Progress Tracker**, and find additional resources in the **Resource Bank** and **Test Generator**.

## Accessing the app

To access Navio:

1. Go to www.MacmillanNavio.com/givemefive
2. Follow the onscreen instructions

If you haven't got a Macmillan Education account, you need to create a profile. Then you can enter your access code and download the app for your device (see System Requirements: www.macmillannavio.com/system-requirements).

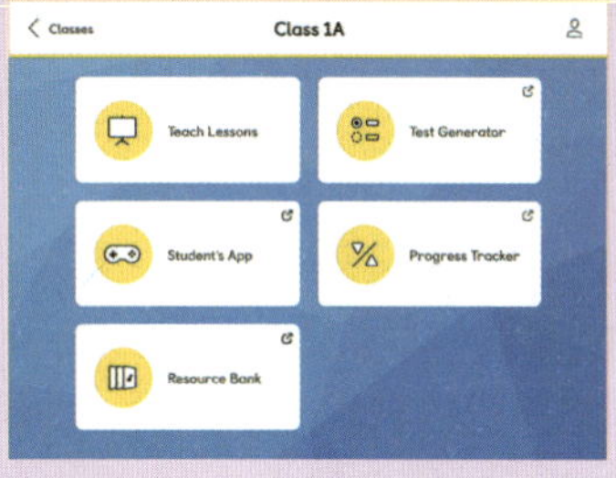


## Setting up a class

You, or your school administrator, will need to set up a class and register pupils with their names and the email address of their parents or guardians. Once the class is created, login details can be given to parents. Parents can then log in to the Pupil's App and enter the access code from the inside cover of the Pupil's Book to access the 3D worlds and practice content.

## Managing your downloads

Navio makes it easy to manage the storage space on your device, as you can control how much material you download at one time. Navio makes it clear how much storage space your chosen content will need. You can download the complete Teacher's and Pupil's Apps at once, or, if your device has limited storage capacity, you can choose to download only one or two units. And after you finish a unit, you can safely delete the content from your device. You won't lose your pupils' data, as this information is stored online.

## Using the Progress Tracker

All the work your pupils complete in the app is recorded in the **Progress Tracker**. You can monitor the progress of a whole class or any individual pupil. Every activity in the app is mapped against the course Learning Outcomes and Skills, so you can easily identify where your pupils need extra support.

## Teaching a lesson

Navio makes it easy to plan and teach your lessons with fully interactive **Tap and Teach Lessons** for every lesson in *Give Me Five! 5*. Go to your Class Dashboard and choose **Teach Lessons**. Find the lesson you want to teach and click to open it. Click on the **Toolbar** along the bottom of the screen to expand it to Thumbnail view. The Toolbar also contains the **Tap and Teach tools** you need to teach heads-up, whole-class activities, including a Timer, Pen tool and Mask tool.

Lessons follow the lesson plans in the Teacher's Book, and provide everything you need to teach from your device in one place. They include digital versions of all the activities in the Pupil's Book and Activity Book with their answer keys. They also include all the audio and video you need for the lesson, as well as some extra tools such as digital Flashcards. All relevant pages from both books are also provided so that you can project them in class, to help your pupils and to encourage heads-up participation.

When you teach, move through the lesson slide by slide using the arrows, or double click on a thumbnail to jump straight to a particular activity. If you prefer, you can **Filter activities** to customise the lesson so it includes only the content you want to teach.

## Using the Rewards tool

Navio's new **Rewards tool** is a great way to keep your pupils engaged in class. Much more than just a record of attendance, you can also use it to award points for good behaviour or success in activities. You can even organise your class into teams, and you can award points to individuals, groups or the whole class at any time. When pupils earn points, they appear in the Pupil's App next time they log in, so parents can see their performance.

## Pupil's App

As a teacher you can also access a version of the Pupil's App from the Class Dashboard. This has all the same content that your pupils can access at home, but your version is set in **Teacher Mode**. This means that all the activities and worlds are already unlocked, and the App does not record any marks to the Progress Tracker.

We recommend using Teacher Mode when pupils share devices to avoid mixing up pupils' grades and progress. However, if pupils have individual devices or are using the app at home, they should always log in with their own username and password. In this way they can earn points and badges, set up and customise their avatar and build a record of their progress in the Progress Tracker.

# Flashcards and Word cards games bank

## Flashcard games

**1 *Keep talking***

Organise the class into teams. Show the class your first flashcard and elicit the vocabulary item. Then give the card to the first team and ask them to make a sentence about what is on the card, for example *It's yellow.* (a banana) If the sentence is acceptable the team wins a point and the card is passed on to the next team who must think up another sentence, e.g. *It gives you light.* (a torch) Continue the activity until the groups run out of things to say. Then repeat the procedure with another card.

**2 *Chain game***

Hold up one of the flashcards (e.g. rock climbing) and say **Yesterday was a very busy day! I went rock climbing** ... Give a different flashcard to another pupil (e.g. hiking). They have to say *Yesterday was a very busy day! I went rock climbing and I went hiking ...* Keep handing out flashcards. The pupils continue to add new activities each time. When you start to hand out objects, the pupils can say *I took a torch*, etc.

## Word card games

**1 *Word card classification***

Use the word cards to organise and classify vocabulary items. You can use the cards to create a mind map, writing the name of the topic in the centre of the board and then asking the class to organise the word cards into sub-topics around the topic. You can also create Venn diagrams, for example classifying food into food groups according to whether it is eaten hot or cold, or organising activities on a line according to how boring or exciting they are.

**2 *Mime the card***

Invite a pupil to come to the front of the room. Stand behind the pupil and show a word card to the rest of the class. The class mimes this activity or item and the pupil at the front should try to guess the word. Repeat the procedure with the other word cards, choosing a different pupil to come to the front of the class each time.

**3 *Yes or No?***

Divide the class into teams. A pupil from one team has to pick a word card from the lexical set and challenge the rest of their team to guess the word. Invite three different team members to ask yes/no questions, e.g. *Is it bigger than my hand? Can you see it in this room?* After three questions, a fourth pupil has to guess what it is.

## Classroom games

**1 *Opposites game***

Use this activity to practise opposites. Write a row of numbers (1–8) on the board and below it a row of letters (a-h). Explain that each number and each letter is an adjective. The pupils must find and match the opposite adjectives. Organise the class into two teams. The teams should take turns to say a number and letter. Read out the corresponding adjectives (below). If the adjectives are opposites, write them on the board and award the team a point. Then continue the game.

1 2 3 4 5 6 7 8
heavy strong noisy long
near hard rough expensive
A B C D E F G H
soft light far weak short
cheap smooth quiet

**2 *Sharing sentences***

Use this activity to practise the past continuous and past simple tenses. Hand out a piece of paper to each pupil and ask them to fold the page in half (vertically). Then write a prompt for the first half of the sentence on the board ***I was ... when ...*** The pupils should copy and complete it, e.g. swimming, eating a pizza, on the left side of the paper. They should then fold the paper so you can only see the blank right side and pass it to a partner. Elicit different ways to complete the sentence using the past simple tense, e.g. *I saw a ghost.* The partners should write the second part of the sentence without looking at the first part and then pass it back for the original pupil to read. Repeat the procedure several times.

**3 *No one can go to the cinema***

Use this activity to practise modal verbs of obligation. Invite a pupil to come to the front of the class and prompt them to ask another pupil *Can you go to the cinema with me?* Prompt the second pupil to give an excuse, e.g. *Sorry, I have to do my homework.* The first pupil should then say to a third pupil *(Pablo) has to do his homework. Can you go to the cinema with me?* Once again, the third pupil should give an excuse.

**4 *Connections***

Explain to the pupils that you will go around the class asking them to say a word connected with the topic. If someone thinks that there isn't a connection, they can 'challenge' and the person who has said the word has to explain the connection to the topic. Repeat the activity with different topics.

**5 *Freeze!***

Use this activity to practise the past continuous tense. Invite a pupil to come to the front of the class and close his / her eyes. Ask the rest of the class to stand up and mime doing an action. After the class have been miming for a few seconds say 3, 2, 1 ... FREEZE! The pupils should freeze in the middle of their action. Ask the pupil at the front of the class to open his / her eyes and identify what action each pupil was doing. The classmates sit down when the pupil guesses their actions correctly.

# Using the Pupil's Book and Activity Book

## Lesson 1

**Clear objectives** set the scene for learning and provide a suggestion for evaluation criteria.

Exciting and engaging photographs are used to activate the pupils' existing knowledge and encourage whole-class discussion.

Twelve items of vocabulary are introduced using **photographic flashcards** and **word cards**.

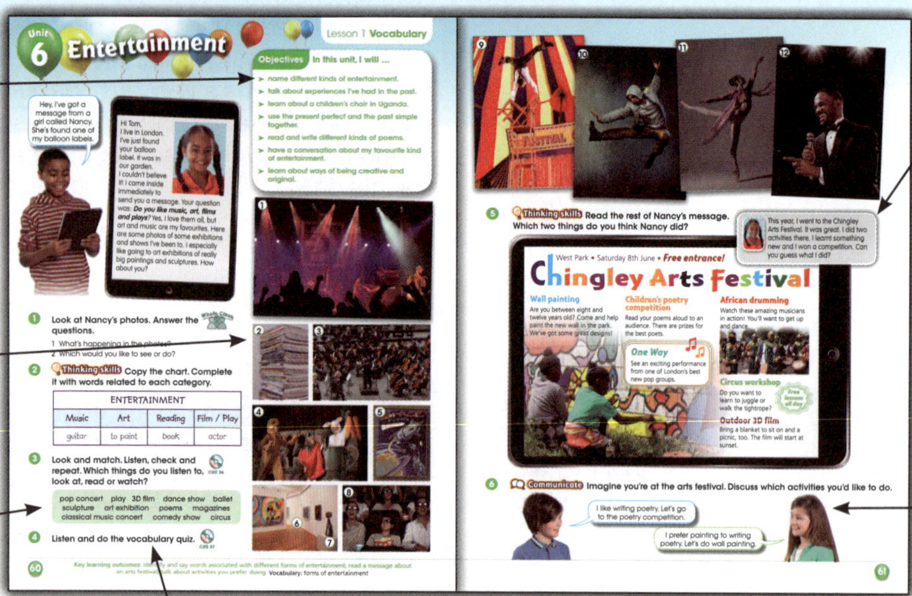


A **real-world reading text** helps contextualise new vocabulary and develop reading skills.

The pupils use a recycled structure to do a **personalised speaking task** in pairs.

A definitions **vocabulary quiz** reinforces understanding of the new vocabulary and develops listening skills.

Fun, game-like activities **motivate the pupils to write** the new vocabulary items.

The pupils **practise reading and writing** definitions of the new vocabulary.

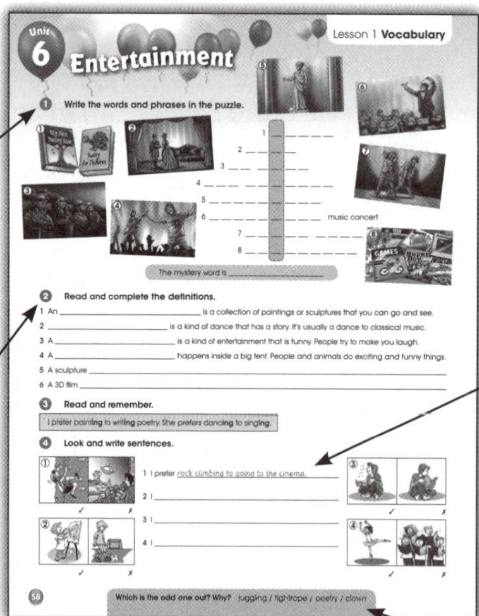


The pupils **review** a language structure and use it in a **personalised writing task**.

An odd-one-out activity on each Activity Book page allows children to have fun while developing **critical thinking skills**.

## Digital resources

**Teacher's Digital:** Don't forget you can teach these lessons using the Teacher's App on Navio.

**Pupil's Digital:** Encourage your pupils to use the Pupil's App on Navio to practise the vocabulary from these lessons.

Powered By NAVIO

## Lessons 2 and 3

A short text-message exchange places **grammar in a fun and familiar context**.

The **Grammar wall** highlights language patterns.

**Think about grammar** encourages the pupils to reflect on language.

The pupils work in pairs to do a **communicative speaking task** using the new grammar.

**Thinking skills** activities invite the pupils to activate previous knowledge before reading an exciting **factual** or **fictional** story with a **cultural** focus.

The story reinforces language introduced in Lessons 1 and 2 and previews language from Lesson 4.

Attractive and age-appropriate artwork and an exciting audio recording support the pupils' understanding of the story.

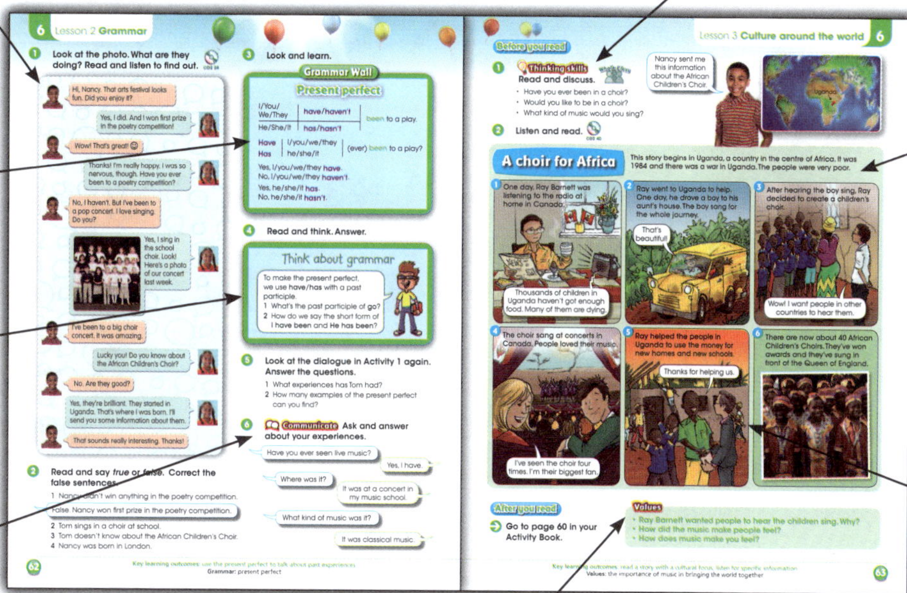


The *Give Me Five!* **values** section encourages the pupils to reflect on the story and relate a personal, social or civic value to their own lives.

A varied range of activities give the pupils **practice in manipulating** the **form** of the new grammar.

Understanding of the content is consolidated through a listening activity type found in the ***Cambridge English Key for Schools Test***.

Activities check the pupils' understanding of the story.

**Comprehension is reinforced** through a listening activity.

The pupils are encouraged to give a **personal response** to the story.

A fun and motivating investigation task encourages pupils to develop their **digital skills**.

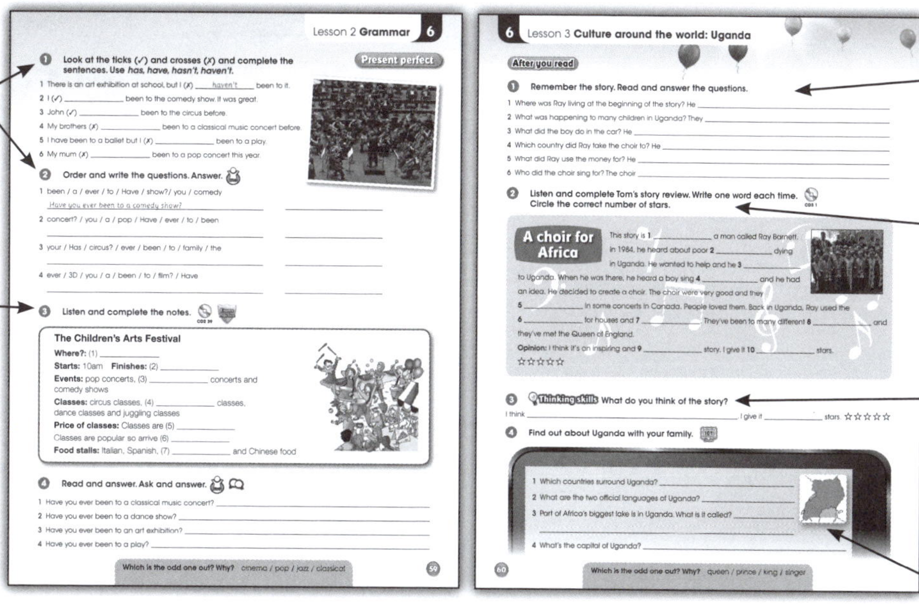


## Digital resources

**Teacher's Digital:** Don't forget you can teach this lesson using the Teacher's App on Navio.

**Pupil's Digital:** Encourage your pupils to use the Pupil's App on Navio to practise the vocabulary from these lessons.

Powered By NAVIO

# Using the Pupil's Book and Activity Book

## Lessons 4 and 5

The pupils listen, read and act out a short dialogue which **contextualises new language**.

Between eight and ten new items of vocabulary are introduced and practised using **pictures** and **photos**.

The **Grammar wall** encourages the pupils to think analytically about new language.

**Oral fluency** is developed through practice of connected speech, stress, rhythm and intonation.

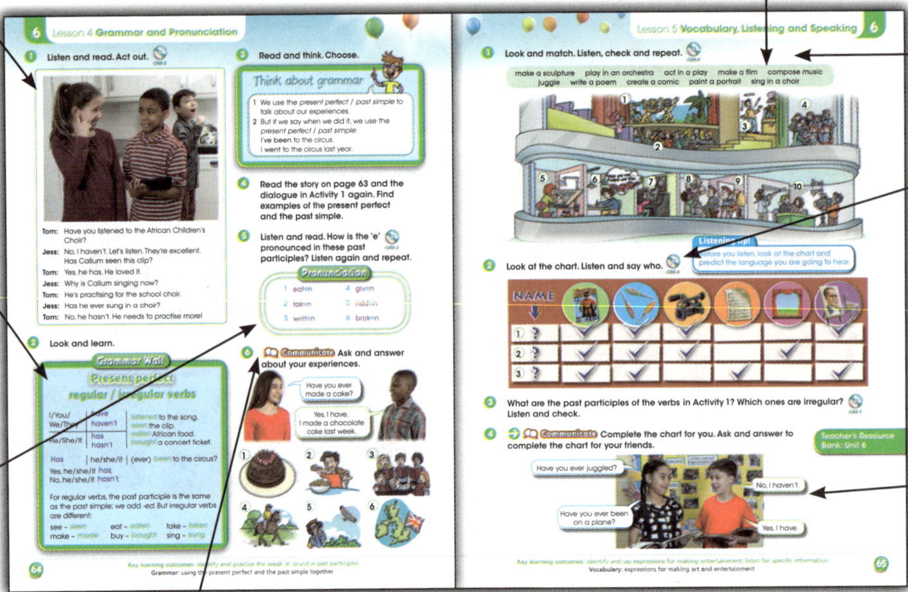


A listening task **prepares pupils for a communicative game**. The pupils listen for global and then specific comprehension.

The pupils play a communicative game in pairs. Each pupil has different information, providing the pupils with a genuine reason for speaking. The supporting material for these types of activities can be found on the Teacher's Resource Bank.

Communication icons indicate when the pupils have the opportunity to practise speaking in pairs. These activities build confidence and ensure full participation.

Reading and writing activities are **carefully staged** to build the pupils' confidence and ensure success.

Activities help consolidate and practise **pronunciation**.

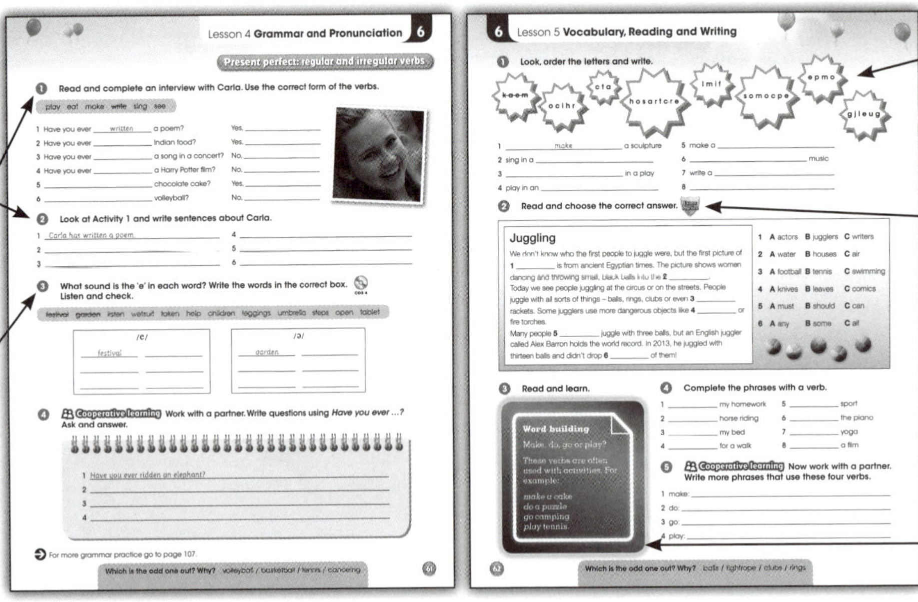


Activities encourage the pupils to recognise and practise the Lesson 5 vocabulary.

Understanding of the content is consolidated through a reading and writing activity type found in the ***Cambridge English Key for Schools Test***.

The **Word building** section introduces and practises strategies for developing, recording and remembering vocabulary.

## Digital resources

**Teacher's Digital:** Don't forget you can teach these lessons using the Teacher's App on Navio.

**Pupil's Digital:** Encourage your pupils to use the Pupil's App on Navio to practise the vocabulary from these lessons.

Powered By NAVIO

## Lessons 6 and 7

The pupils are introduced to a wide **range of reading text types**. These are selected to **reflect the interests and experiences** of the age group and have an **authentic appearance** that will appeal to learners.

A variety of tasks help the pupils to understand the **purpose of a text**, **the intended audience** or what is **appropriate content**.

The **Before you read** activities help prepare the pupils to read. These include activating pupils' existing knowledge, exploiting visuals, asking questions to raise interest and making predictions.

The pupils are given the opportunity to communicate information and **express ideas**, **opinions**, **feelings and interpretations** of the text.

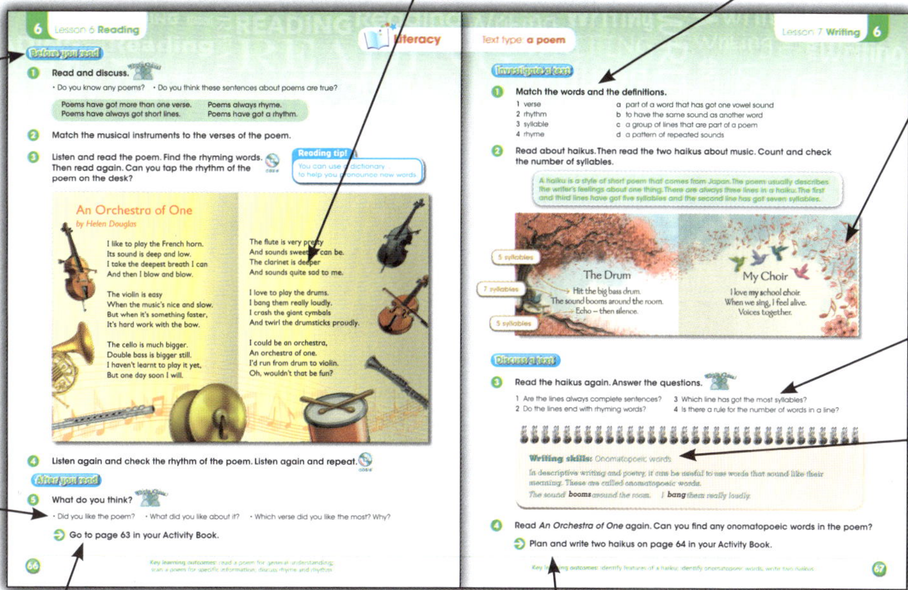


A shorter text provides a **writing model** for the pupils to follow.

**Guided questions** help the pupils **identify key text features** such as titles and captions.

The **Writing skills** section highlights a discrete writing skill such as time connectors.

The pupils are directed to the **After you read activities** in the Activity Book.

The pupils are directed to the Activity Book to prepare their piece of writing.

A range of activities reinforce and check the pupils' understanding of the literacy text.

Reading skills such as **skimming** and **scanning** are actively developed.

Understanding of the content is consolidated through a listening activity.

A variety of **enjoyable activities** allows the pupils to respond to the text in a personal and creative way.

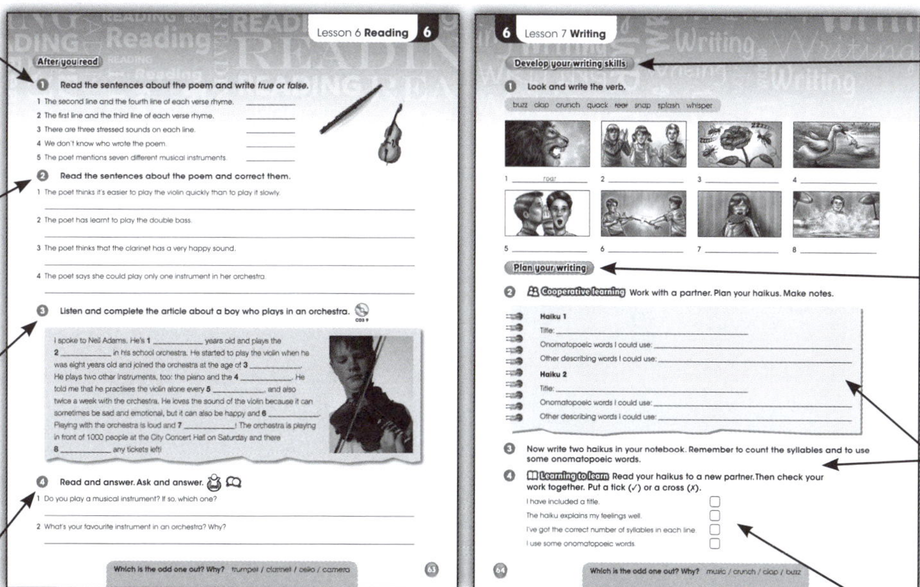


The pupils have the opportunity to practise and consolidate a discrete writing skill such as time connectors, adverbs of manner or the use of direct speech.

The pupils **work with a partner** to **plan**, **draft** and **revise** their writing.

**Step-by-step instructions** provide the pupils with plenty of support in the planning stage.

The pupils **share their work** with another student and use **self-assessment criteria** to check their work.

## Digital resources

**Teacher's Digital:** Don't forget you can teach this lesson using the Teacher's App on Navio.

**Pupil's Digital:** Encourage your pupils to use the Pupil's App on Navio to practise the vocabulary from these lessons.

Powered By NAVIO

# Using the Pupil's Book and Activity Book

## Lesson 8, Review and Video and 21st Century Skills

There is a focus on the speaking skills needed for **external exams success** or real-life needs.

The pupils learn to communicate in different situations working on individual **presentation skills**, **conversation skills** or **cooperative speaking** tasks.

The pupils are encouraged to **reflect** upon their learning based on the **objectives** set at the beginning of the unit.

The pupils are directed to the Song Bank at the back of the Pupil's Book in Units 1, 3, 4, 6, 7 and 9.

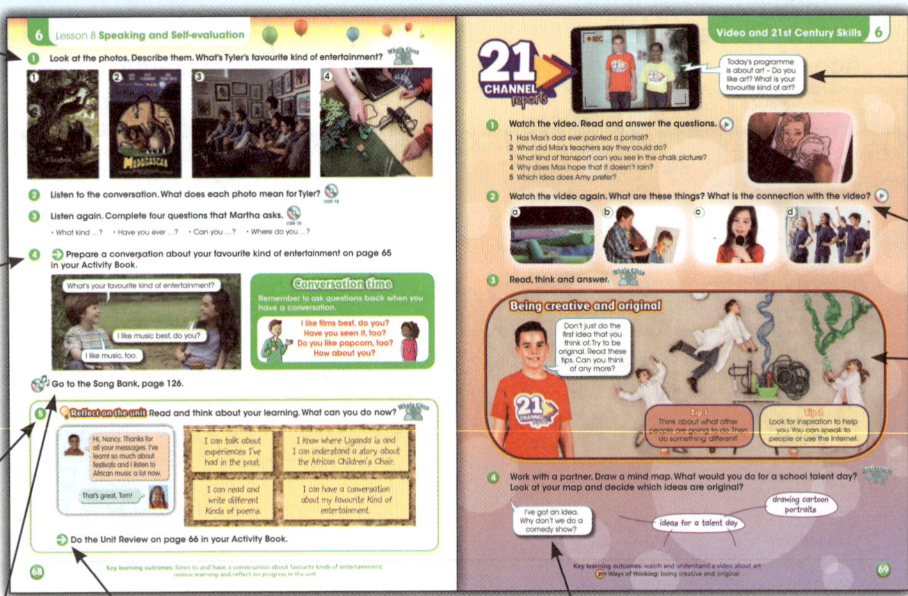

The children introduce the video lesson and spark the pupils' interest in a wide range of topics.

The pupils watch an engaging **video** related to the topic of the unit and 21st Century Skills.

Encouraging the pupils to be creative and original is a good way to practise **21st Century Skills**. Pupils are fostered to reflect on a different skill in each unit.

The pupils are directed to the Activity Book to do the **Unit Review**.

Pupils are set fascinating tasks to promote the skills needed in the modern world.

A **framework** helps the pupils organise their ideas and select language for the speaking task.

The pupils are encouraged to organise their thoughts and ideas by making notes to **prepare a conversation** about a different topic in every unit.

The pupils reflect on their learning and set a **personal learning objective for the next unit**.

The pupils complete a **listening task** related to a 21st Century Skill.

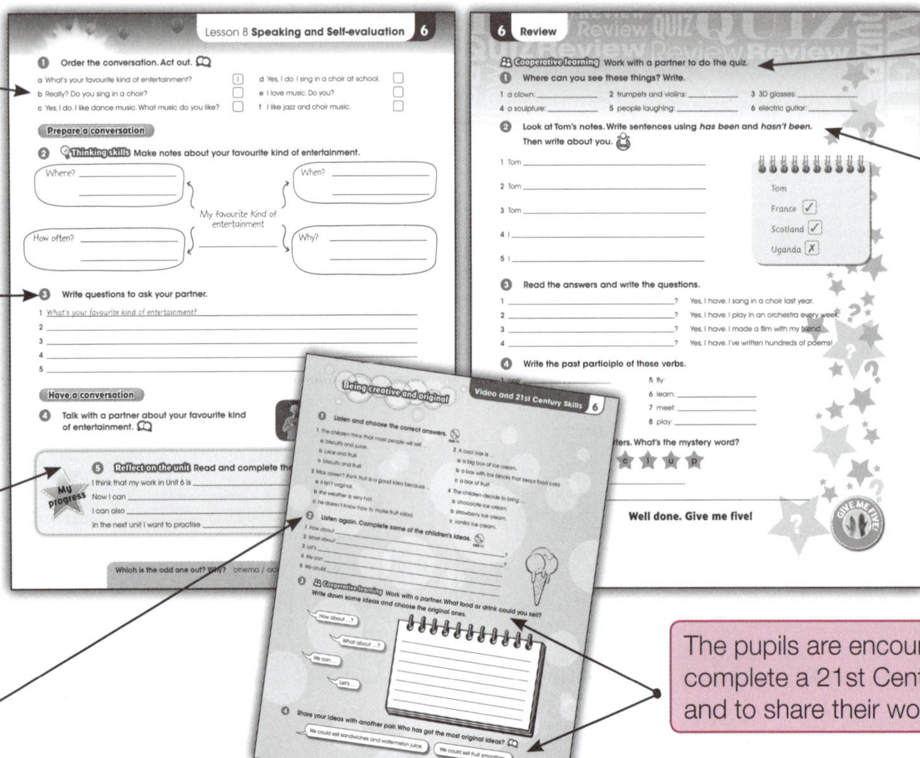

The pupils **work cooperatively** to check their learning.

A full page review **checks and reinforces** all of the unit vocabulary and grammar.

The pupils are encouraged to complete a 21st Century Skills task and to share their work with a partner.

## Digital resources

**Teacher's Digital:** Don't forget you can teach these lessons using the Teacher's App on Navio.

**Pupil's Digital:** Encourage your pupils to use the Pupil's App on Navio to practise the vocabulary from these lessons.

Powered By NAVIO

# Using the projects

*Give Me Five! 5* provides three fun and highly doable **projects**. A healthy life digital poster (Term 1), A film script (Term 2) and An eco tourist attraction (Term 3). These provide an opportunity for the pupils to **work cooperatively** in a structured way, building autonomy and promoting creativity.

The pupils have the opportunity to **share existing knowledge** about the topic.

A group investigation task develops the pupils' listening and **note-taking** skills.

**Project tips** help develop research and presentation and digital skills.

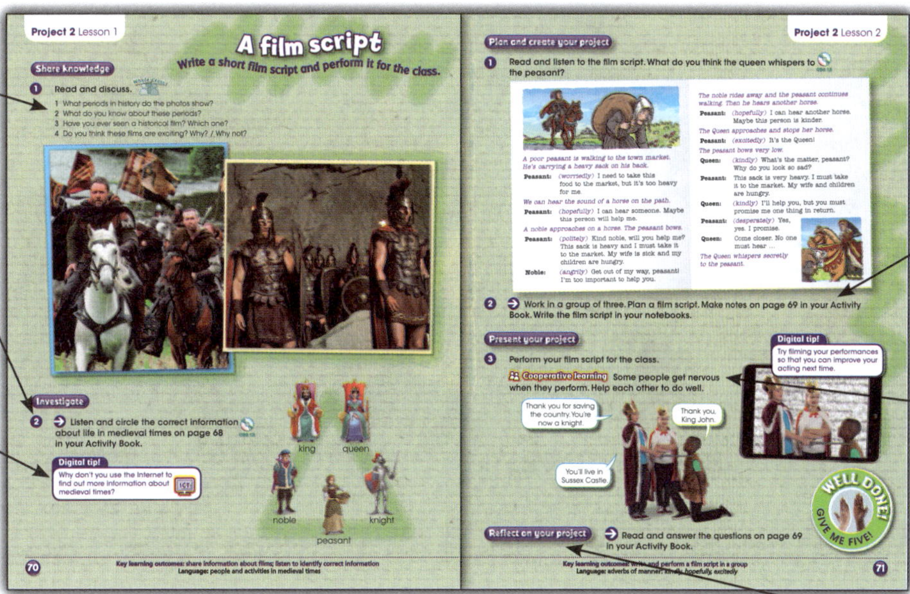


The pupils have an opportunity to work together to **plan and create** their project. Working together encourages the pupils to **talk meaningfully** about the task.

Tasks create **positive interdependence**. Each member's contribution is essential in order to complete the group's task.

The pupils have the opportunity to **reflect on what they have learnt** and their final piece of work.

The pupils develop their listening and **note-taking** skills.

The pupils also prepare their **investigation task** in the Activity Book.

**Thinking skills** are developed by prompting the students to reflect about their findings and give an opinion.

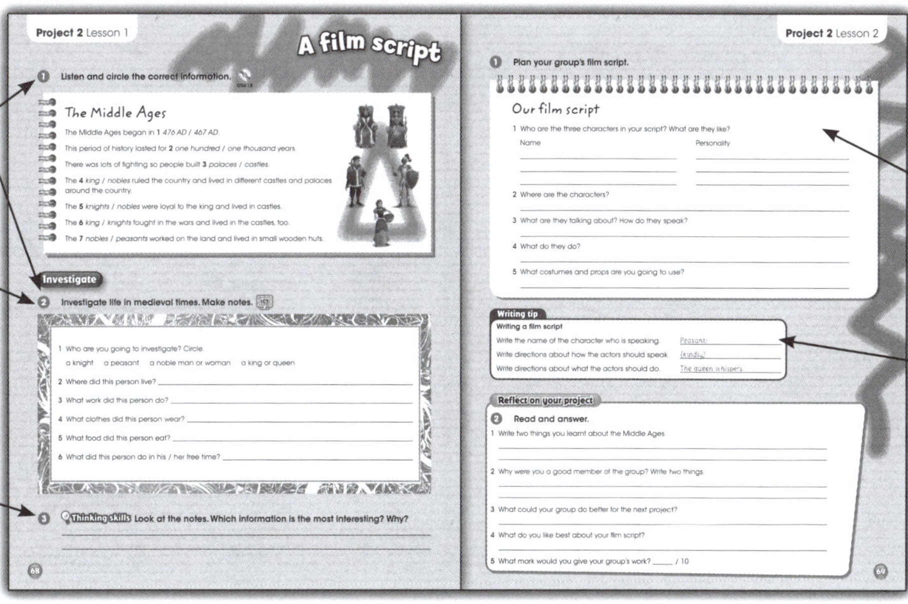


The pupils go to the Activity Book to **record their decisions** for the group task.

**The writing tip** supports and helps the pupils to organise their thoughts and ideas in logical manner. It also supports the development of discrete writing skills across the units.

## Digital resources

**Teacher's Digital:** Don't forget you can teach this lesson using the Teacher's App on Navio.

**Pupil's Digital:** Encourage your pupils to use the Pupil's App on Navio to practise the vocabulary from these lessons.

Powered By NAVIO

# Using the Exams Practice

The **Cambridge Exams Practice** section at the back of both the Pupil's Book and Activity Book introduces the pupils to the activity types found in the different parts of the three papers of the ***Cambridge English Key for Schools Tests***: Listening, Reading and Writing and Speaking.

The nine Cambridge Exams Practice pages at the back of the Pupil's Book will help the pupils to **develop the necessary skills** to do the Reading and Writing papers.

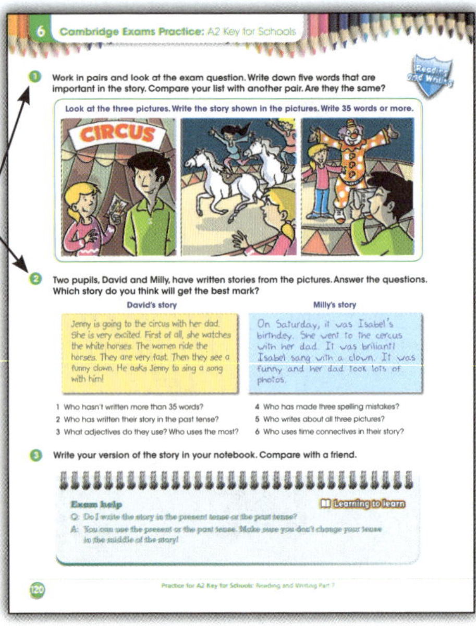
Cambridge Exams Practice: A2 Key for Schools

1 Work in pairs and look at the exam question. Write down five words that are important in the story. Compare your list with another pair. Are they the same?

Look at the three pictures. Write the story shown in the pictures. Write 35 words or more.

2 Two pupils, David and Milly, have written stories from the pictures. Answer the questions. Which story do you think will get the best mark?

3 Write your version of the story in your notebook. Compare with a friend.

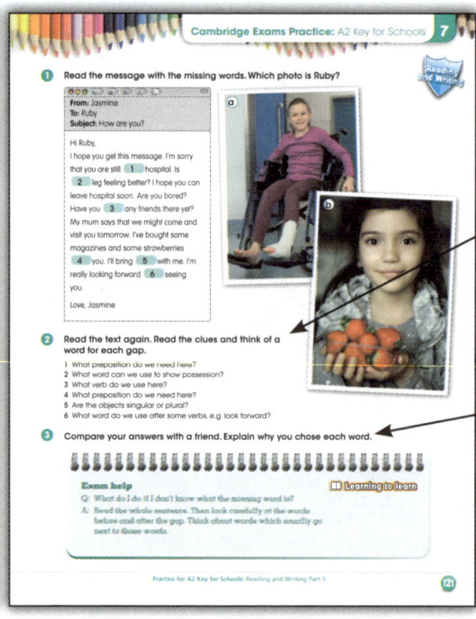
Cambridge Exams Practice: A2 Key for Schools

1 Read the message with the missing words. Which photo is Ruby?

2 Read the text again. Read the clues and think of a word for each gap.

3 Compare your answers with a friend. Explain why you chose each word.

The pupils practise simple and effective **reading strategies** such as guessing the meaning of words or reading the clues to think of words.

An **Exam help** section supports the pupils by providing answers to common questions and concerns.

For further practice, watch the **Cambridge Exams Video** which you can find in the Teacher's Resource Bank.

The nine Cambridge Exams Practice pages at the back of the Activity Book will help the pupils to **develop the necessary skills** to do the Listening and Reading and Writing papers.

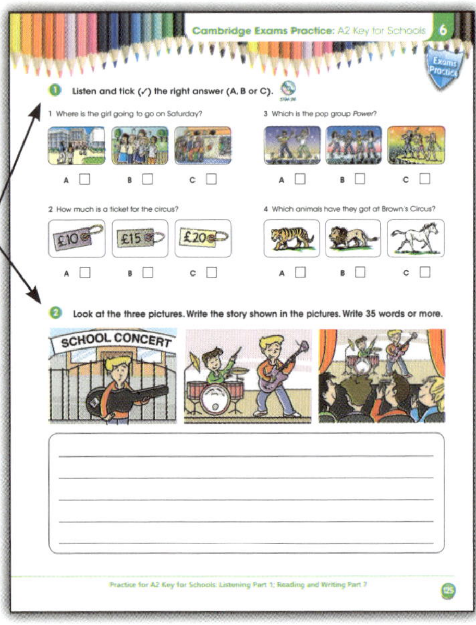
Cambridge Exams Practice: A2 Key for Schools

1 Listen and tick (✓) the right answer (A, B or C).

2 Look at the three pictures. Write the story shown in the pictures. Write 35 words or more.

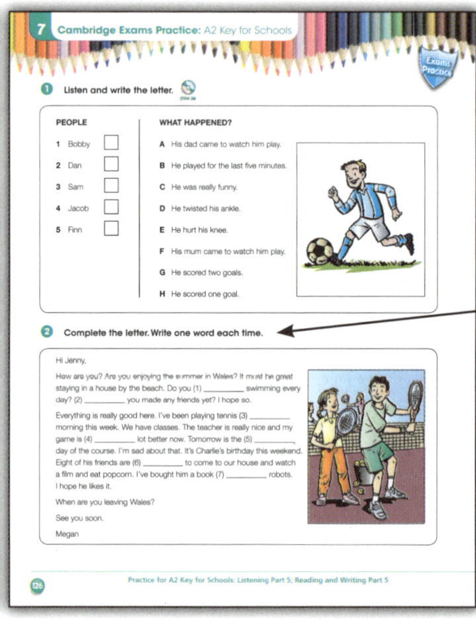
Cambridge Exams Practice: A2 Key for Schools

1 Listen and write the letter.

2 Complete the letter. Write one word each time.

Pupils are encouraged to develop their reading and writing skills by practising activities found in the Reading and Writing papers.

## Digital resources

**Teacher's Digital:** Don't forget you can teach these lessons using the Teacher's App on Navio.

**Pupil's Digital:** Encourage your pupils to use the Pupil's App on Navio to practise the vocabulary from these lessons.

Powered By NAVIO

Exams Practice

# *Give Me Five! 5* and the external exams

*Give Me Five! 5* provides a wide range of material to support teachers who are preparing their pupils for the ***Cambridge English Key for Schools Test***. Reading, writing and listening activity types found in the ***Cambridge English Key for Schools Test*** are integrated into the material and both the Pupil's Book and the Activity Book end with a section full of Cambridge Exams Practice lessons. This material is adapted to match the linguistic and cognitive level of the pupils and language is systematically extended as the course progresses.

There is also the **External Exams Resources** which contain videos of children doing speaking practice, and provide detailed Teacher's Notes on how to exploit these videos in the classroom. The resources, which are part of the Teacher's Resource Bank, also include additional External exams practice material and practice tests for both the Cambridge English Key for Schools and the Trinity Graded Exam in Spoken English (Elementary Stage, Grade 6), and a set of Trinity Exams Practice cards.

## Trinity Exams Practice cards

The **Trinity Exams Practice cards** are a set of downloadable and photocopiable cards. They can be used to build the pupils' confidence in asking and answering questions. On each card is a question based on the ***Trinity Graded Exam in Spoken English*** syllabus. These introduce questions from the Elementary Stage (Grade 6) and recycle questions from earlier grades. These cards should be printed out, laminated if possible and filed by unit. They can then be used during the Starting the lesson stage which systematically recycles language, transferring it to the pupils' long-term memory. For the Trinity Exams Practice cards routine, the teacher selects several cards from previous units. The teacher should choose a different set of cards for each lesson, and tricky questions and recent topics should be revisited more frequently. The teacher then uses the cards to practise asking and answering questions by doing one of the following suggested activities.

## Trinity Exams Practice cards activity bank

***1 Ask and answer in pairs***

Ask the class to get into pairs. Then hold up one of the selected Trinity Exams Practice cards and ask the question. Invite a pupil to answer and repeat their answer for the class. The pupils then ask and answer the same question with their partner. Repeat the procedure with other cards.

***2 Three-step interview***

Follow the procedure for activity 1. When the pupils have asked and answered all the questions on the Trinity Exams Practice cards, ask them to get into different pairs. They should then share information about their first partner's responses.

***3 Moving questions***

Select eight Trinity Exams Practice cards and stick them on the board, writing a number (1–8) above each one. Organise the class into small groups of three or four. One pupil from each group should come to the board and read and memorise the first question. They should then return to the group and ask the question. Once everyone in the group has answered, a second pupil should repeat the procedure, reading and memorising the second question. Continue until all eight questions have been asked and answered.

***4 Mix Pair Share***

The pupils should move silently around the room. When you call out the word **pair**, they should form a pair with the person closest to them. The pupils who haven't found a partner should raise their hands to find each other. Read out a question on one of the Trinity Exams Practice cards and give the pupils a moment to think. The pupils then tell each other their answers. Encourage the pupils to keep talking as long as possible. When all the pupils have finished, repeat the procedure with other cards.

***5 Card swap***

Hand out a Trinity Exams Practice card to each pupil. The pupils should move silently around the room. When you call out the word **pair**, they should form a pair with the person closest to them. The pupils who haven't found a partner should raise their hands to find each other. The pupils should then take turns to ask and answer their question with their partners. When each pair has finished, the pupils should swap cards, find new partners and repeat the procedure. Stress the importance of giving complete answers to the different questions each time.

***6 Card survey***

Hand out a Trinity Exams Practice card to each pupil and explain that they are going to ask their question to six classmates. The pupils should move silently around the room. When you call out the word **pair**, they should form a pair with the person closest to them and ask their question. They may take notes as they listen to their partners' answers. When each pair has finished, the pupils should find new partners and repeat the procedure. At the end of the activity, ask different pupils to report their findings to the rest of the class.

***7 Class question box***

Make extra copies of the Trinity Exams Practice cards that you have practised in class. Laminate these, if possible, and store them in a class question box. Fast finishers can use these cards to review and practise language, working individually to write the answers in their notebooks or asking and answering the questions with a partner.

# Using the Teacher's Book

The Teacher's Notes have a clear, user-friendly design, offering both an **At a Glance Lesson Plan** and a **Detailed Lesson Plan**. These mirror each other, enabling teachers to move between the two lesson plans with ease.

This box clearly shows the learning objectives, key active language and materials required for the lesson. The objectives are mapped to the **Key Competences and Key Learning Outcomes**.

The **At a Glance Lesson Plan** provides a brief overview of all the activities in the lesson, including **Starting** and **Ending the lesson activities** and **Extra activities**. Class audio references are also provided.

**Fast forward icons** indicate the **fast route** through for teachers who have shorter lessons or fewer hours of English.

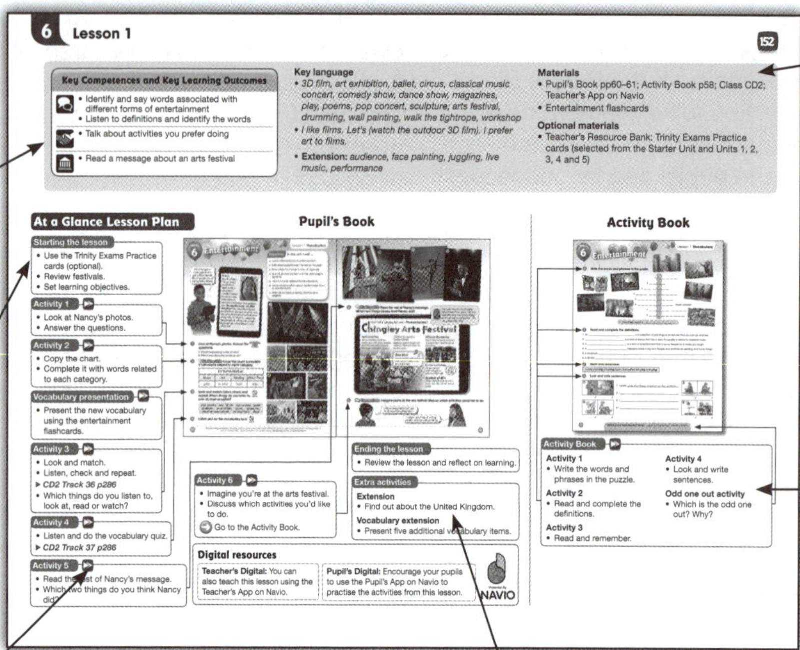


The required and optional materials for each lesson are included in the panel.

An optional **Link to Science** to reinforce learning from the Science curriculum is included in some lessons.

There is also a brief overview of the Activity Book activities.

Each lesson includes optional **Extra activities** to reinforce and extend learning. The **Vocabulary** extension suggests additional vocabulary to extend the lexical set.

The **Detailed Lesson Plan** provides more detailed **step-by-step instructions** for each activity.

The activities for **Starting the lesson** include optional use of the **Trinity Exams Practice cards** and set the learning objectives and outcomes of the lesson.

A clear layout and clear stages make the plan very easy to follow.

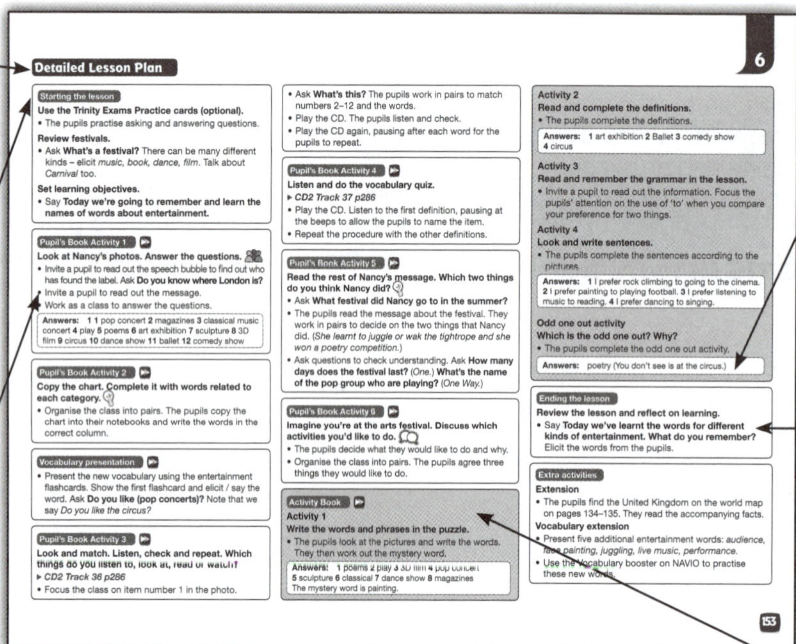


Answers are provided for most Pupil's Book and Activity Book activities.

The activities for **Ending the lesson** include reviewing the lesson and reflecting on learning.

**Activity Book teaching notes** always appear in a shaded box so they can be easily identified. The answers to the Activity Book tasks are also provided.

Unit S

# The school fair

## Unit overview

### Key Competences and Key Learning Outcomes

- Understand and act out a dialogue (Lesson 3)

- Listen and read information about a balloon race (Lesson 4)
- Review countries of the world (Lesson 4)

- Review vocabulary: school subjects, character adjectives, transport, fruit and verbs (Lessons 1 and 2)
- Review the use of relative pronouns (Lesson 2)
- Review superlative adjectives (Lesson 3)
- Review 'must' and 'mustn't' for obligation (Lesson 4)

- Read personal descriptions and write a personal profile (Lesson 1)

- Work in pairs or small groups to practise and reinforce learning (all lessons)

- Learn about school fairs and balloon races (Lessons 2 and 3)

### Vocabulary

**Core vocabulary**
*balloon race, school fair; borrow, cook, drink, eat, sell tickets, sing, throw*

**Other vocabulary**
*air, at the same time, coconut shy, email address, heavy, helium, kilometres, latex, light, organic, paper, rules, winner; burst, degrade, explode, float away, label, land, let go, release, rise, tie the balloons together*

**Recycled vocabulary**
*brother, sister; bananas, chocolate, coconut, eggs, flour, pasta, pineapple, pizza, smoothies, sugar, tomatoes; Art, Geography, History, ICT, Maths, Science; active, confident, friendly, lazy, noisy, quiet, shy, tidy, unfriendly, untidy;* dates; *black / blonde / short / straight hair; guitar, Brazil, China, France, Germany, Italy, Mexico, Portugal, Russia*

### Structures

**Core structures**
*What's (Tom) like? He's (a bit untidy, quiet and shy). What does (Jess) look like? She's got (straight blonde hair and brown eyes). She's (tall). He's / She's the person who's (buying a smoothie and has got straight blonde hair). It's the place where (you can win a coconut). It's a food that's (made from flour, eggs and sugar). It's something which (you use to take photos). You mustn't tie the balloons together. The balloons must be made of latex.*

**Other structures**
*There's going to be a balloon race. What's your favourite item of clothing? What do you like doing in your free time? Where do you live? What interesting things can you see there? How often do you use a computer? Which wild animals can you see in your country? Do you like music, art, films and plays? How do you help others? How do you look after the environment? What are your favourite natural places?*

### Thinking skills

Hypothesising (Lesson 1); Finding information (Lesson 1); Matching words and pictures (Lessons 1 and 2); Ordering information (Lesson 3); Analysing and applying rules (Lesson 4); Logical thinking (Lesson 4); Reflecting on learning (Lesson 4)

### Cooperative learning

Working together (Lessons 1–4); Collaborating (Lessons 1–4); Checking learning (Lessons 1–4); Participating (Lessons 1–4); Helping and encouraging (Lessons 1–4); Reflecting and setting goals (Lesson 1–4)

### Key Competences and Key Learning Outcomes

- Review vocabulary: school subjects and character adjectives
- Read personal descriptions and find information
- Write a personal profile
- Ask and answer questions about the course characters

### Key language

- *chocolate, eggs, pasta, pizza, smoothies, tomatoes; Art, Geography, History, ICT, Maths, Science; active, confident, friendly, lazy, noisy, quiet, shy, tidy, unfriendly, untidy; brown / black / blonde / short hair; brother, sister, school fair;* dates
- *What's (Tom) like? He's (a bit untidy, quiet and a bit shy). What does (Jess) look like? She's got (straight blonde hair and brown eyes). She's tall.*

### Materials

- Pupil's Book pp4–5; Activity Book p2; Class CD1; Teacher's App on Navio

## At a Glance Lesson Plan

### Pupil's Book

**Starting the lesson**

- Greet the class.
- Set learning objectives.

**Activity 1**

- Look at the photos.
- What are the people doing?
- Does your school have a fair?

**Activity 2**

- Read the profiles for Callum, Jess and Tom.
- Who's most like you?

**Activity 3**

- Listen, answer and check.

▶ ***CD1 Track 1 p275***

**Activity 4**

- Ask and answer.

Go to the Activity Book.

**Ending the lesson**

- Review the lesson and reflect on learning.

**Extra activity**

**Extension**

- Write a famous person's profile.

### Digital resources

**Teacher's Digital:** You can also teach this lesson using the Teacher's App on Navio.

**Pupil's Digital:** Encourage your pupils to use the Pupil's App on Navio to practise the activities from this lesson.

Powered By NAVIO

### Activity Book

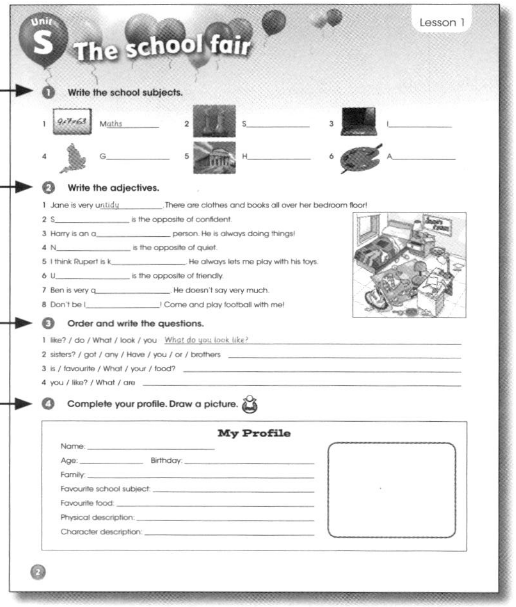

**Activity Book**

**Activity 1**

- Write the school subjects.

**Activity 2**

- Write the adjectives.

**Activity 3**

- Order and write the questions.

**Activity 4**

- Complete your profile. Draw a picture.

# Detailed Lesson Plan

## Starting the lesson

**Greet the class**

- Introduce yourself and ask the pupils to tell you their names.

**Set learning objectives.**

- Say **Today we're going to start our new English book. We're going to meet the main characters in the book and we're going to write about ourselves too.**

## Pupil's Book Activity 1

**Look at the photos. What are the people doing? Does your school have a fair?**

- (Books open.) Ask the pupils to look at the photos. Ask **What's happening?** (*It's a school fair.*) Ask them to look at the photos for one minute and try to remember as much as possible.
- (Books closed.) Ask **What are the people doing? Can you remember? What objects can you remember?**
- (Books open.) The pupils check their answers.
- Ask **Does our school have a fair?** If it does, ask the pupils to describe what happens.

## Pupil's Book Activity 2

**Read the profiles for Callum, Jess and Tom. Who's most like you?**

- Ask the pupils to look at the profiles for Callum, Jess and Tom. Ask them to find each child in the main photos. Ask **What's Tom / Callum / Jess doing?**
- Invite individual pupils to read each profile to the class. Check understanding of some of the words with the class. Ask **What's the opposite of 'confident'? Can you find (smoothies) in the photo?**

## Pupil's Book Activity 3

**Listen, answer and check.**

▶ ***CD1 Track 1 p275***

- Ask the pupils to look at the profiles for Callum, Jess and Tom. Ask **How old is Callum? When's Jess's birthday?**
- Tell the pupils that they are going to hear five more questions. Play the CD. Stop after the beep and ask a pupil the answer. Then play the answer. Repeat with the other questions.

## Pupil's Book Activity 4

**Ask and answer.**

- Invite the pupils to read the speech bubbles.
- Ask the pupils to remember the information in the profiles.
- (Books closed.) In pairs, the pupils ask questions about Tom, Callum and Jess and see how much they can remember.

## Activity Book

### Activity 1

**Write the school subjects.**

- In pairs, ask the pupils to name as many school subjects as they can. Remind the pupils that English school subjects are divided differently to those in Spain. Ask **Can anyone think of ten subjects?**
- Check the answers with the class orally.
- The pupils complete the activity individually.

**Answers:** **1** Maths **2** Science **3** ICT **4** Geography **5** History **6** Art

### Activity 2

**Write the adjectives.**

- Ask **What are Callum, Jess and Tom like? Can you remember the adjectives they use on their profiles?**
- Check the answers with the class orally.
- The pupils complete the activity individually. Check the answers with the class, asking the pupils to spell the words.

**Answers:** **1** untidy **2** Shy **3** active **4** Noisy **5** kind **6** Unfriendly **7** quiet **8** lazy

### Activity 3

**Order and write the questions.**

- Ask the pupils to order the words to make questions.
- Check the answers with the class. The pupils can also ask the questions to each other as a preparation for the next task.

**Answers:** **1** What do you look like? **2** Have you got any brothers or sisters? **3** What is your favourite food? **4** What are you like?

### Activity 4

**Complete your profile. Draw a picture.**

- The pupils complete their own profiles.
- The pupils can ask about each other in pairs. Encourage them to find two things that make them similar, and two things that make them different.

## Ending the lesson

**Review the lesson and reflect on learning.**

- Say **We've learnt about the new characters of our English course and we have read and written personal profiles.**
- Ask **Which was your favourite activity? Which activity was easy / difficult?**

## Extra activity

**Extension**

- Ask the pupils to imagine a famous person, either living or dead. Ask the pupils for a suggestion and work with them to produce a profile for that person. You will need to imagine many of the answers. Ask **What was his / her favourite school subject? What does he / she look like?**
- Now ask the pupils to do the same for someone else. They should write the profile in their notebooks.
- Invite the pupils to present their profiles to the class.

**Key Competences and Key Learning Outcomes**

- Complete a listening and writing task on definitions
- Review vocabulary: transport, fruit, verbs
- Review and practise the use of relative pronouns
- Personalise ideas about a school fair
- Learn about school fairs

**Key language**

- *bananas, coconut, eggs, flour, pineapple, sugar; borrow, cook, drink, eat, sell tickets, sing, throw; guitar; coconut shy*
- *He's / She's the person who's (buying a smoothie and has got straight blonde hair). It's the place where (you can win a coconut). It's a food that's (made from flour, eggs and sugar). It's something which (you use to take photos).*

**Materials**

- Pupil's Book pp4–5; Activity Book p3; Class CD1; Teacher's App on Navio

## At a Glance Lesson Plan

### Pupil's Book

**Starting the lesson**
- Review vocabulary from Lesson 1.
- Set learning objectives.

**Activity 1**
- Read and find.

**Activity 2**
- Listen and find.
- ▶ *CD1 Track 2 p275*

**Activity 3**
- Think of five things that you would like to have at your school fair.
- Go to the Activity Book.

**Extra activity**

**Reinforcement**
- Play a guessing game.

**Ending the lesson**
- Review the lesson and reflect on learning.

### Activity Book

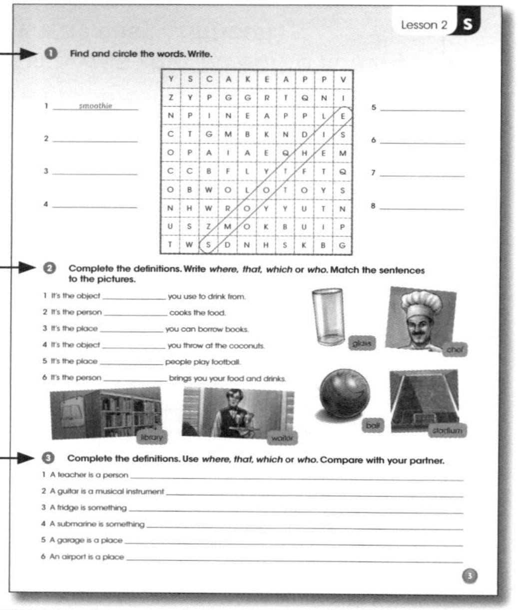

**Activity Book**

**Activity 1**
- Find and circle the words. Write.

**Activity 2**
- Complete the definitions. Write *where, that, which* or *who.*
- Match the sentences to the pictures.

**Activity 3**
- Complete the definitions. Use *where, that, which* or *who.* Compare with your partner.

**Digital resources**

**Teacher's Digital:** You can also teach this lesson using the Teacher's App on Navio.

**Pupil's Digital:** Encourage your pupils to use the Pupil's App on Navio to practise the activities from this lesson.

Powered By NAVIO

# Detailed Lesson Plan

### Starting the lesson

**Review vocabulary from Lesson 1.**

- (Books closed.) Ask questions about the profiles and the photos on Pupil's Book pages 4 and 5. See how much the pupils can remember. Ask **Which child is the oldest? Who likes chocolate? What does Tom look like? What food can you remember? How many people are in the photos?**
- Invite one pupil to open their book and ask more questions.

**Set learning objectives.**

- Say **Today we're going to remember how to use 'who', 'which', 'that' and 'where' in sentences.**

### Pupil's Book Activity 1

**Read and find.**

- Ask the pupils to read the sentences and find all five things in the photos. When they have all finished, they compare answers in pairs.
- Check the answers with the class. Check the meaning of 'coconut'. Ask **What colour is the inside of a coconut?** Explain that the place is called a 'coconut shy'.
- Ask **What is the relative pronoun in sentence 1? Why is it 'who'?** (*Because it is a person*.) Ask the same question for the other sentences. Make it clear to the pupils that 'that' and 'which' can be used interchangeably in these examples.

### Pupil's Book Activity 2

**Listen and find.**

▶ ***CD1 Track 2 p275***

- Tell the pupils that they are now going to hear some more definitions.
- Play the CD. Pause, if necessary, after each definition.
- Play the CD again. Invite different pupils to give the answer. Ask **What is the relative pronoun in the sentence? Why?**

### Pupil's Book Activity 3

**Think of five things that you would like to have at your school fair.**

- Ask about school fairs. Ask **Why do schools have fairs?** (*To raise money for the school or for charity*.) Ask what 'charity' means. (*People do activities to collect money for people who need it more than we do*.) Schools also have fairs to have fun!
- The pupils think of five things they would like to have at a school fair in pairs.
- Ask the pupils to get into groups of four and compare lists. They agree which five things they would like to do. Encourage the pupils to make suggestions using 'Let's …'.
- Ask the groups to share their ideas with the class.

### Activity Book

**Activity 1**

**Find and circle the words. Write.**

- The pupils find, circle and write words from the lesson.
- Check the answers as a class.

**Answers:** **1** smoothie **2** coconut **3** balloon **4** cake **5** pineapple **6** toys **7** books **8** camera

**Activity 2**

**Complete the definitions. Write *where, that, which* or *who*. Match the sentences to the pictures.**

- The pupils complete the sentences with the correct relative pronoun. Then they match them to the pictures.

**Answers:** **1** which / that; glass **2** who; chef **3** where; library **4** which / that; ball **5** where; stadium **6** who; waiter

**Activity 3**

**Complete the definitions. Use *where, that, which* or *who*. Compare with your partner.**

- The pupils write definitions of the words and compare them with a partner.
- Invite the pupils to read their definitions to the class.

### Ending the lesson

**Review the lesson and reflect on learning.**

- Say **We've learnt about relative pronouns and writing definitions.**
- Ask **Which was your favourite activity today? Which activity was easy / difficult?**

### Extra activity

**Reinforcement**

- Ask the pupils to work in pairs. They should write definitions of objects, people or places in the classroom for others to guess. *(It's something which … It's the person who …)* Ask each pair to write three sentences.
- Ask one pair to choose another pair. They each say three sentences and see which pair gets the most correct answers.

## Key Competences and Key Learning Outcomes

- Listen to and act out a conversation about balloon races
- Review superlative adjectives
- Ask and answer personal information questions
- Learn about balloon races

## Key language

- *confident / most confident, far / furthest, fast / fastest, funny / funniest, good / best, hot / hottest; balloon race, email address, float away, label, land, winner*
- *There's going to be a balloon race. What's your favourite item of clothing? What do you like doing in your free time? Where do you live? What interesting things can you see there? How often do you use a computer? Which wild animals can you see in your country? Do you like music, art, films and plays? How do you help others? How do you look after the environment? What are your favourite natural places?*

## Materials

- Pupil's Book p6; Activity Book p4; Class CD1; Teacher's App on Navio

# At a Glance Lesson Plan

## Pupil's Book

### Starting the lesson

- Review relative pronouns.
- Set learning objectives.

### Activity 1

- Listen and read.
- ▶ ***CD1 Track 3 p275***
- Act out.

### Activity 2

- Say the sentences in the correct order.

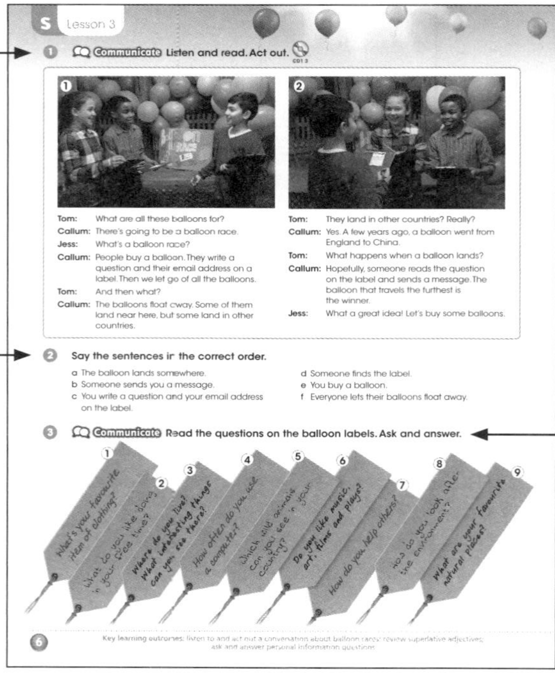

S Lesson 3

1 Communicate Listen and read. Act out.

Tom: What are all these balloons for?
Callum: There's going to be a balloon race.
Jess: What's a balloon race?
Callum: People buy a balloon. They write a question and their email address on a label. Then we let go of all the balloons.
Tom: And then what?
Callum: The balloons float away. Some of them land near here, but some land in other countries.
Tom: They land in other countries? Really?
Callum: Yes. A few years ago, a balloon went from England to China.
Tom: What happens when a balloon lands?
Callum: Hopefully, someone reads the question on the label and sends a message. The balloon that travels the furthest is the winner.
Jess: What a great idea! Let's buy some balloons.

2 Say the sentences in the correct order.

a The balloon lands somewhere.
b Someone sends you a message.
c You write a question and your email address on the label.
d Someone finds the label.
e You buy a balloon.
f Everyone lets their balloons float away.

3 Communicate Read the questions on the balloon labels. Ask and answer.



6

### Activity 3

- Read the questions on the balloon labels.
- Ask and answer.
- Go to the Activity Book.

### Ending the lesson

- Review the lesson and reflect on learning.

### Extra activity

**Extension**

- Write and draw a sequence of balloon race instructions.

## Activity Book

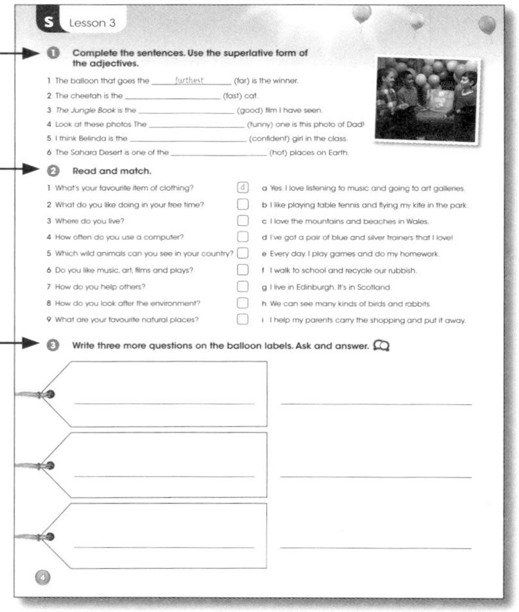

S Lesson 3

1 Complete the sentences. Use the superlative form of the adjectives.

1 The balloon that goes the furthest (far) is the winner.
2 The cheetah is the ______ (fast) cat.
3 The Jungle Book is the ______ (good) film I have seen.
4 Look at these photos. The ______ (funny) one is this photo of Dad!
5 I think Belinda is the ______ (confident) girl in the class.
6 The Sahara Desert is one of the ______ (hot) places on Earth.

2 Read and match.

1 What's your favourite item of clothing? [d]
2 What do you like doing in your free time?
3 Where do you live?
4 How often do you use a computer?
5 Which wild animals can you see in your country?
6 Do you like music, art, films and plays?
7 How do you help others?
8 How do you look after the environment?
9 What are your favourite natural places?

a Yes. I love listening to music and going to art galleries.
b I like playing table tennis and flying my kite in the park.
c I love the mountains and beaches in Wales.
d I've got a pair of blue and silver trainers that I love!
e Every day I play games and do my homework.
f I walk to school and recycle our rubbish.
g I live in Edinburgh. It's in Scotland.
h We can see many kinds of birds and rabbits.
i I help my parents carry the shopping and put it away.

3 Write three more questions on the balloon labels. Ask and answer.

4

### Activity Book

**Activity 1**

- Complete the sentences. Use the superlative form of the adjectives.

**Activity 2**

- Read and match.

**Activity 3**

- Write three more questions on the balloon labels. Ask and answer.

## Digital resources

**Teacher's Digital:** You can also teach this lesson using the Teacher's App on Navio.

**Pupil's Digital:** Encourage your pupils to use the Pupil's App on Navio to practise the activities from this lesson.

Powered By NAVIO

# Detailed Lesson Plan

## Starting the lesson

**Review relative pronouns.**

- Play a point and say game. Say **Point to something that is orange.** Then say **Point to someone who's got long hair.**
- Invite a pupil to say the sentences.
- Then change the sentence to **Say something that is bigger than an aeroplane**. Children put up their hands to answer.
- Invite the pupils to say other sentences using 'say' and 'point'.

**Set learning objectives.**

- Say **Today we're going to learn about balloon races.**

## Pupil's Book Activity 1

**Listen and read. Act out.**

▶ ***CD1 Track 3 p275***

- (Books closed.) Write **Balloon Race** on the board. Ask the pupils to guess what it is. Ask for a lot of detail from the pupils and let them discuss and disagree between themselves. Write a few of the ideas on the board.
- (Books open.) Look at the photos with the pupils. Invite a pupil to describe Callum. Ask another two pupils to describe Jess and Tom.
- Say **Let's listen to see if our ideas about balloon races are correct.** Play the CD.
- Play the CD again if necessary. Ask the pupils if their ideas were correct.
- Put the pupils into groups of three. They read and act out the dialogue. Invite a group to perform it to the class.

## Pupil's Book Activity 2

**Say the sentences in the correct order.**

- Ask the pupils to look at the sentences individually. They put the sentences in the correct order.
- Invite the pupils to share their answers.

**Answers:** e c f a d b

## Pupil's Book Activity 3

**Read the questions on the balloon labels. Ask and answer.**

- Explain that each child writes a question on their balloon label. Say **Here are nine of the balloon labels.**
- Read the questions with the class and explain any difficult words. Ask **What is another way to say 'spare time'? What's the difference between a wild animal and a pet? What's the environment?**
- Ask the pupils to look at the questions for a few minutes and think of some answers.
- The pupils ask and answer the questions about themselves in pairs.
- Check with the class. Invite a pupil to choose another pupil to ask the first question to. That pupil then chooses another pupil to ask the second question to. Continue this chain for all the questions.
- Ask the pupils to decide which is the most interesting question. Ask **Can you think of any more interesting questions to ask?**

## Activity Book

**Activity 1**

**Complete the sentences. Use the superlative form of the adjectives.**

- Ask the pupils to look at the dialogue on page 6 of the Pupil's Book. Ask **Can you find a superlative adjective?** (*Furthest.*)
- To check meaning, ask **Who is the fastest runner in the world?** or **Where is the highest mountain in the world?**
- Remind the pupils that with short adjectives you add '-est' but with longer adjectives you use the word 'most'. For adjectives that end in '-y', you need to remove the '-y' and add '-iest'.
- The pupils complete the sentences.

**Answers:** **1** furthest **2** fastest **3** best **4** funniest **5** most confident **6** hottest

**Activity 2**

**Read and match.**

- The pupils read the questions and answers and match them.
- Check the answers by inviting pairs of pupils to read the questions and answers.

**Answers:** **1** d **2** b **3** g **4** e **5** h **6** a **7** i **8** f **9** c

**Activity 3**

**Write three more questions on the balloon labels. Ask and answer.**

- Individually, the pupils write three more questions.
- The pupils ask a partner their questions and note down the answers they receive.
- Invite some pupils to report back to the class giving the question they wrote and some of the answers they received.

## Ending the lesson

**Review the lesson and reflect on learning.**

- Say **Today we've learnt about balloon races and asked more personal information questions.**
- Ask **Which was your favourite activity today? Which activity was easy / difficult?**

## Extra activity

**Extension**

- Ask the class in pairs or in groups of three to create some visual instructions about how a balloon race works. They can do this as a sequence of pictures with text below.
- Ask the pupils to present their instructions to the class or put some of them up on the wall.

### Key Competences and Key Learning Outcomes

- Read an information text about the science behind balloon races
- Review countries and where they are
- Do a listening and completing task
- Review 'must' and 'mustn't'

### Key language

- *air, at the same time, balloon race, burst, degrade, explode, find / found, gas, heavy, helium, kilometres, label, latex, let go, light, organic, paper, release, rise, rules, tie the balloons together; Brazil, China, France, Germany, Italy, Namibia, Portugal, Russia*
- *You mustn't tie the balloons together. The balloons must be made of latex. There aren't any rules. The balloons usually burst.*

### Materials

- Pupil's Book p7; Activity Book p5; Class CD1; Teacher's App on Navio

## At a Glance Lesson Plan

### Pupil's Book

**Starting the lesson**

- Review countries.
- Set learning objectives.

**Activity 1**

- Listen and read about balloon races.
- ▶ ***CD1 Track 4 p275***
- Find the words in the text with these meanings.

**Activity 2**

- Read and say *true* or *false*.

**Activity 3**

- Name five countries that you think the balloons will go to.

Go to the Activity Book.

**Ending the lesson**

- Review the lesson and reflect on learning.

**Extra activity**

**Reinforcement**

- Play a country guessing game.

### Activity Book

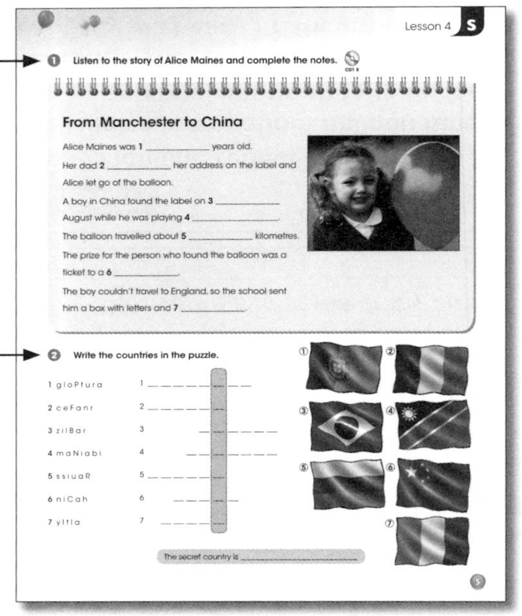

**Activity Book**

**Activity 1**

- Listen to the story of Alice Maines and complete the notes.
- ▶ ***CD1 Track 5 p275***

**Activity 2**

- Write the countries in the puzzle.

### Digital resources

**Teacher's Digital:** You can also teach this lesson using the Teacher's App on Navio.

**Pupil's Digital:** Encourage your pupils to use the Pupil's App on Navio to practise the activities from this lesson.

Powered By NAVIO

# Detailed Lesson Plan

### Starting the lesson

**Review countries.**

- Remind the pupils that the balloons in the balloon race could land in different countries. Ask **How many countries do you know in English?**
- Play a chain game. Say that you are going to go round the class and each pupil has to name a country that has not yet been named. The pupils all stand up and sit down again when they are out. They will be out of the game if they repeat a country. The last pupil standing is the winner.

**Set learning objectives.**

- Say **Today we are going to learn about the science of balloon races and review some countries of the world.**

### Pupil's Book Activity 1

**Listen and read about balloon races. Find the words in the text with these meanings.**

▶ ***CD1 Track 4 p275***

- The pupils look at the photo of the balloons. Ask **What's happening in the photo?** (*The balloons are rising into the air.*) Ask **Why do the balloons rise? Is the material inside the balloons important?** Say that they need to listen and check the answers.
- Play the CD. Ask the pupils to follow the text. Check understanding by repeating the two questions.
- Ask the pupils to look at the text and find the words that are defined above. (*Helium, burst, latex.*)
- Ask **Why are the balloons made of latex and the labels made of paper? How many balloons can there be in a balloon race?**

### Pupil's Book Activity 2

**Read and say *true* or *false*.**

- Invite the pupils to read the sentences. Don't let them say if they think the sentences are true or false yet.
- The pupils do the activity individually.

**Answers:** **1** true **2** true **3** false **4** false **5** true **6** true

### Pupil's Book Activity 3

**Name five countries that you think the balloons will go to.**

- Review some countries by giving the pupils clues. Say **Paris is in this country. People dance the Samba in this country**. Invite some pupils to think of clues for countries too.
- In pairs, ask the pupils to choose five countries where they think the balloons will go to.
- The pupils share their ideas with the class.
- Then ask the pupils to flick through the book to see if they can tell where the balloons go. Ask them to look at the world map on pages 134–135 in the Activity Book and find the five countries that they chose.

### Activity Book

**Activity 1**

**Listen to the story of Alice Maines and complete the notes.**

▶ ***CD1 Track 5 p275***

- Ask the pupils **Can you remember? In 2007, a girl released a balloon in Manchester. Where did it go?** (*China.*) Tell them that they are going to hear some information about this. The pupils need to complete the notes.
- Play the CD. The pupils write the answers. Play the CD again.
- Ask the pupils if they think this is possible. Ask them what some people believe happened. (*The balloon got stuck to a plane.*)

**Answers:** **1** four **2** wrote **3** 25th **4** basketball **5** 9,500 **6** zoo **7** pictures

**Activity 2**

**Write the countries in the puzzle.**

- Discuss using a capital letter. Say that in English a capital letter is also used for the nationality.
- The pupils complete the puzzle and then work out the secret country.

**Answers:** **1** Portugal **2** France **3** Brazil **4** Namibia **5** Russia **6** China **7** Italy The secret country is Germany.

### Ending the lesson

**Review the lesson and reflect on learning.**

- Say **Today we've learnt about the science and rules of balloon races.**
- Ask **Which was your favourite activity today? Which activity was easy / difficult?**

### Extra activity

**Reinforcement**

- Play a country guessing game. Ask the pupils to prepare some facts about a country of their choice. This could be done for homework. They have to write five facts. The first needs to be a difficult clue, the next one a little easier and so on. They can use the Internet to research the facts with their family at home.
- When the pupils bring their facts to class, they will need to read the clues out one by one and see how many clues people need to guess the country. You could do this as a team game with each team having one guess after each clue.

Date: ______________ Unit: __________

**1 What did my pupils learn in this unit?**

**2 How did my pupils work? (✓)**

individually ☐ in pairs ☐ in small groups ☐

in large groups ☐ as a class ☐

**3 Which key competences did my pupils develop? Give a score from 1 to 5 (5 being the highest).**

- Competence in linguistic communication ☐
- Competence in mathematics, science and technology ☐
- Digital competence ☐
- Learning to learn ☐
- Social and civic competences ☐
- Sense of initiative and entrepreneurship ☐
- Cultural awareness and expression ☐

**4 Which lessons / activities were the most successful and why?**

**5 Which lessons / activities did my pupils find the most difficult and why?**

**6 What did I try in the classroom for the first time? How did it go?**

**7 Which resources did I find most useful? (including webpages)**

**8 What could I do differently next time I teach this unit?**

Unit 1

# My clothes

## Unit overview

### Key Competences and Key Learning Outcomes

- Review and learn the names of clothes (Lesson 1)
- Review and contrast the present simple and the present continuous tenses (Lesson 2)
- Learn and practise using 'too' and 'not enough' to say what's wrong (Lesson 4)
- Review and learn adjectives to describe clothing (Lesson 5)
- Learn about and use the linkers 'and', 'also' and 'too' (Lesson 7)
- Talk about your favourite item of clothing (Lesson 8)
- Watch and understand a video about making clothes (Video and 21st Century Skills)

- Learn about different types of materials (Lesson 6)

- Use the Pupil's App on Navio
- Investigate Switzerland (Lesson 3)

- Identify and practise saying the stress in words (Lesson 4)
- Reflect on your own learning (Lesson 8)
- Practise activity types found in the Cambridge Exams: A2 Key for Schools

- Think about the importance of perseverance (Lesson 3)

- Work in pairs and small groups to practise and reinforce learning (all lessons)
- Do a communication task (Lesson 5)
- Design a sports kit (Video and 21st Century Skills)

- Read and understand a story (Lesson 3)
- Learn about Switzerland and a Swiss inventor (Lesson 3)
- Read a magazine article (Lesson 6)
- Write a magazine article (Lesson 7)
- Sing a song (Lesson 8)

### Vocabulary

**Core vocabulary**
*baseball boots, belt, cardigan, jeans, leggings, polo shirt, sweatshirt, tie, tights, top, tracksuit, waistcoat; baggy, flowery, long-sleeved, patterned, plain, short-sleeved, striped, tight*

**Extension vocabulary (optional)**
*blazer, blouse, pyjamas, suit, underwear, uniform; dark blue, light green, gold, silver*

**Other vocabulary**
*bright, casual, dark, fashionable, clear, comfortable, rough, smart, smooth, sticky, uncomfortable, unfair, unfashionable, weak; chemical, cloak, engineer, equipment, hooks, nylon, pocket, seeds, slime, stick, waterproof, zip; creative, fashion designer, interview, research, sew, sewing machine, sketch; smart, spotted*

**Recycled vocabulary**
*clothes, dress, gloves, helmet, T-shirt; big, dirty, dry, happy, healthy, heavy, kind, light, long, noisy, quiet, short, small, soft, strong, tidy, unhappy, unhealthy, unkind, untidy; astronaut, autumn, flowers, fur, invention, inventor, material, natural, watch; cotton, wool*

### Structures

**Core structures**
*I / You / We / They wear (a helmet). He / She / It wears (a helmet). I / You / We / They don't wear (a helmet). He / She / It doesn't wear (a helmet). I am / am not wearing (a hat). He / She / It is / isn't wearing (a helmet). You / We / They are / aren't wearing (a hat). Are you / we / they wearing ( a helmet)? Is he /she / it wearing (a helmet)? Do you / we / they wear (a T-shirt)? Does he / she / it wear (a T-shirt)? The (sweatshirt is) too big. The (sweatshirt isn't) big enough.*

**Recycled structures**
*What's your favourite item of clothing? (Wool) comes from (sheep). I agree with you. I disagree. Let's choose a T-shirt first. What about having some plain shorts?*

### Pronunciation

Stressed syllables in words

### Literacy

**Text type:** a magazine article (information text; writing preparation)
**Reading skills:** scanning
**Writing skills:** adding new information

### Culture ... around the world

The invention of Velcro in Switzerland

### 21st Century Skills

**Ways of thinking:** developing your ideas

### Thinking skills

Categorising (Lesson 1); Problem solving (Lesson 1); Analysing and applying rules (Lessons 2 and 4); Hypothesising (Lesson 3); Logical thinking (Lesson 4); Defining and describing (Lesson 5); Finding information (Lesson 6); Planning, checking and correcting (Lesson 7); Seeing another's point of view (Lesson 8); Reflecting on learning (Lesson 8)

### Cooperative learning

Working together (Lessons 1–8); Collaborating (Lessons 1–8); Checking learning (Lessons 1–8); Peer evaluation and feedback (Lesson 7); Helping and encouraging (Lessons 1–8); Reaching agreement (Lesson 8); Reflecting and setting goals (Lessons 1 and 8)

### Values

The importance of persevering

### Cross-curricular links

**Link to Science**
Properties of materials

**Suggested Arts and Crafts concepts**
Proportion in figure drawing

### Key Competences and Key Learning Outcomes

- Identify and say the names of clothes
- Talk about the clothes you wear
- Read information to solve a problem
- Ask and answer personal questions about clothes

### Key language

- *baseball boots, belt, cardigan, jeans, leggings, polo shirt, sweatshirt, T-shirt, tie, tights, top, tracksuit, waistcoat; bright, casual, dark, fashionable, smart, sporty*
- *What do you usually wear at the weekend? I usually wear (smart clothes). What's your favourite item of clothing? My favourite item of clothing is a (polo shirt). (My friends) prefer / like (casual clothes).*
- **Extension:** *blouse, blazer, suit, uniform, pyjamas, underwear*

### Materials

- Pupil's Book pp8–9; Activity Book p6; Class CD1; Teacher's App on Navio
- Clothes flashcards

### Optional materials

- Teacher's Resource Bank: Trinity Exams Practice cards (selected from the Starter Unit)

## At a Glance Lesson Plan

### Starting the lesson

- Use the Trinity Exam Practice cards (optional).
- Review clothing and appearance.
- Set learning objectives.

### Activity 1

- Look at Nico's photos.
- Answer the questions.

### Activity 2

- Copy the chart.
- Complete it with the clothes you know.

### Vocabulary presentation

- Present the unit vocabulary using the clothes flashcards.

### Activity 3

- Look and match.
- Listen, check and repeat.

▶ *CD1 Track 6 p275*

### Activity 4

- Listen and do the vocabulary quiz.

▶ *CD1 Track 7 p275*

## Pupil's Book

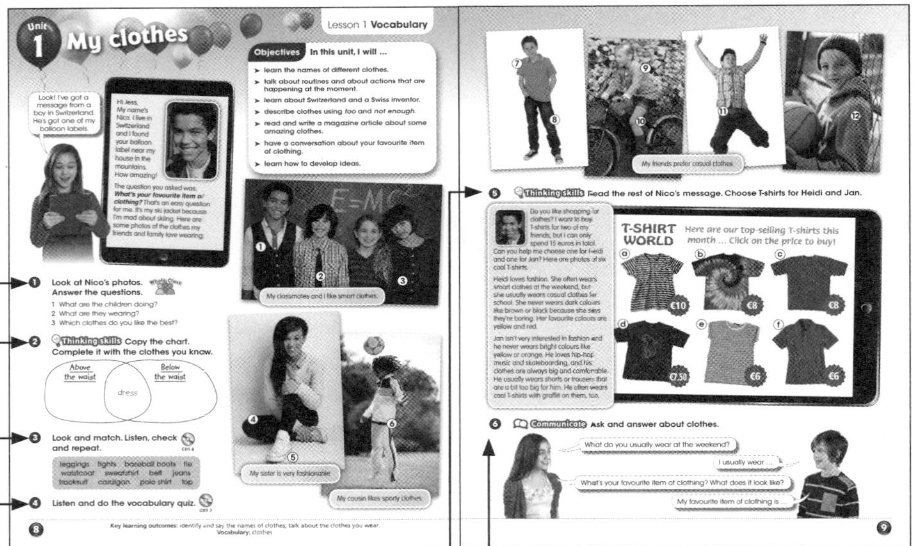

### Activity 5

- Read the rest of Nico's message.
- Choose T-shirts for Heidi and Jan.

### Activity 6

- Ask and answer about clothes.
- Go to the Activity Book.

### Ending the lesson

- Review the lesson and reflect on learning.

### Extra activities

**Extension**

- Find out about Switzerland.
- Present six aditional vocabulary items.

### Digital resources

**Teacher's Digital:** You can also teach this lesson using the Teacher's App on Navio.

**Pupil's Digital:** Encourage your pupils to use the Pupil's App on Navio to practise the activities from this lesson.

Powered By NAVIO

## Activity Book

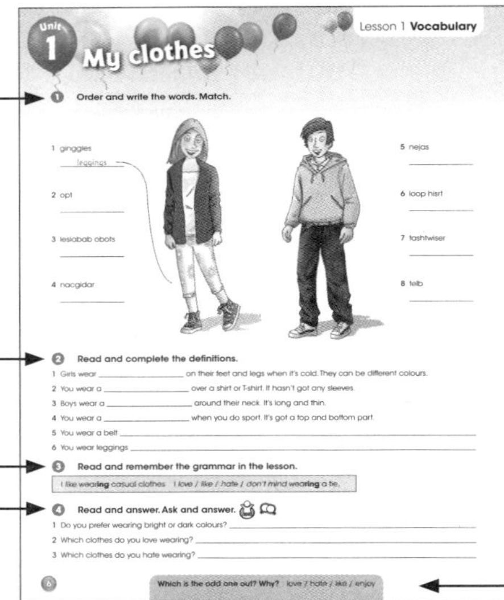

### Activity Book

**Activity 1**
- Order and write the words. Match.

**Activity 2**
- Read and complete the definitions.

**Activity 3**
- Read and remember the grammar in the lesson.

**Activity 4**
- Read and answer. Ask and answer.

**Odd one out activity**
- Which is the odd one out? Why?

# Detailed Lesson Plan

## Starting the lesson

**Use the Trinity Exams Practice cards (optional).**
- The pupils practise asking and answering questions.

**Review clothing and appearance.**
- Say **I'm thinking of a pupil in this room. Who is it?** Describe the pupil's appearance and clothing. Ask the pupils to guess. Repeat the procedure.

**Set learning objectives.**
- Say **Today we're going to remember and learn the names of different clothes.**

## Pupil's Book Activity 1

**Look at Nico's photos. Answer the questions.**
- Invite a pupil to read out the speech bubble to find out who has found the balloon. Ask **Do you know where Switzerland is?**
- Ask a pupil to read out the message. Check understanding.
- Work as a class to answer the questions.

**Answers:** **1** posing for photos, playing sports **2** **1** waistcoat **2** tie **3** cardigan **4** leggings **5** baseball boots **6** tracksuit **7** polo shirt **8** jeans **9** top **10** tights **11** belt **12** sweatshirt

## Pupil's Book Activity 2

**Copy the chart. Complete it with the clothes you know.**
- Copy the Venn diagram onto the board. Check that the class understands how the diagram works.
- The pupils copy the Venn diagram into their notebooks. In pairs, they classify the clothes.

## Vocabulary presentation

- Present the unit vocabulary using the clothes flashcards. Show the first flashcard and elicit / say the word. Ask **Who's wearing a (tie) today? When do you usually wear a (tie)?**
- Invite a pupil to stick the flashcard on the Venn diagram on the board. Repeat with the other flashcards.

## Pupil's Book Activity 3

**Look and match. Listen, check and repeat.**
▶ ***CD1 Track 6 p275***
- Ask the pupils to look at number 1 in the photo. Ask **Which item of clothing is this?** The pupils work in pairs to match numbers 2–12 and the clothes words.
- Play the CD. The pupils listen and check.
- Play the CD again, pausing after each word for the pupils to repeat.

## Pupil's Book Activity 4

**Listen and do the vocabulary quiz.**
▶ ***CD1 Track 7 p275***
- Play the CD. Listen to the first definition, pausing at the beep to allow the pupils to name the item. Play the CD to listen to the answer.
- Repeat the procedure with the other definitions.

## Pupil's Book Activity 5

**Read the rest of Nico's message. Choose T-shirts for Heidi and Jan.**
- Check that the pupils understand the task. The pupils read the information about Heidi and Jan and choose the T-shirts.

**Answers:** T-shirts e and d

## Pupil's Book Activity 6

**Ask and answer about clothes.**
- Ask a pupil the first question. Repeat the procedure with other questions, inviting a different pupil to answer each time.
- The pupils ask and answer questions in pairs.

## Activity Book

**Activity 1**

**Order and write the words. Match.**
- The pupils order, write and match the clothes words.

**Answers:** **1** leggings **2** top **3** baseball boots **4** cardigan **5** jeans **6** polo shirt **7** sweatshirt **8** belt

**Activity 2**

**Read and complete the definitions.**
- The pupils complete the definitions.

**Answers:** **1** leggings **2** waistcoat **3** tie **4** tracksuit

**Activity 3**

**Read and remember the grammar in the lesson.**
- Read the information. Focus on the *-ing* form.
- The pupils create sentences with these verbs.

**Activity 4**

**Read and answer. Ask and answer.**
- The pupils write their answers to the questions.
- The pupils ask and answer the questions.

**Odd one out activity**

**Which is the odd one out? Why?**

**Answers:** hate (It expresses dislike.)

## Ending the lesson

**Review the lesson and reflect on learning.**
- Say **Today we've learnt the names of different clothes. What do you remember?**
- Ask **Which was your favourite activity today? Which activity was easy / difficult?**

## Extra activities

**Extension**
- The pupils find Switzerland on the world map on pages 134–135. They read the accompanying facts.

**Vocabulary extension**
- Present six additional clothes items: *blouse*, *blazer, suit, uniform, pyjamas, underwear.*
- Use the Vocabulary Booster on NAVIO to practise these words.

## Key Competences and Key Learning Outcomes

- Listen to and read a dialogue
- Use the present simple and present continuous to talk about things you usually do and things you're doing now
- Ask and answer questions using the present simple and present continuous tenses

- Practise activity types found in the Cambridge Exams: A2 Key for Schools

**Key language**
- *gloves, goggles, helmet, shorts, ski clothes, T-shirt; autumn, ski station*
- *I / You / We / They wear (a helmet). I / You / We / They don't wear (a helmet). He / She / It wears (a helmet). He / She / It doesn't wear (a helmet). Do you / we / they wear (a T-shirt)? Does he / she / it wear (a T-shirt)? I am / am not wearing (a hat). You / We / They are / aren't wearing (a hat). He / She / It is / isn't wearing (a helmet). Are you / we / they wearing (a helmet)? Is he / she / it wearing (a helmet)?*

**Materials**
- Pupil's Book p10; Activity Book p7; Class CD1; Teacher's App on Navio
- Teacher's Resource Bank: Clothes word cards

**Optional materials**
- Teacher's Resource Bank: Trinity Exams Practice cards (selected from the Starter Unit)

## At a Glance Lesson Plan

### Pupil's Book

**Starting the lesson**
- Use the Trinity Exams Practice cards (optional).
- Review clothes.
- Set learning objectives.

**Activity 1**
- Look at the photo.
- Can Nico ski in the autumn?
- Read and listen to find out.
- ▶ *CD1 Track 8 p276*

**Activity 2**
- Read the dialogue again.
- Ask and answer.

**Activity 3**
- Look and learn – Grammar wall

**Activity 4**
- Read and think.
- Answer.

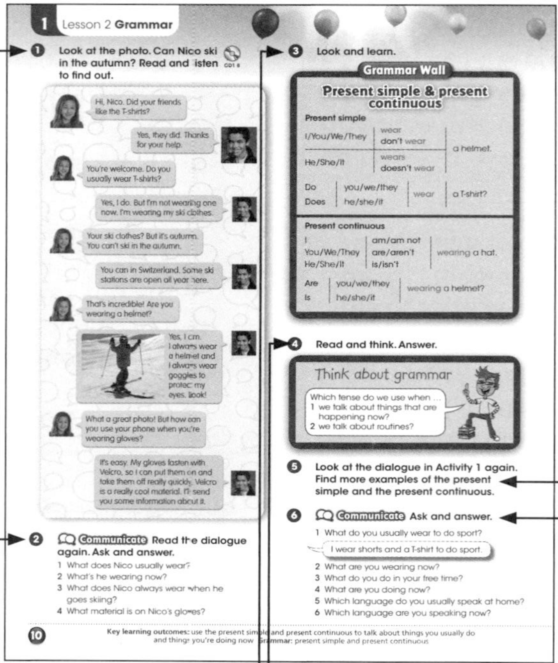


**Activity 5**
- Look at the dialogue in Activity 1 again.
- Find more examples of the present simple and the present continuous.

**Activity 6**
- Ask and answer.
- Go to the Activity Book.

**Ending the lesson**
- Review the lesson and reflect on learning.

**Extra activity**

**Reinforcement**
- Make true and false sentences about your daily routines.

### Digital resources

**Teacher's Digital:** You can also teach this lesson using the Teacher's App on Navio.

**Pupil's Digital:** Encourage your pupils to use the Pupil's App on Navio to practise the activities from this lesson.

Powered By NAVIO

### Activity Book

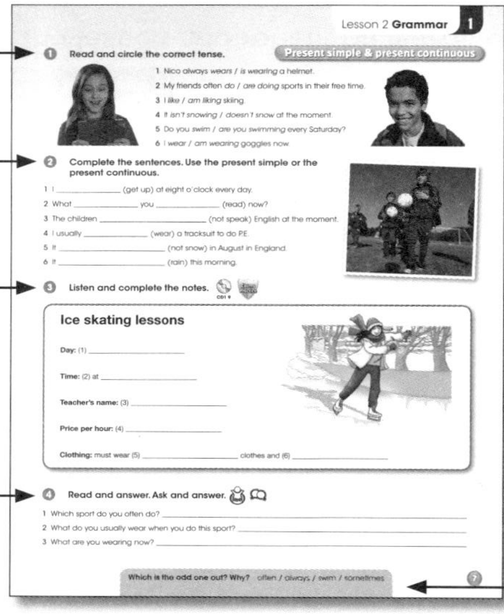


**Activity Book**

**Activity 1**
- Read and circle the correct tense.

**Activity 2**
- Complete the sentences. Use the present simple or the present continuous.

**Activity 3**
- Listen and complete the notes.
- ▶ *CD1 Track 9 p276*

**Activity 4**
- Read and answer. Ask and answer.

**Odd one out activity**
- Which is the odd one out? Why?

# Detailed Lesson Plan

**Starting the lesson**

**Use the Trinity Exams Practice cards (optional).**

- The pupils practise asking and answering questions.

**Review clothes.**

- Play the *Mime the card game* (see p27) with the clothes word cards.

**Set learning objectives.**

- Say **Today we're going to remember how to talk about routines and how to talk about things that are happening at the moment.**

**Pupil's Book Activity 1**

**Look at the photo. Can Nico ski in the autumn? Read and listen to find out.**

▶ *CD1 Track 8 p276*

- Prompt the class to describe what they can see in the photo. Ask **Where's Nico? What's he doing? What's he wearing?**
- Read out the instructions and encourage the pupils to say if they think Nico can ski in the autumn.
- Play the CD. The pupils listen and read the dialogue. (*It is possible to ski all year in some parts of Switzerland.*)

**Pupil's Book Activity 2**

**Read the dialogue again. Ask and answer.**

- The pupils work in pairs to read and answer the questions. They can do this orally or in their notebooks.

**Pupil's Book Activity 3**

**Look and learn – Grammar wall**

- Read the information on the Grammar wall as a class.
- Use questions to encourage the pupils to think about form and identify / remember patterns. Ask **What happens to the verb when we use 'he', 'she' and 'it' in the present simple? Which verb do we add to make the negative? Do we use the verb 'to be' in the present simple or the present continuous? Do we say 'wear' or 'wearing' after the verb 'to be' in the present continuous?**

**Pupil's Book Activity 4**

**Read and think. Answer.**

- Focus the pupils' attention on the Think about grammar box. Read out the sentences as a class. The pupils complete these sentences in their pairs.

**Answers:** **1** present continuous **2** present simple

**Pupil's Book Activity 5**

**Look at the dialogue in Activity 1 again. Find more examples of the present simple and the present continuous.**

- Ask the pupils to find examples of the present simple and the present continuous in the text.
- The pupils share information with the rest of the class.

**Pupil's Book Activity 6**

**Ask and answer.**

- Ask a pupil the first question. Repeat the procedure with the other questions, inviting a different pupil to answer each time.
- The pupils ask and answer questions in pairs.

**Activity Book**

**Activity 1 Read and circle the correct tense.**

- Read out the first sentence. Prompt the class to identify the correct verb. Highlight that the word 'always' is a clue as it tells us that the action is a routine. Then elicit other adverbs of frequency.
- The pupils circle the correct tense in sentences 2–6.

**Answers:** **1** wears **2** do **3** like **4** isn't snowing **5** swim **6** am wearing

**Activity 2 Complete the sentences. Use the present simple or the present continuous.**

- Prompt the class to complete the first sentence.
- The pupils complete the remaining sentences.

**Answers:** **1** get up **2** are/reading **3** aren't speaking **4** wear **5** doesn't snow **6** is raining

**Activity 3**

**Listen and complete the notes.**

▶ *CD1 Track 9 p276*

- Focus the pupils on the picture. Ask them to identify the sport (*ice skating*). Ask **Have you ever tried this sport? What do you need to wear?**
- Ask the class to read the notes. Then play the CD. The pupils listen and follow in their books.
- Play the CD again, pausing after each piece of key information. The pupils say and write the missing information.

**Answers:** **1** Friday **2** 6 o'clock **3** Penny **4** 10 pounds for adults, five pounds for children **5** warm **6** gloves

**Activity 4**

**Read and answer. Ask and answer.**

- Model the activity by asking a pupil the three questions. The pupils then write their own answers.
- The pupils ask and answer questions in pairs.

**Odd one out activity**

**Which is the odd one out? Why?**

- The pupils complete the odd one out activity.

**Answers:** swim (It isn't an adverb of frequency.)

**Ending the lesson**

**Review the lesson and reflect on learning.**

- Say **Today we've learnt how to talk about routines and habits. We've also learnt how to talk about what is happening now.**
- Ask **Which was your favourite activity today? Which activity was easy / difficult?**

**Extra activity**

**Reinforcement**

- Make four statements about your daily routines, using an adverb of frequency each time. Three of the sentences are true and one is false. The pupils listen and guess the false sentence.
- The pupils prepare three true sentences and one false one. They guess the false sentences in pairs.

**Key Competences and Key Learning Outcomes**

- Read a story with a cultural focus
- Listen for specific information
- Use the Internet to investigate Switzerland
- Think about the importance of persevering with difficult tasks
- Learn about a famous Swiss inventor

**Key language**

- *heavy, light, noisy, quiet, rough, smooth, strong, weak; jacket, trousers; astronaut, curious, engineer, flowers, fur, hooks, idea, invent, invention, inventor, material, microscope, nylon, seeds, stick, wild plants, woollen*
- *He's wearing (woollen trousers). This material is too heavy and it isn't pretty enough.*

**Materials**

- Pupil's Book p11; Activity Book p8; Class CD1; Teacher's App on Navio
- Teacher's Resource Bank: Clothes word cards
- Velcro

**Optional materials**

- Teacher's Resource Bank: Trinity Exams Practice cards (selected from the Starter Unit)

## At a Glance Lesson Plan

### Pupil's Book

**Starting the lesson**

- Use the Trinity Exams Practice cards (optional).
- Review clothes.
- Set learning objectives.

**Activity 1: Before you read**

- Read and discuss.

**Activity 2**

- Listen and read.
- ▶ *CD1 Track 10 p276*
- Go to the Activity Book.

**Values**

- Read and discuss.

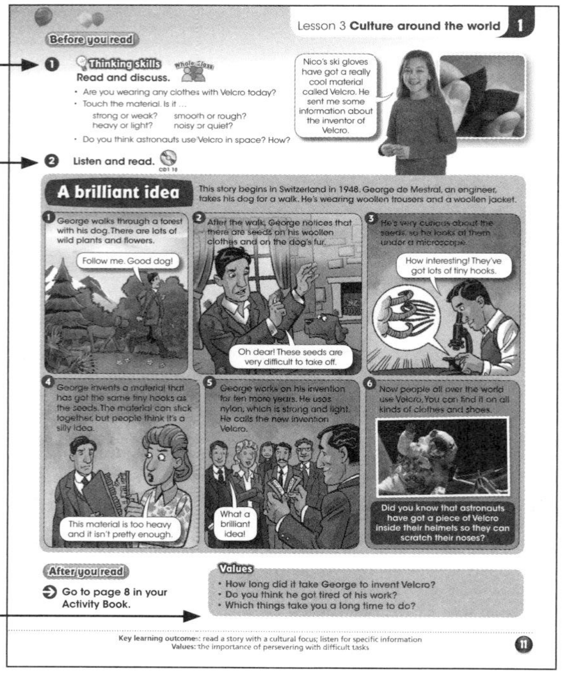


**Ending the lesson**

- Review the lesson and reflect on learning.

**Extra activity**

**Extension**

- Invent different uses for Velcro.

### Activity Book

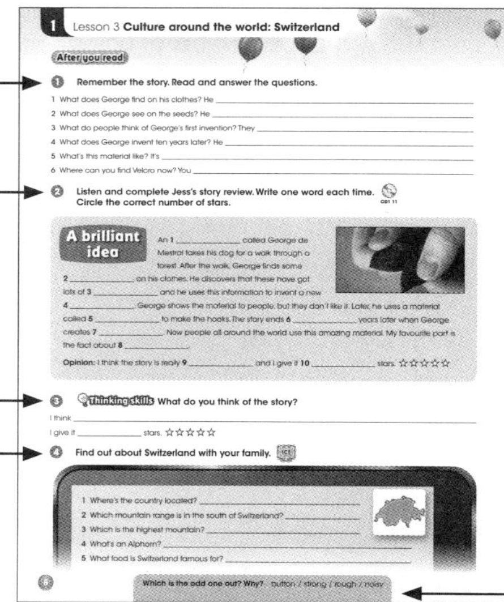


**Activity Book: After you read**

**Activity 1**

- Remember the story. Read and answer the questions.

**Activity 2**

- Listen and complete Jess's story review.
- ▶ *CD1 Track 11 p276*
- Write one word each time. Circle the correct number of stars.

**Activity 3**

- What do you think of the story?

**Activity 4**

- Find out about Switzerland with your family.

**Odd one out activity**

- Which is the odd one out? Why?

**Digital resources**

**Teacher's Digital:** You can also teach this lesson using the Teacher's App on Navio.

**Pupil's Digital:** Encourage your pupils to use the Pupil's App on Navio to practise the activities from this lesson.

Powered By NAVIO

**Starting the lesson**

**Use the Trinity Exams Practice cards (optional).**

- The pupils practise asking and answering questions.

**Review clothes.**

- Hold up the clothes word cards in turn and ask the class to say the words. Highlight any tricky spelling, i.e. double letters, silent letters or alternative spellings. Stick the cards on the board.
- Organise the class into pairs. One pupil should face the board and the other pupil should face away from the board. The pupil facing the board chooses a word for their partner to spell and asks *How do you spell ...?*
- Repeat the procedure several times. Then ask the pupils to swap roles.

**Set learning objectives.**

- Say **Today we're going to read a story from Switzerland.**

**Pupil's Book Activity 1: Before you read**

**Read and discuss.**

- Read the information about Velcro as a class. Encourage the class to touch the Velcro and describe what they can feel.
- Ask **Do you think astronauts use Velcro in space?** Encourage the class to predict and hypothesise about how the material is used.

**Pupil's Book Activity 2**

**Listen and read.**

▶ ***CD1 Track 10 p276***

- Play the CD. The pupils follow in their books. Confirm that astronauts use Velcro to scratch their noses in space.
- Ask questions to check understanding.

**Suggested comprehension questions:**

- Frames 1 and 2: **What sticks on George's clothes?** (*Seeds.*) **Where do the seeds come from?** (*Wild plants and flowers.*)
- Frame 3: **What do the seeds look like?** (*They've got lots of tiny hooks.*)
- Frame 4: **How is George's material similar to the seeds?** (*It has the same tiny hooks.*)
- Frame 5: **How long does he work on his invention?** (*Ten years.*) **What is Velcro like?** (*Strong and light.*)

**Activity Book : After you read**

**Activity 1**

**Remember the story. Read and answer the questions.**

- Read out the first question and invite a pupil to answer it.
- The pupils work on their own or in pairs to read and answer the remaining questions.

**Answers:** **1** finds seeds. **2** sees tiny hooks. **3** think it's a silly idea. **4** invents Velcro. **5** light and strong. **6** can find it on all kinds of clothes and shoes.

**Activity 2**

**Listen and complete Jess's story review. Write one word each time. Circle the correct number of stars.**

▶ ***CD1 Track 11 p276***

- Read out the story review as a class. Ask the pupils to guess the missing words.
- Play the CD without pausing. The pupils should listen and complete as much of the information as possible.
- Play the CD again, pausing after each piece of key information to check the information and spelling. The pupils circle the correct number of stars.

**Answers:** **1** engineer **2** seeds **3** hooks **4** material **5** nylon **6** ten **7** Velcro **8** astronauts **9** interesting **10** five

**Activity 3**

**What do you think of the story?**

- The pupils write their opinion of the story and give a rating.
- Invite the pupils to share their opinions with the rest of the class.

**Activity 4**

**Find out about Switzerland with your family.** ICT

- Read out the questions about Switzerland. Ask **Where can you find out this information?** (*Internet, library, asking friends and family.*) The pupils should complete the activity at home.
- If you prefer to do this activity in the class, connect to a children's website which has information about Switzerland such as: http://kids.nationalgeographic.com (search for 'Switzerland facts and pictures'). Read out the questions. The pupils work as a class to find and write the answers.

**Answers:** **1** It borders with Germany, Italy, France, Austria and Liechtenstein. **2** the Alps **3** Monte Rosa **4** an alpine horn **5** fondue

**Odd one out activity**

**Which is the odd one out? Why?**

- The pupils complete the odd one out activity.

**Answers:** button (It isn't an adjective.)

**Values**

**Read and discuss.**

- The pupils read and discuss the value.
- Encourage the pupils to think about the things they do that require effort and talk about the importance of perseverance.

**Ending the lesson**

**Review the lesson and reflect on learning.**

- Say **Today we've read a story from Switzerland.**
- Ask **Which was your favourite activity today? Which activity was easy / difficult?**

**Extra activity**

**Extension**

- Ask **What does an astronaut use Velcro for?** (*To scratch his / her nose.*) Ask **What other things can we do with Velcro? Let's imagine.** Encourage the class to be as creative as possible with their ideas.

### Key Competences and Key Learning Outcomes

- Act out a short dialogue in pairs
- Learn how to use 'too' and 'not enough' to say what's wrong
- Identify the stress in words and practise saying the words

### Key language

- *big, comfortable, fashionable, long, short, small, uncomfortable, unfashionable; strap, sweatshirt, trousers, watch*
- *The (sweatshirt is) too big. The (sweatshirt isn't) small enough.*

### Materials

- Pupil's Book p12; Activity Book p9; Class CD1; Teacher's App on Navio

### Optional materials

- Teacher's Resource Bank: Trinity Exams Practice cards (selected from the Starter Unit)

## At a Glance Lesson Plan

### Pupil's Book

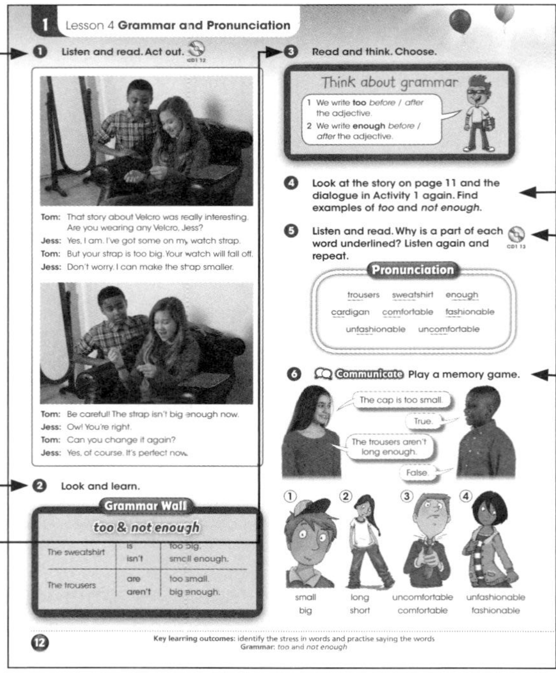

**Starting the lesson**
- Use the Trinity Exams Practice cards (optional).
- Review adjectives.
- Set learning objectives.

**Activity 1**
- Listen and read.
- ▶ *CD1 Track 12 p276*
- Act out.

**Activity 2**
- Look and learn – Grammar wall

**Activity 3**
- Read and think.
- Choose.

**Activity 4**
- Look at the story on page 11 and the dialogue in Activity 1 again.
- Find examples of *too* and *not enough*.

**Activity 5**
- Listen and read.
- ▶ *CD1 Track 13 p276*
- Why is a part of each word underlined?
- Listen again and repeat.

**Activity 6**
- Play a memory game.
- Go to the Activity Book.

**Ending the lesson**
- Review the lesson and reflect on learning.

**Extra activity**

**Extension**
- Identify word stress in other clothes vocabulary.

### Activity Book

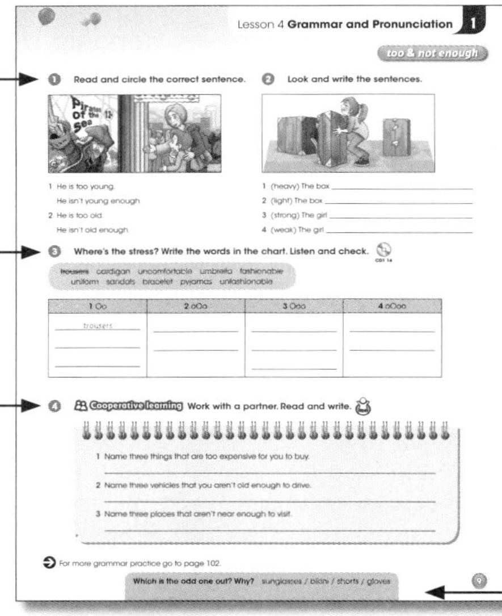

**Activity Book**

**Activity 1**
- Read and circle the correct sentence.

**Activity 2**
- Look and write the sentences.

**Activity 3**
- Where is the stress? Write the words in the chart. Listen and check.

▶ *CD1 Track 14 p276*

**Activity 4**
- Work with a partner. Read and write.

**Odd one out activity**
- Which is the odd one out? Why?

### Digital resources

**Teacher's Digital:** You can also teach this lesson using the Teacher's App on Navio.

**Pupil's Digital:** Encourage your pupils to use the Pupil's App on Navio to practise the activities from this lesson.

Powered By NAVIO

# Detailed Lesson Plan

**Starting the lesson**

**Use the Trinity Exams Practice cards (optional).**
- The pupils practise asking and answering questions.

**Review adjectives.**
- Play *Opposites* (see p32) with: *heavy, light, near, far, strong, weak, hard, soft, noisy, quiet, rough, smooth, long, short, expensive, cheap.*

**Set learning objectives.**
- Say **Today we're going to learn how to say what's wrong with some clothes and we're going to practise our pronunciation.**

**Pupil's Book Activity 1**

**Listen and read. Act out.**

▸ *CD1 Track 12 p276*
- The pupils look at the pictures. Ask **What are Tom and Jess looking at? What's the problem?**
- Play the CD. The pupils listen and read the dialogue. Confirm that they're looking at a watch. The strap is too big and then not big enough. Check understanding by drawing / showing different things that are too big / not big enough.
- Play the CD again, pausing after each sentence for the pupils to repeat.
- The pupils practise the dialogue in pairs.

**Pupil's Book Activity 2**

**Look and learn – Grammar wall**
- Read the information on the Grammar wall as a class.
- Ask **Is a sweatshirt singular or plural? Do we use 'is' or 'are'? Are trousers singular or plural? Do we use 'is' or 'are'?**

**Pupil's Book Activity 3**

**Read and think. Choose.**
- Focus the pupils' attention on the Think about grammar box. Read out the sentences as a class. The pupils complete the sentences in pairs.

**Answers:** 1 before 2 after

**Pupil's Book Activity 4**

**Look at the story on page 11 and the dialogue in Activity 1 again. Find examples of *too* and *not enough*.**
- Ask the pupils to find examples of 'too' and 'not enough' in the dialogue and the story.

**Pupil's Book Activity 5**

**Listen and read. Why is a part of each word underlined? Listen again and repeat.**

▸ *CD1 Track 13 p276*
- Say **Look. Parts of the words are underlined. Let's listen to the words and find out why.** Play the CD, pausing after each word.
- Identify that the underlined parts of words sound stronger / are stressed. The pupils identify the stress pattern.
- Play the CD again. The pupils listen and repeat.

**Pupil's Book Activity 6**

**Play a memory game.**
- Focus the class on the first picture. Elicit what's wrong, using the adjectives to make the sentences.
- Repeat the process with the other three pictures. Ask two pupils to read out the speech bubbles. Make similar true or false sentences about the pictures. The pupils should listen and respond appropriately.
- (Books closed.) The pupils play the game in pairs.

**Activity Book**

**Activity 1**

**Read and circle the correct sentence.**
- Ask a pupil to read out the first pair of sentences. Prompt the class to identify the correct one.
- The pupils circle the second correct sentence.

**Answer:** 1 He is too young. 2 He isn't old enough.

**Activity 2**

**Look and write the sentences.**
- The pupils complete the sentences.

**Answers:** 1 is too heavy. 2 isn't light enough. 3 isn't strong enough. 4 is too weak.

**Activity 3**

**Where is the stress? Write the words in the chart. Listen and check.**

▸ *CD1 Track 14 p276*
- Clap the stress pattern in each column.
- The pupils work in pairs to say and classify the words.
- Play the CD. The pupils check their answers.

**Answers:** 1 trousers, sandals, bracelet 2 umbrella, pyjamas 3 cardigan, fashionable, uniform 4 uncomfortable, unfashionable

**Activity 4**

**Work with a partner. Read and write.**
- Read the sentences as a class and check understanding. Set a time limit, e.g. 3–4 minutes.
- The pupils work in pairs to brainstorm the answers.
- Check answers as a class.

**Odd one out activity**

**Which is the odd one out? Why?**
- The pupils complete the odd one out activity.

**Answers:** gloves (You don't wear them in summer.)

**Ending the lesson**

**Review the lesson and reflect on learning.**
- Say **Today we've learnt how to say what's wrong with clothes and we've practised our pronunciation.**
- Ask **Which was your favourite activity today? Which activity was easy / difficult?**

**Extra activity**

**Extension**
- The pupils add words to the chart in the Activity Book.

**Key Competences and Key Learning Outcomes**

- Identify and say adjectives to describe clothing
- Listen for specific information
- Practise activity types found in the Cambridge Exams: A2 Key for Schools
- Do a communication task

**Key language**

- *baggy, flowery, long-sleeved, patterned, plain, short-sleeved, striped, tight; dress, T-shirt, tie, trousers; comfortable, fair, happy, healthy, kind, tidy, uncomfortable, unfair, unhappy, unhealthy, unkind, untidy*
- *What's (Sally) wearing? (She's) wearing trousers and a T-shirt. Is (she) wearing baggy trousers? Yes, (she) is. No, (she) isn't.*
- **Extension:** *dark (blue), light (green), gold, silver*

**Materials**

- Pupil's Book p13; Activity Book p10; Class CD1; Teacher's App on Navio; Teacher's Resource Bank: Unit 1
- Pictures of famous people

**Optional materials**

- Teacher's Resource Bank: Trinity Exams Practice cards (selected from the Starter Unit)

## At a Glance Lesson Plan

### Pupil's Book

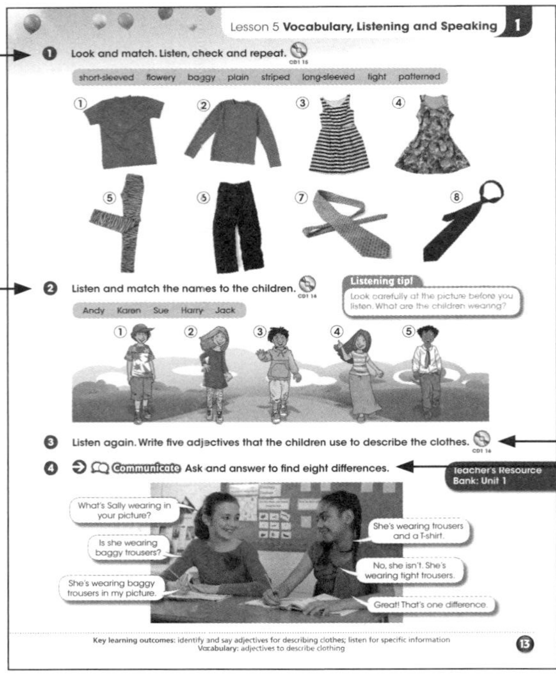


**Starting the lesson**

- Use the Trinity Exams Practice cards (optional).
- Review clothes and adjectives.
- Set learning objectives and use the talk cards.

**Activity 1**

- Look and match.
- Listen, check and repeat.
- ▶ ***CD1 Track 15 p277***

**Activity 2**

- Listen and match the names to the children.
- ▶ ***CD1 Track 16 p277***

**Activity 3**

- Listen again.
- ▶ ***CD1 Track 16 p277***
- Write five adjectives that the children use to describe the clothes.

**Activity 4**

- Ask and answer to find eight differences (Teacher's Resource Bank: Unit 1).

Go to the Activity Book.

**Ending the lesson**

- Review the lesson and reflect on learning.

**Extra activity**

**Reinforcement**

- Have a class fashion show.

**Vocabulary extension**

- Present four additional vocabulary items.

### Activity Book

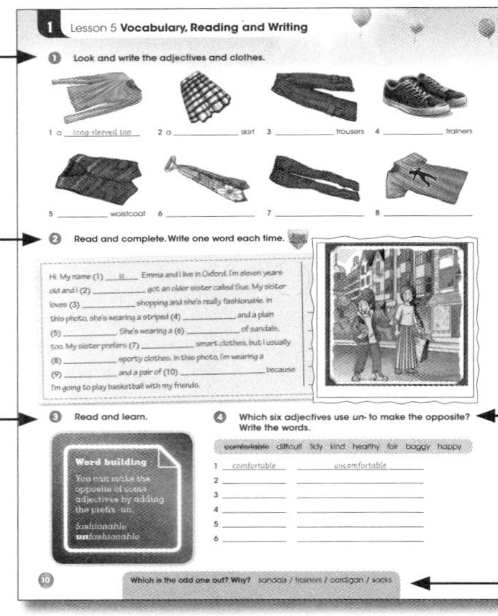


**Activity Book**

**Activity 1**

- Look and write the adjectives and clothes.

**Activity 2**

- Read and complete. Write one word each time.

**Activity 3**

- Read and learn.

**Activity 4**

- Which six adjectives use *un-* to make the opposite? Write the words.

**Odd one out activity**

- Which is the odd one out? Why?

### Digital resources

**Teacher's Digital:** You can also teach this lesson using the Teacher's App on Navio.

**Pupil's Digital:** Encourage your pupils to use the Pupil's App on Navio to practise the activities from this lesson.

Powered By NAVIO

# Detailed Lesson Plan

**Starting the lesson**

**Use the Trinity Exams Practice cards (optional).**

- The pupils practise asking and answering questions.

**Review clothes and adjectives.**

- Organise the class into two groups. Hold up a picture of a famous person. Ask Group A to say a sentence about the clothes the famous person is wearing. The members of the group should confer before they answer. They earn one point if the sentence is correct and another point if the sentence contains an adjective.
- Show the same picture to Group B and award similar points. The groups take turns to make sentences until they have nothing more to say.
- Repeat the procedure with different pictures, starting with a different group each time. At the end of the activity, add up the points.

**Set learning objectives.**

- Say **Today we're going to learn some new adjectives to describe clothes and we're going to do a communication task.**

**Pupil's Book Activity 1**

**Look and match. Listen, check and repeat.**

▶ ***CD1 Track 15 p277***

- Ask the pupils to name the clothes they can see in the photos. They work in pairs to match the adjectives in the box to the clothes.
- Play the CD. The pupils listen, check and repeat.

**Pupil's Book Activity 2**

**Listen and match the names to the children.**

▶ ***CD1 Track 16 p277***

- Ask the pupils to describe what the children are wearing in the picture. Then ask them to write the six names in their notebooks.
- Play the CD. The pupils listen and write the corresponding number next to each name.

**Answers:** Andy 5, Karen 2, Sue 4, Harry 1, Jack 3

**Pupil's Book Activity 3**

**Listen again. Write five adjectives that the children use to describe the clothes.**

▶ ***CD1 Track 16 p277***

- Play the CD again. The pupils write down five adjectives to describe clothing that they hear.

**Answers:** Five from: patterned, plain, smart, casual, flowery, baggy, fashionable, striped, long

**Pupil's Book Activity 4**

**Ask and answer to find eight differences (Teacher's Resource Bank: Unit 1).**

- Invite two pupils to read out the speech bubbles.
- Organise the class into pairs (A and B). Give Pupils A the first worksheet from Teacher's Resource Bank Unit 1, and Pupils B the other worksheet.
- Ask a confident pair to demonstrate the activity by asking and answering questions to find another difference. Then ask the rest of the class to do the same activity in pairs.
- At the end of the activity, the pupils should show each other their pictures and check / identify the differences.

**Activity Book**

**Activity 1**

**Look and write the adjectives and clothes.**

- The pupils work on their own or in pairs to complete the remaining labels.

**Answers:** **1** long-sleeved / plain top **2** striped **3** baggy **4** plain **5** patterned **6** a flowery tie **7** tight jeans **8** short-sleeved T-shirt

**Activity 2**

**Read and complete. Write one word each time.**

- Ask the pupils to describe the picture. Then read out the text as a class. Check comprehension by asking questions.
- Complete the first two sentences as a class.
- The pupils work on their own or in pairs to complete the remaining sentences.

**Answers:** **1** is **2** have **3** going **4** skirt **5** T-shirt **6** pair **7** wearing **8** wear **9** tracksuit **10** trainers

**Activity 3**

**Read and learn.**

- Read the information as a class.

**Activity 4**

**Which six adjectives use *un-* to make the opposite? Write the words.**

- The pupils work on their own or in pairs to identify and write the opposites that begin with 'un-'.

**Answers:** **1** comfortable, uncomfortable **2** tidy, untidy **3** kind, unkind **4** healthy, unhealthy **5** fair, unfair **6** happy, unhappy

**Odd one out activity**

**Which is the odd one out? Why?**

- The pupils complete the odd one out activity.

**Answers:** cardigan (You don't wear it on your feet.)

**Ending the lesson**

**Review the lesson and reflect on learning.**

- Ask **Which was your favourite activity today? Which activity was easy / difficult?**

**Extra activity**

**Reinforcement**

- Invite a pupil to walk in front of the class. Describe his / her clothes as if you were at a fashion show.
- Organise the class into small groups. The pupils work together to write their fashion show script describing what the different pupils in their group are wearing.

**Vocabulary extension**

- Present four additional colours: *dark (blue), light (green), gold, silver*.
- Use the Vocabulary booster on NAVIO to practise these new words.

### Key Competences and Key Learning Outcomes

- Do pre-reading tasks to predict content and raise interest
- Read a magazine article for general understanding
- Scan a text to find specific information

- Learn about different types of materials

- Discuss what magazines you know

- Read and understand a magazine article
- Give an opinion on the text

**Key language**
- *bend, chemical, cloak, clothes, cotton, dirty, light, long, material, natural, plants, sheep, slime, small, smelly, smooth, soft, stain, sticky, stretchy, strong, water, wool*
- *Scientists think that we can use this slime to make strong, soft clothes. Which material is the most (amazing)? (Wool) comes from (sheep).*

**Materials**
- Pupil's Book p14; Activity Book p11; Class CD1; Teacher's App on Navio

**Optional materials**
- Teacher's Resource Bank: Trinity Exams Practice cards (selected from the Starter Unit)

## At a Glance Lesson Plan

**Starting the lesson**
- Use the Trinity Exams Practice cards (optional).
- Review natural materials we wear and where they come from.
- Set learning objectives.

**Activity 1: Before you read**
- Read and discuss.

**Activity 2**
- Look at the title.
- Why do you think these materials are amazing?
- Read and find out.

**Activity 3: After you read**
- What do you think?

Go to the Activity Book.

### Pupil's Book

**Ending the lesson**
- Review the lesson and reflect on learning.

**Extra activity**

**Extension**
- Design a radio advert for one of the materials in the magazine article.

### Activity Book

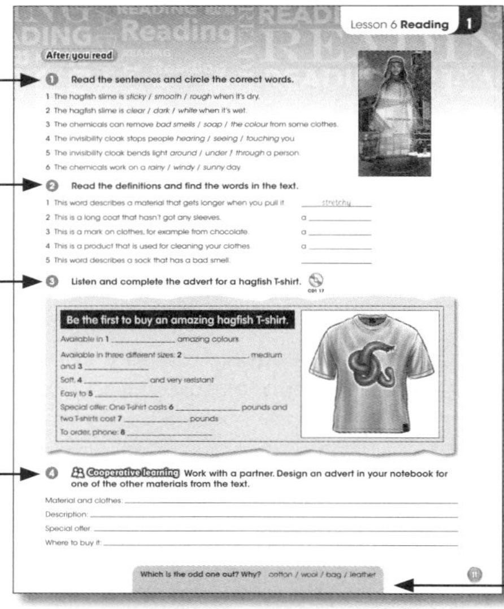


**Activity Book: After you read**

**Activity 1**
- Read the sentences and circle the correct words.

**Activity 2**
- Read the definitions and find the words in the text.

**Activity 3**
- Listen and complete the advert for a hagfish T-shirt.

▶ *CD1 Track 17 p277*

**Activity 4**
- Work with a partner. Design an advert in your notebook for one of the other materials in the text.

**Odd one out activity**
- Which is the odd one out? Why?

### Digital resources

**Teacher's Digital:** You can also teach this lesson using the Teacher's App on Navio.

**Pupil's Digital:** Encourage your pupils to use the Pupil's App on Navio to practise the activities from this lesson.

Powered By NAVIO

# Detailed Lesson Plan

## Starting the lesson

**Use the Trinity Exams Practice cards (optional).**
- The pupils practise asking and answering questions.

**Review natural materials we wear and where they come from.**
- Quickly brainstorm the names of natural materials we wear. Ask **Where does cotton come from?** Repeat the procedure with wool, leather, silk and (some) rubber.

**Set learning objectives.**
- Say **Today we're going to read a magazine article about some amazing materials.**

## Pupil's Book Activity 1: Before you read

**Read and discuss.**
- Read the questions as a class. Prompt the pupils to answer in as much detail as possible.
- Organise the class into pairs. The pupils ask and answer the same questions in their pairs.

## Pupil's Book Activity 2

**Look at the title. Why do you think these materials are amazing? Read and find out.**
- Read out the question and the title of the magazine article. Ask **How can materials be amazing?** Encourage the class to make predictions.
- If pupils need more support, focus their attention on the photos and ask them to describe what they can see and predict what the materials can do.
- The pupils read the texts as a class or in pairs to see if their predictions are correct.
- Quickly check comprehension by asking **Why is the first material amazing?** (*Because it comes from a fish.*) Repeat the procedure with the other two materials.

## Pupil's Book Activity 3: After you read

**What do you think?**
- Read the questions as a class. Prompt the pupils to say which material is the most amazing / useful and why.
- If you wish to do so, have a class vote.

## Activity Book: After you read

### Activity 1

**Read the sentences and circle the correct words.**
- The pupils work on their own or in pairs to read each sentence and circle the correct information. They should refer back to the text in the Pupil's Book when necessary.

**Answers:** **1** smooth **2** clear **3** bad smells **4** seeing **5** around **6** sunny

### Activity 2

**Read the definitions and find the words in the text.**
- The pupils work on their own or in pairs to read the definitions and write the words. They should refer back to the text in the Pupil's Book when necessary.

**Answers:** **1** stretchy **2** cloak **3** stain **4** soap **5** smelly

### Activity 3

**Listen and complete the advert for a hagfish T-shirt.**

▶ *CD1 Track 17 p277*
- Read out the advertisement, pausing at the spaces to allow pupils to predict the missing words.
- Play the CD. The pupils listen and follow the information in their books.
- Play the CD again, pausing after each piece of key information. The pupils should say and write the missing information each time.

**Answers:** **1** six **2** small **3** large **4** light **5** wash **6** ten **7** fifteen **8** 685524

### Activity 4

**Work with a partner. Design an advert in your notebook for one of the other materials from the text.**
- The pupils work in pairs to write an advert. They should use the advert in Activity 3 as a model.

**Odd one out activity**

**Which is the odd one out? Why?**
- The pupils complete the odd one out activity.

**Answers:** bag (It isn't a material.)

## Ending the lesson

**Review the lesson and reflect on learning.**
- Say **Today we've read a magazine article about some amazing materials.**
- Ask **Which was your favourite activity today? Which activity was easy / difficult?**

## Extra activity

**Extension**
- Organise the class into pairs. Each pair should choose the remaining amazing material and create a radio advert.

## Key Competences and Key Learning Outcomes

- Learn about and practise using the linkers 'and', 'also' and 'too'
- Identify the informational content of a magazine article
- Identify features of a magazine article
- Use criteria to check your writing
- Share your writing with another pupil
- Write a magazine article

**Key language**

- *camera, equipment, jacket, light, magnet, map, mobile phone, notebook, pocket, radio, sunglasses, sleeve, waistcoat, waterproof, zip*
- *It's waterproof, too. There's a pocket for your mobile phone and your radio. There are also pockets for a notebook, maps, sunglasses and a camera.*

**Materials**

- Pupil's Book p15; Activity Book p12; Teacher's App on Navio

**Optional materials**

- Teacher's Resource Bank: Trinity Exams Practice cards (selected from the Starter Unit)

## At a Glance Lesson Plan

### Pupil's Book

**Starting the lesson**

- Use the Trinity Exams Practice cards (optional).
- Review the magazine article in Lesson 6.
- Set learning objectives.

**Activity 1: Investigate a text**

- Read the information.
- Think of three questions.

**Activity 2**

- Read the magazine article.
- Does it answer your questions?

**Activity 3: Discuss a text**

- Read the article again.
- Answer the questions.

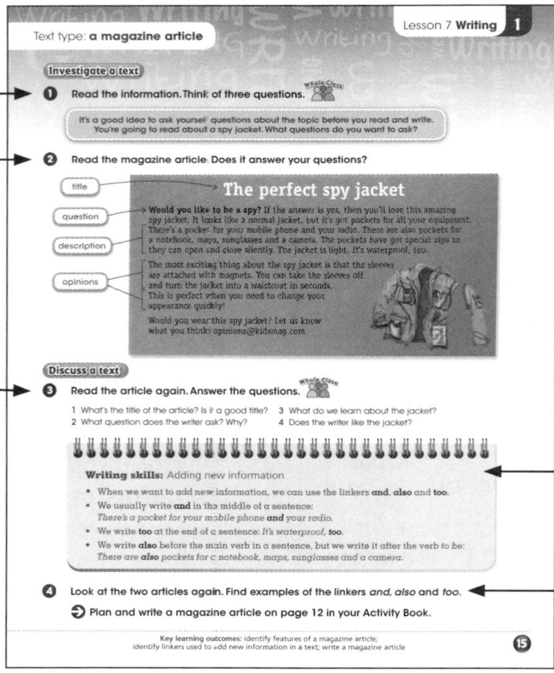


**Writing skills**

- Read about adding new information.

**Activity 4**

- Look at the two articles again.
- Find examples of the linkers *and*, *also* and *too*.

Go to the Activity Book.

**Ending the lesson**

- Review the lesson and reflect on learning.

**Extra activity**

**Extension**

- Draw and label your amazing item of clothing.

### Activity Book

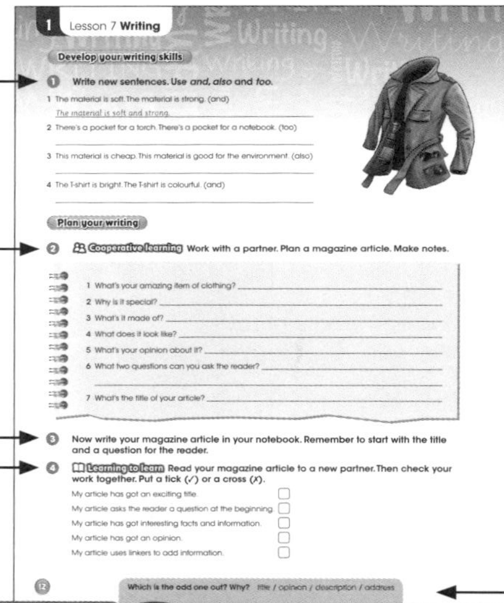


**Activity Book**

**Activity 1: Develop your writing skills**

- Write new sentences. Use *and, also* and *too*.

**Activity 2: Plan your writing**

- Work with a partner. Plan a magazine article. Make notes.

**Activity 3**

- Now write your magazine article in your notebook.
- Remember to start with the title and a question for the reader.

**Activity 4**

- Read your magazine article to a new partner. Then check your work together. Put a tick (✓) or a cross (✗).

**Odd one out activity**

- Which is the odd one out? Why?

## Digital resources

**Teacher's Digital:** You can also teach this lesson using the Teacher's App on Navio.

**Pupil's Digital:** Encourage your pupils to use the Pupil's App on Navio to practise the activities from this lesson.

Powered By NAVIO

# Detailed Lesson Plan

## Starting the lesson

**Use the Trinity Exams Practice cards (optional).**

- The pupils practise asking and answering questions.

**Review the magazine article in Lesson 6.**

- Review information about the three amazing materials in Lesson 6. Ask **Where does the first material come from? What does it look like? Why is it friendly to the environment? What's special about the second material? What does it use to clean the clothes? Why is it friendly to the environment? What happens when you wear the third item of clothing?**

**Set learning objectives.**

- Say **Today we're going to write a magazine article about an amazing item of clothing.**

## Pupil's Book Activity 1: Investigate a text

**Read the information. Think of three questions.**

- Read the information as a class. Brainstorm three questions they want to ask about a spy jacket. If necessary, use prompts to support the class, e.g. **Made from? Look like? Colours?**
- Write the questions on the board.

## Pupil's Book Activity 2

**Read the magazine article. Does it answer your questions?**

- Read the text as a class.
- Check to see if any of the questions on the board are answered.
- The pupils read the text on their own and answer the questions.

## Pupil's Book Activity 3: Discuss a text

**Read the article again. Answer the questions.**

- Read and discuss the questions as a class. Highlight that a magazine article needs a good, eye-catching title. It should also ask a question to get the reader's interest and give plenty of information. Finally, the article needs to give an opinion.

## Writing skills

- Read the information.
- Prompt the pupils to create their own sentences using 'and', 'also' and 'too'. *(I've got brown hair and brown eyes. I've got brown hair. I've also got brown eyes. I've got brown hair. I've got brown eyes, too.)*

## Pupil's Book Activity 4

**Look at the two articles again. Find examples of the linkers *and, also* and *too*.**

- Organise the pupils into pairs. Ask them to find examples of 'and', 'also' and 'too' in Lessons 6 and 7. They can do this orally or write the sentences in their notebook.
- The pupils share information with the rest of the class.

## Activity Book

**Activity 1: Develop your writing skills**

**Write new sentences. Use *and, also* and *too*.**

- The pupils work on their own or in pairs to rewrite the sentences using *and, also* and *too.*

**Answers:** **1** The material is soft and strong. **2** There's a pocket for a torch. There's a pocket for a notebook, too. **3** This material is cheap. This material is also good for the environment. **4** This T-shirt is bright and colourful.

**Activity 2: Plan your writing**

**Work with a partner. Plan a magazine article. Make notes.**

- Read out the question and elicit examples of how pupils can complete each section. If necessary, write these ideas on the board.
- Organise the class into Writing Partners. The pupils think of an amazing piece of clothing and complete their writing notes.

**Activity 3**

**Now write your magazine article in your notebook. Remember to start with the title and a question for the reader.**

- The pupils work with their Writing Partner to write their magazine article in their notebooks.
- Remind the class to write the title at the top of the page and then begin with a question for the reader. The rest of the article should be a description and an opinion.

**Activity 4**

**Read your magazine article to a new partner. Then check your work together. Put a tick (✓) or a cross (✗).** LEARN

- Read through the statements as a class.
- Organise the class into new Writing Partners. One pupil reads aloud their text to their partner. The pupils work together to decide if the text fulfils the criteria and tick the corresponding boxes. The pupils can add, improve or correct the text at this stage.
- The pupils swap roles.

**Odd one out activity**

**Which is the odd one out? Why?**

- The pupils complete the odd one out activity.

**Answers:** address (It isn't used in a magazine article.)

## Ending the lesson

**Review the lesson and reflect on learning.**

- Say **Today we've written a magazine article about some amazing items of clothing.**
- Ask **Which was your favourite activity today? Which activity was easy / difficult?**

## Extra activity

**Extension**

- Ask the pupils to draw and label their amazing item of clothing in their notebooks.
- The pupils copy their article onto a piece of paper and illustrate it with a drawing of the clothing. Make a class display of their work.

**Key Competences and Key Learning Outcomes**

- Talk about your favourite item of clothing

- Listen to a text for general understanding
- Listen to a text and identify key functional language
- Review learning and reflect on progress

- Sing a song

**Key language**
- *baseball boots, grey, hat, soft, T-shirt, warm, wool*
- *What's your favourite item of clothing? What's it like? Really? Is that right? Oh! No way!*

**Materials**
- Pupil's Book p16; Activity Book p13 and 14; Class CD1 and CD4; Teacher's App on Navio

**Optional materials**
- Teacher's Resource Bank: Trinity Exams Practice cards (selected from the Starter Unit)

## At a Glance Lesson Plan

### Pupil's Book

**Starting the lesson**
- Use the Trinity Exams Practice cards (optional).
- Review clothes.
- Set learning objectives.

**Activity 1**
- Describe the clothes.
- What kind of clothes do you think Julia likes?

**Activity 2**
- Listen to the conversation.
- ▶ ***CD1 Track 18 p277***
- What's Julia's favourite item of clothing? Why?

**Activity 3**
- Listen again.
- ▶ ***CD1 Track 18 p277***
- Complete four questions that Anna asks.

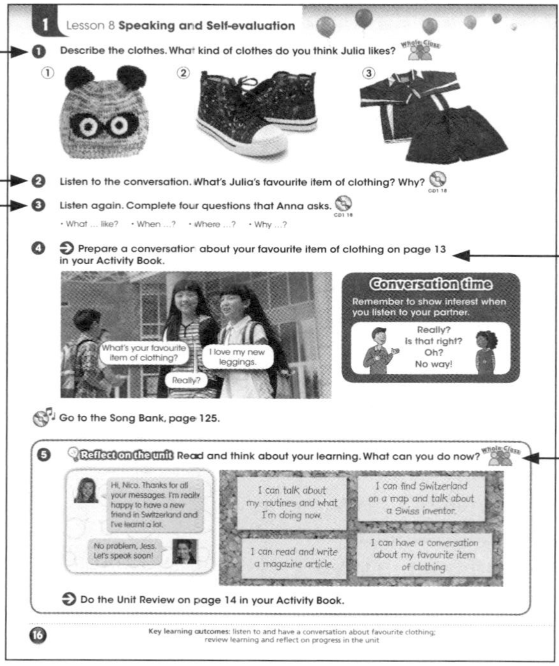

**Activity 4**
- Prepare a conversation about your favourite item of clothing on page 13 in your Activity book.

Go to page 13 in the Activity Book.

**Song**
- ▶ ***CD4 Track 18 p296***
- ▶ ***CD4 Track 19 p297 (optional karaoke version)***

**Activity 5**
- Reflect and think about your learning. What can you do now?

Go to page 14 in the Activity Book.

**Ending the lesson**
- Review the lesson and reflect on learning.

**Extra activity**
- Play a guessing game to review clothes vocabulary.

### Activity Book

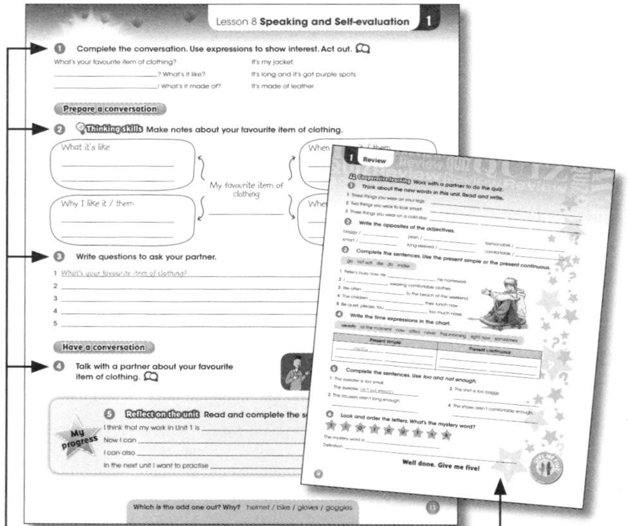

**Activity Book page 14: Review**
- Work with a partner to do the quiz.

**Activity Book**

**Activity 1**
- Complete the conversation.
- Use expressions to show interest.
- Act out.

**Activity 2**
- Make notes about your favourite item of clothing.

**Activity 3**
- Write questions to ask your partner.

**Activity 4**
- Talk with a partner about your favourite item of clothing.

**Activity 5**
- Read and complete the sentences.

**Odd one out activity**
- Which is the odd one out? Why?

## Digital resources

**Teacher's Digital:** You can also teach this lesson using the Teacher's App on Navio.

Powered By NAVIO

# Detailed Lesson Plan

### Starting the lesson

**Use the Trinity Exams Practice cards (optional).**

- The pupils practise asking and answering questions.

**Review words for clothes and clothes adjectives.**

- Invite a pupil to the front. Describe what he/she is wearing, but make some deliberate mistakes. Say **Is that correct?** Elicit the correct description. Pupils repeat the activity in groups.

**Set learning objectives.**

- Say **Today we're going to prepare a conversation about our favourite item of clothing.**

### Pupil's Book Activity 1

**Describe the clothes. What kind of clothes do you think Julia likes?**

- Ask different pupils to describe the clothes. Explain that they are going to hear a girl called Julia talk about her clothes with her friend, Anna. Ask pupils what kind of clothes they think she likes, based on the clothes that they can see.

### Pupil's Book Activity 2

**Listen to the conversation. What's Julia's favourite item of clothing? Why?**

▶ ***CD1 Track 18 p277***

- Play the CD. Ask pupils if all the clothes belong to Julia (*No, the baseball boots belong to Anna*).

**Answer:** Julia's favourite is 1.

### Pupil's Book Activity 3

**Listen again. Complete four questions that Anna asks.**

▶ ***CD1 Track 18 p277***

- Direct pupils to the four question prompts. Ask if they can remember the questions.
- Play the CD. Pupils check in pairs. Then play again and check as a class.

**Answers:** What's it like?; When do you wear the hat?; Where did you buy it?; Why do you like it so much?

### Pupil's Book Activity 4

**Prepare a conversation about your favourite item of clothing on page 13 in your Activity Book.**

- Read the speech bubbles with the pupils. Model the phrases in the Conversation Time box and get the class to repeat. Point out that they should use intonation to sound interested.

### Song

- Go to the Song Bank on page 125 to do the song activities (see p243).

▶ ***CD4 Track 18 p296***

▶ ***CD4 Track 19 p297 (optional karaoke version)***

### Pupil's Book Activity 5

**Read and think about your learning. What can you do now?**

- Read the speech bubbles and notes with the pupils. Then look back through the unit and prompt them to identify things that they have done/learnt.

### Activity Book page 14: Review

**Work with a partner to do the quiz.**

- Organise the class into pairs. Set a time limit for the pupils to do the quiz. This time limit will depend on the ability of the class (10–15 minutes). Stress that the pupils are not competing with each other.
- Read out the six tasks that the pupils have to complete. Check understanding. Then say **Ready, steady ... Go!**
- The pupils work in their pairs to do the quiz.
- Correct the answers as a class.

**Answers:** **1 1** Three from: trousers, leggings, jeans, tracksuit **2** tie, suit **3** Three from: hat, gloves, scarf, coat **2** tight, patterned, unfashionable, casual, short-sleeved, uncomfortable **3 1** is doing **2** like **3** go **4** aren't eating **5** are making **4** Present simple: usually, often, never, sometimes Present continuous: at the moment, now, this morning, right now **5 1** isn't big enough. **2** The trousers are too short. **3** The shirt isn't tight enough. **4** The shoes are too uncomfortable. **6** tracksuit, what you wear to do exercise

### Activity Book

**Activity 1**

**Complete the conversation. Use expressions to show interest. Act out.**

- Demonstrate the dialogue with a pupil. Then pupils complete and perform the dialogue in pairs.

**Activity 2**

**Make notes about your favourite item of clothing.**

- Tell pupils about your favourite item of clothing. Then pupils complete the boxes with their own information.

**Activity 3**

**Write questions to ask your partner.**

- Direct pupils to the five headings in Activity 2 and explain that they need to form questions about them. Then pupils complete the questions alone. Check as a class.

**Answers:** **1** What's your favourite item of clothing? **2** What's it like? **3** Why do you like it/them? **4** When do you wear it/them? **5** Where did you buy it/them?

**Activity 4**

**Talk with a partner about your favourite item of clothing.**

- In pairs, pupils ask and answer the questions from Activity 3.
- Invite one or two pairs to perform their conversations for the class.

**Activity 5**

**Read and complete the sentences.**

- Pupils work alone to review their work in the unit.

**Odd one out activity**

**Which is the odd one out? Why?**

**Answer:** **1** bike (You don't wear it.)

### Ending the lesson

**Review the lesson and reflect on learning.**

- Say **Today we've learnt how to have a conversation about our favourite item of clothing.**

### Key Competences and Key Learning Outcomes

- Watch and understand a video about making clothes
- Design a sports kit

**Key language**

- *comfortable, creative, fashionable, fashion designer, interview, material, sew, sewing machine, sketch, smart, spotted, research*
- *I think shorts are a good idea. I agree. What else? What about having a bag for the sports kit?*

**Materials**

- Pupil's Book p17; Activity Book p15; Class CD1; Teacher's App on Navio
- Teacher's Resource Bank: Talk cards

**Optional materials**

- Teacher's Resource Bank: Trinity Exams Practice cards (selected from the Starter Unit)

## At a Glance Lesson Plan

### Pupil's Book

**Starting the lesson**

- Use the Trinity Exams Practice cards (optional).
- **Think-Pair-Share** Review clothes and clothes adjectives.
- Set learning objectives and use the talk cards.

**Activity 1**

- Before you watch
- Watch the video.

*Unit 1 video p300*

- Read and say the sentences in the correct order.

**Activity 2**

- Watch the video again.

*Unit 1 video*

- What does Amy think about these clothes?
- Do you agree?

**Activity 3**

- Read, think and answer.

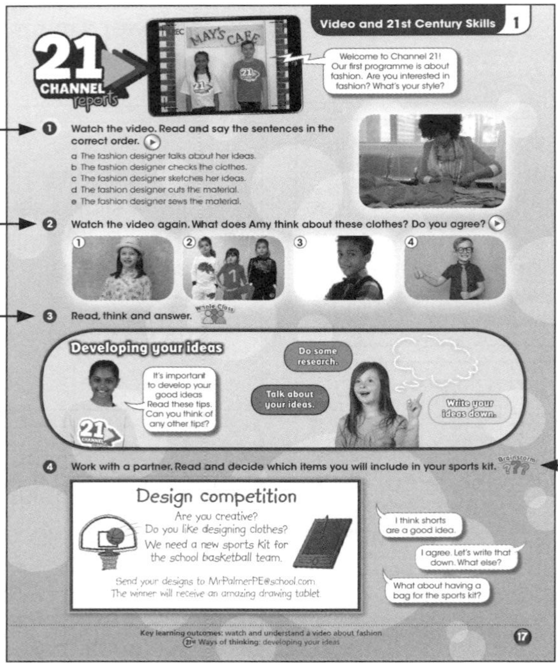

**Activity 4**

- Work with a partner.
- Read and decide which items you will include in your sports kit.

Go to the Activity Book

**Ending the lesson**

- Review the lesson and reflect on learning.

**Extra activity**

- Play a guessing game to review clothes vocabulary.

### Digital resources

**Teacher's Digital:** You can also teach this lesson using the Teacher's App on Navio.

**Pupil's Digital:** Encourage your pupils to use the Pupil's App on Navio to practise the activities from this lesson.

Powered By NAVIO

### Activity Book

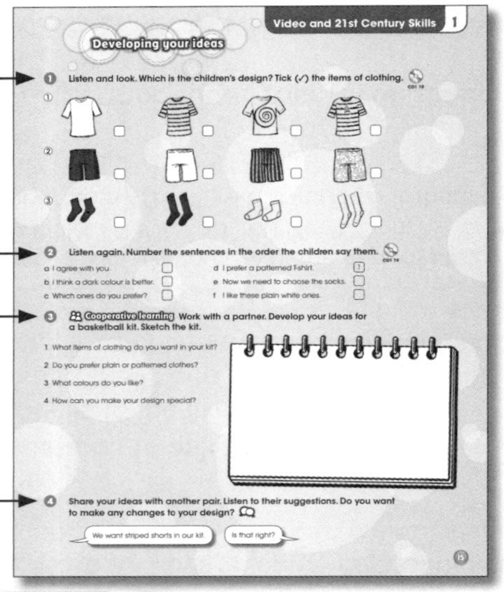

**Activity Book**

**Activity 1**

- Listen and look.
- Which is the children's design? Tick (✓) the items of clothing.

▶ *CD1 Track 19 p277*

**Activity 2**

- Listen again. Number the sentences in the order the children say them.

▶ *CD1 Track 19 p277*

**Activity 3**

- Work with a partner.
- Develop your ideas for a basketball kit.
- Sketch the kit.

**Activity 4**

- Share your ideas with another pair.
- Listen to their suggestions.
- Do you want to make any changes to your design?

# Detailed Lesson Plan

## Starting the lesson

**Think-Pair-Share Review words for clothes and clothes adjectives.**

- Ask **How many different clothes and clothes adjectives can you think of?** The class thinks silently for a minute.
- Then the pupils work with a Talk Partner to name clothes and clothes adjectives.
- Invite different Talk Partners to say a different clothes word or clothes adjective. Hold up the corresponding flashcard and prompt the class to repeat the word.

**Set learning objectives.**

- Say **Today we're going to watch a video and then ask and answer questions about making clothes**.
- Explain to the pupils that in every unit they will watch a TV programme called Channel 21, which is presented by two children called Amy and Max. Each video will cover a different topic.

## Pupil's Book Activity 1

**Before you watch**

- Look at the photo of Amy and Max and explain that these are the presenters of Channel 21.
- Read the speech bubble to pupils. Ask **Are you interested in fashion? What's your style?** Elicit responses from a number of pupils.

**Watch the video. Read and say the sentences in the correct order.** *p300*

- Watch Part 1 of the video. Ask pupils **What are you going to see next?**
- Play Part 2 of the video. Ask general questions to check understanding. Direct pupils to look at the sentences a–e in Activity 1. Say **Which sentence is first?** Pupils offer ideas.
- Play the video again and check answers as a group.

**Answers:** **1** c **2** a **3** d **4** e **5** b

## Pupil's Book Activity 2

**Watch the video again. What does Amy think about these clothes? Do you agree?**

- Explain that you are going to listen for Amy's opinions on the clothes.
- Ask a pupil to describe the clothes in picture 1. Repeat with pictures 2–4.

**Answers:** **1** She thinks these clothes are cool. **2** She doesn't like the flowery design. **3 and 4** She thinks these clothes are smart.

## Pupil's Book Activity 3

**Read, think and answer.**

- Tell pupils that in the last part of the video Amy and Max talk about developing ideas when you design clothes.
- Read the speech bubble with the class. Then read the three tips. Ask if pupils remember any more tips that Amy and Max talk about in the video, and who says it. (*Amy says 'Be practical.'*)
- Tell pupils they are going to design a sports kit in the next activity. Pupils work in pairs to think of more tips for how to develop their ideas before they start designing. Make a class list of all the tips.

## Pupil's Book Activity 4

**Work with a partner. Read and decide which items you will include in your sports kit.**

- Read the poster with the pupils. Ask general questions to check understanding.
- Pupils work in pairs to decide what items they will include in their sports kit. Tell them they can include any items they like.

## Activity Book

**Activity 1**

**Listen and look. Which is the children's design? Tick (✓) the items of clothing.**

▶ *CD1 Track 19 p277*

**Answers:** **1** the fourth T-shirt (striped with a star)
**2** the first pair of shorts (plain and black)
**3** the third pair of socks (short and white)

**Activity 2**

**Listen again. Number the sentences in the order the children say them.**

▶ *CD1 Track 19 p277*

- Read the sentences with the pupils and ask which line the children say first (*d*). Ask if they remember which sentence the children say next. Then play the CD, pausing when each line is said to allow the pupils to write the number.

**Answers:** **1** d **2** a **3** f **4** b **5** e **6** c

**Activity 3**

**Work with a partner. Develop your ideas for a basketball kit. Sketch the kit.**

- Organise the pupils into the same pairs that they worked in for Activity 4 in the Pupil's Book. Ask pupils to remember which clothes items they already chose for their kit.
- Pupils work together to design their kit. Help them to put the ideas for developing their ideas into practice.

**Activity 4**

**Share your ideas with another pair. Listen to their suggestions. Do you want to make any changes to your design?**

- Ask pupils to remember the different items in the children's kit from Activity 1. Tell them you want to make some suggestions about how to change the design. Say **I like the star on the T-shirt, but I think one star is a bit boring. I prefer three stars.** Ask pupils for some different suggestions to change the design.
- Pupils work in groups of four to show each other their designs, and think of suggestions about how to change them.

## Ending the lesson

**Review the lesson and reflect on learning.**

- Say **Today we've watched a video about designing clothes. What have we learnt about developing our ideas?** Elicit ideas from the pupils.

Date: ____________ Unit: ________

1 **What did my pupils learn in this unit?**

2 **How did my pupils work? (✓)**

individually ☐ in pairs ☐ in small groups ☐

in large groups ☐ as a class ☐

3 **Which key competences did my pupils develop? Give a score from 1 to 5 (5 being the highest).**

- Competence in linguistic communication ☐
- Competence in mathematics, science and technology ☐
- Digital competence ☐
- Learning to learn ☐
- Social and civic competences ☐
- Sense of initiative and entrepreneurship ☐
- Cultural awareness and expression ☐

4 **Which lessons / activities were the most successful and why?**

5 **Which lessons / activities did my pupils find the most difficult and why?**

6 **What did I try in the classroom for the first time? How did it go?**

7 **Which resources did I find most useful? (including webpages)**

8 **What could I do differently next time I teach this unit?**

# Unit 2 Adventure holiday
## Unit overview

### Key Competences and Key Learning Outcomes

- Review and learn the names of outdoor activities and equipment (Lesson 1)
- Identify and review the past simple (Lesson 2)
- Review the formation of 'Wh-' questions in the past simple (Lesson 4)
- Review and learn objects in a survival kit (Lesson 5)
- Learn about and practise using time connectives (Lesson 7)
- Talk about your favourite place to visit (Lesson 8)
- Watch and understand a video about adventurous sports (Video and 21st Century Skills)

- Learn about prehistoric art (Lesson 3)

- Use the Pupil's App on Navio
- Investigate France (Lesson 3)

- Identify and practise intonation in questions (Lesson 4)
- Reflect on your own learning (Lesson 8)
- Practise activity types found in the Cambridge Exams: A2 Key for Schools

- Think about the importance of looking after old things (Lesson 3)
- Prepare and give a presentation to the class (Lesson 8)
- Learn about safety equipment (Video and 21st Century Skills)

- Work in pairs and small groups to practise and reinforce learning (all lessons)
- Do a communication task (Lesson 5)

- Read and understand a story (Lesson 3)
- Learn about the Dordogne region of France and the history of cave paintings (Lesson 3)
- Read a travel blog (Lesson 6)
- Write a travel blog (Lesson 7)

### Vocabulary

**Core vocabulary**
*camping, compass, helmet, hiking, lifejacket, map, mountain biking, rock climbing, rucksack, torch, wetsuit, whitewater rafting; binoculars, camping stove, insect repellent, matches, rope, saucepan, sleeping bag, sun cream, walking boots, wildlife guidebooks*

**Extension vocabulary (optional)**
*abseiling, bungee jumping, canoeing, canyoning, kite surfing, snorkelling; alarm clock, water bottle, waterproof jacket, waterproof trousers*

**Other vocabulary**
*bike rack, blog, campsite, caravan, canyoning, clouds, equipment, helicopter, hole, lightening, shower, thunder, treasure; goat, deer; climb, find, explore, get lost, put up a tent; lantern, meanwhile, paintings, secret, spectacular, timeline, tunnels; adventurous, icy, paragliding, race, rocks, scary, skiing, snowboarding, tightrope walking*

**Recycled vocabulary**
*beach, cliff, cow, duck, horse riding, rain, river, rocks, wet, woods; cousins, family, parents; after an hour, at 11 o'clock, at first, finally, first of all, soon, suddenly, then; sunny, tired; tell; had breakfast, cereal, cheese, fried eggs, hot dog, toast*

### Structures

**Core structures**
*I / He / She / It was / wasn't really loud. You / We / They were / weren't really loud. Was I / he / she / it cold? / Were you / we / they cold? I / He / She / It / You / We / They jumped / didn't jump. Did I / you / he / she / it / we / they jump? Where / When / Why did (you) go? What did (you) do? How did (you) get there? Who did (you) go with? How long did (you) go for?*

**Recycled structures**
*Do you want to go whitewater rafting? Yes, because I love water sports. We couldn't see very well. What do you want to take with you?*

### Pronunciation

Intonation in 'Did …?' and 'Wh-' questions in the past

### Literacy

**Text type:** a travel blog (chronological account; writing preparation)
**Reading skills:** skimming
**Writing skills:** using time connectives

### Culture … around the world

The discovery of ancient cave paintings in France

### 21st Century Skills

**Digital skills:** researching a topic online

### Thinking skills

Matching words and pictures (Lesson 1); Analysing and applying rules (Lessons 2 and 4); Predicting (Lesson 2); Hypothesising (Lesson 3); Defining and describing (Lesson 5); Finding information (Lesson 6); Planning, checking and correcting (Lesson 7); Seeing another's point of view (Lesson 8); Reflecting on learning (Lesson 8)

### Cooperative learning

Working together (Lessons 1-8); Collaborating (Lessons 1-8); Checking learning (Lessons 1-8); Peer evaluation and feedback (Lesson 7); Helping and encouraging (Lessons 1-8); Reaching agreement (Lesson 8); Reflecting and setting goals (Lesson 8)

### Values

The importance of looking after old things

### Cross-curricular links

**Links to Science**
Prehistoric art

**Suggested Arts and Crafts concepts**
Scale and proportion

## Key Competences and Key Learning Outcomes

- Identify and say the names of outdoor activities and equipment
- Listen to definitions and identify the words
- Read an adventure holiday itinerary and complete a matching exercise
- Talk about activities you want to do

**Key language**
- *camping, compass, helmet, hiking, lifejacket, map, mountain biking, rock climbing, rucksack, torch, wetsuit, whitewater rafting; campsite, caves, cheese, equipment, get lost, horse riding, picnic, prizes, quiz, relax, spectacular, woods*
- *Do you want to go whitewater rafting? Yes, because I love water sports. What do you want to take with you?*
- **Extension:** *abseiling, bungee jumping, canoeing, canyoning, kite surfing, snorkeling*

**Materials**
- Pupil's Book pp18-19; Activity Book p16; Class CD1; Teacher's App on Navio
- Outdoor activities and equipment flashcards

**Optional materials**
- Teacher's Resource Bank: Trinity Exams Practice cards (selected from the Starter Unit and Unit 1)

## At a Glance Lesson Plan

### Pupil's Book

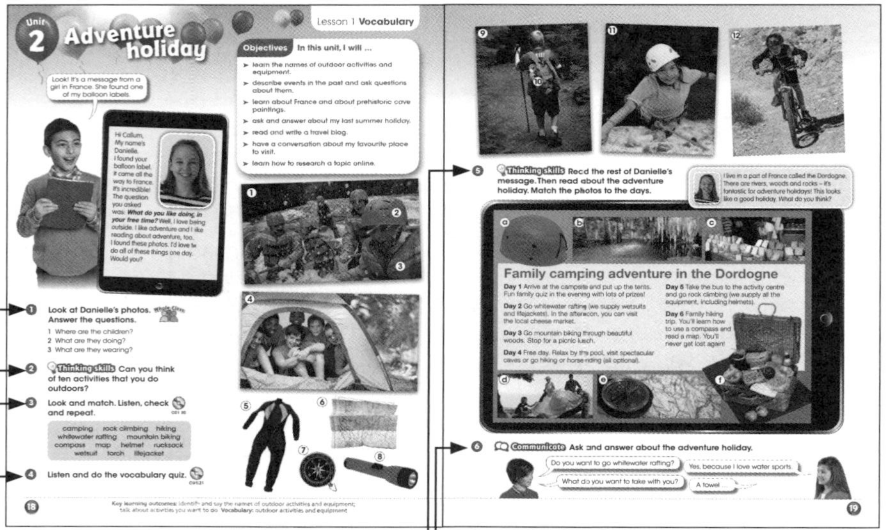


**Starting the lesson**
- Use the Trinity Exams Practice cards (optional).
- Review weather, clothes and outdoor activities.
- Set learning objectives.

**Activity 1**
- Look at Danielle's photos.
- Answer the questions.

**Activity 2**
- Can you think of ten activities that you do outdoors?

**Vocabulary presentation**
- Present the unit vocabulary using the outdoor activities and equipment flashcards.

**Activity 3**
- Look and match.
- Listen, check and repeat.
- ▶ *CD1 Track 20 p277*

**Activity 4**
- Listen and do the vocabulary quiz.
- ▶ *CD1 Track 21 p277*

**Activity 5**
- Read the rest of Danielle's message.
- Then read about the adventure holiday.
- Match the photos to the days.

**Activity 6**
- Ask and answer about the adventure holiday.
- Go to the Activity Book.

**Ending the lesson**
- Review the lesson and reflect on learning.

**Extra activities**

**Extension**
- Find out about France.

**Vocabulary extension**
- Present six additional vocabulary items.

**Digital resources**

**Teacher's Digital:** You can also teach this lesson using the Teacher's App on Navio.

**Pupil's Digital:** Encourage your pupils to use the Pupil's App on Navio to practise the activities from this lesson.

Powered By NAVIO

### Activity Book

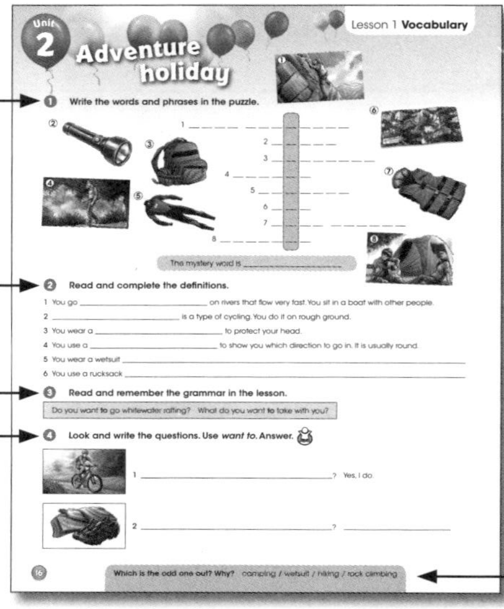


**Activity Book**

**Activity 1**
- Write the words and phrases in the puzzle.

**Activity 2**
- Read and complete the definitions.

**Activity 3**
- Read and remember the grammar in the lesson.

**Activity 4**
- Look and write the questions. Use *want to.* Answer.

**Odd one out activity**
- Which is the odd one out? Why?

# Detailed Lesson Plan

### Starting the lesson

**Use the Trinity Exams Practice cards (optional).**
- The pupils practise asking and answering questions.

**Review weather, clothes and outdoor activities.**
- Ask **What's the weather like today? When it's (rainy / sunny) what clothes do you wear? When it's (rainy / sunny) what activities do you do?**

**Set learning objectives.**
- Say **Today we're going to remember and learn the names of different outdoor activities and some equipment we use for these activities.**

### Pupil's Book Activity 1

**Look at Danielle's photos. Answer the questions.**
- Invite a pupil to read out the speech bubble to find out who has found the balloon. Ask the class if they know where France is and if anyone has been there.
- Invite a pupil to read out the message from Danielle and check understanding.
- Work as a class to read and answer the questions about the photos.

**Answers:** **1** on an adventure holiday **2** whitewater rafting, camping, hiking, rock climbing, mountain biking **3** helmets, lifejackets, rucksacks

### Pupil's Book Activity 2

**Can you think of ten activities that you do outdoors?**
- Say **Write the numbers 1 to 10 in your notebook. In pairs, think of ten activities you do outdoors.**

### Vocabulary presentation

- Present the unit vocabulary using the outdoor activities and equipment flashcards. Write **Activities** and **Equipment** on the board. Show the first flashcard and elicit / say the name of the activity or object.
- Invite a pupil to stick the card on the board under the correct heading. Repeat with the other cards.

### Pupil's Book Activity 3

**Look and match. Listen, check and repeat.**
▶ *CD1 Track 20 p277*
- Focus the class on item number 1 in the photo. Ask **Which object or activity is this?** The pupils work in pairs to match numbers 2–12 and the words.
- Play the CD. The pupils listen and check.
- Play the CD again, pausing after each word for the pupils to repeat.

### Pupil's Book Activity 4

**Listen and do the vocabulary quiz.**
▶ *CD1 Track 21 p277*
- Play the CD. Listen to the first definition, pausing at the beep to allow the pupils to name the item. Continue with the CD to listen to the answer.
- Repeat the procedure with the other definitions.

### Pupil's Book Activity 5

**Read the rest of Danielle's message. Then read about the adventure holiday. Match the photos to the days.**
- Invite a pupil to read the message. Invite another pupil to read the text from the website. The pupils match photos a–e to the days.

### Pupil's Book Activity 6

**Ask and answer about the adventure holiday.**
- Invite two pupils to read out the speech bubbles.
- The pupils ask and answer questions in pairs.

### Activity Book

**Activity 1**

**Write the words and phrases in the puzzle.**
- The pupils look at the pictures and write the words or phrases. They then work out the mystery word.

**Answers:** **1** rock climbing **2** torch **3** rucksack **4** hiking **5** wetsuit **6** map **7** life jacket **8** camping Mystery word: mountain

**Activity 2**

**Read and complete the definitions.**
- The pupils complete the definitions.

**Answers:** **1** whitewater rafting **2** Mountain biking **3** helmet **4** compass **5** to keep you warm. **6** to carry your equipment.

**Activity 3**

**Read and remember the grammar in the lesson.**
- Invite a pupil to read out the information. Focus the group's attention on the 'to' form used after 'want'.

**Activity 4**

**Look and write the questions. Use want to. Answer.**
- The pupils work on their own to complete the dialogue.

**Answers:** **1** Do you want to go mountain biking? **2** Do you want to go hiking? Yes, I do. / No, I don't.

**Odd one out activity**

**Which is the odd one out? Why?**
- The pupils complete the odd one out activity.

**Answers:** wetsuit (It isn't an activity.)

### Ending the lesson

**Review the lesson and reflect on learning.**
- Say **Today we've learnt the names of different activities and objects. What do you remember?**
- Ask **Which was your favourite activity today? Which activity was easy / difficult?**

### Extra activities

**Extension**
- The pupils find France on the world map on pages 134–135. They read the accompanying facts.

**Vocabulary extension**
- Present six additional activities: *abseiling, bungee jumping, canoeing, canyoning, kite surfing, snorkelling.*
- Use the Vocabulary booster on NAVIO to practise these new words.

## Key Competences and Key Learning Outcomes

- Listen to and read a dialogue
- Use the past simple to talk about an event in the past
- Ask and answer questions using the past simple

- Practise activity types found in the Cambridge Exams: A2 Key for Schools

## Key language

- *canyoning, caves, cold, jump, loud, river, rock, quiet, sound, waterproof*
- *I / He / She / It was / wasn't really loud. You / We / They were / weren't really loud. Was I / he / she / it cold? Were you / we / they cold? I / He / She / It / You / We / They jumped / they didn't jump. Did I / you / he / she / it / we / they jump? Danielle went canyoning with her family. Did you play tennis last weekend?*

## Materials

- Pupil's Book p20; Activity Book p17; Class CD1; Teacher's App on Navio
- Teacher's Resource Bank: Outdoor activities and equipment word cards

## Optional materials

- Teacher's Resource Bank: Trinity Exams Practice cards (selected from the Starter Unit and Unit 1)

## At a Glance Lesson Plan

### Pupil's Book

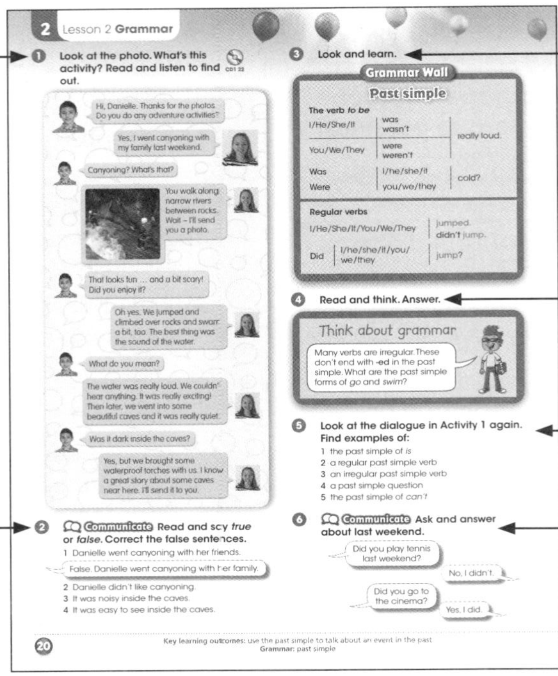
2 Lesson 2 Grammar

1 Look at the photo. What's this activity? Read and listen to find out.

2 Communicate Read and say *true* or *false*. Correct the false sentences.

1 Danielle went canyoning with her friends.

False: Danielle went canyoning with her family.

2 Danielle didn't like canyoning.

3 It was noisy inside the caves.

4 It was easy to see inside the caves.

3 Look and learn.

Grammar Wall

Past simple

4 Read and think. Answer.

Think about grammar

Many verbs are irregular. These don't end with -ed in the past simple. What are the past simple forms of *go* and *swim*?

5 Look at the dialogue in Activity 1 again. Find examples of:

1 the past simple of *is*

2 a regular past simple verb

3 an irregular past simple verb

4 a past simple question

5 the past simple of *can't*

6 Communicate Ask and answer about last weekend.

Did you play tennis last weekend? No, I didn't.

Did you go to the cinema? Yes, I did.

20

Key learning outcomes: use the past simple to talk about an event in the past

Grammar: past simple

**Starting the lesson**

- Use the Trinity Exams Practice cards (optional).
- Review outdoor activities and equipment.
- Set learning objectives.

**Activity 1**

- Look at the photo.
- What's this activity?
- Read and listen to find out.

▶ *CD1 Track 22 p278*

**Activity 2**

- Read and say *true* or *false*.
- Correct the false sentences.

**Activity 3**

- Look and learn – Grammar wall

**Activity 4**

- Read and think.
- Answer.

**Activity 5**

- Look at the dialogue in Activity 1 again.
- Find examples of:

**Activity 6**

- Ask and answer about last weekend.

Go to the Activity Book.

**Ending the lesson**

- Review the lesson and reflect on learning.

**Extra activity**

**Reinforcement**

- Make true and false sentences about your last weekend.

### Activity Book

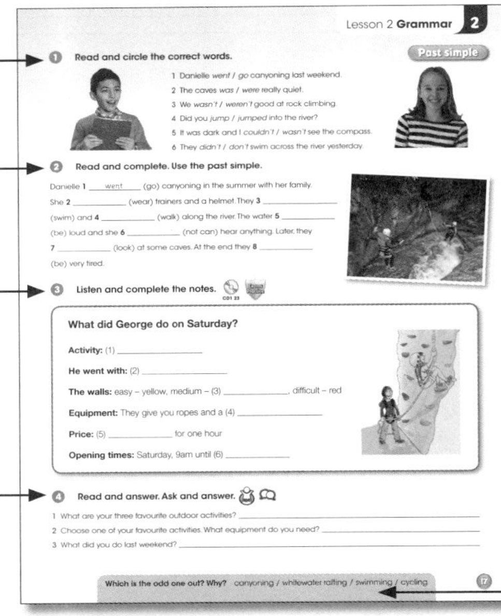
Lesson 2 Grammar 2

Past simple

1 Read and circle the correct words.

1 Danielle went / go canyoning last weekend.

2 The caves was / were really quiet.

3 We wasn't / weren't good at rock climbing.

4 Did you jump / jumped into the river?

5 It was dark and I couldn't / wasn't see the compass.

6 They didn't / don't swim across the river yesterday.

2 Read and complete. Use the past simple.

3 Listen and complete the notes.

What did George do on Saturday?

Activity: (1)

He went with: (2)

The walls: easy – yellow, medium – (3) difficult – red

Equipment: They give you ropes and a (4)

Price: (5) for one hour

Opening times: Saturday, 9am until (6)

4 Read and answer. Ask and answer.

1 What are your three favourite outdoor activities?

2 Choose one of your favourite activities. What equipment do you need?

3 What did you do last weekend?

Which is the odd one out? Why? canyoning / whitewater rafting / swimming / cycling

17

**Activity Book**

**Activity 1**

- Read and circle the correct words.

**Activity 2**

- Read and complete. Use the past simple.

**Activity 3**

- Listen and complete the notes.

▶ *CD1 Track 23 p278*

**Activity 4**

- Read and answer. Ask and answer.

**Odd one out activity**

- Which is the odd one out? Why?

## Digital resources

**Teacher's Digital:** You can also teach this lesson using the Teacher's App on Navio.

**Pupil's Digital:** Encourage your pupils to use the Pupil's App on Navio to practise the activities from this lesson.

Powered By NAVIO

# Detailed Lesson Plan

**Starting the lesson**

**Use the Trinity Exams Practice cards (optional).**
- The pupils practise asking and answering questions.

**Review outdoor activities and equipment.**
- Play the *Mime the card* game (see p27) with the outdoor activities and equipment word cards.

**Set learning objectives and use the talk cards.**
- Say **Today we're going to remember how to talk about things that happened in the past. At the weekend, last week or last summer.**

**Pupil's Book Activity 1**

**Look at the photo. What's this activity? Read and listen to find out.**

▸ *CD1 Track 22 p278*
- Prompt the class to describe what they can see in the photo. Ask **Where's Danielle? What's she doing? What's she wearing?**
- Ask the class if they know the name of this activity.
- Play the CD. The pupils listen and read the dialogue. Confirm that the activity is canyoning.

**Pupil's Book Activity 2**

**Read and say *true* or *false*. Correct the false sentences.**
- Organise the class into pairs. The pupils work together to read and say if the sentences are true or false. They should correct the false sentences in their notebooks.

**Pupil's Book Activity 3**

**Look and learn – Grammar wall**
- Read the information on the Grammar wall as a class.
- Use questions to encourage the pupils to think about form and identify / remember patterns. Ask **What's the past simple form of 'to be'? How many forms are there in the affirmative? What do you add to a regular verb to make a past simple form? Can you think of other regular verbs?**

**Pupil's Book Activity 4**

**Read and think. Answer.**
- Focus the pupils' attention on the Think about grammar box and read out the questions as a class. The pupils answer in pairs. Then check the answers as a class. (*Went, swam.*)

**Pupil's Book Activity 5**

**Look at the dialogue in Activity 1. Find more examples of the past simple.**
- Organise the pupils into pairs. Ask them to find examples of the past simple in the dialogue. They can do this orally or write the sentences in their notebooks.

**Pupil's Book Activity 6**

**Ask and answer about last weekend.**
- Ask a pupil the questions.
- Organise the class into pairs. The pupils ask and answer questions about last weekend.

**Activity Book**

**Activity 1**

**Read and circle the correct words.**
- Read out the first sentence. Prompt the class to identify the correct word. Highlight that the phrase 'last weekend' tells us the sentence is in the past.
- The pupils work on their own or in pairs to circle the correct words in the remaining sentences.

**Answers:** **1** went **2** were **3** weren't **4** jump **5** couldn't **6** didn't

**Activity 2**

**Read and complete. Use the past simple.**
- Explain to the pupils that they write the past simple form of the verb in brackets. Look at the example together.
- The pupils work on their own or in pairs to complete the remaining answers.

**Answers:** **1** went **2** wore **3** swam **4** walked **5** was **6** couldn't hear **7** looked **8** were

**Activity 3**

**Listen and complete the notes.**

▸ *CD1 Track 23 p278*
- Ask **What's he doing?** (*Rock climbing.*) **Have you ever tried this? Where can you do it? What do you need to wear?**
- Ask the class to read the notes. Then play the CD. The pupils listen and follow in their books.
- Play the CD a second time, pausing after each piece of key information. The pupils should write the missing information each time.
- Play the CD a third time, without stopping it.

**Answers:** **1** rock climbing **2** his dad **3** green **4** helmet **5** eight pounds **6** 6pm

**Activity 4**

**Read and answer. Ask and answer.** me
- Model the activity by asking a pupil the three questions. The pupils then write their own answers.
- The pupils ask and answer questions in pairs.

**Odd one out activity**

**Which is the odd one out? Why?**
- The pupils complete the odd one out activity.

**Answers:** cycling (It isn't a water sport.)

**Ending the lesson**

**Review the lesson and reflect on learning.**
- Say **Today we've learnt how to talk about things that we did in the past.**
- Ask **Which was your favourite activity today? Which activity was easy / difficult?**

**Extra activity**

**Reinforcement**
- Tell the class four things that you did last weekend, some true and others false. Ask pupils to guess which are true.
- Pupils write their own true / false sentences to read to their partner.

## Key Competences and Key Learning Outcomes

- Read a story with a cultural focus
- Listen for specific information
- Learn about prehistoric art
- Use the Internet to investigate France
- Think about the importance of looking after old things
- Learn about the discovery of prehistoric cave paintings in France

**Key language**
- *bulls, cave, ceiling, climb / climbed, deer, find / found, hole, lantern, paintings, secret, tell / told, treasure, walls, woods*
- *The boys made the hole bigger. Is it safe? You have to wait your turn.*

**Materials**
- Pupil's Book p21; Activity Book p18; Class CD1; Teacher's App on Navio

**Optional materials**
- Teacher's Resource Bank: Trinity Exams Practice cards (selected from the Starter Unit and Unit 1)

## At a Glance Lesson Plan

**Starting the lesson**
- Use the Trinity Exams Practice cards (optional).
- Review the past simple.
- Set learning objectives.

**Activity 1: Before you read**
- Read and discuss.

**Activity 2**
- Listen and read.
- ▶ *CD1 Track 24 p278*
- Go to the Activity Book.

**Values**
- Read and discuss.

### Pupil's Book

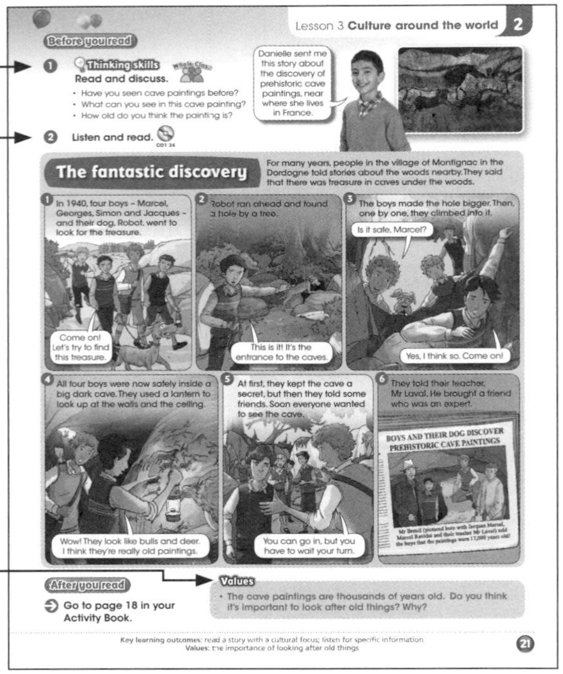

**Ending the lesson**
- Review the lesson and reflect on learning.

**Extra activities**
- Discuss cave paintings in your country.
- Make a list of old buildings, paintings or sculptures around the world.

### Activity Book

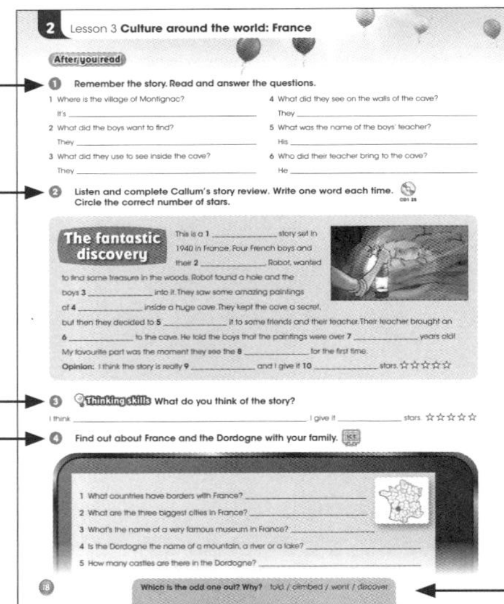

**Activity Book: After you read**

**Activity 1**
- Remember the story. Answer the questions.

**Activity 2**
- Listen and complete Callum's story review.
- ▶ *CD1 Track 25 p278*
- Write one word each time. Circle the correct number of stars.

**Activity 3**
- What do you think of the story?

**Activity 4**
- Find out about France and the Dordogne with your family.

**Odd one out activity**
- Which is the odd one out? Why?

**Digital resources**

**Teacher's Digital:** You can also teach this lesson using the Teacher's App on Navio.

**Pupil's Digital:** Encourage your pupils to use the Pupil's App on Navio to practise the activities from this lesson.

Powered By NAVIO

## Detailed Lesson Plan

### Starting the lesson

**Use the Trinity Exams Practice cards (optional).**

- The pupils practise asking and answering questions.

**Review the past simple.**

- Make a false statement about what you did yesterday. Say **I played tennis yesterday.** The pupils guess if the statement is true or false. Repeat with another two sentences.
- Then invite individual pupils to come to the front of the class and take your role.

**Set learning objectives.**

- Say **Today we're going to read a story from France. We're going to find out about cave paintings.**

### Pupil's Book Activity 1: Before you read

**Read and discuss.**

- Ask the class to look at the cave painting. Ask **What can you see in the painting?**
- Ask **How old do you think the painting is?** Encourage the class to make predictions. Say that they are going to find out the answer in the story.

### Pupil's Book Activity 2

**Listen and read.**

▶ *CD1 Track 24 p278*

- Play the CD. The pupils follow in their books. Confirm that the painting is about 17,000 years old.
- Ask questions to check understanding.

**Suggested comprehension questions:**

- Frame 1: **What are the names of the boys?** (*Marcel, Georges, Simon and Jacques.*)
- Frame 2: **Who found the entrance to the caves?** (*Robot, the dog.*)
- Frame 3: **Who climbed into the hole first?** (*Marcel.*)
- Frame 4: **What did they see?** (*Old paintings on the walls and the ceiling.*)
- Frame 5: **Did they let people into the cave?** (*Yes.*)
- Frame 6: **Who did they tell?** (*Their teacher.*)

### Activity Book: After you read

**Activity 1**

**Remember the story. Read and answer the questions.**

- Ask individual pupils to read out the questions.
- The pupils work on their own to order the sentences.

**Answers:** **1** in the Dordogne. **2** wanted to find treasure. **3** used a lantern. **4** saw old paintings. **5** name was Mr Laval. **6** brought a friend who was an expert.

**Activity 2**

**Listen and complete Callum's story review. Write one word each time. Circle the correct number of stars.**

▶ *CD1 Track 25 p278*

- Read out the story review as a class. Ask the pupils to guess the missing words.
- Play the CD without pausing. The pupils should listen and complete as much of the information as possible.
- Play the CD again, pausing after each piece of key information to check the information and spelling. The pupils circle the correct number of stars.

**Answers:** **1** true **2** dog **3** climbed **4** animals **5** show **6** expert **7** 17,000 **8** paintings **9** exciting **10** four

**Activity 3**

**What do you think of the story?**

- The pupils write their opinion and give a rating.
- Invite the pupils to share their opinions with the class.

**Activity 4**

**Find out about France and the Dordogne with your family.** ICT

- Read out the questions about France. Ask **Where can you find out this information?** (*Internet, library, asking friends and family.*) The pupils complete the activity at home.
- If you prefer to do this activity in the class, connect to a children's website which has information about France such as: www.kids-world-travel-guide.com/france-facts.html. Read out the questions. The pupils work as a class to find the answers.

**Answers:** **1** Germany, Spain, Andorra, Belgium, Luxembourg, Switzerland, Monaco and Italy. **2** Paris, Marseille, Lyon. **3** Louvre **4** A river. **5** More than 1,500.

### Odd one out activity

**Which is the odd one out? Why?**

- The pupils complete the odd one out activity.

**Answers:** discover (It isn't in the past simple.)

### Values

- Read out the statement and the questions. Discuss as a class. Encourage the pupils to think about what people learn from old things. Talk about museums and the discovery of other old things.
- You can also say that the people who ran the caves at Lascaux had many problems with bacteria from visitors visiting the paintings. They built a replica cave for people to visit and they have closed the original cave to protect the paintings.

### Ending the lesson

**Review the lesson and reflect on learning.**

- Say **Today we've read a story from France.**
- Ask **Which was your favourite activity today? Which activity was easy / difficult?**

### Extra activities

**Extension**

- Ask **Do you know any cave paintings in your country?** In Spain, the Altamira caves in Santander are from a similar period.
- If you have time, organise the class into groups to put together a list of old buildings, paintings or sculptures from around the world. Discuss their lists as a class.

## Key Competences and Key Learning Outcomes

- Act out a short dialogue in pairs
- Learn how to form 'Wh-' questions in the past simple
- Identify and practise intonation in questions

### Key language

- *adventure, cousins, explore / explored, go by car, go camping / hiking, go last summer, go to an activity camp, parents*
- *Where / When / Why did (you) go? What did (you) do? How did (you) get there? Who did (you) go with? How long did (you) go for?*

### Materials

- Pupil's Book p22; Activity Book p19; Class CD1; Teacher's App on Navio

### Optional materials

- Teacher's Resource Bank: Trinity Exams Practice cards (selected from the Starter Unit and Unit 1)

## At a Glance Lesson Plan

## Pupil's Book

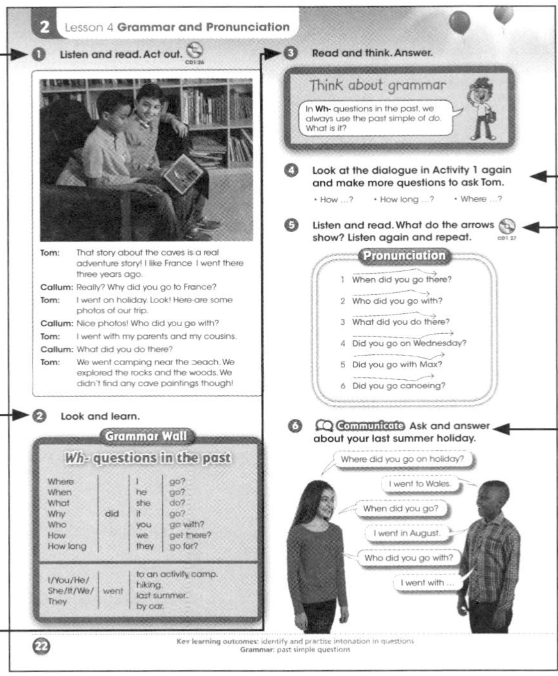


### Starting the lesson

- Use the Trinity Exams Practice cards (optional).
- Review the story from Lesson 3.
- Set learning objectives.

### Activity 1

- Listen and read.
- ▶ ***CD1 Track 26 p278***
- Act out.

### Activity 2

- Look and learn – Grammar wall

### Activity 3

- Read and think.
- Answer.

### Activity 4

- Look at the dialogue in Activity 1 again and make more questions to ask Tom.

### Activity 5

- Listen and read.
- ▶ ***CD1 Track 27 p278***
- What do the arrows show?
- Listen again and repeat.

### Activity 6

- Ask and answer about your last summer holiday.
- Go to the Activity Book.

### Ending the lesson

- Review the lesson and reflect on learning.

### Extra activity

**Extension**

- Create quiz questions about famous people and places.

### Digital resources

**Teacher's Digital:** You can also teach this lesson using the Teacher's App on Navio.

**Pupil's Digital:** Encourage your pupils to use the Pupil's App on Navio to practise the activities from this lesson.

Powered By NAVIO

## Activity Book

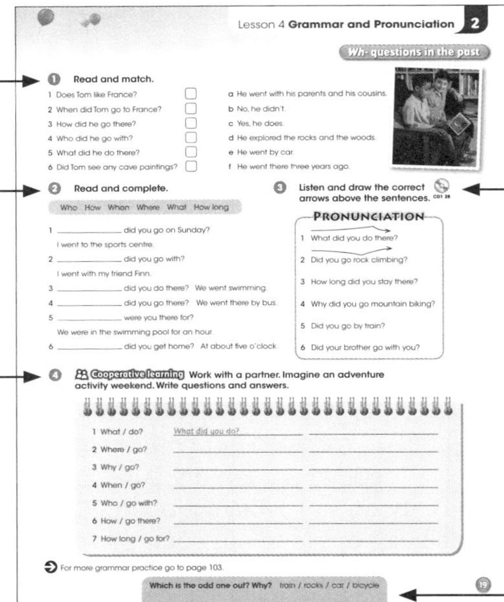


### Activity Book

**Activity 1**

- Read and match.

**Activity 2**

- Read and complete.

**Activity 3**

- Listen and draw the correct arrows above the sentences.
- ▶ ***CD1 Track 28 p279***

**Activity 4**

- Work with a partner. Imagine an adventure activity weekend. Write questions and answers.

**Odd one out activity**

- Which is the odd one out? Why?

# Detailed Lesson Plan

**Starting the lesson**

**Use the Trinity Exams Practice cards (optional).**
- The pupils practise asking and answering questions.

**Review the story from Lesson 3.**
- Ask several yes/no questions about the story from Lesson 3, e.g. **Was the dog called Rupert?** (*No.*)

**Set learning objectives.**
- Say **Today we're going to learn how to ask questions in the past using words like 'What', 'Where' and 'Who'. We're going to practise our pronunciation of these questions too.**

**Pupil's Book Activity 1**

**Listen and read. Act out.**

▶ *CD1 Track 26 p278*
- Ask **What's Tom showing Callum? What do you think the photo shows?**
- Play the CD. The pupils listen and read the dialogue. Confirm that the photo is of Tom's trip to France. Check understanding by asking **Who did he go with?**
- Play the CD again, pausing after each sentence for the pupils to repeat.
- The pupils practise the dialogue in pairs.

**Pupil's Book Activity 2**

**Look and learn – Grammar wall**
- Read the information on the Grammar wall as a class.
- Ask **Which word tells us that the question is in the past?** (*Did.*) **Does 'did' go before or after the subject of the question?** (*Before.*)

**Pupil's Book Activity 3**

**Read and think. Answer.**
- Focus the pupils' attention on the Think about grammar box. Read out the questions as a class. The pupils should decide how to answer in pairs.

**Pupil's Book Activity 4**

**Look at the dialogue in Activity 1 again and make more questions to ask Tom.**
- Ask the pupils to look at the dialogue. They imagine that they are asking Tom more questions about his trip. They use the question prompts.
- Ask two pupils to come to the front of the class. One pupil asks a question and the other pretends to be Tom and answers. Use different pairs for each question.

**Pupil's Book Activity 5**

**Listen and read. What do the arrows show? Listen again and repeat.**

▶ *CD1 Track 27 p278*
- Focus the pupils' attention on the questions and the arrows above the words. Say **Look! The arrow above the questions goes up and down. Let's listen and find out why.** Play the CD. Identify that the intonation goes up and down, or down and up.
- Play the CD again. The pupils listen and repeat the questions. Ask the pupils how the intonation changes if the question begins with 'What' or with 'Did'.

**Pupil's Book Activity 6**

**Ask and answer about your last summer holiday.**
- Say **Think about your last summer holiday.**
- Ask two pupils to read out the speech bubbles.
- The pupils work in pairs to find out about each other's holiday.

**Activity Book**

**Activity 1**

**Read and match.**
- The pupils match the questions and answers.

**Answers:** **1** c **2** f **3** e **4** a **5** d **6** b

**Activity 2**

**Read and complete.**
- Read out the first question. Ask pupils what the missing word is.
- The pupils complete the remaining questions.

**Answers:** **1** Where **2** Who **3** What **4** How **5** How long **6** When

**Activity 3**

**Listen and draw the correct arrows above the sentences.**

▶ *CD1 Track 28 p279*
- Read the first two questions and model the intonation. The pupils practise in pairs as you go round the class and listen to them.
- Play the CD. The pupils draw in the correct arrows.

**Answers:**

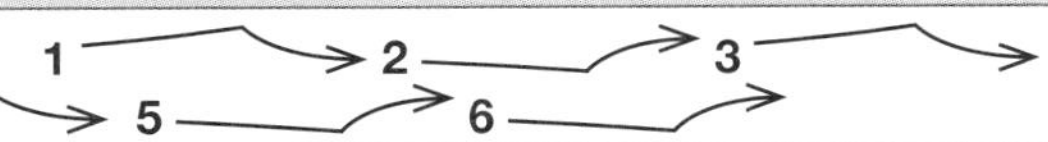


**Activity 4**

**Work with a partner. Imagine an adventure activity weekend. Write questions and answers.**
- The pupils write questions and answers in pairs.

**Answers:** **1** What did you do? **2** Where did you go? **3** Why did you go? **4** When did you do? **5** Who did you go with? **6** How did you go there? **7** How long did you go for?

**Odd one out activity**

**Which is the odd one out? Why?**

**Answers:** rocks (It isn't a vehicle.)

**Ending the lesson**

**Review the lesson and reflect on learning.**
- Say **Today we've learnt how to ask questions in the past and we've practised our pronunciation.**
- Ask **Which was your favourite activity today? Which activity was easy / difficult?**

**Extra activity**

**Extension**
- In pairs, ask the pupils to write three quiz questions about the past, and then have a class quiz.

## Key Competences and Key Learning Outcomes

- Identify and say the names of objects in a survival kit
- Listen for specific information
- Practise activity types found in the Cambridge Exams: A2 Key for Schools
- Do a communication task

**Key language**
- *binoculars, camping stove, insect repellent, matches, rope, saucepan, sleeping bag, sun cream, walking boots, wildlife guidebooks*
- *Where did (Molly) go? She went to Whispering Woods. When did (Patrick) go? What did (Leah) take?*
- **Extension:** *alarm, clock, water bottle, waterproof jacket, waterproof trousers*

**Materials**
- Pupil's Book p23; Activity Book pp20; Class CD1; Teacher's App on Navio; Teacher's Resource Bank: Unit 2
- Outdoor activities and equipment flashcards

**Optional materials**
- Teacher's Resource Bank: Trinity Exams Practice cards (selected from the Starter Unit and Unit 1)
- Pictures of remote but exciting places

## At a Glance Lesson Plan

### Pupil's Book

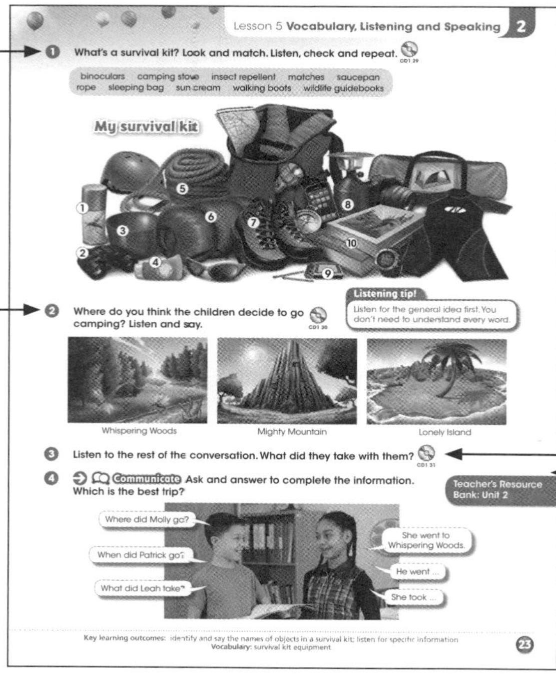


**Starting the lesson**
- Use the Trinity Exams Practice cards (optional).
- Review outdoor activities and equipment.
- Set learning objectives.

**Activity 1**
- What's a survival kit?
- Look and match.
- Listen, check and repeat.

▶ *CD1 Track 29 p279*

**Activity 2**
- Where do you think the children decide to go camping?
- Listen and say.

▶ *CD1 Track 30 p279*

**Activity 3**
- Listen to the rest of the conversation.

▶ *CD1 Track 31 p279*
- What did they take with them?

**Activity 4**
- Ask and answer to complete the information (Teacher's Resource Bank: Unit 2).
- Which is the best trip?

Go to the Activity Book.

**Ending the lesson**
- Review the lesson and reflect on learning.

**Extra activities**

**Reinforcement**
- Create a collage of objects you should take with you on a trip.

**Vocabulary extension**
- Present four additional vocabulary items.

### Activity Book

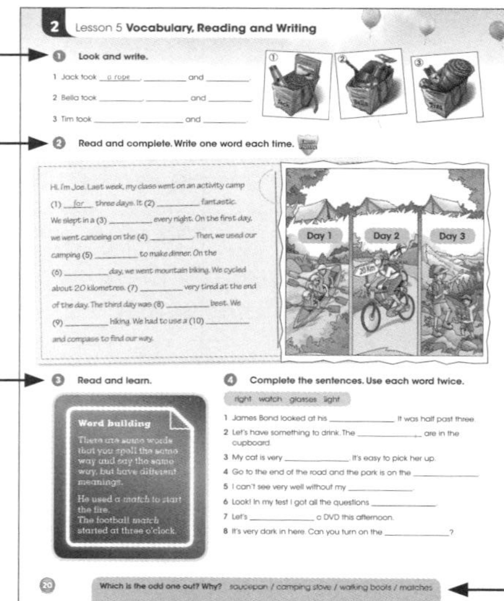


**Activity Book**

**Activity 1**
- Look and write.

**Activity 2**
- Read and complete. Write one word each time.

**Activity 3**
- Read and learn.

**Activity 4**
- Complete the sentences. Use each word twice.

**Odd one out activity**
- Which is the odd one out? Why?

## Digital resources

**Teacher's Digital:** You can also teach this lesson using the Teacher's App on Navio.

**Pupil's Digital:** Encourage your pupils to use the Pupil's App on Navio to practise the activities from this lesson.

Powered By NAVIO

# Detailed Lesson Plan

## Starting the lesson

**Use the Trinity Exams Practice cards (optional).**
- The pupils practise asking and answering questions.

**Review outdoor activities and equipment.**
- Play the *Chain game* (see p27) with the outdoor activities and equipment flashcards.

**Set learning objectives.**
- Say **Today we're going to learn some words for objects you can take on a camping trip and we're going to do a communication task too.**

## Pupil's Book Activity 1

**What's a survival kit? Look and match. Listen, check and repeat.**

▶ ***CD1 Track 29 p279***
- Ask the pupils if they can guess what a survival kit is. Ask **When do people need a survival kit?**
- Ask the pupils to name as many objects as possible in the picture.
- Organise the class into pairs. Ask them to match the words in the box to the items.
- Play the CD. The pupils listen and check.
- Play the CD again, pausing after each word for the pupils to repeat.

## Pupil's Book Activity 2

**Where do you think the children decide to go camping? Listen and say.**

▶ ***CD1 Track 30 p279***
- Focus the class on the three pictures. Ask the pupils to describe each one.
- Ask the pupils to vote for where they think the children have decided to go camping. Say **Let's see who is right.**
- Play the CD. The pupils listen and note down which place the children decide to go to. (*Whispering Woods.*)

## Pupil's Book Activity 3

**Listen to the rest of the conversation. What did they take with them?**

▶ ***CD1 Track 31 p279***
- Say **The children have a tent, sleeping bags, a rucksack and some food.**
- Ask the pupils to listen and write down the objects that the children decide to bring with them. (*Insect repellent, torch, map, compass, sun cream, binoculars, wildlife guidebook.*)
- Play the CD. Play it again if necessary.

## Pupil's Book Activity 4

**Ask and answer to complete the information (Teacher's Resource Bank: Unit 2). Which is the best trip?**
- Invite two pupils to read out the speech bubbles.
- Organise the class into pairs (A and B). Give Pupils A the first worksheet from Teacher's Resource Bank Unit 2 and give Pupils B the other worksheet.
- Ask a confident pair to demonstrate the activity. Then ask the pupils to do the activity in their pairs.

## Activity Book

**Activity 1**

**Look and write.**
- The pupils complete the sentences.

**Answers:** **1** a rope, a wildlife guidebook, sun cream **2** a camping stove, matches, a saucepan **3** a sleeping bag, insect repellent, a torch

**Activity 2**

**Read and complete. Write one word each time.**
- Focus the pupils on the picture. Ask them to describe what they can see. Then read out the text as a class. Check comprehension by asking questions.
- Complete the first two sentences as a class.
- The pupils complete the remaining sentences.

**Answers:** **1** for **2** was **3** tent **4** river **5** stove **6** second **7** was **8** the **9** went **10** map

**Activity 3**

**Read and learn.**
- Read the information as a class. Encourage the pupils to think of other examples.

**Activity 4**

**Complete the sentences. Use each word twice.**
- The pupils work on their own or in pairs to complete the sentences.

**Answers:** **1** watch **2** glasses **3** light **4** right **5** glasses **6** right **7** watch **8** light

**Odd one out activity**

**Which is the odd one out? Why?**
- The pupils complete the odd one out activity.

**Answers:** walking boots (You don't use them to cook.)

## Ending the lesson

**Review the lesson and reflect on learning.**
- Say **Today we've learnt some new objects to take on a camping trip and we've played a communication game.**
- Ask **Which was your favourite activity today? Which activity was easy / difficult?**

## Extra activity

**Reinforcement**
- Show photos of different kinds of places to visit. Ask the pupils to describe the place and then to say which items they would take with them on a trip to this place.
- Put the pupils in groups of three. Ask them to decide on five items that they would take with them.
- Make a collage with the pupils writing descriptions of the places and the survival kit that they would take with them.

**Vocabulary extension**
- Present four additional words: *alarm clock, water bottle, waterproof jacket, waterproof trousers.*
- Use the Vocabulary booster on NAVIO to practise these new words.

**Key Competences and Key Learning Outcomes**

- Do pre-reading tasks to predict content and raise interest
- Read a blog post for general understanding
- Scan a blog post for specific information

- Discuss blogs

- Read and understand a travel blog
- Give an opinion on the text

**Key language**

- *beach, bike rack, blog, campsite, cereal, cliff, coast, cow, cycle, duck, fried eggs, goat, got dressed, halfway, helicopter, hot dog, laptop, put up a tent, ready to go, rescue, rope, safe, sheep, sleeping bags, stuck, tired, toast*
- *My name's Kieron. Welcome to my first ever blog! I'll write my blog at the end of every day.*

**Materials**

- Pupil's Book p24; Activity Book p21; Class CD1; Teacher's App on Navio
- Examples of online blogs

**Optional materials**

- Teacher's Resource Bank: Trinity Exams Practice cards (selected from the Starter Unit and Unit 1)

## At a Glance Lesson Plan

### Pupil's Book

**Starting the lesson**

- Use the Trinity Exams Practice cards (optional).
- Review objects in a survival kit.
- Set learning objectives.

**Activity 1: Before you read**

- Read and discuss.

**Activity 2**

- Read these sentences.
- Then read the travel blog quickly and say if each thing happened on Day 1 or Day 2.
- Read again and check.

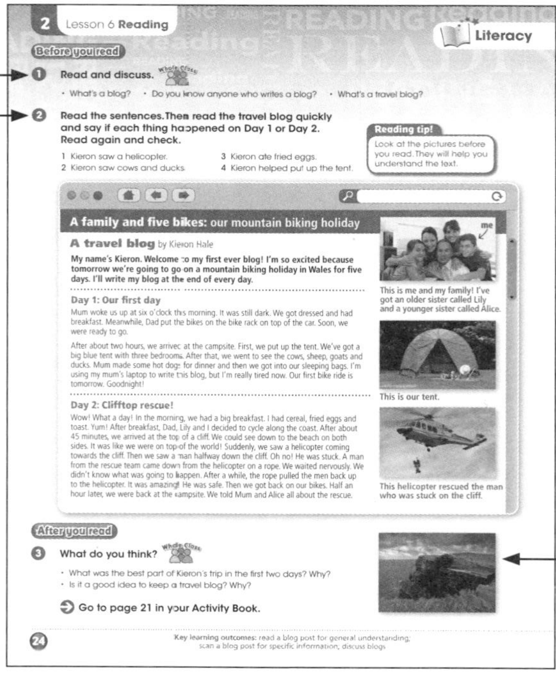

**Activity 3: After you read**

- What do you think?
- Go to the Activity Book.

**Ending the lesson**

- Review the lesson and reflect on learning.

**Extra activity**

**Reinforcement**

- Imagine you are Kieron's mother and write questions about Day 2.

### Activity Book

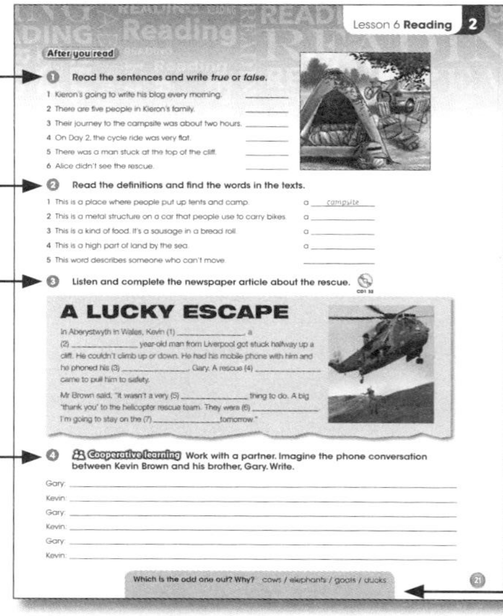

**Activity Book: After you read**

**Activity 1**

- Read the sentences and write *true* or *false*.

**Activity 2**

- Read the definitions and find the words in the texts.

**Activity 3**

- Listen and complete the newspaper article about the rescue.

▶ *CD1 Track 32 p279*

**Activity 4**

- Work with a partner. Imagine the phone conversation between Kevin Brown and his brother, Gary. Write.

**Odd one out activity**

- Which is the odd one out? Why?

**Digital resources**

**Teacher's Digital:** You can also teach this lesson using the Teacher's App on Navio.

**Pupil's Digital:** Encourage your pupils to use the Pupil's App on Navio to practise the activities from this lesson.

Powered By NAVIO

# Detailed Lesson Plan

## Starting the lesson

**Use the Trinity Exams Practice cards (optional).**

- The pupils practise asking and answering questions.

**Review objects in a survival kit.**

- Review objects in a survival kit by playing a guessing game.
- Invite a pupil to think of an object from the previous lesson and then ask yes/no questions. Ask **Is it electrical? Is it in a bottle?** After three questions you have to try and guess the object. Repeat the game with another pupil thinking of an object and pupils asking the questions.

**Set learning objectives.**

- Say **Today we're going to read a travel blog about a boy's mountain biking holiday.**

## Pupil's Book Activity 1: Before you read

**Read and discuss.**

- Read the questions as a class. Prompt the pupils to answer in as much detail as possible. Explain that a blog is similar to a diary that is kept on the Internet. Show the pupils some examples.

## Pupil's Book Activity 2

**Read the sentences. Then read the travel blog quickly and say if each thing happened on Day 1 or Day 2. Read again and check.**

- Look at the photos. Ask **Who is going on the trip? Where are they sleeping? What's in the third photo?**
- Ask a pupil to read the four sentences. Explain that the pupils shouldn't read the blog in detail. They have to skim read the text. Say **You have one minute to find which things Kieron did on Day 1 and which things he did on Day 2.**
- The pupils do the task.
- The pupils read the text again as a class or in pairs to see if their answers are correct.

**Answers:** **1** Day 2 **2** Day 1 **3** Day 2 **4** Day 1

## Pupil's Book Activity 3: After you read

**What do you think?**

- Read the questions as a class. Prompt the pupils to give their views. Find out how many people would like to keep a blog and why.

## Activity Book: After you read

### Activity 1

**Read the sentences and write *true* or *false*.**

- The pupils work on their own or in pairs to read each sentence and decide if it's true or false. The pupils should refer back to the text in the Pupil's Book when necessary.

**Answers:** **1** false **2** true **3** true **4** false **5** false **6** true

### Activity 2

**Read the definitions and find the words in the text.**

- The pupils, on their own or in pairs, read the definitions and write the words. They should refer back to the text in the Pupil's Book when necessary.

**Answers:** **1** a campsite **2** bike rack **3** hot dog **4** cliff **5** stuck

### Activity 3

**Listen and complete the newspaper article about the rescue.**

▶ ***CD1 Track 32 p279***

- Read out the article, pausing at the spaces to allow the pupils to predict what the missing words could be.
- Play the CD. The pupils listen and follow the information in their books.
- Play the CD again, pausing after each piece of key information. The pupils should write the missing information each time.

**Answers:** **1** Brown **2** 30 **3** brother **4** helicopter **5** clever **6** fantastic **7** beach

### Activity 4

**Work with a friend. Imagine the phone conversation between Kevin Brown and his brother, Gary. Write.**

- The pupils think about the phone conversation between Kevin and his brother. Together with the class, think of some things that Kevin could say first of all. (*Hi Gary. I need some help.*)
- In pairs, the pupils complete the dialogue. Ask some pairs to read their dialogue out to the class.

**Odd one out activity**

**Which is the odd one out? Why?**

- The pupils complete the odd one out activity.

**Answers:** elephants (They're wild animals.)

## Ending the lesson

**Review the lesson and reflect on learning.**

- Say **Today we've read a travel blog about a trip to Wales.**
- Ask **Which was your favourite activity today? Which activity was easy / difficult?**

## Extra activity

**Reinforcement**

- Ask the pupils to imagine they are Kieron's mother when Kieron comes back to the tent on Day 2. Kieron says *We saw a man rescued by a helicopter!* The pupils individually or in pairs write questions she asks him about the things he saw, e.g. *How old was the man?*
- The pupils could then ask and answer the questions in pairs in front of the class.

## Key Competences and Key Learning Outcomes

- Identify time connectives
- Identify the order of events in a chronological account
- Plan a blog entry about a trip
- Use criteria to check your writing
- Share your writing with another pupil
- Write a blog post

### Key language

- *after an hour, after breakfast / dinner, at 11 o'clock, at first, at last, finally, first of all, meanwhile, one hour later, straightaway, soon, suddenly, then; clouds, lightning, muddy, rain, shower, sunny, timeline, thunder, wet;*
- *We couldn't see very well. He put on some sun cream.*

### Materials

- Pupil's Book p25; Activity Book p22; Teacher's App on Navio

### Optional materials

- Teacher's Resource Bank: Trinity Exams Practice cards (selected from the Starter Unit and Unit 1)

## At a Glance Lesson Plan

### Pupil's Book

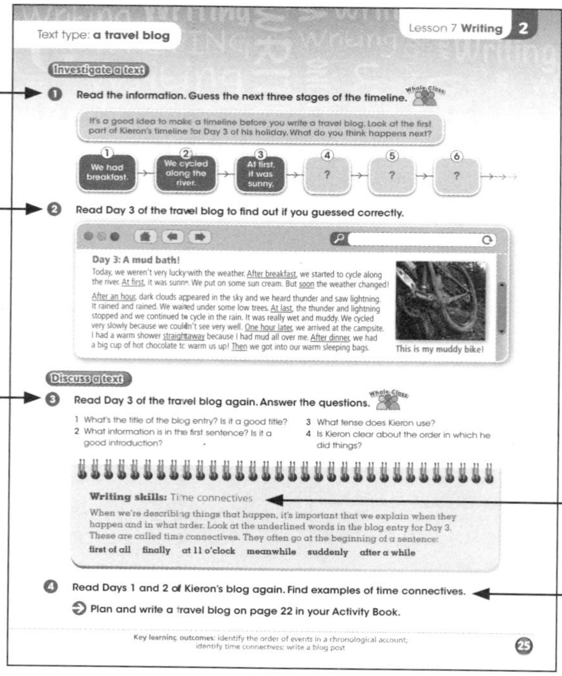

**Starting the lesson**

- Use the Trinity Exams Practice cards (optional).
- Review past simple verbs.
- Set learning objectives.

**Activity 1: Investigate a text**

- Read the information.
- Guess the next three stages of the timeline.

**Activity 2**

- Read Day 3 of the travel blog to find out if you guessed correctly.

**Activity 3: Discuss a text**

- Read Day 3 of the travel blog again.
- Answer the questions.

**Writing skills**

- Read about using time connectives.

**Activity 4**

- Read Days 1 and 2 of Keiron's blog again.
- Find examples of time connectives.

Go to the Activity Book.

**Ending the lesson**

- Review the lesson and reflect on learning.

**Extra activity**

**Reinforcement**

- Write a timeline for your friend's travel blog.

### Activity Book

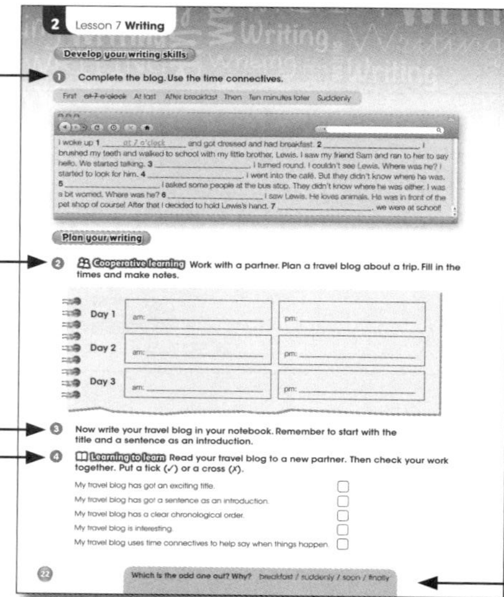

**Activity Book**

**Activity 1: Develop your writing skills**

- Complete the blog. Use the time connectives.

**Activity 2: Plan your writing**

- Work with a partner. Plan a travel blog about a trip. Fill in the times and make notes.

**Activity 3**

- Now write your travel blog in your notebook. Remember to start with the title and a sentence as an introduction.

**Activity 4**

- Read your travel blog to a new partner. Then check your work together. Put a tick (✓) or a cross (✗).

**Odd one out activity**

- Which is the odd one out? Why?

## Digital resources

**Teacher's Digital:** You can also teach this lesson using the Teacher's App on Navio.

**Pupil's Digital:** Encourage your pupils to use the Pupil's App on Navio to practise the activities from this lesson.

Powered By NAVIO

# Detailed Lesson Plan

### Starting the lesson

**Use the Trinity Exams Practice cards (optional).**

- The pupils practise asking and answering questions.

**Review past simple verbs.**

- Review some past simple verbs that will be used in the lesson. Write these verbs on the board: *start, put on, change, appear, hear, see, wait, stop, continue, have.*
- Ask the pupils to write the ten verbs in the past simple tense. Ask if they think the verbs are regular or irregular.

**Set learning objectives.**

- Say **Today we're going to write a travel blog and we're going to use a timeline.**

### Pupil's Book Activity 1: Investigate a text

**Read the information. Guess the next three stages of the timeline.**

- Introduce the idea of a timeline by writing four sentences on the board: *I went to the shops. I got dressed. I got up. I bought some bread.* Ask the pupils to put the sentences in order. Then rewrite the sentences with arrows between them. Say **This is a timeline. It shows the order that things happen.**
- Read the three sentences of the timeline in Activity 1. Ask the pupils to think about what happened next and write down some ideas.

### Pupil's Book Activity 2

**Read Day 3 of the travel blog to find out if you guessed correctly.**

- Read the text as a class.
- Check to see if anyone predicted correctly.
- Check understanding of the text by asking questions. Ask **What did they do when it was sunny? What did they do when there was thunder and lightning? What was the first thing Kieron did when he arrived at the campsite? What did they do after dinner?**

### Pupil's Book Activity 3: Discuss a text

**Read Day 3 of the travel blog again. Answer the questions.**

- Read and discuss the questions as a class. Highlight that using an introductory sentence is a good way to start a blog entry.

### Writing skills

**Read the information.**

- Give some example sentences with the time connectives. Then ask the pupils to give some too. You may need to explain 'meanwhile'. It means 'at the same time'.

### Pupil's Book Activity 4

**Read Days 1 and 2 of Kieron's blog again. Find examples of time connectives.**

- Ask the pupils to look at Kieron's blog and find more examples of time connectives.

### Activity Book

**Activity 1: Develop your writing skills**

**Complete the blog. Use the time connectives.**

- The pupils work on their own or in pairs to complete the blog using the time connectives from the box.

**Answers:** **1** at 7 o'clock **2** After breakfast **3** Suddenly **4** First **5** Then **6** At last **7** Ten minutes later

**Activity 2: Plan your writing**

**Work with a partner. Plan a travel blog entry about a trip. Fill in the times and make notes.**

- Remind the pupils about how a timeline works. They have to write notes about a trip. This can be a trip they have been on or one that they are imagining. You can give an example: **got on train / stopped for lunch.**
- Organise the class into Writing Partners. The pupils complete the timeline.

**Activity 3**

**Now write your travel blog in your notebook. Remember to start with the title and a sentence as an introduction.**

- The pupils work with a Writing Partner to write their travel blog in their notebooks. Remind the class to write a title at the top of the page and then begin with an introductory sentence. The rest of the blog should follow the order of the timeline.

**Activity 4**

**Read your travel blog to a new partner. Then check your work together. Put a tick (✓) or a cross (✗).**

- Read through the statements as a class.
- Organise the class into new Writing Partners. One pupil reads aloud their text to their partner. The other pupil listens. The pupils work together to decide if the text fulfils the criteria and tick the corresponding boxes. The pupils can add, improve or correct the text at this stage.
- The pupils swap roles.

**Odd one out activity**

**Which is the odd one out? Why?**

- The pupils complete the odd one out activity.

**Answers:** breakfast (It isn't a time connective.)

### Ending the lesson

**Review the lesson and reflect on learning.**

- Say **Today we've written a travel blog entry about a trip and learnt to use time connectives.**
- Ask **Which was your favourite activity today? Which activity was easy / difficult?**

### Extra activity

**Reinforcement**

- Ask the pupils to read another pupil's travel blog and try to guess the timeline that they had for their plan. They should write it in note form.
- The pupils compare their guess with the timeline that was used.

### Key Competences and Key Learning Outcomes

- Listen to and have a conversation about your favourite place to visit
- Listen to a text for general understanding
- Prepare a presentation
- Review learning and reflect on progress in the unit
- Write questions with a partner

### Key language

- *beach, boat trip, cafe, caravan, cliffs, coast, hotel, surfing, swimming*
- *Where is it? When did you last go there? What can you eat there?*

### Materials

- Pupil's Book p26; Activity Book p23 and 24; Class CD1; Teacher's App on Navio

### Optional materials

- Teacher's Resource Bank: Trinity Exams Practice cards (selected from the Starter Unit and Unit 1)

## At a Glance Lesson Plan

### Pupil's Book

**Starting the lesson**
- Use the Trinity Exams Practice cards (optional).
- Review outdoor activities.
- Set learning objectives.

**Activity 1**
- Describe the photos.
- What's Mike's favourite place to visit?

**Activity 2**
- Listen to the conversation.
- ▶ *CD1 Track 33 p279*
- What does Mike like doing there?

**Activity 3**
- Listen again.
- ▶ *CD1 Track 33 p279*
- Complete five questions that Hannah asks.

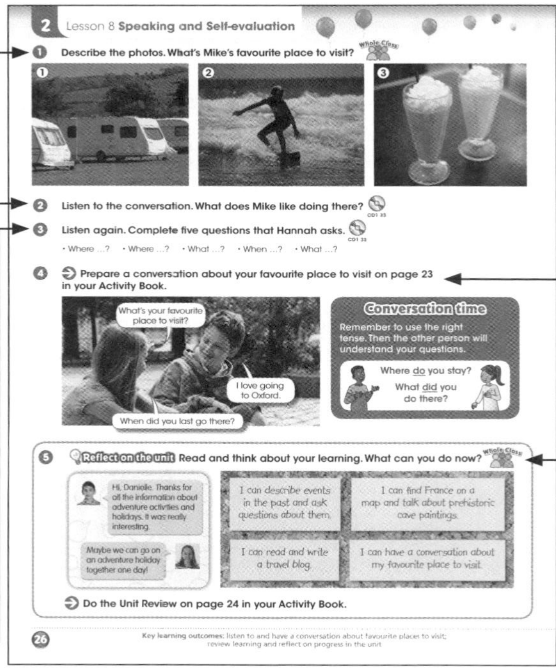

**Activity 4**
- Prepare a conversation about your favourite place to visit on page 23 in your Activity book.

Go to page 23 in the Activity Book.

**Activity 5**
- Read and think about your learning. What can you do now?

Go to page 24 in the Activity Book.

**Ending the lesson**
- Review the lesson and reflect on learning.

**Extra activity**
- Play a guessing game about a place in your country.

### Activity Book

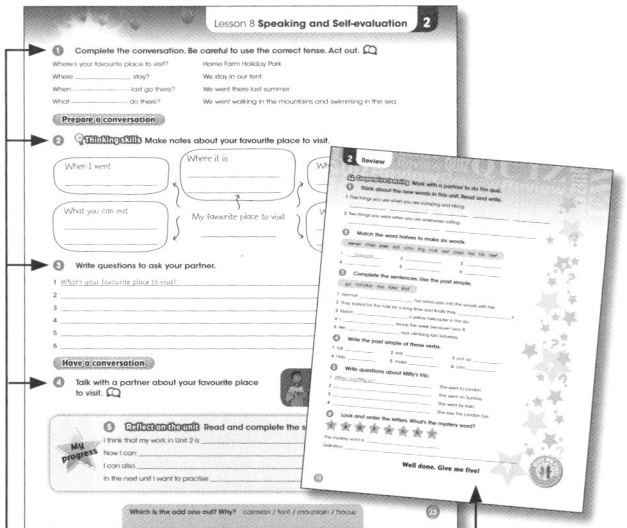

**Activity Book page 24: Review**
- Work with a partner to do the quiz.

**Activity Book**

**Activity 1**
- Complete the conversation.
- Be careful to use the correct tense
- Act out.

**Activity 2**
- Make notes about your favourite place to visit.

**Activity 3**
- Write questions to ask your partner.

**Activity 4**
- Talk with a partner about your favourite place to visit.

**Activity 5**
- Read and complete the sentences.

**Odd one out activity**
- Which is the odd one out? Why?

## Digital resources

**Teacher's Digital:** You can also teach this lesson using the Teacher's App on Navio.

Powered By NAVIO

# Detailed Lesson Plan

**Starting the lesson**

**Use the Trinity Exams Practice cards (optional).**

- The pupils practise asking and answering questions.

**Review outdoor equipment.**

- Describe one of the outdoor equipment words, for example **We use this if we're lost.** Pupils choose and describe other words in pairs.

**Set learning objectives.**

- Say **Today we're going to prepare a conversation about our favourite place to visit.**

**Pupil's Book Activity 1**

**Describe the clothes. What's Mike's favourite place to visit?**

- Ask different pupils to describe the photos. Explain that they are all different things that you can find in Mike's favourite place. Ask pupils what sort of place it is.

**Pupil's Book Activity 2**

**Listen to the conversation. What does Mike like doing there?**

▶ ***CD1 Track 33 p279***

- Play the CD. As well as the activities that Mike likes, ask if pupils remember the name of the place (Land's End in Cornwall).

**Answer:** Mike likes walking in the cliffs, swimming and surfing in the sea, going to the café in the village and doing on a boat trip.

**Pupil's Book Activity 3**

**Listen again. Complete five questions that Hannah asks.**

▶ ***CD1 Track 33 p279***

- Direct pupils to the four question prompts. Ask if they can remember the questions.
- Play the CD. Pupils check in pairs. Then play again and check as a class.

**Answers:** Where is it?; Where do you stay?; What can you eat there?; When did you last go there, What did you do there?

**Pupil's Book Activity 4**

**Prepare a conversation about your favourite place to visit on page 23 in your Activity Book.**

- Read the speech bubbles with the pupils. Model the phrases in the Conversation Time box and get the class to repeat.

**Pupil's Book Activity 5**

**Read and think about your learning. What can you do now?**

- Read the speech bubbles and notes with the pupils. Then look back through the unit and prompt them to identify things that they have done/learnt.

**Activity Book page 24: Review**

**Work with a partner to do the quiz.**

- Organise the class into pairs. Set a time limit for the pupils to do the quiz (10–15 minutes). Stress that the pupils are not competing with each other.
- Read out the six tasks. Check understanding. Then say **Ready, steady ... Go!**
- The pupils work in their pairs to do the quiz.
- Correct the answers as a class.

**Answers:** **1** Five from: binoculars, camping stove, insect repellent, matches, rope, saucepan, sleeping bag, sun cream, torch, walking boots, wildlife guidebooks **2** Helmet, life jacket **2 1** saucepan **2** wetsuit **3** helmet **4** hiking **5** compass **6** matches **3 1** took **2** found **3** saw **4** didn't play **5** went **4 1** fell **2** ate **3** put up **4** helped **5** made **6** could **5 1** Where did Milly go? **2** When did Milly go? **3** How did Milly go? **4** What did Milly see? **6** rucksack, something you wear on your back to carry things

**Activity Book**

**Activity 1**

**Complete the conversation. Be careful to use the correct tense. Act out.**

- Demonstrate the dialogue with a pupil. Ask him/her the questions. Then pupils perform the dialogue in pairs.

**Activity 2**

**Make notes about your favourite place to visit.**

- Tell pupils about your favourite place to visit. Then pupils complete the boxes with their own information.

**Activity 3**

**Write questions to ask your partner.**

- Direct pupils to the six headings in Activity 2 and explain that they need to form questions about them. Then pupils complete the questions alone. Check as a class.

**Answers:** **1** What's your favourite place to visit? **2** When did you go there? **3** Where is it? **4** What can you do (there)? **5** Who did you go with? **6** What did you do (there)?

**Activity 4**

**Talk with a partner about your favourite place to visit.**

- In pairs, pupils ask and answer the questions from Activity 3.
- Invite one or two pairs to perform their conversations for the class.

**Activity 5**

**Read and complete the sentences.**

- Pupils to review their work in the unit.

**Odd one out activity**

**Which is the odd one out? Why?**

**Answer:** mountain (You can't sleep in it.)

**Ending the lesson**

**Review the lesson and reflect on learning.**

- Say **Today we've learnt how to have a conversation about our favourite place to visit.**
- Ask **Which was your favourite activity today? Which activity was easy / difficult?**

### Key Competences and Key Learning Outcomes

- Watch and understand a video about adventurous sports
- Learn about safety equipment when doing dangerous activities

**Key language**

- *adventurous, icy, paragliding, race, rocks, scary, skiing, snowboarding, tightrope walking*
- *Where did she live? Why was he famous? When were they born?*

**Materials**

- Pupil's Book p27; Activity Book p25; Class CD1; Teacher's App on Navio
- Teacher's Resource Bank: Talk cards

**Optional materials**

- Teacher's Resource Bank: Trinity Exams Practice cards (selected from the Starter Unit and Unit 1)

## At a Glance Lesson Plan

### Pupil's Book

**Starting the lesson**

- Use the Trinity Exams Practice cards (optional).
- **Think-Pair-Share** Review outdoor activities vocabulary.
- Set learning objectives and use the talk cards.

**Activity 1**

- Before you watch
- Watch the video.
  *Unit 2 video p300*
- Read and answer the questions.

**Activity 2**

- Match the words to the pictures.
- Then watch the video again.
  *Unit 2 video*
- Which activities does Max mention?

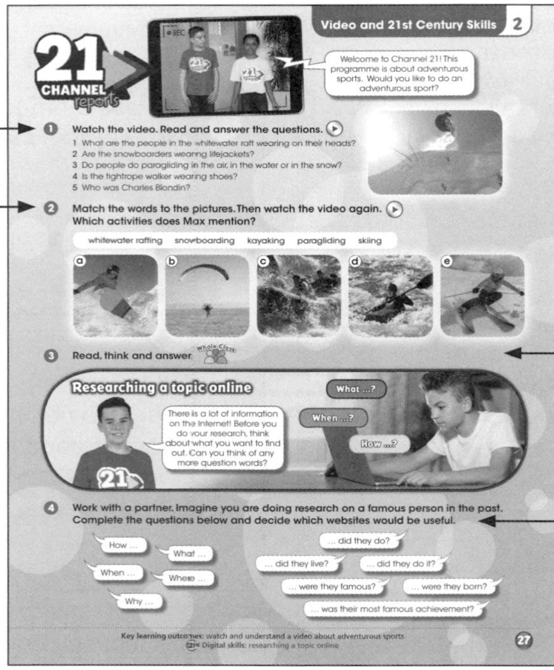

**Activity 3**

- Read, think and answer.

**Activity 4**

- Work with a partner.
- Imagine you are doing research on a famous person in the past.
- Complete the questions below and decide which websites would be useful.

Go to the Activity Book

**Ending the lesson**

- Review the lesson and reflect on learning.

**Extra activity**

- Play a mime game to revise outdoor activities vocabulary.

### Activity Book

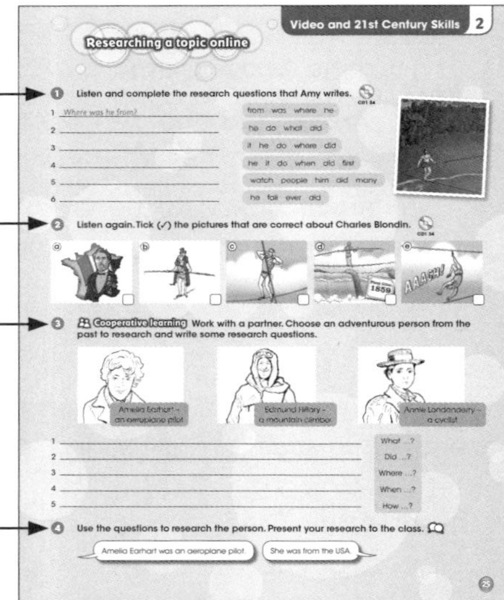

**Activity Book**

**Activity 1**

- Listen and repeat the research questions that Amy writes.

▶ ***CD1 Track 34 p279***

**Activity 2**

- Listen again.
- Tick (✓) the pictures that are correct about Charles Blondin.

▶ ***CD1 Track 34 p279***

**Activity 3**

- Work with a partner.
- Choose an adventurous person from the past to research and write some research questions.

**Activity 4**

- Use the questions to research the person.
- Present your research to the class.

### Digital resources

**Teacher's Digital:** You can also teach this lesson using the Teacher's App on Navio.

**Pupil's Digital:** Encourage your pupils to use the Pupil's App on Navio to practise the activities from this lesson.

Powered By NAVIO

### Starting the lesson

**Think-Pair-Share Review outdoor activities vocabulary.**

- Ask **How many different clothes and clothes adjectives can you think of?** The class thinks silently for a minute.
- Then the pupils work with a Talk Partner to name outdoor activities.
- Invite different Talk Partners to say different outdoor activities. Hold up the corresponding flashcard and prompt the class to repeat the word.
- Finally, repeat the procedure, asking different pairs of Talk Partners each time, until all the ideas have been recorded.

**Set learning objectives and use the talk cards.**

- Say **Today we're going to watch a video and then ask and answer questions about adventurous sports.**
- Point to the talk cards to show the pupils the different ways they will be working in the lesson.

### Pupil's Book Activity 1

**Before you watch**

- Read the speech bubble to pupils. Ask **Would you like to do an adventurous sport?** Elicit responses from a number of pupils.

**Watch the video. Read and answer the questions.**

*p300*

- Watch Part 1 of the video. Ask pupils **What are you going to see next?**
- Play Part 2 of the video. Direct pupils to the sentences in Activity 1, and ask **What are the people in the whitewater raft wearing on their heads?** Pupils offer ideas.
- Play the video again. Pupils answer the questions. Check answers as a group.

**Answers:** **1** helmets **2** No, they aren't. **3** in the air **4** No, he isn't. **5** a famous tightrope walker

### Pupil's Book Activity 2

**Match the words to the pictures. Then watch the video again. Which activities does Max mention?**

- Ask pupils **What activities does Max mention?** Pupils offer ideas.
- Play the video. Check the answers as a class.

**Answers:** Max mentions whitewater rafting, skiing, snowboarding and paragliding.

### Pupil's Book Activity 3

**Read, think and answer.**

- Read the speech bubble with the class. Ask pupils what letters question words most words in English start with (*Wh* – the only exception is *How*).
- Pupils work in pairs to think of questions beginning with the question words. They ask each other the questions.

### Pupil's Book Activity 4

**Work with a partner. Imagine you are doing research on a famous person in the past. Complete the questions below and decide which websites would be useful.**

- Ask pupils to think of famous people in the past who they want to learn more about.
- Pupils work in pairs to complete the questions.

**Answers:** What did they do? Where/When did they live? Where did they do it? Why were they famous? Where/When were they born? What was their most famous achievement?

### Activity Book

**Activity 1**

**Listen and complete the research questions that Amy writes.**

▶ ***CD1 Track 34 p279***

- Ask pupils if they remember which famous person Amy wants to research and why he was famous (*Charles Blondin; he was a famous tightrope walker*).
- Pupils can try and order the questions before they listen.

**Answers:** **1** Where was he from? **2** What did he do? **3** Where did he do it? **4** When did he first do it? **5** Did many people watch him? **6** Did he ever fall?

**Activity 2**

**Listen again. Tick (✓) the pictures that are correct about Charles Blondin.**

▶ ***CD1 Track 34 p279***

**Answers:** a, b, d

- Ask the pupils to explain why pictures c and e are incorrect. (*Picture c – He didn't cover his ears. He covered his eyes. Picture e – He never fell.*)

**Activity 3**

**Work with a partner. Choose an adventurous person from the past to research and write some research questions.**

- Pupils work together. Tell them to choose one of the people and write five questions together.

**Activity 4**

**Use the questions to research the person. Present your research to the class.**

- Remind the pupils of websites where they can research the information they need.
- Encourage pupils to look for the information on two different websites, not just one, so they can be sure that it's correct.
- Invite pairs of pupils to come to the class to talk about the person that they researched.

### Ending the lesson

**Review the lesson and reflect on learning.**

- Say **Today we've watched a video about adventurous sports. What have we learnt about researching information online?** Elicit ideas from the pupils.

Date: ______________ Unit: ________

**1 What did my pupils learn in this unit?**

**2 How did my pupils work? (✓)**

individually ☐ in pairs ☐ in small groups ☐

in large groups ☐ as a class ☐

**3 Which key competences did my pupils develop? Give a score from 1 to 5 (5 being the highest).**

- Competence in linguistic communication ☐
- Competence in mathematics, science and technology ☐
- Digital competence ☐
- Learning to learn ☐
- Social and civic competences ☐
- Sense of initiative and entrepreneurship ☐
- Cultural awareness and expression ☐

**4 Which lessons / activities were the most successful and why?**

**5 Which lessons / activities did my pupils find the most difficult and why?**

**6 What did I try in the classroom for the first time? How did it go?**

**7 Which resources did I find most useful? (including webpages)**

**8 What could I do differently next time I teach this unit?**

Unit 3

# I ♥ my city

## Unit overview

### Key Competences and Key Learning Outcomes

- Review and learn the names of places in a city (Lesson 1)
- Identify and practise the past continuous (Lesson 2)
- Identify and practise using the past continuous with the past simple (Lesson 4)
- Review and learn activities you do in a city (Lesson 5)
- Review and practise using adverbs of manner (Lesson 7)
- Talk about your favourite place in town (Lesson 8)
- Watch and understand a video about other people's favourite cities (Video and 21st Century Skills)

---

- Learn about volcanic activity (Lesson 3)
- Learn about Venn diagrams (Video and 21st Century Skills)

---

- Use the Pupil's App on Navio
- Investigate Italy (Lesson 3)

---

LEARN

- Identify and practise the weak and strong forms of 'was' (Lesson 4)
- Identify and use expressions to ask for repetition and clarification (Lesson 5)
- Reflect on your own learning (Lesson 8)
- Practise activity types found in the Cambridge Exams: A2 Key for Schools

---

- Think about things you must and mustn't do in an emergency (Lesson 3)

---

- Work in pairs and small groups (all lessons)
- Do a communication task (Lesson 5)

---

- Read a story (Lesson 3)
- Learn about Italy and the ancient city of Pompeii (Lesson 3)
- Read a story opener (Lesson 6)
- Write a story opener (Lesson 7)
- Sing a song (Lesson 8)
- Learn about the city of Venice (Video and 21st Century Skills)

### Vocabulary

**Core vocabulary**
*bridge, castle, crossroads, fountain, pavement, pedestrian crossing, square, statue, steps, tower, town hall, traffic lights; catch a taxi, cross the road, get off the bus, get on the bus, go sightseeing, have a snack, meet a friend, wait for a bus*

**Extension vocabulary (optional)**
*cycle path, post box, phone box, underpass, signpost, tunnel; miss a bus, take the underground, wait at a crossing, wait in a queue*

**Other vocabulary**
*adventure / fairy / mystery / science fiction / sports / spy story; archaeologist, ash, Colosseum, emergency, erupt, fire alarm, gladiator, monuments, rescue, ruins, shield, sword, tragedy, volcano; characters, genre, setting; exciting, floating, islands, gondola, guide book, relaxing, traditional, water bus, water taxi*

**Recycled vocabulary**
*cooking, drinking, reading, running, scary, sleeping, speaking, studying; cloud, coast, newspaper, planet, woollen hat; boat trip, costume, half past, o'clock, ride a horse, scientists*

### Structures

**Core structures**
*I / He / She / It was / wasn't eating at 2pm. You / We / They were / weren't eating at 2pm. Was I / he / she / it eating at 2pm? Were you / we / they eating at 2pm? Yes, I / he / she / it was. No, I / he / she / it wasn't. Yes, you / we / they were. No, you / we / they weren't. I / He / She / It was reading when it rang. You / We / They were reading when it rang. What was I / he / she / it doing when it rang? What were you / we / they doing when it rang?*

**Recycled structures**
*Where are they going to be at ten o'clock? They're going to be at the Trevi Fountain. What are they going to do there? They're going to throw a coin into the fountain. We can't turn back now. We must help my friends. The sea is too dangerous. The setting is the place where the story happens. The characters are the people who appear in the story.*

### Pronunciation

Weak and strong forms of 'was'

### Literacy

**Text type:** a story opener (text to entertain; writing preparation)
**Reading skills:** predicting content from pictures
**Writing skill:** using adverbs of manner

### Culture ... around the world

The tragedy of Pompeii in Italy

### 21st Century Skills

**Ways of working:** making detailed comparisons

### Thinking skills

Categorising (Lesson 1); Analysing and applying rules (Lessons 2 and 4); Creating (Lesson 4); Defining and describing (Lesson 5); Finding and classifying information (Lesson 6); Planning, checking and correcting (Lesson 7); Seeing another's point of view (Lesson 8); Reflecting on learning (Lesson 8)

### Cooperative learning

Working together (Lessons 1–8); Collaborating (Lessons 1–8); Checking learning (Lessons 1–8); Peer evaluation and feedback (Lesson 7); Participating (Lessons 1–8); Helping and encouraging (Lessons 1–8); Reaching agreement (Lesson 8); Reflecting and setting goals (Lessons 1 and 8)

### Values

The importance of knowing safety procedures at school

### Cross-curricular links

**Link to Science**
Volcanic activity

**Suggested Arts and Crafts concepts**
Contour lines

## Key Competences and Key Learning Outcomes

- Identify and say the names of places in a city
- Listen to definitions and identify the words
- Read an email for general understanding
- Talk about a city tour

**Key language**

- *bridge, castle, crossroads, fountain, pavement, pedestrian crossing, square, statue, steps, tower, town hall, traffic lights; boat trip, buildings, climb, gladiator, historical, lunch, monuments, pizza, public, restaurants, shops, throw a coin, town, views*
- *Where are they going to be at ten o'clock? They're going to be at the Trevi Fountain. What are they going to do there? They're going to throw a coin into the fountain.*
- **Extension:** *cycle path, phone box, post box, signpost, tunnel, underground*

**Materials**

- Pupil's Book pp28–29; Activity Book p26; Class CD1; Teacher's App on Navio
- Places in a city flashcards

**Optional materials**

- Teacher's Resource Bank: Trinity Exams Practice cards (selected from the Starter Unit and Units 1 and 2)

## At a Glance Lesson Plan

### Pupil's Book

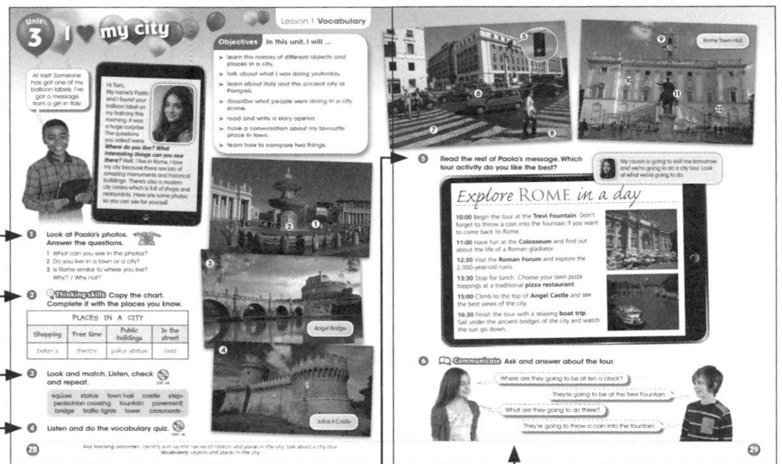


**Starting the lesson**

- Use the Trinity Exams Practice cards (optional).
- Review favourite places in your town or city.
- Set learning objectives.

**Activity 1**

- Look at Paola's photos.
- Answer the questions.

**Activity 2**

- Copy the chart.
- Complete it with the places you know.

**Vocabulary presentation**

- Present the unit vocabulary using the places in a city flashcards.

**Activity 3**

- Look and match.
- Listen, check and repeat.
- ▶ *CD1 Track 35 p279*

**Activity 4**

- Listen and do the vocabulary quiz.
- ▶ *CD1 Track 36 p280*

**Activity 5**

- Read the rest of Paola's message.
- Which tour activity do you like the best?

**Activity 6**

- Ask and answer about the tour.
- Go to the Activity Book.

**Ending the lesson**

- Review the lesson and reflect on learning.

**Extra activities**

**Extension**

- Find out about Italy.

**Vocabulary extension**

- Present six additional vocabulary items.

**Digital resources**

**Teacher's Digital:** You can also teach this lesson using the Teacher's App on Navio.

**Pupil's Digital:** Encourage your pupils to use the Pupil's App on Navio to practise the activities from this lesson.

Powered By NAVIO

### Activity Book

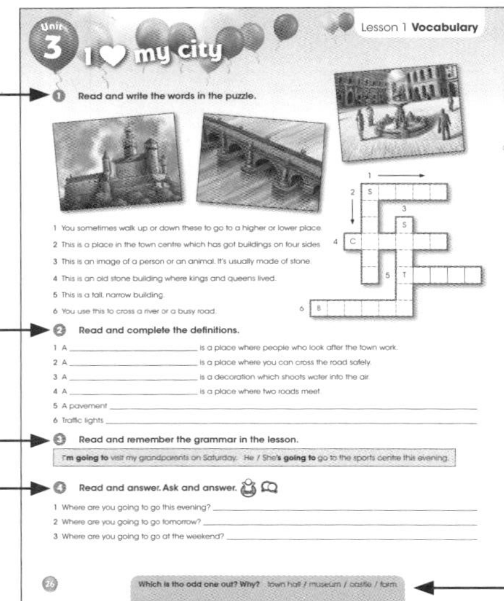


**Activity Book**

**Activity 1**

- Read and write the words in the puzzle.

**Activity 2**

- Read and complete the definitions.

**Activity 3**

- Read and remember the grammar in the lesson.

**Activity 4**

- Read and answer. Ask and answer.

**Odd one out activity**

- Which is the odd one out? Why?

# Detailed Lesson Plan

## Starting the lesson

**Use the Trinity Exams Practice cards (optional).**
- The pupils practise asking and answering questions.

**Review favourite places in your town or city.**
- Ask **Do we live in a village, a town or a city?** Check understanding of the three places. Ask **What's your favourite place in (name of your town / city)? What do you do there? Who do you go there with? How often do you go there?**

**Set learning objectives.**
- Say **Today we're going to remember and learn the names of different places in a city.**

## Pupil's Book Activity 1

**Look at Paola's photos. Answer the questions.**
- Invite a pupil to read out the speech bubble to find out who has found the balloon. Ask the class if they know where Italy is and if anyone has been there.
- Invite a pupil to read out the message from Paola and check understanding.
- Work as a class to read and answer the questions about the photos.

**Answers:** **1** Navona Square, Angel bridge, Julius II Castle, street scene, Rome Town Hall

## Pupil's Book Activity 2

**Copy the chart. Complete it with places you know.**
- Copy the chart onto the board. Elicit an example for each column.
- Organise the class into pairs. The pupils copy the chart into their notebooks and classify the places they know.
- Invite different pairs of pupils to say the places they have written in their chart.

## Vocabulary presentation

- Present the unit vocabulary using the places in a city flashcards. Show the first flashcard and elicit / say the word. Check understanding.
- Invite a pupil to stick the card on the chart on the board. Repeat the procedure with the other cards.

## Pupil's Book Activity 3

**Look and match. Listen, check and repeat.**
▶ ***CD1 Track 35 p279***
- Focus the class on item 1 in the photo. Ask **What's this?** The pupils work in pairs to match numbers 2–12 and the words.
- Play the CD. The pupils listen and check.
- Play the CD again, pausing after each word for the pupils to repeat.

## Pupil's Book Activity 4

**Listen and do the vocabulary quiz.**
▶ ***CD1 Track 36 p280***
- Play the CD. Listen to the first definition, pausing at the beep to allow the pupils to name the item. Continue with the CD to listen to the answer.
- Repeat the procedure with the other definitions.

## Pupil's Book Activity 5

**Read the rest of Paola's message. Which tour activity do you like the best?**
- Invite a pupil to read out the message. The pupils read the information about the tour and choose the activity they like best. The pupils report their answers to a partner and then to the class.

## Pupil's Book Activity 6

**Ask and answer about the tour.**
- Invite two pupils to read out the speech bubbles.
- The pupils ask and answer questions in pairs.

## Activity Book

**Activity 1**

**Read and write the words in the puzzle.**
- The pupils write the words in the puzzle.

**Answers:** **1** steps **2** square **3** statue **4** castle **5** tower **6** bridge

**Activity 2**

**Read and complete the definitions.**
- The pupils complete the definitions.

**Answers:** **1** town hall **2** pedestrian crossing **3** fountain **4** crossroads

**Activity 3**

**Read and remember the grammar in the lesson.**
- Invite a pupil to read out the information. Remind the class that we use 'to be + going to' for future plans.
- Encourage the class to use the structure to talk about what they are going to do after class / lunch, etc.

**Activity 4**

**Read and answer. Ask and answer.**
- The pupils work on their own to write their answers.
- The pupils then work in pairs to ask and answer.

**Odd one out activity**

**Which is the odd one out? Why?**
- The pupils complete the odd one out activity.

**Answers:** farm (It isn't in the city.)

## Ending the lesson

**Review the lesson and reflect on learning.**
- Say **Today we've learnt the names of places in the city. What do you remember?**
- Ask **Which was your favourite activity today? Which activity was easy / difficult?**

## Extra activities

**Extension**
- The pupils find Italy on the world map on pages 134-135. They read the accompanying facts.

**Vocabulary extension**
- Present six additional places: *cycle path, phone box, post box, signpost, tunnel, underground.*

### Key Competences and Key Learning Outcomes

- Listen to and read a dialogue
- Identify the past continuous tense
- Use the past continuous to talk about what you were doing yesterday

- Practise activity types found in the Cambridge Exams: A2 Key for Schools

### Key language

- *actor, Ancient History, Colosseum, costume, gladiator, half past, o'clock; carry a sword, make a film, ride a horse, wear a costume*
- *I / He / She / It was eating at 2pm. I / He / She / It wasn't eating at 2pm. You / We / They were eating at 2pm. You / We / They weren't eating at 2pm. Was I / he / she / it eating at 2pm? Were you / we / they eating at 2pm? Yes, I / he / she / it was. No, I / he / she / it wasn't. Yes, you / we / they were. No, you / we / they weren't. What were you doing at eight o'clock yesterday morning?*

### Materials

- Pupil's Book p30; Activity Book p27; Class CD1; Teacher's App on Navio
- Teacher's Resource Bank: Places in a city word cards

### Optional materials

- Teacher's Resource Bank: Trinity Exams Practice cards (selected from the Starter Unit and Units 1 and 2)

## At a Glance Lesson Plan

### Pupil's Book

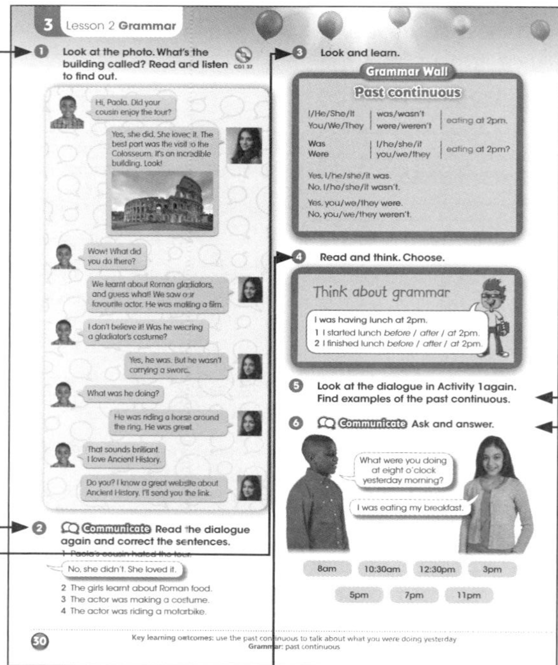

**Starting the lesson**

- Use the Trinity Exams Practice cards (optional).
- Review places in a city.
- Set learning objectives.

**Activity 1**

- Look at the photo.
- What's the building called?
- Read and listen to find out.

▶ ***CD1 Track 37 p280***

**Activity 2**

- Read the dialogue again and correct the sentences.

**Activity 3**

- Look and learn – Grammar wall

**Activity 4**

- Read and think.
- Choose.

**Activity 5**

- Look at the dialogue in Activity 1 again.
- Find examples of the past continuous.

**Activity 6**

- Ask and answer.
- Go to the Activity Book.

**Ending the lesson**

- Review the lesson and reflect on learning.

**Extra activity**

**Reinforcement**

- Play a mime game.

### Digital resources

**Teacher's Digital:** You can also teach this lesson using the Teacher's App on Navio.

**Pupil's Digital:** Encourage your pupils to use the Pupil's App on Navio to practise the activities from this lesson.

Powered By NAVIO

### Activity Book

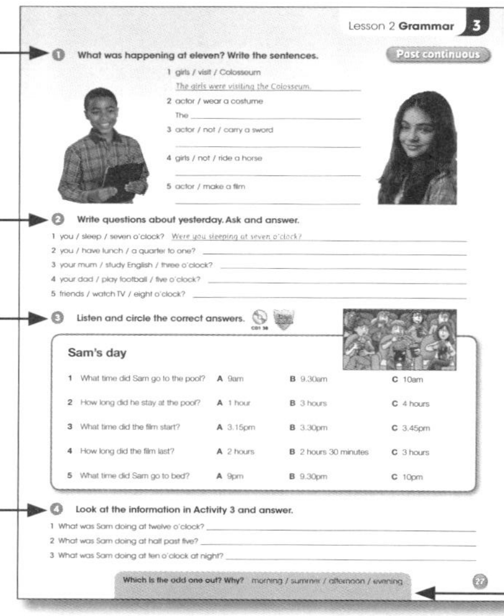

**Activity Book**

**Activity 1**

- What was happening at eleven? Write the sentences.

**Activity 2**

- Write questions about yesterday. Ask and answer.

**Activity 3**

- Listen and circle the correct answers.

▶ ***CD1 Track 38 p280***

**Activity 4**

- Look at the information in Activity 3 and answer.

**Odd one out activity**

- Which is the odd one out? Why?

# Detailed Lesson Plan

**Starting the lesson**

**Use the Trinity Exams Practice cards (optional).**
- The pupils practise asking and answering questions.

**Review places in a city.**
- Hold up one of the places in a city word cards so that the class can't see it and give the definition. The pupils say the word.
- Then ask **How do you spell (the word on the card)?** Invite a pupil to write the word on the board.

**Set learning objectives.**
- Say **Today we're going to learn how to talk about actions in the past.**

**Pupil's Book Activity 1**

**Look at the photo. What's the building called? Read and listen to find out.**

▶ *CD1 Track 37 p280*
- Prompt the class to describe the photo.
- Ask **Do you know what the building is called?**
- Play the CD. The pupils listen and read the dialogue. Confirm that the building is called the Colosseum.

**Pupil's Book Activity 2**

**Read the dialogue again and correct the sentences.**
- The pupils work in pairs to read and correct the sentences.

**Pupil's Book Activity 3**

**Look and learn – Grammar wall**
- Read the information on the Grammar wall as a class.
- Ask **Can you see the past of the verb 'to be'? When do we use 'was' / 'were'? Do we say 'have or 'having' after the verb 'to be'?**
- Explain that we use the past continuous to describe an action that was happening at a point in the past.
- Draw a timeline on the board with 'Past' and 'Now' at either end. Mark 'two o'clock' with a cross in the middle of the timeline. Write 'having lunch' and indicate that this started before two o'clock and ended afterwards.

**Pupil's Book Activity 4**
- Read and think. Choose.
- Focus the pupils' attention on the Think about grammar box. Read out the sentences as a class. The pupils choose the answers.

**Answers:** **1** before **2** after

**Pupil's Book Activity 5**

**Look at the dialogue in Activity 1 again. Find examples of the past continuous.**
- Ask the pupils to find examples of the past continuous in pairs.

**Pupil's Book Activity 6**

**Ask and answer.**
- Invite two pupils to read out the speech bubbles. Ask and answer questions about the other times.
- The pupils ask and answer the questions in pairs.

**Activity Book**

**Activity 1**

**What was happening at eleven? Write the sentences.**
- The pupils write the sentences in the past continuous.

**Answers: 1** The girls were visiting the Colosseum. **2** The actor was wearing a costume. **3** The actor wasn't carrying a sword. **4** The girls weren't riding a horse. **5** The actor was making a film.

**Activity 2**

**Write questions about yesterday. Ask and answer.**
- The pupils write the questions.
- Ask a pair of pupils to demonstrate the activity. Review short answers if necessary.
- The pupils take it in turns to ask and answer the questions in pairs.

**Answers: 1** Were you sleeping at seven o'clock? **2** Were you having lunch at quater to one? **3** Was your mum studying English at three o'clock? **4** Was your dad playing football at five o'clock? **5** Were your friends watching TV at eight o'clock?

**Activity 3**

**Listen and circle the correct answers.**

▶ *CD1 Track 38 p280*
- Read out the questions and answers as a class. Check understanding of 'am' and 'pm'.
- Play the CD. The pupils listen and follow in their books.
- Play the CD again, pausing after each piece of key information. The pupils circle the correct information.

**Answers:** **1** C **2** B **3** C **4** C **5** A

**Activity 4**

**Look at the information in Activity 3 and answer.**
- The pupils write the answers to the questions.

**Answers:** **1** He was swimming / playing in the pool. **2** He was watching a film. **3** He was sleeping.

**Odd one out activity**

**Which is the odd one out? Why?**
- The pupils complete the odd one out activity.

**Answers:** summer (It's a season.)

**Ending the lesson**

**Review the lesson and reflect on learning.**
- Say **Today we've learnt how to talk about actions we were doing in the past.** Elicit sentences in the past continuous from the pupils.
- Ask **Which was your favourite activity today? Which activity was easy / difficult?**

**Extra activity**

**Reinforcement**
- Ask **What was I doing at six o'clock last night?** Then mime doing a daily routine and prompt the class to ask the question *Were you ... at six o'clock?* Continue until a pupil guesses correctly. Invite the pupil to the front of the class and ask him / her to take your role. Repeat the procedure with different pupils.

### Key Competences and Key Learning Outcomes

- Read a story with a cultural focus
- Listen for specific information
- Learn about volcanic activity
- Use the Internet to investigate Italy
- Think about things you must and mustn't do in an emergency
- Learn about the ancient city of Pompeii

**Key language**

- *archaeologist, ash, cloud, coast, erupt, rescue, rocks, shake, tragedy, volcano*
- *We can't turn back now. We must help my friends. Many people were leaving and the ground was shaking. The sea is too dangerous. It was baking in the oven when Vesuvius erupted.*

**Materials**

- Pupil's Book p31; Activity Book p28; Class CD1; Teacher's App on Navio

**Optional materials**

- Teacher's Resource Bank: Trinity Exams Practice cards (selected from the Starter Unit and Units 1 and 2)

## At a Glance Lesson Plan

### Pupil's Book

**Starting the lesson**

- Use the Trinity Exams Practice cards (optional).
- Review the past continuous.
- Set learning objectives.

**Activity 1: Before you read**

- Read and discuss.

**Activity 2**

- Listen and read.

▶ *CD1 Track 39 p280*

Go to the Activity Book.

**Values**

- Read and discuss.

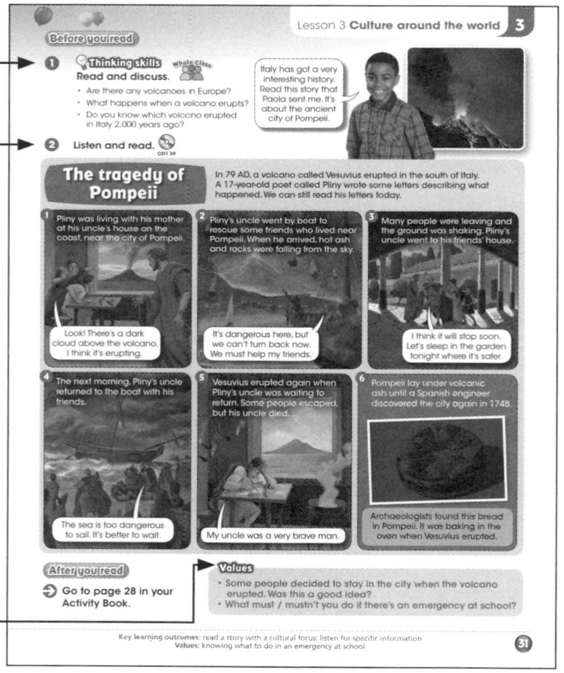
Lesson 3 Culture around the world 3

Before you read

1 Thinking skills Whole Class Read and discuss.

- Are there any volcanoes in Europe?
- What happens when a volcano erupts?
- Do you know which volcano erupted in Italy 2,000 years ago?

Italy has got a very interesting history. Read this story that Paola sent me. It's about the ancient city of Pompeii.

2 Listen and read. CD1 39

**The tragedy of Pompeii**

In 79 AD, a volcano called Vesuvius erupted in the south of Italy. A 17-year-old poet called Pliny wrote some letters describing what happened. We can still read his letters today.

1 Pliny was living with his mother at his uncle's house on the coast, near the city of Pompeii.

Look! There's a dark cloud above the volcano. I think it's erupting.

2 Pliny's uncle went by boat to rescue some friends who lived near Pompeii. When he arrived, hot ash and rocks were falling from the sky.

It's dangerous here, but we can't turn back now. We must help my friends.

3 Many people were leaving and the ground was shaking. Pliny's uncle went to his friends' house.

I think it will stop soon. Let's sleep in the garden tonight where it's safer.

4 The next morning, Pliny's uncle returned to the boat with his friends.

The sea is too dangerous to sail. It's better to wait.

5 Vesuvius erupted again when Pliny's uncle was waiting to return. Some people escaped, but his uncle died.

My uncle was a very brave man.

6 Pompeii lay under volcanic ash until a Spanish engineer discovered the city again in 1748.

Archaeologists found this bread in Pompeii. It was baking in the oven when Vesuvius erupted.

After you read

Go to page 28 in your Activity Book.

Values

- Some people decided to stay in the city when the volcano erupted. Was this a good idea?
- What must / mustn't you do if there's an emergency at school?

Key learning outcomes: read a story with a cultural focus; listen for specific information
Values: knowing what to do in an emergency at school

31

**Ending the lesson**

- Review the lesson and reflect on learning.

**Extra activity**

**Extension**

- Create different eye witness accounts of the eruption of Mount Vesuvius.

### Activity Book

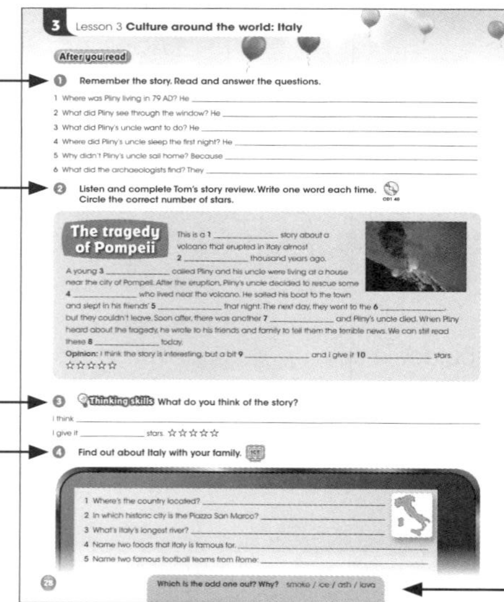
3 Lesson 3 Culture around the world: Italy

After you read

1 Remember the story. Read and answer the questions.

1 Where was Pliny living in 79 AD? He ________
2 What did Pliny see through the window? He ________
3 What did Pliny's uncle want to do? He ________
4 Where did Pliny's uncle sleep the first night? He ________
5 Why didn't Pliny's uncle sail home? Because ________
6 What did the archaeologists find? They ________

2 Listen and complete Tom's story review. Write one word each time. Circle the correct number of stars. CD1 40

**The tragedy of Pompeii**

This is a 1 ________ story about a volcano that erupted in Italy almost 2 ________ thousand years ago. A young 3 ________ called Pliny and his uncle were living at a house near the city of Pompeii. After the eruption, Pliny's uncle decided to rescue some 4 ________ who lived near the volcano. He sailed his boat to the town and slept in his friends' 5 ________ that night. The next day, they went to the 6 ________, but they couldn't leave. Soon after, there was another 7 ________ and Pliny's uncle died. When Pliny heard about the tragedy, he wrote to his friends and family to tell them the terrible news. We can still read these 8 ________ today.

Opinion: I think the story is interesting, but a bit 9 ________ and I give it 10 ________ stars. ☆☆☆☆☆

3 Thinking skills What do you think of the story?

I think ________
I give it ________ stars. ☆☆☆☆☆

4 Find out about Italy with your family. ICT

1 Where's the country located? ________
2 In which historic city is the Piazza San Marco? ________
3 What's Italy's longest river? ________
4 Name two foods that Italy is famous for. ________
5 Name two famous football teams from Rome: ________

28

Which is the odd one out? Why? smoke / ice / ash / lava

**Activity Book: After you read**

**Activity 1**

- Remember the story. Read and answer the questions.

**Activity 2**

- Listen and complete Tom's story review.

▶ *CD1 Track 40 p280*

- Write one word each time. Circle the correct number of stars.

**Activity 3**

- What do you think of the story?

**Activity 4**

- Find out about Italy with your family.

**Odd one out activity**

- Which is the odd one out? Why?

### Digital resources

**Teacher's Digital:** You can also teach this lesson using the Teacher's App on Navio.

**Pupil's Digital:** Encourage your pupils to use the Pupil's App on Navio to practise the activities from this lesson.

Powered By NAVIO

# Detailed Lesson Plan

## Starting the lesson

**Use the Trinity Exams Practice cards (optional).**
- The pupils practise asking and answering questions.

**Review the past continuous.**
- Make a false statement about what you were doing yesterday evening. Say **I was horse riding at (six o'clock) yesterday evening.** The pupils say if the statement is true or false.
- Repeat the procedure with different actions and times.
- Then invite different pupils to the front of the class to take your role.

**Set learning objectives.**
- Say **Today we're going to read a story from Italy.**

## Pupil's Book Activity 1: Before you read

**Read and discuss.**
- Read the questions as a class. Encourage the pupils to share the information they know.
- Ask **Do you think that we can read some letters about an eruption 2,000 years ago?** Encourage the class to say if they think that it's possible.

## Pupil's Book Activity 2

**Listen and read.**
▶ *CD1 Track 39 p280*
- Play the CD. The pupils follow in their books. Confirm that a poet called Pliny wrote some letters about an eruption in 79 AD and we can still read them today.
- Ask questions to check understanding.

**Suggested comprehension questions:**
- Frame 1: **Where were Pliny and his mother living in this story?** (*At his uncle's house near Pompeii.*)
- Frame 2: **What did Pliny's uncle do?** (*He went to rescue some friends.*)
- Frame 3: **Why did Pliny's uncle and his friends sleep outside?** (*It was too dangerous to sleep inside.*)
- Frame 4: **Where did they go the next morning?** (*To the boat.*)
- Frame 5: **What happened while Pliny's uncle was on the beach?** (*The volcano erupted again.*)
- Frame 6: **What have archaeologists found under the ash?** (*Bread.*)

## Activity Book: After you read

### Activity 1

**Remember the story. Read and answer the questions.**
- Read out the first question and invite a pupil to answer it.
- The pupils work on their own or in pairs to read and answer the remaining questions.
- Check the answers as a class.

**Answers:** **1** was living in his uncle's house in Pompeii. **2** saw a dark cloud above the volcano. **3** wanted to help his friends. **4** slept in the garden. **5** the sea was too dangerous. **6** found bread.

### Activity 2

**Listen and complete Tom's story review. Write one word each time. Circle the correct number of stars.**
▶ *CD1 Track 40 p280*
- Read out the story review as a class. Ask the pupils to guess the missing words.
- Play the CD without pausing. The pupils should listen and complete as much of the information as possible.
- Play the CD a second time, pausing after each piece of key information to check the information and spelling. The pupils should also circle the correct number of stars.

**Answers:** **1** true **2** two **3** poet **4** friends **5** garden **6** beach **7** eruption **8** letters **9** sad **10** four

### Activity 3

**What do you think of the story?**
- The pupils write their opinion of the story and give a rating.
- Invite different pupils to share their opinions with the rest of the class.

### Activity 4

**Find out about Italy with your family.**
- Read out the questions about Italy. Ask **Where can you find out this information?** (*Internet, library, asking friends and family.*) The pupils complete the activity at home.
- If you prefer to do this activity in the class, connect to a children's website which has information about Italy such as: www.kids-world-travel-guide.com/italy-facts.html. Read out the questions. The pupils work as a class to find and write the answers.

**Answers:** **1** Southern Europe **2** Venice **3** Po river **4** pizza and pasta **5** Lazio and Roma

**Odd one out activity**

**Which is the odd one out? Why?**
- The pupils complete the odd one out activity.

**Answers:** ice (It doesn't come from a volcano.)

## Values

- Read out each question and discuss it as a class.
- Encourage the pupils to think about what they must and mustn't do if there's an emergency in the school. (*Get in a line, follow the teacher, leave their bags, don't run, don't shout.*)

## Ending the lesson

**Review the lesson and reflect on learning.**
- Say **Today we've read a story from Italy.**
- Ask **Which was your favourite activity today? Which activity was easy / difficult?**

## Extra activity

**Extension**
- Explain to the class that when Mount Vesuvius erupted the people in the town were living their normal lives. Say **There was a baker in the town. What do you think he was doing when the volcano erupted?** Elicit different sentences.
- Organise the class into pairs. Invite them to think of five different people in the town. They create eye witness accounts of what they were doing when the volcano erupted.

## Key Competences and Key Learning Outcomes

- Act out a short dialogue in pairs
- Learn and practise using the past simple and past continuous together
- Identify and practise saying weak and strong forms of *was*

## Key language

- *emergency, fire alarm, scary, scientists; cooking, drinking, open my eyes, reading, running, sleeping, speaking, studying (Maths)*
- *I / He / She / It was reading when it rang. You / We / They were reading when it rang. What was I / he / she / it doing when it rang? What were you / we / they doing when it rang? Was he sleeping? Yes, he was.*

## Materials

- Pupil's Book p32; Activity Book p29; Class CD1; Teacher's App on Navio

## Optional materials

- Teacher's Resource Bank: Trinity Exams Practice cards (selected from the Starter Unit and Units 1 and 2)

# At a Glance Lesson Plan

## Pupil's Book

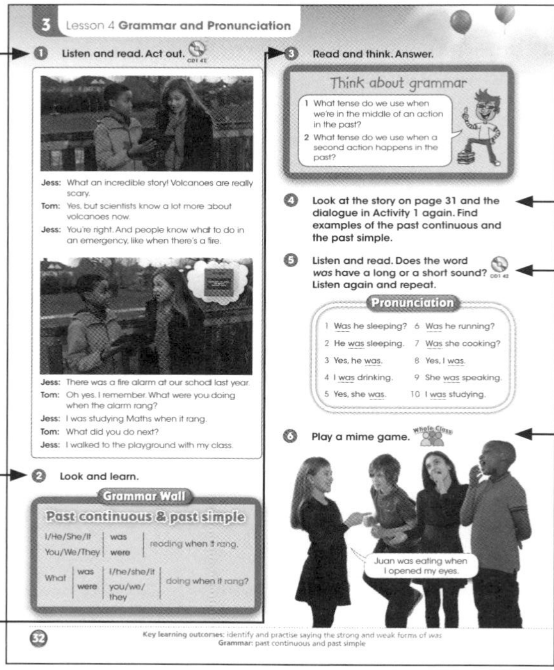


### Starting the lesson

- Use the Trinity Exams Practice cards (optional).
- Review verbs.
- Set learning objectives.

### Activity 1

- Listen and read.
- ▶ ***CD1 Track 41 p281***
- Act out.

### Activity 2

- Look and learn – Grammar wall

### Activity 3

- Read and think.
- Answer.

### Activity 4

- Look at the story on page 31 and the dialogue in Activity 1 again.
- Find examples of the past continuous and the past simple.

### Activity 5

- Listen and read.
- ▶ ***CD1 Track 42 p281***
- Does the word *was* have a long or a short sound?
- Listen again and repeat.

### Activity 6

- Play a mime game.
- Go to the Activity Book.

### Ending the lesson

- Review the lesson and reflect on learning.

### Extra activity

**Reinforcement**

- Play *Sharing a story*.

## Activity Book

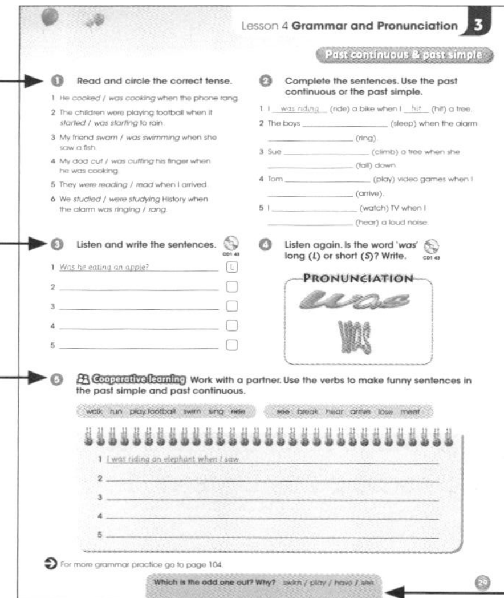


### Activity Book

**Activity 1**

- Read and circle the correct tense.

**Activity 2**

- Complete the sentences. Use the past continuous or the past simple.

**Activity 3**

- Listen and write the sentences.
- ▶ ***CD1 Track 43 p281***

**Activity 4**

- Listen again. Is the word *'was' long* (L) or *short* (S)?

**Activity 5**

- Work with a partner. Use the verbs to make funny sentences in the past simple and past continuous.

**Odd one out activity**

- Which is the odd one out? Why?

## Digital resources

**Teacher's Digital:** You can also teach this lesson using the Teacher's App on Navio.

**Pupil's Digital:** Encourage your pupils to use the Pupil's App on Navio to practise the activities from this lesson.

Powered By NAVIO

# Detailed Lesson Plan

**Starting the lesson**

**Use the Trinity Exams Practice cards (optional).**
- The pupils practise asking and answering questions.

**Review verbs.**
- Write the alphabet on the board in three or four columns. The pupils work together to write as many verbs on the board as possible for each letter.

**Set learning objectives.**
- Say **Today we're going to learn how to use the past simple and past continuous tenses together.**

**Pupil's Book Activity 1**

**Listen and read. Act out.**
▶ *CD1 Track 41 p281*
- Ask **What are Tom and Jess looking at? What do you think they are talking about?**
- Play the CD. The pupils listen and read the dialogue. Ask **What was Jess doing when the alarm rang?**
- Play the CD again, pausing after each sentence for the pupils to repeat.
- The pupils practise the dialogue in pairs.

**Pupil's Book Activity 2**

**Look and learn – Grammar wall**
- Read the information on the Grammar wall as a class.
- Ask **What was happening first? What happened next?**

**Pupil's Book Activity 3**

**Read and think. Answer.**
- Focus the pupils' attention on the Think about grammar box. Read out the questions as a class. The pupils answer the questions in pairs.

**Pupil's Book Activity 4**

**Look at the story on page 31 and the dialogue in Activity 1 again. Find examples of the past continuous and the past simple.**
- Ask the pupils to find examples of the past simple and past continuous used together.

**Pupil's Book Activity 5**

**Listen and read. Does the word *was* have a long or a short sound? Listen again and repeat.**
▶ *CD1 Track 42 p281*
- Say **Let's listen to the sentences. Does the word 'was' have a long or a short sound?** Play the CD, pausing after each sentence.
- Identify that 'was' is longer when it's at the beginning of a question or when it's at the end of a short answer. It's shorter when it's in the middle of a sentence.
- Play the CD again. The pupils listen and repeat.

**Pupil's Book Activity 6**

**Play a mime game.**
- Read out the speech bubble. Then invite a pupil to come to the front of the class and close his / her eyes.
- The pupils play *Freeze* (see p32) with actions.

**Activity Book**

**Activity 1**
**Read and circle the correct tense.**
- The pupils circle the correct verb in each sentence.

**Answers:** **1** was cooking **2** started **3** was swimming **4** cut **5** were reading **6** were studying, rang

**Activity 2**
**Complete the sentences. Use the past continuous or the past simple.**
- Read out the first sentence and identify which action began first and which action happened next.
- The pupils complete the remaining sentences.

**Answers:** **1** was riding, hit **2** were sleeping, rang **3** was climbing, fell **4** was playing, arrived **5** was watching, heard

**Activity 3**
**Listen and write the sentences.**
▶ *CD1 Track 43 p281*
- Play the CD, pausing after each sentence. The pupils should listen and write down what they hear.

**Answers:** **1** Was he eating an apple? **2** She was crossing the road. **3** He was getting off the bus. **4** Was he taking a photo? **5** He was wearing a pair of jeans.

**Activity 4**
**Listen again. Is the word '*was*' long *(L)* or short *(S)*?**
▶ *CD1 Track 43 p281*
- Review when 'was' has a long or a short sound.
- Play the CD again. The pupils write 'L' or 'S' for each sentence.

**Answers:** **1** L **2** S **3** S **4** L **5** S

**Activity 5**
**Work with a partner. Use the verbs to make funny sentences in the past simple and past continuous.**
- Read out the first half of the sentence. Prompt the class to think of different ways of finishing it.
- The pupils work in pairs to write funny sentences.

**Odd one out activity**
**Which is the odd one out? Why?**
- The pupils complete the odd one out activity.

**Answers:** play (It's a regular past simple verb.)

**Ending the lesson**

**Review the lesson and reflect on learning.**
- Say **Today we've learnt how to use the past simple and past continuous tenses together.**
- Ask **Which was your favourite activity today? Which activity was easy / difficult?**

**Extra activity**

**Reinforcement**
- The pupils play *Sharing sentences* (see p32) in pairs using the prompt **I was ... when ...**

### Key Competences and Key Learning Outcomes

- Identify and say the names of activities you do in a city

- Listen for specific information
- Identify and use expressions to ask for repetition / clarification
- Practise activity types found in the Cambridge Exams: A2 Key for Schools

- Do a communication task

### Key language

- *catch a taxi, cross the road, get off the bus, get on the bus, go sightseeing, have a snack, meet a friend, wait for a bus*
- *What was (Gloria) doing when it started to rain? (She) was having a snack. Was (she) having an ice cream? Yes, (she) was. No, (she) wasn't. Pardon? What did you say? I'm sorry. Could you say that again, please?*
- **Extension:** *miss a bus, take the underground, wait at a crossing, wait in a queue*

### Materials

- Pupil's Book p33; Activity Book p30; Class CD1 and CD2; Teacher's App on Navio; Teacher's Resource Bank: Unit 3

### Optional materials

- Teacher's Resource Bank: Trinity Exams Practice cards (selected from the Starter Unit and Units 1 and 2)
- Photos of city scenes

## At a Glance Lesson Plan

## Pupil's Book

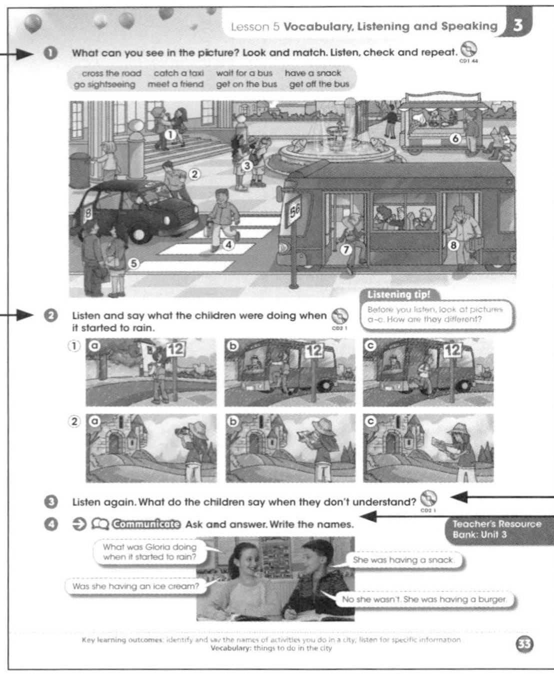


### Starting the lesson

- Use the Trinity Exams Practice cards (optional).
- Review activities you do in a city.
- Set learning objectives.

### Activity 1

- What can you see in the picture?
- Look and match.
- Listen, check and repeat.

▶ ***CD1 Track 44 p281***

### Activity 2

- Listen and say what the children were doing when it started to rain.

▶ ***CD2 Track 1 p281***

### Activity 3

- Listen again.

▶ ***CD2 Track 1 p281***

- What do the children say when they don't understand?

### Activity 4

- Ask and answer.
- Write the names (Teacher's Resource Bank: Unit 3).

Go to the Activity Book.

### Ending the lesson

- Review the lesson and reflect on learning.

### Extra activities

**Reinforcement**

- Describe photos of city scenes.

**Vocabulary extension**

- Present four additional vocabulary items.

### Digital resources

**Teacher's Digital:** You can also teach this lesson using the Teacher's App on Navio.

**Pupil's Digital:** Encourage your pupils to use the Pupil's App on Navio to practise the activities from this lesson.

Powered By NAVIO

## Activity Book

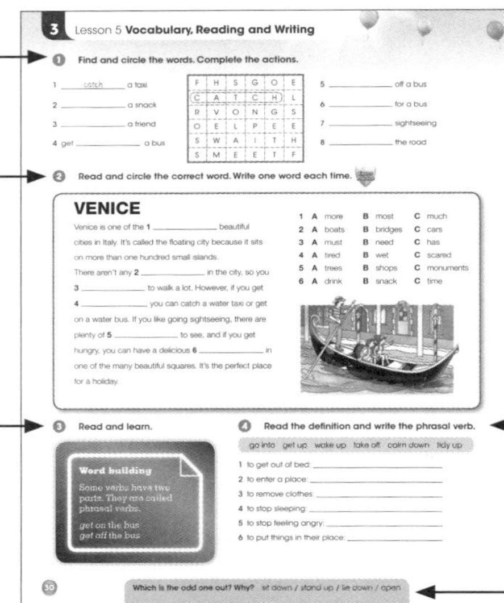


### Activity Book

**Activity 1**

- Find and circle the words. Complete the actions.

**Activity 2**

- Read and circle the correct word. Write one word each time.

**Activity 3**

- Read and learn.

**Activity 4**

- Read the definition and write the phrasal verb.

**Odd one out activity**

- Which is the odd one out? Why?

**Starting the lesson**

**Use the Trinity Exams Practice cards (optional).**
- The pupils practise asking and answering questions.

**Review activities you do in the city.**
- Ask **What do you do when you are in a city?** Encourage the class to describe different activities, e.g. *go shopping, go to the park, have an ice cream.*

**Set learning objectives.**
- Say **Today we're going to learn the names of more activities we do in a city and we're going to do a communication task.**

**Pupil's Book Activity 1**

**What can you see in the picture? Look and match. Listen, check and repeat.**
▶ ***CD1 Track 44 p281***
- Ask the pupils to describe the picture.
- Organise the class into pairs. Ask them to match the actions in the box to the people in the picture.
- Play the CD. The pupils listen and check.
- Play the CD again, pausing after each action for the pupils to repeat.

**Pupil's Book Activity 2**

**Listen and say what the children were doing when it started to rain.**
▶ ***CD2 Track 1 p281***
- Ask the pupils to describe what they can see in the first three pictures.
- Play the CD. The pupils listen and identify the correct picture. (b)
- Repeat with the second set of pictures. (a)

**Pupil's Book Activity 3**

**Listen again. What do the children say when they don't understand?**
▶ ***CD2 Track 1 p281***
- Play the first recording on the CD again. The pupils identify *Pardon? What did you say?* Ask the class to repeat the sentence.
- Repeat the procedure with the second recording. (*I'm sorry. Could you say that again, please?*)

**Pupil's Book Activity 4**

**Ask and answer. Write the names (Teacher's Resource Book: Unit 3).**
- Invite two pupils to read out the speech bubbles.
- Organise the class into pairs (A and B). Give Pupils A the first worksheet from Teacher's Resource Bank Unit 3 and give Pupils B the other worksheet.
- Ask a confident pair to demonstrate the activity with another person in the picture. Then ask the pupils to do the activity in their pairs.
- At the end of the activity, the pupils should show each other their pictures and check the names.

**Activity Book**

**Activity 1**
**Find and circle the words. Complete the actions.**
- The pupils work on their own or in pairs to find and circle the words in the puzzle and then complete the phrases.

**Answers:** **1** catch **2** have **3** meet

**Activity 2**
**Read and circle the correct word. Write one word each time.**
- Ask the pupils to describe what they can see in the picture. Check comprehension by asking questions.
- Identify the first two missing words as a class. Prompt the pupils to explain why the other options don't fit.
- The pupils work on their own or in pairs to identify the remaining missing words.

**Answers:** **1** B **2** C **3** B **4** A **5** C **6** B

**Activity 3**
**Read and learn.**
- Invite a pupil to read out the information. Encourage the class to think of other phrasal verbs they know.

**Activity 4**
**Read the definition and write the phrasal verb.**
- Read out the list of phrasal verbs as a class.
- The pupils work on their own or in pairs to write the phrasal verb next to each definition.

**Answers:** **1** get up **2** go into **3** take off **4** wake up **5** calm down **6** tidy up

**Odd one out activity**
**Which is the odd one out? Why?**
- The pupils complete the odd one out activity.

**Answers:** open (It isn't a phrasal verb.)

**Ending the lesson**

**Review the lesson and reflect on learning.**
- Say **Today we've learnt the names of activities we do in the city and we've played a communication game.**
- Ask **Which was your favourite activity today? Which activity was easy / difficult?**

**Extra activities**

**Reinforcement**
- If you have Internet access in the classroom, find a photo of a busy city scene and project it onto the board. Challenge the class to make as many sentences about what they can see in the scene as possible. (*There's a man who is crossing the road. There are two children who are having a snack.*)
- If you don't have internet access in the classroom, find and print out several scenes before class. The pupils work in small groups to describe the photos.

**Vocabulary extension**
- Present four additional phrases: *miss a bus, take the underground, wait at a crossing, wait in a queue.*
- Use the Vocabulary booster on NAVIO to practise these new words.

## Key Competences and Key Learning Outcomes

- Do pre-reading tasks to predict content and raise interest
- Read three story openers for general understanding
- Scan stories to find specific information

- Talk about the type of stories you like

- Read and understand three story openings
- Give an opinion on the text

**Key language**

- *adventure / fairy / mystery / science fiction / sports / spy story; ancient, blinded, bored, deliver, get off a ferry, guidebook, knock loudly, newspaper, monuments, narrow, shield, shivered, soldier, square, statue, sweating, sword, warm light, woollen hat*
- *A warm light was shining at the window. It was smiling.*

**Materials**

- Pupil's Book p34; Activity Book p31; Class CD2; Teacher's App on Navio

**Optional materials**

- Teacher's Resource Bank: Trinity Exams Practice cards (selected from the Starter Unit and Units 1 and 2)

## At a Glance Lesson Plan

### Pupil's Book

**Starting the lesson**

- Use the Trinity Exams Practice cards (optional).
- Review the five senses.
- Set learning objectives.

**Activity 1: Before you read**

- Read and discuss.

**Activity 2**

- Look at the pictures.
- Which three story types do you think these are?
- Read the story openers and find out.

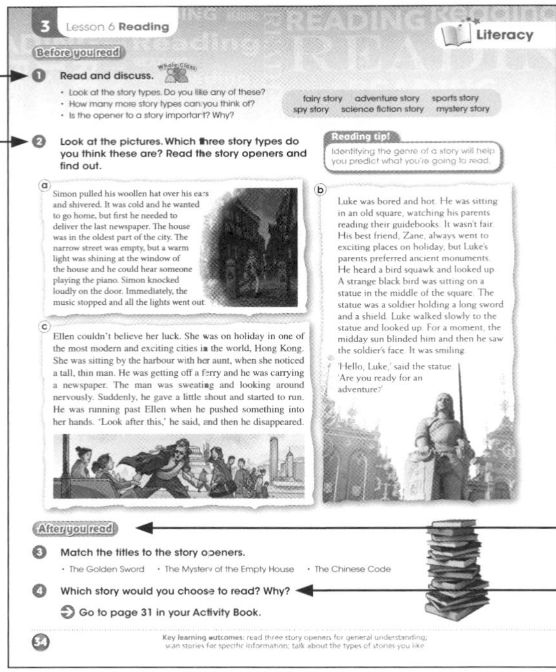


**Activity 3: After you read**

- Match the titles to the story openers.

**Activity 4**

- Which story would you choose to read?
- Why?
- Go to the Activity Book.

**Ending the lesson**

- Review the lesson and reflect on learning.

**Extra activity**

**Extension**

- Continue the dialogue in the adventure story.

### Activity Book

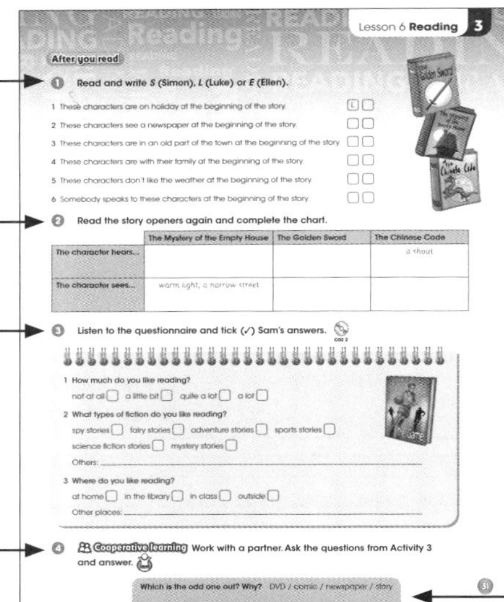


**Activity Book: After you read**

**Activity 1**

- Read and write *S* (Simon), *L* (Luke) or *E* (Ellen).

**Activity 2**

- Read the story openers again and complete the chart.

**Activity 3**

- Listen to the questionnaire and tick (✓) Sam's answers.

▶ *CD2 Track 2 p281*

**Activity 4**

- Work with a friend. Ask the questions from Activity 3 and answer.

**Odd one out activity**

- Which is the odd one out? Why?

## Digital resources

**Teacher's Digital:** You can also teach this lesson using the Teacher's App on Navio.

**Pupil's Digital:** Encourage your pupils to use the Pupil's App on Navio to practise the activities from this lesson.

Powered By NAVIO

# Detailed Lesson Plan

**Starting the lesson**

**Review the five senses.**

- Explain to the class that writers often use the five senses when they describe a place. Elicit the senses. Say **Let's describe our school. What can you see in the school?** Encourage the class to give detailed answers. Then ask **What can you hear / touch / smell / taste?**

**Set learning objectives.**

- Say **Today we're going to read the beginning of three stories. These are called story openers.**

**Pupil's Book Activity 1: Before you read**

**Read and discuss.**

- Read the questions as a class. Prompt the pupils to answer in as much detail as possible.

**Pupil's Book Activity 2**

**Look at the pictures. Which three story types do you think these are? Read the story openers and find out.**

- Read out the list of story types in Activity 1. Elicit the names of books that the pupils have read from each type.
- Focus the pupils on the first picture. Ask them to describe what they can see. Then ask them to predict what story type the accompanying text will belong to. Repeat the procedure with the other pictures.
- The pupils read the texts to see if their predictions are correct. Ask questions to check comprehension.

**Answers:** **a** mystery story **b** adventure story **c** spy story

**Pupil's Book Activity 3: After you read**

**Match the titles to the story openers.**

- Read the story titles as a class. Prompt the pupils to match a title to each story opener.

**Answers:** **a** The Mystery of the Empty House **b** The Golden Sword **c** The Chinese Code

**Pupil's Book Activity 4**

**Which story would you choose to read? Why?**

- Read the questions as a class. Prompt the pupils to tell a partner which story they would choose and why.
- Have a class vote on the most popular story.

**Activity Book: After you read**

**Activity 1**

**Read and write *S* (Simon), *L* (Luke) or *E* (Ellen).**

- The pupils work on their own or in pairs to read each statement and write the initial of the main character in the story. The pupils should refer back to the text in the Pupil's Book when necessary.

**Answers:** **1** L, E **2** S, E **3** S, L **4** L, E **5** S, L **6** L, E

**Activity 2**

**Read the story openers again and complete the chart.**

- The pupils work on their own or in pairs to complete the chart. They scan the story openers and note down the things the characters can see and hear.

**Answers:** **The Mystery of the Empty House** hears: playing piano; sees: a warm light, narrow street, old house **The Golden Sword** hears: a bird squawk; sees: his parents reading guidebooks, a statue **The Chinese Code** hears: a shout; sees: a tall thin man, the man running

**Activity 3**

**Listen to the questionnaire and tick (✓) Sam's answers.**

▶ *CD2 Track 2 p281*

- Read out the questionnaire as a class.
- Play the CD. The pupils listen and follow the information in their books.
- Play the CD again, pausing after each piece of key information. The pupils tick the corresponding box each time.

**Answers:** **1** quite a lot **2** spy stories, adventure stories, mystery stories Others: horror stories, scary stories **3** at home, in class Others: in the living room, in bed

**Activity 4**

**Work with a partner. Ask the questions from Activity 3 and answer.**

- Ask the pupils to take out a different coloured pen or pencil. The pupils should do the questionnaire in pairs, recording their partner's answers each time.

**Odd one out activity**

**Which is the odd one out? Why?**

- The pupils complete the odd one out activity.

**Answers :** DVD (You can't read it.)

**Ending the lesson**

**Review the lesson and reflect on learning.**

- Say **Today we've read some story openers.**
- Ask **Which was your favourite activity today? Which activity was easy / difficult?**

**Extra activity**

**Extension**

- Ask the class to look at the ending of the adventure story. Write the dialogue on the board as if it were a film script.
  *Statue: Hello, Luke. Are you ready for an adventure?*
  *Luke:*
- Prompt the class to imagine what Luke says in reply. The pupils work in pairs to continue the dialogue.
- The pupils act out their dialogues for the class.

## Key Competences and Key Learning Outcomes

- Review and practise using adverbs of manner

- Identify adverbs of manner in a story
- Identify features of a good story opener
- Use criteria to check your writing

- Share your writing with another pupil

- Choose a story genre and write a story opener

### Key language

- *characters, genre, setting; beeped, dry, flashed, galactic sensor, helmet, lava, life, planet, smoke, spacesuit, sun, volcano*
- *The setting is the place where the story happens. The characters are the people who appear in the story. She looked calmly at the information.*

### Materials

- Pupil's Book p35; Activity Book p32; Teacher's App on Navio

### Optional materials

- Teacher's Resource Bank: Trinity Exams Practice cards (selected from the Starter Unit and Units 1 and 2)
- Sheets of A5 and A4 paper

## At a Glance Lesson Plan

### Pupil's Book

**Starting the lesson**

- Use the Trinity Exams Practice cards (optional).
- Review story types.
- Set learning objectives.

**Activity 1: Investigate a text**

- Read and complete the definitions with the words in the box.

**Activity 2**

- Read the story opener.
- What's the genre and the setting?
- Who are the characters?

**Activity 3: Discuss a text**

- Read the story opener again.
- Answer the questions.

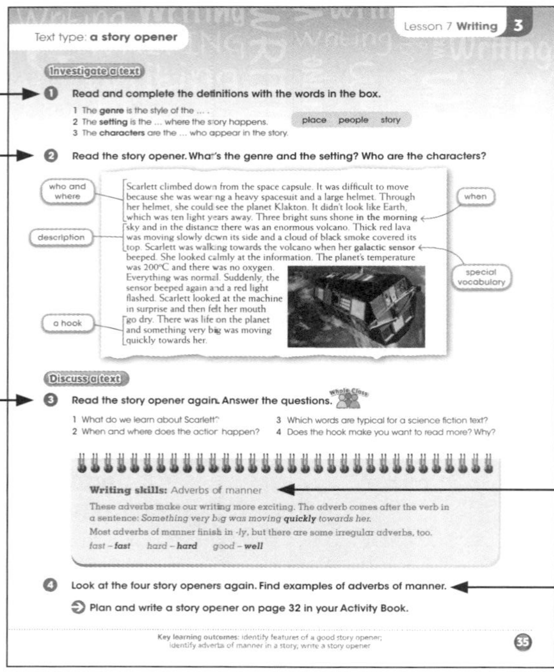
Lesson 7 Writing 3

Text type: a story opener

Investigate a text

1 Read and complete the definitions with the words in the box.

place people story

Read the story opener. What's the genre and the setting? Who are the characters?

Discuss a text

3 Read the story opener again. Answer the questions.

Writing skills: Adverbs of manner

4 Look at the four story openers again. Find examples of adverbs of manner.

Plan and write a story opener on page 32 in your Activity Book.

35

**Writing skills**

- Read about using adverbs of manner.

**Activity 4**

- Look at the four story openers again.
- Find examples of adverbs of manner.

Go to the Activity Book.

**Ending the lesson**

- Review the lesson and reflect on learning.

**Extra activity**

**Reinforcement**

- Make a book cover for your story opener.

### Activity Book

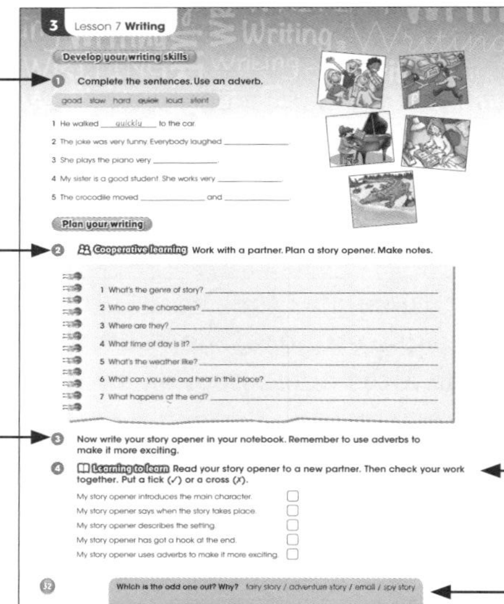
3 Lesson 7 Writing

Develop your writing skills

1 Complete the sentences. Use an adverb.

Plan your writing

2 Cooperative learning Work with a partner. Plan a story opener. Make notes.

3 Now write your story opener in your notebook. Remember to use adverbs to make it more exciting.

4 Learning to learn Read your story opener to a new partner. Then check your work together. Put a tick (✓) or a cross (✗).

Which is the odd one out? Why?

**Activity Book**

**Activity 1: Develop your writing skills**

- Complete the sentences. Use an adverb.

**Activity 2: Plan your writing**

- Work with a partner. Plan a story opener. Make notes.

**Activity 3**

- Now write your story opener in your notebook. Remember to use adverbs to make it more exciting.

**Activity 4**

- Read your story opener to a new partner. Then check your work together. Put a tick (✓) or a cross (✗).

**Odd one out activity**

- Which is the odd one out? Why?

## Digital resources

**Teacher's Digital:** You can also teach this lesson using the Teacher's App on Navio.

**Pupil's Digital:** Encourage your pupils to use the Pupil's App on Navio to practise the activities from this lesson.

Powered By NAVIO

# Detailed Lesson Plan

**Starting the lesson**

**Use the Trinity Exams Practice cards (optional).**
- The pupils practise asking and answering questions.

**Review story types.**
- Review the different story types from Lesson 6. Then ask the class **What's your favourite book? Which book are you reading at the moment?** Prompt the class to give as much information as possible about the books they read.

**Set learning objectives.**
- Say **Today we're going to write a story opener.**

**Pupil's Book Activity 1: Investigate a text**

**Read and complete the definitions.**
- Read and complete the definitions as a class.

**Pupil's Book Activity 2**

**Read the story opener. What's the genre and the setting? Who are the characters?**
- Read the text as a class.
- Check understanding. Identify the genre (*science fiction*), the setting (*a distant planet*) and the main character (*Scarlett, an astronaut*).

**Pupil's Book Activity 3: Discuss a text**

**Read the story opener again. Answer the questions.**
- Read and discuss the questions as a class. Highlight that a good story opener introduces the main character or characters and says when the action takes place. It also describes the setting and often uses the different senses to do that. Highlight that some genres have special vocabulary and all good story openers have a hook to make the reader want to read more.

**Writing skills**
- Read the information.
- Brainstorm different adverbs of manner by asking the pupils to complete the sentences. *He speaks ... He drives ... He works ...*

**Pupil's Book Activity 4**

**Look at the four story openers again. Find examples of adverbs of manner.**
- Organise the pupils into pairs. Ask them to find examples of adverbs of manner in Lessons 6 and 7. They can do this orally or write the sentences in their notebooks.
- The pupils share information with the rest of the class.

**Activity Book**

**Activity 1: Develop your writing skills**

**Complete the sentences. Use an adverb.**
- The pupils work on their own or in pairs to complete the sentences with an adverb of manner.

**Answers:** **1** quickly **2** loudly **3** well **4** hard **5** slowly, silently

**Activity 2: Plan your writing**

**Work with a partner. Plan a story opener. Make notes.**
- Read out the notes and elicit examples of how the pupils can complete each section. If necessary, write these ideas on the board.
- Organise the class into Writing Partners. The pupils work with their partner to plan their story.

**Activity 3**

**Now write your story opener in your notebook. Remember to use adverbs to make it more exciting.**
- The pupils work with a Writing Partner to write their story opener in their notebooks.

**Activity 4**

**Read your story opener to a new partner. Then check your work together. Put a tick (✓) or a cross (✗).**
- Read through the statements as a class.
- Organise the class into new Writing Partners. One pupil reads aloud their text to their partner. The other pupil listens. The pupils work together to decide if the text fulfils the criteria and tick the corresponding boxes. The pupils can add, improve or correct the text at this stage.
- The pupils swap roles.

**Odd one out activity**

**Which is the odd one out? Why?**
- The pupils complete the odd one out activity.

**Answers:** email (It isn't a story genre.)

**Ending the lesson**

**Review the lesson and reflect on learning.**
- Say **Today we've written a story opener.**
- Ask **Which was your favourite activity today? Which activity was easy / difficult?**

**Extra activity**

**Reinforcement**
- Ask the pupils to copy their corrected story opener onto a piece of A5 paper. Then hand out a piece of A4 paper to each pupil and fold it in half to make a front and back cover. The pupils should design and draw their book's cover. Staple the stories inside the A4 paper and use them to create a class display.

# Lesson 8 and Review

### Key Competences and Key Learning Outcomes

- Listen to and have a conversation about favourite places in town
- Listen to a text for general understanding
- Listen to a text and identify key functional language
- Review learning and reflect on progress in the unit
- Sing a song

### Key language

- *go swimming, indoor pool, outdoor pool, sports centre, 3D cinema*
- *What do you think of the 3D cinema? Do you know it? What about you?*

### Materials

- Pupil's Book p36; Activity Book p33 and 34; Class CD2 and CD4; Teacher's App on Navio

### Optional materials

- Teacher's Resource Bank: Trinity Exams Practice cards (selected from the Starter Unit and Units 1 and 2)

## At a Glance Lesson Plan

### Pupil's Book

**Starting the lesson**

- Use the Trinity Exams Practice cards (optional).
- Review objects and places in a city.
- Set learning objectives.

**Activity 1**

- Describe the photos.
- What can you do in these places?

**Activity 2**

- Listen to the conversation.
- ▶ ***CD2 Track 3 p281***
- Which is Sam's favourite place? Why?

**Activity 3**

- Listen again.
- ▶ ***CD2 Track 3 p281***
- Complete four questions that Lucy asks.

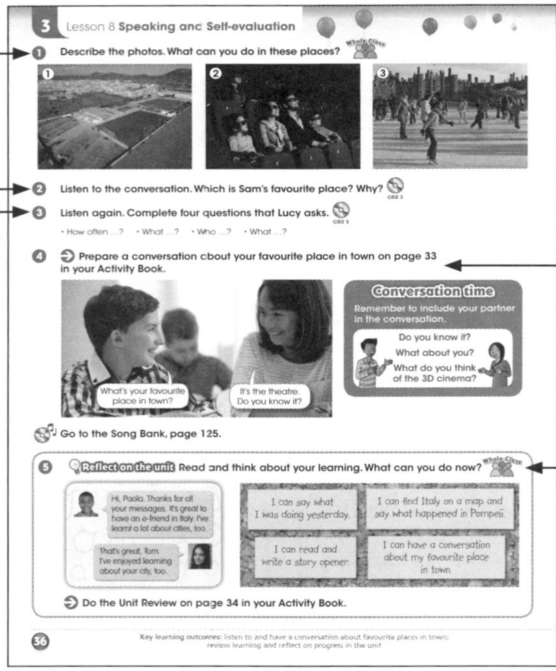

**Activity 4**

- Prepare a conversation about your favourite place in town on page 33 in your Activity book.

Go to page 33 in the Activity Book.

**Song**

- ▶ ***CD4 Track 20 p297***
- ▶ ***CD4 Track 21 p297 (optional karaoke version)***

**Activity 5**

- Read and think about your learning. What can you do now?

Go to page 34 in the Activity Book.

**Ending the lesson**

- Review the lesson and reflect on learning.

**Extra activity**

- Play a drawing game to review objects and places in a city.

### Activity Book

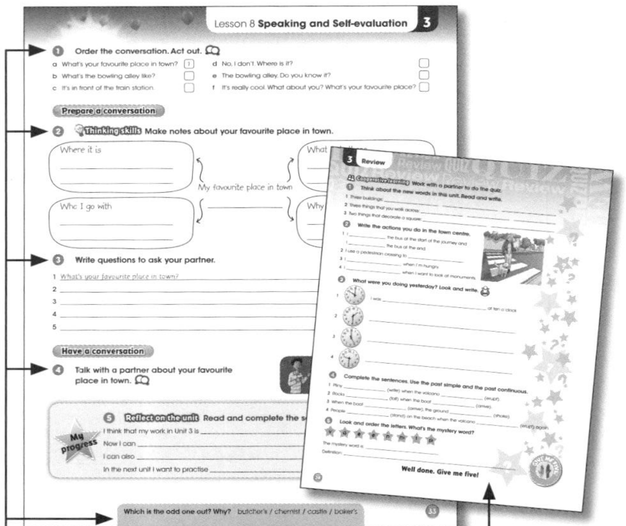

**Activity Book page 34: Review**

- Work with a partner to do the quiz.

**Activity Book**

**Activity 1**

- Order the conversation.
- Act out.

**Activity 2**

- Make notes about your favourite place in town.

**Activity 3**

- Write questions to ask your partner.

**Activity 4**

- Talk with a partner about your favourite place in town.

**Activity 5**

- Read and complete the sentences.

**Odd one out activity**

- Which is the odd one out? Why?

### Digital resources

**Teacher's Digital:** You can also teach this lesson using the Teacher's App on Navio.

Powered By NAVIO

# Detailed Lesson Plan

### Starting the lesson

**Use the Trinity Exams Practice cards (optional).**

- The pupils practise asking and answering questions.

**Review objects and places in the city.**

- Say **I'm a tourist and I'm visiting (your town/city). What should I see?** Pupils suggest different places of interest in the city. In pairs, ask them to prepare a tourist itinerary for a day or weekend.

**Set learning objectives.**

- Say **Today we're going to prepare a conversation about our favourite place in town.**

### Pupil's Book Activity 1

**Describe the photos. What can you do in these places?**

- Ask different pupils to describe the places and what you can do there. Ask if your town/city has these places.

### Pupil's Book Activity 2

**Listen to the conversation. What is Sam's favourite place? Why?**

▸ *CD2 Track 3 p281*

- Play the CD. Ask pupils if the children talk about all the places in Activity 1 (*No, they don't talk about the ice rink*).

**Answer:** Sam's favourite is **1** because it's got a brilliant indoor pool and outdoor pool.

### Pupil's Book Activity 3

**Listen again. Complete four questions that Lucy asks.**

▸ *CD2 Track 3 p281*

- Direct pupils to the four question prompts. Ask if they can remember the questions.
- Play the CD. Pupils check in pairs. Then play again and check as a class.

**Answers:** How often do you do there?; What do you do there?; Who do you usually go with?; What do you think of it?

### Pupil's Book Activity 4

**Prepare a conversation about your favourite place in town on page 33 in your Activity Book.**

- Read the speech bubbles with the pupils. Model the phrases in the Conversation Time box. The class repeats.

### Song

- Go to the Song Bank on page 125 to do the song activities (see p243).

***CD4 Track 20 p297***

***CD4 Track 21 p297 (optional karaoke version)***

### Pupil's Book Activity 5

**Read and think about your learning. What can you do now?**

- Read the speech bubbles and notes with the pupils. Then look back through the unit and prompt them to identify things that they have done/learnt.

### Activity Book page 34: Review

**Work with a partner to do the quiz.**

- Organise the class into pairs. Set a time limit for the pupils to do the quiz (10–15 minutes). Stress that the pupils are not competing with each other.
- Read out the tasks and check understanding. Then say **Ready, steady ... Go!**
- The pupils work in their pairs to do the quiz.
- Correct the answers as a class.

**Answers:** **1** castle, tower, town hall **2** Three from: bridge, pavement, pedestrian crossing, square **3** fountain, statue **2 1** get on, get off **2** cross the road **3** have a snack **4** go sightseeing **4 1** was writing, erupted **2** were falling, arrived **3** arrived, was shaking **4** were standing, erupted **5** pavement, where pedestrians walk

### Activity Book

**Activity 1**

**Order the conversation. Act out.**

- In pairs, pupils order the conversation and act it out.

**Answers:** **1** a **2** e **3** d **4** c **5** b **6** f

**Activity 2**

**Make notes about your favourite place in town.**

- Tell pupils about your favourite place in your town. Then pupils complete the boxes with their own information.

**Activity 3**

**Write questions to ask your partner.**

- Direct pupils to the five headings in Activity 2 and explain that they need to form questions about them. Then pupils complete the questions. Check as a class.

**Answers:** **1** What's your favourite item of clothing? **2** Where is it? **3** Who do you go with? **4** What do you do there? **5** Why do you like it?

**Activity 4**

**Talk with a partner about your favourite place in town.**

- In pairs, pupils ask and answer the questions from Activity 3.
- Invite one or two pairs to perform their conversations for the class.

**Activity 5**

**Read and complete the sentences.**

- Pupils review their work in the unit.

**Odd one out activity**

**Which is the odd one out? Why?**

**Answer:** castle (It isn't a shop.)

### Ending the lesson

**Review the lesson and reflect on learning.**

- Say **Today we've learnt how to have a conversation about our favourite item of clothing.**

### Key Competences and Key Learning Outcomes

- Watch and understand a video about other people's favourite cities
- Learn how to make detailed comparisons using Venn diagrams
- Learn about the city of Venice

### Key language

- *exciting, floating, islands, gondola, guide book, relaxing, traditional, water bus, water taxi*
- *The city is more exciting than the countryside. I think I prefer the city.*

### Materials

- Pupil's Book p37; Activity Book p35; Class CD2; Teacher's App on Navio
- Teacher's Resource Bank: Talk cards

### Optional materials

- Teacher's Resource Bank: Trinity Exams Practice cards (selected from the Starter Unit and Units 1 and 2)

## At a Glance Lesson Plan

### Pupil's Book

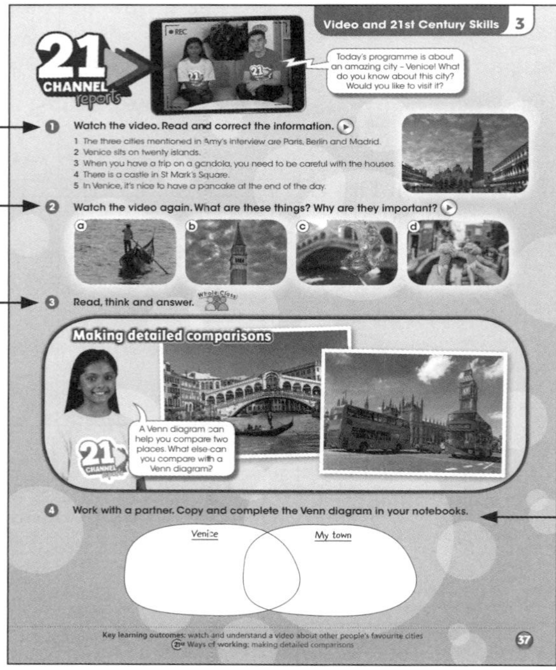


**Starting the lesson**

- Use the Trinity Exams Practice cards (optional).
- **Think-Pair-Share** Review vocabulary for objects and places in a city.
- Set learning objectives and use the talk cards.

**Activity 1**

- Before you watch
- Watch the video.
- *Unit 3 video p301*
- Read and correct the information.

**Activity 2**

- Watch the video again.
- *Unit 3 video*
- What are these things?
- Why are they important?

**Activity 3**

- Read, think and answer.

**Activity 4**

- Work with a partner.
- Copy and complete the Venn diagram in your notebooks.
- Go to the Activity Book.

**Ending the lesson**

- Review the lesson and reflect on learning.

**Extra activity**

- Create a Venn diagram about you and your partner.

### Digital resources

**Teacher's Digital:** You can also teach this lesson using the Teacher's App on Navio.

**Pupil's Digital:** Encourage your pupils to use the Pupil's App on Navio to practise the activities from this lesson.

Powered By NAVIO

### Activity Book

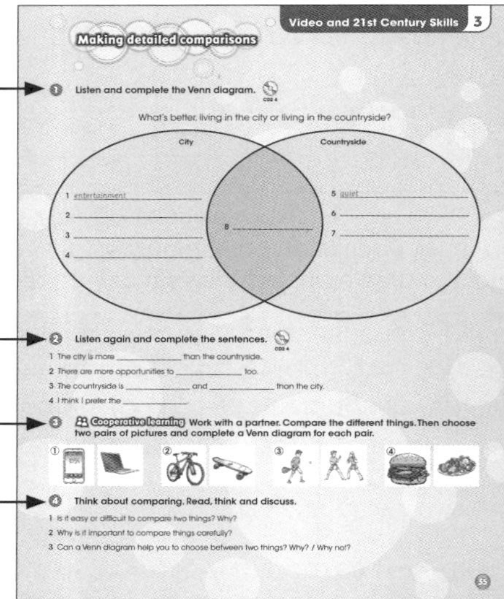


**Activity Book**

**Activity 1**

- Listen and complete the Venn diagram.

▶ *CD2 Track 4 p281*

**Activity 2**

- Listen again and complete the sentences.

▶ *CD2 Track 4 p281*

**Activity 3**

- Work with a partner. Compare the different things.
- Then choose two pairs of pictures and complete a Venn diagram for each pair.

**Activity 4**

- Think about comparing.
- Read, think and discuss.

# Detailed Lesson Plan

## Starting the lesson

**Think-Pair-Share Review vocabulary for places in a city.**

- Ask **How many different clothes and clothes adjectives can you think of?** The class thinks silently for a minute.
- Then the pupils work with a Talk Partner to name places in a city.
- Invite different Talk Partners to say different objects and places in a city. Hold up the corresponding flashcard and prompt the class to repeat the word.
- Finally, repeat the procedure, asking different pairs of Talk Partners each time, until all the ideas have been recorded.

**Set learning objectives and use the talk cards.**

- Say **Today we're going to watch a video and then ask and answer questions about Venice.**
- Point to the talk cards to show the pupils the different ways they will be working in the lesson.

## Pupil's Book Activity 1

**Before you watch**

- Read the speech bubble to pupils. Ask **What do you know about Venice? Would you like to visit it?** Elicit responses from a number of pupils.

**Watch the video. Read and correct the information.**
*p301*

- Watch Part 1 of the video. Ask pupils **What are you going to see next?**
- Play Part 2 of the video. Pupils correct the sentence in Activity 1 if they can.
- Play the video again. Pupils correct the information. Check answers as a group.

**Answers:** **1** The three cities are Paris, Istanbul and Madrid. **2** Venice sits on more than one hundred islands. **3** You need to be careful with the bridges. **4** There is a tower in St Mark's Square. **5** It's nice to have an ice cream at the end of the day.

## Pupil's Book Activity 2

**Watch the video again. What are these things? Why are they important?**

- Ask a pupil **What can you see in picture a?** Ask a different pupil **Why are gondolas important in Venice?** Pupils offer answers.

**Answers:** **a** A Gondola. Many tourists have a trip on a gondola in Venice. **b** The Tower in St Mark's Square. Thousands of people climb the tower every day. **c** A mask. Tourists often buy a mask as a souvenir. **d** Ice cream. Venice is famous for its amazing ice cream.

## Pupil's Book Activity 3

**Read, think and answer.**

- Ask pupils what two cities they can see in the photos (*Venice and London*). Ask if they remember what comparison Amy makes about them (*London is a capital city; Venice isn't*).
- Read the speech bubble with the class. Give pupils some ideas if necessary (*You can compare two countries, two people, two animals, two types of food, etc*). In pairs, pupils think of more things that they can compare.

## Pupil's Book Activity 4

**Work with a partner. Copy and complete the Venn diagram in your notebooks.**

- Ask a pupil **Are there gondolas in your town?** They write things that Venice has on the left, things that their town has on the right and things that both have in the middle.
- Pupils work in pairs to complete the Venn diagram with as many ideas as possible.

**Answers:** Pupils' own answers

## Activity Book

**Activity 1**

**Listen and complete the Venn diagram.**
▶ *CD2 Track 4 p281*

- Ask **What's better, living in the city or living in the countryside?** Pupils answer.

**Answers:** **1** entertainment **2** universities **3** traffic **4** pollution **5** quiet **6** clean air **7** friendly people **8** good food

**Activity 2**

**Listen again and complete the sentences.**
▶ *CD2 Track 4 p281*

**Answers:** **1** exciting **2** study **3** cleaner; quieter **4** city

- Ask the pupils why Amy prefers the city (*There's more entertainment; She loves going to the cinema and to museums.*)

**Activity 3**

**Work with a partner. Compare the different things. Then choose two pairs of pictures and complete a Venn diagram for each pair.**

- Ask the pupils what they can see in each picture.
- Pupils work in pairs. They compare the items using a venn diagram for each pair. Remind them that they don't have to write full sentences in the diagrams, only key words.

**Activity 4**

**Think about comparing. Read, think and discuss.**

- In pairs, pupils discuss the questions.
- Do a class vote: How many pupils think that Venn diagrams are helpful?

## Ending the lesson

**Review the lesson and reflect on learning.**

- Say **Today we've watched a video about Venice. What have we learnt about Venn diagrams?** Elicit ideas from the pupils.

# Project 1: A healthy life digital poster



**Key Competences and Key Learning Outcomes**

- Learn about healthy lives
- Investigate healthy living habits
- Listen for specific information and take notes
- Interview a partner about their lifestyle
- Make suggestions about how they can live more healthily

**Key language**

- *brush your teeth, campaign, doctor, do exercise, drink water, eat breakfast, fast food, feel tired, fizzy drinks, have a check-up, healthy, nutritionist, questionnaire, sports coach, stay up late, sun cream, walk to school, watch TV*
- *How often do you (have a check-up at the dentist)? I have a check-up once a year.*

**Materials**

- Pupil's Book p38; Activity Book p36; Class CD2; Teacher's App on Navio
- Teacher's Resource Bank: Talk cards (optional)

## At a Glance Lesson Plan

**Starting the lesson**

- Set learning objectives.

**Activity 1: Share knowledge**

- Read and discuss.

**Activity 2: Investigate**

- Listen and complete the notes about healthy lives on page 36 in your Activity Book.

*CD2 Track 5 p282*

Go to the Activity Book.

**Activity 3**

- Work with a partner.
- Find out if they are healthy.
- Ask and answer the questions.
- Listen carefully.

**Activity 4**

- What do you remember about your partner's answers?
- Complete the information on page 36 of your Activity Book.

Go to the Activity Book.

## Pupil's Book

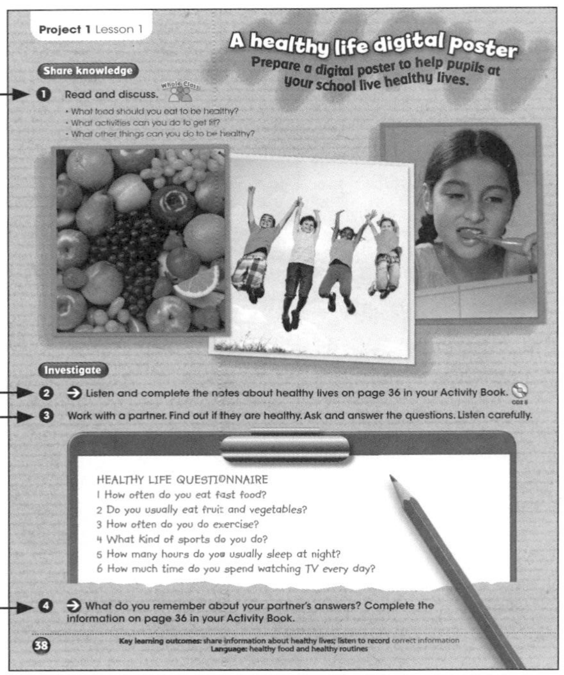


**Ending the lesson**

- Review the lesson and reflect on learning.

**Extension activity**

- Do further research.

**Link to Science**

- **The human body:** Review the importance of being healthy.

## Digital resources

**Teacher's Digital:** You can also teach this lesson using the Teacher's App on Navio.

**Pupil's Digital:** Encourage your pupils to use the Pupil's App on Navio to practise the activities from this lesson.

Powered By NAVIO

## Activity Book

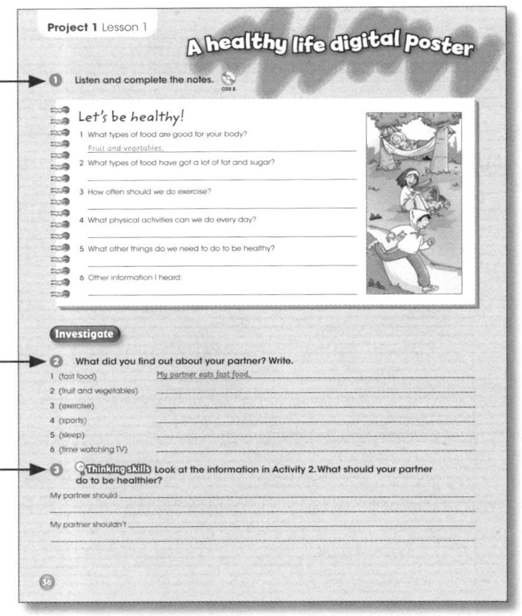


**Activity Book**

**Activity 1**

- Listen and complete the notes.

▶ *CD2 Track 5 p282*

**Activity 2**

- What did you find out about your partner? Write.

**Activity 3**

- Look at the information in Activity 2. What should your partner do to be healthier?

# Detailed Lesson Plan

### Starting the lesson

**Set learning objectives.**

- Say **Today we're going to begin a project.**
- Focus the group's attention on the project description at the top of the page. Read the text as a class.

### Pupil's Book Activity 1: Share knowledge

**Read and discuss.**

- Work as a class to read and discuss the questions. The pupils share what they know about healthy living.
- Prompt the class to give more information. Ask **Why is it important to (eat fruit and vegetables)? What kind of exercise can you do? How can we protect our bodies?**

### Pupil's Book Activity 2: Investigate

**Listen and complete the notes about healthy lives on page 36 in your Activity Book.**

- Read the instructions. Ask the pupils to open their Activity Books (page 36).
- Invite a pupil to read the Digital tip.

### Activity Book

**Activity 1**

**Listen and complete the notes.**

▸ *CD2 Track 5 p282*

- Read the questions as a class and predict the answers. Then play the CD. The pupils listen and follow the information in their books.
- Play the CD again, pausing after each piece of key information. The pupils say and write the answer each time.

**Answers:** **1** Fruit and vegetables, cheese and yogurts, meat and eggs, pasta and rice **2** cakes and sweets **3** three times a week **4** walk the dog / walk to school **5** wash your hands / brush your teeth

### Pupil's Book Activity 3

**Work with a partner. Find out of they are healthy. Ask and answer the questions. Listen carefully.**

- Focus the pupils on the first question in the questionnaire. Ask several pupils for their answer. Then ask different pupils what their classmates answered, to check that they are listening carefully.
- Pupils continue the questionnaire in pairs.

### Pupil's Book Activity 4

**What do you remember about your partner's answers? Complete the information on page 36 of your Activity Book.**

- Direct pupils to the example in their Activity Books. Ask several pupils what their partners said about fast food.

### Activity Book

**Activity 2**

**What did you find out about your partner? Write.**

- Pupils work alone to write their information.
- Ask them to compare the information with their partners and check if it's correct. They can correct it if necessary.

**Activity 3**

**Look at the information in Activity 2. What should your partner do to be healthier?**

- Give the class an example about you - something you should do to be healthier.
- Pupils work alone to write about their partners. Then they compare in pairs.
- Ask some pupils if they agree with the advice that their partners have written.

### Ending the lesson

**Review the lesson and reflect on learning.**

- Say **Today we've learnt about how to be healthy.**
- Ask **Which was your favourite activity today? Which activity was easy / difficult?**

**Extension activity**

- Organise the class into groups of three. Ask them to use the Internet to investigate healthy lifestyles further. The pupils record extra information in their Activity Books (page 36, Activity 1). Sources of information include:
  www.bbc.co.uk/schools/scienceclips/ages/9_10/keeping_healthy_fs.shtml

### Link to Science

- If you are studying the Science topic of the human body, review the importance of hygiene for preventing infections. Teach the expression *Coughs and sneezes spread diseases.* Ask the class to think about what this expression means and what we should do to protect ourselves and others. (*Hand washing, covering your mouth when you cough or sneeze, using a tissue and throwing it in the bin.*)

# Project 1: A healthy life digital poster



## Key Competences and Key Learning Outcomes

- Present your digital poster in a group
- Reflect on what you've learnt and how you've worked together
- Create your digital poster in a group

## Key language

- *brush your teeth, campaign, do exercise, eat fruit, look after our teeth*
- *You should brush your teeth two or three times a day. You need (nine hours' sleep every night). Why don't we (make a poster)? What about (writing an article)? We need to (look for pictures). I can do that.*

## Materials

- Pupil's Book p39; Activity Book p37; Teacher's App on Navio
- Materials depend on the task chosen (poster / PowerPoint presentation / article for school magazine / article for school web page)

## At a Glance Lesson Plan

### Starting the lesson

- Set learning objectives.

### Activity 1: Plan and create your project

- In pairs or groups, discuss the questions.
- Write the information on page 37 in your Activity Book.

Go to the Activity Book.

### Activity 2

- Design and create a digital poster.

### Activity 3: Present your project

- Present your digital poster to the class.
- Take turns to answer any questions.

## Pupil's Book

### Reflect on your project

- Read and answer the questions on page 37 in your Activity Book.

Go to the Activity Book.

### Ending the lesson

- Review the lesson and reflect on learning.

**Extension activity**

- Display your campaign for a wider audience.

## Digital resources

**Teacher's Digital:** You can also teach this lesson using the Teacher's App on Navio.

**Pupil's Digital:** Encourage your pupils to use the Pupil's App on Navio to practise the activities from this lesson.

Powered By NAVIO

## Activity Book

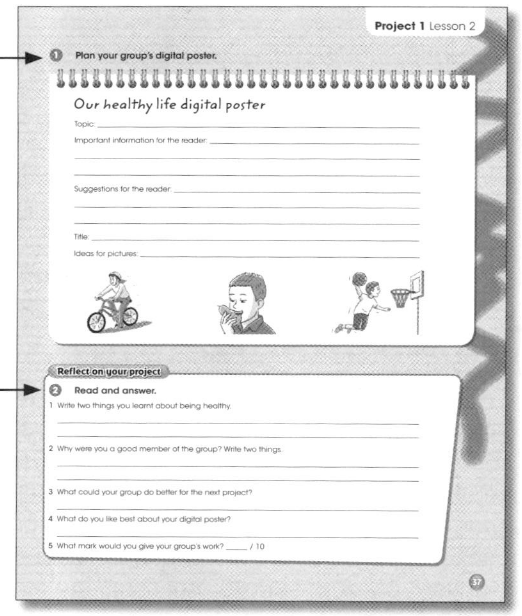


### Activity Book

**Activity 1**

- Plan your group's digital poster.

**Activity 2: Reflect on your project**

- Read and answer.

### Starting the lesson

**Set learning objectives.**

- Say **Today we're going to continue the project**. Ask the class to tell you what they did in the last lesson.

### Pupil's Book Activity 1: Plan and create your project

**In pairs or groups, discuss the questions. Write the information on page 37 in your Activity Book.**

- Put the class into pairs or groups. Tell them now they are going to plan their own digital poster.
- Direct pupils to the Language bank. Read through the phrases and elicit some different ways to complete them.

### Activity Book

**Activity 1**

**Plan your group's digital poster.**

- The pupils record their decisions about the campaign.

### Pupil's Book Activity 2

**Design and create a digital poster.**

- Show the class how to create a simple poster on a computer. Show them how to select different colours, fonts and sizes, and how to add simple pictures.
- In their pairs of groups, pupils create their posters.

### Pupil's Book Activity 3: Present your project

**Present your digital poster to the class. Take turns to answer any questions.**

- The class looks at the posters and talks about what they can see. Ask **What are these groups' posters about?** Then ask a pupil to read out the speech bubbles.
- Invite different groups in turn to present their posters to the rest of the class. At the end of each presentation, ask the group a question and encourage the rest of the class to think of questions they'd like to ask. The group giving the presentation answer the questions.

### Reflect on your project

**Read and answer the questions on page 37 of your Activity Book.**

- The pupils answer the questions in the Activity Book.

### Activity Book

**Activity 2: Reflect on your project**

**Read and answer.**

- The pupils write their answers.

### Ending the lesson

**Review the lesson and reflect on learning.**

- Say **Today we've done a project about being healthy.**
- Ask **Which was your favourite activity today? Which activity was easy / difficult?**

**Extension activity**

- Make a display of the pupils' work so that other classes can enjoy and learn from it. Posters can be displayed in the corridor or library. PowerPoint presentations can be uploaded onto the class or school web page.

Date: ____________ Unit: ____________

1 What did my pupils learn in this unit?

______________________________

______________________________

______________________________

______________________________

2 How did my pupils work? (✓)

individually ☐ in pairs ☐ in small groups ☐

in large groups ☐ as a class ☐

3 Which key competences did my pupils develop? Give a score from 1 to 5 (5 being the highest).

- Competence in linguistic communication ☐
- Competence in mathematics, science and technology ☐
- Digital competence ☐
- Learning to learn ☐
- Social and civic competences ☐
- Sense of initiative and entrepreneurship ☐
- Cultural awareness and expression ☐

4 Which lessons / activities were the most successful and why?

______________________________

______________________________

______________________________

______________________________

5 Which lessons / activities did my pupils find the most difficult and why?

______________________________

______________________________

______________________________

______________________________

6 What did I try in the classroom for the first time? How did it go?

______________________________

______________________________

______________________________

______________________________

7 Which resources did I find most useful? (including webpages)

______________________________

______________________________

______________________________

______________________________

______________________________

______________________________

8 What could I do differently next time I teach this unit?

______________________________

______________________________

______________________________

______________________________

Unit 4

# My technology

## Unit overview

### Key Competences and Key Learning Outcomes

- Review and learn words related to technology (Lesson 1)
- Learn the similarity between 'must' and 'have to' and the difference between 'mustn't' and 'don't have to' (Lesson 2)
- Learn and practise how to use 'if' and 'when' in zero conditional (Lesson 4)
- Review and practise using the present simple and the past simple (Lesson 7)
- Talk about your favourite object (Lesson 8)
- Watch and understand a video about new technology (Video and 21st Century Skills)

---

- Learn about webcams (Lesson 3)
- Learn about augmented reality glasses (Video and 21st Century Skills)
- Learn expressions for using touchscreen devices (Lesson 5)

---

- Use the Pupil's App on Navio
- Investigate Germany (Lesson 3)

---

- Read a message and a list of rules for specific information (Lesson 1)
- Identify and practise intonation in zero conditional sentences (Lesson 4)
- Reflect on your own learning (Lesson 8)
- Practise activity types found in the Cambridge Exams: A2 Key for Schools

---

- Think about the importance of acting quickly in an emergency (Lesson 3)
- Prepare and give a short presentation to the class (Lesson 8)

---

- Do a communication task (Lesson 5)
- Discuss ways technology can help us (Video and 21st Century Skills)

---

- Read and understand a story (Lesson 3)
- Learn about Germany (Lesson 3)
- Read and write reviews (Lessons 6 and 7)
- Sing a song (Lesson 8)

### Vocabulary

**Core vocabulary**
*camera, CD player, computer game, interactive whiteboard, karaoke, laptop, MP3 player, mobile phone, tablet, video call, webcam, website; move down, move left, move right, move up, pause the game, start the game, swipe the screen, tap the screen, tilt the screen*

**Extension vocabulary (optional)**
*charger, download, share, the cloud, upload, USB; download a game, get a high score, get a low score, read the instructions*

**Other vocabulary**
*shore, sunset; careful, lost, safe, useful; car lights, flash, get dark; article, brain, electric currents, entertainment, news, quizzes, sections, sport; computer company / game / programmer / screen, description, experience, facts, introduction, rating, swipe; app, augmented reality, cardboard, e-reader, headset, robotic, virtual reality*

**Recycled vocabulary**
*beach, foggy, future, ice, masks, police, help, science; play music / online, press the button, record a video, take a photo; after that, first, then; drawing, gallery, paintbrush, painting, sculptures*

### Structures

**Core structures**
*I / You / We / They have to (use the Internet). He / She / It has to (use the Internet). I / You / He / She / It / We / They had to (carry CDs). I / You / We / They don't have to (carry CDs). He / She / It doesn't have to (carry CDs). I / You / He / She / It / We / They didn't have to (leave). What happens if you heat ice? It changes to water. If you press here, you take a photo. When you turn it off, the screen goes black.*

**Recycled structures**
*I can use (the Internet for my homework). I must (share my passwords with my parents). I mustn't (send photos). A tourist was walking. Jennifer wants to work on games about football.*

### Pronunciation

Intonation in zero conditional sentences

### Literacy

**Text type:** a review (information text; writing preparation)
**Reading skill:** identifying opinions
**Writing skill:** using the present and the past simple

### Culture ... around the world

How a man's life was saved by a webcam in Germany

### 21st Century Skills

**Digital skills:** using technology to help us

### Thinking skills

Expanding on lexical sets (Lesson 1); Matching words and pictures (Lesson 1); Analysing and applying rules (Lessons 2, 4 and 7); Hypothesising and thinking laterally (Lesson 3); Logical thinking (Lesson 5); Finding information (Lesson 6); Planning, checking and correcting (Lesson 7); Seeing another's point of view (Lesson 8); Reflecting on learning (Lesson 8)

### Cooperative learning

Working together (Lessons 1–8); Collaborating (Lessons 1–8); Checking learning (Lessons 1–8); Peer evaluation and feedback (Lessons 7 and 8); Participating (Lessons 1–8); Helping and encouraging (Lessons 1–8); Reflecting and setting goals (Lesson 8)

### Values

Acting quickly in an emergency

### Cross-curricular links

**Link to Science**
Technology

**Suggested Arts and Crafts concepts**
Tints and shades

## Key Competences and Key Learning Outcomes

- Identify and say words associated with technology
- Listen to definitions and identify the words
- Read a message and a list of rules for specific information
- Talk about computer rules at home

### Key language

- *camera, CD player, computer game, interactive whiteboard, karaoke, laptop, MP3 player, mobile phone, tablet, video call, webcam, website*
- *I can use (the Internet for my homework). I must (share my passwords with my parents). I mustn't (send photos).*
- **Extension:** *charger, download, share, the cloud, upload, USB*

### Materials

- Pupil's Book pp40–41; Activity Book p38; Class CD2; Teacher's App on Navio
- Technology flashcards

### Optional materials

- Teacher's Resource Bank: Trinity Exams Practice cards (selected from the Starter Unit and Units 1, 2 and 3)

## At a Glance Lesson Plan

### Starting the lesson

- Use the Trinity Exams Practice cards (optional).
- Set learning objectives.

### Activity 1

- Look at Lena's photos.
- Answer the questions.

### Activity 2

- Think of five ways that people use technology to communicate with each other.

### Vocabulary presentation

- Present the new vocabulary using the technology flashcards.

### Activity 3

- Look and match.
- Listen, check and repeat.

▶ *CD2 Track 6 p282*

### Activity 4

- Listen and do the vocabulary quiz.

▶ *CD2 Track 7 p282*

## Pupil's Book

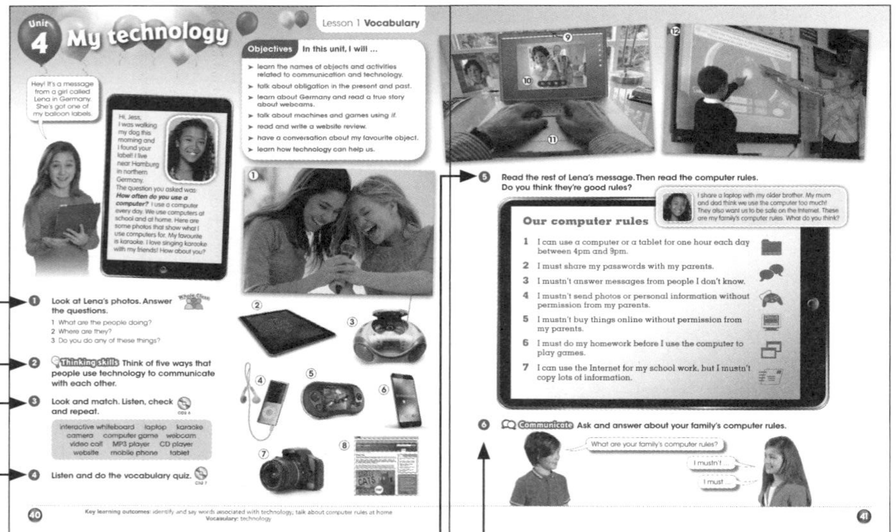

### Activity 5

- Read the rest of Lena's message.
- Then read the computer rules.
- Do you think they're good rules?

### Activity 6

- Ask and answer about your family's computer rules.

Go to the Activity Book.

### Ending the lesson

- Review the lesson and reflect on learning.

### Extra activities

**Extension**

- Find out about Germany.

**Vocabulary extension**

- Present six additional vocabulary items.

### Digital resources

**Teacher's Digital:** You can also teach this lesson using the Teacher's App on Navio.

**Pupil's Digital:** Encourage your pupils to use the Pupil's App on Navio to practise the activities from this lesson.

## Activity Book

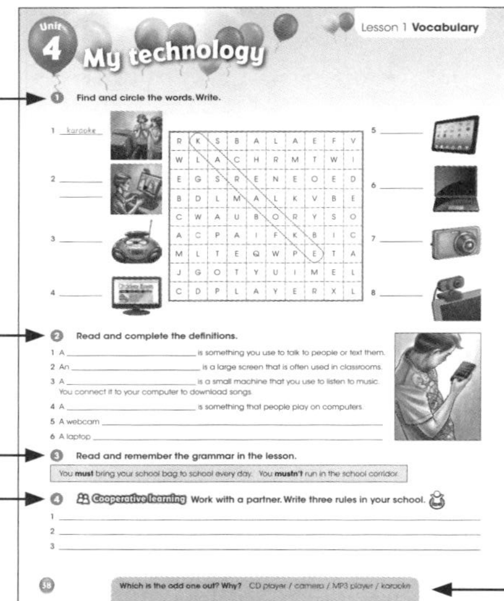

### Activity Book

**Activity 1**

- Find and circle the words. Write.

**Activity 2**

- Read and complete the definitions.

**Activity 3**

- Read and remember the grammar in the lesson.

**Activity 4**

- Work with a partner. Write three rules in your school.

**Odd one out activity**

- Which is the odd one out? Why?

# Detailed Lesson Plan

**Starting the lesson**

**Use the Trinity Exams Practice cards (optional).**

- The pupils practise asking and answering questions.

**Set learning objectives.**

- Say **Today we're going to learn words about technology and talk about using computers.**

**Pupil's Book Activity 1**

**Look at Lena's photos. Answer the questions.**

- Invite a pupil to read out the speech bubble to find out who has found the label. Ask **Do you know where Germany is?**
- Invite a pupil to read out the message. Check understanding.
- Read and answer the questions about the photos.

**Answers:** 1 singing karaoke, using a laptop, using an interactive whiteboard **2** at home, at home / the office, at school

**Pupil's Book Activity 2**

**Think of five ways that people use technology to communicate with each other.**

- Ask **How do we communicate with each other?** Say **Some ways use technology.**
- Organise the class into pairs. The pupils think of five ways that we use technology to communicate.

**Vocabulary presentation**

- Present the new vocabulary using the technology flashcards. Show the first flashcard and elicit / say the word. Then ask **Can we communicate using this?**
- Repeat the procedure with the other flashcards.

**Pupil's Book Activity 3**

**Look and match. Listen, check and repeat.**

▶ ***CD2 Track 6 p282***

- Focus the class on item number 1 in the photo. Ask **What's this?** The pupils work in pairs to match numbers 2–12 and the words.
- Play the CD. The pupils listen and check.
- Play the CD again, pausing after each word for the pupils to repeat.

**Pupil's Book Activity 4**

**Listen and do the vocabulary quiz.**

▶ ***CD2 Track 7 p282***

- Play the CD. Listen to the first definition, pausing at the beep to allow the pupils to name the item. Continue with the CD to listen to the answer.
- Repeat the procedure with the other definitions.

**Pupil's Book Activity 5**

**Read the rest of Lena's message. Then read the computer rules. Do you think they're good rules?**

- Invite a pupil to read out the message and rules. Tell the pupils that you are going to read out some of Lena's actions. The pupils need to write down 'good' if she didn't break a rule and 'bad' if she breaks a rule. **1 I used the computer at 5pm.** (*Good.*) **2 I sent an email and then did my homework after that.** (*Bad.*) **3 I sent my photo to you but I didn't ask my parents.** (*Bad.*) **4 I got a message from someone that I don't know. I'm not going to answer it.** (*Good.*)
- The pupils discuss the question in pairs.
- Discuss with the class. Encourage the pupils to give reasons for their opinions.

**Pupil's Book Activity 6**

**Ask and answer about your family's computer rules.**

- Invite two pupils to read out the speech bubbles.
- The pupils ask and answer in pairs.

**Activity Book**

**Activity 1**

**Find and circle the words. Write.**

- The pupils look at the pictures. They find and write the words.

**Answers:** 1 karaoke **2** video call **3** CD player **4** website **5** tablet **6** laptop **7** camera **8** webcam

**Activity 2**

**Read and complete the definitions.**

- The pupils complete the definitions.

**Answers:** 1 mobile phone **2** interactive whiteboard **3** MP3 player **4** computer game

**Activity 3**

**Read and remember the grammar in the lesson.**

- Read the information.

**Activity 4**

**Work with a partner.**
**Write three rules in your school.**

- The pupils write three rules.

**Odd one out activity**

**Which is the odd one out? Why?**

- The pupils complete the odd one out activity.

**Answers:** camera (It doesn't play music.)

**Ending the lesson**

**Review the lesson and reflect on learning.**

- Say **Today we've learnt words about technology and talked about rules. What do you remember?**
- Ask **Which was your favourite activity today? Which activity was easy / difficult?**

**Extra activities**

**Extension**

- The pupils find Germany on the world map on pages 134–135. They read the accompanying facts.

**Vocabulary extension**

- Present six additional technology words: *charger, download, share, the cloud, upload, USB.*

## Key Competences and Key Learning Outcomes

- Listen to and read a dialogue
- Identify the use of 'have to' in the present and past
  - Learn the similarity between 'must' and 'have to' and the difference between 'mustn't' and 'don't have to'
- Practise activity types found in the Cambridge Exams: A2 Key for Schools
- Talk about what you have to do

## Key language

- *CD player, interactive whiteboard, internet connection, MP3 player, play music, video call, webcam*
- *I / You / We / They have to (use the Internet). He / She / It has to (use the Internet). I / You / He / She / It / We / They had to (carry CDs). I / You / We / They don't have to (carry CDs). He / She / It doesn't have to (carry CDs). I / You / He / She / It / We / They didn't have to (leave).*

## Materials

- Pupil's Book p42; Activity Book p39; Class CD2; Teacher's App on Navio
- Teacher's Resource Bank: Technology word cards

## Optional materials

- Teacher's Resource Bank: Trinity Exams Practice cards (selected from the Starter Unit and Units 1, 2 and 3)

# At a Glance Lesson Plan

## Pupil's Book

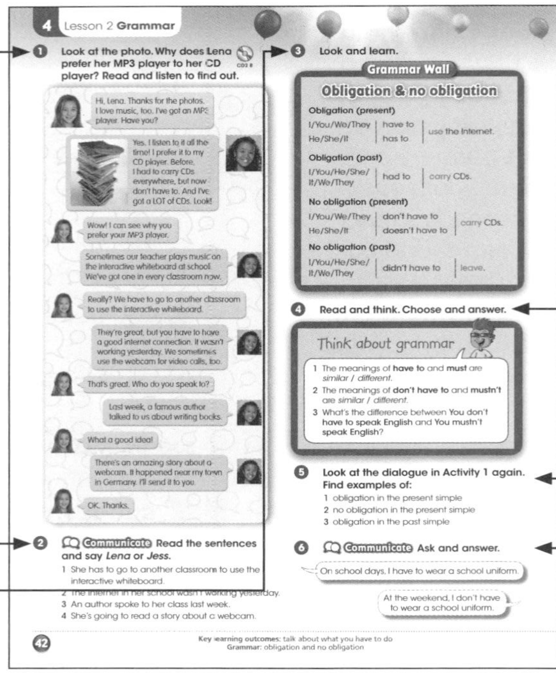

### Starting the lesson

- Use the Trinity Exams Practice cards (optional).
- Review technology objects.
- Set learning objectives.

### Activity 1

- Look at the photo.
- Why does Lena prefer her MP3 player to her CD player?
- Read and listen to find out.

▶ *CD2 Track 8 p282*

### Activity 2

- Read the sentences and say *Lena* or *Jess.*

### Activity 3

- Look and learn – Grammar wall

### Activity 4

- Read and think.
- Choose and answer.

### Activity 5

- Look at the dialogue in Activity 1 again.
- Find examples of:

### Activity 6

- Ask and answer.

Go to the Activity Book.

### Ending the lesson

- Review the lesson and reflect on learning.

### Extra activity

**Reinforcement**

- Think about what your family had to, or didn't have to do when they were younger.

## Activity Book

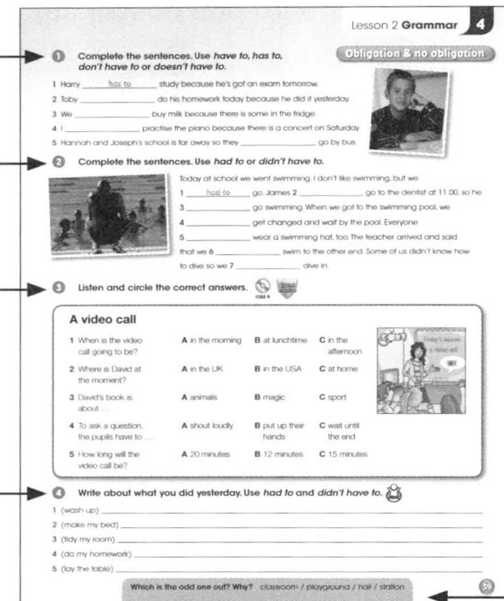

### Activity Book

**Activity 1**

- Complete the sentences. Use *have to, has to, don't have to* or *doesn't have to.*

**Activity 2**

- Complete the sentences. Use *had to* or *didn't have to.*

**Activity 3**

- Listen and circle the correct answers.

▶ *CD2 Track 9 p282*

**Activity 4**

- Write about what you did yesterday. Use *had to* and *didn't have to*.

**Odd one out activity**

- Which is the odd one out? Why?

## Digital resources

**Teacher's Digital:** You can also teach this lesson using the Teacher's App on Navio.

**Pupil's Digital:** Encourage your pupils to use the Pupil's App on Navio to practise the activities from this lesson.

Powered By NAVIO

# Detailed Lesson Plan

**Starting the lesson**

**Use the Trinity Exams Practice cards (optional).**
- The pupils practise asking and answering questions.

**Review technology objects.**
- Hold up one of the technology word cards so that the class can't see it and describe it. Describe its shape, size, use and material. When the class guesses the item, show the card.
- Repeat the procedure several times.

**Set learning objectives.**
- Say **Today we're going to learn how to use 'have to' to talk about things that are necessary.**

**Pupil's Book Activity 1**

**Look at the photo. Why does Lena prefer her MP3 player to her CD player? Read and listen to find out.**
▶ *CD2 Track 8 p282*
- The pupils describe what they can see in the photo.
- Ask for ideas why Lena prefers her MP3 player.
- Play the CD. The pupils listen and read the dialogue. Confirm that Lena prefers her MP3 player because it means she doesn't have to carry CDs.

**Pupil's Book Activity 2**

**Read the sentences and say *Lena* or *Jess*.**
- Organise the class into pairs. The pupils read the sentences and decide which girl each sentence refers to.

**Pupil's Book Activity 3**

**Look and learn – Grammar wall**
- Read the information on the Grammar wall as a class.
- Use questions to encourage the pupils to think about form and identify / remember patterns. Ask **Do we use 'have to' with 'He' and 'She'? How does it change in the past tense?**

**Pupil's Book Activity 4**

**Read and think. Choose and answer.**
- Read out the sentences in the Think about grammar box. The pupils complete the sentences in pairs. Then check the answers as a class.

**Answers:** **1** similar **2** different **3** In the first sentence, you can speak English if you want to but it isn't necessary. In the second sentence, you aren't allowed to speak English.

**Pupil's Book Activity 5**

**Look at the dialogue in Activity 1 again. Find examples of:**
- Organise the pupils into pairs. Ask them to find the examples in the text. They can do this orally or write the sentences in their notebooks.
- The pupils share information with the rest of the class.

**Pupil's Book Activity 6**

**Ask and answer.**
- Invite two pupils to read out the speech bubbles. In pairs, the pupils make sentences about school days and weekends using 'have to' and 'don't have to'

**Activity Book**

**Activity 1**

**Complete the sentences. Use *have to, has to, don't have to* or *doesn't have to*.**
- The pupils complete the sentences.

**Answers:** **1** has to **2** doesn't have to **3** don't have to **4** have to **5** have to

**Activity 2**

**Complete the sentences. Use *had to* or *didn't have to*.**
- The pupils complete the paragraph in the past tense.

**Answers:** **1** had to **2** had to **3** didn't have to **4** had to **5** had to **6** had to **7** didn't have to

**Activity 3**

**Listen and circle the correct answers.**
▶ *CD2 Track 9 p282*
- Ask the pupils if they have had a video call. Ask **Who do you have video calls with? Do we have video calls at school?**
- Remind the pupils that Lena spoke to a famous author. Explain that they are going to hear a teacher talking to her class about a video call.
- Play the CD, pausing after each piece of key information if you wish. The pupils circle the answers.

**Answers:** **1** C **2** B **3** B **4** B **5** A

**Activity 4**

**Write about what you did yesterday. Use *had to* and *didn't have to*.**
- Ask a pupil to read the activities.
- Make it clear that the pupils are thinking about yesterday. Do the first sentence as an example about you (*I had to wash up yesterday*).

**Odd one out activity**

**Which is the odd one out? Why?**
- The pupils complete the odd one out activity.

**Answers:** station (It isn't at school.)

**Ending the lesson**

**Review the lesson and reflect on learning.**
- Say **Today we've learnt how to use 'have to'.** Elicit examples of the language from the pupils.
- Ask **Which was your favourite activity today? Which activity was easy / difficult?**

**Extra activity**

**Reinforcement**
- As a homework task, the pupils talk to their family about the things they had to do, or didn't have to do, when they were younger.
- The pupils write down three examples of each.

### Key Competences and Key Learning Outcomes

- Read a story with a cultural focus
- Listen for specific information
- Learn about webcams
- Use the Internet to investigate Germany
- Think about the importance of acting quickly in an emergency
- Learn about Germany

### Key language

- *camera, computer screen, webcam, photo; beach, shore; careful, safe; car lights, flash, foggy, get dark, ice, lost, maybe, police, sunset*
- *A tourist was walking. He wanted to (take photos). If I (take photos, the camera flashes). The police used their car lights to help the man.*

### Materials

- Pupil's Book p43; Activity Book p40; Class CD2; Teacher's App on Navio

### Optional materials

- Teacher's Resource Bank: Trinity Exams Practice cards (selected from the Starter Unit and Units 1, 2 and 3)

## At a Glance Lesson Plan

### Pupil's Book

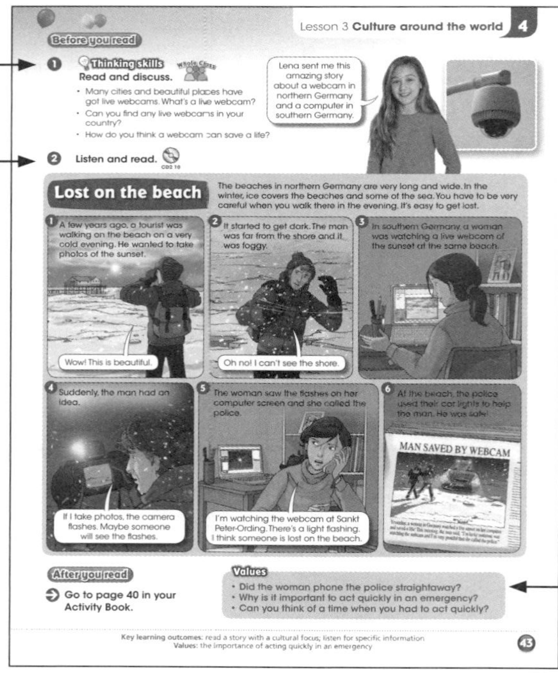


**Starting the lesson**

- Use the Trinity Exams Practice cards (optional).
- Review 'have to'.
- Set learning objectives.

**Activity 1: Before you read**

- Read and discuss.

**Activity 2**

- Listen and read.
- ▶ *CD2 Track 10 p283*
- Go to the Activity Book.

**Values**

- Read and discuss.

**Ending the lesson**

- Review the lesson and reflect on learning.

**Extra activity**

**Reinforcement**

- Research a live webcam in your country.

### Activity Book

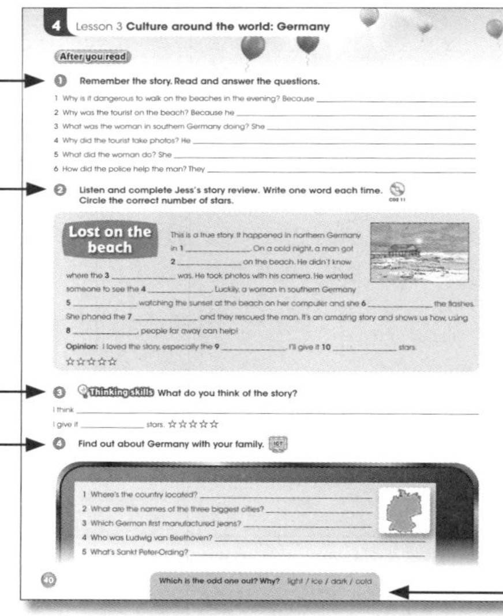


**Activity Book: After you read**

**Activity 1**

- Remember the story. Read and answer the questions.

**Activity 2**

- Listen and complete Jess's story review.
- ▶ *CD2 Track 11 p283*
- Write one word each time. Circle the correct number of stars.

**Activity 3**

- What do you think of the story?

**Activity 4**

- Find out about Germany with your family.

**Odd one out activity**

- Which is the odd one out? Why?

### Digital resources

**Teacher's Digital:** You can also teach this lesson using the Teacher's App on Navio.

**Pupil's Digital:** Encourage your pupils to use the Pupil's App on Navio to practise the activities from this lesson.

Powered By NAVIO

# Detailed Lesson Plan

**Starting the lesson**

**Use the Trinity Exams Practice cards (optional).**
- The pupils practise asking and answering questions.

**Review 'have to'.**
- Ask the class to think about the last time they used a webcam. Ask **What did you have to do?** Elicit sentences with 'I had to'.
- Invite different pupils to report the information to the rest of the class.

**Set learning objectives.**
- Say **Today we're going to read a true story from Germany.**

**Pupil's Book Activity 1: Before you read**

**Read and discuss.**
- Read the first two questions as a class. Encourage the pupils to share information about live webcams. Then ask the class to hypothesise about how a webcam could save a life. The pupils can do this in pairs.
- The pupils report back their ideas to the class. Write down some of these ideas on the board.

**Pupil's Book Activity 2**

**Listen and read.**
▶ *CD2 Track 10 p283*
- Play the CD. The pupils follow in their books. Confirm how the webcam saved a life. (*The woman saw the flashes on her webcam and called the police.*)
- Ask questions to check understanding.

**Suggested comprehension questions:**
- Frame 1: **Why was the tourist on the beach?** (*To take photos of the sunset.*)
- Frames 1 and 2: **What was the weather like?** (*Very cold and foggy.*)
- Frame 3: **Where was the woman watching the sunset?** (*In southern Germany, on a live webcam.*)
- Frame 4: **What did the man decide to do?** (*Take photos and maybe someone will see the flashes.*)
- Frame 5: **What did the woman do when she saw the flashes?** (*She called the police.*)
- Frame 6: **How did the police save the man?** (*They used their car lights.*)

**Activity Book: After you read**

**Activity 1**

**Remember the story. Read and answer the questions.**
- Read out the first question and invite a pupil to answer it.
- The pupils read and answer the remaining questions.

**Answers:** **1** ice covers the beaches and some of the sea and it's easy to get lost. **2** wanted to take photos of the sunset. **3** was watching a live webcam of the sunset. **4** wanted people to see the flashes from his camera. **5** called the police. **6** used their car lights to help the man.

**Activity 2**

**Listen and complete Jess's story review. Write one word each time. Circle the correct number of stars.**
▶ *CD2 Track 11 p283*
- Read out the story review as a class. Ask the pupils to guess the missing words.
- Play the CD without pausing. The pupils listen and complete as much of the information as possible.
- Play the CD again, pausing after each piece of key information to check the information and spelling. The pupils circle the correct number of stars.

**Answers:** **1** 2010 **2** lost **3** shore **4** flashes **5** was **6** saw **7** police **8** technology **9** end **10** five

**Activity 3**

**What do you think of the story?**
- The pupils write their opinion and give it a rating.
- Invite the pupils to share their opinions.

**Activity 4**

**Find out about Germany with your family.** ICT
- Read out the questions about Germany. Ask **Where can you find out this information?** (*Internet, library, asking friends and family*) The pupils complete the activity at home.
- If you prefer to do this activity in the class, connect to a children's website which has information about Germany such as: http://kids.nationalgeographic.com/kids/places/find/germany or www.sciencekids.co.nz/sciencefacts/countries/germany.html.
- Read out the questions. The pupils work as a class to find and write the answers.

**Answers:** **1** In Central Europe **2** Berlin, Hamburg, Munich **3** Levis Straus **4** a composer **5** a seaside spa

**Odd one out activity**

**Which is the odd one out? Why?**
- The pupils complete the odd one out activity.

**Answers:** ice (It isn't an adjective.)

**Values**

**Read and discuss.**
- Read out each question and discuss it as a class.
- Explain to the class that it is better to act quickly even if it turns out that it wasn't an emergency. 'It's better to be safe than sorry!' is an English expression.

**Ending the lesson**

**Review the lesson and reflect on learning.**
- Say **Today we've read a story from Germany.**
- Ask **Which was your favourite activity today? Which activity was easy / difficult?**

**Extra activity**

**Extension**
- The pupils research a live webcam in their country. They answer these questions: *Where's the webcam? What does it show? Why would people watch this webcam? What was the webcam showing when you watched it?*

## Key Competences and Key Learning Outcomes

- Act out a short dialogue in pairs
- Learn how to use 'if' and 'when' in zero conditional sentences
- Identify and practise intonation in zero conditional sentences

### Key language

- *camera, machine; play music, press the button, record a video, take a photo; cry, hungry, rain, useful, wet*
- *What happens if you heat ice? It changes to water. If you press here, you take a photo. When you turn it off, the screen goes black.*

### Materials

- Pupil's Book p44; Activity Book p41; Class CD2; Teacher's App on Navio

### Optional materials

- Teacher's Resource Bank: Trinity Exams Practice cards (selected from the Starter Unit and Units 1, 2 and 3)

## At a Glance Lesson Plan

### Pupil's Book

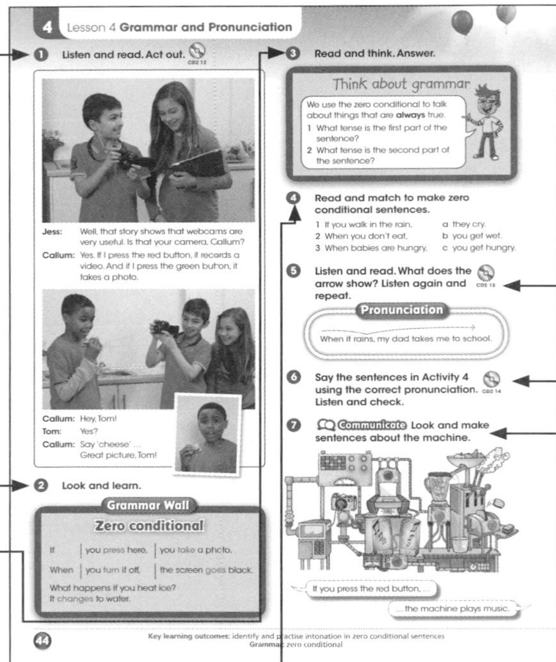

**Starting the lesson**

- Review 'have to'.
- Set learning objectives.

**Activity 1**

- Listen and read.
- Act out.
- ▶ *CD2 Track 12 p283*

**Activity 2**

- Look and learn – Grammar wall

**Activity 3**

- Read and think.
- Answer.

**Activity 4**

- Read and match to make zero conditional sentences.

**Activity 5**

- Listen and read.
- ▶ *CD2 Track 13 p283*
- What does the arrow show?
- Listen again and repeat.

**Activity 6**

- Say the sentences in Activity 4 using the correct pronunciation.
- Listen and check.
- ▶ *CD2 Track 14 p283*

**Activity 7**

- Look and make sentences about the machine.

Go to the Activity Book.

**Ending the lesson**

- Review the lesson and reflect on learning.

**Extra activity**

**Reinforcement**

- Make a poster of your crazy machine.

### Activity Book

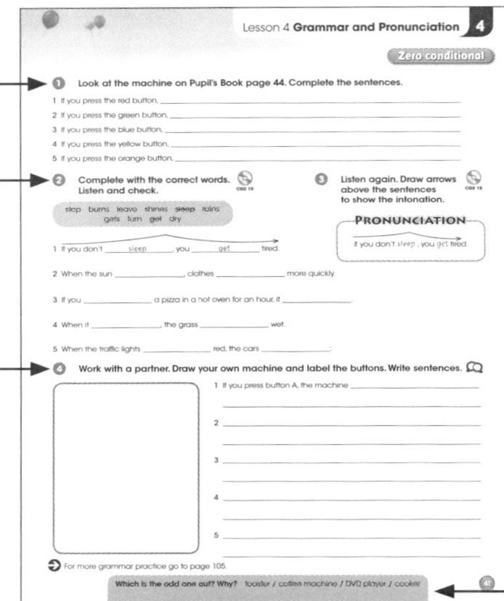

**Activity Book**

**Activity 1**

- Look at the machine on Pupil's Book page 44. Complete the sentences

**Activity 2**

- Complete with the correct words. Listen and check.
- ▶ *CD2 Track 15 p283*

**Activity 3**

- Listen again. Draw arrows above the sentences to show the intonation.
- ▶ *CD2 Track 15 p283*

**Activity 4**

- Work with a partner. Draw your own machine and label the buttons. Write sentences.

**Odd one out activity**

- Which is the odd one out? Why?

## Digital resources

**Teacher's Digital:** You can also teach this lesson using the Teacher's App on Navio.

**Pupil's Digital:** Encourage your pupils to use the Pupil's App on Navio to practise the activities from this lesson.

Powered By NAVIO

# Detailed Lesson Plan

## Starting the lesson

**Use the Trinity Exams Practice cards (optional).**
- The pupils practise asking and answering questions.

**Review 'have to'.**
- Play the *No one can go to the cinema* game (p27).

**Set learning objectives.**
- Say **Today we're going to learn how to use sentences with 'if' and 'when'.**

## Pupil's Book Activity 1

**Listen and read. Act out.**
▶ *CD2 Track 12 p283*
- Ask **What's Callum holding? What do you think they are talking about? What's happening in the second picture?**
- Play the CD. The pupils listen and read the dialogue. Check understanding. Ask **Whose camera is it? What happens if Callum presses the (red) button?**
- Play the CD again. Pause after each sentence for the pupils to repeat.
- The pupils practise the dialogue in pairs.

## Pupil's Book Activity 2

**Look and learn – Grammar wall**
- Read the information on the Grammar wall as a class.
- Ask questions about the verbs. Ask **What verbs can you see? What tense are they?**

## Pupil's Book Activity 3

**Read and think. Answer.**
- Read the Think about grammar box as a class. The pupils answer the questions in pairs.

## Pupil's Book Activity 4

**Read and match to make zero conditional sentences.**
- Ask a pupil to read the sentence halves.
- The pupils match the sentence halves.

## Pupil's Book Activity 5

**Listen and read. What does the arrow show? Listen again and repeat.**
▶ *CD2 Track 13 p283*
- Focus the pupils on the sentence and the arrow above the words. Say **Look! The arrow above the sentences goes down and up. Listen and check.** Play the CD and identify that the intonation goes down and then up.
- Play the CD again. The pupils listen and repeat.

## Pupil's Book Activity 6

**Say the sentences in Activity 4 using the correct pronunciation. Listen and check.**
▶ *CD2 Track 14 p283*
- In pairs, ask the pupils to practise in pairs saying the three sentences correctly. Remind them how the sentence in Activity 5 is pronounced.
- Play the CD. Ask the pupils to repeat each sentence.

## Pupil's Book Activity 7

**Look and make sentences about the machine.**
- Look at the picture with the class. Ask **What can you see?**
- Invite two pupils to read the text in the speech bubbles.
- Ask two pupils to make another sentence together. Correct the intonation if necessary.
- The pupils work in pairs to make more sentences.

## Activity Book

**Activity 1**

**Look at the machine on Pupil's Book page 44. Complete the sentences.**
- The pupils look at the machine on page 44 of the Pupil's Book and complete the sentences.

**Answers:** **1** the machine plays music. **2** the machine makes toast. **3** the machine prints a photo. **4** the machine takes a photo. **5** the machine makes a fruit smoothie.

**Activity 2**

**Complete with the correct words. Listen and check.**
▶ *CD2 Track 15 p283*
- The pupils complete the sentences.
- Play the CD, pausing after each sentence. Check the sentences as a class.

**Answers:** **1** sleep, get **2** shines, dry **3** leave, burns **4** rains, gets **5** turns, stop

**Activity 3**

**Listen again. Draw arrows above the sentences to show the intonation.**
▶ *CD2 Track 15 p283*
- Ask the pupils to listen again and draw arrows above the sentences showing the intonation.

**Answers:**
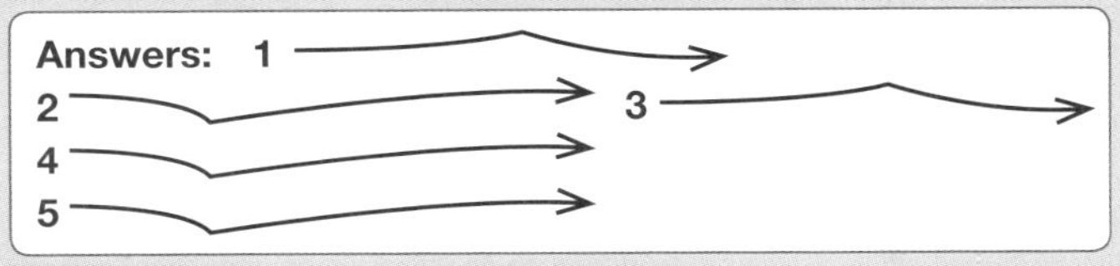


**Activity 4**

**Work with a partner. Draw your own machine and label the buttons. Write sentences.**
- The pupils draw their machine and write sentences about it.

**Odd one out activity**

**Which is the odd one out? Why?**
- The pupils complete the odd one out activity.

**Answers:** DVD player (It doesn't make food or drink.)

## Ending the lesson

**Review the lesson and reflect on learning.**
- Say **Today we've learnt how to use 'if' and 'when'.**
- Ask **Which was your favourite activity today? Which activity was easy / difficult?**

## Extra activity

**Reinforcement**
- The pupils make a poster about their machine.

## Key Competences and Key Learning Outcomes

- Identify and say expressions for using touchscreen devices
- Listen for specific information
- Practise activity types found in the Cambridge Exams: A2 Key for Schools
- Do a communication task

**Key language**

- *move down, move left, move right, move up, pause the game, start the game, swipe the screen, tap the screen, tilt the screen*
- *What do you have to do? You have to eat all the cakes in the maze. What are the controls? If you swipe left, you go left.*
- **Extension:** *download a game, get a high score, get a low score, read the instructions*

**Materials**

- Pupil's Book p45; Activity Book p42; Class CD2; Teacher's App on Navio; Teacher's Resource Bank: Unit 4

**Optional materials**

- Teacher's Resource Bank: Trinity Exams Practice cards (selected from the Starter Unit and Units 1, 2 and 3)

## At a Glance Lesson Plan

### Pupil's Book

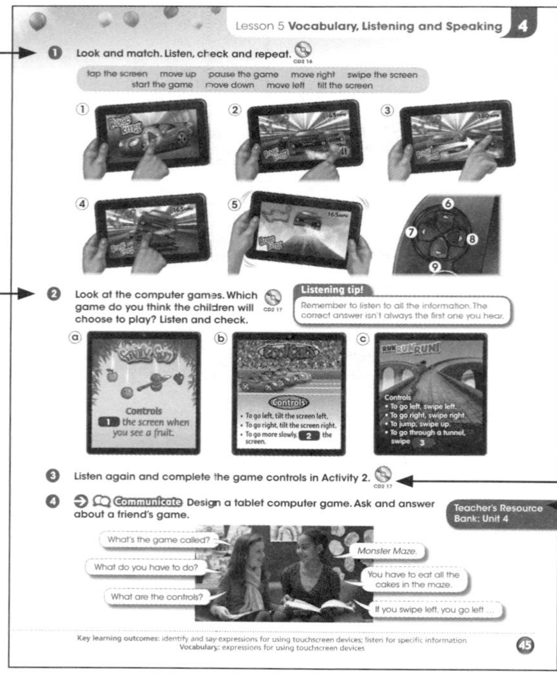

**Starting the lesson**

- Use the Trinity Exams Practice cards (optional).
- Review the zero conditional.
- Set learning objectives.

**Activity 1**

- Look and match.
- Listen, check and repeat.

▶ *CD2 Track 16 p283*

**Activity 2**

- Look at the computer games.
- Which game do you think the children will choose to play?
- Listen and check.

▶ *CD2 Track 17 p283*

**Activity 3**

- Listen again and complete the game controls in Activity 2.

▶ *CD2 Track 17 p283*

**Activity 4**

- Design a tablet computer game.
- Ask and answer about a friend's game (Teacher's Resource Bank: Unit 4).

Go to the Activity Book.

**Ending the lesson**

- Review the lesson and reflect on learning.

**Extra activities**

**Reinforcement**

- Describe a real computer game.

**Vocabulary extension**

- Present four additional vocabulary items.

### Activity Book

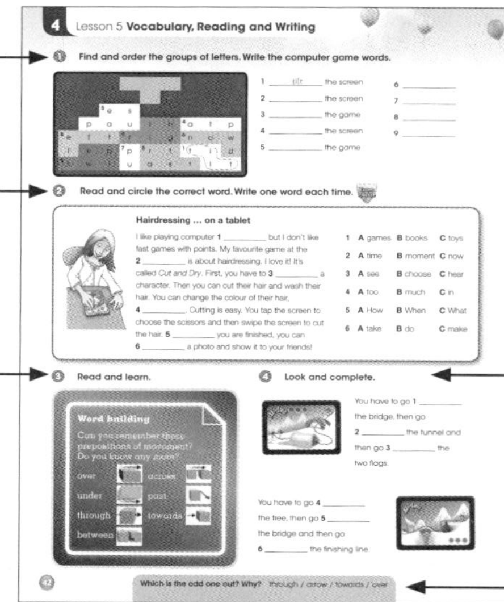

**Activity Book**

**Activity 1**

- Find and order the groups of letters. Write the computer game words.

**Activity 2**

- Read and circle the correct word. Write one word each time.

**Activity 3**

- Read and learn.

**Activity 4**

- Look and complete.

**Odd one out activity**

- Which is the odd one out? Why?

## Digital resources

**Teacher's Digital:** You can also teach this lesson using the Teacher's App on Navio.

**Pupil's Digital:** Encourage your pupils to use the Pupil's App on Navio to practise the activities from this lesson.

Powered By NAVIO

# Detailed Lesson Plan

## Starting the lesson

**Use the Trinity Exams Practice cards (optional).**

- The pupils practise asking and answering questions.

**Review the zero conditional.**

- Look at the Activity Book drawings of the machines that the pupils drew in Lesson 4. The pupils make sentences about the machines. Ask **If you press the red button, what happens?** Encourage the pupils to use the zero conditional.

**Set learning objectives.**

- Say **Today we're going to learn some words we use when we talk about computer games.**

## Pupil's Book Activity 1

**Look and match. Listen, check and repeat.**

▶ *CD2 Track 16 p283*

- (Books closed.) Ask the pupils if they have ever played computer games on a tablet. Ask **Which games have you played?**
- (Books open.) Organise the class into pairs. They match the words and phrases in the box to the pictures.
- Play the CD. The pupils listen and check.
- Play the CD again, pausing after each word or phrase for the pupils to repeat.

## Pupil's Book Activity 2

**Look at the computer games. Which game do you think the children will choose to play? Listen and check.**

▶ *CD2 Track 17 p283*

- Focus the pupils' attention on the three pictures. Ask them to describe each game. Ask **Which game would you like to play most? Which game do you think the children will choose?**
- Play the CD. The pupils listen and note down which game the children decide to play. (*Cool Cars.*)

## Pupil's Book Activity 3

**Listen again and complete the game controls in Activity 2.**

▶ *CD2 Track 17 p283*

- Tell the pupils to look at the controls for the games. In pairs, the pupils predict what words go in the spaces.
- Play the CD.

**Answers:** **1** Swipe **2** tap **3** down

## Pupil's Book Activity 4

**Design a tablet computer game. Ask and answer about a friend's game (Teacher's Resource Bank: Unit 4).**

- Invite two pupils to read out the speech bubbles.
- Organise the class into pairs (A and B). Give Pupils A the first worksheet from Teacher's Resource Bank Unit 4 and give Pupils B the other worksheet.
- Pupils A complete the details about their computer game. Then Pupils B ask their partner questions about their game in order to complete the empty chart.
- The pupils show their pages to their partner and check their answers.

## Activity Book

**Activity 1**

**Find and order the groups of letters. Write the computer game words.**

- Ask the pupils if they know the game that this word puzzle looks like. Ask **What do you have to do in that game?** (*The bricks fall and you have to turn the bricks round to build a wall.*)
- The pupils arrange the letters in each brick to make nine words.

**Answers:** **1** tilt **2** swipe **3** start **4** tap **5** pause **6** down **7** up **8** left **9** right

**Activity 2**

**Read and circle the correct word. Write one word each time.**

- Complete the first answer as a class. Remind the pupils to try out all three words in the space before deciding what the answer should be.
- The pupils complete the remaining words.

**Answers:** **1** A **2** B **3** B **4** A **5** B **6** A

**Activity 3**

**Read and learn.**

- Read the information as a class.

**Activity 4**

**Look and complete.**

- The pupils complete the instructions.

**Answers:** **1** under **2** through **3** between **4** past **5** across / over **6** towards / across

**Odd one out activity**

**Which is the odd one out? Why?**

**Answers:** arrow (It isn't a preposition.)

## Ending the lesson

**Review the lesson and reflect on learning.**

- Say **Today we've learnt some new words to use with computer games and we've described different computer games.**

## Extra activities

**Reinforcement**

- Pupils write about a computer game they like. Ask about a computer game the pupils have **What do you have to do? What are the game controls?** The pupils can also draw a screen from the game.

**Vocabulary extension**

- Present four additional gaming words: *download a game, get a high score, get a low score, read the instructions.*
- Use the Vocabulary booster on NAVIO to practise these new words.

## Key Competences and Key Learning Outcomes

- Do pre-reading tasks to predict content and raise interest
- Read the text for general understanding
- Scan the text to find specific information

- Discuss and share what you know about this type of text

- Read and understand two reviews
- Give an opinion on the text

## Key language

- *after that, first, then; drawing, gallery, paintbrush, painting, sculptures, webcam, website; article, electric currents, entertainment, news, quizzes, sections, sport, videos; animals, brain, future, masks, science, technology, turn on, wave*
- *What website do you prefer?*

## Materials

- Pupil's Book p46; Activity Book p43; Class CD2; Teacher's App on Navio
- Teacher's Resource Bank: Technology word cards

## Optional materials

- Teacher's Resource Bank: Trinity Exams Practice cards (selected from the Starter Unit and Units 1, 2 and 3)

## At a Glance Lesson Plan

### Pupil's Book

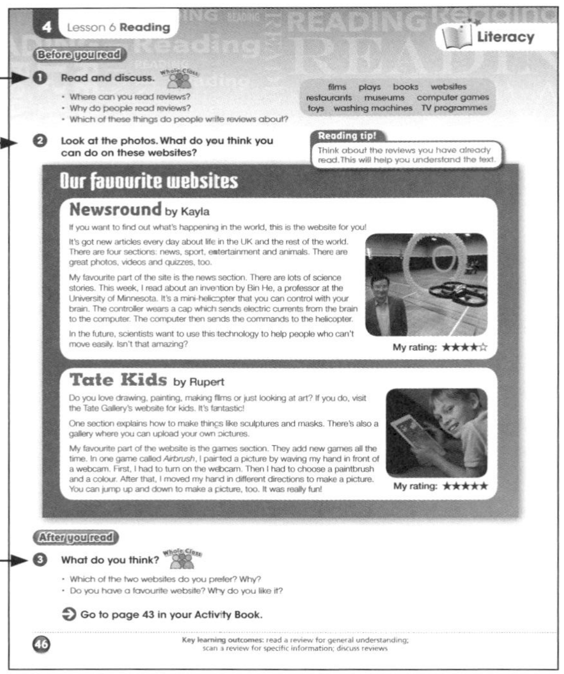


**Starting the lesson**

- Use the Trinity Exams Practice cards (optional).
- Review technology vocabulary.
- Set learning objectives.

**Activity 1: Before you read**

- Read and discuss.

**Activity 2**

- Look at the photos.
- What do you think you can do on these websites?

**Activity 3: After you read**

- What do you think?
- Go to the Activity Book.

**Ending the lesson**

- Review the lesson and reflect on learning.

**Extra activity**

**Extension**

- Find reviews.

## Digital resources

**Teacher's Digital:** You can also teach this lesson using the Teacher's App on Navio.

**Pupil's Digital:** Encourage your pupils to use the Pupil's App on Navio to practise the activities from this lesson.

Powered By NAVIO

### Activity Book

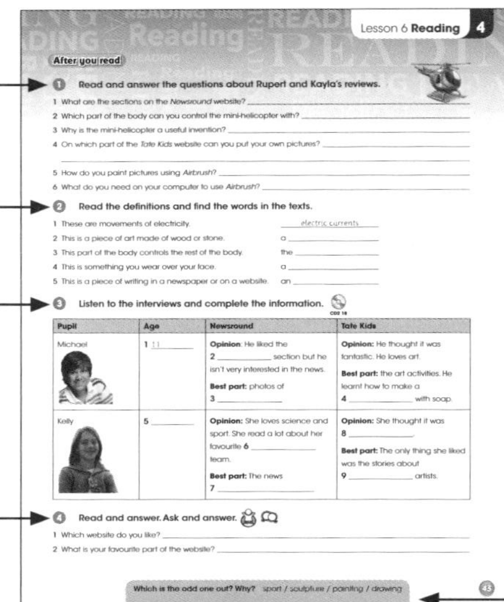


**Activity Book: After you read**

**Activity 1**

- Read and answer the questions about Rupert and Kayla's reviews.

**Activity 2**

- Read the definitions and find the words in the texts.

**Activity 3**

- Listen to the interviews and complete the information.

▶ *CD2 Track 18 p283*

**Activity 4**

- Read and answer. Ask and answer.

**Odd one out activity**

- Which is the odd one out? Why?

# Detailed Lesson Plan

## Starting the lesson

**Use the Trinity Exams Practice cards (optional).**

- The pupils practise asking and answering questions.

**Review technology vocabulary.**

- Review technology vocabulary. Play the *Yes or No* game (see p27) with the technology word cards.

**Set learning objectives.**

- Say **Today we're going to read about two different websites.**

## Pupil's Book Activity 1: Before you read

**Read and discuss.**

- Read the questions as a class. Prompt the pupils to answer in as much detail as possible. Explain that almost anything can have a review. All of the words in the box have reviews written by people. Ask **When is it useful to read a review of (a museum)?**

## Pupil's Book Activity 2

**Look at the photos. What do you think you can do on these websites?**

- Look at the photos. Ask **What are the websites about?**
- The pupils make predictions about what people can do on each website.
- The pupils read the reviews. They check their predictions.

## Pupil's Book Activity 3: After you read

**What do you think?**

- Read the questions as a class. Prompt the pupils to give their views. Ask the pupils to think about whether their opinions changed after reading the reviews.
- Encourage the pupils to visit the websites. They give their own star rating and explain why.

## Activity Book: After you read

### Activity 1

**Read and answer the questions about Rupert and Kayla's reviews.**

- The pupils read each sentence and answer the questions. They refer back to the text in the Pupil's Book when necessary.

**Answers:** **1** news, sport, entertainment and animals **2** the brain **3** Scientists can use the technology to help people who can't move easily. **4** the gallery **5** by moving your hand in front of the webcam **6** a webcam

### Activity 2

**Read the definitions and find the words in the texts.**

- The pupils read the definitions and write the words. They refer back to the text in the Pupil's Book when necessary.

**Answers:** **1** electric currents **2** sculpture **3** brain **4** mask **5** article

### Activity 3

**Listen to the interviews and complete the information.**

▶ *CD2 Track 18 p283*

- Show the pupils the chart. Ask the pupils what it shows. *(Two more children's opinions on the websites.)* Invite the pupils to read out the text. The pupils predict what the missing words may be.
- Play the CD. The pupils listen and complete the information in their books.
- Play the CD again.

**Answers:** **1** 11 **2** animals **3** snakes **4** sculpture **5** 10 **6** football **7** quiz **8** boring **9** famous

### Activity 4

**Read and answer. Ask and answer.**

- The pupils think about their own opinions on the two websites. It would be good if the pupils have an opportunity to look at the two websites.
- The pupils complete the information.

## Odd one out activity

**Which is the odd one out? Why?**

- The pupils complete the odd one out activity.

**Answers:** sport (It isn't related to art.)

## Ending the lesson

**Review the lesson and reflect on learning.**

- Say **Today we've read reviews about two websites.**
- Ask **Which was your favourite activity today? Which activity was easy / difficult?**

## Extra activity

**Extension**

- Ask the pupils, at school or with their families at home, to find an example of a review for each of the categories in Pupil's Book Activity 1. The reviews don't have to be in English but say that it is better if they are. There are ten reviews to find.

## Key Competences and Key Learning Outcomes

- Identify the use of present simple and past simple
- Learn a structure for writing reviews
- Distinguish between facts and opinions in texts
- Use criteria to check your writing
- Share your writing with another pupil
- Write a review

**Key language**
- *explorers, equipment, planets, robot, rockets, scientist, space; description, experience, facts, introduction, rating*
- *I sent SpaceAce a question about Mars. You can write to the magazine with questions about a planet.*

**Materials**
- Pupil's Book p47; Activity Book p44; Teacher's App on Navio

**Optional materials**
- Teacher's Resource Bank: Trinity Exams Practice cards (selected from the Starter Unit and Units 1, 2 and 3)

## At a Glance Lesson Plan

### Pupil's Book

**Starting the lesson**
- Use the Trinity Exams Practice cards (optional).
- Review past simple verbs.
- Set learning objectives.

**Activity 1: Investigate a text**
- Look at the labels for each section of the review.
- In which section can you find the answers to these questions?

**Activity 2**
- Read the review to check your answers.

**Activity 3: Discuss a text**
- Read the review again.
- Answer the questions.

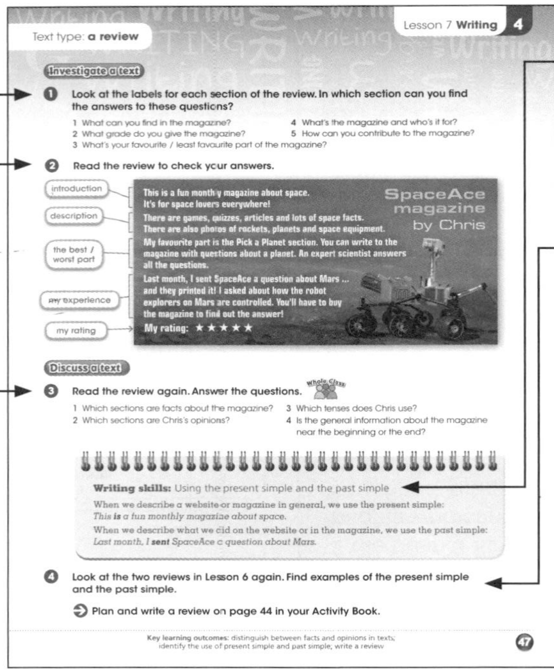

**Writing skills**
- Read about using the present simple and past simple.

**Activity 4**
- Look at the two reviews in Lesson 6 again.
- Find examples of the present simple and the past simple.

Go to the Activity Book.

**Ending the lesson**
- Review the lesson and reflect on learning.

**Extra activity**

**Extension**
- Read other reviews and choose a website you would like to visit.

**Digital resources**

**Teacher's Digital:** You can also teach this lesson using the Teacher's App on Navio.

**Pupil's Digital:** Encourage your pupils to use the Pupil's App on Navio to practise the activities from this lesson.

Powered By NAVIO

### Activity Book

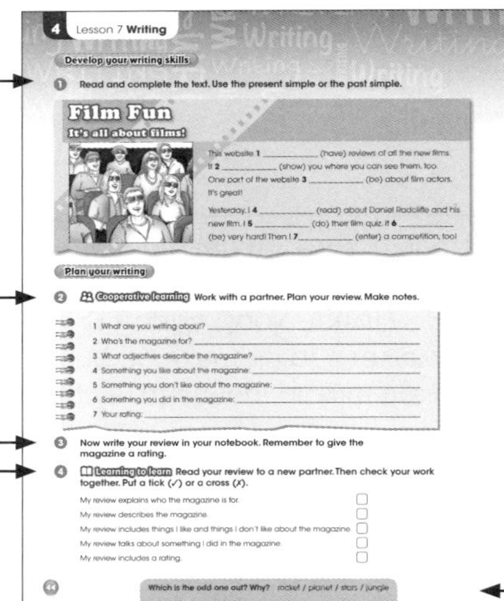

**Activity Book**

**Activity 1: Develop your writing skills**
- Read and complete the text. Use the present simple or the past simple.

**Activity 2: Plan your writing**
- Work with a partner. Plan your website review. Make notes.

**Activity 3**
- Now write your review in your notebook. Remember to give the magazine a rating.

**Activity 4**
- Read your review to a new partner. Then check your work together. Put a tick (✓) or a cross (✗).

**Odd one out activity**
- Which is the odd one out? Why?

# Detailed Lesson Plan

## Starting the lesson

**Use the Trinity Exams Practice cards (optional).**

- The pupils practise asking and answering questions.

**Review past simple verbs.**

- Review some past simple verbs that will be used in the lesson. Write these verbs on the board: *send, put, read, do, be, enter, have, show, ask.*
- The pupils write down the verbs in the past simple tense. Invite the pupils to come up and write the words next to the infinitives. Check with the class if they think the verbs are regular or irregular.

**Set learning objectives.**

- Say **Today we're going to write a review for a website.**

## Pupil's Book Activity 1: Investigate a text

**Look at the labels for each section of the review. In which sections can you find the answers to these questions?**

- (Books closed.) Ask the pupils to explain what a review is. Ask **Why do people want to read a review? What information should you put in a review to make it useful?**
- (Books open.) Ask a pupil to read the five questions to the class. Then look at the review. Make sure that the pupils only look at the labels. They don't need to read the review yet. Ask **In which part of the review will you find the answer to each question?**

## Pupil's Book Activity 2

**Read the review to check your answers.**

- Read the text as a class.
- Check to see if the pupils were right about where the questions in Activity 1 were answered.
- Check understanding of the text by asking questions. Ask **What's the name of the magazine? What's it about? What kinds of photos are there?**

## Pupil's Book Activity 3: Discuss a text

**Read the review again. Answer the questions.**

- Read and discuss the questions as a class. Ask the pupils to explain the difference between a fact and an opinion. (*A fact is something that is always true; an opinion is what one person thinks.*)
- Recap the functions of the different sections of the review.

## Writing skills

- Read the information.
- Explain that in a review it's good to give some general information (present tense) and also some examples of what you did (past simple).

## Pupil's Book Activity 4

**Look at the two reviews in Lesson 6 again. Find examples of the present simple and the past simple.**

- Ask the pupils to look at the reviews and find more examples of the present simple and the past simple.

## Activity Book

### Activity 1: Develop your writing skills

**Read and complete the text. Use the present simple or the past simple.**

- The pupils look at the picture and guess what the review is about. (*Film website.*)
- They complete the text with the correct form of the verbs.

**Answers:** **1** has / has got **2** shows **3** is **4** read **5** did **6** was **7** entered

### Activity 2: Plan your writing

**Work with a partner. Plan your website review. Make notes.**

- The pupils think of a website that they would like to review. If you prefer, you could give them a specific website to review.
- The pupils complete the plan with a Writing Partner.

### Activity 3

**Now write your review in your notebook. Remember to give the magazine a rating.**

- The pupils write their review in their notebooks.
- Remind the class to begin with an introduction and to include a description and their opinions. They need to give the website a rating too.

### Activity 4

**Read your review to a new partner. Then check your work together. Put a (✓) or a cross (✗).**

- Read through the statements as a class.
- Organise the class into new Writing Partners. One pupil reads aloud their review to their partner. The pupils work together to decide if the review fulfils the criteria and tick the corresponding boxes. The pupils can add, improve or correct the review at this stage.
- The pupils swap roles.

### Odd one out activity

**Which is the odd one out? Why?**

- The pupils complete the odd one out activity.

**Answers:** jungle (It isn't in space.)

## Ending the lesson

**Review the lesson and reflect on learning.**

- Say **Today we've written a review.**
- Ask **Which was your favourite activity today? Which activity was easy / difficult?**

## Extra activity

**Extension**

- Ask the pupils to leave their notebooks open on their desks so that other pupils can read their reviews. Ask the pupils to choose one website that they would definitely like to visit.

## Key Competences and Key Learning Outcomes

- Talk about your favourite object

- Listen to and have a conversation about favourite objects
- Prepare for and carry out a conversation
- Review learning and reflect on progress in the unit

- Sing a song

## Key language

- *bright, dance music, headphones, jazz MP3 player, pop music, silver, watch*
- *Why do you like it so much? What does it look like? Actually, my favourite object is my MP3 player. In fact, it's red.*

## Materials

- Pupil's Book p48; Activity Book p45 and 46; Class CD2 and CD4; Teacher's App on Navio

## Optional materials

- Teacher's Resource Bank: Trinity Exams Practice cards (selected from the Starter Unit and Units 1, 2 and 3)

# At a Glance Lesson Plan

## Pupil's Book

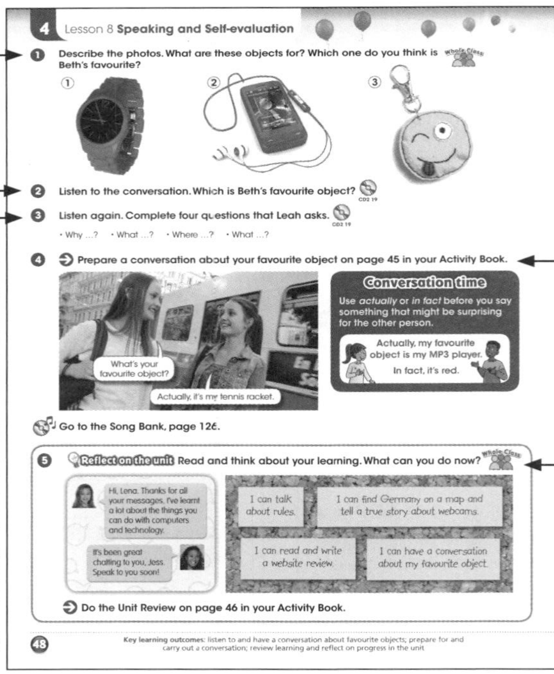


### Starting the lesson

- Use the Trinity Exams Practice cards (optional).
- Review technology vocabulary.
- Set learning objectives.

### Activity 1

- Describe the photos.
- What are these objects for?
- Which one do you think is Beth's favourite?

### Activity 2

- Listen to the conversation.
- ▶ ***CD2 Track 19 p284***
- Which is Beth's favourite object?

### Activity 3

- Listen again.
- ▶ ***CD2 Track 19 p284***
- Complete four questions that Leah asks.

### Activity 4

- Prepare a conversation about your favourite object on page 45 in your Activity book.

Go to page 45 in the Activity Book.

### Song

- ▶ ***CD4 Track 22 p297***
- ▶ ***CD4 Track 23 p297 (optional karaoke version)***

### Activity 5

- Read and think about your learning. What can you do now?

Go to page 46 in the Activity Book.

### Ending the lesson

- Review the lesson and reflect on learning.

### Extra activity

- Pupils describe real objects belonging to each other.

## Activity Book

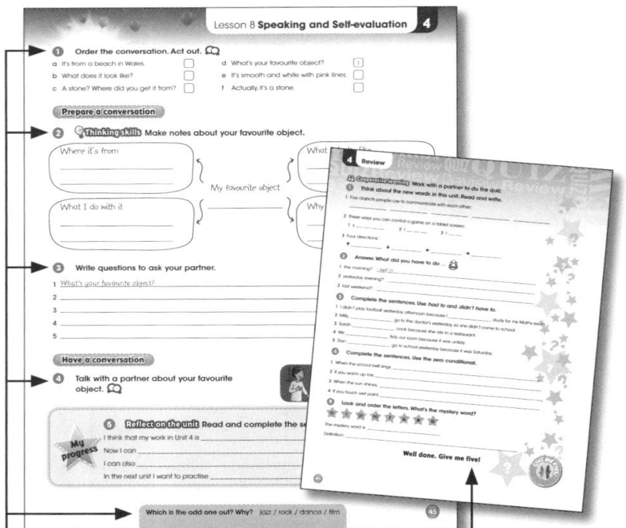


### Activity Book page 46: Review

- Work with a partner to do the quiz.

### Activity Book

**Activity 1**
- Order the conversation.
- Act out.

**Activity 2**
- Make notes about your favourite object.

**Activity 3**
- Write questions to ask your partner.

**Activity 4**
- Talk with a partner about your favourite object.

**Activity 5**
- Read and complete the sentences.

**Odd one out activity**
- Which is the odd one out? Why?

## Digital resources

**Teacher's Digital:** You can also teach this lesson using the Teacher's App on Navio.

Powered By NAVIO

# Detailed Lesson Plan

## Starting the lesson

**Use the Trinity Exams Practice cards (optional).**
- The pupils practise asking and answering questions.

**Review words for technology.**
- Ask pupils **What technology do you use every day? What technology do you use sometimes?** Pupils offer ideas. Ask them how often they use the items in the technology vocabulary set.

**Set learning objectives.**
- Say **Today we're going to prepare a conversation about our favourite object.**

## Pupil's Book Activity 1

**Describe the photos. What are these objects for? Which one do you think is Beth's favourite?**
- Ask different pupils to describe the objects. Explain that they are going to hear a girl called Beth talk about objects with her friend, Leah. Ask pupils which is their favourite of the three objects.

## Pupil's Book Activity 2

**Listen to the conversation. Which is Beth's favourite object?**

▶ ***CD2 Track 19 p284***
- Play the CD. Ask pupils if Beth and Leach talk about all the objects (*No, they don't talk about the keyring*).

**Answer:** Beth's favourite object is 2.

## Pupil's Book Activity 3

**Listen again. Complete four questions that Leah asks.**

▶ ***CD2 Track 19 p284***
- Direct pupils to the four question prompts. Ask if they can remember the questions.
- Play the CD. Pupils check in pairs. Then play again and check as a class.

**Answers:** Why do you like it so much?; What does it look like?; Where did you get it from?; What music do you listen to?

## Pupil's Book Activity 4

**Prepare a conversation about your favourite object on page 45 in your Activity Book.**
- Read the speech bubbles with the pupils. Model the phrases in the Conversation Time box and get the class to repeat.

## Song

- Go to the Song Bank on page 126 to do the song activities (see p244).

***CD4 Track 22 p297***

***CD4 Track 23 p297 (optional karaoke version)***

## Pupil's Book Activity 5

**Read and think about your learning. What can you do now?**
- Read the speech bubbles and notes with the pupils. Then look back through the unit and prompt them to identify things that they have done/learnt.

## Activity Book page 46: Review

**Work with a partner to do the quiz.**
- Organise the class into pairs. Set a time limit for the pupils to do the quiz (10–15 minutes). Stress that the pupils are not competing with each other.
- Read out the six tasks. Check understanding. Then say **Ready, steady ... Go!**
- The pupils work in their pairs to do the quiz.
- Correct the answers as a class.

**Answers:** **1** Five from: laptop, webcam, video call, website, mobile phone, tablet **2** **1** start / swipe **2** turn **3** tap **3** up, down, left, right **3** **1** had to **2** had to **3** didn't have to **4** had to **5** didn't have to **5** computer, an electronic machine

## Activity Book

**Activity 1**

**Order the conversation. Act out.**
- In pairs, pupils order the conversation and act it out.

**Answers:** **1** d **2** f **3** c **4** a **5** b **6** e

**Activity 2**

**Make notes about your favourite object.**
- Tell pupils about your favourite object. Then pupils work alone to complete the boxes with their own information.

**Activity 3**

**Write questions to ask your partner.**
- Direct pupils to the five headings in Activity 2 and explain that they need to form questions about them. Elicit the second question. Then pupils complete the questions alone. Check as a class.

**Answers:** **1** What's your favourite object? **2** Where's it from? **3** What do you do with it? **4** What does it look like? **5** Why do you like it?

**Activity 4**

**Talk with a partner about your favourite object.**
- In pairs, pupils ask and answer the questions from Activity 3.
- Invite one or two pairs to perform their conversations for the class.

**Activity 5**

**Read and complete the sentences.**
- Pupils review their work in the unit.

**Odd one out activity**

**Which is the odd one out? Why?**

**Answer:** film (It isn't a type of music.)

## Ending the lesson

**Review the lesson and reflect on learning.**
- Say **Today we've learnt how to have a conversation about our favourite object.**

## Extra activity

**Reinforcement**
- Ask 10 pupils to give you an object from their bags or pockets. Give each object to a different pupil. Each pupil describes the object you have given them, and the class guesses who they belong to.

# Video and 21st Century Skills

**Key Competences and Key Learning Outcomes**

- Watch and understand a video about new technology
- Learn about augmented reality glasses
- Think about new ways in which technology can help us

**Key language**

- *app, augmented reality, carboard, e-reader, headset, laptop, robotic, swipe, virtual reality*
- *It can help doctors practise operations. Smartphones are useful for making videos.*

**Materials**

- Pupil's Book p49; Activity Book p47; Class CD2; Teacher's App on Navio
- Teacher's Resource Bank: Talk cards

**Optional materials**

- Teacher's Resource Bank: Trinity Exams Practice cards (selected from the Starter Unit and Units 1–3)

## At a Glance Lesson Plan

### Pupil's Book

**Starting the lesson**

- Use the Trinity Exams Practice cards (optional).
- **Think-Pair-Share** Review technology words.
- Set learning objectives and use the talk cards.

**Activity 1**

- Before you watch
- Watch the video.
- *Unit 4 video p301*
- Read and say *true* or *false*.
- Correct the false sentences.

**Activity 2**

- Watch the video again.
- *Unit 4 video*
- What are these things?
- What is the connection with the video?

**Activity 3**

- Read, think and answer.

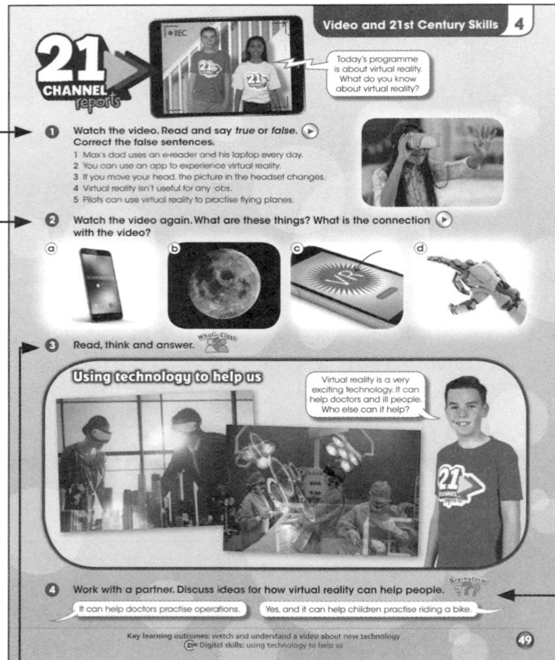


**Activity 4**

- Work with a partner.
- Discuss ideas for how virtual reality can help people.
- Go to the Activity Book.

**Ending the lesson**

- Review the lesson and reflect on learning.

**Extra activity**

- Imagine technology in 100 years' time and draw a picture.

### Activity Book

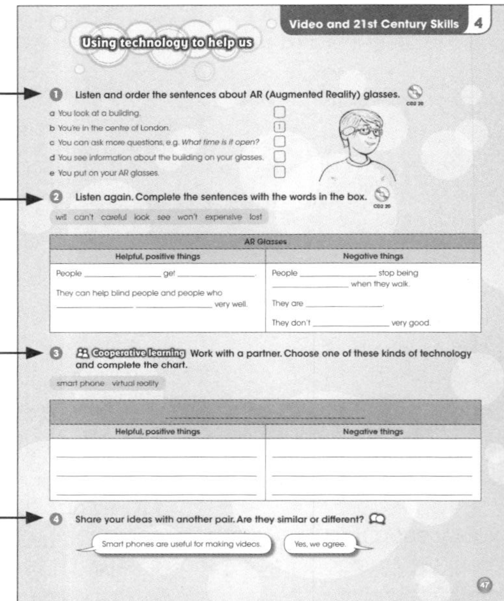


**Activity Book**

**Activity 1**

- Listen and order the sentences about AR (Augmented Reality) glasses.

▶ ***CD2 Track 20 p284***

**Activity 2**

- Listen again.
- Complete the sentences with the words in the box.

▶ ***CD1 Track 20 p284***

**Activity 3**

- Work with a partner.
- Choose one of these kinds of technology and complete the chart.

**Activity 4**

- Share your ideas with another pair.
- Are they similar or different?

**Digital resources**

**Teacher's Digital:** You can also teach this lesson using the Teacher's App on Navio.

**Pupil's Digital:** Encourage your pupils to use the Pupil's App on Navio to practise the activities from this lesson.

Powered By NAVIO

# Detailed Lesson Plan

## Starting the lesson

**Use the Trinity Exams Practice cards (optional).**

- The pupils practise asking and answering questions.

**Think-Pair-Share Review words for technology.**

- Ask **How many different technology words can you think of?** The class thinks silently for a minute.
- Then the pupils work with a Talk Partner to name technology words.
- Invite different Talk Partners to say a different technology words. Hold up the corresponding flashcard and prompt the class to repeat the word.
- Finally, repeat the procedure, asking different pairs of Talk Partners each time, until all the ideas have been recorded.

**Set learning objectives and use the talk cards.**

- Say **Today we're going to watch a video and then ask and answer questions about virtual reality**.
- Point to the talk cards to show the pupils the different ways they will be working in the lesson.

## Pupil's Book Activity 1

**Before you watch**

- Read the speech bubble to pupils. Ask **What do you know about virtual reality?** Elicit responses from a number of pupils.

**Watch the video. Read and say *true* or *false*. Correct the false sentences.** *p301*

- Watch Part 1 of the video. Ask pupils **What are you going to see next?**
- Play Part 2 of the video. Ask general questions to check understanding. Direct pupils to look at the sentences 1–5. Say **Max's dad uses an e-reader and his laptop every day. True or false?** (*False*). Elicit why it is false. (*His mum uses an e-reader every day, not his dad*.)
- Play the video again and check answers as a group. Ask why the false sentences are false.

**Answers:** **1** False (His mum uses an e-reader.) **2** True **3** True **4** False (It's important for many jobs.) **5** False (Scientists can use virtual reality do practise doing things.)

## Pupil's Book Activity 2

**Watch the video again. What are these things? What is the connection with the video?**

- Ask a pupil **What can you see in picture a?** Ask a different pupil **What is the connection with the video?**

**Answers:** **a** A mobile phone. You can use a mobile phone in a carboard headset. **b** The moon. You can use a headset to imagine that you're on the moon. **c** Virtual reality. Virtual reality is important for many jobs. **d** A robotic hand. You can use a virtual reality headset to control a robotic hand.

## Pupil's Book Activity 3

**Read, think and answer.**

- Read the speech bubble with the class. Then ask pupils to describe what they can see in the photos. Ask them how they think virtual reality is helping the people.
- Elicit some ideas of different people who virtual reality can help. At this stage, pupils don't need to think about exactly how it can help. Make a class list.

## Pupil's Book Activity 4

**Work with a partner. Discuss ideas for how virtual reality can help people.**

- Say **What things do children need to learn?** Then ask **Can virtual reality help them to do any of those things?**
- In pairs, pupils discuss ways in which virtual reality can help other people from the list in Activity 3.

## Activity Book

### Activity 1

**Listen and order the sentences about AR (Augmented Reality) glasses.**

▶ *CD2 Track 20 p284*

- Pupils look at the boy in Activity 1. Tell them his glasses are called AR, or Augmented Reality glasses and explain that this means that they give you information that you might need as you walk around.
- Play the CD again without pausing and check answers.

**Answers:** **a** 3 **b** 1 **c** 5 **d** 4 **e** 2

### Activity 2

**Listen again. Complete the sentences with the words in the box.**

▶ *CD2 Track 20 p284*

**Answers:** Helpful, positive things: People won't get lost; They can help blind people and people who can't see very well. Negative things: People will stop being careful when they walk; They are expensive' They don't look very good.

### Activity 3

**Work with a partner. Choose one of these kinds of technology and complete the chart.**

- In pairs, pupils think of as many ways in which smart phones can help people as possible.
- In the same pairs, pupils complete the table for one of the types of technology in the box.

### Activity 4

**Share your ideas with another pair. Are they similar or different?**

- Put pupils into groups of four – preferably with a pair who chose a different type of technology. They take turns to tell each other their ideas, and respond.

## Ending the lesson

**Review the lesson and reflect on learning.**

- Say **Today we've watched a video about virtual reality. What have we learnt about how technology can help people?** Elicit ideas from the pupils.
- Ask **Which was your favourite activity today? Which activity was easy / difficult?**

Date: ____________ Unit: ____________

1 What did my pupils learn in this unit?

2 How did my pupils work? (✓)

individually ☐ in pairs ☐ in small groups ☐

in large groups ☐ as a class ☐

3 Which key competences did my pupils develop? Give a score from 1 to 5 (5 being the highest).

- Competence in linguistic communication ☐
- Competence in mathematics, science and technology ☐
- Digital competence ☐
- Learning to learn ☐
- Social and civic competences ☐
- Sense of initiative and entrepreneurship ☐
- Cultural awareness and expression ☐

4 Which lessons / activities were the most successful and why?

5 Which lessons / activities did my pupils find the most difficult and why?

6 What did I try in the classroom for the first time? How did it go?

7 Which resources did I find most useful? (including webpages)

8 What could I do differently next time I teach this unit?

Unit 5

# Amazing animals

## Unit overview

### Key Competences and Key Learning Outcomes

- Learn the names of parts of an animal's body (Lesson 1)
- Learn and practise making deductions using modal verbs (Lesson 2)
- Learn and practise describing things with the verbs of senses (Lesson 4)
- Learn and practise the names of new animals (Lesson 5)
- Learn adjectives to describe animals (Lesson 5)
- Review and practise using direct speech (Lesson 7)
- Watch and understand a video about animals in danger (Video and 21st Century Skills)

---

- Review and categorise animals (Lesson 1)
- Compare and describe different animals (Lesson 5)
- Learn about the habitat and diet of the koala (Video and 21st Century Skills)

---

- Use the Pupil's App on Navio
- Investigate Australia (Lesson 3)

---

LEARN

- Identify and practise rising and falling intonation in questions (Lesson 4)
- Reflect on your own learning (Lesson 8)
- Practise activity types found in the Cambridge Exams: A2 Key for Schools

---

- Work in a group to choose the best pets for people (Lesson 8)
- Think about the importance of helping to protect endangered species (Video and 21st Century Skills)

---

- Work in pairs and small groups to practise and reinforce learning (all lessons)
- Do a communication task (Lesson 5)

---

- Read and understand a story (Lesson 3)
- Learn about Australia (Lesson 3)
- Read and write a newspaper report (Lessons 6 and 7)

### Vocabulary

**Core vocabulary**
*beak, claws, fangs, feathers, fins, fur, jaw, scales, spikes, tail, whiskers, wings; bull, donkey, eagle, grasshopper, mole, praying mantis, silkworm, swan*

**Extension vocabulary (optional)**
*gills, hoof, horn, paw, shell, tentacle; deer, fox, wasp, wolf*

**Other vocabulary**
*length, speed, weight; budgie, creepy crawlies, eel, great white shark, hamster, kitten, mammals, platypus, puppy, reptiles, saltwater crocodile, Tasmanian devil, tropical fish, white-bellied sea eagle; colourful, domestic, enormous, fierce, harmless, lucky, mysterious, poisonous, wild; creature, flippers, headline, hero; cut down, eucalyptus, forest, gas, habitat, joey, leaves, marsupial, power station*

**Recycled vocabulary**
*birds, cat, dog, dolphin, fish, guinea pig, hippo, koala, lion, lizard, pony, seal, snake, spider, whale; scary, strange; bones, teeth; news, newspaper, noise, pet, skeleton; lake, river*

### Structures

**Core structures**
*It must / may / might / could / can't be a (koala). What does it look / smell / taste / feel / sound like? It (looks) like a snake. It (sounds) dangerous. Does it (look) scary? Does it (smell) like a dog? Yes, it does. No, it doesn't.*

**Other structures**
*Emma's mum said 'Sandy isn't a big dog , but she's very brave'. Tropical fish are a good idea. I agree. I think he'd like a budgie more. I don't think that's a good idea. That could be a possibility.*

**Recycled structures**
*The great white shark is the heaviest animal. The saltwater crocodile has got the most teeth. What happened? Why / When / Where did it happen? Who was there?*

### Pronunciation

Rising and falling intonation in questions

### Literacy

**Text type:** a newspaper report (non-chronological report, writing preparation)
**Reading skill:** predicting content from headlines
**Writing skill:** direct speech

### Culture ... around the world

The myth of the bunyip in Australia

### 21st Century Skills

**Living in the world:** protecting animals in danger

### Thinking skills

Categorising (Lesson 1); Comparing and contrasting (Lesson 1); Analysing and applying rules (Lessons 2 and 4); Logical thinking (Lessons 2 and 5); Finding and classifying information (Lesson 6); Planning, checking and correcting (Lesson 7); Seeing another's point of view (Lesson 8); Reflecting on learning (Lesson 8)

### Cooperative learning

Working together (Lessons 1–8); Collaborating (Lessons 1–8); Checking learning (Lessons 1–8); Peer evaluation and feedback (Lesson 7); Participating (Lessons 1–8); Helping and encouraging (Lessons 1–8); Reflecting and setting goals (Lessons 1 and 8)

### Values

Recognising and learning to deal with fears

### Cross-curricular links

**Link to Science**
The five classes of vertebrates

**Suggested Arts and Crafts concepts**
Light and shadows

## Key Competences and Key Learning Outcomes

- Identify and say the names of parts of an animal's body
- Listen to definitions and identify the words
- Review and categorise wild animals
- Read a message for general information
- Play a game about Australian wild animals

**Key language**
- *beak, claws, fangs, feathers, fins, fur, jaw, scales, spikes, tail, whiskers, wings; birds, fish, mammals, reptiles; great white shark, saltwater crocodile, Tasmanian devil, white-bellied sea eagle; length, speed, weight; teeth*
- *The great white shark is the heaviest animal. The saltwater crocodile has got the most teeth.*
- **Extension:** *gills, hoof, horn, paw, shell, tentacle*

**Materials**
- Pupil's Book pp50–51; Activity Book p48; Class CD2; Teacher's App on Navio
- Parts of an animal's body flashcards

**Optional materials**
- Teacher's Resource Bank: Trinity Exams Practice cards (selected from the Starter Unit and Units 1, 2, 3 and 4)

## At a Glance Lesson Plan

### Pupil's Book

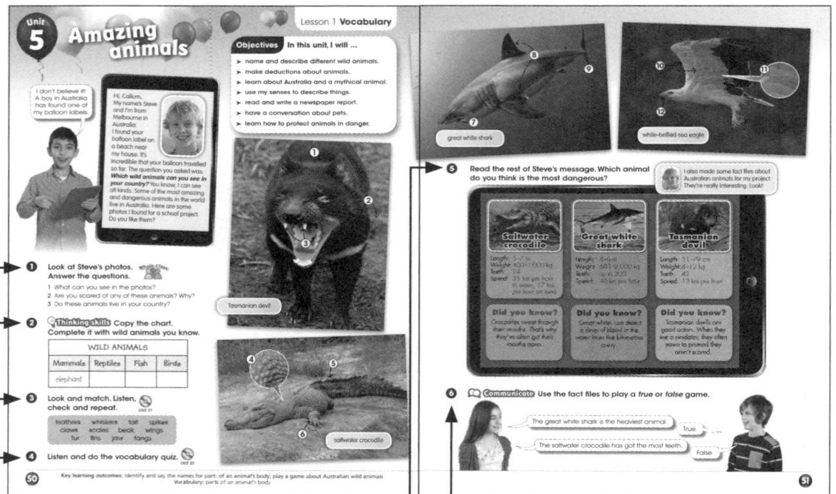

**Starting the lesson**
- Use the Trinity Exams Practice cards (optional).
- Review wild animals.
- Set learning objectives.

**Activity 1**
- Look at Steve's photos.
- Answer the questions.

**Activity 2**
- Copy the chart.
- Complete it with wild animals you know.

**Vocabulary presentation**
- Present the unit vocabulary using the parts of an animal's body flashcards.

**Activity 3**
- Look and match.
- Listen, check and repeat.

▶ *CD2 Track 21 p284*

**Activity 4**
- Listen and do the vocabulary quiz.

▶ *CD2 Track 22 p284*

**Activity 5**
- Read the rest of Steve's message.
- Which animal do you think is the most dangerous?

**Activity 6**
- Use the fact files to play a *true* or *false* game.

Go to the Activity Book.

**Ending the lesson**
- Review the lesson and reflect on learning.

**Extra activities**

**Extension**
- Find out about Australia.

**Vocabulary extension**
- Present six additional vocabulary items.

**Digital resources**

**Teacher's Digital:** You can also teach this lesson using the Teacher's App on Navio.

**Pupil's Digital:** Encourage your pupils to use the Pupil's App on Navio to practise the activities from this lesson.

Powered By NAVIO

### Activity Book

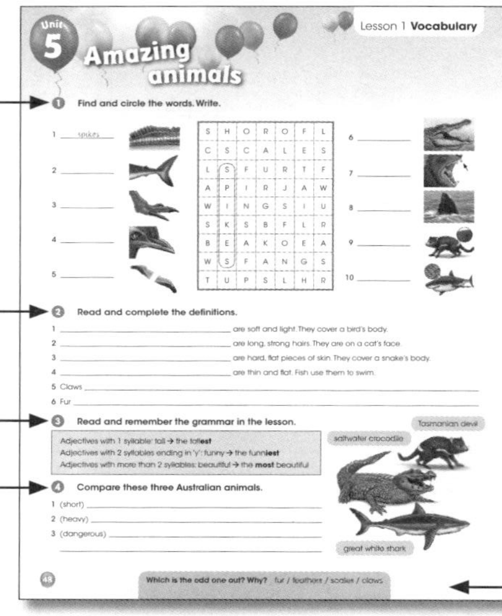

**Activity Book**

**Activity 1**
- Find and circle the words. Write.

**Activity 2**
- Read and complete the definitions.

**Activity 3**
- Read and remember the grammar in the lesson.

**Activity 4**
- Compare these three Australian animals.

**Odd one out activity**
- Which is the odd one out? Why?

# Detailed Lesson Plan

## Starting the lesson

**Review wild animals.**

- Ask **Which are your favourite wild animals?** Encourage the pupils to name and describe their favourite wild animals. Prompt the pupils to say where these animals live and if they have ever seen one.

**Set learning objectives.**

- Say **Today we're going to remember the names of wild animals and learn the names of parts of their body.**

## Pupil's Book Activity 1

**Look at Steve's photos. Answer the questions.**

- Invite a pupil to read out the speech bubble to find out who has found the label. Ask **Do you know where Australia is?**
- Invite a pupil to read out the message. Check understanding.
- Read and answer the questions about the photos.

## Pupil's Book Activity 2

**Copy the chart. Complete it with wild animals you know.**

- Copy the chart onto the board. Elicit examples.
- Organise the class into pairs. The pupils copy the chart into their notebooks and classify the wild animals they know.
- Invite different pairs of pupils to say the animals they have written in their chart. Check spelling and write the words in the chart on the board.

## Vocabulary presentation

- Present the new vocabulary using the parts of an animal's body flashcards. Show the first flashcard and elicit / say the word. Ask **What's this? / What are these? Which animals have got (scales)?**
- Repeat the procedure with the other cards.

## Pupil's Book Activity 3

**Look and match. Listen, check and repeat.**

▶ *CD2 Track 21 p284*

- The class look at item number 1. Ask **What part of the animal is this?** The pupils work in pairs to match numbers 2–12 and the words.
- Play the CD. The pupils listen and check.
- Play the CD again, pausing after each word for the pupils to repeat.

## Pupil's Book Activity 4

**Listen and do the vocabulary quiz.**

▶ *CD2 Track 22 p284*

- Play the CD. Listen to the first definition, pausing at the beep to allow the pupils to name the item. Continue with the CD to listen to the answer.
- Repeat the procedure with the other definitions.

## Pupil's Book Activity 5

**Read the rest of Steve's message. Which animal do you think is the most dangerous?**

- Invite a pupil to read out the message. Check that the pupils understand the task. The pupils read the information and choose the most dangerous animal.
- Discuss with the class. Encourage the pupils to give reasons for their answers.

## Pupil's Book Activity 6

**Use the fact files to play a *true* or *false* game.**

- Invite a pair of pupils to read out the speech bubbles.
- (Books closed.) The pupils play the game in pairs.

## Activity Book

**Activity 1**

**Find and circle the words. Write.**

- The pupils find and circle the words. They then label the pictures.

**Answers:** **1** spikes **2** tail **3** claws **4** beak **5** wings **6** jaw **7** fangs **8** fin **9** fur **10** scales

**Activity 2**

**Read and complete the definitions.**

- The pupils complete the definitions.

**Answers:** **1** Feathers **2** Whiskers **3** Scales **4** Fins

**Activity 3**

**Read and remember the grammar in the lesson.**

- Read out the information. Remind the class that we use the superlative form to compare more than two things.
- The pupils make comparisons about animals.

**Activity 4**

**Compare these three Australian animals.**

- The pupils work on their own to write the sentences.

**Odd one out activity**

**Which is the odd one out? Why?**

- The pupils complete the odd one out activity.

**Answers:** claws (They don't cover an animal's body.)

## Ending the lesson

**Review the lesson and reflect on learning.**

- Say **Today we've remembered the names of wild animals and learnt the names of parts of their body. What do you remember?**
- Ask **Which was your favourite activity today? Which activity was easy / difficult?**

## Extra activities

**Extension**

- The pupils find Australia on the world map on pages 134–135. They read the accompanying facts.

**Vocabulary extension**

- Present six additional animal words: *gills, hoof, horn, paw, shell, tentacle.*
- Use the Vocabulary booster on NAVIO to practise these new words.

### Key Competences and Key Learning Outcomes

- Listen to and read a dialogue
- Use modal verbs to make deductions

- Make deductions about different wild animals

### Key language

- *beak, fangs, fur, scales, spikes; dolphin, koala, lizard, mammal, platypus, reptile, seal, snake; clue, poisonous*
- *It must / may / might / could / can't be a (koala).*

### Materials

- Pupil's Book p52; Activity Book p49; Class CD2; Teacher's App on Navio
- Teacher's Resource Bank: Parts of an animal's body word cards

### Optional materials

- Teacher's Resource Bank: Trinity Exams Practice cards (selected from the Starter Unit and Units 1, 2, 3 and 4)
- Photos of wild animals

## At a Glance Lesson Plan

## Pupil's Book

### Starting the lesson

- Use the Trinity Exams Practice cards (optional).
- Review parts of an animal's body.
- Set learning objectives.

### Activity 1

- Look at the photo.
- What's this animal called?
- Read and listen to find out.

▶ *CD2 Track 23 p283*

### Activity 2

- Read and say *true* or *false*.
- Correct the false sentences.

### Activity 3

- Look and learn – Grammar wall

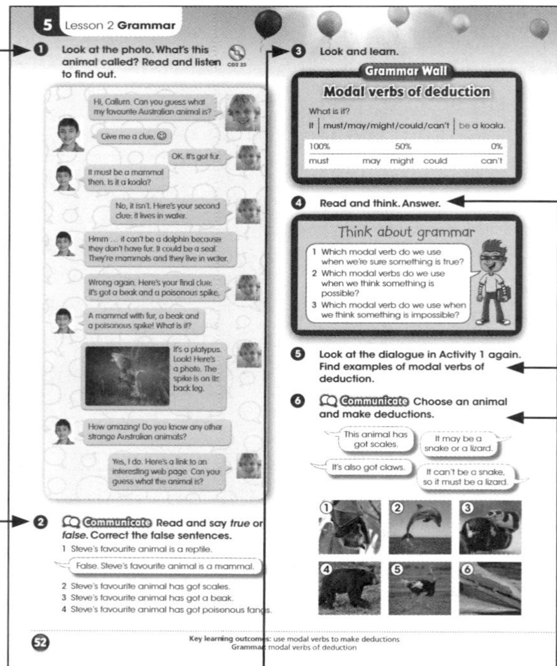

### Activity 4

- Read and think.
- Answer.

### Activity 5

- Look at the dialogue in Activity 1 again.
- Find examples of modal verbs of deduction.

### Activity 6

- Choose an animal and make deductions.

Go to the Activity Book.

### Ending the lesson

- Review the lesson and reflect on learning.

### Extra activity

**Reinforcement**

- Play a deductions game with photos of wild animals.

### Digital resources

**Teacher's Digital:** You can also teach this lesson using the Teacher's App on Navio.

**Pupil's Digital:** Encourage your pupils to use the Pupil's App on Navio to practise the activities from this lesson.

Powered By NAVIO

## Activity Book

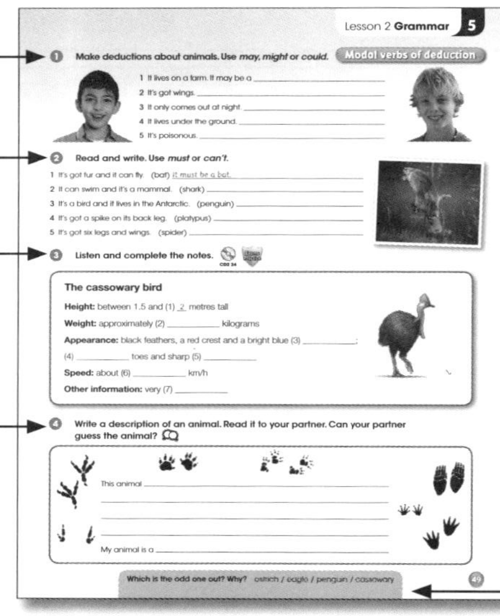

### Activity Book

**Activity 1**

- Make deductions about animals. Use *may, might* or *could.*

**Activity 2**

- Read and write. Use *must* or *can't.*

**Activity 3**

- Listen and complete the notes.

▶ *CD2 Track 24 p285*

**Activity 4**

- Write a description of an animal. Read it to your partner. Can your partner guess the animal?

**Odd one out activity**

- Which is the odd one out? Why?

# Detailed Lesson Plan

**Starting the lesson**

**Use the Trinity Exams Practice cards (optional).**

- The pupils practise asking and answering questions.

**Review parts of an animal's body.**

- Organise the class into small groups.
- Hold up one of the parts of an animal's body word cards and ask the class to read it out, e.g. *claws*. Say **Think of five animals which have got claws.** The pupils work in their groups to list the animals.
- Repeat the procedure with other word cards.

**Set learning objectives.**

- Say **Today we're going to learn how to make deductions.**

**Pupil's Book Activity 1**

**Look at the photo. What's this animal called? Read and listen to find out.**

▶ *CD2 Track 23 p283*

- Ask the class to describe the photo.
- Read out the instructions and ask the class if they know what the animal is called.
- Play the CD. The pupils listen and read the dialogue. Confirm that the animal is a platypus.

**Pupil's Book Activity 2**

**Read and say *true* or *false*. Correct the false sentences.**

- Organise the class into pairs. The pupils work together to identify and correct the false sentences.

**Pupil's Book Activity 3**

**Look and learn – Grammar wall**

- Read the information on the Grammar wall as a class.
- Ask **What comes after 'must' and the other modal verbs of deduction?** (*Another verb / the infinitive form.*) **Do the modal verbs change when we use 'it', 'he' or 'she'?** (*No.*) **When we make a deduction, is the opposite of 'must', 'mustn't'?** (*No, it's 'can't'.*)

**Pupil's Book Activity 4**

**Read and think. Answer.**

- Focus the pupils' attention on the Think about grammar box and read out the questions as a class. The pupils answer in pairs.

**Answer:** **1** must **2** may / might / could **3** can't

**Pupil's Book Activity 5**

**Look at the dialogue in Activity 1 again. Find examples of modal verbs of deduction.**

- Organise the pupils into pairs. Ask them to find examples of modal verbs of deduction in the text.

**Pupil's Book Activity 6**

**Choose an animal and make deductions.**

- Identify and describe the animals as a class.
- Invite two pupils to read out the speech bubbles. Then make a similar statement. Say **It's got claws.** Prompt the class to make deductions.
- The pupils play the game in pairs.

**Activity Book**

**Activity 1**

**Make deductions about animals. Use *may, might* or *could.***

- The pupils make deductions and write sentences.

**Activity 2**

**Read and write. Use *must* or *can't.***

- The pupils make deductions and write the sentences.

**Answers:** **1** It must be a bat. **2** It can't be a shark. **3** It must be a penguin. **4** It must be a platypus. **5** It can't be a spider.

**Activity 3**

**Listen and complete the notes.**

▶ *CD2 Track 24 p285*

- Ask the class to identify the animal in the picture. Ask **Where does it live? What does it look like?**
- Ask the class to read the notes. Then play the CD. The pupils listen and follow the information in their books.
- Play the CD again, pausing after each piece of key information. The pupils say and write the missing information each time.

**Answers:** **1** 2 **2** 58 **3** neck **4** 3 **5** claws **6** 50 **7** dangerous

**Activity 4**

**Write a description of an animal. Read it to your partner. Can your partner guess the animal?**

- The pupils work on their own to choose a wild animal and write a description.
- Invite a pupil to read out their description. Prompt the rest of the class to make deductions.
- Organise the pupils into pairs. Ask them to do the same activity.

**Odd one out activity**

**Which is the odd one out? Why?**

- The pupils complete the odd one out activity.

**Answers:** eagle (It can fly.)

**Ending the lesson**

**Review the lesson and reflect on learning.**

- Say **Today we've learnt how to make deductions.** Elicit examples of the language from the pupils.
- Ask **Which was your favourite activity today? Which activity was easy / difficult?**

**Extra activity**

**Reinforcement**

- Place a piece of paper over a photo of a wild animal and reveal a small part of it. Ask **What could it be?** The pupils should make deductions. Repeat the procedure with other photos.

### Key Competences and Key Learning Outcomes

- Read a story with a cultural focus
- Listen for specific information
- Use the Internet to investigate Australia
- Think about what you are scared of and how to deal with fears
- Learn about Australia and a mythical Australian animal

### Key language

- *billabong, lake, river; beast, bunyip, hippo, monster, prehistoric animal, seal; bones, fur, fangs, skeleton; scary, strange; newspaper, noise, theories*
- *It sounds like a lion. This skeleton looks like a hippo. What did it look like? Bunyips (could be real monsters).*

### Materials

- Pupil's Book p53; Activity Book p50; Class CD2; Teacher's App on Navio

### Optional materials

- Teacher's Resource Bank: Trinity Exams Practice cards (selected from the Starter Unit and Units 1, 2, 3 and 4)

## At a Glance Lesson Plan

### Pupil's Book

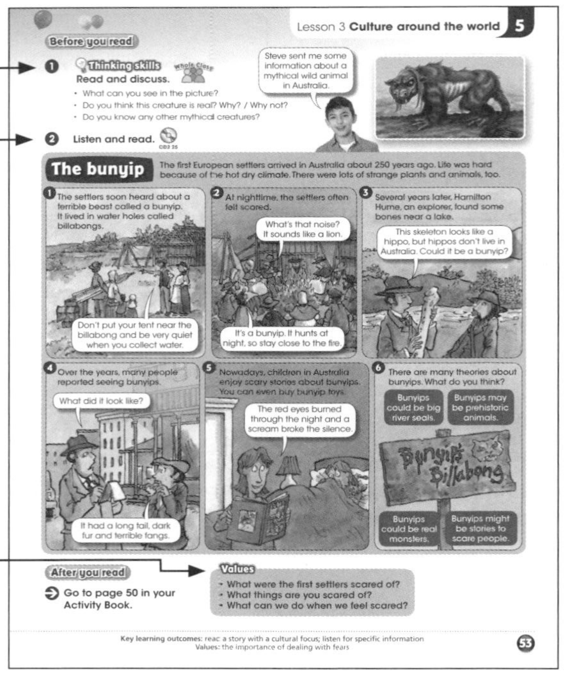

#### Starting the lesson

- Use the Trinity Exams Practice cards (optional).
- Review parts of an animal's body.
- Set learning objectives.

#### Activity 1: Before you read

- Read and discuss.

#### Activity 2

- Listen and read.
- ▶ *CD2 Track 25 p285*
- Go to the Activity Book.

#### Values

- Read and discuss.

#### Ending the lesson

- Review the lesson and reflect on learning.

#### Extra activity

**Reinforcement**

- Create your own mythical creature.

### Activity Book

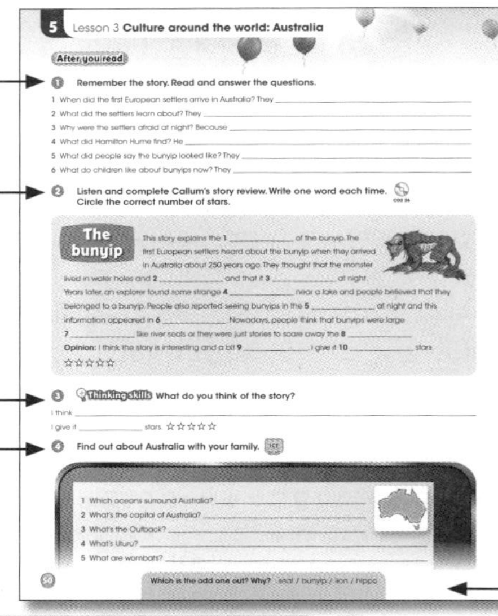

#### Activity Book: After you read

**Activity 1**

- Remember the story. Read and answer the questions.

**Activity 2**

- Listen and complete Callum's story review.
- ▶ *CD2 Track 26 p285*
- Write one word each time. Circle the correct number of stars.

**Activity 3**

- What do you think of the story?

**Activity 4**

- Find out about Australia with your family.

**Odd one out activity**

- Which is the odd one out? Why?

### Digital resources

**Teacher's Digital:** You can also teach this lesson using the Teacher's App on Navio.

**Pupil's Digital:** Encourage your pupils to use the Pupil's App on Navio to practise the activities from this lesson.

Powered By NAVIO

### Starting the lesson

**Use the Trinity Exams Practice cards (optional).**
- The pupils practise asking and answering questions.

**Review parts of an animal's body.**
- Think of an animal and begin to describe it using the key vocabulary from Lesson 1. Prompt the pupils to make a deduction about what the animal could be after each statement. Repeat the procedure until the pupils have worked out what the animal must be.
- Invite different pupils to come to the front of the class and take your role.

**Set learning objectives.**
- Say **Today we're going to read a story from Australia.**

### Pupil's Book Activity 1: Before you read

**Read and discuss.**
- Read the questions as a class. Encourage the pupils to share information about other mythical creatures they know. They may have heard of Big Foot or the Loch Ness monster. Encourage the pupils to use the modals of deduction in their response, e.g. *It can't be real.*

### Pupil's Book Activity 2

**Listen and read.**
▶ ***CD2 Track 25 p285***
- Play the CD. The pupils follow in their books. Confirm that the picture in Activity 1 is a bunyip.
- Ask questions to check understanding.

**Suggested comprehension questions:**
- Frame 1: **Where did people think the bunyip lived?** (*In water holes called billabongs.*)
- Frame 2: **What did people tell the settlers about the bunyip?** (*It hunts at night.*)
- Frame 3: **Why did the explorer think the bones belonged to a bunyip?** (*They were near a lake, it looked like a hippo, but hippos don't live in Australia.*)
- Frame 4: **How did people describe the bunyip?** (*Long tail, dark fur, terrible fangs.*)
- Frame 5: **Do people believe in the bunyip now?** (*No.*)

### Activity Book: After you read

**Activity 1**
**Remember the story. Read and answer the questions.**
- Read out the first question and invite a pupil to answer it.
- The pupils read and answer the remaining questions.

**Answers: 1** arrived about 250 years ago. **2** learnt about binyups. **3** the binyups hunted at night. **4** found bones near a lake. **5** said that it had a long tail, dark fur and terrible fangs. **6** like the scary stories.

**Activity 2**
**Listen and complete Callum's story review. Write one word each time. Circle the correct number of stars.**
▶ ***CD2 Track 26 p285***
- Read out the story review as a class. Ask the pupils to guess the missing words.
- Play the CD without pausing. The pupils listen and complete as much of the information as possible.
- Play the CD again, pausing after each piece of key information to check the information and spelling. The pupils circle the correct number of stars.

**Answers: 1** myth **2** rivers **3** hunted **4** bones **5** countryside **6** newspapers **7** mammals **8** settlers **9** scary **10** four

**Activity 3**
**What do you think of the story?**
- The pupils write their opinion and give a rating.
- Invite different pupils to share their opinions with the rest of the class.

**Activity 4**
**Find out about Australia with your family.** ICT
- Read out the questions about Australia. Ask **Where can you find out this information?** (*Internet, library, asking friends and family.*) The pupils should do the activity at home.

- If you prefer to do this activity in the class, connect to a children's website which has information about Australia such as: http://kids.nationalgeographic.com/kids/places/find/australia/. Read out the questions. The pupils work as a class to find and write the answers.

**Answers: 1** Pacific Ocean, Indian Ocean **2** Canberra **3** vast and arid area of Australia **4** a sandstone rock formation **5** marsupials

**Odd one out activity**
**Which is the odd one out? Why?**
- The pupils complete the odd one out activity.

**Answers:** bunyip (It's a mythical creature.)

### Values

**Read and discuss.**
- Read out each question and discuss it as a class.
- Explain to the pupils that it's normal to feel afraid sometimes and encourage them to think about techniques for dealing with fears. Strategies include talking about your fears, breathing deeply, thinking happy thoughts, creating silly images of the scary thing in your head or counting.

### Ending the lesson

**Review the lesson and reflect on learning.**
- Say **Today we've read a story from Australia.**
- Ask **Which was your favourite activity today? Which activity was easy / difficult?**

### Extra activity

**Reinforcement**
- The pupils create mythical creatures for their neighbourhood. They work individually to draw their animals. They then write a brief description of its appearance, habitat and diet.

### Key Competences and Key Learning Outcomes

- Act out a short dialogue in pairs
- Learn and practise describing things with verbs of the senses
- Compare and describe different animals
- Identify and practise rising and falling intonation in questions

### Key language

- *long hair, pointed ears, red eyes, sharp fangs; hard, rectangular, scary, soft; dog, lion, snake*
- *What does it look / smell / taste / feel / sound like? It (looks) like a snake. It (sounds) dangerous. Does it (look) scary? Does it (smell) like a dog? Yes, it does. No, it doesn't.*

### Materials

- Pupil's Book p54; Activity Book p51; Class CD2; Teacher's App on Navio

### Optional materials

- Teacher's Resource Bank: Trinity Exams Practice cards (selected from the Starter Unit and Units 1, 2, 3 and 4)

## At a Glance Lesson Plan

### Pupil's Book

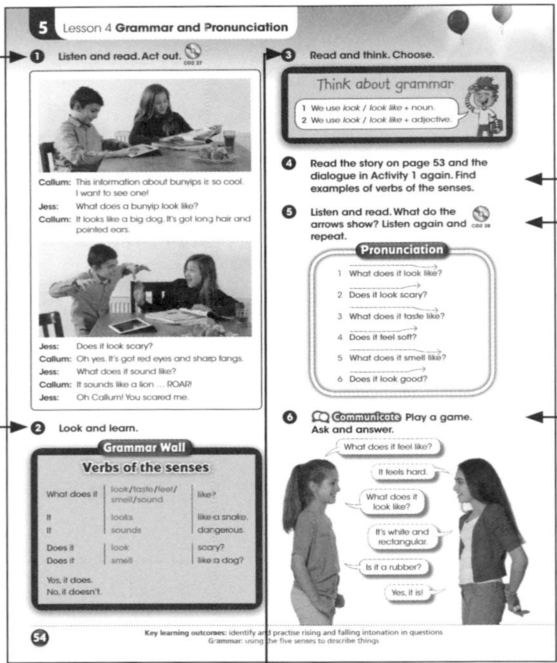

**Starting the lesson**

- Use the Trinity Exams Practice cards (optional).
- Review the senses.
- Set learning objectives.

**Activity 1**

- Listen and read.
- Act out.

▶ *CD2 Track 27 p285*

**Activity 2**

- Look and learn – Grammar wall

**Activity 3**

- Read and think.
- Choose.

**Activity 4**

- Read the story on page 53 and the dialogue in Activity 1 again.
- Find examples of verbs of the senses.

**Activity 5**

- Listen and read.
- What do the arrows show?
- Listen again and repeat.

▶ *CD2 Track 28 p285*

**Activity 6**

- Play a game.
- Ask and answer.

Go to the Activity Book.

**Ending the lesson**

- Review the lesson and reflect on learning.

**Extra activity**

**Extension**

- Play some thinking games on the board as a class.

### Digital resources

**Teacher's Digital:** You can also teach this lesson using the Teacher's App on Navio.

**Pupil's Digital:** Encourage your pupils to use the Pupil's App on Navio to practise the activities from this lesson.

Powered By NAVIO

### Activity Book

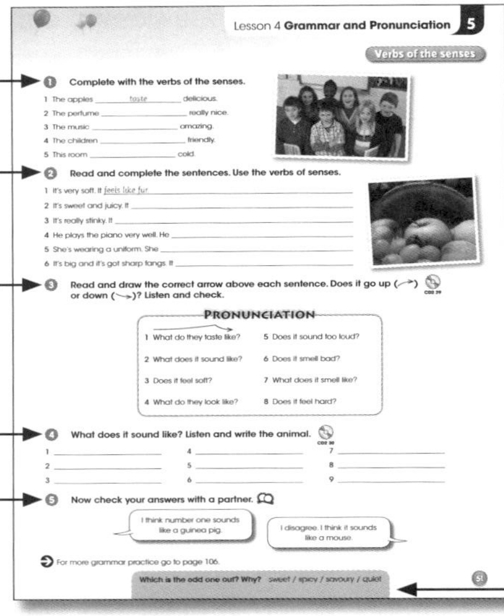

**Activity Book**

**Activity 1**

- Complete with the verbs of the senses.

**Activity 2**

- Read and complete the sentences. Use the verbs of the senses.

**Activity 3**

- Read and draw the correct arrow above each sentence. Does it go up (↗) or down (↘)?
- Listen and check.

▶ *CD2 Track 29 p285*

**Activity 4**

- What does it sound like? Listen and write the animal.

▶ *CD2 Track 30 p286*

**Activity 5**

- Now check your answers with a partner.

**Odd one out activity**

- Which is the odd one out? Why?

**Starting the lesson**

**Use the Trinity Exams Practice cards (optional).**

- The pupils practise asking and answering questions.

**Review the senses.**

- Ask **What can you smell / see / hear / feel?** The pupils describe their school. Ask the pupils which is the fifth sense. (*Taste*.)

**Set learning objectives.**

- Say **Today we're going to practise using verbs of the senses to describe things.**

**Pupil's Book Activity 1**

**Listen and read. Act out.**

▸ *CD2 Track 27 p285*

- The pupils look at the photos. Ask **What do you think they're talking about in the first photo? What's happening in the second photo?**
- Play the CD. The pupils listen and read the dialogue. Ask **What does the bunyip look / sound like?**
- Play the CD again, pausing after each sentence for the pupils to repeat.
- The pupils practise the dialogue in pairs.

**Pupil's Book Activity 2**

**Look and learn – Grammar wall**

- Read the information on the Grammar wall as a class.
- Ask questions about different objects using the verbs of the senses.

**Pupil's Book Activity 3**

**Read and think. Choose.**

- Read out the Think about grammar box as a class. The pupils complete the sentences.

**Answers:** **1** look like **2** look

**Pupil's Book Activity 4**

**Read the story on page 53 and the dialogue in Activity 1 again. Find examples of verbs of the senses.**

- The pupils find examples with the verbs of the senses.

**Pupil's Book Activity 5**

**Listen and read. What do the arrows show? Listen again and repeat.**

▸ *CD2 Track 28 p285*

- Say **Let's listen to the questions. Does the intonation go up or down?** Play the CD, pausing after each question.
- Ask **When does the intonation go up? When does the intonation go down?** The pupils identify the intonation pattern. (*The intonation goes down when the sentence begins with a 'Wh' question word, but goes up when a question is answered with 'yes' or 'no'.*)
- Play the CD again. The pupils listen and repeat the sentences.

**Pupil's Book Activity 6**

**Play a game. Ask and answer.**

- The pupils play the game in pairs.

**Activity Book**

**Activity 1**

**Complete with the verbs of the senses.**

- The pupils complete each sentence.

**Answers:** **1** taste **2** smells **3** sounds **4** look **5** feels

**Activity 2**

**Read and complete the sentences. Use the verbs of senses.**

- The pupils complete each sentence.

**Activity 3**

**Read and draw the correct arrow above each sentence. Does it go up (↗) or down (↘) ? Listen and check.**

▸ *CD2 Track 29 p285*

- Invite a pupil to read out the first question with a clear falling intonation. The pupils read the remaining questions and draw the arrows.
- Play the CD. The pupils listen and check.

**Answers:** **Down:** 1, 2, 4, 7 **Up:** 3, 5, 6, 8

**Activity 4**

**What does it sound like? Listen and write the animal.**

▸ *CD2 Track 30 p286*

- Play the CD, pausing after the each animal sound. The pupils write the animal they think it is.

**Answers:** **1** guinea pig **2** elephant **3** whale **4** owl **5** wolf **6** seal **7** snake **8** chicken **9** mosquito

**Activity 5**

**Now check your answers with a partner.**

- The pupils check their answers to Activity 4 in pairs.

**Odd one out activity**

**Which is the odd one out? Why?**

- The pupils complete the odd one out activity.

**Answers:** quiet (It doesn't describe a taste.)

**Ending the lesson**

**Review the lesson and reflect on learning.**

- Say **Today we've learnt how to use verbs of the senses to describe things.**
- Ask **Which was your favourite activity today? Which activity was easy / difficult?**

**Extra activity**

**Extension**

- Draw a picture on the board. Ask **What does it look like?** Encourage the pupils to answer with *It looks like*.
- Repeat the procedure with other pictures.
- Then play a game with doodles. Find doodles by searching on websites such as: www.folklore.ee/Droodles/

## Key Competences and Key Learning Outcomes

- Say and identify the names of animals
- Review and learn adjectives to describe animals

- Listen for specific information
- Practise activity types found in the Cambridge Exams: A2 Key for Schools

- Do a communication task

### Key language

- *bull, donkey, eagle, grasshopper, mole, praying mantis, silkworm, swan; colourful, dangerous, domestic, fierce, harmless, poisonous, wild; cat, dog, hamster; long tail, pointed ears, sharp claws*
- *What does it look like? It (must) be a domestic animal.*
- **Extension:** *deer, fox, wasp, wolf*

### Materials

- Pupil's Book p55; Activity Book p52; Class CD2; Teacher's App on Navio; Teacher's Resource Bank: Unit 5

### Optional materials

- Teacher's Resource Bank: Trinity Exams Practice cards (selected from the Starter Unit and Units 1, 2, 3 and 4)

## At a Glance Lesson Plan

### Starting the lesson

- Use the Trinity Exams Practice cards (optional).
- Review animals.
- Set learning objectives.

### Activity 1

- Look and match.
- Listen, check and repeat.

▶ *CD2 Track 31 p286*

### Activity 2

- Listen and say which animals the children are talking about.

▶ *CD2 Track 32 p286*

### Activity 3

- Listen again.

▶ *CD2 Track 32 p286*

- Which four adjectives do you hear?

## Pupil's Book

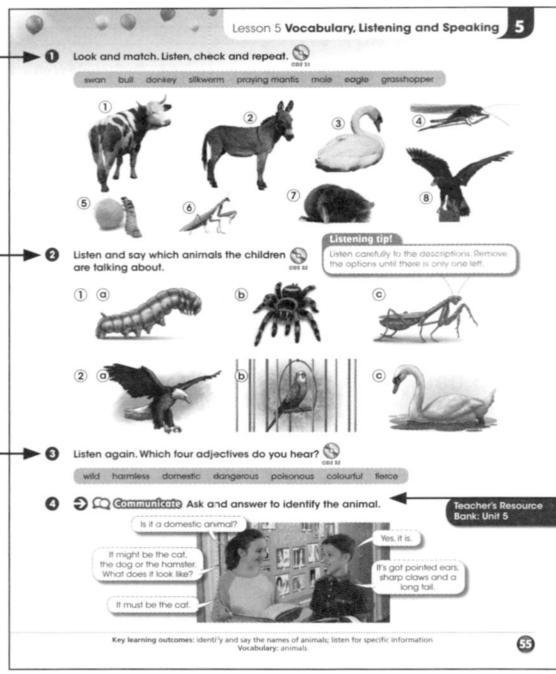


### Activity 4

- Ask and answer to identify the animal (Teacher's Resource Bank: Unit 5).

Go to the Activity Book.

### Ending the lesson

- Review the lesson and reflect on learning.

### Extra activities

**Extension**

- Create a synonym word wall.

**Vocabulary extension**

- Present four additional vocabulary items.

## Digital resources

**Teacher's Digital:** You can also teach this lesson using the Teacher's App on Navio.

**Pupil's Digital:** Encourage your pupils to use the Pupil's App on Navio to practise the activities from this lesson.

Powered By NAVIO

## Activity Book

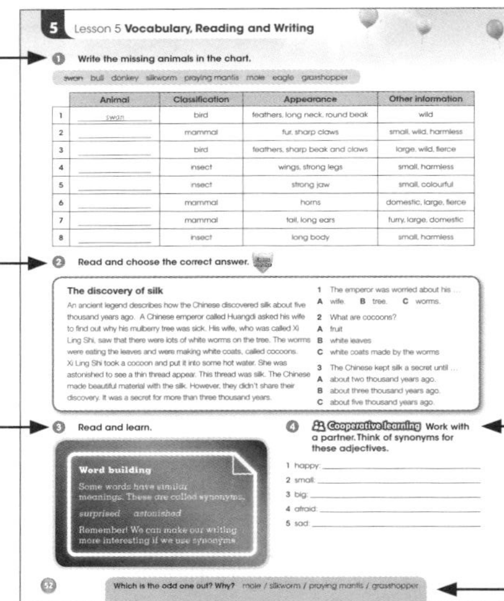


### Activity Book

**Activity 1**

- Write the missing animals in the chart.

**Activity 2**

- Read and choose the correct answer.

**Activity 3**

- Read and learn.

**Activity 4**

- Work with a partner. Think of synonyms for these adjectives.

**Odd one out activity**

- Which is the odd one out? Why?

**Starting the lesson**

**Use the Trinity Exams Practice cards (optional).**
- The pupils practise asking and answering questions.

**Review animals.**
- Write the alphabet on the board, leaving a space next to each letter.
- Challenge the class to think of an animal that begins with each letter. Set a time limit for this task.
- The pupils write an animal's name next to each letter. A list of animals can be found at the website http://a-z-animals.com/animals/.

**Set learning objectives.**
- Say **Today we're going to learn the names of more animals and we're going to play a communication game.**

**Pupil's Book Activity 1**

**Look and match. Listen, check and repeat.**
▸ ***CD2 Track 31 p286***
- Ask the pupils to describe the animals that they can see in the activity.
- Organise the class into pairs. Ask the pupils to work together to try to match the words and pictures.
- Play the CD. The pupils listen and check.
- Play the CD again, pausing after each word or phrase for the pupils to repeat.

**Pupil's Book Activity 2**

**Listen and say which animals the children are talking about.**
▸ ***CD2 Track 32 p286***
- Focus the class on the first row of pictures. Ask the pupils to describe what they can see.
- Play the CD. The pupils listen and identify the matching drawing. (*Picture c.*)
- Repeat the procedure with the second row of pictures. (*Picture a.*)

**Pupil's Book Activity 3**

**Listen again. Which four adjectives do you hear?**
▸ ***CD2 Track 32 p286***
- Read out the list of adjectives and check understanding.
- Play the first recording on the CD again. The pupils identify the two adjectives that the children use.
- Repeat the procedure with the second recording.

**Answers:** **1** colourful, dangerous **2** domestic, fierce

**Pupil's Book Activity 4**

**Ask and answer to identify the animal (Teacher's Resource Bank: Unit 5).**
- Invite two pupils to read out the speech bubbles.
- Organise the class into pairs (A and B). Give Pupils A the first worksheet from Teacher's Resource Bank Unit 5 and give Pupils B the other worksheet. All the pupils choose five animals that appear on the page and write the names in the column 'My animals'.
- Demonstrate the activity by asking a pupil questions to discover the first animal on his / her list.
- The pupils then play the game, taking turns to ask and answer questions about the animals.
- At the end of the activity, the pairs show their partners their lists.

**Activity Book**

**Activity 1**

**Write the missing animals in the chart.**
- Read out the information in the first row of the chart as a class.
- Read out the information in the second row and elicit the missing animal.
- The pupils read the rest of the information and write the animals.

**Answers:** **1** swan **2** mole **3** eagle **4** grasshopper **5** praying mantis **6** bull **7** donkey **8** silkworm

**Activity 2**

**Read and choose the correct answer.**
- Ask the class to share what they know about silk.
- Read out the text as a class. Check comprehension.
- Read out the first question and options and identify where the information is in the text.
- The pupils read the remaining questions and choose the correct answers

**Answers:** **1** B **2** C **3** A

**Activity 3**

**Read and learn.**
- Read the information as a class.

**Activity 4**

**Work with a partner. Think of synonyms for these adjectives.**
- Read out the adjectives as a class. The pupils work in pairs to think of synonyms for each adjective.

**Odd one out activity**

**Which is the odd one out? Why?**
- The pupils complete the odd one out activity.

**Answers:** mole (It isn't an insect.)

**Ending the lesson**

**Review the lesson and reflect on learning.**
- Say **Today we've learnt the names of some more animals and we've played a communication game.**
- Ask **Which was your favourite activity today? Which activity was easy / difficult?**

**Extra activities**

**Extension**
- Make a classroom display of useful synonyms. Write the different words on cards and group the synonyms around the high frequency word.

**Vocabulary extension**
- Present four additional animal words: *deer, fox, wasp, wolf*.
- Use the Vocabulary booster on NAVIO to practise these new words.

### Key Competences and Key Learning Outcomes

- Do pre-reading tasks to predict content and raise interest
- Read a newspaper report for general understanding
- Scan a newspaper report for specific information

- Discuss newspapers

- Read and understand a newspaper report
- Give an opinion on the text

### Key language

- *enormous, mysterious, prehistoric, terrified; creature, dark shape, eel, flippers, headline, hide, lake, Loch Ness, news, newspaper, surprise, tail, underwater cave*
- *It looked dangerous.*

### Materials

- Pupil's Book p56; Activity Book p53; Class CD2; Teacher's App on Navio

### Optional materials

- Teacher's Resource Bank: Trinity Exams Practice cards (selected from the Starter Unit and Units 1, 2, 3 and 4)

## At a Glance Lesson Plan

### Starting the lesson

- Use the Trinity Exams Practice cards (optional).
- Review the myth of the bunyip.
- Set learning objectives.

### Activity 1: Before you read

- Read and discuss.

### Activity 2

- Read the headline.
- What do you think the report is about?
- Read and find out.

## Pupil's Book

5 Lesson 6 Reading

Literacy

Before you read

1 Read and discuss.
- Who reads a newspaper in your home?
- What topics are in the news at the moment?
- Which newspapers do you know?

2 Read the headline. What do you think the report is about? Read and find out.

Reading tip!
Read the text quickly to get a general idea. Don't worry if you don't understand all the words.

The Daily News

Family sees mysterious creature

A family from London had a surprise last Tuesday when they saw a mysterious creature in the Scottish lake, Loch Ness.

The Peter family at Loch Ness

Mr and Mrs Peter were fishing with their sons on a quiet part of the lake when they saw something strange in the water. It was a large dark shape and it was moving towards them. At first, the family thought that it was a big fish or a long eel, but when it got closer, they saw that it was much bigger.

'It was enormous,' said Mr Peter. 'It had four flippers in the middle of its body.'

His ten-year-old son, Patrick, said, 'It had a long tail and a small head like a snake. It was really cool. I can't wait to tell my friends about it.'

Mrs Peter wasn't as happy as her son. She said, 'I was terrified. The creature swam under the boat and it looked dangerous.'

Many local people believe that the lake is home to a prehistoric reptile called a plesiosaurus. Mr Smith, who owns the rental boats on the lake, said, 'Loch Ness is one of the deepest freshwater lakes in the world and it's got many underwater caves. It's the perfect place for a prehistoric monster to hide.'

Did the Peter family really see the Loch Ness monster?

An artist's impression of the mysterious creature

After you read

3 What do you think?
- Is this an interesting report?
- Which information is the most interesting?
- Do you think the Loch Ness monster exists?

Go to page 53 in your Activity Book.

Key learning outcomes: read a newspaper report for general understanding; scan a newspaper report for specific information; discuss newspapers

56

### Activity 3: After you read

- What do you think?
- Go to the Activity Book.

### Ending the lesson

- Review the lesson and reflect on learning.

### Extra activity

**Reinforcement**
- Practise and record your interview.

## Activity Book

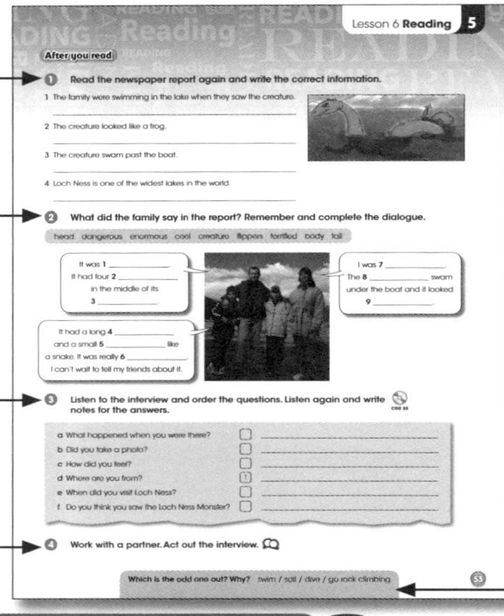
Lesson 6 Reading 5

After you read

1 Read the newspaper report again and write the correct information.
1 The family were swimming in the lake when they saw the creature.
2 The creature looked like a frog.
3 The creature swam past the boat.
4 Loch Ness is one of the widest lakes in the world.

2 What did the family say in the report? Remember and complete the dialogue.
head dangerous enormous cool creature flippers terrified body tail

3 Listen to the interview and order the questions. Listen again and write notes for the answers.
a What happened when you were there?
b Did you take a photo?
c How did you feel?
d Where are you from?
e When did you visit Loch Ness?
f Do you think you saw the Loch Ness Monster?

4 Work with a partner. Act out the interview.

Which is the odd one out? Why? swim / sail / dive / go rock climbing

53

### Activity Book: After you read

**Activity 1**
- Read the newspaper report again and write the correct information.

**Activity 2**
- What did the family say in the report? Remember and complete the dialogue.

**Activity 3**
- Listen to the interview and order the questions.

▶ *CD2 Track 33 p286*
- Listen again and write notes for the answers.

**Activity 4**
- Work with a partner. Act out the interview.

**Odd one out activity**
- Which is the odd one out? Why?

## Digital resources

**Teacher's Digital:** You can also teach this lesson using the Teacher's App on Navio.

**Pupil's Digital:** Encourage your pupils to use the Pupil's App on Navio to practise the activities from this lesson.

Powered By NAVIO

# Detailed Lesson Plan

## Starting the lesson

**Use the Trinity Exams Practice cards (optional).**
- The pupils practise asking and answering questions.

**Review the myth of the bunyip.**
- Ask **Do you remember what a bunyip is?** Encourage the class to recount what they learnt about this mythical creature in Lesson 3. Ask **What does it look like? What does it sound like?**

**Set learning objectives.**
- Say **Today we're going to read a newspaper report about another mythical creature.**

## Pupil's Book Activity 1: Before you read

**Read and discuss.**
- Read the questions as a class. Prompt the pupils to answer in as much detail as possible.

## Pupil's Book Activity 2

**Read the headline. What do you think the report is about? Read and find out.**
- Read out the headline. Ask the class to predict what will appear in the newspaper report. Ask **Do you think the report will describe the mysterious creature? What other things do you think the report will give us information about?**
- The pupils read the text as a class or in pairs to see if their predictions are correct. Ask questions about the content of the report to check general comprehension.

## Pupil's Book Activity 3: After you read

**What do you think?**
- Read the questions as a class. Prompt the pupils to say which information is the most interesting.
- Ask the pupils if they think the monster exists and, if you wish to do so, have a class vote.

## Activity Book: After you read

**Activity 1**

**Read the newspaper report again and write the correct information.**
- Read and correct the first sentence as a class.
- The pupils correct the remaining sentences.

**Answers:** **1** The family were fishing. **2** The creature looked like an eel. **3** The creature swam under the boat. **4** The Loch Ness is one of the deepest lakes in the world.

**Activity 2**

**What did the family say in the report? Remember and complete the dialogue.**
- The pupils complete what the family said in the text.

**Answers:** **1** enormous **2** flippers **3** body **4** tail **5** head **6** cool **7** terrified **8** creature **9** dangerous

**Activity 3**

**Listen to the interview and order the questions. Listen again and write notes for the answers.**

▶ *CD2 Track 33 p286*
- Read out the questions as a class.
- Play the CD. The pupils listen and order the questions.
- Play the CD again, pausing after each piece of key information. The pupils write the answers to the questions in note form.

**Answers:** 3, 5, 4, 1, 2, 6; **1** from Saltney **2** last week **3** saw something in the water **4** a little bit afraid **5** no **6** yes

**Activity 4**

**Work with a partner. Act out the interview.**
- Organise the class into pairs. The pupils use the information in Activity 3 to act out the interview.

**Odd one out activity**

**Which is the odd one out? Why?**
- The pupils complete the odd one out activity.

**Answers:** go rock climbing (It isn't a water sport.)

## Ending the lesson

**Review the lesson and reflect on learning.**
- Say **Today we've read a newspaper report.**
- Ask **Which was your favourite activity today? Which activity was easy / difficult?**

## Extra activity

**Reinforcement**
- Ask the pupils to present their interviews. If you have access to a recording device, make an audio or video recording of the pupils acting out their interviews. Then play the recordings to the class.

## Key Competences and Key Learning Outcomes

- Identify direct speech in a newspaper article
- Identify the five 'Wh' questions that are answered in a newspaper report
- Identify features of a newspaper article
- Use criteria to check your writing
- Share your writing with another pupil
- Invent a story and write a newspaper article

## Key language

- *brave, deadly, lucky; fangs, fight, hero, poison, slithered, snake*
- *What happened? Why / When / Where did it happen? Who was there? Emma was playing with her dog, Sandy, when the snake appeared. Emma's mum said, 'Sandy isn't a big dog, but she's very brave.'*

## Materials

- Pupil's Book p57; Activity Book p54; Teacher's App on Navio
- A coloured pen or pencil

## Optional materials

- Teacher's Resource Bank: Trinity Exams Practice cards (selected from the Starter Unit and Units 1, 2, 3 and 4)
- Sheets of A3 paper

## At a Glance Lesson Plan

### Pupil's Book

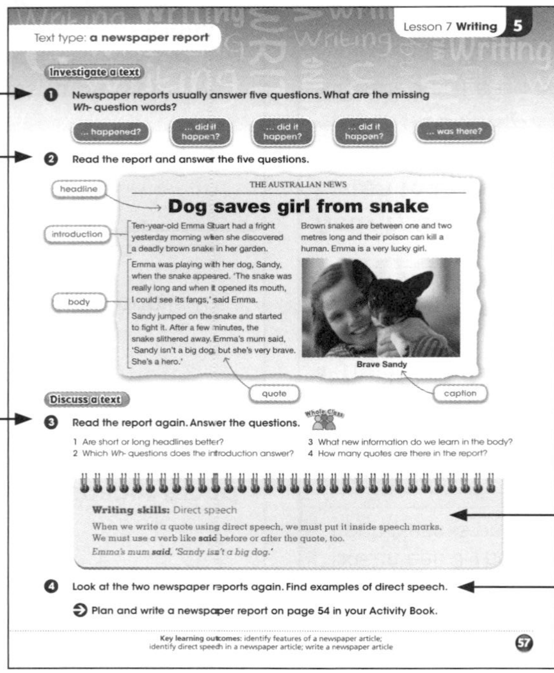
Lesson 7 Writing 5

Text type: a newspaper report

Investigate a text

1 Newspaper reports usually answer five questions. What are the missing *Wh-* question words?

... happened? ... did it happen? ... did it happen? ... did it happen? ... was there?

2 Read the report and answer the five questions.

headline / introduction / body

THE AUSTRALIAN NEWS

**Dog saves girl from snake**

Ten-year-old Emma Stuart had a fright yesterday morning when she discovered a deadly brown snake in her garden. Brown snakes are between one and two metres long and their poison can kill a human. Emma is a very lucky girl.

Emma was playing with her dog, Sandy, when the snake appeared. 'The snake was really long and when it opened its mouth, I could see its fangs,' said Emma.

Sandy jumped on the snake and started to fight it. After a few minutes, the snake slithered away. Emma's mum said, 'Sandy isn't a big dog, but she's very brave. She's a hero.'

Brave Sandy

quote / caption

Discuss a text

3 Read the report again. Answer the questions.

1 Are short or long headlines better?
2 Which *Wh-* questions does the introduction answer?
3 What new information do we learn in the body?
4 How many quotes are there in the report?

**Writing skills:** Direct speech

When we write a quote using direct speech, we must put it inside speech marks. We must use a verb like **said** before or after the quote, too.

*Emma's mum **said**, 'Sandy isn't a big dog.'*

4 Look at the two newspaper reports again. Find examples of direct speech.

Plan and write a newspaper report on page 54 in your Activity Book.

Key learning outcomes: identify features of a newspaper article; identify direct speech in a newspaper article; write a newspaper article

57

### Starting the lesson

- Use the Trinity Exams Practice cards (optional).
- Review newspaper headlines.
- Set learning objectives.

### Activity 1: Investigate a text

- Newspaper reports usually answer five questions.
- What are the missing *Wh-* question words?

### Activity 2

- Read the report and answer the five questions.

### Activity 3: Discuss a text

- Read the report again.
- Answer the questions.

### Writing skills

- Read about using direct speech.

### Activity 4

- Look at the two newspaper reports again.
- Find examples of direct speech.
- Go to the Activity Book.

### Ending the lesson

- Review the lesson and reflect on learning.

### Extra activity

**Reinforcement**

- Combine the newspaper reports to make a class newspaper.

## Digital resources

**Teacher's Digital:** You can also teach this lesson using the Teacher's App on Navio.

**Pupil's Digital:** Encourage your pupils to use the Pupil's App on Navio to practise the activities from this lesson.

Powered By NAVIO

### Activity Book

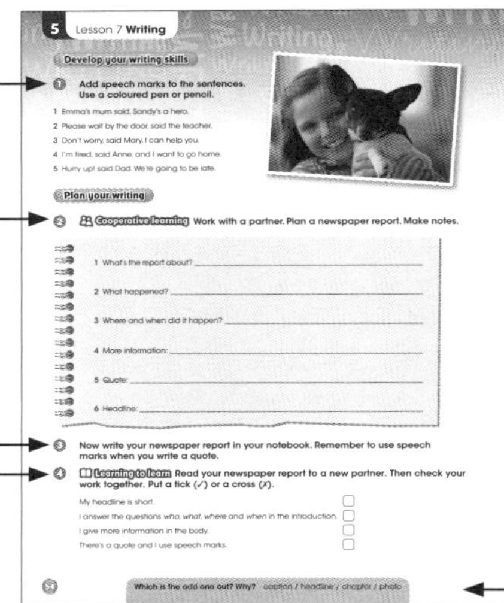
5 Lesson 7 Writing

Develop your writing skills

1 Add speech marks to the sentences. Use a coloured pen or pencil.

Plan your writing

2 Cooperative learning Work with a partner. Plan a newspaper report. Make notes.

3 Now write your newspaper report in your notebook. Remember to use speech marks when you write a quote.

4 Learning to learn Read your newspaper report to a new partner. Then check your work together. Put a tick (✓) or a cross (✗).

Which is the odd one out? Why? caption / headline / chapter / photo

### Activity Book

**Activity 1: Develop your writing skills**

- Add speech marks to the sentences. Use a coloured pen or pencil.

**Activity 2: Plan your writing**

- Work with a partner. Plan a newspaper report. Make notes.

**Activity 3**

- Now write your newspaper report in your notebook.

Remember to use speech marks when you write a quote.

**Activity 4**

- Read your newspaper report to a new partner. Then check your work together. Put a tick (✓) or a cross (✗).

**Odd one out activity**

- Which is the odd one out? Why?

# Detailed Lesson Plan

### Starting the lesson

**Use the Trinity Exams Practice cards (optional).**
- The pupils practise asking and answering questions.

**Review newspaper headlines.**
- Write a headline on the board *Dog bites man.* Then prompt the class to create the story by asking **Who was the man? What kind of dog was it? Where was the man? When did the dog bite him? Where did the dog bite him? Why did the dog bite him?**
- Write a second headline on the board. Ask the pupils to imagine the story in pairs. The pupils work together to invent the story details. Ideas for headlines: *Treasure found in school. Pop star surprises children. Police rescue boy.*

**Set learning objectives.**
- Say **Today we're going to write a newspaper report.**

### Pupil's Book Activity 1: Investigate a text

**Newspaper reports usually answer five questions. What are the missing *Wh-* question words?**
- Explain that all newspaper reports answer five questions. These questions begin with 'Wh-' question words.
- Read and complete the questions as a class.

**Answers:** What happened? When did it happen? Where did it happen? Why did it happen? Who was there?

### Pupil's Book Activity 2

**Read the report and answer the five questions.**
- Read and discuss the headline and photo caption as a class. Encourage the pupils to predict what will appear in the report.
- Read the newspaper report as a class. The pupils answer the five questions.

### Pupil's Book Activity 3: Discuss a text

**Read the report again. Answer the questions.**
- Read and discuss the questions as a class. Highlight that a good newspaper report has got a short headline to attract the reader's attention and that the introduction answers the questions who, what, where and when. The body of the article gives more information and often answers the questions why and how. A newspaper report also frequently contains quotes.

### Writing skills

- Read about using direct speech.

### Pupil's Book Activity 4

**Look at the two newspaper reports again. Find examples of direct speech.**
- Organise the pupils into pairs. Ask them to find examples of direct speech in Lessons 6 and 7.

### Activity Book

**Activity 1: Develop your writing skills**

**Add speech bubbles to the sentences. Use a coloured pen or pencil.**
- The pupils identify the direct speech and add the speech marks to the sentences.

**Answers:** **1** Emma's mum said, 'Sandy's a hero.' **2** 'Please wait by the door,' said the teacher. **3** 'Don't worry,' said Mary. 'I can help you.' **4** 'I'm tired,' said Anne, 'and I want to go home.' **5** 'Hurry up!' said dad. 'We're going to be late.'

**Activity 2: Plan your writing**

**Work with a partner. Plan a newspaper report. Make notes.**
- Read out the notes and elicit examples of how the pupils can complete each section.
- Organise the class into Writing Partners. The pupils think of a news story and plan their newspaper report.

**Activity 3**

**Now write your newspaper report in your notebook. Remember to use speech marks when you write a quote.**
- The pupils write their newspaper reports in their notebooks.

**Activity 4**

**Read your newspaper report to a new partner. Then check your work together. Put a tick (✓) or a cross (✗).** LEARN
- Read through the statements as a class.
- Organise the class into new partners. One pupil reads aloud their text to their partner. The other pupil listens. The pupils work together to decide if the text fulfils the criteria and tick the corresponding boxes. The pupils can add, improve or correct the text at this stage.
- The pupils swap roles.

**Odd one out activity**

**Which is the odd one out? Why?**
- The pupils complete the odd one out activity.

**Answers:** chapter (It isn't in newspaper reports.)

### Ending the lesson

**Review the lesson and reflect on learning.**
- Say **Today we've written a newspaper report.**
- Ask **Which was your favourite activity today? Which activity was easy / difficult?**

### Extra activity

**Reinforcement**
- Ask the pupils to copy their corrected newspaper reports onto a piece of paper. Collect them and stick them onto sheets of A3 paper to make a class newspaper. The pupils choose a name for their newspaper and write the title, date and price on the front page.
- Alternatively, ask the class to use a word processing programme to write their newspaper articles and then send the electronic version to you.

### Key Competences and Key Learning Outcomes

- Listen to and have a conversation about pets

LEARN
- Listen to a text for general understanding
- Listen to a text and identify language for making choices and giving opinions
- Review learning and reflect on progress in the unit

### Key language

- *boring, exercise, friendly, fun, puppy, striped, take (them) for a walk, tropical fish*
- *Did you have a pet when you were small, Eva? What were they like? What do you think? Do you agree? How do you feel about that?*

### Materials

- Pupil's Book p58; Activity Book p55 and 56; Class CD2; Teacher's App on Navio
- Teacher's Resource Bank: Talk cards (optional)

### Optional materials

- Teacher's Resource Bank: Trinity Exams Practice cards (selected from the Starter Unit and Units 1, 2, 3 and 4)

## At a Glance Lesson Plan

### Pupil's Book

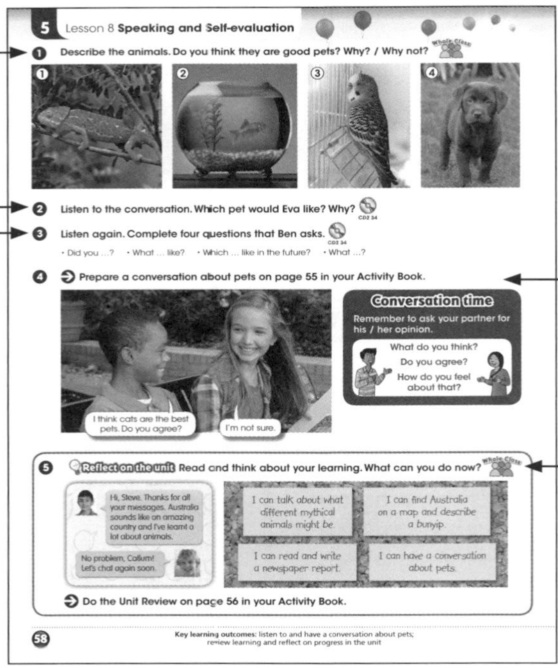

**Starting the lesson**
- Use the Trinity Exams Practice cards (optional).
- Review parts of an animal's body.
- Set learning objectives.

**Activity 1**
- Describe the animals.
- Do you think they are good pets? Why? / Why not?

**Activity 2**
- Listen to the conversation.
- ▶ *CD2 Track 34 p286*
- Which pet would Eva like?

**Activity 3**
- Listen again.
- ▶ *CD2 Track 34 p286*
- Complete four questions that Ben asks.

**Activity 4**
- Prepare a conversation about your pets on page 55 in your Activity book.

Go to page 55 in the Activity Book.

**Activity 5**
- Read and think about your learning. What can you do now?

Go to page 56 in the Activity Book.

**Ending the lesson**
- Review the lesson and reflect on learning.

**Extra activity**
- A class discussion about wild animals and pets.

### Activity Book

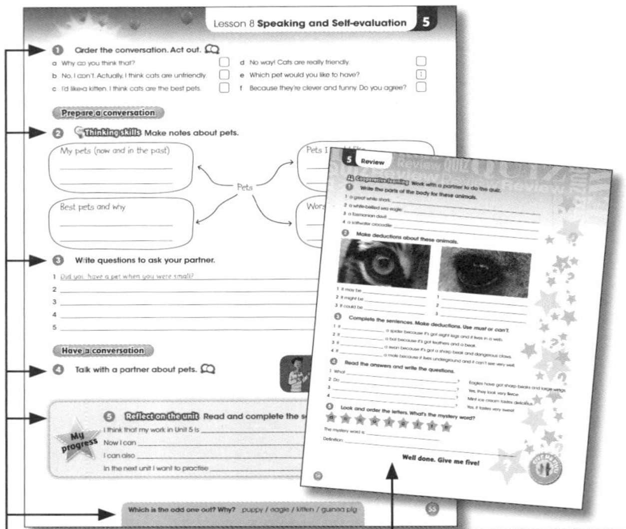

**Activity Book page 56: Review**
- Work with a partner to do the quiz.

**Activity Book**

**Activity 1**
- Order the conversation.
- Act out.

**Activity 2**
- Make notes about pets.

**Activity 3**
- Write questions to ask your partner.

**Activity 4**
- Talk with a partner about pets.

**Activity 5**
- Read and complete the sentences.

**Odd one out activity**
- Which is the odd one out? Why?

### Digital resources

**Teacher's Digital:** You can also teach this lesson using the Teacher's App on Navio.

Powered By NAVIO

# Detailed Lesson Plan

**Starting the lesson**

**Use the Trinity Exams Practice cards (optional).**
- The pupils practise asking and answering questions.

**Review parts of an animal's body.**
- Think of an animal, and describe it by saying **It's got (whiskers and a tail). It hasn't got (scales).** Pupils guess the animal. Then pupils repeat the activity in pairs.

**Set learning objectives.**
- Say **Today we're going to prepare a conversation about pets.**

**Pupil's Book Activity 1**

**Describe the animals. Do you think they are good pets? Why? / Why not?**
- Ask different pupils to describe the objects. Ask if any pupils have these pets, and if they are good pets. Ask if any pupils have different pets, if they are good pets, and why / why not.

**Pupil's Book Activity 2**

**Listen to the conversation. Which pet would Eva like?**

▶ *CD2 Track 34 p286*
- Play the CD. Ask pupils which pets Eva had in the past (*tropical fish*), and if she would like some more now (*no, they're a bit boring*).

**Answer:** Eva would like 4.

**Pupil's Book Activity 3**

**Listen again. Complete four questions that Ben asks.**

▶ *CD2 Track 34 p286*
- Pupils look at Activity 3. They think of the questions Ben asked.
- Play the CD. Pupils check in pairs. Then play again and check as a class.

**Answers:** Did you have a pet when you were small, Eva?; What were they like?; Which pet would you like in the future?; What do they need?

**Pupil's Book Activity 4**

**Prepare a conversation about your favourite object on page 55 in your Activity Book.**
- Read the speech bubbles with the pupils. Model the phrases in the Conversation Time box and get the class to repeat.

**Pupil's Book Activity 5**

**Read and think about your learning. What can you do now?**
- Read the speech bubbles and notes with the pupils. Then look back through the unit and prompt them to identify things that they have done/learnt.

**Activity Book page 56: Review**

**Work with a partner to do the quiz.**
- Organise the class into pairs. Set a time limit for the pupils to do the quiz (10–15 minutes). Stress that the pupils are not competing with each other.
- Read out the five tasks. Check understanding. Then say **Ready, steady … Go!**
- The pupils work in their pairs to do the quiz.
- Correct the answers as a class.

**Answers: 3 1** must be **2** can't be **3** can't be **4** must be **4 1** do eagles look like? **2** they look very fierce? **3** What does mint ice cream taste like? **4** Does it taste sweet? **5** crocodile, a reptile

**Activity Book**

**Activity 1**

**Order the conversation. Act out.**
- Ask pupils to find the second line in the conversation (c). Then in pairs, pupils order the rest the conversation and act it out.

**Answers:** **1** e **2** c **3** a **4** f **5** b **6** d

**Activity 2**

**Make notes about pets.**
- Tell pupils about your pets and your opinions on them. Then pupils work alone to complete the boxes with their own information.

**Activity 3**

**Write questions to ask your partner.**
- Direct pupils to the five headings in Activity 2 and explain that they need to form questions about them. Elicit the second question. Then pupils complete the questions alone. Check as a class.

**Answers:** **1** Did you have a pet when you were small? **2** Do you have a pet now? **3** Which pets do you think are best? Why? **4** Which pets would you like? **5** Which pets do you think are worst? Why?

**Activity 4**

**Talk with a partner about pets.**
- In pairs, pupils ask and answer the questions from Activity 3.
- Invite one or two pairs to perform their conversations for the class.

**Activity 5**

**Read and complete the sentences.**
- Pupils work alone to review their work in the unit.

**Odd one out activity**

**Which is the odd one out? Why?**

**Answer:** eagle (it isn't a pet)

**Ending the lesson**

**Review the lesson and reflect on learning.**
- Say **Today we've learnt how to have a conversation about pets.**
- Ask **Which was your favourite activity today? Which activity was easy / difficult?**

## Key Competences and Key Learning Outcomes

- Watch and understand a video about animals that are in danger
- Learn about the habitat and diet of the koala
- Think about the importance of helping to protect endangered species

### Key language

- *cut down, eucalyptus, forest, gas, habitat, koala, joey, leaves, marsupial, power station*
- *The house sparrow is in danger because of urbanisation. We can help by making nestboxes.*

### Materials

- Pupil's Book p59; Activity Book p57; Class CD2; Teacher's App on Navio
- Teacher's Resource Bank: Talk cards

### Optional materials

- Teacher's Resource Bank: Trinity Exams Practice cards (selected from the Starter Unit and Units 1–4)

# At a Glance Lesson Plan

## Pupil's Book

### Starting the lesson

- Use the Trinity Exams Practice cards (optional).
- **Think-Pair-Share** Review animal body part words.
- Set learning objectives and use the talk cards.

### Activity 1

- Before you watch
- Watch the video.
  ▶ *Unit 5 video p302*
- Read and answer the questions.

### Activity 2

- Watch the video again.
  ▶ *Unit 5 video*
- What are these things?
- Why are they important?

### Activity 3

- Read, think and answer.

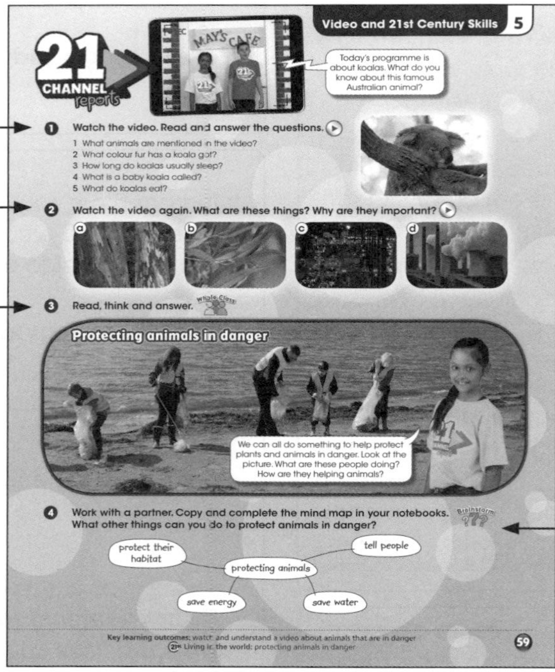


### Activity 4

- Work with a partner.
- Copy and complete the mind map in your notebooks.
- What other things can you do to protect animals in danger?

Go to the Activity Book

### Ending the lesson

- Review the lesson and reflect on learning.

### Extra activity

- Play a guessing game to review vocabulary about animals.

## Activity Book

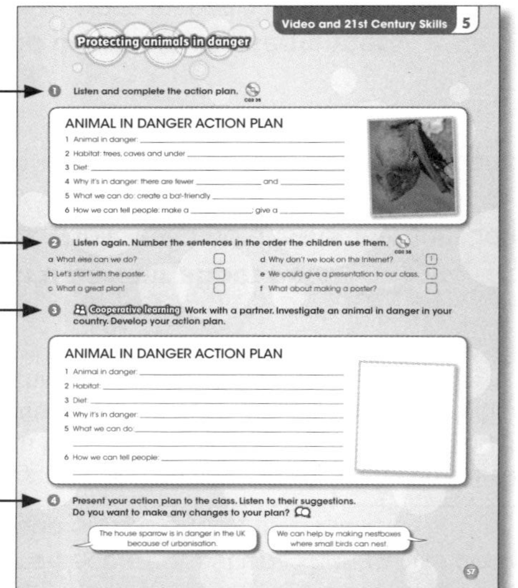


### Activity Book

**Activity 1**

- Listen and complete the action plan.

▶ *CD2 Track 35 p286*

**Activity 2**

- Listen again.
- Number the sentences in the order the children use them.

▶ *CD2 Track 35 p286*

**Activity 3**

- Work with a partner.
- Investigate an animal in danger in your country.
- Develop your action plan.

**Activity 4**

- Present your action plan to the class.
- Listen to their suggestions.
- Do you want to make any changes to your plan?

## Digital resources

**Teacher's Digital:** You can also teach this lesson using the Teacher's App on Navio.

**Pupil's Digital:** Encourage your pupils to use the Pupil's App on Navio to practise the activities from this lesson.

Powered By NAVIO

# Detailed Lesson Plan

### Starting the lesson

**Use the Trinity Exams Practice cards (optional).**

- The pupils practise asking and answering questions.

**Think-Pair-Share Review words for animal body parts.**

- Ask **How many different animal body parts can you think of?** The class thinks silently for a minute.
- Then the pupils work with a Talk Partner to name animal body parts.
- Invite different Talk Partners to say a different animal body part. Hold up the corresponding flashcard and prompt the class to repeat the word.
- Finally, repeat the procedure, asking different pairs of Talk Partners each time, until all the ideas have been recorded.

**Set learning objectives and use the talk cards.**

- Say **Today we're going to watch a video and then ask and answer questions about an endangered animal.**
- Point to the talk cards to show the pupils the different ways they will be working in the lesson.

### Pupil's Book Activity 1

**Before you watch**

- Read the speech bubble to pupils. Ask **What do you know about koalas?**

**Watch the video. Read and answer the questions.**
*p302*

- Watch Part 1 of the video. Ask pupils **What are you going to see next?**
- Play Part 2 of the video. Ask general questions to check understanding. Direct pupils to look at the sentences 1–5. Ask if they can remember any of the answers before they watch again.
- Play the video again and check answers.

**Answers:** **1** Blue whales, mountain gorillas, koalas **2** grey and cream **3** about 18 hours a day **4** a joey **5** leaves from the eucalyptus tree

### Pupil's Book Activity 2

**Watch the video again. What are these things? Why are they important?**

- Ask a pupil **What can you see in picture a?** (a eucalyptus tree) Ask a different pupil **Why is it important?** (Koalas have long claws and they can climb eucalyptus trees.) Repeat with pictures b–d.

**Answers:** **1a** A Eucalyptus tree. Koalas have long claws for climbing trees. **b** Eucalyptus leaves. Koalas need to eat a lot of these. **c** A city in Australia. The forests where koalas live are disappearing because humans cut down the trees to build roads. **d** A power station. The gas from power stations can harm eucalyptus trees.

### Pupil's Book Activity 3

**Read, think and answer.**

- Read the speech bubble with the class. Then direct pupils to the photo and ask them to discuss the two questions in the speech bubble in pairs. Ask them an additional question **Which animals are the people helping?**

### Pupil's Book Activity 4

**Work with a partner. Copy and complete the mind map in your notebooks. What other things can you do to protect animals in danger?**

- Ask pupils what dangers the koala faces (*humans are destroying its habitat and food*).
- In pairs, pupils think of as many ways as possible to protect koalas and other animals.

### Activity Book

**Activity 1**

**Listen and complete the action plan.**

▸ *CD2 Track 35 p286*

- Ask pupils what animal they can see in the photo (*a bat*). Ask a pupil to give a fact about bats.
- Read through the action plan and check pupils understand what information they need.
- Play the CD and check answers.

**Answers:** **1** bat **2** bridges **3** insects **4** trees; insects **5** garden **6** poster; presentation

**Activity 2**

**Listen again. Number the sentences in the order the children use them.**

▸ *CD2 Track 35 p286*

**Answers:** **1** d **2** f **3** a **4** e **5** b **6** c

- Ask the pupils which of the ideas they prefer.

**Activity 3**

**Work with a partner. Investigate an animal in danger in your country. Develop your action plan.**

- Ask pupils if they know any animals in danger in their country. Each pair chooses an animal.
- Pupils work in pairs to research the information to complete their action plan.

**Activity 4**

**Present your action plan to the class. Listen to their suggestions. Do you want to make any changes to your plan?**

- Invite a pair to the front of the class to present their action plan. Alternatively, the pairs could present their action plan to another pair or a small group.

### Ending the lesson

**Review the lesson and reflect on learning.**

- Say **Today we've watched a video about an endangered animal. What have we learnt about protecting animals?** Elicit ideas from the pupils.
- Ask **Which was your favourite activity today? Which activity was easy / difficult?**

Date: ______________________ Unit: __________

1 What did my pupils learn in this unit?

2 How did my pupils work? (✓)

individually ☐ in pairs ☐ in small groups ☐

in large groups ☐ as a class ☐

3 Which key competences did my pupils develop? Give a score from 1 to 5 (5 being the highest).

- Competence in linguistic communication ☐
- Competence in mathematics, science and technology ☐
- Digital competence ☐
- Learning to learn ☐
- Social and civic competences ☐
- Sense of initiative and entrepreneurship ☐
- Cultural awareness and expression ☐

4 Which lessons / activities were the most successful and why?

5 Which lessons / activities did my pupils find the most difficult and why?

6 What did I try in the classroom for the first time? How did it go?

7 Which resources did I find most useful? (including webpages)

8 What could I do differently next time I teach this unit?

# Unit 6 Entertainment

## Unit overview

### Key Competences and Key Learning Outcomes

- Review and learn words associated with different forms of entertainment (Lesson 1)
- Talk about past experiences using the present perfect simple (Lesson 2)
- Learn how to use the present perfect simple with regular and irregular verbs (Lesson 4)
- Learn expressions for making art and entertainment (Lesson 5)
- Learn about onomatopoeic words (Lesson 7)
- Watch and understand a video about art (Video and 21st Century Skills)

- Use a mind map to brainstorm ideas (Video and 21st Century Skills)

- Use the Pupil's App on Navio
- Investigate Uganda (Lesson 3)

- Identify and practise the weak sound 'e' in past participles (Lesson 4)
- Practise activity types found in the Cambridge Exams: A2 Key for Schools

- Think about the importance of music in bringing the world together (Lesson 3)
- Prepare and carry out a conversation about a topic (Lesson 8)

- Work in pairs and small groups to practise and reinforce learning (all lessons)
- Think about activities and products for a talent day (Video and 21st Century Skills)

- Read and understand a story (Lesson 3)
- Learn about Uganda and the African Children's Choir (Lesson 3)
- Write two haikus (Lesson 7)
- Sing a song (Lesson 8)

### Vocabulary

**Core vocabulary**
*3D film, art exhibition, ballet, circus, classical music concert, comedy show, dance show, magazines, play, poems, pop concert, sculpture; act in a play, create a comic, compose music, juggle, make a film, make a sculpture, paint a portrait, play in an orchestra, sing in a choir, write a poem*

**Extension vocabulary (optional)**
*audience, face painting, juggling, live music, performance; dance in a dance troupe, direct a play, perform in a show, play in a band*

**Other vocabulary**
*lines, onomatopoeic, rhyme, rhythm, sound, syllable, verse; bow, cello, clarinet, cymbals, double bass, drums, drumsticks, flute, French horn, orchestra, violin; arts festival, drumming, poetry competition, wall painting, walk the tightrope, workshop; art gallery, cartoon, chalk, colour in, playground, talent day*

**Recycled vocabulary**
*been, bought, broken, decided, eaten, given, made, ridden, seen, sung, taken, went, written; bigger, deep, deeper, loudly, low, pretty, sad, slow, sweet; adventure / action / comedy films, cinema, environment, film director, nature, painting, restaurant, TV, zoo*

### Structures

**Core structures**
*I / You / We / They have / haven't been to a play. He / She / It has / hasn't been to a play. Have I / you / we / they (ever) been to a play? Has he / she / it (ever) been to a play? Yes, I / you / we / they have. No, I / you / we / they haven't. Yes, he / she / it has. No, he / she / it hasn't. I / You / We / They have / haven't listened to the song. He / She / It has / hasn't bought a concert ticket. Has he / she / it (ever) been to the circus? Yes, he / she / it has. No, he / she / it hasn't.*

**Recycled structures**
*I like films. I've made films with my friend, Ben. Can you repeat the question, please? Let's (watch an outdoor 3D film).*

### Pronunciation

The weak sound 'e' in past participles

### Literacy

**Text type:** a poem (text to express; writing preparation)
**Reading skill:** reading with rhythm
**Writing skill:** onomatopoeic words

### Culture … around the world

The creation of the African Children's Choir in Uganda

### 21st Century Skills

**Ways of thinking:** being creative and original

### Thinking skills

Categorising (Lesson 1); Analysing and applying rules (Lessons 2 and 4); Predicting (Lesson 2); Hypothesising (Lesson 3); Logical thinking (Lesson 5); Defining and describing (Lesson 5); Finding information (Lesson 6); Planning, checking and correcting (Lesson 7); Seeing another's point of view (Lesson 8); Reflecting on learning (Lesson 8)

### Cooperative learning

Working together (Lessons 1–8); Collaborating (Lessons 1–8); Checking learning (Lessons 1–8); Peer evaluation and feedback (Lesson 7); Participating (Lessons 1–8); Helping and encouraging (Lessons 1–8); Reflecting and setting goals (Lesson 8)

### Values

How music helps people and how it makes you feel

### Cross-curricular links

**Link to Science**
Urban and rural populations

**Suggested Arts and Crafts concepts**
Shade and shadow

### Key Competences and Key Learning Outcomes

- Identify and say words associated with different forms of entertainment
- Listen to definitions and identify the words
- Talk about activities you prefer doing
- Read a message about an arts festival

**Key language**

- *3D film, art exhibition, ballet, circus, classical music concert, comedy show, dance show, magazines, play, poems, pop concert, sculpture; arts festival, drumming, wall painting, walk the tightrope, workshop*
- *I like films. Let's (watch the outdoor 3D film). I prefer art to films.*
- **Extension:** *audience, face painting, juggling, live music, performance*

**Materials**

- Pupil's Book pp60–61; Activity Book p58; Class CD2; Teacher's App on Navio
- Entertainment flashcards

**Optional materials**

- Teacher's Resource Bank: Trinity Exams Practice cards (selected from the Starter Unit and Units 1, 2, 3, 4 and 5)

## At a Glance Lesson Plan

### Pupil's Book

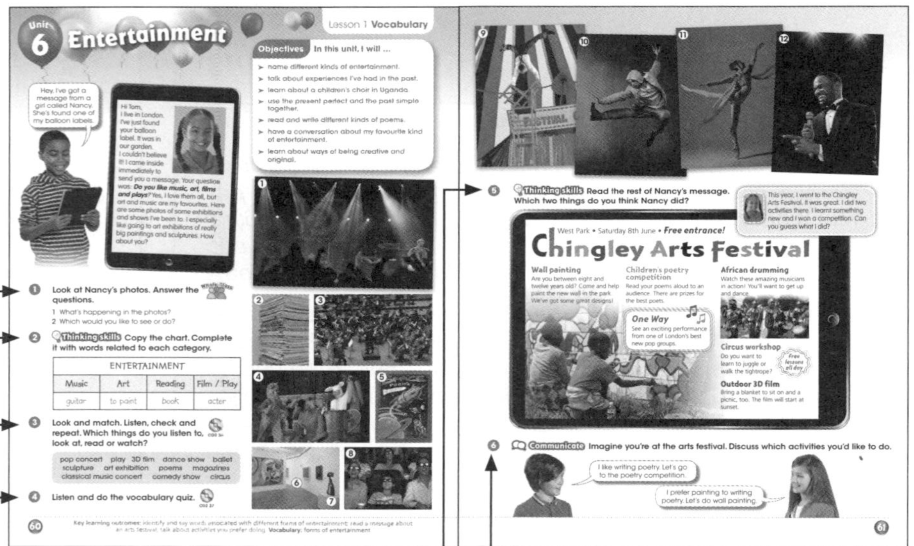


**Starting the lesson**
- Use the Trinity Exams Practice cards (optional).
- Review festivals.
- Set learning objectives.

**Activity 1**
- Look at Nancy's photos.
- Answer the questions.

**Activity 2**
- Copy the chart.
- Complete it with words related to each category.

**Vocabulary presentation**
- Present the new vocabulary using the entertainment flashcards.

**Activity 3**
- Look and match.
- Listen, check and repeat.

▶ *CD2 Track 36 p286*
- Which things do you listen to, look at, read or watch?

**Activity 4**
- Listen and do the vocabulary quiz.

▶ *CD2 Track 37 p286*

**Activity 5**
- Read the rest of Nancy's message.
- Which two things do you think Nancy did?

**Activity 6**
- Imagine you're at the arts festival.
- Discuss which activities you'd like to do.

Go to the Activity Book.

**Ending the lesson**
- Review the lesson and reflect on learning.

**Extra activities**

**Extension**
- Find out about the United Kingdom.

**Vocabulary extension**
- Present five additional vocabulary items.

**Digital resources**

**Teacher's Digital:** You can also teach this lesson using the Teacher's App on Navio.

**Pupil's Digital:** Encourage your pupils to use the Pupil's App on Navio to practise the activities from this lesson.

Powered By NAVIO

### Activity Book

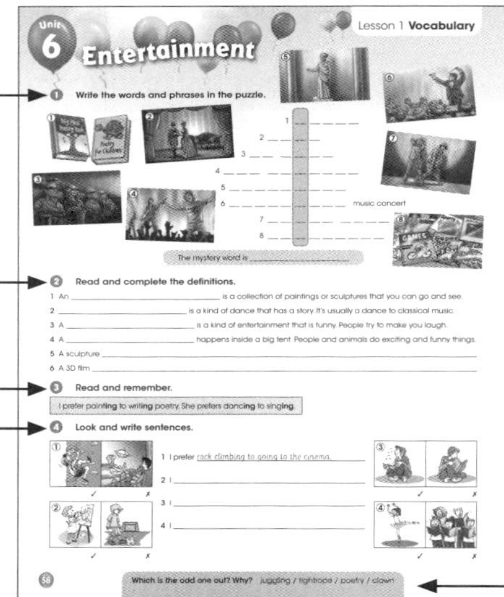


**Activity Book**

**Activity 1**
- Write the words and phrases in the puzzle.

**Activity 2**
- Read and complete the definitions.

**Activity 3**
- Read and remember.

**Activity 4**
- Look and write sentences.

**Odd one out activity**
- Which is the odd one out? Why?

# Detailed Lesson Plan

**Starting the lesson**

**Use the Trinity Exams Practice cards (optional).**
- The pupils practise asking and answering questions.

**Review festivals.**
- Ask **What's a festival?** There can be many different kinds – elicit *music, book, dance, film*. Talk about *Carnival* too.

**Set learning objectives.**
- Say **Today we're going to remember and learn the names of words about entertainment.**

**Pupil's Book Activity 1**

**Look at Nancy's photos. Answer the questions.**
- Invite a pupil to read out the speech bubble to find out who has found the label. Ask **Do you know where London is?**
- Invite a pupil to read out the message.
- Work as a class to answer the questions.

**Answers:** **1** **1** pop concert **2** magazines **3** classical music concert **4** play **5** poems **6** art exhibition **7** sculpture **8** 3D film **9** circus **10** dance show **11** ballet **12** comedy show

**Pupil's Book Activity 2**

**Copy the chart. Complete it with words related to each category.**
- Organise the class into pairs. The pupils copy the chart into their notebooks and write the words in the correct column.

**Vocabulary presentation**
- Present the new vocabulary using the entertainment flashcards. Show the first flashcard and elicit / say the word. Ask **Do you like (pop concerts)?** Note that we say *Do you like the circus?*

**Pupil's Book Activity 3**

**Look and match. Listen, check and repeat. Which things do you listen to, look at, read or watch?**
▸ ***CD2 Track 36 p286***
- Focus the class on item number 1 in the photo.
- Ask **What's this?** The pupils work in pairs to match numbers 2–12 and the words.
- Play the CD. The pupils listen and check.
- Play the CD again, pausing after each word for the pupils to repeat.

**Pupil's Book Activity 4**

**Listen and do the vocabulary quiz.**
▸ ***CD2 Track 37 p286***
- Play the CD. Listen to the first definition, pausing at the beeps to allow the pupils to name the item.
- Repeat the procedure with the other definitions.

**Pupil's Book Activity 5**

**Read the rest of Nancy's message. Which two things do you think Nancy did?**
- Ask **What festival did Nancy go to in the summer?**
- The pupils read the message about the festival. They work in pairs to decide on the two things that Nancy did. (*She learnt to juggle or wak the tightrope and she won a poetry competition.*)
- Ask questions to check understanding. Ask **How many days does the festival last?** (*One.*) **What's the name of the pop group who are playing?** (*One Way.*)

**Pupil's Book Activity 6**

**Imagine you're at the arts festival. Discuss which activities you'd like to do.**
- The pupils decide what they would like to do and why.
- Organise the class into pairs. The pupils agree three things they would like to do.

**Activity Book**

**Activity 1**

**Write the words and phrases in the puzzle.**
- The pupils look at the pictures and write the words. They then work out the mystery word.

**Answers:** **1** poems **2** play **3** 3D film **4** pop concert **5** sculpture **6** classical **7** dance show **8** magazines
The mystery word is painting.

**Activity 2**

**Read and complete the definitions.**
- The pupils complete the definitions.

**Answers:** **1** art exhibition **2** Ballet **3** comedy show **4** circus

**Activity 3**

**Read and remember the grammar in the lesson.**
- Invite a pupil to read out the information. Focus the pupils' attention on the use of 'to' when you compare your preference for two things.

**Activity 4**

**Look and write sentences.**
- The pupils complete the sentences according to the pictures.

**Answers:** **1** I prefer rock climbing to going to the cinema. **2** I prefer painting to playing football. **3** I prefer listening to music to reading. **4** I prefer dancing to singing.

**Odd one out activity**

**Which is the odd one out? Why?**
- The pupils complete the odd one out activity.

**Answers:** poetry (You don't see is at the circus.)

**Ending the lesson**

**Review the lesson and reflect on learning.**
- Say **Today we've learnt the words for different kinds of entertainment. What do you remember?** Elicit the words from the pupils.

**Extra activities**

**Extension**
- The pupils find the United Kingdom on the world map on pages 134–135. They read the accompanying facts.

**Vocabulary extension**
- Present five additional entertainment words: *audience, face painting, juggling, live music, performance.*
- Use the Vocabulary booster on NAVIO to practise these new words.

## Key Competences and Key Learning Outcomes

- Listen to and read a dialogue
- Use the present perfect to talk about past experiences
- Practise activity types found in the Cambridge Exams: A2 Key for Schools
- Ask and answer questions using 'Have you been ...?'

**Key language**

- *arts festival, classical music, choir, play, poetry competition, pop concert*
- *I / You / We / They have / haven't been to a play. He / She / It has / hasn't been to a play. Have I / you / we / they (ever) been to a play? Has he / she / it (ever) been to a play? Yes, I / you / we / they have. No, I / you / we / they haven't. Yes, he / she / it has. No, he / she / it hasn't.*

**Materials**

- Pupil's Book p62; Activity Book p59; Class CD2; Teacher's App on Navio
- Teacher's Resource Bank: Entertainment word cards

**Optional materials**

- Teacher's Resource Bank: Trinity Exams Practice cards (selected from the Starter Unit and Units 1, 2, 3, 4 and 5)

## At a Glance Lesson Plan

### Pupil's Book

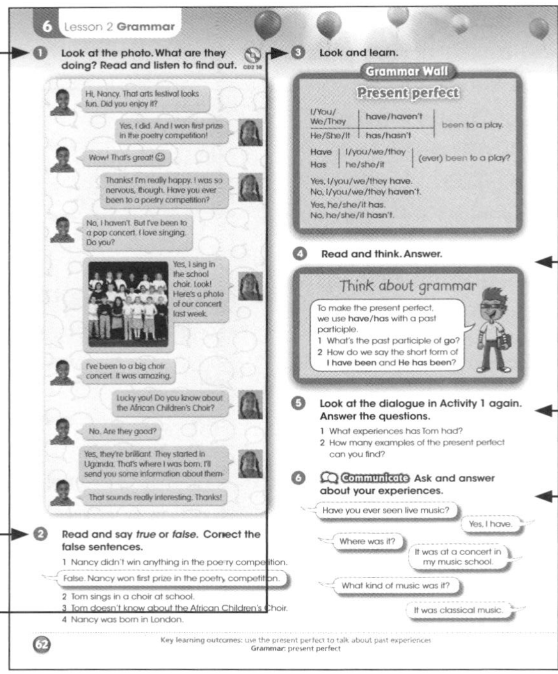

**Starting the lesson**

- Use the Trinity Exams Practice cards (optional).
- Review entertainment vocabulary.
- Set learning objectives.

**Activity 1**

- Look at the photo.
- What are they doing?
- Read and listen to find out.

▶ *CD2 Track 38 p287*

**Activity 2**

- Read and say *true* or *false*.
- Correct the false sentences.

**Activity 3**

- Look and learn – Grammar wall

**Activity 4**

- Read and think.
- Answer.

**Activity 5**

- Look at the dialogue in Activity 1 again.
- Answer the questions.

**Activity 6**

- Ask and answer about your experiences.

Go to the Activity Book.

**Ending the lesson**

- Review the lesson and reflect on learning.

**Extra activity**

**Reinforcement**

- Form a question chain.

### Activity Book

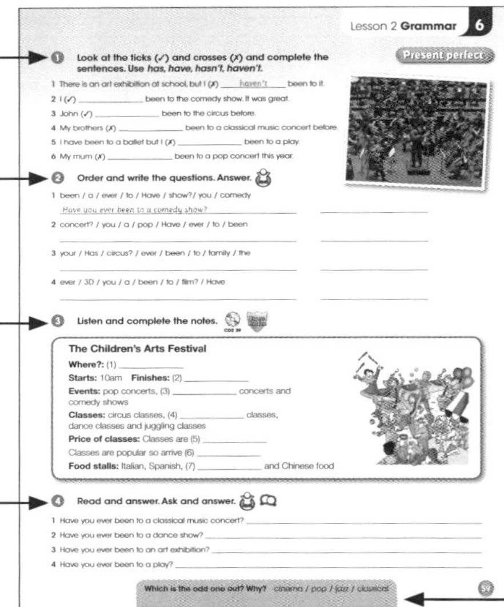

**Activity Book**

**Activity 1**

- Look at the ticks (✓) and crosses (✗) and complete the sentences. Use *has, have, hasn't, haven't.*

**Activity 2**

- Order and write the questions. Answer

**Activity 3**

- Listen and complete the notes.

▶ *CD2 Track 39 p287*

**Activity 4**

- Read and answer. Ask and answer.

**Odd one out activity**

- Which is the odd one out? Why?

**Digital resources**

**Teacher's Digital:** You can also teach this lesson using the Teacher's App on Navio.

**Pupil's Digital:** Encourage your pupils to use the Pupil's App on Navio to practise the activities from this lesson.

Powered By NAVIO

# Detailed Lesson Plan

**Starting the lesson**

**Review entertainment words.**

- Play the *Mime the card* game (see p27) with the entertainment word cards.

**Set learning objectives.**

- Say **Today we're going to learn how to talk about places we have been to using the present perfect tense.**

**Pupil's Book Activity 1**

**Look at the photo. What are they doing? Read and listen to find out.**

▶ *CD2 Track 38 p287*

- Prompt the class to describe what they can see in the photo. Ask **Where are they? What are they doing?**
- Play the CD. The pupils listen and read the dialogue. (*They are singing in a choir.*)

**Pupil's Book Activity 2**

**Read and say *true* or *false*. Correct the false sentences.**

- Organise the class into pairs. The pupils decide if the sentences are true or false. They correct the false sentences in their notebooks.

**Pupil's Book Activity 3**

**Look and learn – Grammar wall**

- Read the information on the Grammar wall as a class.
- Encourage the pupils to think about form and identify / remember patterns. Ask **Can you see the two parts of the present perfect tense? Which verb is first? What changes when we use 'he / she / it'? Where do we put 'ever'?**
- Explain that 'been' is a past participle of a verb and that they will learn more of these in the next few lessons. 'Been' is the past participle of 'go'.

**Pupil's Book Activity 4**

**Read and think. Answer.**

- Focus the pupils' attention on the Think about grammar box. Read out the sentences as a class. The pupils complete the sentences in their pairs.

**Answers:** **1** gone **2** I've been / He's been

**Pupil's Book Activity 5**

**Look at the dialogue in Activity 1 again. Answer the questions.**

- The pupils answer the two questions.

**Pupil's Book Activity 6**

**Ask and answer about your experiences.**

- Organise the class into pairs. The pupils ask and answer questions about their experiences.

**Activity Book**

**Activity 1**

**Look at the ticks (✓) and crosses (✗) and complete the sentences. Use *has, have, hasn't, haven't.***

- Read out the first sentence. Prompt the class to identify the correct form of 'have'. Point out that the crosses and ticks show if the sentence is affirmative or negative.
- The pupils complete the sentences.

**Answers:** **1** haven't **2** have **3** has **4** haven't **5** haven't **6** hasn't

**Activity 2**

**Order and write the questions. Answer.**

- The pupils order the words to make a question. They then write answers about themselves.

**Answers:** **1** Have you ever been to a comedy show? **2** Have you ever been to a pop concert? **3** Has your family ever been to the circus? **4** Have you ever been to a 3D film?

**Activity 3**

**Listen and complete the notes.**

▶ ***CD2 Track 39 p287***

- The pupils look at the picture and say what is happening.
- Ask the class to read the notes. Then play the CD. The pupils listen and follow the information in their books.
- Play the CD again, pausing after each piece of key information. The pupils write the missing information each time.

**Answers:** **1** London **2** 9pm **3** orchestra / classical **4** singing **5** free **6** early **7** Mexican

**Activity 4**

**Read and answer. Ask and answer.**

- Organise the class into pairs. The pupils ask and answer questions.

**Odd one out activity**

**Which is the odd one out? Why?**

- The pupils complete the odd one out activity.

**Answers:** cinema (It isn't music.)

**Ending the lesson**

**Review the lesson and reflect on learning.**

- Say **Today we've learnt how to talk about experiences.** Elicit sentences using 'I've been' from the pupils.
- Ask **Which was your favourite activity today? Which activity was easy / difficult?**

**Extra activity**

**Reinforcement**

- Ask 'Have you ever been' questions as a chain around the class.

### Key Competences and Key Learning Outcomes

- Read a story with a cultural focus
- Use the Internet to investigate Uganda
- Listen for specific information
- Practise activity types found in the Cambridge Exams: A2 Key for Schools
- Think about the importance of music in bringing the world together
- Learn about the African Children's Choir

### Key language

- *awards, choir, concerts, decided, drove, fan, poor, sang, war, went*
- *I've seen the choir four times. Thanks for helping us.*

### Materials

- Pupil's Book p63; Activity Book p60; Class CD2 and CD3; Teacher's App on Navio

### Optional materials

- Teacher's Resource Bank: Trinity Exams Practice cards (selected from the Starter Unit and Units 1, 2, 3, 4 and 5)
- Music extracts

## At a Glance Lesson Plan

### Starting the lesson

- Use the Trinity Exams Practice cards (optional).
- Review kinds of music.
- Set learning objectives.

### Activity 1: Before you read

- Read and discuss.

### Activity 2

- Listen and read
- ▶ *CD2 Track 40 p287*
- Go to the Activity Book.

### Values

Read and discuss.

## Pupil's Book

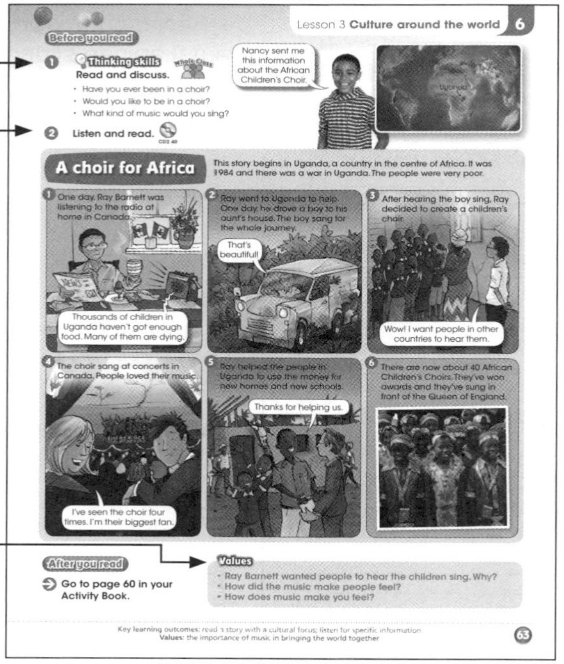

### Ending the lesson

- Review the lesson and reflect on learning.

### Extra activities

**Extension**

- Find out about music from different countries.
- Listen to music.

## Activity Book

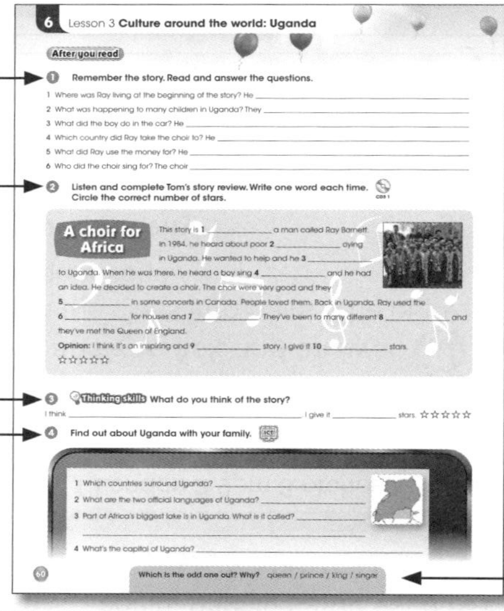

### Activity Book: After you read

**Activity 1**

- Remember the story. Read and answer the questions.

**Activity 2**

- Listen and complete Tom's story review.
- ▶ *CD3 Track 1 p287*
- Write one word each time. Circle the correct number of stars

**Activity 3**

- What do you think of the story?

**Activity 4**

- Find out about Uganda with your family.

**Odd one out activity**

- Which is the odd one out? Why?

### Digital resources

**Teacher's Digital:** You can also teach this lesson using the Teacher's App on Navio.

**Pupil's Digital:** Encourage your pupils to use the Pupil's App on Navio to practise the activities from this lesson.

Powered By NAVIO

# Detailed Lesson Plan

## Starting the lesson

**Review kinds of music.**

- Discuss different kinds of music with the class. Ask the pupils to tell you different kinds of music along with some examples. Ask **What's your favourite kind of music?**

**Set learning objectives.**

- Say **Today we're going to read a story about Uganda. We're going to find out about a children's choir.**

## Pupil's Book Activity 1: Before you read

**Read and discuss.**

- Ask the class to look at the pictures. Ask **What can you see?**
- Remind the pupils that a choir is a group of people who sing together. Note the spelling of the word.
- Look at the questions. Ask the pupils to answer the questions in pairs.

## Pupil's Book Activity 2

**Listen and read.**

▶ *CD2 Track 40 p287*

- Look at the photo at the end of the story. Ask **What do you see?**
- Play the CD. The pupils follow in their books.
- Ask questions to check understanding.

**Suggested comprehension questions:**

- Frame 1: **Why did Ray Barnett decide to go to Uganda?** (*Thousands of children didn't have enough food.*)
- Frame 2: **Did he like the song that the boy sang?** (*Yes.*)
- Frame 3: **Why did he create a children's choir?** (*He wanted people in other countries to hear them.*)
- Frame 4: **Where did the choir sing concerts?** (*Canada.*)
- Frame 5: **What did Ray use the money for?** (*To build new homes and schools in Uganda.*)
- Frame 6: **Who have the choir sang for?** (*They've sung for the Queen of England.*)

## Activity Book: After you read

**Activity 1**

**Remember the story. Read and answer the questions.**

- Ask the pupils to read out the questions.
- The pupils work on their own to write the answers.

**Answers:** **1** was living in Canada. **2** were dying. **3** sang beautifully. **4** took the choir to Canada. **5** built new homes and schools. **6** sang for the Queen of England.

**Activity 2**

**Listen and complete Tom's story review. Write one word each time. Circle the correct number of stars.**

▶ *CD3 Track 1 p287*

- Read out the story review as a class. Ask the pupils to guess the missing words.
- Play the CD without pausing. The pupils listen and complete as much of the information as possible.
- Play the CD again, pausing after each piece of key information to check the information and spelling.

**Answers:** **1** about **2** children **3** flew / went **4** beautifully **5** sang **6** money **7** schools **8** countries **9** happy **10** four

**Activity 3**

**What do you think of the story?**

- The pupils write their opinion and give a rating.
- Invite different pupils to share their opinions with the class.

**Activity 4**

**Find out about Uganda with your family.** ICT

- Read out the questions about Uganda. Ask **Where can you find out this information?** (*Internet, library, asking friends and family.*) The pupils complete the activity at home.
- If you prefer to do this activity in the class, connect to a children's website which has information about Uganda such as: www.timeforkids.com/destination/uganda or http://travel.nationalgeographic.co.uk/travel/countries/uganda-facts/. Read out the questions. The pupils work as a class to find and write the answers.

**Answers:** **1** Sudan, Democratic Republic of the Congo, Kenya, Rwanda, Tanzania **2** English and Luganda **3** Lake Victoria **4** Kampala

**Odd one out activity**

**Which is the odd one out? Why?**

- The pupils complete the odd one out activity.

**Answers:** singer (It isn't royalty.)

## Values

**Read and discuss.**

- Read out the statement and the questions and discuss them as a class.
- Encourage the pupils to think about the special qualities of music and why people enjoy it so much.

## Ending the lesson

**Review the lesson and reflect on learning.**

- Say **Today we've read a story about Uganda.**
- Ask **Which was your favourite activity today? Which activity was easy / difficult?**

## Extra activities

**Extension**

- The pupils find out about music from another country. They present their findings to the class.
- Play music in class. Discuss what the pupils like or don't like about the music. Ask them to describe the music and name the instruments used.

**Key Competences and Key Learning Outcomes**

- Act out a short dialogue in pairs
- Learn how to use the present perfect simple with regular and irregular verbs
- Use the present perfect simple and past simple together
- Identify and practise weak 'e' sound in past participles

**Key language**

- *been, bought, broken, eaten, given, made, ridden, seen, sung, taken, written*
- *I / You / We / They have / haven't listened to the song. He / She / It has / hasn't bought a concert ticket. Has he / she / it (ever) been to the circus? Yes, he / she / it has. No, he / she / it hasn't.*

**Materials**

- Pupil's Book p64; Activity Book p61; Class CD3; Teacher's App on Navio

**Optional materials**

- Teacher's Resource Bank: Trinity Exams Practice cards (selected from the Starter Unit and Units 1, 2, 3, 4 and 5)

## At a Glance Lesson Plan

### Pupil's Book

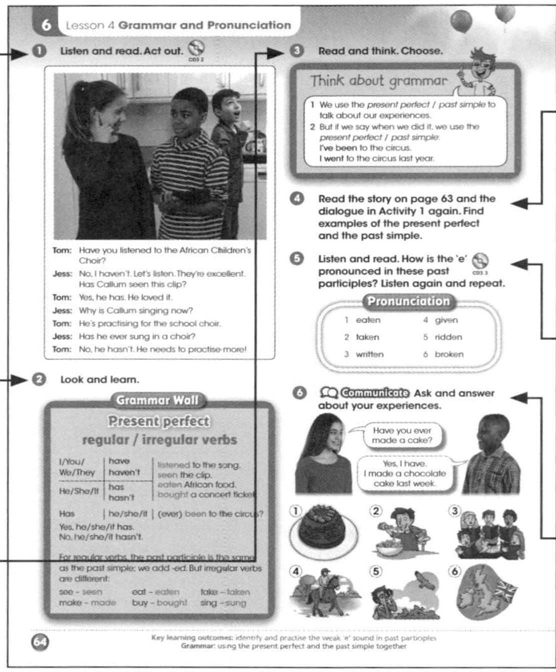

**Starting the lesson**

- Use the Trinity Exams Practice cards (optional).
- Review the story from Lesson 3.
- Set learning objectives.

**Activity 1**

- Listen and read.
- Act out.
- ▶ *CD3 Track 2 p287*

**Activity 2**

- Look and learn – Grammar wall

**Activity 3**

- Read and think.
- Choose.

**Activity 4**

- Read the story on page 63 and the dialogue in Activity 1 again.
- Find examples of the present perfect simple and the past simple.

**Activity 5**

- Listen and read.
- ▶ *CD3 Track 3 p288*
- How is the 'e' pronounced in these past participles?
- Listen again and repeat.

**Activity 6**

- Ask and answer about your experiences.

Go to the Activity Book.

**Ending the lesson**

- Review the lesson and reflect on learning.

**Extra activity**

**Reinforcement**

- Play a chain game.

### Digital resources

**Teacher's Digital:** You can also teach this lesson using the Teacher's App on Navio.

**Pupil's Digital:** Encourage your pupils to use the Pupil's App on Navio to practise the activities from this lesson.

Powered By NAVIO

### Activity Book

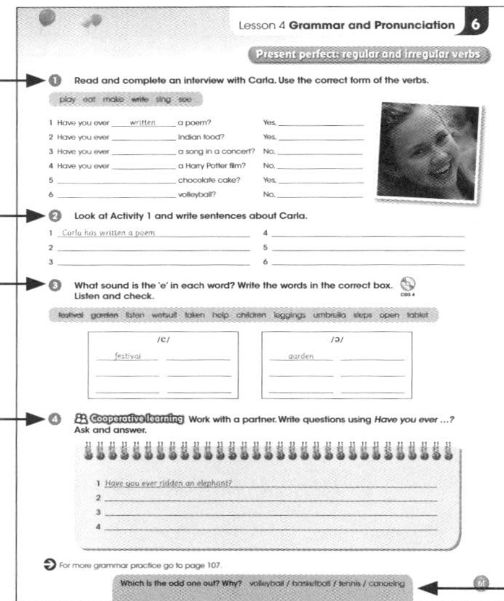

**Activity Book**

**Activity 1**

- Read and complete an interview with Carla. Use the correct form of the verbs.

**Activity 2**

- Look at Activity 1 and write sentences about Carla.

**Activity 3**

- What sound is the 'e' in each word?

Write the words in the correct box. Listen and check.

▶ *CD3 Track 4 p288*

**Activity 4**

- Work with a partner. Write some questions using *Have you ever…?* Ask and answer.

**Odd one out activity**

- Which is the odd one out? Why?

# Detailed Lesson Plan

**Starting the lesson**

**Use the Trinity Exams Practice cards (optional).**

- The pupils practise asking and answering questions.

**Review the story from Lesson 3.**

- Ask yes/no questions about the story from Lesson 3.

**Set learning objectives.**

- Say **Today we're going to learn how to use the present perfect simple with other verbs. We have used 'been' and 'seen'.**

**Pupil's Book Activity 1**

**Listen and read. Act out.**

▶ *CD3 Track 2 p287*

- The pupils look at the photo. Ask **What's Callum doing? Why do you think he's singing?**
- Play the CD. The pupils listen and read the dialogue.
- Play the CD again, pausing after each sentence for the pupils to repeat.
- The pupils practise the dialogue in pairs.

**Pupil's Book Activity 2**

**Look and learn – Grammar wall**

- Read the information on the Grammar wall as a class.
- Ask questions about the grammar. Ask **Which verb is the auxiliary verb?** (*Have.*) **Which verb is the past participle?** Point out that a regular verb is the same in the past simple as the past participle. Some irregular verbs have different past participles.

**Pupil's Book Activity 3**

**Read and think. Choose.**

- The pupils look at the Think about Grammar box. They decide which tense to choose for each sentence.

**Answers:** **1** present perfect **2** past simple

**Pupil's Book Activity 4**

**Read the story on page 63 and the dialogue in Activity 1 again. Find examples of the present perfect simple and the past simple.**

- The pupils find examples of the present perfect simple and the past simple tenses.

**Pupil's Book Activity 5**

**Listen and read. How is the 'e' pronounced in these past participles? Listen again and repeat.**

▶ *CD3 Track 3 p288*

- Write the letter 'e' on the board. Focus the pupils' attention on the words in the box.
- Play the CD. Confirm that the sound is a weak 'er' sound.
- Play the CD again. The pupils listen and repeat the words.

**Pupil's Book Activity 6**

**Ask and answer about your experiences.**

- The pupils ask and answer questions in pairs using the pictures.

**Activity Book**

**Activity 1**

**Read and complete an interview with Carla. Use the correct form of the verbs.**

- The pupils write the correct form of the verbs in the questions. They then complete the short answer too.

**Answers:** **1** written, I have **2** eaten / made, I have **3** sung, I haven't **4** seen, I haven't **5** Have you ever made / eaten, I have **6** Have you ever played, I haven't

**Activity 2**

**Look at Activity 1 and write sentences about Carla.**

- The pupils write sentences.

**Answers:** **1** Carla has written a poem. **2** Carla has eaten / made Indian food. **3** Carla hasn't sung in a concert. **4** Carla hasn't seen a Harry Potter film. **5** Carla has made / eaten a chocolate cake. **6** Carla hasn't played volleyball.

**Activity 3**

**What sound is the 'e' in each word? Write the words in the correct box. Listen and check.**

▶ *CD3 Track 4 p288*

- The pupils read the words and write them in the correct box. As an example, pronounce 'garden' and 'festival'. Invite the pupils to say these words too.
- Play the CD. The pupils write the words in the correct box.

**Answers:** **/e/** festival, wetsuit, help, leggings, umbrella, steps, tablet **/ə/** garden, listen, taken, children, open

**Activity 4**

**Work with a partner. Write some questions using *Have you ever…?* Ask and answer.**

- The pupils work in pairs. They decide on five questions that they think all the class will answer 'no' to. They try and use different verbs each time.

**Odd one out activity**

**Which is the odd one out? Why?**

- The pupils complete the odd one out activity.

**Answers:** canoeing (You don't use a ball to play it.)

**Ending the lesson**

**Review the lesson and reflect on learning.**

- Say **Today we've learnt how to use the present perfect tense with regular and irregular verbs and also how to use the present perfect simple and the past simple together.**
- Ask **Which was your favourite activity today? Which activity was easy / difficult?**

**Extra activity**

**Reinforcement**

- Play a chain game using *Have you ever eaten ...?*

### Key Competences and Key Learning Outcomes

- Identify and say expressions for making entertainment
- Listen for specific information
- Practise activity types found in the Cambridge Exams: A2 Key for Schools
- Do a communication task

### Key language

- *act in a play, create a comic, compose music, juggle, make a film, make a sculpture, paint a portrait, play in an orchestra, sing in a choir, write a poem*
- *Have you ever juggled? Yes, I have. / No, I haven't.*
- **Extension:** *dance in a dance troupe, direct a play, perform in a show, play in a band*

### Materials

- Pupil's Book p65; Activity Book p62; Class CD3; Teacher's App on Navio; Teacher's Resource Bank: Unit 6
- Teacher's Resource Bank: Entertainment word cards

### Optional materials

- Teacher's Resource Bank: Trinity Exams Practice cards (selected from the Starter Unit and Units 1, 2, 3, 4 and 5)

## At a Glance Lesson Plan

### Pupil's Book

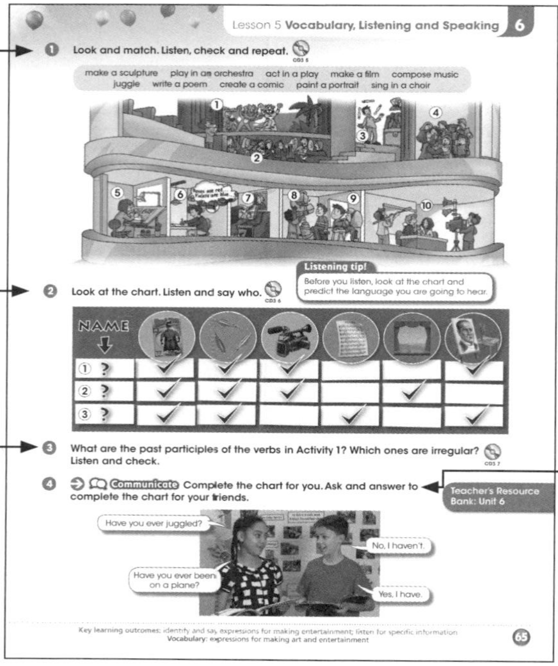


**Starting the lesson**

- Use the Trinity Exams Practice cards (optional).
- Review entertainment words.
- Set learning objectives.

**Activity 1**

- Look and match.
- Listen, check and repeat.
- ▶ *CD3 Track 5 p288*

**Activity 2**

- Look at the chart.
- Listen and say who.
- ▶ *CD3 Track 6 p288*

**Activity 3**

- What are the past participles of the verbs in Activity 1?
- Which ones are irregular?
- Listen and check.
- ▶ *CD3 Track 7 p288*

**Activity 4**

- Complete the chart for you.
- Ask and answer to complete the chart for your friends (Teacher's Resource Bank: Unit 6).

Go to the Activity Book.

**Ending the lesson**

- Review the lesson and reflect on learning.

**Extra activities**

**Extension**

- Present your data in a pie chart or bar chart.

**Vocabulary extension**

- Present four additional vocabulary items.

### Digital resources

**Teacher's Digital:** You can also teach this lesson using the Teacher's App on Navio.

**Pupil's Digital:** Encourage your pupils to use the Pupil's App on Navio to practise the activities from this lesson.

Powered By NAVIO

### Activity Book

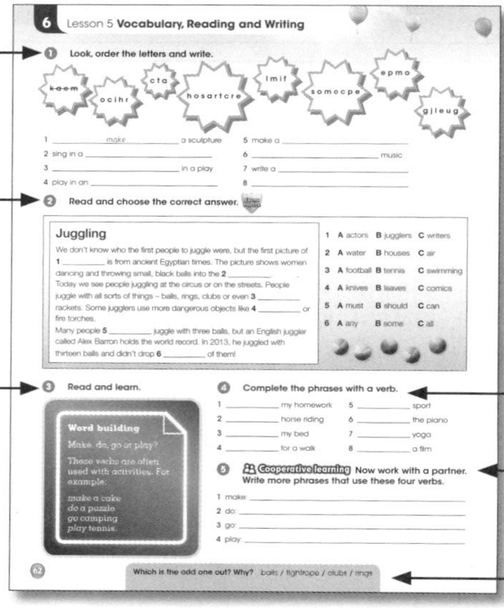


**Activity Book**

**Activity 1**

- Look, order the letters and write.

**Activity 2**

- Read and choose the correct answer.

**Activity 3**

- Read and learn.

**Activity 4**

- Complete the phrases with a verb.

**Activity 5**

- Now work with a partner. Write more phrases that use these four verbs.

**Odd one out activity**

- Which is the odd one out? Why?

# Detailed Lesson Plan

### Starting the lesson

**Use the Trinity Exams Practice cards (optional).**
- The pupils practise asking and answering questions.

**Review entertainment words.**
- Play a game with the entertainment word cards. The pupils act out words for their partner to guess.

**Set learning objectives.**
- Say **Today we're going to learn some new phrases for different kinds of entertainment.**

### Pupil's Book Activity 1

**Look and match. Listen, check and repeat.**

▸ *CD3 Track 5 p288*
- Organise the class into pairs. The pupils match the phrases in the box to the pictures.
- Play the CD. The pupils listen and check.
- Play the CD again, pausing after each phrase for the pupils to repeat.

### Pupil's Book Activity 2

**Look at the chart. Listen and say who.**

▸ *CD3 Track 6 p288*
- Focus the class on the chart and the six pictures along the top. Ask **What does the chart show?** The pupils name the six activities.
- Ask the pupils to guess which child is which. Say **Let's listen and find out.**
- Play the CD. The pupils listen and note down which child is in which row. (*1 Tim 2 Polly 3 Robbie*)

### Pupil's Book Activity 3

**What are the past participles of the verbs in Activity 1? Which ones are irregular? Listen and check.**

▸ *CD3 Track 7 p288*
- The pupils look at the verbs at the top of the page. Ask **Which are irregular verbs?**
- The pupils write down the past participle of all ten verbs.
- Play the CD. The pupils make any corrections they wish to their work.

### Pupil's Book Activity 4

**Complete the chart for you. Ask and answer to complete the chart for your friends. (Teacher's Resource Bank: Unit 6).**
- Invite two pupils to read out the speech bubbles.
- Organise the class into pairs (A and B). Give Pupils A the first worksheet from Teacher's Resource Bank Unit 6 and give Pupils B the other worksheet. Check pupils know which activities are shown.
- The pupils complete the chart for themselves.
- Then the pupils ask four other pupils the questions.

### Activity Book

**Activity 1**

**Look, order the letters and write.**
- The pupils order the letters. They write the words in the gap.

**Answers:** **1** make **2** choir **3** act **4** orchestra **5** film **6** compose **7** poem **8** juggle

**Activity 2**

**Read and choose the correct answer.**
- Read the text as a class. Read the first sentence. Explain why the answer is 'B'.
- The pupils work on their own to choose the remaining answers.

**Answers:** **1** B **2** C **3** B **4** A **5** C **6** A

**Activity 3**

**Read and learn.**
- Read the information as a class.

**Activity 4**

**Complete the phrases with a verb.**
- The pupils complete the phrases with one of the four verbs.

**Answers:** **1** do **2** go **3** make **4** go **5** do **6** play **7** do **8** make

**Activity 5**

**Now work with a partner. Write more phrases that use these four verbs.**
- The pupils work in pairs to think of other phrases that use these four verbs.
- Write the four verbs on the board at the top of four separate columns. Invite the pupils to make suggestions and add the correct ones to the board.
- The pupils complete the activity in their books.

**Odd one out activity**

**Which is the odd one out? Why?**
- The pupils complete the odd one out activity.

**Answers:** tightrope (You can't juggle it.)

### Ending the lesson

**Review the lesson and reflect on learning.**
- Say **Today we've learnt some verb phrases for different kinds of entertainment.**

### Extra activities

**Extension**
- The pupils present the data from Pupil's Book Activity 4 as a pie chart or a bar chart.

**Vocabulary extension**
- Present four additional vocabulary items: *dance in a dance troupe, direct a play, perform in a show, play in a band.*
- Use the Vocabulary booster on NAVIO to practise these new words.

## Key Competences and Key Learning Outcomes

- Do pre-reading tasks to identify features of poems
- Read a poem for general understanding
- Scan a poem for specific information
- Recognise and discuss rhyme and rhythm in a poem

- Read and understand a poem
- Give an opinion on the poem

**Key language**
- *lines, rhyme, rhythm, verse; bow, cello, clarinet, cymbals, double bass, drums, drumsticks, flute, French horn, orchestra, violin; bigger, deep, deeper, loudly, low, pretty, sad, slow, sweet; bang, crash, twirl*
- *I could be an orchestra. Did you like the poem? What did you like about it?*

**Materials**
- Pupil's Book p66; Activity Book p63; Class CD3; Teacher's App on Navio

**Optional materials**
- Teacher's Resource Bank: Trinity Exams Practice cards (selected from the Starter Unit and Units 1, 2, 3, 4 and 5)

## At a Glance Lesson Plan

### Pupil's Book

**Starting the lesson**
- Use the Trinity Exams Practice cards (optional).
- Review musical instruments.
- Set learning objectives.

**Activity 1: Before you read**
- Read and discuss.

**Activity 2**
- Match the musical instruments to the verses of the poem.

**Activity 3**
- Listen and read the poem.
- ▶ ***CD3 Track 8 p288***
- Find the rhyming words.
- Then read again.
- Can you tap the rhythm of the poem on the desk?

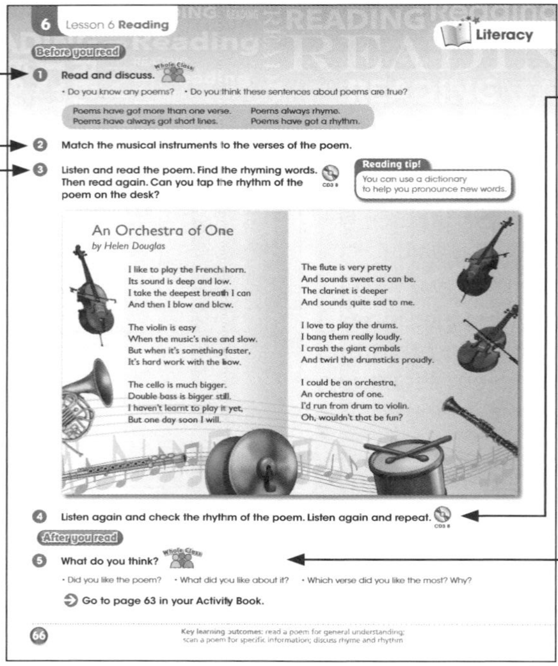

**Activity 4**
- Listen again and check the rhythm of the poem
- ▶ ***CD3 Track 8 p288***
- Listen again and repeat.

**Activity 5: After you read**
- What do you think?
- Go to the Activity Book.

**Ending the lesson**
- Review the lesson and reflect on learning.

**Extra activity**

**Reinforcement**
- Play a rhyming words game.

### Activity Book

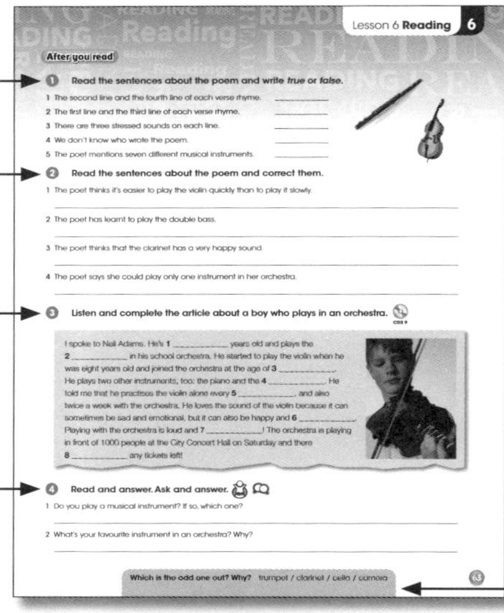

**Activity Book: After you read**

**Activity 1**
- Read the sentences about the poem and write *true* or *false*.

**Activity 2**
- Read the sentences about the poem and correct them.

**Activity 3**
- Listen and complete the magazine article about a boy who plays in an orchestra.
- ▶ ***CD3 Track 9 p288***

**Activity 4**
- Read and answer. Ask and answer.

**Odd one out activity**
- Which is the odd one out? Why?

### Digital resources

**Teacher's Digital:** You can also teach this lesson using the Teacher's App on Navio.

**Pupil's Digital:** Encourage your pupils to use the Pupil's App on Navio to practise the activities from this lesson.

Powered By NAVIO

# Detailed Lesson Plan

## Starting the lesson

**Use the Trinity Exams Practice cards (optional).**
- The pupils practise asking and answering questions.

**Review musical instruments.**
- Review musical instruments by playing *Mime the card* game (see p32).

**Set learning objectives.**
- Say **Today we're going to read a poem.**

## Pupil's Book Activity 1: Before you read

**Read and discuss.**
- Read the first question as a class. Ask **Can anyone recite a poem? Do you like poems?**
- Ask the pupils to read the sentences and discuss each in pairs or small groups. You may need to explain rhyme, rhythm and verse. Then go through the sentences one by one inviting the pupils to give their opinions.

## Pupil's Book Activity 2

**Match the musical instruments to the verses of the poem.**
- Look at the pictures. Ask **What kind of poem do you think it is? What instruments can you see?**
- Ask the pupils to quickly match the musical instruments to the verses of the poem by skimming the text.

## Pupil's Book Activity 3

**Listen and read the poem. Find the rhyming words. Then read again. Can you tap the rhythm of the poem on the desk?**
▶ *CD3 Track 8 p288*
- The pupils read the poem to see if they can identify the rhyming words.
- Read out the first verse yourself, tapping out the rhythm as you do. (You should be tapping on *like, play, French, horn, sound, deep, low, take, deep-, breath, can, then, blow, blow.*) The pupils repeat the verse. They then try to tap the rhythm for the other verses.

## Pupil's Book Activity 4

**Listen again and check the rhythm of the poem. Listen again and repeat.**
▶ *CD3 Track 8 p288*
- Play the CD. The pupils listen and see if their rhythm was correct. Play the CD again and the pupils repeat the lines.

## Pupil's Book Activity 5: After you read

**What do you think?**
- Read the questions as a class. Ask the pupils to give their views.

## Activity Book: After you read

**Activity 1**
**Read the sentences about the poem and write *true* or *false*.**
- The pupils read each sentence and decide if it's true or false.

**Answers:** **1** true **2** false **3** false **4** false **5** false

**Activity 2**
**Read the sentences about the poem and correct them.**
- The pupils read the sentences and write correct versions.

**Answers:** **1** The writer thinks it is easier to play the violin slowly than to play it quickly. **2** The writer hasn't learnt to play the double bass yet. **3** The writer thinks that the clarinet has a sad sound. **4** The writer says she could play all the instruments in her orchestra.

**Activity 3**
**Listen and complete the article about a boy who plays in an orchestra.**
▶ *CD3 Track 9 p288*
- Read out the article, pausing at the spaces to allow the pupils to predict the missing words.
- Play the CD. The pupils listen and follow the information in their books.
- Play the CD again, pausing after each piece of key information. The pupils write the missing information.

**Answers:** **1** 15 **2** violin **3** 10 **4** cello **5** day **6** fun **7** exciting **8** aren't

**Activity 4**
**Read and answer. Ask and answer.**
- The pupils read the questions individually and write answers.
- They then ask the same questions to a partner.

**Odd one out activity**
**Which is the odd one out? Why?**
- The pupils complete the odd one out activity.

**Answers:** camera (It isn't a musical intrument.)

## Ending the lesson

**Review the lesson and reflect on learning.**
- Say **Today we've read a poem about musical instruments.**
- Ask **Which was your favourite activity today? Which activity was easy / difficult?**

## Extra activity

**Reinforcement**
- Play a rhyming words game. Say **Let's see how many rhyming words we can think of. I'll say the first word 'low'.**
- The pupils take it in turns to say another word that rhymes. Count up how many words they thought of.

## Key Competences and Key Learning Outcomes

- Define words relating to poetry
- Identify onomatopoeic words
- Identify features of a haiku
- Use criteria to check your writing
- Share your writing with another pupil
- Write two haikus

### Key language

- *feelings, line, meaning, onomatopoeic, rhyme, rhythm, sentence, sound, syllable, verse, vowel*
- *The sound booms around the room.*

### Materials

- Pupil's Book p67; Activity Book p64; Teacher's App on Navio

### Optional materials

- Teacher's Resource Bank: Trinity Exams Practice cards (selected from the Starter Unit and Units 1, 2, 3, 4 and 5)

## At a Glance Lesson Plan

### Pupil's Book

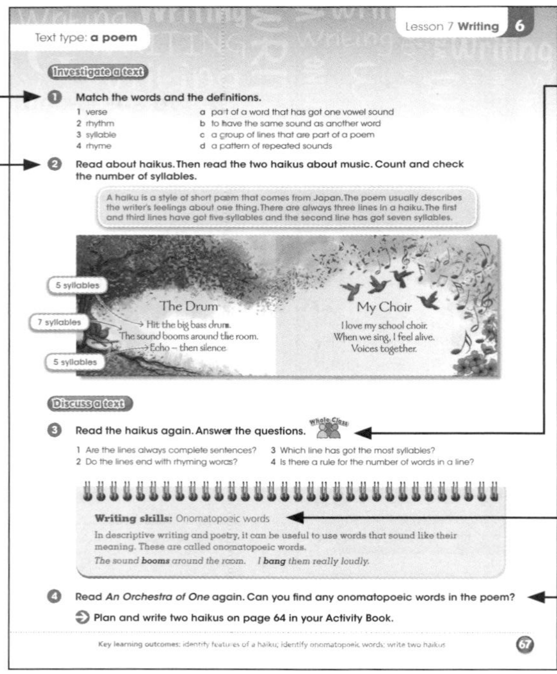

**Starting the lesson**

- Use the Trinity Exams Practice cards (optional).
- Review the features of a poem.
- Set learning objectives.

**Activity 1: Investigate a text**

- Match the words and the definitions.

**Activity 2**

- Read about haikus.
- Then read the two haikus about music.
- Count and check the number of syllables.

**Activity 3: Discuss a text**

- Read the haikus again.
- Answer the questions.

**Writing skills**

- Read about onomatopoeic words.

**Activity 4**

- Read *An Orchestra of One* again.
- Can you find any onomatopoeic words in the poem?

Go to the Activity Book.

**Ending the lesson**

- Review the lesson and reflect on learning.

**Extra activity**

**Extension**

- Practise counting syllables.

### Activity Book

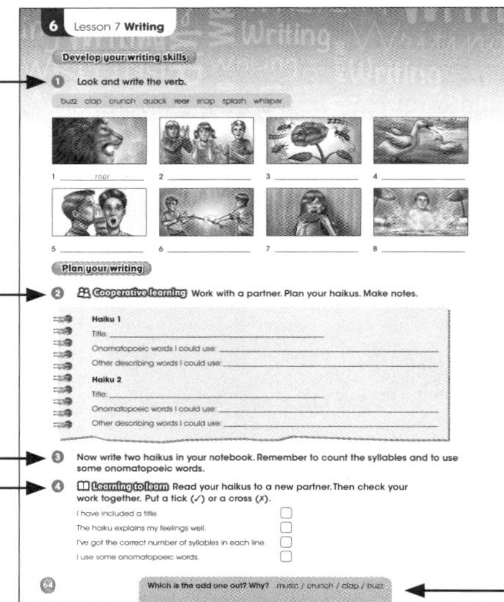

**Activity Book**

**Activity 1: Develop your writing skills**

- Look and write the verb.

**Activity 2: Plan your writing**

- Work with a partner. Plan your haikus. Make notes.

**Activity 3**

- Now write two haikus in your notebook. Remember to count the syllables and to use some onomatopoeic words.

**Activity 4**

- Read your haikus to a new partner. Then check your work together. Put a tick (✓) or a cross (✗).

**Odd one out activity**

- Which is the odd one out? Why?

## Digital resources

**Teacher's Digital:** You can also teach this lesson using the Teacher's App on Navio.

**Pupil's Digital:** Encourage your pupils to use the Pupil's App on Navio to practise the activities from this lesson.

Powered By NAVIO

# Detailed Lesson Plan

### Starting the lesson

**Use the Trinity Exams Practice cards (optional).**

- The pupils practise asking and answering questions.

**Review the features of a poem.**

- Ask the pupils questions about the poem in Lesson 6. Ask **What was the title? Can you remember any lines? Can you remember any rhyming words? Which musical instruments were in the poem?**
- Invite the pupils to ask questions about the poem to other pupils.

**Set learning objectives.**

- Say **Today we're going to write some Japanese poems called haikus.**

### Pupil's Book Activity 1: Investigate a text

**Match the words and the definitions.**

- Read the words and sentences as a class. In pairs, ask the pupils to match the words and definitions.
- Give examples to help explain 'syllable'. Check they understand by asking **How many syllables are there in (drum)?**

### Pupil's Book Activity 2

**Read about haikus. Then read the two haikus about music. Count and check the number of syllables.**

- Read the text about haikus as a class.
- Check understanding of the text by asking questions. Ask **Where do haikus come from? How many lines are in a haiku? How many syllables are there in a haiku in total?**
- Read the example haikus and count the syllables together. Check the understanding of 'echo' and 'boom'.
- Ask the pupils to decide, in pairs, which haiku they prefer and why.

### Pupil's Book Activity 3: Discuss a text

**Read the haikus again. Answer the questions.**

- The pupils read the haikus again. Discuss the questions as a class.

### Writing skills

- Read about onomatopoeic words. The pupils think of more examples in English.

### Pupil's Book Activity 4

**Read *An Orchestra* of *One* again. Can you find any onomatopoeic words in the poem?**

- The pupils look back at the poem on page 68 and find any more onomatopoeic words. (*Crash and twirl.*)
- The pupils think of onomatopoeic words in their own language.

### Activity Book

**Activity 1: Develop your writing skills**

**Look and write the verb.**

- (Books closed.) Read the eight words out to the pupils. Say that they are all onomatopoeic words. Can they guess the meaning of any of them from the sound?
- (Books open.) The pupils do the matching activity on their own.

**Answers:** **1** roar **2** clap **3** buzz **4** quack **5** whisper **6** snap **7** crunch **8** splash

**Activity 2: Plan your writing**

**Work with a partner. Plan your haikus. Make notes.**

- The pupils work with a Writing Partner. They think of two different topics or themes to write about. They list verbs, nouns and adjectives for the first haiku. They then start to think of some phrases with five or seven syllables.
- The pupils do the same for the second haiku.

**Activity 3**

**Now write two haikus in your notebook. Remember to count the syllables and to use some onomatopoeic words.**

- The pupils, still working with a Writing Partner, write two haikus. Encourage them to include onomatopoeic words. Make sure they check that the number of syllables is correct.

**Activity 4**

**Read your haikus to a new partner. Then check your work together. Put a tick (✓) or a cross (✗).**

- Read through the statements as a class.
- Organise the class into new partners. One pupil reads aloud their text to their partner. The other pupil listens. The pupils work together to decide if the text fulfils the criteria and tick the corresponding boxes. The pupils can add, improve or correct the text at this stage.
- The pupils swap roles.

**Odd one out activity**

**Which is the odd one out? Why?**

- The pupils complete the odd one out activity.

**Answers:** music (It isn't an onomatopoeic word.)

### Ending the lesson

**Review the lesson and reflect on learning.**

- Say **Today we've written haikus and learnt to use onomatopoeic words.**
- Ask **Which was your favourite activity today? Which activity was easy / difficult?**

### Extra activity

**Extension**

- Counting syllables of words is difficult but it is a good way to help the pupils listen carefully to the sound of words and also to improve pronunciation.
- The pupils look at the poem on page 68 of the Pupil's Book. They find five words with two syllables and two words with three syllables.

### Key Competences and Key Learning Outcomes

- Listen to and have a conversation about favourite kinds of entertainment
- Listen to a conversation for general and specific understanding
- Prepare a conversation about a topic
- Review learning and reflect on progress in the unit
- Carry out a conversation about a topic
- Sing a song

### Key language

- *adventure films, action films, animated films, characters, comedies, music, film director, popcorn, scary, theatre, video camera*
- *What's your favourite kind of entertainment? Have you ever seen a 3D film? I like films, best, do you? Have you seen it, too? Do you like popcorn, too? How about you?*

### Materials

- Pupil's Book p68; Activity Book p65 and 66; Class CD3 and CD4; Teacher's App on Navio

### Optional materials

- Teacher's Resource Bank: Trinity Exams Practice cards (selected from the Starter Unit and Units 1, 2, 3, 4 and 5)

## At a Glance Lesson Plan

### Pupil's Book

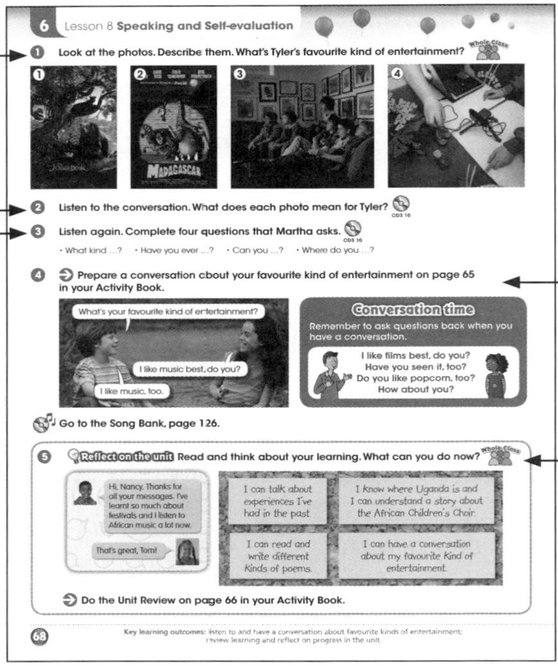

#### Starting the lesson

- Use the Trinity Exams Practice cards (optional).
- Review forms of entertainment.
- Set learning objectives.

#### Activity 1

- Look at the photos.
- Describe them.
- What's Tyler's favourite kind of entertainment?

#### Activity 2

- Listen to the conversation.
- ▶ *CD3 Track 10 p288*
- What does each photo mean for Tyler?

#### Activity 3

- Listen again.
- ▶ *CD3 Track 10 p288*
- Complete four questions that Martha asks.

#### Activity 4

- Prepare a conversation about your favourite kind of entertainment on page 65 in your Activity book.

Go to page 65 in the Activity Book.

#### Song

- ▶ *CD4 Track 24 p297*
- ▶ *CD4 Track 25 p297 (optional karaoke version)*

#### Activity 5

- Read and think about your learning. What can you do now?

Go to page 66 in the Activity Book.

#### Ending the lesson

- Review the lesson and reflect on learning.

#### Extra activity

- Describe a time when you saw some entertainment that you really enjoyed.

### Digital resources

**Teacher's Digital:** You can also teach this lesson using the Teacher's App on Navio.

Powered By NAVIO

### Activity Book

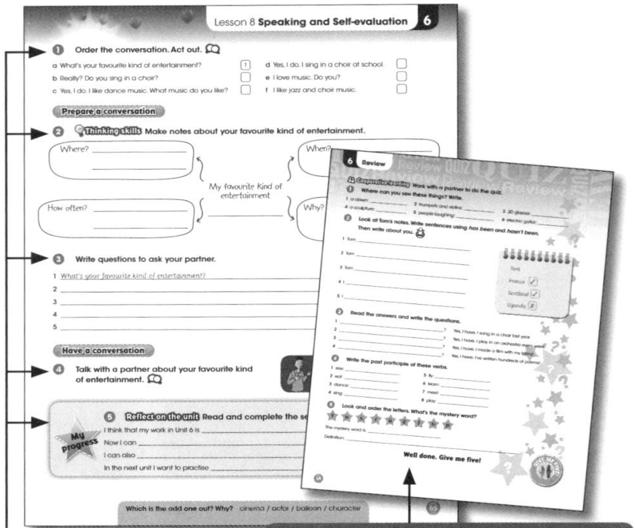

#### Activity Book page 66: Review

- Work with a partner to do the quiz.

#### Activity Book

**Activity 1**
- Order the conversation.
- Act out.

**Activity 2**
- Make notes about your favourite kind of entertainment.

**Activity 3**
- Write questions to ask your partner.

**Activity 4**
- Talk with a partner about your favourite kind of entertainment.

**Activity 5**
- Read and complete the sentences.

**Odd one out activity**
- Which is the odd one out? Why?

# Detailed Lesson Plan

**Starting the lesson**

**Use the Trinity Exams Practice cards (optional).**

- The pupils practise asking and answering questions.

**Review forms of entertainment.**

- Tell students to name different kinds of music. Throw a ball for a pupil. The pupil catches it and says a type of music. The pupil throws it to a new pupil who says a different type. Repeat with kinds of film, kinds of dance, kinds of magazine and materials for creating art.

**Set learning objectives.**

- Say **Today we're going to prepare a conversation about our favourite kind of entertainment.**

**Pupil's Book Activity 1**

**Look at the photos. Describe them. What's Tyler's favourite kind of entertainment?**

- Ask different pupils to describe the pictures. Elicit ideas about what Tyler's favourite kind of entertainment might be.

**Pupil's Book Activity 2**

**Listen to the conversation. What does each photo mean for Tyler?**

▶ ***CD3 Track 10 p288***

- Play the CD. In pairs, pupils explain why the photos are important for Tyler.

**Answer:** **1** *The Jungle Book* is his favourite film at the moment. **2** *Madagascar* was the first film he saw. **3** His favourite thing is to watch films at home with his friends. **4** He's made some short films with his friend.

**Pupil's Book Activity 3**

**Listen again. Complete four questions that Ben asks.**

▶ ***CD3 Track 10 p288***

- Direct pupils to the four question prompts. Ask if they can remember the questions.
- Play the CD. Check answers as a class.

**Answers:** What kind of films do you like?; Have you ever seen a 3D film?; Can you remember the first film you saw?; Where do you usually go to watch films?

**Pupil's Book Activity 4**

**Prepare a conversation about your favourite kind of entertainment on page 65 in your Activity Book.**

- Read the speech bubbles with the pupils. Model the phrases in the Conversation Time box and get the class to repeat.

**Song**

- Go to the Song Bank on page 126 to do the song activities (see p244).

***CD4 Track 24 p297***

***CD4 Track 25 p297 (optional karaoke version)***

**Pupil's Book Activity 5**

**Read and think about your learning. What can you do now?**

- Read the speech bubbles and notes with the pupils. They look back through the unit and identify things that they have done/learnt.

**Activity Book page 66: Review**

**Work with a partner to do the quiz.**

- Organise the class into pairs. Set a time limit for the pupils to do the quiz (10–15 minutes).
- Read out the five tasks. Check understanding. Then say **Ready, steady ... Go!**
- The pupils work in their pairs to do the quiz.
- Correct the answers as a class.

**Answers:** **1** **1** a circus **2** a classical music concert **3** a cinema **4** an art exhibition **5** a comedy show **6** a pop concert **2** **1** has been to France. **2** has been to Scotland. **3** hasn't been to Uganda. **3** **1** Have you sung in a choir? **2** Have you played in an orchestra? **3** Have you made a film? **4** Have you written poems? **4** **1** seen **2** eaten **3** danced **4** sung **5** flown **6** learnt / learned **7** met **8** played **6** painting, a picture you hang on the wall

**Activity Book**

**Activity 1**

**Order the conversation. Act out.**

- In pairs, pupils order the conversation and act it out.

**Answers:** **1** a **2** e **3** c **4** f **5** b **6** d

**Activity 2**

**Make notes about your favourite kind of entertainment.**

- Tell pupils about your favourite kind of entertainment. Then pupils complete the boxes with their own information.

**Activity 3**

**Write questions to ask your partner.**

- Direct pupils to the five headings in Activity 2 and explain that they need to form questions about them. Elicit the second question. Then pupils complete the questions alone. Check as a class.

**Answers:** **1** What's your favourite kind of entertainment? **2** Where do you usually go to see/do it? **3** How often do you see/do it? **4** When do you usually see/do it? Why do you like it?

**Activity 4**

**Talk with a partner about your favourite kind of entertainment.**

- In pairs, pupils ask and answer the questions from Activity 3.
- Invite one or two pairs to perform their conversations for the class.

**Activity 5**

**Read and complete the sentences.**

- Pupils work alone to review their work in the unit.

**Odd one out activity**

**Which is the odd one out? Why?**

**Answer:** balloon (It isn't a person.)

**Ending the lesson**

**Review the lesson and reflect on learning.**

- Say **Today we've learnt how to have a conversation about our favourite kind of entertainment.**

# Video and 21st Century Skills

**Key Competences and Key Learning Outcomes**

- Watch and understand a video about art
- Use a mind map to brainstorm ideas for a talent day
- Think about activities and products for a talent day

**Key language**

- *art gallery, cartoon, chalk, colour in, playground, talent day*
- *Why don't we do a comedy show? What about selling ice cream?*

**Materials**

- Pupil's Book p69; Activity Book p67; Class CD3; Teacher's App on Navio
- Teacher's Resource Bank: Talk cards

**Optional materials**

- Teacher's Resource Bank: Trinity Exams Practice cards (selected from the Starter Unit and Units 1–5)

## At a Glance Lesson Plan

### Pupil's Book

**Starting the lesson**

- Use the Trinity Exams Practice cards (optional).
- **Think-Pair-Share** Review forms of entertainment vocabulary.
- Set learning objectives and use the talk cards.

**Activity 1**

- Before you watch
- Watch the video.
- *Unit 6 video p302*
- Read and answer the questions.

**Activity 2**

- Watch the video again.
- *Unit 6 video*
- What are these things?
- What is the connection with the video?

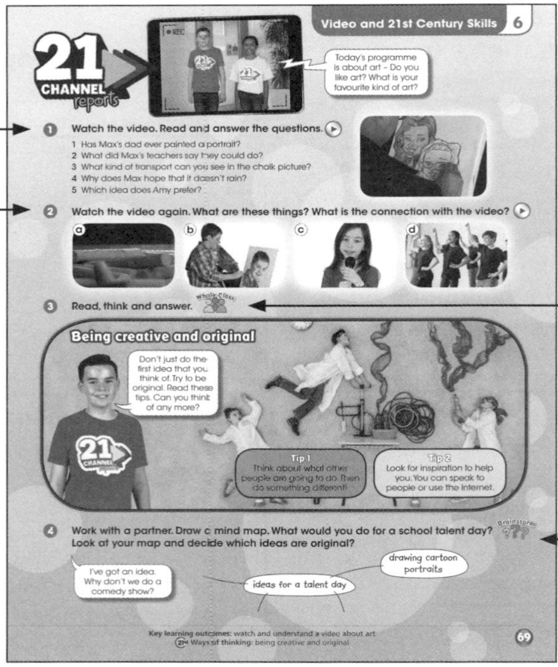


**Activity 3**

- Read, think and answer.

**Activity 4**

- Work with a partner.
- Draw a mind map.
- What would you do for a school talent day?
- Look at your map and decide which ideas are original.

Go to the Activity Book.

**Ending the lesson**

- Review the lesson and reflect on learning.

**Extra activity**

- Plan your ideal volunteering project.

### Activity Book

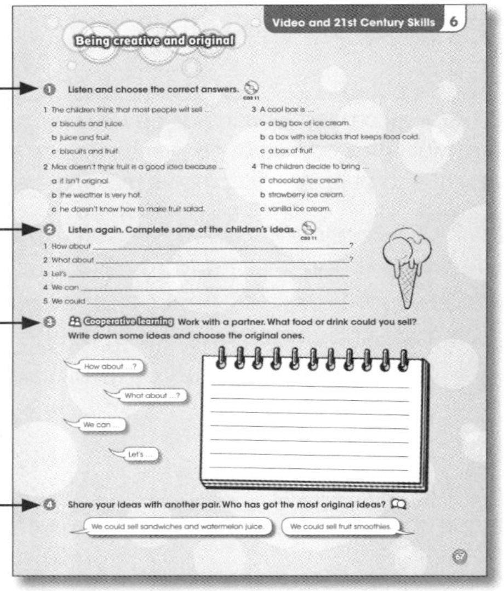


**Activity Book**

**Activity 1**

- Listen and choose the correct answers.

▶ *CD3 Track 11 p289*

**Activity 2**

- Listen again.
- Complete some of the children's ideas.

▶ *CD3 Track 11 p289*

**Activity 3**

- Work with a partner.
- What food or drink could you sell?
- Write down some ideas and choose the original ones.

**Activity 4**

- Share your ideas with another pair.
- Who has got the most original ideas?

**Digital resources**

**Teacher's Digital:** You can also teach this lesson using the Teacher's App on Navio.

**Pupil's Digital:** Encourage your pupils to use the Pupil's App on Navio to practise the activities from this lesson.

Powered By NAVIO

# Detailed Lesson Plan

**Starting the lesson**

**Use the Trinity Exams Practice cards (optional).**

- The pupils practise asking and answering questions.

**Think-Pair-Share Review forms of entertainment vocabulary.**

- Ask **Can you remember the forms of entertainment vocabulary?** The class thinks silently for a minute.
- Then the pupils work with a Talk Partner to name forms of entertainment.
- Invite different Talk Partners to say different types of entertainment and entertainment activities. Hold up the corresponding flashcard and prompt the class to repeat the word.
- Finally, repeat the procedure, asking different pairs of Talk Partners each time, until all the ideas have been recorded.

**Set learning objectives and use the talk cards.**

- Say **Today we're going to watch a video and then ask and answer questions about different types of drawing.**
- Point to the talk cards to show the pupils the different ways they will be working in the lesson.

**Pupil's Book Activity 1**

**Before you watch**

- Read the speech bubble to pupils. Ask **Would you like to do an adventurous sport?** Elicit responses from a number of pupils.

**Watch the video. Read and answer the questions.**
*p302*

- Watch Part 1 of the video. Ask pupils **What are you going to see next?**
- Play Part 2 of the video. Ask general questions to check understanding. Direct pupils to the sentences in Activity 1, and ask **Has Max's dad ever painted a portrait?** Pupils offer ideas.
- Play the video again. Pupils answer the questions.

**Answers:** **1** Yes, he has. **2** Max's teachers said they could draw on the playground. **3** motorbike **4** He hopes that it doesn't rain because the rain would wash away the chalk. **5** She prefers cartoon portraits.

**Pupil's Book Activity 2**

**Watch the video again. What are these things? What is the connection with the video?**

- Ask a pupil **What can you see in picture a?** Ask a different pupil **What is the connection with the video?**

**Answers:** **a** Chalk. You can use chalk to draw on the playground. **b** A portrait. Max's dad has drawn a portrait of Max. **c** A girl singing. Everyone is going to sing or dance on the talent day. **d** Some children dancing. Everyone is going to sing or dance on the talent day.

**Pupil's Book Activity 3**

**Read, think and answer.**

- Read the speech bubble and the tips with the class. Can they remember who said each tip? (*Max said Tip 1; Amy said Tip 2*)
- Pupils work in pairs to think of more tips for being creative and original. Then check ideas as a class.

**Pupil's Book Activity 4**

**Work with a partner. Draw a mind map. What would you do for a school talent day? Look at your map and decide which ideas are original.**

- Ask pupils for all the ideas that Max and Amy mention for their school talent day. Pupils add the ideas to their mind maps.
- Pupils work in pairs to think of more ideas.

**Activity Book**

**Activity 1**

**Listen and choose the correct answers.**

▶ *CD3 Track 11 p289*

- As a class, look through the options. Ask **What different food and drink words can you find in the questions?** (*biscuits*, *juice*, *fruit*, *fruit salad*, *ice cream*, *chocolate*, *strawberry*, *vanilla*)
- Play the CD. Pupils choose the correct answers.

**Answers:** **1** a **2** b **3** b **4** c

**Activity 2**

**Listen again. Complete some of the children's ideas.**

▶ *CD3 Track 11 p289*

- Play the CD again. Pupils complete the sentences.

**Answers:** **1** How about vanilla ice cream? **2** What about orange juice?; What about some fruit? **3** Let's be different and original; Let's think of something different; Let's have chocolate ice cream. **4** We can sell strawberries or melon; We can bring some ice cream. **5** We could make fruit salad.

**Activity 3**

**Work with a partner. What food or drink could you sell? Write down some ideas and choose the original ones.**

- Pupils imagine they are having a food sale like Amy and Max. In pairs, pupils think of ideas for food and drink to sell. When they agree, they can write down their ideas. Remind them to be as creative and original as possible.

**Activity 4**

**Share your ideas with another pair. Who has got the most original ideas?**

- Pupils share their ideas in groups of four.
- They present their final list of food and drink to the class. Ask the class which group has got the most original list.

**Ending the lesson**

**Review the lesson and reflect on learning.**

- Say **Today we've watched a video about different types of drawing. What have we learnt about being creative and original?** Elicit ideas from the pupils.
- Ask **Which was your favourite activity today? Which activity was easy / difficult?**

# Project 2: A film script



## Key Competences and Key Learning Outcomes

- Investigate how people lived in the Middle Ages
- Listen to and identify correct information
- Share information about films
- Learn about life in the Middle Ages

**Key language**

- *castle, characters, go hunting, have a banquet, have a tournament, historical film, jester, king, knight, medieval times, Middle Ages, noble, palace, peasant, queen, suit of armour, TV show, wooden hut*

**Materials**

- Pupil's Book pp70; Activity Book p68; Class CD3; Teacher's App on Navio

## At a Glance Lesson Plan

### Starting the lesson

- Set learning objectives.

### Activity 1: Share knowledge

- Read and discuss.

### Activity 2: Investigate

- Listen and circle the correct information about life in medieval times on page 68 in your Activity Book.

▶ *CD3 Track 12 p289*

Go to the Activity Book.

## Pupil's Book

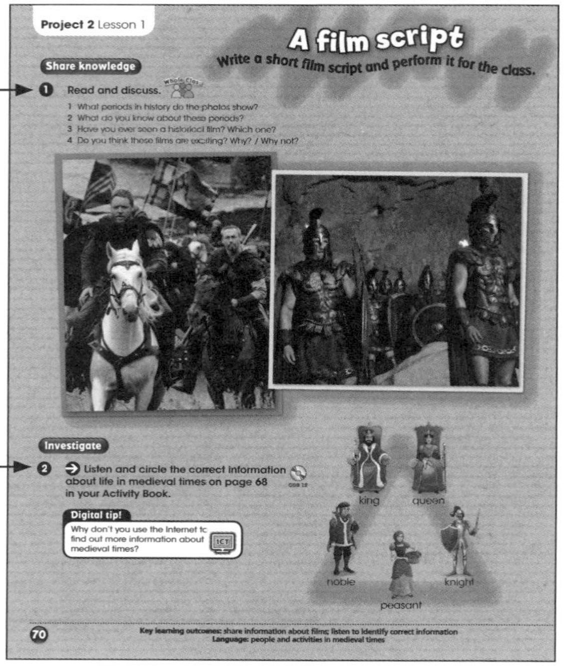


### Ending the lesson

- Review the lesson and reflect on learning.

**Extension activity**

- Do further research on life in medieval times.

### Link to Science

- **The Middle Ages:** Review the feudal system.

## Activity Book

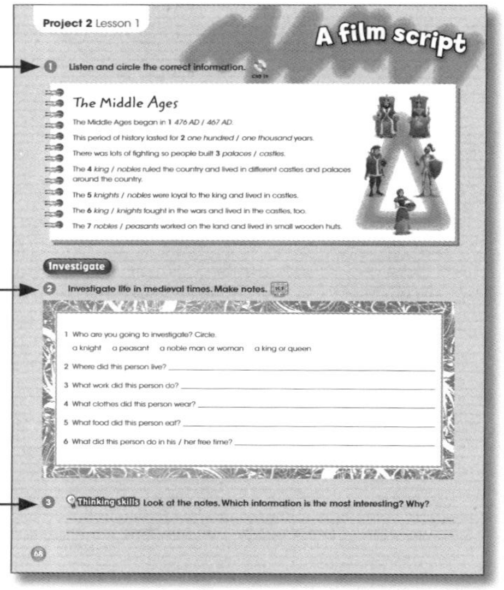


### Activity Book

**Activity 1**

- Listen and circle the correct information.

▶ *CD3 Track 12 p289*

**Activity 2**

- Investigate life in medieval times. Make notes.

**Activity 3**

- Look at the notes. Which information is the most interesting? Why?

## Digital resources

**Teacher's Digital:** You can also teach this lesson using the Teacher's App on Navio.

**Pupil's Digital:** Encourage your pupils to use the Pupil's App on Navio to practise the activities from this lesson.

Powered By NAVIO

# Detailed Lesson Plan

## Starting the lesson

**Set learning objectives.**

- Say **Today we're going to begin another project.**
- Focus the group's attention on the Task box at the top of the page. Read the text as a class.

## Pupil's Book Activity 1: Share knowledge

**Read and discuss.**

- Read and discuss the questions as a class.
- Encourage the pupils to talk about historical films and TV shows they've seen. Prompt the pupils to give as much information as possible. Provide key vocabulary when necessary. Write any relevant vocabulary on the side of the board.

## Pupil's Book Activity 2: Investigate

**Listen and circle the correct information about life in medieval times on page 68 in your Activity Book.**

▶ *CD3, Track 12 p289*

- Ask **What do you know about medieval times? Was life easy or hard? Where did people live? Was it a time of peace or war?** Encourage the pupils to report what they know.
- Direct students to the pictures Check the meaning of the people and elicit what their position in the diagram might mean.
- Invite a pupil to read the Digital tip.

## Activity Book

### Activity 1

**Listen and circle the correct information.**

▶ *CD3 Track 12 p289*

- Read the information as a class. Predict the answers. Then play the CD. The pupils listen and circle the correct information in their books.
- Play the CD again, pausing after each piece of key information. The pupils give the answer each time.

**Answers:** **1** 476 AD **2** one thousand **3** castles **4** king **5** nobles **6** knights **7** peasants

### Activity 2

**Investigate life in medieval times. Make notes.**

- Ask the pupils to write the social group they are going to investigate at the top of the activity. They then investigate what life was like for this group.
- If the pupils have access to computers, they can research the information online. Sources of information include: www.english-online.at/history/middle-ages/life-in-the-middle-ages.htm. Alternatively, they can use reference books and the information in the Activity Book (Activity 1, page 68).

### Activity 3

**Look at the notes. Which information is the most interesting? Why?**

- Organise the class into groups. The pupils decide which information is the most interesting and why.

## Ending the lesson

**Review the lesson and reflect on learning.**

- Say **Today we've learnt about medieval times.**
- Ask **Which was your favourite activity today? Which activity was easy / difficult?**

## Extension activity

- Organise the class into groups of four. Ask them to use the Internet to investigate life in medieval times.

## Link to Science

- If you are studying the Science topic of **Medieval times**, you could review the feudal system. Draw a large triangle on the board and divide it into four sections. Elicit the different social groups as in the first diagram. Then use arrows to elicit and explain the interdependent relationships as in the second diagram.

**European Feudal System**

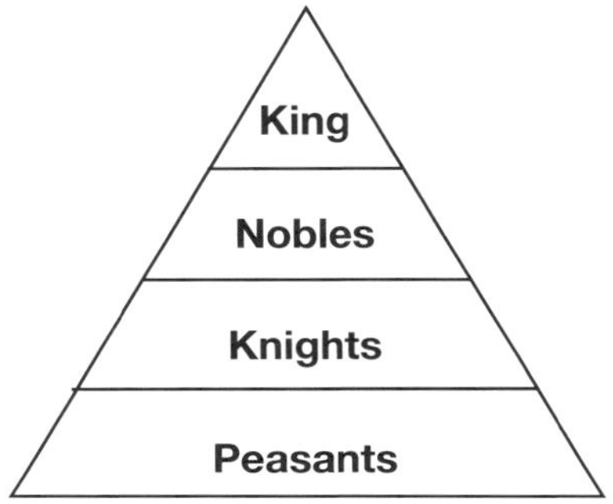


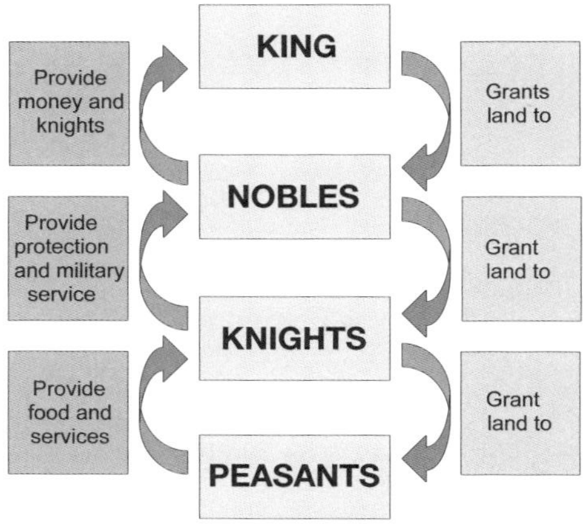

# Project 2: A film script



### Key Competences and Key Learning Outcomes

- Perform the script for the class

- Reflect on what you've learnt and how you've worked together

- Work in groups to plan and write a script
- Rehearse performing your script in groups

- Learn about scripts for films and TV shows

**Key language**

- *king, noble, peasant, queen; angrily, desperately, hopefully, kindly, politely, worriedly; children, directions, heavy, hungry, market, sack, script, sick, wife*
- *Will you help me? If I don't take it to market, my wife and children will be hungry. I am too important to help you. I can't sing and I can't tell jokes.*

**Materials**

- Pupil's Book pp71; Activity Book p69; Class CD3; Teacher's App on Navio

**Optional materials**

- The pupils' props and costumes

## At a Glance Lesson Plan

**Starting the lesson**

- Set learning objectives.

**Activity 1: Plan and create your project**

- Read and listen to the film script.
- What do you think the queen whispers to the peasant?

▶ ***CD3 Track 13 p289***

**Activity 2**

- Work in a group of three.
- Plan a film script.
- Make notes on page 69 in your Activity Book.
- Write the film script in your notebooks.

Go to the Activity Book.

**Activity 3: Present your project**

- Perform your film script for the class.

## Pupil's Book

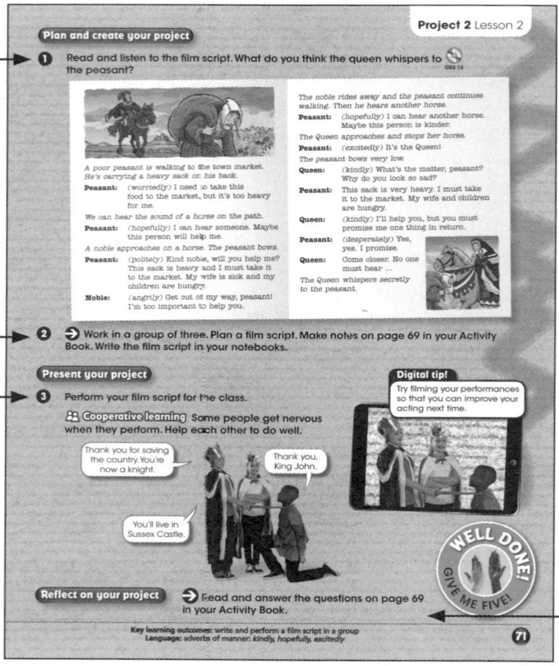
Project 2 Lesson 2

Plan and create your project

1 Read and listen to the film script. What do you think the queen whispers to the peasant?

*A poor peasant is walking to the town market. He's carrying a heavy sack on his back.*

**Peasant:** *(worriedly)* I need to take this food to the market, but it's too heavy for me.

*We can hear the sound of a horse on the path.*

**Peasant:** *(hopefully)* I can hear someone. Maybe this person will help me.

*A noble approaches on a horse. The peasant bows.*

**Peasant:** *(politely)* Kind noble, will you help me? This sack is heavy and I must take it to the market. My wife is sick and my children are hungry.

**Noble:** *(angrily)* Get out of my way, peasant! I'm too important to help you.

*The noble rides away and the peasant continues walking. Then he hears another horse.*

**Peasant:** *(hopefully)* I can hear another horse. Maybe this person is kinder.

*The Queen approaches and stops her horse.*

**Peasant:** *(excitedly)* It's the Queen!

*The peasant bows very low.*

**Queen:** *(kindly)* What's the matter, peasant? Why do you look so sad?

**Peasant:** This sack is very heavy. I must take it to the market. My wife and children are hungry.

**Queen:** *(kindly)* I'll help you, but you must promise me one thing in return.

**Peasant:** *(desperately)* Yes, yes. I promise.

**Queen:** Come closer. No one must hear ...

*The Queen whispers secretly to the peasant.*

2 Work in a group of three. Plan a film script. Make notes on page 69 in your Activity Book. Write the film script in your notebooks.

Present your project

3 Perform your film script for the class.

Cooperative learning Some people get nervous when they perform. Help each other to do well.



Reflect on your project

Read and answer the questions on page 69 in your Activity Book.

Key learning outcomes: write and perform a film script in a group
Language: adverbs of manner: *kindly, hopefully, excitedly*

71

**Reflect on your project**

- Read and answer the questions on page 69 in your Activity Book.

Go to the Activity Book.

**Ending the lesson**

- Review the lesson and reflect on learning.

**Reinforcement activity**

- Make a class display of your work.

## Activity Book

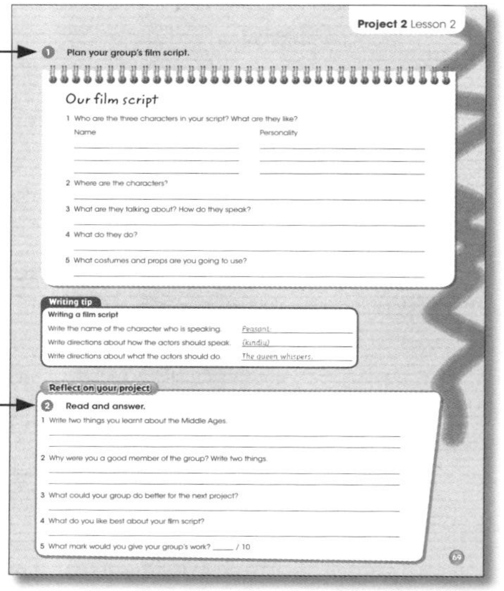
Project 2 Lesson 2

1 Plan your group's film script.

Our film script

1 Who are the three characters in your script? What are they like?

| Name | Personality |
| --- | --- |
| | |
| | |
| | |

2 Where are the characters?

3 What are they talking about? How do they speak?

4 What do they do?

5 What costumes and props are you going to use?

Writing tip

Writing a film script

Write the name of the character who is speaking. *Peasant:*

Write directions about how the actors should speak. *(kindly)*

Write directions about what the actors should do. *The queen whispers.*

Reflect on your project

2 Read and answer.

1 Write two things you learnt about the Middle Ages.

2 Why were you a good member of the group? Write two things.

3 What could your group do better for the next project?

4 What do you like best about your film script?

5 What mark would you give your group's work? ____ / 10

69

**Activity Book**

**Activity 1**

- Plan your group's film script.

**Activity 2: Reflect on your project**

- Read and answer.

### Digital resources

**Teacher's Digital:** You can also teach this lesson using the Teacher's App on Navio.

**Pupil's Digital:** Encourage your pupils to use the Pupil's App on Navio to practise the activities from this lesson.

Powered By NAVIO

# Detailed Lesson Plan



### Starting the lesson

**Set learning objectives.**

- Say **Today we're going to continue the project.** Prompt the class to tell you what they did in the last lesson.
- Highlight that the pupils will be working in small groups again. Prompt the pupils to tell you what they must do when they work in groups: listen, take turns, respect different opinions, etc.

### Pupil's Book Activity 1: Plan and create your project

**Read and listen to the film script. What do you think the queen whispers to the peasant?**

- Focus the class on the script. Explain to the pupils that the first time they read they should try to understand what the people say.

▸ ***CD3 Track 13 p289***

- Play the CD and read the text as a class. Check understanding. Ask the pupils to imagine what they think the queen whispers to the peasant.
- Ask the pupils to read the text another time. This time the pupils focus on understanding the stage directions to the actors and director. Once again, check understanding as a class.

### Pupil's Book Activity 2

**Work in a group of three. Plan a film script. Make notes on page 69 in your Activity Book. Write the film script in your notebooks.**

- Organise the class into their groups of three. Ask the pupils to turn to page 69 in their Activity Book.

### Activity Book

**Activity 1**

**Plan your group's film script.**

- Focus the class on the activity. Invite a pupil to read out the first question. Encourage the class to think of possible characters, i.e. a cruel king, a brave knight, a clever peasant. Write the pupils' suggestions on the board so they can refer to them later. Repeat the procedure with the other questions.
- Ask the pupils to work in their groups to discuss the questions and record their ideas in their Activity Books. Read the Writing tip with the class.
- Finally, each group should work together to write their scripts in their notebooks.

### Pupil's Book Activity 3: Present your project

**Perform your film script for the class.**

- Focus the class on the photo. Encourage the pupils to talk about what they can see. Ask **Who are the characters?** Then ask four pupils to read out the three speech bubbles. Read the Cooperative learning tip with the class.
- Organise the classroom so that each group has got a small space to practise acting out their script. The pupils should just practise reading their parts first. Later, when they are confident, they can begin to add movement.
- Remind the class of the importance of speaking clearly and slowly when they perform. Then invite different groups in turn to act out their script for the rest of the class. Ensure that the rest of the class applauds at the end.

### Pupil's Book: Reflect on your project

**Read and answer the questions on page 69 in your Activity Book.**

- The pupils answer the questions in the Activity Book.

### Activity Book

**Activity 2: Reflect on your project**

**Read and answer.**

- The pupils write the answers to the questions.

### Ending the lesson

**Review the lesson and reflect on learning.**

- Say **We've written and performed a scene for a film.**
- Ask **Which was your favourite activity today? Which activity was easy / difficult?**

**Reinforcement activity**

- Take photos of the groups performing their scripts. Ask each group to copy their script onto a piece of paper. Make a display of the scripts and photos so that other classes can enjoy and learn from the work.

Date: ____________________ Unit: __________

1 **What did my pupils learn in this unit?**

______________________________________

______________________________________

______________________________________

______________________________________

2 **How did my pupils work? (✓)**

individually ☐ in pairs ☐ in small groups ☐

in large groups ☐ as a class ☐

3 **Which key competences did my pupils develop? Give a score from 1 to 5 (5 being the highest).**

- Competence in linguistic communication ☐
- Competence in mathematics, science and technology ☐
- Digital competence ☐
- Learning to learn ☐
- Social and civic competences ☐
- Sense of initiative and entrepreneurship ☐
- Cultural awareness and expression ☐

4 **Which lessons / activities were the most successful and why?**

______________________________________

______________________________________

______________________________________

______________________________________

5 **Which lessons / activities did my pupils find the most difficult and why?**

______________________________________

______________________________________

______________________________________

______________________________________

6 **What did I try in the classroom for the first time? How did it go?**

______________________________________

______________________________________

______________________________________

______________________________________

7 **Which resources did I find most useful? (including webpages)**

______________________________________

______________________________________

______________________________________

______________________________________

______________________________________

______________________________________

8 **What could I do differently next time I teach this unit?**

______________________________________

______________________________________

______________________________________

______________________________________

Unit 7

# A helping hand

## Unit overview

### Key Competences and Key Learning Outcomes

- Name different ways of preparing for a party (Lesson 1)
- Learn and practise the present perfect with 'yet' and 'already' (Lesson 2)
- Learn and practise the present perfect with 'just' (Lesson 4)
- Learn phrases related to accidents (Lesson 5)
- Practise using questions to make your writing more interesting (Lesson 7)
- Talk about an activity to raise money (Lesson 8)
- Watch and understand a video about volunteering (video and 21st Century Skills)

- Learn about the discovery of insulin (Lesson 3)

- Use the Pupil's App on Navio
- Investigate Canada (Lesson 3)

- Practise intonation of sentences in the present perfect (Lesson 4)
- Review the present perfect for present evidence of a past action (Lesson 5)
- Review and practise the past continuous tense (Lesson 5)
- Reflect on your own learning (Lesson 8)
- Practise activity types found in the Cambridge Exams: A2 Key for Schools

- Think about the importance of being optimistic (Lesson 3)
- Learn about ways to help your community (Video and 21st Century Skills)

- Work in pairs and small groups to practise and reinforce learning (all lessons)
- Do a communication task (Lesson 5)

- Read and understand a story (Lesson 3)
- Learn about Canada (Lesson 3)
- Read a publicity leaflet (Lesson 6)
- Write a publicity leaflet (Lesson 7)
- Sing a song (Lesson 8)

### Vocabulary

**Core vocabulary**
*blow up balloons, choose the music, clean the furniture, decorate the room, go shopping, make a cake, make posters, put out the food, sell tickets, send invitations, serve drinks, sweep the floor; break my arm, bruise my arm, burn my hand, cut my finger, hurt my knee, scratch my leg, twist my ankle*

**Extension vocabulary (optional)**
*give directions, invite a band, put up banners, sell raffle tickets, set up stalls, write thank you letters; bang my head, feel sick, have a fever, have a sore throat*

**Other vocabulary**
*amount, blood, control, cure, diabetes, insulin, medicine, pancreas; fundraising event, volunteer; strapline, testimonials, title; animal care home, community, rubbish, rugby, tyre, volunteering*

**Recycled vocabulary**
*do my homework, feed (Charlie), have a party, tidy up my room, water the plants; been, bought, broken, eaten, finished, met, read*

### Structures

**Core structures**
*I / You / We / They have already made a cake. He / She / It has already made a cake. I / You / We / They haven't made a cake yet. He / She / It hasn't made a cake yet. Have I / you / we / they made a cake yet? Has he / she / it made a cake yet? No, I / you / we / they haven't. Yes, he / she / it has. No, he / she / it hasn't. I / You / We / They have just eaten an apple. He / She / It has just eaten an apple. Have I / you / we / they just eaten an apple? Has he / she / it just eaten an apple? Yes, I / you / we / they have.*

**Recycled structures**
*Elizabeth Hughes was living with her family. If she eats very little food, she can live for longer. What's happened to you? I've twisted my ankle. What were you doing? I was playing basketball.*

### Pronunciation

Intonation of sentences in the present perfect

### Literacy

**Text type:** a publicity leaflet (text to persuade; writing preparation)
**Reading skill:** predicting content from pictures
**Writing skill:** using questions to create interest

### Culture ... around the world

The discovery of a cure for diabetes in Canada

### 21st Century Skills

**Ways of working:** being a leader

### Thinking skills

Categorising (Lesson 1); Analysing and applying rules (Lessons 2 and 4); Creating (Lesson 4); Defining and describing (Lesson 5); Finding and classifying information (Lesson 6); Planning, checking and correcting (Lesson 7); Seeing another's point of view (Lesson 8); Reflecting on learning (Lesson 8)

### Cooperative learning

Working together (Lessons 1–8); Collaborating (Lessons 1–8); Checking learning (Lessons 1–8); Peer evaluation and feedback (Lesson 7); Participating (Lessons 1–8); Helping and encouraging (Lessons 1–8); Reaching agreement (Lesson 8); Reflecting and setting goals (Lessons 1 and 8)

### Values

The importance of being optimistic

### Cross-curricular links

**Link to Science**
The tertiary sector

**Suggested Arts and Crafts concepts**
Depth in landscapes

## Key Competences and Key Learning Outcomes

- Identify and say words associated with preparing for a party
- Listen to definitions and identify the words
- Talk about preparing for a party
- Read a message for general understanding
- Review different ways of helping others
- Discuss and agree how to help at a party

**Key language**

- *blow up balloons, choose the music, clean the furniture, decorate the room, go shopping, make a cake, make posters, put out the food, sell tickets, send invitations, serve drinks, sweep the floor*
- *What shall we do a week before the party? We could make posters. What will we need? We'll need pens.*
- **Extension:** *give directions, invite a band, put up banners, sell raffle tickets, set up stalls, write thank you letters*

**Materials**

- Pupil's Book pp72–73; Activity Book p70; Class CD3; Teacher's App on Navio
- Preparing for a party flashcards

**Optional materials**

- Teacher's Resource Bank: Trinity Exams Practice cards (selected from the Starter Unit and Units 1, 2, 3, 4, 5 and 6)

## At a Glance Lesson Plan

### Pupil's Book

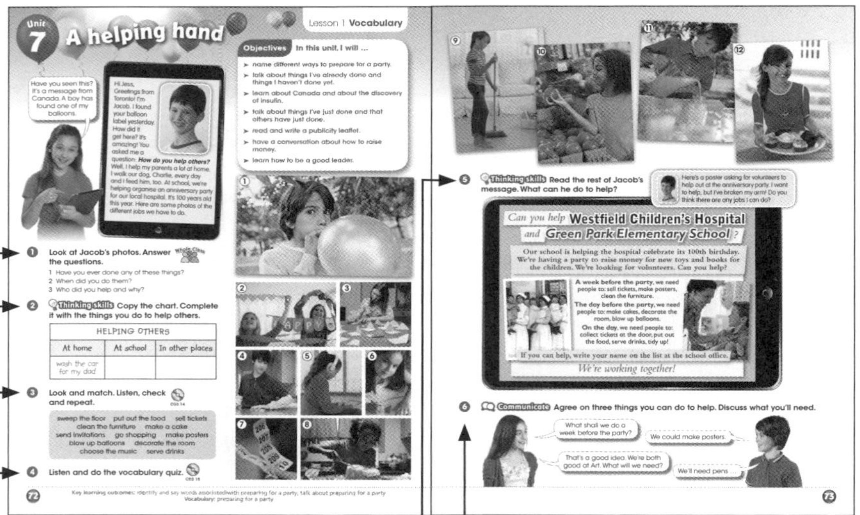


**Starting the lesson**

- Review helping at home.
- Set learning objectives.

**Activity 1**

- Look at Jacob's photos.
- Answer the questions.

**Activity 2**

- Copy the chart.
- Complete it with the things you do to help others.

**Vocabulary presentation**

- Present the new vocabulary using the preparing for a party flashcards.

**Activity 3**

- Look and match.
- Listen, check and repeat.

▶ *CD3 Track 14 p289*

**Activity 4**

- Listen and do the vocabulary quiz.

▶ *CD3 Track 15 p289*

**Activity 5**

- Read the rest of Jacob's message.
- What can he do to help?

**Activity 6**

- Agree on three things you can do to help.
- Discuss what you'll need.
- Go to the Activity Book.

**Ending the lesson**

- Review the lesson and reflect on learning.

**Extra activities**

**Extension**

- Find out about Canada.

**Vocabulary extension**

- Present six additional vocabulary items.

**Digital resources**

**Teacher's Digital:** You can also teach this lesson using the Teacher's App on Navio.

**Pupil's Digital:** Encourage your pupils to use the Pupil's App on Navio to practise the activities from this lesson.

Powered By NAVIO

### Activity Book

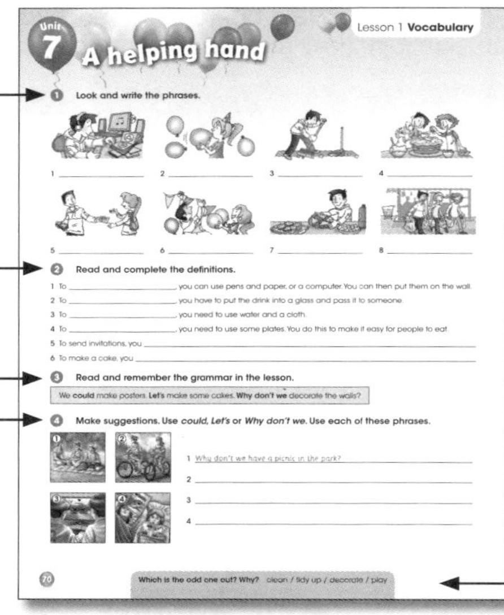


**Activity Book**

**Activity 1**

- Look and write the phrases.

**Activity 2**

- Read and complete the definitions.

**Activity 3**

- Read and remember the grammar in the lesson.

**Activity 4**

- Make suggestions. Use *could*, *Let's* or *Why don't we*. Use each of these phrases.

**Odd one out activity**

- Which is the odd one out? Why?

**Starting the lesson**

**Use the Trinity Exams Practice cards (optional).**
- The pupils practise asking and answering questions.

**Review helping at home.**
- Ask **Do you help at home? What did you do to help at home this morning?**

**Set learning objectives.**
- Say **Today we're going to learn some ways of helping to prepare for a party.**

**Pupil's Book Activity 1**

**Look at Jacob's photos. Answer the questions.**
- Invite a pupil to read out the speech bubble to find out who has found the balloon. Ask **Do you know where Canada is?**
- Invite a pupil to read out the message. Check understanding.
- Work as a class to answer the questions.

**Answers:** **1** blow up a balloon. **2** decorate the room **3** send invitations **4** clean the furniture **5** choose the music **6** make posters **7** sell tickets **8** make a cake

**Pupil's Book Activity 2**

**Copy the chart. Complete it with the things you do to help others.**
- Copy the chart onto the board. Elicit an example for each column.
- Organise the class into pairs. The pupils copy the chart into their notebooks and classify the activities that they think of.

**Vocabulary presentation**

- Present the new vocabulary using the preparing for a party flashcards. Show the first flashcard and elicit / say the phrase. Ask **When do you have to (sweep the floor)? What do you use to (sweep the floor)?**

**Pupil's Book Activity 3**

**Look and match. Listen, check and repeat.**
▶ *CD3 Track 14 p289*
- Ask the pupils to look at number 1 in the photo. Ask **What activity is this?** The pupils work in pairs to match numbers 2–12 and the phrases.
- Play the CD. The pupils listen and check.
- Play the CD again, pausing after each phrase for the pupils to repeat.

**Pupil's Book Activity 4**

**Listen and do the vocabulary quiz.**
▶ *CD3 Track 15 p289*
- Play the CD. Listen to the first definition, pausing at the beep to allow the pupils to name the activity. Play the CD to listen to the answer.
- Repeat the procedure with the other definitions.

**Pupil's Book Activity 5**

**Read the rest of Jacob's message. What can he do to help?**
- Invite a pupil to read out the message. Check that the pupils understand the task. The pupils read the information and choose the activities for Jacob to do.

**Pupil's Book Activity 6**

**Agree on three things you can do to help. Discuss what you'll need.**
- Invite two pupils to read the speech bubbles.
- The pupils work in pairs. They agree on three things they could do. They make notes in their notebooks.
- The pupils then agree on what they will need.

**Activity Book**

**Activity 1**

**Look and write the phrases.**
- The pupils write the phrases to match the pictures.

**Answers:** **1** choose the music **2** blow up balloons **3** sweep the floor **4** make a cake **5** sell tickets **6** decorate the room **7** put out the food **8** go shopping

**Activity 2**

**Read and complete the definitions.**
- The pupils complete the definitions.

**Answers:** **1** make a poster **2** serve drinks **3** clean the furniture **4** put out the food

**Activity 3**

**Read and remember the grammar in the lesson.**
- Invite a pupil to read out the information. Remind the class that we use these expressions when we are trying to decide, with other people, what to do.
- Ask **How can we change our classroom?** The pupils make suggestions using the structures.

**Activity 4**

**Make suggestions. Use *could*, *Let's* or *Why don't we*. Use each of these phrases.**
- The pupils make suggestions based on the pictures.

**Odd one out activity**

**Which is the odd one out? Why?**
- The pupils complete the odd one out activity.

**Answers:** play (It isn't something you do to prepare for a party.)

**Ending the lesson**

**Review the lesson and reflect on learning.**
- Say **Today we've learnt the names of activities to help prepare for a party. What do you remember?**
- Ask **Which was your favourite activity today? Which activity was easy / difficult?**

**Extra activities**

**Extension**
- The pupils find Canada on the world map on pages 134–135. They read the accompanying facts.

**Vocabulary extension**
- Present six additional expressions: *give directions, invite a band, put up banners, sell raffle tickets, set up stalls, write thank you letters.*
- Use the Vocabulary booster on NAVIO to practise these new words.

## Key Competences and Key Learning Outcomes

- Listen to and read a dialogue
- Use *already* and *yet* to talk about things that have and haven't been done
- Identify the use of the present perfect in the dialogue

## Key language

- *do my homework, feed (Charlie), make a cake / cupcakes, raise money, sell all the tickets, tidy up my room, water the plants; bowl, mixture, stir; medical discovery*
- *I / You / We / They have already made a cake. He / She / It has already made a cake. I / You / We / They haven't made a cake yet. He / She / It hasn't made a cake yet. Have I / you / we / they made a cake yet? Has he / she / it made a cake yet? No, I / you / we / they haven't. Yes, he / she / it has. No, he / she / it hasn't.*

## Materials

- Pupil's Book p74; Activity Book p71; Class CD3; Teacher's App on Navio
- Teacher's Resource Bank: Preparing for a party word cards

## Optional materials

- Teacher's Resource Bank: Trinity Exams Practice cards (selected from the Starter Unit and Units 1, 2, 3, 4, 5 and 6)

# At a Glance Lesson Plan

## Pupil's Book

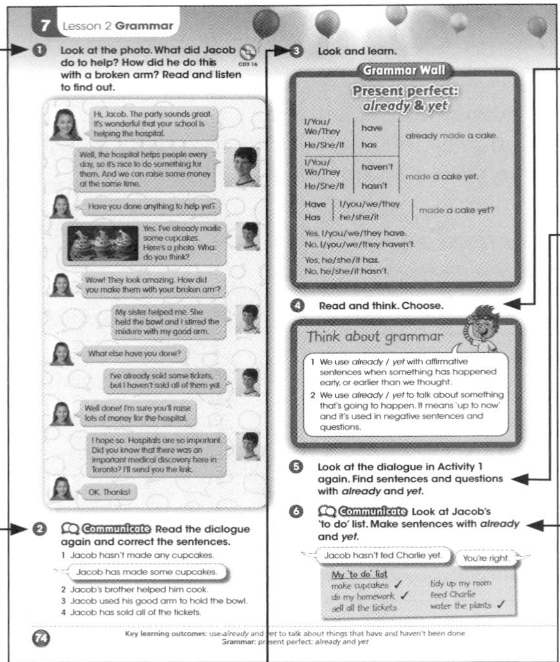

### Starting the lesson

- Use the Trinity Exams Practice cards (optional).
- Review the activities for helping to prepare for a party.
- Set learning objectives.

### Activity 1

- Look at the photo.
- What did Jacob do to help?
- How did he do this with a broken arm?
- Read and listen to find out.

▶ ***CD3 Track 16 p290***

### Activity 2

- Read the dialogue again and correct the sentences.

### Activity 3

- Look and learn – Grammar wall

### Activity 4

- Read and think.
- Choose.

### Activity 5

- Look at the dialogue in Activity 1 again.
- Find sentences and questions with *already* and *yet*.

### Activity 6

- Look at Jacob's 'to do' list.
- Make sentences with *already* and *yet*.

Go to the Activity Book.

### Ending the lesson

- Review the lesson and reflect on learning.

### Extra activity

**Reinforcement**

- Play a chain game.

## Digital resources

**Teacher's Digital:** You can also teach this lesson using the Teacher's App on Navio.

**Pupil's Digital:** Encourage your pupils to use the Pupil's App on Navio to practise the activities from this lesson.

Powered By NAVIO

## Activity Book

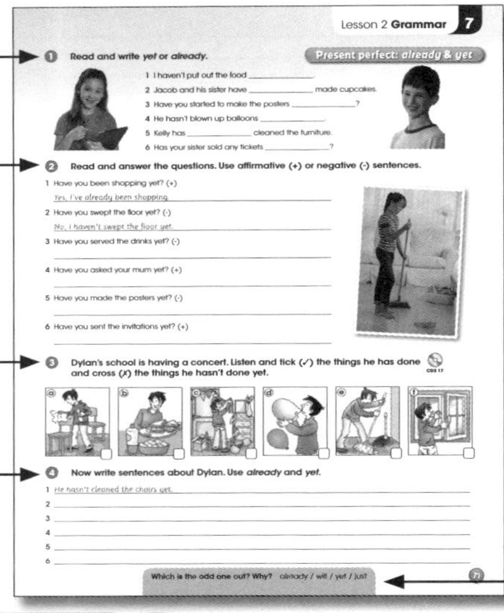

### Activity Book

**Activity 1**

- Read and write *yet* or *already*.

**Activity 2**

- Read and answer the questions. Use affirmative (+) or negative (-) sentences.

**Activity 3**

- Dylan's school is having a concert. Listen and tick (✓) the things he has done and cross (✗) the things he hasn't done yet.

▶ ***CD3 Track 17 p290***

**Activity 4**

- Now write sentences about Dylan. Use *already* and *yet*.

**Odd one out activity**

- Which is the odd one out? Why?

# Detailed Lesson Plan

**Starting the lesson**

**Use the Trinity Exams Practice cards (optional).**
- The pupils practise asking and answering questions.

**Review the activities for preparing for a party.**
- The pupils play the *Yes or No?* game (see p27) with the preparing for a party word cards.

**Set learning objectives.**
- Say **Today we're going to learn how to use 'yet' and 'already' to talk about things we have done and things we haven't done.**

**Pupil's Book Activity 1**

**Look at the photo. What did Jacob do to help? How did he do this with a broken arm? Read and listen to find out.**

▸ ***CD3 Track 16 p290***
- Prompt the class to describe the photo.
- Read out the questions. Ask the class if they can predict the answers without reading the text.
- Play the CD. The pupils listen and read the dialogue. They answer the questions. (*Jacob has made some cupcakes and his sister helped him.*)

**Pupil's Book Activity 2**

**Read the dialogue again and correct the sentences.**
- The pupils read and correct the sentences in pairs.

**Pupil's Book Activity 3**

**Look and learn – Grammar wall**
- Read the information on the Grammar wall as a class.
- Ask **Do we use 'already' with the affirmative or the negative? Does 'already' go before or after the main verb? With what kind of sentences do we use 'yet'? Where do we put 'yet' in the sentence?**

**Pupil's Book Activity 4**

**Read and think. Choose.**
- Focus the pupils' attention on the Think about grammar box. Read out the sentences as a class. The pupils complete the sentences in pairs.

**Answer:** **1** already **2** yet

**Pupil's Book Activity 5**

**Look at the dialogue in Activity 1 again. Find sentences and questions with *already* and *yet*.**
- Organise the pupils into pairs. They look at the dialogue and find examples with 'already' or 'yet'.

**Pupil's Book Activity 6**

**Look at Jacob's 'to do' list. Make sentences with *already* and *yet*.**
- Invite two pupils to read out the speech bubbles and Jacob's 'to do' list.
- In pairs, the pupils take turns to make sentences about the things on the list.

**Activity Book**

**Activity 1**

**Read and write *yet* or *already*.**
- The pupils complete the sentences.

**Answers:** **1** yet **2** already **3** yet **4** yet **5** already **6** yet

**Activity 2**

**Read and answer the questions. Use affirmative (+) or negative (-) sentences.**
- The pupils write the answers to the questions.
- The pupils ask and answer the questions in pairs.

**Answers:** **1** Yes, I've already been shopping. **2** No, I haven't swept the floor yet. **3** No, I haven't served the drinks yet. **4** Yes, I've already asked my mum. **5** No, I haven't made the posters yet. **6** Yes, I've already sent the invitations.

**Activity 3**

**Dylan's school is having a concert. Listen and tick (✓) the things he has done and cross (✗) the things he hasn't done yet.**

▸ ***CD3 Track 17 p290***
- Ask the pupils to describe each picture.
- Play the CD. The pupils listen and tick or cross.
- Play the CD again, pausing after each piece of key information. The pupils complete their answers.

**Answers:** **1** cleaned the chairs ✗ **2** put out food ✗ **3** decorated the room ✓ **4** blown up the balloons ✓ **5** swept the floor ✗ **6** closed the windows ✓

**Activity 4**

**Now write sentences about Dylan. Use *already* and *yet*.**
- The pupils write the sentences.

**Answers:** **1** He hasn't cleaned the chairs yet. **2** He hasn't put out the food yet. **3** He has already decorated the room. **4** He has already blown up the balloons. **5** He hasn't swept the floor yet. **6** He has already closed the windows.

**Odd one out activity**

**Which is the odd one out? Why?**
- The pupils complete the odd one out activity.

**Answers:** will (You don't use it with the present perfect.)

**Ending the lesson**

**Review the lesson and reflect on learning.**
- Say **Today we've learnt how to talk about actions that we have already done and actions that we haven't done yet.**
- Ask **Which was your favourite activity today? Which activity was easy / difficult?**

**Extra activity**

**Reinforcement**
- Play a chain game with *Have I ... yet?*

## Key Competences and Key Learning Outcomes

- Read a story with a cultural focus
- Learn about the discovery of insulin
- Use the Internet to investigate Canada
- Listen for specific information
- Think about the importance of being optimistic
- Learn about Canada

**Key language**
- *amount, become ill, blood, chemical, control, cure, dangerous, diabetes, discover, famous politician, hope, hungry, insulin, medicine, Nobel Prize, optimistic, pancreas, scientist, sugar, twice*
- *Elizabeth Hughes was living with her family. If she eats very little food, she can live for longer. She's just eaten, but she's still hungry. We haven't finished testing it yet. Elizabeth took insulin twice a day.*

**Materials**
- Pupil's Book p75; Activity Book p72; Class CD3; Teacher's App on Navio

**Optional materials**
- Teacher's Resource Bank: Trinity Exams Practice cards (selected from the Starter Unit and Units 1, 2, 3, 4, 5 and 6)

## At a Glance Lesson Plan

### Starting the lesson
- Use the Trinity Exams Practice cards (optional).
- Review 'already' and 'yet'.
- Set learning objectives.

### Activity 1: Before you read
- Read and discuss.

### Activity 2
- Listen and read.

▶ *CD3 Track 18 p290*

Go to the Activity Book.

### Values
- Read and discuss.

## Pupil's Book

### Ending the lesson
- Review the lesson and reflect on learning.

### Extra activity
**Reinforcement**
- Make sentences about Elizabeth Hughes.

## Activity Book

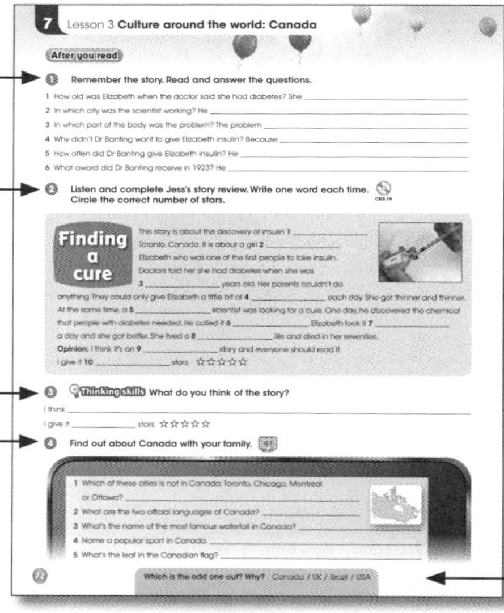


### Activity Book: After you read

**Activity 1**
- Remember the story. Read and answer the questions.

**Activity 2**
- Listen and complete Jess's story review.

▶ *CD3 Track 19 p290*
- Write one word each time. Circle the correct number of stars.

**Activity 3**
- What do you think of the story?

**Activity 4**
- Find out about Canada with your family.

**Odd one out activity**
- Which is the odd one out? Why?

## Digital resources

**Teacher's Digital:** You can also teach this lesson using the Teacher's App on Navio.

**Pupil's Digital:** Encourage your pupils to use the Pupil's App on Navio to practise the activities from this lesson.

Powered By NAVIO

# Detailed Lesson Plan

## Starting the lesson

**Use the Trinity Exams Practice cards (optional).**
- The pupils practise asking and answering questions.

**Review 'already' and 'yet'.**
- The pupils make three sentences using 'already' or 'yet'. One of them has to be false.
- The pupils read out their three sentences. The other pupils guess which sentence is false.

**Set learning objectives.**
- Say **Today we're going to read a story from Canada. We're going to find out about a famous discovery.**

## Pupil's Book Activity 1: Before you read

**Read and discuss.**
- Ask the class to look at the photo. Ask **What can you see?**
- Ask the pupils to answer the questions in pairs. Then discuss ideas as a class.

## Pupil's Book Activity 2

**Listen and read.**

▶ *CD3 Track 18 p290*
- Ask the pupils to listen to the story to find out why diabetes can be dangerous.
- Play the CD. The pupils follow in their books.
- Ask questions to check understanding.

**Suggested comprehension questions:**
- Frame 1: **How old was Elizabeth when she became ill?** (*11.*)
- Frame 2: **Who was working to find a cure for diabetes?** (*Frederick Banting.*)
- Frame 3: **What's it dangerous to do if you have diabetes?** (*To eat too much food.*)
- Frame 4: **What did Dr Banting discover in 1922?** (*The chemical he called insulin.*)
- Frame 5: **Did Dr Banting help Elizabeth?** (*Yes.*)
- Frame 6: **What happened to Elizabeth?** (*She took insulin twice a day.*)

## Activity Book: After you read

### Activity 1

**Remember the story. Read and answer the questions.**
- Read out the first question and invite a pupil to answer it.
- The pupils read and answer the remaining questions.

**Answers:** **1** was 11 years old. **2** was working in Toronto. **3** was in the pancreas. **4** they hadn't finished testing it yet. **5** gave her insulin twice a day. **6** received the Nobel Prize.

### Activity 2

**Listen and complete Jess's story review. Write one word each time. Circle the correct number of stars.**

▶ *CD3 Track 19 p290*
- Read out the story review as a class. Ask the pupils to guess the missing words.
- Play the CD without pausing. The pupils listen and complete as much of the information as possible.
- Play the CD again, pausing after each piece of key information to check the information and spelling. The pupils circle the correct number of stars.

**Answers:** **1** in **2** called **3** 11 **4** food **5** Canadian **6** insulin **7** twice **8** long **9** important **10** five

### Activity 3

**What do you think of the story?**
- The pupils write their opinion and give a rating.
- Invite different pupils to share their opinions.

### Activity 4

**Find out about Canada with your family.** ICT
- Read out the questions about Canada. Ask **Where can you find out this information?** (*Internet, library, asking friends and family.*) The pupils complete the activity at home.
- If you prefer to do this activity in the class, connect to a children's website which has information about Canada such as: www.kids-world-travel-guide.com/canada-facts.html.
- Read out the questions. The pupils work as a class to find and write the answers.

**Answers:** **1** Chicago **2** English and French **3** Niagara (although there are many others too) **4** ice hockey **5** the maple leaf

## Odd one out activity

**Which is the odd one out? Why?**
- The pupils complete the odd one out activity.

**Answers:** Brazil (They don't have English as an official language.)

## Values

**Read and discuss.**
- Read out the statement and questions. Discuss as a class.
- Encourage the pupils to think about people who don't lose hope. Ask **Can you think of other famous people who didn't lose hope?**

## Ending the lesson

**Review the lesson and reflect on learning.**
- Say **Today we've read a story from Canada.**
- Ask **Which was your favourite activity today? Which activity was easy / difficult?**

## Extra activity

**Reinforcement**
- Ask the class to think about Elizabeth and how she felt before she had insulin and how she began to feel after she had insulin. They write sentences, e.g. *Elizabeth was very weak before she had insulin. She became stronger after she had insulin.*

### Key Competences and Key Learning Outcomes

- Act out a short dialogue in pairs
- Learn and practise using the present perfect with 'just'

- Identify and practise sentence stress in the present perfect tense with *just*, *already* and *yet*

### Key language

- *been, bought, broken, eaten, finished, met, read; inject insulin, healthy food*
- *I / You / We / They have just eaten an apple. He / She / It has just eaten an apple. Have I / you / we / they just eaten an apple? Has he / she / it just eaten an apple? Yes, I / you / we / they have.*

### Materials

- Pupil's Book p76; Activity Book p73; Class CD3; Teacher's App on Navio

### Optional materials

- Teacher's Resource Bank: Trinity Exams Practice cards (selected from the Starter Unit and Units 1, 2, 3, 4, 5 and 6)

## At a Glance Lesson Plan

### Pupil's Book

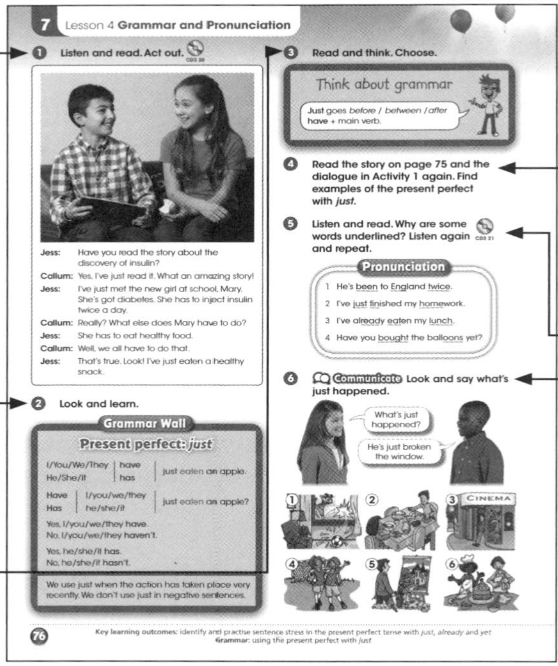
7 Lesson 4 Grammar and Pronunciation

1 Listen and read. Act out.

Jess: Have you read the story about the discovery of insulin?
Callum: Yes. I've just read it. What an amazing story!
Jess: I've just met the new girl at school, Mary. She's got diabetes. She has to inject insulin twice a day.
Callum: Really? What else does Mary have to do?
Jess: She has to eat healthy food.
Callum: Well, we all have to do that.
Jess: That's true. Look! I've just eaten a healthy snack.

2 Look and learn.

Grammar Wall

Present perfect: *just*

| | | |
|---|---|---|
| I/You/We/They | have | just eaten an apple. |
| He/She/It | has | |
| Have | I/you/we/they | just eaten an apple? |
| Has | he/she/it | |

Yes, I/you/we/they have. No, I/you/we/they haven't.
Yes, he/she/it has. No, he/she/it hasn't.

We use just when the action has taken place very recently. We don't use just in negative sentences.

3 Read and think. Choose.

Think about grammar

Just goes before / between / after have + main verb.

4 Read the story on page 75 and the dialogue in Activity 1 again. Find examples of the present perfect with *just*.

5 Listen and read. Why are some words underlined? Listen again and repeat.

Pronunciation

1 He's been to England twice.
2 I've just finished my homework.
3 I've already eaten my lunch.
4 Have you bought the balloons yet?

6 Communicate Look and say what's just happened.

What's just happened?
He's just broken the window.

76

Key learning outcomes: identify and practise sentence stress in the present perfect tense with just, already and yet
Grammar: using the present perfect with just

#### Starting the lesson

- Use the Trinity Exams Practice cards (optional).
- Review past participles.
- Set learning objectives.

#### Activity 1

- Listen and read.
- Act out.
- ▶ *CD3 Track 20 p290*

#### Activity 2

- Look and learn – Grammar wall

#### Activity 3

- Read and think.
- Choose.

#### Activity 4

- Read the story on page 75 and the dialogue in Activity 1 again.
- Find examples of the present perfect simple with *just*.

#### Activity 5

- Listen and read.
- ▶ *CD3 Track 21 p290*
- Why are some words underlined?
- Listen again and repeat.

#### Activity 6

- Look and say what's just happened.
- Go to the Activity Book.

#### Ending the lesson

- Review the lesson and reflect on learning.

#### Extra activity

**Reinforcement**
- Play a mime game.

### Digital resources

**Teacher's Digital:** You can also teach this lesson using the Teacher's App on Navio.

**Pupil's Digital:** Encourage your pupils to use the Pupil's App on Navio to practise the activities from this lesson.

Powered By NAVIO

### Activity Book

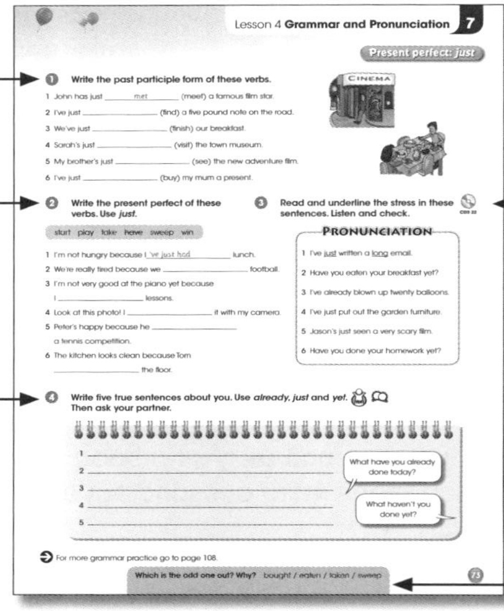
Lesson 4 Grammar and Pronunciation 7

Present perfect: just

1 Write the past participle form of these verbs.

1 John has just met (meet) a famous film star.
2 I've just ______ (find) a five pound note on the road.
3 We've just ______ (finish) our breakfast.
4 Sarah's just ______ (visit) the town museum.
5 My brother's just ______ (see) the new adventure film.
6 I've just ______ (buy) my mum a present.

2 Write the present perfect of these verbs. Use *just*.

start play take have sweep win

1 I'm not hungry because I 've just had lunch.
2 We're really tired because we ______ football.
3 I'm not very good at the piano yet because I ______ lessons.
4 Look at this photo! I ______ it with my camera.
5 Peter's happy because he ______ a tennis competition.
6 The kitchen looks clean because Tom ______ the floor.

3 Read and underline the stress in these sentences. Listen and check.

PRONUNCIATION

1 I've just written a long email.
2 Have you eaten your breakfast yet?
3 I've already blown up twenty balloons.
4 I've just put out the garden furniture.
5 Jason's just seen a very scary film.
6 Have you done your homework yet?

4 Write five true sentences about you. Use *already*, *just* and *yet*. Then ask your partner.

What have you already done today?
What haven't you done yet?

For more grammar practice go to page 108.

Which is the odd one out? Why? bought / eaten / taken / sweep

73

#### Activity Book

**Activity 1**
- Write the the past participle form of these verbs.

**Activity 2**
- Write the present perfect of these verbs. Use *just*.

**Activity 3**
- Read and underline the stress in these sentences. Listen and check.
- ▶ *CD3 Track 22 p291*

**Activity 4**
- Write five true sentences about you. Use *already*, *just* and *yet*. Then ask your partner.

**Odd one out**
- Which is the odd one out? Why?

# Detailed Lesson Plan

**Starting the lesson**

**Use the Trinity Exams Practice cards (optional).**
- The pupils practise asking and answering questions.

**Review past participles.**
- Play *Tic Tac Toe* (*Noughts and crosses*) to review past participles of *read, meet, eat, buy, finish, break, write, make, go*. Use the question ***What have you done?***

**Set learning objectives.**
- Say **Today we're going to learn how to use the present perfect simple tense with 'just' to talk about very recent actions.**

**Pupil's Book Activity 1**

**Listen and read. Act out.**

▶ *CD3 Track 20 p290*
- The pupils look at the photo. Ask **What do you think Jess and Callum are talking about? What can you see in the photo?**
- Play the CD. The pupils listen and read the dialogue.
- Play the CD again, pausing after each sentence for the pupils to repeat.
- The pupils practise the dialogue in pairs.

**Pupil's Book Activity 2**

**Look and learn – Grammar wall**
- Read the information on the Grammar wall as a class.
- Use questions to encourage the pupils to think about the position of 'just' in the present perfect simple sentence. Ask **Do we put 'just' before or after the main verb?** Focus on meaning too. Ask **If we use 'just' when did the action happen?**

**Pupil's Book Activity 3**

**Read and think. Choose.**
- Focus the pupils' attention on the Think about grammar box. Read out the sentence as a class. The pupils decide how to complete the sentence correctly in pairs.

**Answer:** between

**Pupil's Book Activity 4**

**Read the story on page 75 and the dialogue in Activity 1 again. Find examples of the present perfect simple with *just*.**
- Organise the pupils into pairs. They find examples of the present perfect simple with 'just' in the dialogue and the story.

**Pupil's Book Activity 5**

**Listen and read. Why are some words underlined? Listen again and repeat.**

▶ *CD3 Track 21 p290*
- Ask the pupils which tense the sentences are in. Say **Let's listen to the sentences. Why are some words underlined?** (*To show the stress.*)
- Play the CD again. The pupils listen and repeat the sentences.

**Pupil's Book Activity 6**

**Look and say what's just happened.**
- Ask two pupils to read the speech bubbles. Ask **Which picture are they talking about?**
- Organise the class into pairs. One pupil asks the question and the other chooses a picture (without saying which) and answers according to that picture. The first pupil guesses the picture.

**Activity Book**

**Activity 1**

**Write the past participle of these verbs.**
- The pupils complete the sentences.

**Answers:** **1** met **2** found **3** finished **4** visited **5** seen **6** bought

**Activity 2**

**Write the present perfect of these verbs. Use *just*.**
- The pupils complete the sentences.

**Answers:** **1** I've just had **2** 've just played **3** 've just started **4** 've just taken **5** 's just won **6** 's just swept

**Activity 3**

**Read and underline the stress in these sentences. Listen and check.**

▶ *CD3 Track 22 p291*
- Invite a pupil to read the first sentence stressing the underlined words.
- Play the CD, pausing after each sentence. The pupils listen and mark the stress.

**Answers:** **1** just, long **2** eaten, breakfast, yet **3** already, twenty **4** just, garden **5** just, very **6** done, homework, yet

**Activity 4**

**Write some true sentences about you. Use *already*, *just* and *yet*. Then ask your partner.**
- The pupils write sentences about what they have and haven't done today. They then ask a partner the questions in the speech bubbles.

**Odd one out activity**

**Which is the odd one out? Why?**
- The pupils complete the odd one out activity.

**Answers:** sweep (It isn't a past participle.)

**Ending the lesson**

**Review the lesson and reflect on learning.**
- Say **Today we've learnt how to use the present perfect simple tense with 'just'.**
- Ask **Which was your favourite activity today? Which activity was easy / difficult?**

**Extra activity**

**Reinforcement**
- Play a mime game with *What have I just done?*

## Key Competences and Key Learning Outcomes

- Identify and say expressions related to accidents

- Listen for specific information
- Review and practise the present perfect simple for present evidence of a past action
  - Review and practise the past continuous tense
  - Practise activity types found in the Cambridge Exams: A2 Key for Schools

- Do a communication task

## Key language

- *break my arm, bruise my arm, burn my hand, cut my finger, hurt my knee, scratch my leg, twist my ankle*
- *What's happened to you? I've twisted my ankle. What were you doing? I was playing basketball.*
- **Extension:** *bang my head, feel sick, have a fever, have a sore throat*

## Materials

- Pupil's Book p77; Activity Book p74; Class CD3; Teacher's App on Navio; Teacher's Resource Bank: Unit 7

## Optional materials

- Teacher's Resource Bank: Trinity Exams Practice cards (selected from the Starter Unit and Units 1, 2, 3, 4, 5 and 6)

# At a Glance Lesson Plan

## Pupil's Book

### Starting the lesson

- Use the Trinity Exams Practice cards (optional).
- Review parts of the body.
- Set learning objectives.

### Activity 1

- Look and match.
- Listen, check and repeat.
- ▶ *CD3 Track 23 p291*

### Activity 2

- Listen and look.
- ▶ *CD3 Track 24 p291*
- What were the children in Activity 1 doing when they hurt themselves?

### Activity 3

- Listen again.
- ▶ *CD3 Track 24 p291*
- Write the past participle of the verbs in Activity 1 in your notebook.

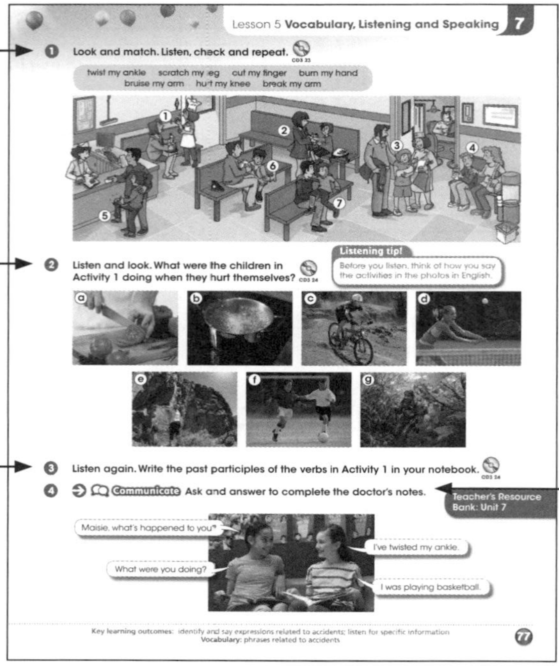

### Activity 4

- Ask and answer to complete the doctor's notes (Teacher's Resource Bank: Unit 7).
- Go to the Activity Book.

### Ending the lesson

- Review the lesson and reflect on learning.

### Extra activities

**Extension**

- Role play a conversation.

**Vocabulary extension**

- Present four additional vocabulary items.

## Digital resources

**Teacher's Digital:** You can also teach this lesson using the Teacher's App on Navio.

**Pupil's Digital:** Encourage your pupils to use the Pupil's App on Navio to practise the activities from this lesson.

Powered By NAVIO

## Activity Book

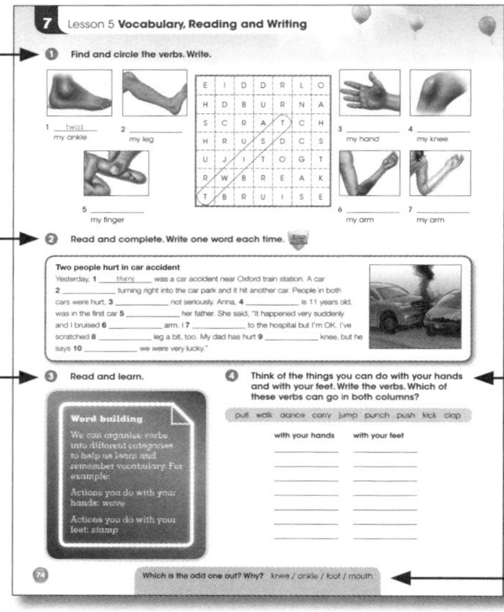

### Activity Book

**Activity 1**

- Find and circle the verbs. Write.

**Activity 2**

- Read and complete. Write one word each time.

**Activity 3**

- Read and learn.

**Activity 4**

- Think of the things you can do with your hands and with your feet. Write the verbs. Which of these verbs can go in both columns?

**Odd one out activity**

- Which is the odd one out? Why?

# Detailed Lesson Plan

## Starting the lesson

**Use the Trinity Exams Practice cards (optional).**
- The pupils practise asking and answering questions.

**Review parts of the body.**
- Ask **Have you ever broken a bone?** Encourage any pupils who answer 'yes' to say where they broke a bone. Ask **What other parts of the body do you know?**

**Set learning objectives.**
- Say **Today we're going to learn phrases to describe ways we can hurt ourselves and we're going to do a communication task.**

## Pupil's Book Activity 1

**Look and match. Listen, check and repeat.**
▶ ***CD3 Track 23 p291***
- The pupils look at the picture. Ask **Where are the children?** They describe what they can see.
- Organise the class into pairs. The pupils match the phrases in the box to the children in the scene.
- Play the CD. The pupils listen and check.
- Play the CD again, pausing after each action for the pupils to repeat.

## Pupil's Book Activity 2

**Listen and look. What were the children in Activity 1 doing when they hurt themselves?**
▶ ***CD3 Track 24 p291***
- The pupils look at number 1 in Activity 1 again. Say **She's burnt her hand. What was she doing when she burnt her hand?**
- Ask the pupils to look at the photos in Activity 2. Invite the pupils to name the activities. Explain that they have to listen to the children in Activity 1 who are explaining what they were doing. The pupils need to decide which child was doing which activity.
- Play the CD. The pupils listen and match. Repeat if necessary, pausing after each short dialogue.

## Pupil's Book Activity 3

**Listen again. Write the past participles of the verbs in Activity 1 in your notebook.**
▶ ***CD3 Track 24 p291***
- The pupils write the past participles in their notebooks.

## Pupil's Book Activity 4

**Ask and answer to complete the doctor's notes (Teacher's Resource Bank: Unit 7).**
- Invite two pupils to read out the speech bubbles.
- Organise the class into pairs (A and B). Give Pupils A the first worksheet from Teacher's Resource Bank Unit 7 and give Pupils B the other worksheet.
- Explain that Pupil A is the doctor and Pupil B is the different children. The doctor is completing their notes. When Pupil A has finished asking questions, Pupil B can be the doctor and complete their notes.
- At the end of the activity, the pupils show their notes to each other and check that the information is correct.

## Activity Book

**Activity 1**
**Find and circle the verbs. Write.**
- The pupils find and circle the words in the puzzle. They then complete the phrases.

**Answers:** **1** twist **2** scratch **3** burn **4** hurt **5** cut **6** bruise **7** break

**Activity 2**
**Read and complete. Write one word each time.**
- The pupils look at the picture and describe what they can see. Ask **What's just happened?**
- Look at the example as a class. The pupils write one word in each gap.

**Answers:** **1** there **2** was **3** but **4** who **5** with **6** my **7** went **8** my **9** his **10** that

**Activity 3**
**Read and learn.**
- Read the information as a class.

**Activity 4**
**Think of the things you can do with your hands and with your feet. Write the verbs. Which of these verbs can go in both columns?**
- Read out the list of verbs.
- The pupils write the verbs in the correct columns.

**Answers:** **with your hands:** pull, carry, punch, push, clap
**with your feet:** walk, dance, jump, kick
**both:** walk, push

**Odd one out activity**
**Which is the odd one out? Why?**
- The pupils complete the odd one out activity.

**Answers:** mouth (It isn't part of your leg.)

## Ending the lesson

**Review the lesson and reflect on learning.**
- Say **Today we've learnt to describe ways we can hurt ourselves and we've played a communication game.**
- Ask **Which was your favourite activity today? Which activity was easy / difficult?**

## Extra activities

**Extension**
- Put the pupils into pairs. Ask them to prepare a conversation between a patient and a doctor. Remind them of the question *What's happened to you?* and teach them *What's the matter?* On the board you could write the following prompts: *say hello, ask what's the matter, ask how it happened, say what you are going to do, say goodbye.*

**Vocabulary extension**
- Present four additional phrases: *bang my head, feel sick, have a fever, have a sore throat.*
- Use the Vocabulary booster on NAVIO to practise these new words.

## Key Competences and Key Learning Outcomes

- Do pre-reading tasks to predict content and raise interest
- Read a leaflet for general understanding
- Scan a leaflet for specific information

- Discuss and share what you know about this type of text

- Read and understand a publicity leaflet
- Give an opinion on the text
- Talk about volunteering in the community

**Key language**

- *bring, broke my leg, care home, clean up, coats, community, environment, homeless people, hospital, lake, local animal shelter, picture frames, scared, volunteer (v), volunteers*
- *When I was seven, I (broke my leg). We've (spoken to lots of children). You can (help animals). What could you do to help?*

**Materials**

- Pupil's Book p78; Activity Book p75; Class CD3; Teacher's App on Navio
- Teacher's Resource Bank: Preparing for a party word cards

**Optional materials**

- Teacher's Resource Bank: Trinity Exams Practice cards (selected from the Starter Unit and Units 1, 2, 3, 4, 5 and 6)

## At a Glance Lesson Plan

### Pupil's Book

**Starting the lesson**

- Use the Trinity Exams Practice cards (optional).
- Review ways of preparing for a party.
- Set learning objectives.

**Activity 1: Before you read**

- Read and discuss.

**Activity 2**

- Look at the photos.
- What's volunteering?
- What things can we volunteer to do in our community?
- Read and find out.

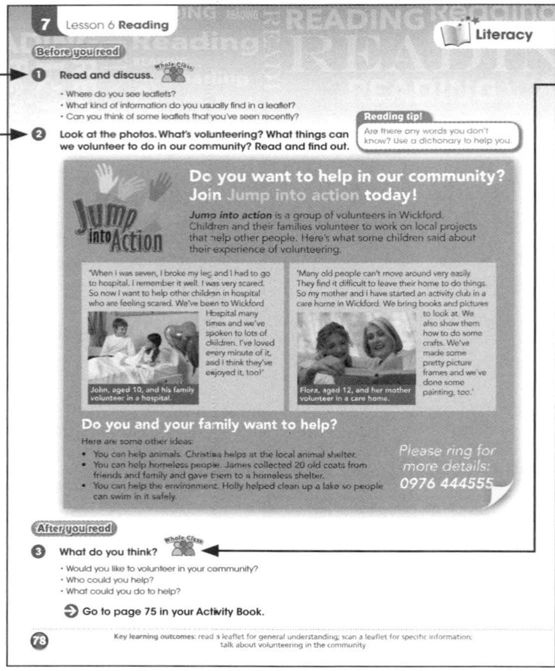


**Activity 3: After you read**

- What do you think?
- Go to the Activity Book.

**Ending the lesson**

- Review the lesson and reflect on learning.

**Extra activity**

**Extension**

- Imagine what the other volunteers on the leaflet have done.

### Activity Book

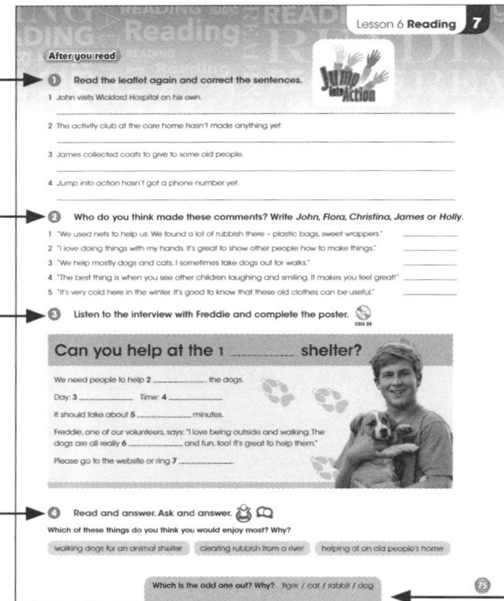


**Activity Book: After you read**

**Activity 1**

- Read the leaflet again and correct the sentences.

**Activity 2**

- Who do you think made these comments? Write *John, Flora, Cristina, James* or *Holly.*

**Activity 3**

- Listen to the interview with Freddie and complete the poster.

▶ ***CD3 Track 25 p291***

**Activity 4**

- Read and answer. Ask and answer.

**Odd one out activity**

- Which is the odd one out? Why?

## Digital resources

**Teacher's Digital:** You can also teach this lesson using the Teacher's App on Navio.

**Pupil's Digital:** Encourage your pupils to use the Pupil's App on Navio to practise the activities from this lesson.

Powered By NAVIO

# Detailed Lesson Plan

## Starting the lesson

**Use the Trinity Exams Practice cards (optional).**
- The pupils practise asking and answering questions.

**Review ways of preparing for a party.**
- Use the preparing for a party word cards to play the *Mime the card* game (see p27).

**Set learning objectives.**
- Say **Today we're going to read a leaflet about volunteering.**

## Pupil's Book Activity 1: Before you read

**Read and discuss.**
- Read the questions as a class. Prompt the pupils to answer in as much detail as possible. Talk about leaflets they see at the doctors, at cinemas, in shops or at school, or through the door at home. Explain that the leaflets are for publicity. People are trying to give you some information or sell you something.

## Pupil's Book Activity 2

**Look at the photos. What's volunteering? What things can we volunteer to do in our community? Read and find out.**
- (Books closed.) Write 'volunteering' on the board. Ask the pupils to explain what it is. Ask the pupils to give you some examples and write these on the board.
- (Books open.) Ask the pupils to describe the photos. Ask **What's happening?** Ask what they think the leaflet is about. Say that they will discover some different ways to volunteer.
- Ask the pupils to read and find the five ways of volunteering with *Jump into Action.*

## Pupil's Book Activity 3: After you read

**What do you think?**
- Read the first question as a class. Prompt the pupils to give their thoughts.
- The pupils work in pairs to think about what they could do to help people in the community.

## Activity Book: After you read

### Activity 1

**Read the leaflet again and correct the sentences.**
- The pupils read each sentence and correct it.

**Answers:** **1** John visits Wickford Hospital with his family. **2** The activity club at the care home has made picture frames. **3** James collected coats to give to a homeless shelter. **4** *Jump into action* has got a phone number.

### Activity 2

**Who do you think made these comments? Write *John, Flora, Cristina, James* or *Holly.***
- Read the statements together as a class. Help with any difficult vocabulary.
- The pupils decide which of the children made which statement.

**Answers:** **1** Holly **2** Flora **3** Christina **4** John **5** James

### Activity 3

**Listen to the interview with Freddie and complete the poster.**

▶ ***CD3 Track 25 p291***
- Look at the poster as a class. Read the text together.
- Play the CD. The pupils listen and try to complete the gaps in the poster.
- Play the CD again, pausing after each piece of key information.

**Answers:** **1** Animal **2** walk **3** Saturday **4** 11.00 **5** 45 **6** friendly **7** 357682

### Activity 4

**Read and answer. Ask and answer.**
- The pupils ask and answer the questions in pairs.

**Odd one out activity**

**Which is the odd one out? Why?**
- The pupils complete the odd one out activity.

**Answers:** tiger (It isn't a pet.)

## Ending the lesson

**Review the lesson and reflect on learning.**
- Say **Today we've read a leaflet about volunteering.**
- Ask **Which was your favourite activity today? Which activity was easy / difficult?**

## Extra activity

**Extension**
- Ask the pupils to look again at the leaflet. In pairs, they choose one of the children and imagine what other things they have done to answer the question *What else have you done with Jump into Action?*

## Key Competences and Key Learning Outcomes

- Identify the use of questions to create interest
- Learn a structure for writing a text to persuade
- Make predictions about texts from headlines
- Use criteria to check your writing
- Share your writing with another pupil
- Write a leaflet

## Key language

- *detailed information, football club, healthy, historic, lifesaver, make new friends, on foot, portions, practise, skills, strapline, testimonials, title, vegetables*
- *Do you want to learn new skills and make new friends? I've (learnt new football skills).*

## Materials

- Pupil's Book p79; Activity Book p76; Teacher's App on Navio
- Publicity leaflet

## Optional materials

- Teacher's Resource Bank: Trinity Exams Practice cards (selected from the Starter Unit and Units 1, 2, 3, 4, 5 and 6)

# At a Glance Lesson Plan

## Pupil's Book

### Starting the lesson

- Use the Trinity Exams Practice cards (optional).
- Review volunteering activities.
- Set learning objectives.

### Activity 1: Investigate a text

- Look at the title and the text on these leaflets.
- What are they about?

### Activity 2

- Read.
- Where would you find this kind of leaflet?

### Activity 3: Discuss a text

- Read the leaflet again.
- Answer the questions.

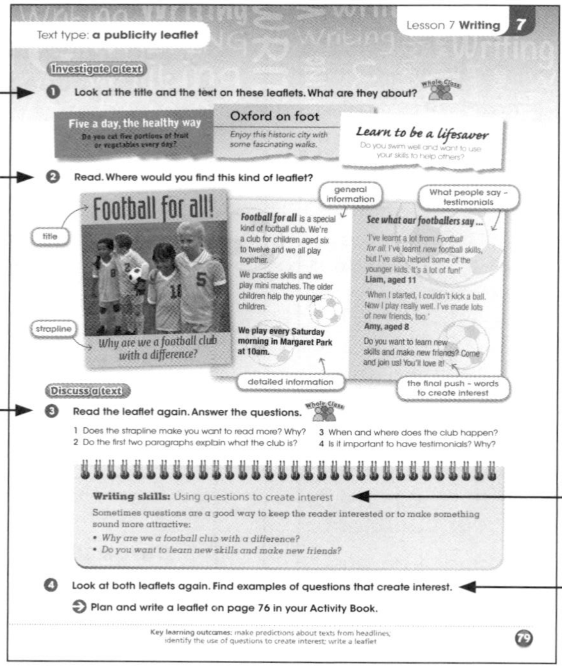


### Writing skills

- Read about using questions to create interest.

### Activity 4

- Look at both leaflets again.
- Find examples of questions that create interest.

Go to the Activity Book.

### Ending the lesson

- Review the lesson and reflect on learning.

### Extra activity

**Reinforcement**

- Make more pages for your leaflet and include photos or illustrations.

## Activity Book

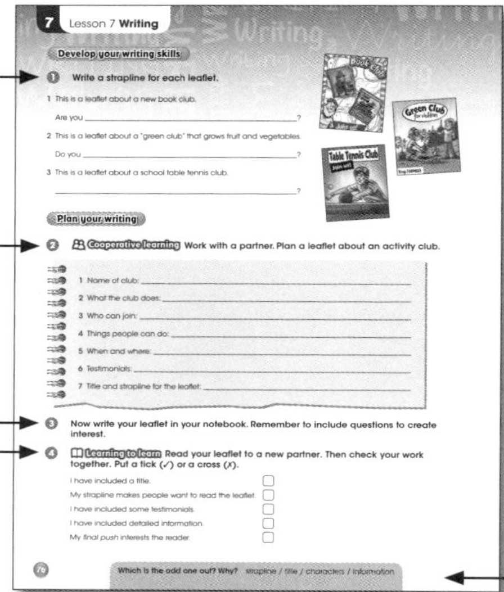


### Activity Book

**Activity 1: Develop your writing skills**

- Write a strapline for each leaflet.

**Activity 2: Plan your writing**

- Work with a partner. Plan a leaflet about an activity club.

**Activity 3**

- Now write your leaflet in your notebook. Remember to include questions to create interest.

**Activity 4**

- Read your leaflet to a new partner. Then check your work together. Put a tick (✓) or a cross (✗).

**Odd one out activity**

- Which is the odd one out? Why?

## Digital resources

**Teacher's Digital:** You can also teach this lesson using the Teacher's App on Navio.

**Pupil's Digital:** Encourage your pupils to use the Pupil's App on Navio to practise the activities from this lesson.

Powered By NAVIO

# Detailed Lesson Plan

## Starting the lesson

**Use the Trinity Exams Practice cards (optional).**

- The pupils practise asking and answering questions.

**Review volunteering activities.**

- Play the *Mime the card* game (see p27) to review volunteering activities from Lesson 6. If necessary, give the pupils a few minutes to make a list of volunteering activities.

**Set learning objectives.**

- Say **Today we're going to write a leaflet for an activity club.**

## Pupil's Book Activity 1: Investigate a text

**Look at the title and the text on these leaflets. What are they about?**

- Read the extracts from the three leaflets. After each one, ask **What's the leaflet about?** Encourage the pupils to give reasons for their views. Ask the pupils which one they find the most interesting.

## Pupil's Book Activity 2

**Read. Where would you find this kind of leaflet?**

- Read the text as a class. Explain any difficult language.
- Check understanding. Agree where you might find it. Ask if it is the kind of club the pupils would like to join. Ask **Does it sound fun? Why?**

## Pupil's Book Activity 3: Discuss a text

**Read the leaflet again. Answer the questions.**

- Read and discuss the questions as a class. Highlight the importance of a good title and strapline. If someone is bored, they will stop reading! Talk about why there are testimonials from some children. Most people who read a leaflet like this want to hear about some people who are actually in the club.

## Writing skills

- Read about using questions to create interest. The class discusses why the questions make you want to read more. (*You want to find out the answers to the questions.*)

## Pupil's Book Activity 4

**Look at both the leaflets. Find examples of questions that create interest.**

- Read the information.
- Organise the pupils into pairs. Ask them to find more examples of questions in the leaflets.

## Activity Book

**Activity 1: Develop your writing skills**

**Write a strapline for each leaflet.**

- The pupils complete the questions in the straplines for the leaflets.
- Check the answers as a class. Write some of them on the board. Encourage the pupils to say which ones are good straplines and why.

**Activity 2: Plan your writing**

**Work with a partner. Plan a leaflet about an activity club.**

- Read out the categories. If you wish, you can make notes for some of the categories as an example.
- Organise the class into Writing Partners. The pupils think of a club and plan their leaflet. Remind them that they only need to write notes at this stage.

**Activity 3**

**Now write your leaflet on your notebook. Remember to include questions to create interest.**

- The pupils work with a Writing Partner to write their leaflet in their notebooks.

**Activity 4**

**Read your leaflet to a new partner. Then check your work together. Put a tick (✓) or a cross (✗).**

- Read through the statements as a class.
- Organise the class into new Writing Partners. One pupil reads aloud their text to their partner. The other pupil listens. The pupils work together to decide if the text fulfils the criteria and tick the corresponding boxes. The pupils can add, improve or correct the text at this stage.
- The pupils swap roles.

**Odd one out activity**

**Which is the odd one out? Why?**

- The pupils complete the odd one out activity.

**Answers:** characters (They aren't included in a publicity leaflet.)

## Ending the lesson

**Review the lesson and reflect on learning.**

- Say **Today we've written a publicity leaflet.**
- Ask **Which was your favourite activity today? Which activity was easy / difficult?**

## Extra activity

**Reinforcement**

- Ask the pupils, in pairs or in larger groups, to plan the layout of their leaflet. They can think about how it might fold up (if it does fold up) and what more information could be added. Ask the pupils to draw where the pictures would go and where the text would go. They could use examples of real leaflets to help them. If they wish, they can use a computer to lay out the leaflet and include photos or other pictures.

# Lesson 8 and Review

## Key Competences and Key Learning Outcomes

- Listen to and have a conversation about how to raise money

- Listen to a text for general understanding
- Listen to a text and identify key functional language
- Review learning and reflect on progress in the unit

- Sing a song

## Key language

- *competition, costumes, drama club, prize, raise money, talent show, winner*
- *Have you decided how to raise money yet? A talent show? How does that work? A prize? What's the prize?*

## Materials

- Pupil's Book p80; Activity Book pp77 and 78; Class CD3 and CD4; Teacher's App on Navio
- Preparing for a party flashcards
- Teacher's Resource Bank: Talk cards (optional)

## Optional materials

- Teacher's Resource Bank: Trinity Exams Practice cards (selected from the Starter Unit and Units 1, 2, 3, 4, 5 and 6)

## At a Glance Lesson Plan

### Starting the lesson

- Use the Trinity Exams Practice cards (optional).
- Think about good causes in the local community.
- Set learning objectives.

### Activity 1

- What are the people doing in the pictures?
- Why do you think they are doing these things?

### Activity 2

- Listen to the conversation.
- ▶ ***CD3 Track 26 p291***
- Which activity do Philip and his friends decide to do?

### Activity 3

- Listen again.
- ▶ ***CD3 Track 26 p291***
- Complete five questions that Luke asks.

## Pupil's Book

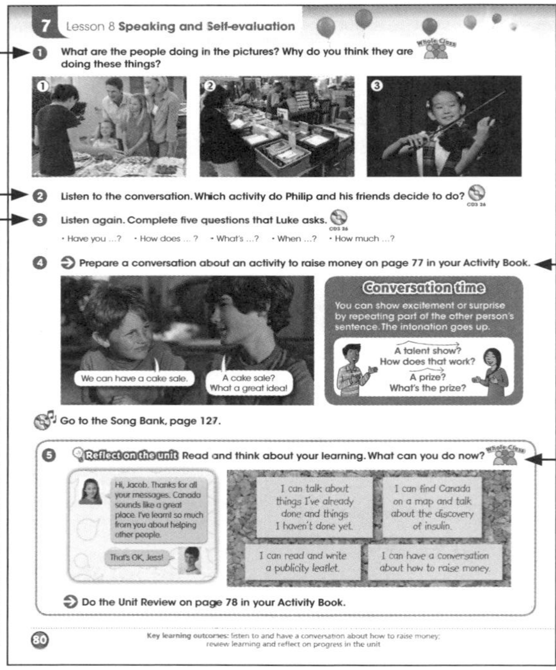


### Activity 4

- Prepare a conversation about your favourite kind of entertainment on page 77 in your Activity book.
- Go to page 77 in the Activity Book.

### Song

- ▶ ***CD4 Track 26 p297***
- ▶ ***CD4 Track 27 p297 (optional karaoke version)***

### Activity 5

- Read and think about your learning. What can you do now?
- Go to page 78 in the Activity Book.

### Ending the lesson

- Review the lesson and reflect on learning.

### Extra activity

- Describe a possession that you could sell to raise money.

## Activity Book

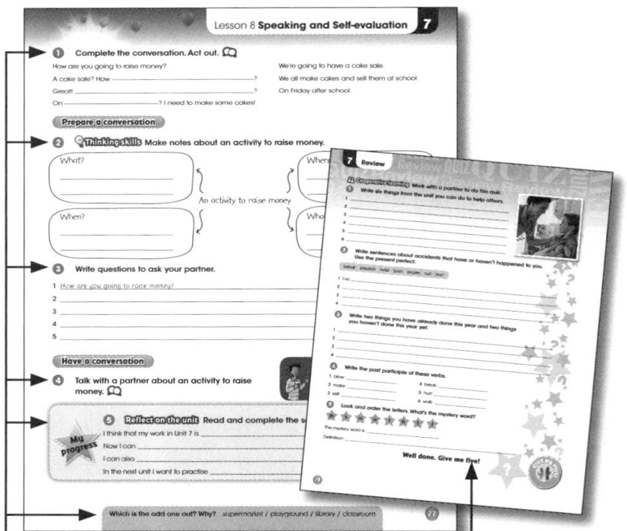


### Activity Book page 78: Review

- Work with a partner to do the quiz.

### Activity Book

**Activity 1**
- Complete the conversation.
- Act out.

**Activity 2**
- Make notes about an activity to raise money.

**Activity 3**
- Write questions to ask your partner.

**Activity 4**
- Talk with a partner about an activity to raise money.

**Activity 5**
- Read and complete the sentences.

**Odd one out activity**
- Which is the odd one out? Why?

## Digital resources

**Teacher's Digital:** You can also teach this lesson using the Teacher's App on Navio.

Powered By NAVIO

# Detailed Lesson Plan

### Starting the lesson

**Use the Trinity Exams Practice cards (optional).**
- The pupils practise asking and answering questions.

**Think about good causes in the local community.**
- Tell students to imagine they have 500 euros. They must spend it on something to help the local community or your school. In pairs, they think of ideas for how to spend it.

**Set learning objectives.**
- Say **Today we're going to prepare a conversation about an activity to raise money.**

### Pupil's Book Activity 1

**What are the people doing in the pictures? Why do you think they are doing these things?**
- Ask different pupils to describe the pictures. Ask if people ever do these things in your school or community.

**Answers: 1** A family is selling food. **2** People are looking at old books. **3** A girl is playing the violin.

### Pupil's Book Activity 2

**Listen to the conversation. Which activity do Philip and his friends decide to do?**

▶ ***CD3 Track 26 p291***
- Play the CD. Ask which picture from Activity 1 is mentioned. Ask how this will raise money (*People have to buy tickets to come to the show*).

**Answer:** 3

### Pupil's Book Activity 3

**Listen again. Complete five questions that Luke asks.**

▶ ***CD3 Track 26 p291***
- Direct pupils to the five question prompts. Ask if they can remember the questions.
- Play the CD. Check answers as a class.

**Answers:** Have you decided how to raise money yet?; How does that work?; What's the prize?; When is the competition?; How much do the tickets cost?

### Pupil's Book Activity 4

**Prepare a conversation about your favourite kind of entertainment on page 77 in your Activity Book.**
- Read the speech bubbles with the pupils. Model the phrases in the Conversation Time box and get the class to repeat. Check their intonation is correct – they should stress *talent* and *prize*.

### Song

- Go to the Song Bank on page 127 to do the song activities (see p245).

▶ ***CD4 Track 26 p297***

▶ ***CD4 Track 27 p297 (optional karaoke version)***

### Pupil's Book Activity 5

**Read and think about your learning. What can you do now?**
- Read the speech bubbles and notes with the pupils. Then look back through the unit and prompt them to identify things that they have done/learnt.

### Activity Book page 78: Review

**Work with a partner to do the quiz.**
- Organise the class into pairs. Set a time limit for the pupils to do the quiz (10–15 minutes). Stress that the pupils are not competing with each other.
- Read out the five tasks that the pupils have to complete. Check understanding. Then say **Ready, steady ... Go!**
- Pupils work in pairs to do the quiz.
- Check answers as a class.

**Answers: 1** Six from: blow up balloons, choose the music, clean the furniture, decorate the room, go shopping, make a cake, make posters, put out the food, sell tickets, send invitations, serve drinks, sweep the floor **4 1** blown **2** made **3** sold **4** broken **5** hurt **6** walked **5** hospital, where you go if you're sick

### Activity Book

**Activity 1**

**Complete the conversation. Act out.**
- Pupils complete and perform the dialogue in pairs.

**Activity 2**

**Make notes about an activity to raise money.**
- Give students example of a way to raise money, such as making and selling cakes. Then pupils complete the boxes with their own information.

**Activity 3**

**Write questions to ask your partner.**
- Direct pupils to the four headings in Activity 2 and explain that they need to form questions about them. Then pupils complete the questions alone. Check as a class.

**Answers: 1** How are you going to raise money? **2** What are you going to do? **3** When are you going to do it? **4** Where are you going to do it? **5** Who are you going to do it with?

**Activity 4**

**Talk with a partner about an activity to raise money.**
- In pairs, pupils ask and answer the questions from Activity 3. Encourage them to use expressions to show interest.
- Invite one or two pairs to perform their conversations for the class.

**Activity 5**

**Read and complete the sentences.**
- Pupils review their work in the unit.

**Odd one out activity**

**Which is the odd one out? Why?**

**Answer:** supermarket (It isn't part of a school.)

### Ending the lesson

**Review the lesson and reflect on learning.**
- Say **Today we've learnt how to have a conversation about an activity to raise money.**

## Key Competences and Key Learning Outcomes

- Watch and understand a video about volunteering
- Learn about volunteering and ways to help your community and environment
- Think about the qualities of a leader

## Key language

- *animal care home, community, rubbish, rugby, tyre, volunteer, volunteering*
- *Are you happy to do that? What would you like to do, Amy?*

## Materials

- Pupil's Book p81; Activity Book p79; Class CD3; Teacher's App on Navio
- Teacher's Resource Bank: Talk cards

## Optional materials

- Teacher's Resource Bank: Trinity Exams Practice cards (selected from the Starter Unit and Units 1–6)

# At a Glance Lesson Plan

## Pupil's Book

### Starting the lesson

- Use the Trinity Exams Practice cards (optional).
- **Think-Pair-Share** Review vocabulary related to preparing for a party.
- Set learning objectives and use the talk cards.

### Activity 1

- Before you watch
- Watch the video.
- *Unit 7 video p303*
- Say the sentences in the correct order.

### Activity 2

- Watch the video again.
- *Unit 7 video*
- What are these things?
- What is the connection with the video?

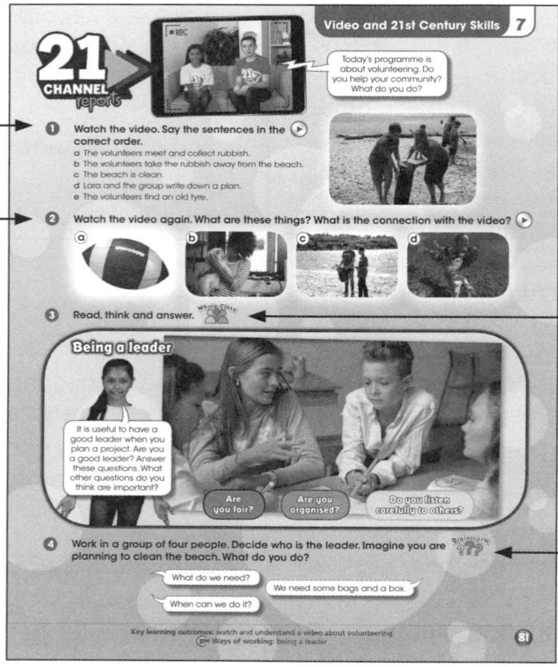


### Activity 3

- Read, think and answer.

### Activity 4

- Work in a group of four people.
- Decide who is the leader.
- Imagine you are planning to clean the beach.
- What do you do?
- Go to the Activity Book.

### Ending the lesson

- Review the lesson and reflect on learning.

### Extra activity

- Play a memory game.

## Activity Book

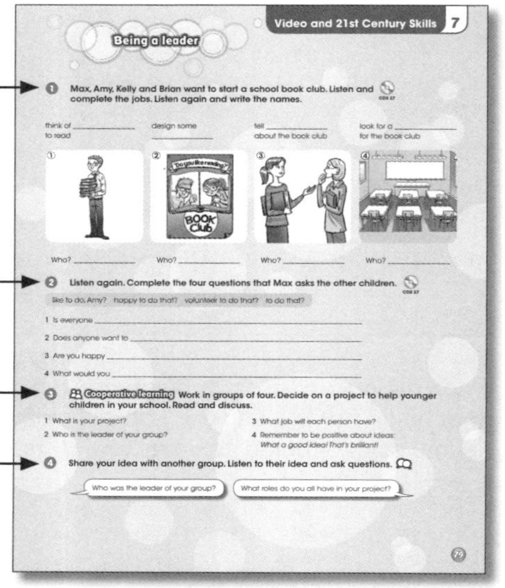


### Activity Book

**Activity 1**

- Max, Amy, Kelly and Brian want to start a school book club.
- Listen and complete the jobs.
- Listen again and write the names.

▶ *CD3 Track 27 p291*

**Activity 2**

- Listen again.
- Complete the four questions that Max asks the other children.

▶ *CD3 Track 27 p291*

**Activity 3**

- Work in groups of four.
- Decide on a project to help younger children in your school.
- Read and discuss.

**Activity 4**

- Share your idea with another group.
- Listen to their idea and ask questions.

## Digital resources

**Teacher's Digital:** You can also teach this lesson using the Teacher's App on Navio.

**Pupil's Digital:** Encourage your pupils to use the Pupil's App on Navio to practise the activities from this lesson.

Powered By NAVIO

# Detailed Lesson Plan

## Starting the lesson

**Think-Pair-Share Review vocabulary related to preparing for a party.**

- Ask **Which phrases for preparing for a party can you remember?** The class thinks silently for a minute.
- Then the pupils work with a Talk Partner to name phrases for preparing for a party.
- Invite different Talk Partners to say a different phrase for preparing for a party. Hold up the corresponding flashcard and prompt the class to repeat the word.
- Finally, repeat the procedure, asking different pairs of Talk Partners each time, until all the phrases have been recorded.

**Set learning objectives and use the talk cards.**

- Say **Today we're going to watch a video and then ask and answer questions about volunteering.**
- Point to the talk cards to show the pupils the different ways they will be working in the lesson.

## Pupil's Book Activity 1

**Before you watch**

- Read the speech bubble to pupils. Ask **Do you help your community? What do you do?** Elicit responses from a number of pupils.

**Watch the video. Say the sentences in the correct order.** *p303*

- Watch Part 1 of the video. Ask pupils **What are you going to see next?**
- Play Part 2 of the video. Ask general questions to check understanding. Direct pupils to look at the sentences a–e in Activity 1. Say **Which sentence is first?** Pupils offer ideas.

**Answers:** d, a, e, c, b

## Pupil's Book Activity 2

**Watch the video again. What are these things? What is the connection with the video?**

- Ask a pupil **What can you see in picture a?** Ask a different pupil **What is the connection with the video?**
- Play the video. Check the answers as a class.

**Answers:** **a** A rugby ball. The woman helps her son's rugby team every Saturday. **b** A girl holding a cat. The woman would like to help at an animal care home. **c** Two boys cleaning up the beach. They are volunteers. **d** Two people swimming in the sea. It's safe for people to go swimming now.

## Pupil's Book Activity 3

**Read, think and answer.**

- Read the speech bubble and the questions with the class. Can they remember who Max and Amy talked about, and what they said about him/her? (*They talked about Max. Max said that he thinks he's fair. Amy said that he's organised and he listens to others.*)
- Pupils ask the questions in pairs.
- Pupils think of more questions that are important for being a good leader in pairs. Share ideas as a class.

## Pupil's Book Activity 4

**Work in a group of four people. Decide who is the leader. Imagine you are planning to clean up the beach. What do you do?**

- In groups of four, pupils decide who is the best leader, based on their answers in Activity 3.
- Tell the class that the leaders should ask the questions, listen to their group members' ideas, and choose the ideas that they think are best.
- After the activity, leaders talk about what their groups decided. Ask other pupils if their leaders were good leaders.

## Activity Book

**Activity 1**

**Max, Amy, Kelly and Brian want to start a school book club. Listen and complete the jobs. Listen again and write the names.**

▸ *CD3 Track 27 p291*

- Ask different pupils to describe the four pictures. Play the CD. Tell pupils only to listen for the missing information, not the names.
- Ask pupils who is the leader of the group (*Max*). Play the CD again. This time, pupils listen for the names. Check all answers.

**Answers:** **1** some good books; Brian **2** posters; Kelly **3** teachers of the younger children; Amy **4** room; Max

**Activity 2**

**Listen again. Complete the four questions that Max asks the other children.**

▸ *CD3 Track 27 p291*

**Answers:** **1** happy to do that? **2** volunteer to do that? **3** to do that? **4** like to do, Amy?

- Ask the pupils **Do you think Max is a good leader? Why / Why not?**

**Activity 3**

**Work in groups of four. Decide on a project to help younger children in your school. Read and discuss.**

- In the same groups of four as Activity 4 in the Pupil's Book, pupils choose one of the ideas.
- Pupils discuss the project. Group members suggest jobs, and the leader assigns the jobs to the members, based on their skills.

**Activity 4**

**Share your idea with another group. Listen to their ideas and ask questions.**

- Tell pupils to imagine that they are part of Max, Kelly, Amy and Brian's group. Ask **Who was your leader? What roles did each person have? Did the younger children enjoy the project?**
- Put each group with another group. They take turns to present their own projects and ask questions.

## Ending the lesson

**Review the lesson and reflect on learning.**

- Say **Today we've watched a video about volunteering. What have we learnt about being a leader?** Elicit ideas from the pupils.
- Ask **Which was your favourite activity today? Which activity was easy / difficult?**

Date: ______________ Unit: ________

1 **What did my pupils learn in this unit?**

2 **How did my pupils work? (✓)**

individually ☐ in pairs ☐ in small groups ☐

in large groups ☐ as a class ☐

3 **Which key competences did my pupils develop? Give a score from 1 to 5 (5 being the highest).**

- Competence in linguistic communication ☐
- Competence in mathematics, science and technology ☐
- Digital competence ☐
- Learning to learn ☐
- Social and civic competences ☐
- Sense of initiative and entrepreneurship ☐
- Cultural awareness and expression ☐

4 **Which lessons / activities were the most successful and why?**

5 **Which lessons / activities did my pupils find the most difficult and why?**

6 **What did I try in the classroom for the first time? How did it go?**

7 **Which resources did I find most useful? (including webpages)**

8 **What could I do differently next time I teach this unit?**

Unit 8

# Green technology

## Unit overview

### Key Competences and Key Learning Outcomes

- Name recyclable objects and materials (Lesson 1)
- Use the present passive (Lesson 2)
- Learn and practise asking questions using the present passive (Lesson 4)
- Learn phrases to describe how different materials are recycled (Lesson 5)
- Review and practise using the imperative (Lesson 7)
- Talk about the environment (Lesson 8)
- Watch and understand a video about recycling (Video and 21st Century Skills)

- Learn about the technology of marine robots (Lesson 3)
- Describe a recycling process (Lesson 5)
- Read and write instructions (Lessons 6 and 7)
- Learn about the process of recycling plastic (Video and 21st Century Skills)

- Use the Pupil's App on Navio
- Investigate Japan (Lesson 3)

- Identify and practise placing the stress correctly in countries' names (Lesson 4)
- Practise activity types found in the Cambridge Exams: A2 Key for Schools

- Think about the importance of protecting the oceans (Lesson 3)
- Think about why recycling helps the planet (Video and 21st Century Skills)

- Work in pairs and small groups to practise and reinforce learning (all lessons)
- Do a communication task (Lesson 5)
- Use a digital poster to persuade (Video and 21st Century Skills)

- Read and understand a story (Lesson 3)
- Learn about Japan (Lesson 3)
- Design an object made of recycled materials (Lesson 7)

### Vocabulary

**Core vocabulary**
*bottle top, button, can, cardboard box, cardboard tube, carton, elastic band, fabric, lolly stick, plastic bottle, straw, string; add water, collect paper, cut paper, remove ink, roll paper, transport paper, use paper, wash paper*

**Extension vocabulary (optional)**
*egg carton, jar, packet, paper bag, tin, tub; recycling bin, recycling containers, recycling lorry, recycling plant*

**Other vocabulary**
*absolutely (not), definitely, not at all, not really, of course; battery, collect, container, environment, factories, felt-tip pens, recycling plant, screws, spray cans; being green, plant a tree, switch off lights, throw away; bury, melt, recycling container, recycling lorry, reduce*

**Recycled vocabulary**
*rice, vegetables; Argentina, Egypt, Japan, Brazil, Canada, Germany, Italy, Japan, Switzerland; cut out, draw, glue, stick; card, paper, scissors; bin, cameras, computers, glass, metal, plastic, printers, recycle, robot, rubbish, technology; after that, first, next*

### Structures

**Core structures**
*Rice is / isn't grown in (Japan). Robots are / aren't produced in (the UK). Is rice grown in (Japan)? Yes, it is. No, it isn't. Are cars produced in (Japan)? Yes, they are. No, they aren't. Where are robots produced? They are produced in Japan. Where is rice grown? It is grown in Japan. What is made / produced / grown in Japan?*

**Recycled structures**
*What are the toys made of? Have you ever made something with recycled materials? Do you recycle batteries at home? How do you recycle them? Be creative.*

### Pronunciation

Stress in countries' names

### Literacy

**Text type:** instructions (text to instruct; writing preparation)
**Reading skill:** inferring meaning
**Writing skill:** imperatives

### Culture ... around the world

Robotic fish made from recycled objects in Japan

### 21st Century Skills

**Digital skills:** using a digital poster to persuade

### Thinking skills

Categorising (Lesson 1); Analysing and applying rules (Lessons 2 and 4); Questioning (Lesson 4); Forming conceptual links (Lesson 5); Making inferences (Lesson 6); Logical thinking (Lesson 7); Planning, checking and correcting (Lesson 7); Reflecting on learning (Lesson 8)

### Cooperative learning

Working together (Lessons 1–8); Collaborating (Lessons 1–8); Checking learning (Lessons 1–8); Peer evaluation and feedback (Lesson 7); Participating (Lessons 1–8); Helping and encouraging (Lessons 1–8); Reflecting and setting goals (Lessons 1 and 8)

### Values

Protecting our oceans and sea animals

### Cross-curricular links

**Link to Science**
Recycling

**Suggested Arts and Crafts concepts**
Linear perspective

### Key Competences and Key Learning Outcomes

- Identify and say the names of objects and materials you can recycle
- Listen to definitions and identify the words
- Read a message for specific information
- Talk about how you recycle

### Key language

- *bottle top, button, can, cardboard box, cardboard tube, carton, elastic band, fabric, lolly stick, plastic bottle, straw, string; collect, recycle, throw away; battery, bin, container, environment, glass, metal, paper, plastic, rubbish, spray cans*
- *What are the toys made of? Have you ever made something with recycled materials? Do you recycle batteries at home? How do you recycle them?*
- **Extension:** *egg carton, jar, packet, paper bag, tin, tub*

### Materials

- Pupil's Book pp82–83; Activity Book p80; Class CD3; Teacher's App on Navio
- Recyclable objects and materials flashcards

### Optional materials

- Teacher's Resource Bank: Trinity Exams Practice cards (selected from the Starter Unit and Units 1, 2, 3 4, 5, 6 and 7)

## At a Glance Lesson Plan

### Pupil's Book

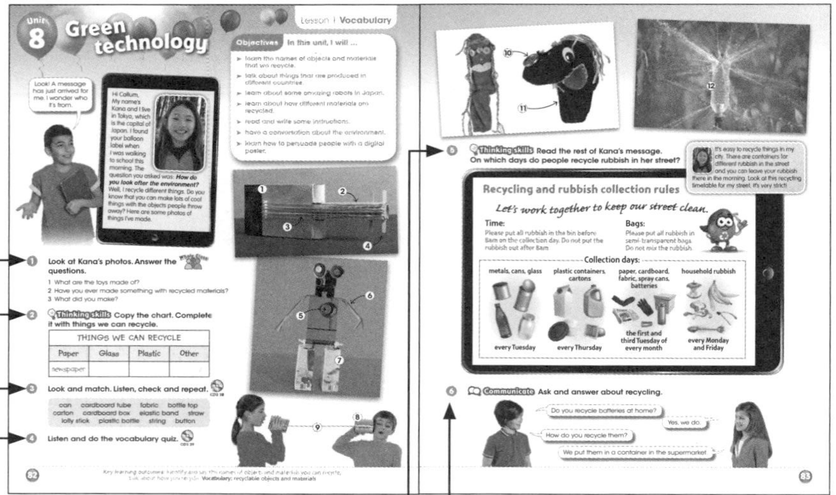

**Starting the lesson**
- Use the Trinity Exams Practice cards (optional).
- Review materials for arts and crafts.
- Set learning objectives.

**Activity 1**
- Look at Kana's photos.
- Answer the questions.

**Activity 2**
- Copy the chart.
- Complete it with things we can recycle.

**Vocabulary presentation**
- Present the new vocabulary using the recyclable objects and materials flashcards.

**Activity 3**
- Look and match.
- Listen, check and repeat.
- ▶ *CD3 Track 28 p291*

**Activity 4**
- Listen and do the vocabulary quiz.
- ▶ *CD3 Track 29 p292*

**Activity 5**
- Read the rest of Kana's message.
- On which days do people recycle rubbish in her street?

**Activity 6**
- Ask and answer about recycling.
- Go to the Activity Book.

**Ending the lesson**
- Review the lesson and reflect on learning.

**Extra activities**

**Extension**
- Find out about Japan.

**Vocabulary extension**
- Present six additional vocabulary items.

### Digital resources

**Teacher's Digital:** You can also teach this lesson using the Teacher's App on Navio.

**Pupil's Digital:** Encourage your pupils to use the Pupil's App on Navio to practise the activities from this lesson.

Powered By NAVIO

### Activity Book

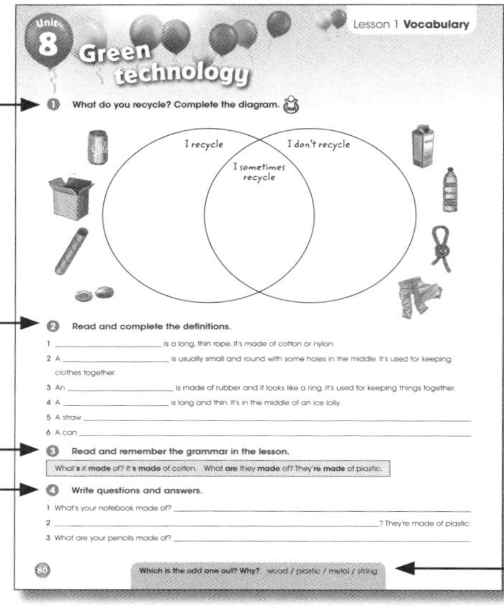

**Activity Book**

**Activity 1**
- What do you recycle? Complete the diagram.

**Activity 2**
- Read and complete the definitions.

**Activity 3**
- Read and remember the grammar in the lesson.

**Activity 4**
- Write questions and answers.

**Odd one out activity**
- Which is the odd one out? Why?

# Detailed Lesson Plan



### Starting the lesson

**Use the Trinity Exams Practice cards (optional).**
- The pupils practise asking and answering questions.

**Review materials for arts and crafts.**
- Ask **Do you like arts and crafts?** The pupils talk about the things they have produced and the materials they used to make them.

**Set learning objectives.**
- Say **Today we're going to remember and learn the names of things we recycle.**

### Pupil's Book Activity 1

**Look at Kana's photos. Answer the questions.**
- Invite a pupil to read out the speech bubble and the message to find out who has found the balloon. Check understanding. Ask **Do you know where Japan is?**
- Invite a pupil to read out the message from Kana. Check understanding.
- Work as a class to answer the questions.

**Answer:** **1** recycled rubbish

### Pupil's Book Activity 2

**Copy the chart. Complete it with things we can recycle.**
- Copy the chart onto the board. Elicit an example for each column.
- Organise the class into pairs. The pupils copy the chart into their notebooks and classify the words they know.
- Invite the pupils to say the objects they have written in their chart. Check spelling and write the words on the board.

### Vocabulary presentation

- Present the new vocabulary using the recyclable objects and materials flashcards. Show the first flashcard and elicit / say the word. Ask **Can we recycle this?** Ask a pupil to stick the card in the correct chart column on the board.
- Repeat the procedure with the other cards.

### Pupil's Book Activity 3

**Look and match. Listen, check and repeat.**
▶ *CD3 Track 28 p291*
- The class look at item number 1 in the photo. Ask **What's this?** The pupils work in pairs to match numbers 2–12 and the words.
- Play the CD. The pupils listen and check.
- Play the CD again, pausing after each word for the pupils to repeat.

### Pupil's Book Activity 4

**Listen and do the vocabulary quiz.**
▶ *CD3 Track 29 p292*
- Play the CD. Listen to the first definition, pausing at the beep to allow the pupils to name the item. Play the CD to listen to the answer.
- Repeat the procedure with the other definitions.

### Pupil's Book Activity 5

**Read the rest of Kana's message. On which days do people recycle rubbish in her street?**
- Invite a pupil to read out the message. Check that the pupils understand the task. The pupils read the information and identify the days that people recycle rubbish in Kana's street.

**Answers:** Monday, Tuesday, Thursday and Friday

### Pupil's Book Activity 6

**Ask and answer about recycling.**
- Invite two pupils to read out the speech bubbles.
- The pupils ask and answer the questions in pairs.

### Activity Book

**Activity 1**
**What do you recycle? Complete the diagram.**
- Ask the pupils to name the items in the activity and say whether they recycle the different items or not.
- The pupils write the words in the diagram.

**Activity 2**
**Read and complete the definitions.**
- The pupils complete the definitions.

**Answer:** **1** String **2** button **3** elastic band **4** lolly stick

**Activity 3**
**Read and remember the grammar in the lesson.**
- Invite a pupil to read out the information. Review the different materials they know. Then the class says what different objects in the room are made of.

**Activity 4**
**Write questions and answers.**
- The pupils write the missing question and answers.

**Odd one out activity**
**Which is the odd one out? Why?**
- The pupils complete the odd one out activity.

**Answers:** string (It isn't a material.)

### Ending the lesson

**Review the lesson and reflect on learning.**
- Say **Today we've learnt the names of things we recycle. What do you remember?**

### Extra activities

**Extension**
- The pupils find Japan on the world map on pages 134–135. They read the accompanying facts.

**Vocabulary extension**
- Present six additional items: *egg carton, jar, packet, paper bag, tin, tub.*
- Use the Vocabulary booster on NAVIO to practise these new words.

## Key Competences and Key Learning Outcomes

- Listen to and read a dialogue
- Use the present passive to talk about the things that are grown and produced in your country

LEARN
- Identify examples of the present passive in the dialogue
- Practise activity types found in the Cambridge Exams: A2 Key for Schools

### Key language

- *cameras, computers, countryside, factories, printers, rice, robot, technology, vegetables*
- *Rice is / isn't grown in (Japan). Robots are / aren't produced in (the UK). Is rice grown in (Japan)? Yes, it is. No, it isn't. Are robots produced in (Japan)? Yes, they are. No, they aren't.*

### Materials

- Pupil's Book p84; Activity Book p81; Class CD3; Teacher's App on Navio
- Teacher's Resource Bank: Recycled objects and materials word cards

### Optional materials

- Teacher's Resource Bank: Trinity Exams Practice cards (selected from the Starter Unit and Units 1, 2, 3, 4, 5, 6 and 7)

## At a Glance Lesson Plan

### Pupil's Book

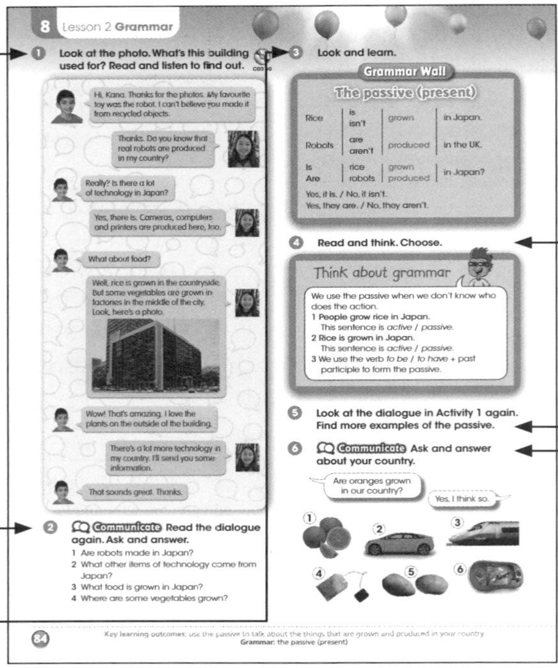


**Starting the lesson**
- Use the Trinity Exams Practice cards (optional).
- Review reyclable objects and materials.
- Set learning objectives.

**Activity 1**
- Look at the photo.
- What's this building used for?
- Read and listen to find out.
- ▶ *CD3 Track 30 p292*

**Activity 2**
- Read the dialogue again.
- Ask and answer.

**Activity 3**
- Look and learn – Grammar wall

**Activity 4**
- Read and think.
- Choose.

**Activity 5**
- Look at the dialogue in Activity 1 again.
- Find more examples of the passive.

**Activity 6**
- Ask and answer about your country.
- Go to the Activity Book.

**Ending the lesson**
- Review the lesson and reflect on learning.

**Extra activity**

**Reinforcement**
- Find out where different items are grown / produced.

### Activity Book

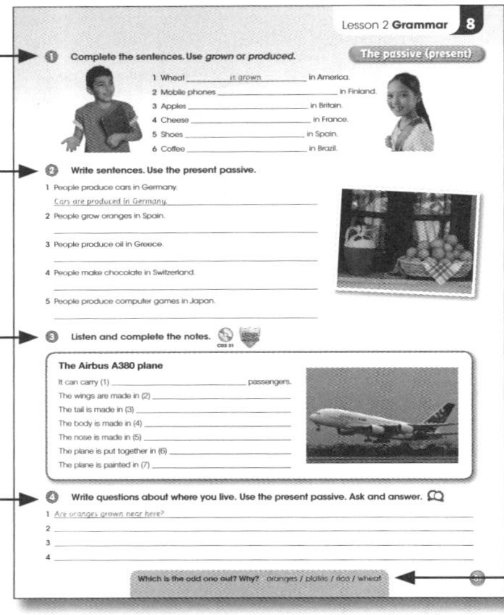


**Activity Book**

**Activity 1**
- Complete the sentences. Use *grown* or *produced.*

**Activity 2**
- Write the sentences. Use the present passive.

**Activity 3**
- Listen and complete the notes.
- ▶ *CD3 Track 31 p292*

**Activity 4**
- Write questions about where you live. Use the present passive. Ask and answer.

**Odd one out activity**
- Which is the odd one out? Why?

### Digital resources

**Teacher's Digital:** You can also teach this lesson using the Teacher's App on Navio.

**Pupil's Digital:** Encourage your pupils to use the Pupil's App on Navio to practise the activities from this lesson.

Powered By NAVIO

**Starting the lesson**

**Use the Trinity Exams Practice cards (optional).**
- The pupils practise asking and answering questions.

**Review recyclable objects and materials.**
- Hold up one of the recyclable objects and materials word cards so that the class can't see it. Describe the object. Describe its shape, size, use and material. When the pupils have named the item, show them the card.
- Repeat the procedure several times.

**Set learning objectives.**
- Say **Today we're going to learn how to talk about where things come from.**

**Pupil's Book Activity 1**

**Look at the photo. What's this building used for? Read and listen to find out.**

▶ *CD3 Track 30 p292*
- Prompt the pupils to describe what they can see in the photo.
- Ask the pupils if they can guess what the building is used for. Play the CD. The pupils listen and read the dialogue.
- Confirm that the building is used for growing vegetables.

**Pupil's Book Activity 2**

**Read the dialogue again. Ask and answer.**
- Organise the pupils into pairs. They read the questions and find the answers in the dialogue.

**Pupil's Book Activity 3**

**Look and learn – Grammar wall**
- Read the information on the Grammar wall as a class.
- Use questions to encourage the pupils to think about form and identify / remember patterns. Ask **Which verb is 'is / are'? What form of the verb is 'grown'?** Remind the pupils that they used the past participle form with the present perfect in Units 6 and 7.

**Pupil's Book Activity 4**

**Read and think. Choose.**
- Focus the pupils' attention on the Think about grammar. Read out the sentences as a class. The pupils complete the sentences in their pairs.

**Answer:** **1** active **2** passive **3** to be

**Pupil's Book Activity 5**

**Look at the dialogue in Activity 1 again. Find more examples of the passive.**
- Organise the pupils into pairs. They find examples of the passive in the text.

**Pupil's Book Activity 6**

**Ask and answer about your country.**
- Name the food and objects that appear in the photos as a class.
- Invite two pupils to read out the speech bubbles to demonstrate the activity. Review or introduce the negative form 'I don't think so'.
- The pupils work in pairs to ask and answer questions about their country.

**Activity Book**

**Activity 1**

**Complete the sentences. Use *grown* or *produced*.**
- The pupils complete the sentences.

**Answers:** **1** is grown **2** are produced **3** are grown **4** is produced **5** are produced **6** is grown

**Activity 2**

**Write the sentences. Use the present passive.**
- The pupils change the active sentences into the passive.

**Answers:** **1** Cars are produced in Germany. **2** Oranges are grown in Spain. **3** Oil is produced in Greece. **4** Chocolate is made in Switzerland. **5** Computer games are produced in Japan.

**Activity 3**

**Listen and complete the notes.**

▶ *CD3 Track 31 p292*
- Focus the class on the photo of the plane. Ask **Where is this plane made?** Listen to the pupils' suggestions.
- Ask the class to quickly read the notes. Then play the CD. The pupils listen and follow in their books.
- Play the CD again, pausing after each piece of key information. The pupils say and write the missing information each time.

**Answers:** **1** 850 **2** the UK **3** Spain **4** Germany **5** France **6** France **7** Germany

**Activity 4**

**Write questions about where you live. Use the present passive. Ask and answer.**
- The pupils write questions about what is grown or produced where they live.
- The pupils then work in pairs to ask and answer the questions.

**Odd one out activity**

**Which is the odd one out? Why?**
- The pupils complete the odd one out activity.

**Answers:** plates (You can't grow them.)

**Ending the lesson**

**Review the lesson and reflect on learning.**
- Say **Today we've learnt how to talk about where things are made or grown.** Elicit examples of the language from the pupils.
- Ask **Which was your favourite activity today? Which activity was easy / difficult?**

**Extra activity**

**Reinforcement**
- As a homework task, the pupils look around their homes and write down where different things are made.

**Key Competences and Key Learning Outcomes**

- Read a story with a cultural focus
- Learn about the technology of marine robots
- Use the Internet to investigate Japan
- Listen for specific information
- Think about the importance of protecting the oceans
- Learn about Japan

**Key language**

- *artificial prey, beach, collect, food containers, marine biologist, ocean, plastic bottles, protect, raincoat, recycled, recycling, remote control, robotic fish, rubbish, technology, turtle*
- *They're operated by remote control. Hayashi has made over 100 robots from recycled rubbish.*

**Materials**

- Pupil's Book p85; Activity Book p82; Class CD3; Teacher's App on Navio

**Optional materials**

- Teacher's Resource Bank: Trinity Exams Practice cards (selected from the Starter Unit and Units 1, 2, 3, 4, 5, 6 and 7)

## At a Glance Lesson Plan

### Pupil's Book

**Starting the lesson**

- Use the Trinity Exams Practice cards (optional).
- Review rubbish that we throw away.
- Set learning objectives.

**Activity 1: Before you read**

- Read and discuss.

**Activity 2**

- Listen and read.

▶ *CD3 Track 32 p292*

Go to the Activity Book.

**Values**

- Read and discuss.

**Ending the lesson**

- Review the lesson and reflect on learning.

**Extra activity**

**Extension**

- Design your own robot.

### Activity Book

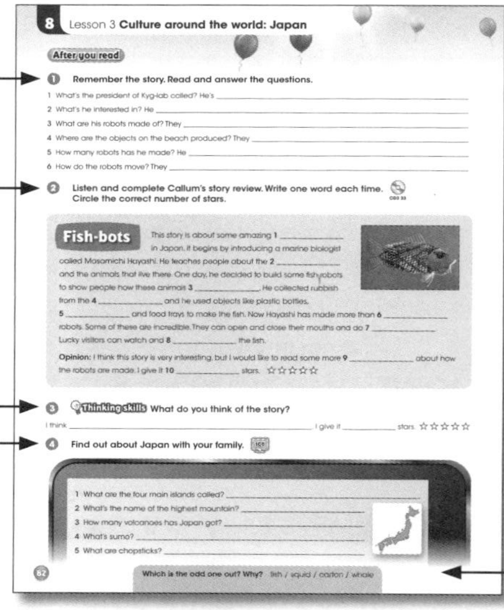


**Activity Book: After you read**

**Activity 1**

- Remember the story. Read and answer the questions.

**Activity 2**

- Listen and complete Callum's story review.

▶ *CD3 Track 33 p292*

- Write one word each time. Circle the correct number of stars.

**Activity 3**

- What do you think of the story?

**Activity 4**

- Find out about Japan with your family.

**Odd one out activity**

- Which is the odd one out? Why?

### Digital resources

**Teacher's Digital:** You can also teach this lesson using the Teacher's App on Navio.

**Pupil's Digital:** Encourage your pupils to use the Pupil's App on Navio to practise the activities from this lesson.

Powered By NAVIO

### Starting the lesson

**Use the Trinity Exams Practice cards (optional).**

- The pupils practise asking and answering questions.

**Review rubbish that we throw away.**

- Ask the class to think about what they threw in the bin yesterday. They list the items in pairs.

**Set learning objectives.**

- Say **Today we're going to read a story from Japan.**

### Pupil's Book Activity 1: Before you read

**Read and discuss.**

- Read the first two questions as a class. Encourage the pupils to share information about rubbish they have seen on the beach. Then ask the class if they think that it's possible to make a robot out of this rubbish.

### Pupil's Book Activity 2

**Listen and read.**

▶ ***CD3 Track 32 p292***

- Play the CD. The pupils follow in their books. Confirm that a biologist in Japan has made robots from recycled rubbish.
- Ask questions to check understanding.

**Suggested comprehension questions:**

- Frame 1: **Who is Masamichi Hayashi?** (*A marine biologist.*) **What's he interested in?** (*Technology.*)
- Frame 2: **What does he teach people about?** (*Recycling.*)
- Frame 3: **Where did this rubbish come from?** (*Other countries.*) **How did it arrive to Japan?** (*It floated.*)
- Frame 4: **How many robots has he made now?** (*Over 100.*)
- Frame 5: **How do they work?** (*By remote control.*)

### Activity Book: After you read

**Activity 1**

**Remember the story. Read and answer the questions.**

- Read out the first question and invite a pupil to answer it.
- The pupils work on their own or in pairs to read and answer the remaining questions

**Answers:** **1** Masamichi Hayashi. **2** is interested in technology. **3** are made of recycled rubbish. **4** are produced in other countries. **5** has made over 100. **6** are operated by remote control.

**Activity 2**

**Listen and complete Callum's story review. Write one word each time. Circle the correct number of stars.**

▶ ***CD3 Track 33 p292***

- Read out the story review as a class. Ask the pupils to guess the missing words.
- Play the CD without pausing. The pupils listen and complete as much of the information as possible.
- Play the CD again, pausing after each piece of key information to check the information and spelling. The pupils circle the correct number of stars.

**Answers:** **1** robots **2** oceans **3** move **4** beaches **5** fabric **6** 100 **7** tricks **8** touch **9** information **10** four

**Activity 3**

**What do you think of the story?**

- The pupils write their opinion and give a rating.
- Invite the pupils to share their opinions with the class.

**Activity 4**

**Find out about Japan with your family.** ICT

- Read out the questions about Japan. Ask **Where can you find out this information?** (*Internet, library, asking friends and family.*) The pupils complete the activity at home.
- If you prefer to do this activity in the class, connect to a children's website which has information about Japan such as: www.sciencekids.co.nz/sciencefacts/countries/japan.html or http://kids.nationalgeographic.com/kids/places/find/japan/.
- Read out the questions. The pupils work as a class to find and write the answers.

**Answers:** **1** Hokaido, Honshu, Shikoku, Kyushu **2** Mount Fuji **3** 124 **4** A wrestling sport. **5** Wooden sticks used for eating.

**Odd one out activity**

**Which is the odd one out? Why?**

- The pupils complete the odd one out activity.

**Answers:** carton (It isn't an animal.)

### Values

**Read and discuss.**

- Read out each question and discuss it as a class.
- Explain to the class that animals can get trapped or eat the rubbish in the sea. Rubbish like batteries and chemicals in the rivers can also contaminate / poison the oceans.

### Ending the lesson

**Review the lesson and reflect on learning.**

- Say **Today we've read a story from Japan.**
- Ask **Which was your favourite activity today? Which activity was easy / difficult?**

### Extra activity

**Extension**

- The pupils design a robot from recycled objects. The pupils draw and write about their robot (*Its head is made of a can.*) They also say what the robot can do.

## Key Competences and Key Learning Outcomes

- Act out a short dialogue in pairs
- Learn and practise asking questions using the present passive

LEARN
- Identify stress in country names and practise saying the words

**Key language**

- *olives, plastic bottles, rice, robotic fish, rubbish, T-shirt; Argentina, Brazil, Canada, Egypt, Germany, Italy, Japan, Switzerland*
- *Where are robots produced? They are produced in Japan. Where is rice grown? It is grown in Japan. What is made / produced / grown in Japan?*

**Materials**

- Pupil's Book p86; Activity Book p83; Class CD3; Teacher's App on Navio

**Optional materials**

- Teacher's Resource Bank: Trinity Exams Practice cards (selected from the Starter Unit and Units 1, 2, 3, 4, 5, 6 and 7)
- A world map

## At a Glance Lesson Plan

### Pupil's Book

**Starting the lesson**

- Use the Trinity Exams Practice cards (optional).
- Review countries.
- Set learning objectives.

**Activity 1**

- Listen and read.

▶ *CD3 Track 34 p293*

- Act out.

**Activity 2**

- Look and learn – Grammar wall

**Activity 3**

- Read and think.
- Choose.

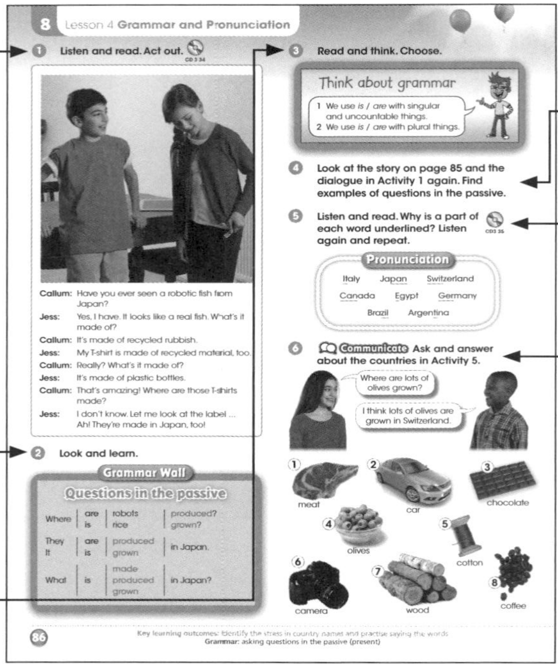


**Activity 4**

- Look at the story on page 85 and the dialogue in Activity 1 again.
- Find examples of questions in the passive.

**Activity 5**

- Listen and read.

▶ *CD3 Track 35 p293*

- Why is a part of each word underlined?
- Listen again and repeat.

**Activity 6**

- Ask and answer about the countries in Activity 5.

Go to the Activity Book.

**Ending the lesson**

- Review the lesson and reflect on learning.

**Extra activity**

**Reinforcement**

- Play a game with a world map.

### Activity Book

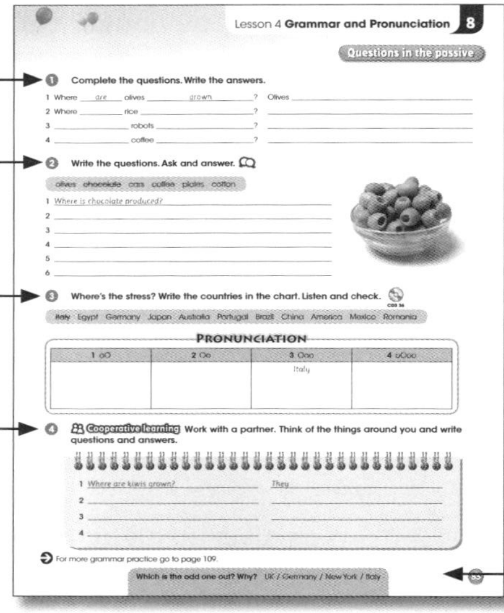


**Activity Book**

**Activity 1**

- Complete the questions. Write the answers.

**Activity 2**

- Write the questions. Ask and answer.

**Activity 3**

- Where's the stress? Write the countries in the chart. Listen and check.

▶ *CD3 Track 36 p293*

**Activity 4**

- Work with a partner. Think of the things around you and write questions and answers.

**Odd one out activity**

- Which is the odd one out? Why?

## Digital resources

**Teacher's Digital:** You can also teach this lesson using the Teacher's App on Navio.

**Pupil's Digital:** Encourage your pupils to use the Pupil's App on Navio to practise the activities from this lesson.

Powered By NAVIO

# Detailed Lesson Plan

**Starting the lesson**

**Use the Trinity Exams Practice cards (optional).**
- The pupils practise asking and answering questions.

**Review countries.**
- Brainstorm the names of different countries.
- Ask **Have you ever been to another country?** Encourage the pupils who have travelled abroad to say where they have been.

**Set learning objectives.**
- Say **Today we're going to ask questions about where things are made and learn the names of different countries in English.**

**Pupil's Book Activity 1**

**Listen and read. Act out.**

▸ *CD3 Track 34 p293*
- The pupils look at the photo. Ask **What do you think Jess and Callum are talking about?**
- Play the CD. The pupils listen and read the dialogue. Check understanding. Ask **What's the robotic fish made of? Where are the T-shirts made?**
- Play the CD again, pausing after each sentence for the pupils to repeat.
- The pupils practise the dialogue in pairs.

**Pupil's Book Activity 2**

**Look and learn – Grammar wall.**
- Read the information on the Grammar wall as a class.
- Ask more questions, using the key structure and encourage the class to answer. Ask **Where is pasta produced?** (*Pasta is produced in Italy.*)

**Pupil's Book Activity 3**

**Read and think. Choose.**
- Focus the pupils' attention on the Think about grammar box. Read out the sentences. The pupils decide how to complete these sentences.

**Pupil's Book Activity 4**

**Look at the story on page 85 and the dialogue in Activity 1 again. Find examples of questions in the passive.**
- The pupils work in pairs to find examples of questions in the passive in the dialogue and the story.

**Pupil's Book Activity 5**

**Listen and read. Why is a part of each word underlined? Listen again and repeat.**

▸ *CD3 Track 35 p293*
- Play the CD, pausing after each country's name. The class identify the stress each time. Confirm that the underlined part of the word is where the stress falls.
- Play the CD again. The pupils listen and repeat.

**Pupil's Book Activity 6**

**Ask and answer about the countries in Activity 5.**
- Invite two pupils to read out the speech bubbles. Prompt them to talk about other items pictured.
- The class work in pairs to ask and answer questions.

**Activity Book**

**Activity 1**

**Complete the questions. Write the answers.**
- The pupils complete each question and write the answers.

**Answers:** 1 are, grown Olives are grown in Spain. **2** is, grown Rice is grown in Japan. **3** Where are, produced Robots are produced in Japan. **4** Where is, grown Coffee is grown in Brazil.

**Activity 2**

**Write the questions. Ask and answer.**
- The pupils write the questions. Then they work in pairs to ask and answer the questions.

**Answers:** 1 Where is chocolate produced? **2** Where are olives grown? **3** Where are cars produced? **4** Where is coffee produced? **5** Where are plates produced? **6** Where is cotton produced?

**Activity 3**

**Where's the stress? Write the countries in the chart. Listen and check.**

▸ *CD3 Track 36 p293*
- In pairs, the pupils categorise the words, based on the stress pattern of each word.
- Play the CD. The pupils listen and check their answers.

**Answers:** 1 Japan, Brazil **2** Egypt, China **3** Italy, Germany, Portugal, Mexico **4** Australia, America, Romania

**Activity 4**

**Work with a partner. Think of the things around you and write questions and the answers.**
- The pupils brainstorm products and food that they see and use. They then write the questions.
- Invite different pupils to read out their questions. Ask if anyone knows the answers.

**Odd one out activity**

**Which is the odd one out? Why?**
- The pupils complete the odd one out activity.

**Answers:** New York (It isn't a country.)

**Ending the lesson**

**Review the lesson and reflect on learning.**
- Say **Today we've asked questions about where things are made and learnt the names of different countries in English.**

**Extra activity**

**Reinforcement**
- Stick a large map of the world on the board. Ask **Where's (France)?** The pupils play a game, and try to be the first to find and point to the countries on the map.

## Key Competences and Key Learning Outcomes

- Learn phrases to describe how different materials are recycled
- Identify and say the parts of the process for recycling paper
- Listen for specific information
- Practise activity types found in the Cambridge Exams: A2 Key for Schools
- Do a communication task

## Key language

- *add water, collect paper, cut paper, remove ink, roll paper, transport paper, use paper, wash paper; bottle, recycling plant, soft, wet; after that, first, next*
- *Do you know how paper is recycled? What happens next? The paper is collected. The bottles are collected.*
- **Extension:** *recycling bin, recycling containers, recycling lorry, recycling plant*

## Materials

- Pupil's Book p87; Activity Book p84; Class CD3; Teacher's App on Navio; Teacher's Resource Bank Unit 8

## Optional materials

- Teacher's Resource Bank: Trinity Exams Practice cards (selected from the Starter Unit and Units 1, 2, 3, 4, 5, 6 and 7)

# At a Glance Lesson Plan

## Pupil's Book

### Starting the lesson

- Use the Trinity Exams Practice cards (optional).
- Review recyclable objects and materials.
- Set learning objectives.

### Activity 1

- Do you know how paper is recycled?
- Look and match.
- Listen, check and repeat.
- ▶ *CD3 Track 37 p293*

### Activity 2

- Look at the chart.
- Listen and say the missing stages.
- ▶ *CD3 Track 38 p293*

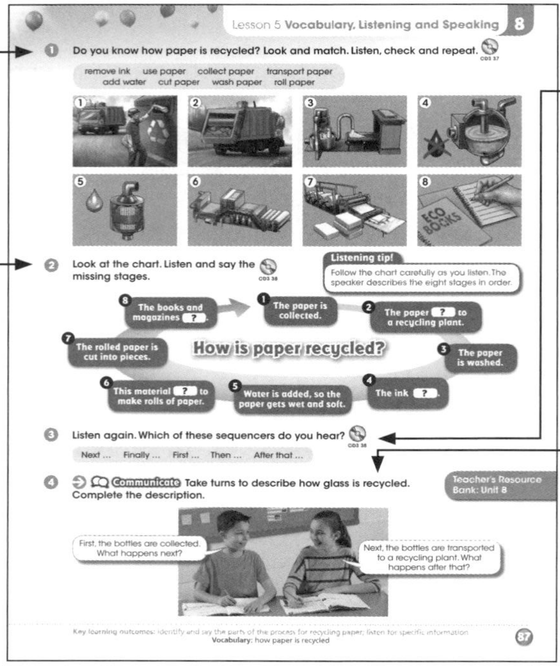


### Activity 3

- Listen again. Which of these sequencers do you hear?
- ▶ *CD3 Track 38 p293*

### Activity 4

- Take turns to describe how glass is recycled.
- Complete the description (Teacher's Resource Bank: Unit 8).

Go to the Activity Book.

### Ending the lesson

- Review the lesson and reflect on learning.

### Extra activities

**Reinforcement**

- Design a poster for a recycling campaign.

**Vocabulary extension**

- Present four additional vocabulary items.

## Activity Book

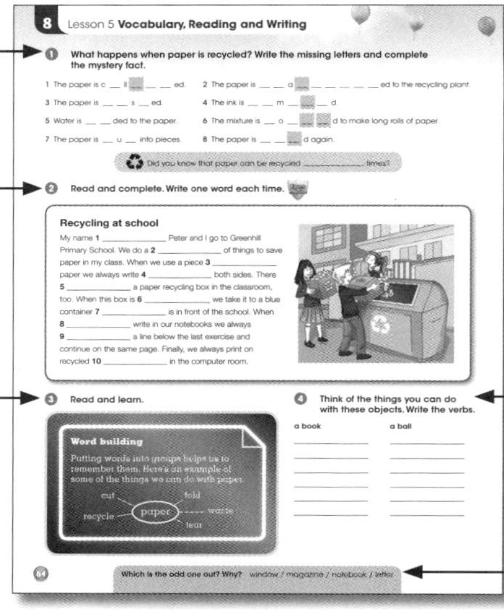


### Activity Book

**Activity 1**

- What happens when paper is recycled? Write the missing letters and complete the mystery fact.

**Activity 2**

- Read and complete. Write one word each time.

**Activity 3**

- Read and learn.

**Activity 4**

- Think of the things you can do with these objects. Write the verbs.

**Odd one out activity**

- Which is the odd one out? Why?

## Digital resources

**Teacher's Digital:** You can also teach this lesson using the Teacher's App on Navio.

**Pupil's Digital:** Encourage your pupils to use the Pupil's App on Navio to practise the activities from this lesson.

Powered By NAVIO

**Starting the lesson**

**Use the Trinity Exams Practice cards (optional).**
- The pupils practise asking and answering questions.

**Review recyclable objects and materials.**
- Review recyclable objects and materials.

**Set learning objectives.**
- Say **Today we're going to learn what happens when paper and glass are recycled.**

**Pupil's Book Activity 1**

**Do you know how paper is recycled? Look and match. Listen, check and repeat.**

▶ ***CD3 Track 37 p293***
- Read the question. Encourage the pupils to share what they think happens to the paper that they put in the recycling bin.
- Explain to the class that the pictures show what happens to paper when it is recycled.
- Organise the pupils into pairs. Ask them to match the words and pictures.
- Play the CD. The pupils listen and check.
- Play the CD again, pausing after each word for the pupils to repeat.

**Pupil's Book Activity 2**

**Look at the chart. Look and say the missing stages.**

▶ ***CD3 Track 38 p293***
- Focus the class on the diagram. Play the CD. The pupils listen to the description of the recycling process and follow the diagram.
- Play the CD again. The pupils say which stages are missing.

**Answers:** **2** is transported **4** is removed **6** is rolled **8** are used again

**Pupil's Book Activity 3**

**Listen again. Which of these sequencers do you hear?**

▶ ***CD3 Track 38 p293***
- Focus pupils on the sequencers and check that they understand what they mean.
- Play the CD. Tell pupils to say when they hear one of the sequencers.

**Answers:** First; Next; After that

**Pupil's Book Activity 4**

**Take turns to describe how glass is recycled. Complete the description (Teacher's Resource Bank: Unit 8).**
- Explain to the pupils that they are going to work together to complete a description of how glass is recycled. Invite two pupils to read out the speech bubbles.
- Organise the class into pairs (A and B). Ask Pupils A to open their Activity Books at page 131 and Pupils B at page 132.
- Invite two pupils to demonstrate the activity. The rest of the class then do the same in their pairs.

**Activity Book**

**Activity 1**

**What happens when paper is recycled? Write the missing letters and complete the mystery fact.**
- The pupils write the missing letters in the words. They order the highlighted letters to find the mystery word and complete the recycling fact.

**Answers:** **1** collected **2** transported **3** washed **4** removed **5** added **6** rolled **7** cut **8** used mystery word: eleven

**Activity 2**

**Read and complete. Write one word each time.**
- Read out the text as a class. Check comprehension by asking questions.
- Complete the first two sentences as a class.
- The pupils complete the remaining sentences.

**Answers:** **1** is **2** lot **3** of **4** on **5** is **6** full **7** which / that **8** we **9** draw **10** paper

**Activity 3**

**Read and learn.**
- Read the information as a class.

**Activity 4**

**Think of the things you can do with these objects. Write the verbs.**
- The pupils work on their own or in pairs to think of different things you can do with the objects.

**Possible answers:** **a book:** open, close, buy, sell, read, lend, borrow **a ball:** kick, throw, catch, bounce, save

**Odd one out activity**

**Which is the odd one out? Why?**
- The pupils complete the odd one out activity.

**Answers:** window (It isn't made of paper.)

**Ending the lesson**

**Review the lesson and reflect on learning.**
- Say **Today we've learnt what happens when paper and glass are recycled.**
- Ask **Which was your favourite activity today? Which activity was easy / difficult?**

**Extra activities**

**Reinforcement**
- Organise the pupils into pairs or small groups. Ask them to design a poster to tell other pupils about the importance of recycling.

**Vocabulary extension**
- Present four additional recycling words: *recycling bin, recycling containers, recycling lorry, recycling plant*
- Use the Vocabulary booster on NAVIO to practise these new words.

## Key Competences and Key Learning Outcomes

- Read and understand a set of instructions
- Do pre-reading tasks to predict content and raise interest
- Read a set of instructions for general understanding
- Scan a set of instructions for specific information
- Discuss and share what you know about this type of text
- Give an opinion on the text

### Key language
- *garden canes, plastic bottles, screws, stapler, wooden posts; collect, cut, dig, fix, make, remove, screw (v), use, wash*
- *Have you ever read instructions for (a game)? Why is it a good idea to ask an adult to help you?*

### Materials
- Pupil's Book p88; Activity Book p85; Class CD3; Teacher's App on Navio
- A drawing of a series of shapes

### Optional materials
- Teacher's Resource Bank: Trinity Exams Practice cards (selected from the Starter Unit and Units 1, 2, 3, 4, 5, 6 and 7)

## At a Glance Lesson Plan

### Pupil's Book

**Starting the lesson**
- Use the Trinity Exams Practice cards (optional).
- Review giving instructions.
- Set learning objectives.

**Activity 1: Before you read**
- Read and discuss.

**Activity 2**
- Look at the photo and read the list of materials.
- How do you think this greenhouse is made?
- Read and find out.

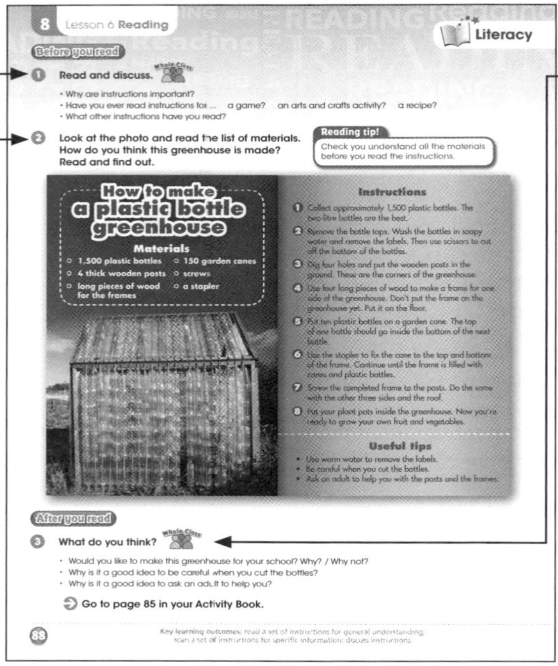


**Activity 3: After you read**
- What do you think?
- Go to the Activity Book.

**Ending the lesson**
- Review the lesson and reflect on learning.

**Extra activity**

**Reinforcement**
- Collect examples of instructions.

### Activity Book

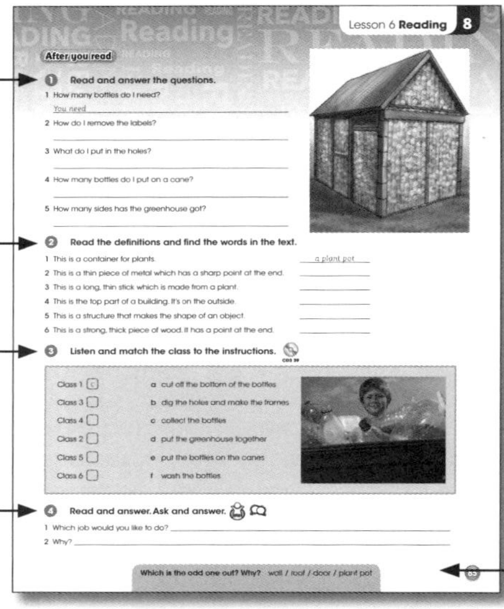


**Activity Book: After you read**

**Activity 1**
- Read and answer the questions.

**Activity 2**
- Read the definitions and find the words in the text.

**Activity 3**
- Listen and match the class to the instructions
- ▶ *CD3 Track 39 p293*

**Activity 4**
- Read and answer. Ask and answer.

**Odd one out activity**
- Which is the odd one out? Why?

## Digital resources

**Teacher's Digital:** You can also teach this lesson using the Teacher's App on Navio.

**Pupil's Digital:** Encourage your pupils to use the Pupil's App on Navio to practise the activities from this lesson.

Powered By NAVIO

# Detailed Lesson Plan

### Starting the lesson

**Use the Trinity Exams Practice cards (optional).**

- The pupils practise asking and answering questions.

**Review giving instructions.**

- Draw a series of shapes on a piece of paper. Then invite a pupil to come to the front of the room and give them the drawing. This pupil instructs the rest of the class on how to draw the picture. (*Draw a large circle. Draw a triangle inside the circle. Draw a line through the circle and the triangle.*) The class follows the instructions and draw the picture in their notebooks. If necessary, review the names of shapes before doing this activity.
- At the end of the activity, the pupils can compare their drawings with the original picture.

**Set learning objectives.**

- Say **Today we're going to read some instructions.**

### Pupil's Book Activity 1: Before you read

**Read and discuss.**

- Read the questions as a class. Prompt the pupils to answer in as much detail as possible.

### Pupil's Book Activity 2

**Look at the photo and read the list of materials. How do you think this greenhouse is made? Read and find out.**

- Describe and discuss the photo of the greenhouse as a class. Clarify what a greenhouse is used for and elicit / explain that a greenhouse is usually made of glass.
- Read the list of materials. Make predictions about how this greenhouse is made as a class. Then read the instructions and useful tips.

### Pupil's Book Activity 3: After you read

**What do you think?**

- Read the first questions as a class. Prompt the pupils to give their opinions. Encourage the pupils to give a reason for their opinions.
- Read the remaining questions. Prompt the class to infer that the activity is dangerous and that you can hurt yourself.

### Activity Book: After you read

**Activity 1**

**Read and answer the questions.**

- Read and answer the first question as a class.
- The pupils answer the remaining questions.

**Answers:** **1** need 1,500 bottles. **2** You wash the bottles in soapy water. **3** You put the wooden posts in the holes. **4** You put ten bottles on a cane. **5** It has four sides.

**Activity 2**

**Read the definitions and find the words in the text.**

- The pupils read the definitions and match each one to a word in the text.

**Answers:** **1** a plant pot **2** a screw **3** a garden cane **4** a roof **5** a frame **6** a wooden post

**Activity 3**

**Listen and match the class to the instructions.**

▶ *CD3 Track 39 p293*

- Read the information as a class.
- Play the CD. The pupils listen and match the class to a job.
- Play the CD again, pausing after each piece of key information to check the answers.

**Answers:** **1** c **2** f **3** a **4** e **5** b **6** d

**Activity 4**

**Read and answer. Ask and answer.**

- The pupils write the job they would like to do and why.
- Then they ask and answer in pairs.

### Odd one out activity

**Which is the odd one out? Why?**

- The pupils complete the odd one out activity.

**Answers:** plant pot (It isn't part of a building.)

### Ending the lesson

**Review the lesson and reflect on learning.**

- Say **Today we've read some instructions.**
- Ask **Which was your favourite activity today? Which activity was easy / difficult?**

### Extra activity

**Reinforcement**

- The pupils use the library or the Internet to find examples of written instructions in English. The pupils copy a section of the instructions and say where the excerpt came from, e.g. *a recipe* or *a computer game*. These instructions can be displayed in a class scrapbook or on a poster.

## Key Competences and Key Learning Outcomes

- Practise using imperatives to give instructions
- Write instructions for making a decoration
- Identify features of a set of instructions
- Use criteria to check your writing
- Share your writing with another pupil
- Design an object made of recycled materials

### Key language

- *CD, coloured card, decoration, felt-tip pens, fins, glue, instructions, materials, mouth, permanent, plastic eye, scales, scissors, string, tail, useful tips; cut out, draw, hang, mark, stick*
- *Be creative. Don't touch the scales when the ink is wet.*

### Materials

- Pupil's Book p89; Activity Book p86; Teacher's App on Navio

### Optional materials

- Teacher's Resource Bank: Trinity Exams Practice cards (selected from the Starter Unit and Units 1, 2, 3, 4, 5, 6 and 7)

## At a Glance Lesson Plan

### Pupil's Book

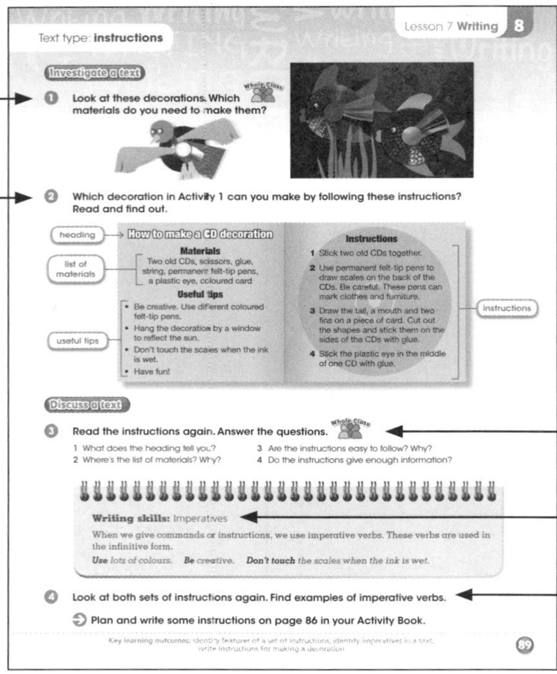
Lesson 7 Writing 8
Text type: instructions
Investigate a text
1 Look at these decorations. Which materials do you need to make them?
2 Which decoration in Activity 1 can you make by following these instructions? Read and find out.
heading / list of materials / useful tips / instructions
How to make a CD decoration
Materials: Two old CDs, scissors, glue, string, permanent felt-tip pens, a plastic eye, coloured card
Useful tips: Be creative. Use different coloured felt-tip pens. Hang the decoration by a window to reflect the sun. Don't touch the scales when the ink is wet. Have fun!
Instructions: 1 Stick two old CDs together. 2 Use permanent felt-tip pens to draw scales on the back of the CDs. Be careful. These pens can mark clothes and furniture. 3 Draw the tail, a mouth and two fins on a piece of card. Cut out the shapes and stick them on the sides of the CDs with glue. 4 Stick the plastic eye in the middle of one CD with glue.
Discuss a text
3 Read the instructions again. Answer the questions.
1 What does the heading tell you? 2 Where's the list of materials? Why? 3 Are the instructions easy to follow? Why? 4 Do the instructions give enough information?
Writing skills: Imperatives
When we give commands or instructions, we use imperative verbs. These verbs are used in the infinitive form.
Use lots of colours. Be creative. Don't touch the scales when the ink is wet.
4 Look at both sets of instructions again. Find examples of imperative verbs.
Plan and write some instructions on page 86 in your Activity Book.
89

#### Starting the lesson

- Use the Trinity Exams Practice cards (optional).
- Review arts and crafts activities.
- Set learning objectives.

#### Activity 1: Investigate a text

- Look at these decorations.
- Which materials do you need to make them?

#### Activity 2

- Which decoration in Activity 1 can you make by following these instructions?
- Read and find out.

#### Activity 3: Discuss a text

- Read the instructions again.
- Answer the questions.

#### Writing skills

- Read about using imperatives.

#### Activity 4

- Look at both sets of instructions again.
- Find examples of imperative verbs.

Go to the Activity Book.

#### Ending the lesson

- Review the lesson and reflect on learning.

#### Extra activity

**Reinforcement**

- Choose the decoration made from recycled materials that you'd like to make.

### Activity Book

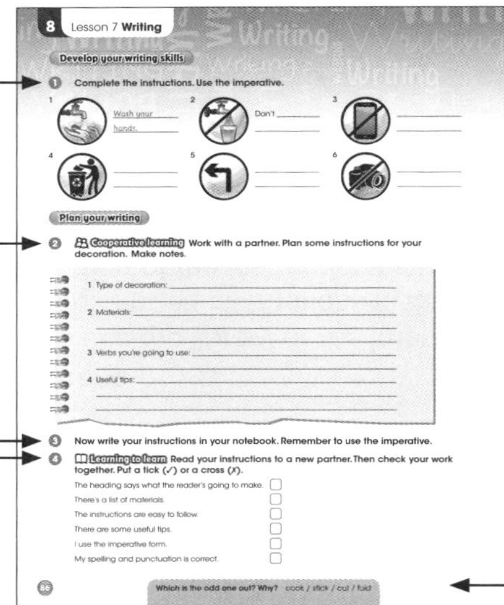
8 Lesson 7 Writing
Develop your writing skills
1 Complete the instructions. Use the imperative.
1 Wash your hands. 2 Don't
Plan your writing
2 Cooperative learning Work with a partner. Plan some instructions for your decoration. Make notes.
1 Type of decoration: 2 Materials: 3 Verbs you're going to use: 4 Useful tips:
3 Now write your instructions in your notebook. Remember to use the imperative.
4 Learning to learn Read your instructions to a new partner. Then check your work together. Put a tick (✓) or a cross (✗).
The heading says what the reader's going to make.
There's a list of materials.
The instructions are easy to follow.
There are some useful tips.
I use the imperative form.
My spelling and punctuation is correct.
Which is the odd one out? Why? cook / stick / cut / fold

#### Activity Book

**Activity 1: Develop your writing skills**

- Complete the instructions. Use the imperative.

**Activity 2: Plan your writing**

- Work with a partner. Plan some instructions for your decoration. Make notes.

**Activity 3**

- Now write your instructions in your notebook. Remember to use the imperative.

**Activity 4**

- Read your instructions to a new partner. Then check your work together. Put a tick (✓) or a cross (✗).

**Odd one out activity**

- Which is the odd one out? Why?

## Digital resources

**Teacher's Digital:** You can also teach this lesson using the Teacher's App on Navio.

**Pupil's Digital:** Encourage your pupils to use the Pupil's App on Navio to practise the activities from this lesson.

Powered By NAVIO

# Detailed Lesson Plan

### Starting the lesson

**Use the Trinity Exams Practice cards (optional).**

- The pupils practise asking and answering questions.

**Review arts and crafts activities.**

- Work as a class to discuss the activities the pupils do in their arts and crafts lesson. Ask **When do you have arts and crafts at school? What things do you do in the lesson? Have you ever made a model or decoration?**

**Set learning objectives.**

- Say **Today we're going to write some instructions.**

### Pupil's Book Activity 1: Investigate a text

**Look at these decorations. Which materials do you need to make them?**

- Focus the class on the pictures. Encourage the pupils to identify and name the materials that the two objects are made of. Then ask the class to think about what actions the reader needs to do to make the decorations.

### Pupil's Book Activity 2

**Which decoration in Activity 1 can you make by following these instructions? Read and find out.**

- Read the instructions as a class and match them to one of the pictures (the fish decoration).
- The pupils look back at the text and find the words that helped them match the instructions to the fish decoration.

### Pupil's Book Activity 3: Discuss a text

**Read the instructions again. Answer the questions.**

- Read and discuss the questions as a class. Highlight that good instructions state the purpose of the activity in the heading and list the materials at the beginning so that the reader can prepare what they need. Good instructions are also easy to follow. They use short sentences and numbers or sequencers to break the activity into clear stages. There is also enough detail with information on shape, size, colour and quantity.

### Writing skills

- Read about using imperatives to give commands or questions.
- Encourage the pupils to think of the imperatives they hear and read every day. Ask **What instructions do your parents / teachers give you? What instructions can you read in a library / at the swimming pool / in the street?**

### Pupil's Book Activity 4

**Look at both sets of instructions again. Find examples of imperative verbs.**

- The pupils look at the sets of instructions in Lessons 6 and 7 to find examples of imperative verbs.

### Activity Book

**Activity 1: Develop your writing skills**

**Complete the instructions. Use the imperative.**

- Focus the class on the signs. Elicit where they are found and what they mean.
- The pupils complete the instructions using the imperative form.

**Answer:** **1** Wash your hands. **2** Don't drink the water. **3** Don't use your phone. **4** Put the rubbish in the bin. **5** Turn left. **6** Don't take photos.

**Activity 2: Plan your writing**

**Work with a partner. Plan some instructions for your decoration. Make notes.**

- Read out the notes. Elicit ideas for decorations that are made from recycled materials. If necessary, review the vocabulary from Lesson 1.
- Organise the class into Writing Partners. The pupils choose a decoration and plan their instructions.

**Activity 3**

**Now write your instructions in your notebook. Remember to use the imperative.**

- The pupils work with their partner to write their instructions in their notebooks.

**Activity 4**

**Read your instructions to a new partner. Then check your work together. Put a tick (✓) or a cross (✗).**

- Read through the statements as a class.
- Organise the class into new Writing Partners. One pupil reads aloud their text to their partner. The other pupil listens. The pupils work together to decide if the text fulfils the criteria and tick the corresponding boxes. The pupils can add, improve or correct the text at this stage.
- The pupils swap roles.

**Odd one out activity**

**Which is the odd one out? Why?**

- The pupils complete the odd one out activity.

**Answers:** cook (It isn't used in instructions for making a decoration.)

### Ending the lesson

**Review the lesson and reflect on learning.**

- Say **Today we've written some instructions for a decoration.**
- Ask **Which was your favourite activity today? Which activity was easy / difficult?**

### Extra activity

**Reinforcement**

- Ask the pupils to leave their notebooks open on their desk so that other pupils can read their instructions. Ask the pupils to move around the class, reading the different instructions. They decide which decoration they would most like to make.

## Key Competences and Key Learning Outcomes

- Talk about the environment
- Listen to a conversation about the environment
- Review learning and reflect on progress in the unit
- Learn different ways of saying 'yes' or 'no' in a conversation
- Have a conversation about the environment

### Key language

- *go to school by car, protect the environment, save energy, recycle rubbish, switch off lights / the TV, walk*
- *What do you do to save energy?, Do you usually switch off the TV, too? Absolutely! Of course! Absolutely not! Not at all!*

### Materials

- Pupil's Book p90; Activity Book p87; Class CD3; Teacher's App on Navio

### Optional materials

- Teacher's Resource Bank: Trinity Exams Practice cards (selected from the Starter Unit and Units 1, 2, 3, 4, 5, 6 and 7)

## At a Glance Lesson Plan

### Pupil's Book

**Starting the lesson**

- Use the Trinity Exams Practice cards (optional).
- Review recyclable objects and materials.
- Set learning objectives.

**Activity 1**

- What are the people doing in the photos? Why?

**Activity 2**

- Listen to the conversation.
- ▶ *CD3 Track 40 p293*
- Which of these activities does Robin do to protect the environment?

**Activity 3**

- Listen again.
- ▶ *CD3 Track 40 p293*
- Complete four questions that Anthony asks.

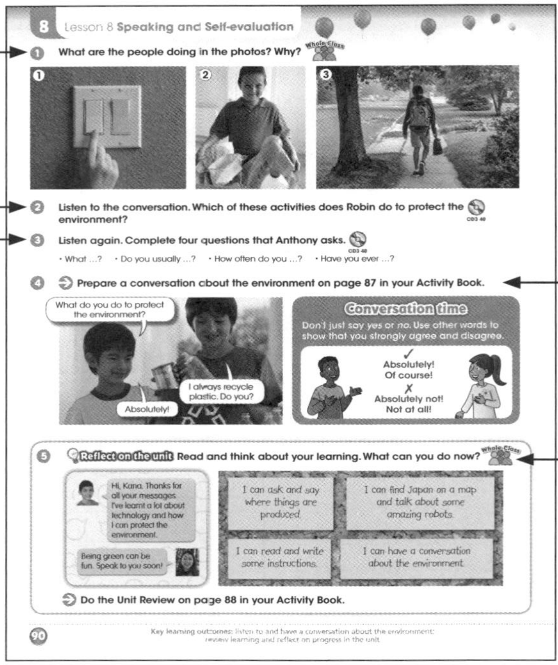


**Activity 4**

- Prepare a conversation about the environment on page 87 in your Activity Book.
- Go to page 87 in the Activity Book.

**Activity 5**

- Read and think about your learning. What can you do now?
- Go to page 88 in the Activity Book.

**Ending the lesson**

- Review the lesson and reflect on learning.

**Extra activity**

- Revise expressions for strongly agreeing and disagreeing.

### Activity Book

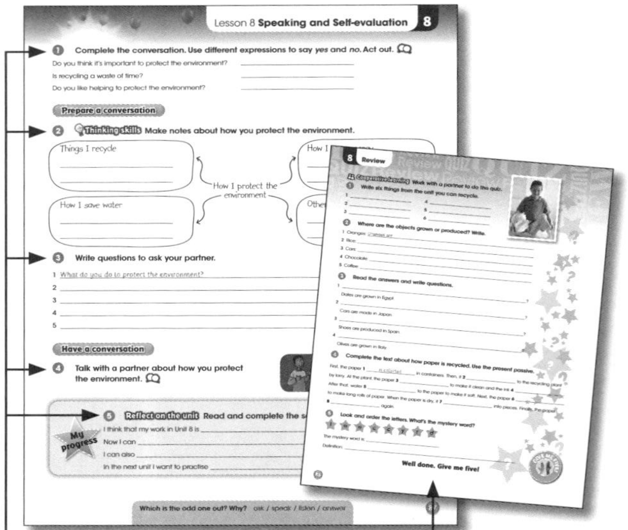


**Activity Book page 88: Review**

- Work with a partner to do the quiz.

**Activity Book**

**Activity 1**

- Complete the conversation.
- Use different expressions to say *yes* and *no*.
- Act out.

**Activity 2**

- Make notes about how you protect the environment.

**Activity 3**

- Write questions to ask your partner.

**Activity 4**

- Talk with a partner about how you protect the environment.

**Activity 5**

- Read and complete the sentences.

**Odd one out activity**

- Which is the odd one out? Why?

### Digital resources

**Teacher's Digital:** You can also teach this lesson using the Teacher's App on Navio.

Powered By NAVIO

# Detailed Lesson Plan

## Starting the lesson

**Use the Trinity Exams Practice cards (optional).**

- The pupils practise asking and answering questions.

**Review recyclable materials and objects.**

- Tell pupils to name everyday objects, such as: a mobile phone, a pair of trainers, a book, a rucksack. For each object, ask **What's it made of? Can you recycle those materials?**

**Set learning objectives.**

- Say **Today we're going to prepare a conversation about protecting the environment.**

## Pupil's Book Activity 1

**What are the people doing in the photos? Why?**

- Ask different pupils to describe the pictures. Ask pupils if they do these activities.

**Answers: 1** Someone is switching off a light. **2** A boy is holding a box of recyclable rubbish. **3** A boy is walking to school.

## Pupil's Book Activity 2

**Listen to the conversation. Which of these activities does Robin do to protect the environment?**

▶ *CD3 Track 40 p293*

- Play the CD. Ask which pictures from Activity 1 are mentioned (*all of them*). Ask for more details about each activity.

**Answer:** Robin does all of them.

## Pupil's Book Activity 3

**Listen again. Complete four questions that Anthony asks.**

▶ *CD3 Track 40 p293*

- Direct pupils to the four question prompts. Ask if they can remember the questions.
- Play the CD. Pupils check in pairs. Then play again and check as a class.

**Answers:** What do you do to save energy?; Do you usually switch off the TV too?; How often do you go to school by car?; Have you ever recycled rubbish before?

## Pupil's Book Activity 4

**Prepare a conversation about the environment on page 87 in your Activity Book.**

- Read the speech bubbles with the pupils. Model the phrases in the Conversation Time box and get the class to repeat.

## Pupil's Book Activity 5

**Read and think about your learning. What can you do now?**

- Read the speech bubbles and notes with the pupils. Then look back through the unit and prompt them to identify things that they have done/learnt.

## Activity Book page 88: Review

**Work with a partner to do the quiz.**

- Organise the class into pairs. Set a time limit for the pupils to do the quiz (10–15 minutes). Stress that the pupils are not competing with each other.
- Read out the five tasks that the pupils have to complete. Check understanding. Then say **Ready, steady ... Go!**
- The pupils work in their pairs to do the quiz.
- Correct the answers as a class.

**Answers: 1** Six from: bottle top, button, can, cardboard box, cardboard tube, carton, elastic band, fabric, lolly stick, plastic bottle, straw, string **3 1** Where are dates grown? **2** Where are cars made? **3** Where are shoes produced? **4** Where are olives grown? **4** is collected, is transported, is washed, is removed, is added, is rolled, is cut, is used **5** recycled, to use materials and objects again.

## Activity Book

**Activity 1**

**Complete the conversation. Use different expressions to say *yes* and *no*. Act out.**

- Ask a pupil to ask you the questions – respond with expressions from Conversation time on the Pupil's Book page. Then pupils perform the dialogue in pairs.

**Activity 2**

**Make notes about how you protect the environment.**

- Talk about how you protect the environment. Then pupils complete the boxes with their own information.

**Activity 3**

**Write questions to ask your partner.**

- Direct pupils to the five headings in Activity 2 and explain that they need to form questions about them. Then pupils complete the questions alone. Check as a class.

**Answers: 1** What do you do to protect the environment? **2** What things do you recycle? **3** How do you save water? **4** How do you save energy? **5** What other things do you do?

**Activity 4**

**Talk with a partner about how you protect the environment.**

- In pairs, pupils ask and answer the questions from Activity 3. Encourage them to use expressions to show interest.
- Invite one or two pairs to perform their conversations for the class.

**Activity 5**

**Read and complete the sentences.**

- Pupils review their work in the unit.

**Odd one out activity**

**Which is the odd one out? Why?**

**Answer:** listen (You don't talk when you do it.)

## Ending the lesson

**Review the lesson and reflect on learning.**

- Say **Today we've learnt how to have a conversation about how you protect the environment.**
- Ask **Which was your favourite activity today? Which activity was easy / difficult?**

## Key Competences and Key Learning Outcomes

- Watch and understand a video about recycling
- Use a digital poster to persuade
- Think about why recycling is important and helps the planet

**Key language**
- *bury, collect, melt, recycled, recycling container, recycling lorry, reduce*
- *I want people to recycle paper. Our poster is for adults.*

**Materials**
- Pupil's Book p91; Activity Book p89; Class CD3; Teacher's App on Navio
- Recyclable objects and materials flashcards
- Teacher's Resource Bank: Talk cards

**Optional materials**
- Teacher's Resource Bank: Trinity Exams Practice cards (selected from the Starter Unit and Units 1–7)

## At a Glance Lesson Plan

### Pupil's Book

**Starting the lesson**
- Use the Trinity Exams Practice cards (optional).
- **Think-Pair-Share** Review recyclable objects and materials vocabulary.
- Set learning objectives and use the talk cards.

**Activity 1**
- Before you watch
- Watch the video.
  *Unit 8 video p303*
- Read and say *true* or *false*.
- Correct the false sentences.

**Activity 2**
- Watch the video again.
  *Unit 8 video*
- What are these things?
- What is the connection with the video?

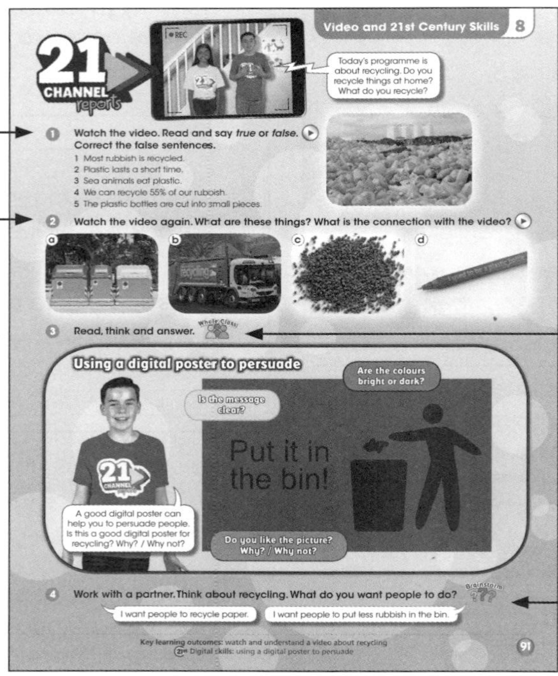

**Activity 3**
- Read, think and answer.

**Activity 4**
- Work with a partner.
- Think about recycling.
- What do you want people to do?

Go to the Activity Book.

**Ending the lesson**
- Review the lesson and reflect on learning.

**Extra activity**
- Make a list of presents made of recycled materials.

### Activity Book

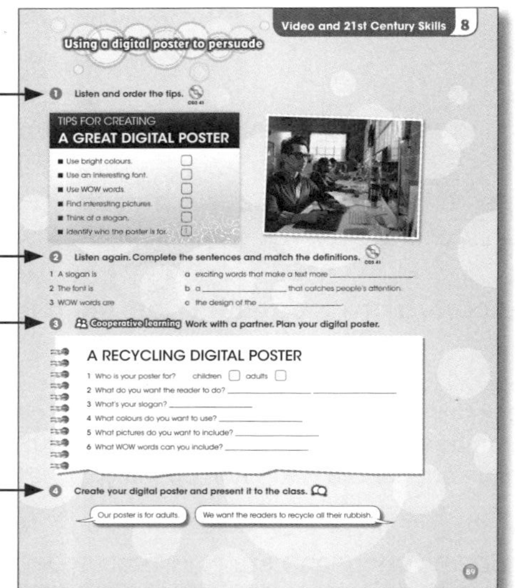

**Activity Book**

**Activity 1**
- Listen and order the tips.

▶ *CD3 Track 41 p293*

**Activity 2**
- Listen again.
- Complete the sentences and match the definitions.

▶ *CD3 Track 41 p293*

**Activity 3**
- Work with a partner.
- Plan your digital poster.

**Activity 4**
- Create your digital poster and present it to the class.

**Digital resources**

**Teacher's Digital:** You can also teach this lesson using the Teacher's App on Navio.

**Pupil's Digital:** Encourage your pupils to use the Pupil's App on Navio to practise the activities from this lesson.

Powered By NAVIO

### Starting the lesson

**Use the Trinity Exams Practice cards (optional).**

- The pupils practise asking and answering questions.

**Think-Pair-Share Review recyclable objects and materials vocabulary.**

- Ask **Can you remember the recyclable objects and materials words?** The class thinks silently for a minute.
- Then the pupils work with a Talk Partner to name recyclable objects and materials.
- Invite different Talk Partners to say different recyclable objects and materials. Hold up the corresponding flashcard and prompt the class to repeat the word.
- Finally, repeat the procedure, asking different pairs of Talk Partners each time, until all the ideas have been recorded.

**Set learning objectives and use the talk cards.**

- Say **Today we're going to watch a video and then ask and answer questions about recycling.**
- Point to the talk cards to show the pupils the different ways they will be working in the lesson.

### Pupil's Book Activity 1

**Before you watch**

- Read the speech bubble to pupils. Ask **Do you recycle things at home? What do you recycle?** Elicit responses from a number of pupils.

**Watch the video. Read and say *true* or *false*. Correct the false sentences.** *p303*

- Watch Part 1 of the video. Ask pupils **What are you going to see next?**
- Play Part 2 of the video. Ask general questions to check understanding. Direct pupils to look at the sentences 1–5. Say **Most rubbish is recycled. True or false?** (*False*). Elicit why it is false. (*Most rubbish is buried under the ground.*)
- Play the video again and check answers as a group.

**Answers:** **1** False (Most rubbish is buried under the ground). **2** False (It lasts a long time.) **3** True **4** False (We can recycle 75% of our rubbish.) **5** True

### Pupil's Book Activity 2

**Watch the video again. What are these things? What is the connection with the video?**

- Ask a pupil **What can you see in picture a?** Ask a different pupil **What is the connection with the video?**
- Play the video. Check the answers as a class.

**Answers:** **a** Recycling containers. Max's mum is taking plastic bottles to them. **b** A recycling lorry. It collects rubbish from the bins. **c** Small pieces of plastic. They are melted to make small balls. **d** A pen. It's made from recycled plastic.

### Pupil's Book Activity 3

**Read, think and answer.**

- Read the speech bubble and ask the class what they think of the poster. Revise *too* and *not enough* and elicit ideas with both structures, such as *It's too dark. It isn't bright enough.*
- Ask pupils to discuss the three questions in pairs, and think of ways to improve the poster.

### Pupil's Book Activity 4

**Work with a partner. Think about recycling. What do you want people to do?**

- Pupils work in pairs to think of more ways to persuade people to recycle. Direct them to the structure *I want people to* + infinitive in the speech bubbles.
- Pupils share their ideas with the class. Have a class vote for the most creative or original ideas.

### Activity Book

**Activity 1**

**Listen and order the tips.**

▶ ***CD3 Track 41 p293***

- Ask pupils to describe what the people in the picture are doing.
- Play the CD. Pause after each sentence so pupils can write the number.

**Answers:** **1** Identify who the poster is for. **2** Use bright colours. **3** Find interesting pictures. **4** Think of a slogan. **5** Use WOW words. **6** Use an interesting font.

**Activity 2**

**Listen again. Complete the sentences and match the definitions.**

▶ ***CD3 Track 41 p293***

- Ask pupils to try and define *slogan*, *font* and *WOW words* in their own words.

**Answers:** **1** b; short phrase **2** c; letters and numbers **3** a; interesting

**Activity 3**

**Work with a partner. Plan your digital poster.**

- Read through the poster with the class. Ask **Is Max and Amy's poster for children or adults?** (*Children*) **What do they want the reader to do?** (*To recycle more*) **What slogans do Uncle Pete and Amy suggest?** (*'Stop, think, recycle!' and 'Go green!'*) **What bright colours does Uncle Pete mention?** (*red and orange*) **What WOW words does he mention?** (*amazing, brilliant*)
- Pupils complete the information in pairs to plan their poster.

**Activity 4**

**Create your digital poster and present it to the class.**

- Pupils create their posters using the digital resources available.
- If possible, allow pupils to display their posters on the interactive whiteboard.

### Ending the lesson

**Review the lesson and reflect on learning.**

- Say **Today we've watched a video about recycling. What have we learnt about using a digital poster to persuade?** Elicit ideas from the pupils.
- Ask **Which was your favourite activity today? Which activity was easy / difficult?**

Date: ____________________ Unit: __________

1 What did my pupils learn in this unit?

2 How did my pupils work? (✓)

individually ☐ in pairs ☐ in small groups ☐

in large groups ☐ as a class ☐

3 Which key competences did my pupils develop? Give a score from 1 to 5 (5 being the highest).

- Competence in linguistic communication ☐
- Competence in mathematics, science and technology ☐
- Digital competence ☐
- Learning to learn ☐
- Social and civic competences ☐
- Sense of initiative and entrepreneurship ☐
- Cultural awareness and expression ☐

4 Which lessons / activities were the most successful and why?

5 Which lessons / activities did my pupils find the most difficult and why?

6 What did I try in the classroom for the first time? How did it go?

7 Which resources did I find most useful? (including webpages)

8 What could I do differently next time I teach this unit?

Unit 9

# Amazing places

## Unit overview

### Key Competences and Key Learning Outcomes

- Name natural places in the world (Lesson 1)
- Learn and use the present continuous for future plans (Lesson 2)
- Learn and use the first conditional (Lesson 4)
- Review and name items to take on a trip (Lesson 5)
- Review and use prepositions of time (Lesson 7)
- Talk about a trip to a place near where you live (Lesson 8)
- Watch and understand a video about different places where people live (Video and 21st Century Skills)

- Categorise natural and man-made things (Lesson 1)

- Use the Pupil's App on Navio
- Investigate Brazil (Lesson 3)

- Identify and practise correct pronunciation of contracted forms in first conditional sentences (Lesson 4)
- Reflect on your own learning (Lesson 8)
- Practise activity types found in the Cambridge Exams: A2 Key for Schools

- Think about importance of sharing stories (Lesson 3)
- Show curiosity about the lives of people who live in different places (Video and 21st Century Skills)

- Work in pairs or small groups (all lessons)
- Do a communication task (Lesson 5)

- Read and understand a story (Lesson 3)
- Learn about Brazil and the legend of Vitória Régia water lily (Lesson 3)
- Read a tourist website (Lesson 6)
- Write a travel itinerary (Lesson 7)
- Sing a song (Lesson 8)
- Learn about life in Alaska (Video and 21st Century Skills)

### Vocabulary

**Core vocabulary**
*canyon, coast, desert, island, lake, ocean, plain, rainforest, reef, valley, volcano, waterfall; anorak, dictionary, money, passport, suitcase, ticket, towel, umbrella, wallet*

**Extension vocabulary (optional)**
*bay, cliff, creek, geyser, lagoon, oasis; puzzle book, sun hat, toothbrush, washbag*

**Other vocabulary**
*canoe trip, dive, equator, full moon, legend, reflection, search on the Internet, water lily, wildlife;* variety of wildlife; *climate, glacier, fishing, moose, otter, snow storm, state*

**Recycled vocabulary**
*binoculars, camera, celebration, climb, cousins, guidebook, MP3 player, pencils, sketchpad, stars, summer, swimming pool, touch, winter; Brazil, England, the UK; at 9:00, for two hours, in the morning, on Saturday*

### Structures

**Core structures**
*I am / am not going camping. You / We / They are / aren't going camping. He / She / It is / isn't going camping. Are you / we / they going camping? Is he / she / it going camping? If you search on the Internet, you'll find lots of great photos. If you play a lot of sport, you'll keep fit. If we're late, they won't let us in. If you don't wear a coat, you'll be cold.*

**Other structures**
*If we go on the trip to Legoland, when will we leave? Which place would you most like to visit?*

**Recycled structures**
*Brazil has won the World Cup more times than any other country. Have you ever been to (an island)? Which (island) did you go to? She loved looking at the stars. Arrive at Waterloo Station.*

### Pronunciation

Contracted forms in first conditional sentences

### Literacy

**Text type:** a travel itinerary (text to inform; writing preparation)
**Reading skill:** scanning text for information
**Writing skill:** using prepositions of time

### Culture ... around the world

The legend of Vitória Régia water lily in Brazil

### 21st Century Skills

**Ways of thinking:** thinking about how other people live

### Thinking skills

Categorising (Lesson 1); Analysing and applying rules (Lessons 2 and 4); Defining and describing (Lesson 5); Finding and classifying (Lesson 6); Planning, checking and correcting (Lesson 7); Seeing another's point of view (Lesson 8); Reflecting on learning (Lesson 8) Working together (Lessons 1–8)

### Cooperative learning

Collaborating (Lessons 1–8); Checking learning (Lessons 1–8); Peer evaluation and feedback (Lesson 7); Helping and encouraging (Lessons 1–8); Reaching agreement (Lesson 8); Reflecting and setting goals (Lessons 1 and 8)

### Values

The importance of sharing stories

### Cross-curricular links

**Link to Science**
Ecosystems

**Suggested Arts and Crafts concepts**
Points of view

## Key Competences and Key Learning Outcomes

- Identify and say words about natural places
- Listen to definitions and identify the words
- Categorise natural and man-made things
- Read a message and some facts for general understanding
- Talk about places you have been to

**Key language**
- *canyon, coast, desert, island, lake, ocean, plain, rainforest, reef, valley, volcano, waterfall; airport, bird, celebration, insect, 17 times bigger, swimming pool, take part, wildlife*
- *Brazil has won the World Cup more times than any other country. Brazil is the fifth biggest country in the world. Have you ever been to (an island)? Which (island) did you go to?*
- **Extension:** *bay, cliff, creek, geyser, lagoon, oasis*

**Materials**
- Pupil's Book pp92–93; Activity Book p90; Class CD4; Teacher's App on Navio
- Natural places flashcards

**Optional materials**
- Teacher's Resource Bank: Trinity Exams Practice cards (selected from the Starter Unit and Units 1, 2, 3, 4, 5, 6, 7 and 8)

## At a Glance Lesson Plan

### Pupil's Book

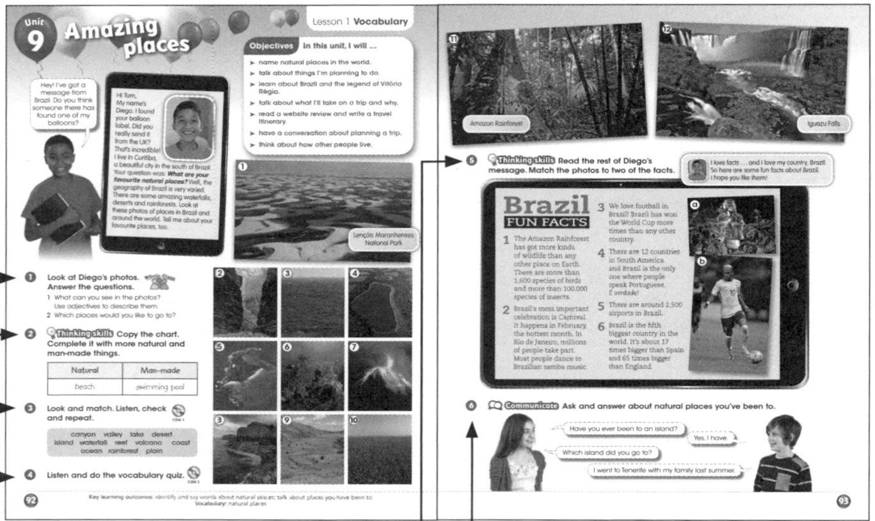


**Starting the lesson**
- Use the Trinity Exams Practice cards (optional).
- Review places in the coountryside.
- Set learning objectives.

**Activity 1**
- Look at Diego's photos.
- Answer the questions.

**Activity 2**
- Copy the chart.
- Complete it with more natural and man-made things.

**Vocabulary presentation**
- Present the new vocabulary using the natural places flashcards.

**Activity 3**
- Look and match.
- Listen, check and repeat.
- ▶ *CD4 Track 1 p294*

**Activity 4**
- Listen and do the vocabulary quiz.
- ▶ *CD4 Track 2 p294*

**Activity 5**
- Read the rest of Diego's message.
- Match the photos to two of the facts.

**Activity 6**
- Ask and answer about natural places you've been to.
- Go to the Activity Book.

**Ending the lesson**
- Review the lesson and reflect on learning.

**Extra activities**

**Extension**
- Find out about Brazil.

**Vocabulary extension**
- Present six additional vocabulary items.

**Digital resources**

**Teacher's Digital:** You can also teach this lesson using the Teacher's App on Navio.

**Pupil's Digital:** Encourage your pupils to use the Pupil's App on Navio to practise the activities from this lesson.

Powered By NAVIO

### Activity Book

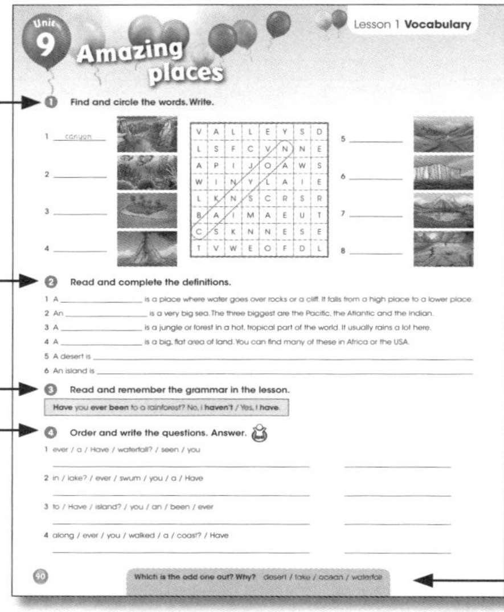


**Activity Book**

**Activity 1**
- Find and circle the words. Write.

**Activity 2**
- Read and complete the definitions.

**Activity 3**
- Read and remember the grammar in the lesson.

**Activity 4**
- Order and write the questions. Answer.

**Odd one out activity**
- Which is the odd one out? Why?

# Detailed Lesson Plan

### Starting the lesson

**Use the Trinity Exams Practice cards (optional).**
- The pupils practise asking and answering questions.

**Review places in the countryside.**
- Ask the class about their favourite places in the countryside. Make a list on the board.

**Set learning objectives.**
- Say **Today we're going to remember and learn the names of natural places in the world.**

### Pupil's Book Activity 1

**Look at Diego's photos. Answer the questions.**
- Invite a pupil to read out the speech bubble to find out who has found the balloon. Ask **Do you know where Brazil is?**
- Invite a pupil to read out the message from Diego. Check understanding.
- Work as a class to answer the questions.

### Pupil's Book Activity 2

**Copy the chart. Complete it with more natural and man-made things.**
- Copy the chart onto the board. Elicit an example for each column.
- Organise the class into pairs. The pupils copy the chart into their notebooks and complete it.

### Vocabulary presentation

- Present the new vocabulary using the natural places flashcards. Show the first flashcard and elicit / say the word. Ask **Is there (a waterfall) near our town / city? Are there (rainforests) in our country?**
- Write *In this country* and *Not in this country* on the board. As the flashcard words are named, the pupils place them in the correct category.

### Pupil's Book Activity 3

**Look and match. Listen, check and repeat.**

▶ ***CD4 Track 1 p294***
- The class looks at photo number 1. Ask **What's this?** The pupils work in pairs to match numbers 2–12 with the words.
- Play the CD. The pupils listen and check.
- Play the CD again, pausing after each word for the pupils to repeat.

### Pupil's Book Activity 4

**Listen and do the vocabulary quiz.**

▶ ***CD4 Track 2 p294***
- Play the CD. Listen to the first definition, pausing at the beep to allow the pupils to name the item. Play the CD to listen to the answer.
- Repeat the procedure with the other definitions.

### Pupil's Book Activity 5

**Read the rest of Diego's message.**
**Match the photos to two of the facts.**
- Invite a pupil to read out the message. Check that the pupils understand the task. The pupils read the facts and match the photos with two of the facts.
- Check understanding. Ask **Are there more species of insects in the Amazon Rainforest than species of birds? When does Carnival happen in Rio?**

### Pupil's Book Activity 6

**Ask and answer about natural places you've been to.**
- The pupils ask and answer in pairs.

### Activity Book

**Activity 1**

**Find and circle the words. Write.**
- The pupils look at the pictures, find the words in the wordsearch and write them.

**Answers:** **1** canyon **2** reef **3** island **4** volcano **5** valley **6** coast **7** lake **8** desert

**Activity 2**

**Read and complete the definitions.**
- The pupils complete the definitions.

**Answers:** **1** waterfall **2** ocean **3** rainforest **4** plain

**Activity 3**

**Read and remember the grammar in the lesson.**
- Invite a pupil to read out the information. Remind the class that we use the present perfect tense to talk about our experiences in the past.

**Activity 4**

**Order and write the questions. Answer.**
- The pupils write the questions and then answer them.

**Answers:** **1** Have you ever seen a waterfall? **2** Have you ever swum in a lake? **3** Have you ever been to an island? **4** Have you ever walked along a coast?

**Odd one out activity**

**Which is the odd one out? Why?**
- The pupils complete the odd one out activity.

**Answers:** desert (It isn't a natural water feature.)

### Ending the lesson

**Review the lesson and reflect on learning.**
- Say **Today we've learnt the names of natural places in the world. What do you remember?**
- Ask **Which was your favourite activity today? Which activity was easy / difficult?**

### Extra activities

**Extension/Reinforcement**
- The pupils find Brazil on the world map on pages 134–135. They read the accompanying facts.

**Vocabulary extension**
- Present six additional natural places: *bay, cliff, creek, geyser, lagoon, oasis.*
- Use the Vocabulary booster on NAVIO to practise these new words.

## Key Competences and Key Learning Outcomes

- Listen to and read a dialogue
- Use the present continous to talk about future plans

- Identify examples of the present continuous for future plans in the dialogue
- Practise activity types found in the Cambridge Exams: A2 Key for Schools

**Key language**

- *summer, winter; camping, canoe trip, cousins, equator, legend, rainforest*
- *I am / am not going camping. You / We / They are / aren't going camping. He / She / It is / isn't going camping. Are you / we / they going camping? Is he / she / it going camping?*

**Materials**

- Pupil's Book p94; Activity Book p91; Class CD4; Teacher's App on Navio
- Teacher's Resource Bank: Natural places word cards

**Optional materials**

- Teacher's Resource Bank: Trinity Exams Practice cards (selected from the Starter Unit and Units 1, 2, 3, 4, 5, 6, 7 and 8)

## At a Glance Lesson Plan

### Pupil's Book

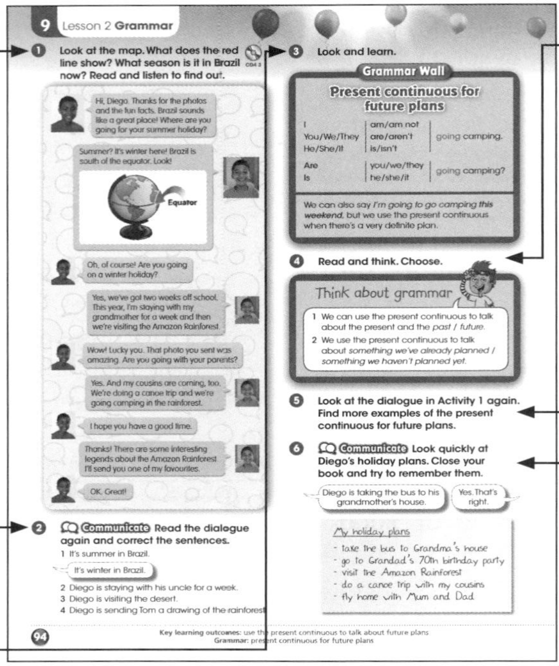

**Starting the lesson**

- Use the Trinity Exams Practice cards (optional).
- Review natural places.
- Set learning objectives.

**Activity 1**

- Look at the map.
- What does the red line show?
- What season is it in Brazil now?
- Read and listen to find out.

▶ *CD4 Track 3 p294*

**Activity 2**

- Read the dialogue again and correct the sentences.

**Activity 3**

- Look and learn – Grammar wall

**Activity 4**

- Read and think.
- Choose.

**Activity 5**

- Look at the dialogue in Activity 1 again.
- Find more examples of the present continuous for future plans.

**Activity 6**

- Look quickly at Diego's holiday plans.
- Close your book and try to remember them.

Go to the Activity Book.

**Ending the lesson**

- Review the lesson and reflect on learning.

**Extra activity**

**Reinforcement**

- Write more holiday plans.

**Digital resources**

**Teacher's Digital:** You can also teach this lesson using the Teacher's App on Navio.

**Pupil's Digital:** Encourage your pupils to use the Pupil's App on Navio to practise the activities from this lesson.

Powered By NAVIO

### Activity Book

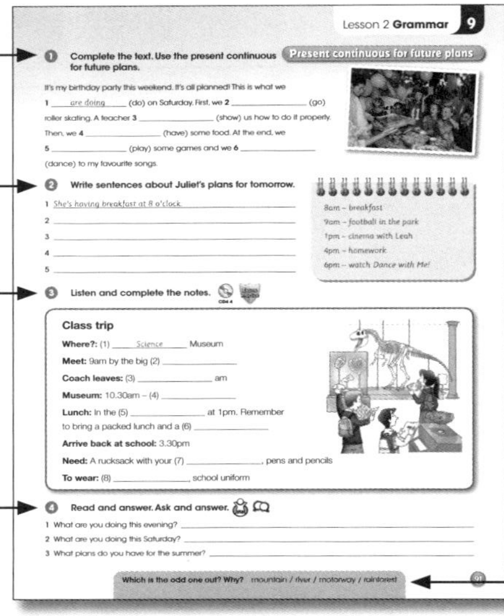

**Activity Book**

**Activity 1**

- Complete the text. Use the present continuous for future plans.

**Activity 2**

- Write sentences about Juliet's plans for tomorrow.

**Activity 3**

- Listen and complete the notes.

▶ *CD4 Track 4 p294*

**Activity 4**

- Read and answer. Ask and answer.

**Odd one out activity**

- Which is the odd one out? Why?

# Detailed Lesson Plan

### Starting the lesson

**Use the Trinity Exams Practice cards (optional).**
- The pupils practise asking and answering questions.

**Review natural places.**
- Hold up the natural places word cards so that the class can't see them. Give the definitions. The pupils listen and say the words, and then check the spellings.

**Set learning objectives.**
- Say **Today we're going to learn how to talk about future plans using the present continuous tense.**

### Pupil's Book Activity 1

**Look at the map. What does the red line show? What season is it in Brazil now? Read and listen to find out.**

▶ *CD4 Track 3 p294*
- Prompt the class to describe what they can see in the picture.
- Ask **What is the red line called? Are the seasons the same above the line and below it?**
- Play the CD. The pupils listen and read the dialogue. Confirm that the red line is the equator and the seasons are not the same above and below the line.

### Pupil's Book Activity 2

**Read the dialogue again and correct the sentences.**
- Organise the class into pairs. The pupils work together to read and correct the sentences.

### Pupil's Book Activity 3

**Look and learn – Grammar wall**
- Read the information on the Grammar wall as a class.
- Use questions to encourage the pupils to think about form and identify / remember patterns. Ask **When do we normally use the present continuous tense?** Make it clear that the form is exactly the same, but the meaning is different.

### Pupil's Book Activity 4

**Read and think. Choose.**
- Focus the pupils' attention on the Think about grammar box. Read out the sentences as a class. The pupils complete the sentences in pairs.

**Answers:** **1** future **2** something we've already planned

### Pupil's Book Activity 5

**Look at the dialogue in Activity 1 again. Find more examples of the present continuous for future plans.**
- Organise the pupils into pairs. Ask them to find examples of the present continuous for future plans in the text.

### Pupil's Book Activity 6

**Look quickly at Diego's holiday plans. Close your books and try to remember them.**
- Ask the pupils to look at the list and read it with the class. Invite two pupils to read out the speech bubbles.
- (Books closed.) Organise the class into pairs. The pupils remember Diego's plans and make sentences using the present continuous for future plans.

### Activity Book

**Activity 1**

**Complete the text. Use the present continuous for future plans.**
- The pupils complete the text with the correct form of the verbs in brackets.

**Answers:** **1** are doing **2** are going **3** is showing **4** are having **5** are playing **6** are dancing

**Activity 2**

**Write sentences about Juliet's plans for tomorrow.**
- The pupils write sentences about Juliet's plans.

**Answers:** **1** She's having breakfast at 8 o'clock. **2** She's playing football in the park at 9 o'clock. **3** She's going to the cinema with Leah at 1 o'clock. **4** She's doing homework at 4 o'clock. **5** She's watching *Dance with Me!* at 6 o'clock.

**Activity 3**

**Listen and complete the notes.**

▶ *CD4 Track 4 p294*
- Read out the notes as a class.
- Play the CD. The pupils listen and follow the information in their books.
- Play the CD again, pausing after each piece of key information. The pupils complete the information.

**Answers:** **1** Science **2** tree **3** 9.15 **4** 12.30pm **5** park **6** drink **7** notebook **8** a coat

**Activity 4**

**Read and answer. Ask and answer.**
- The pupils write answers to the questions. They then ask a partners the questions.

**Odd one out activity**

**Which is the odd one out? Why?**
- The pupils complete the odd one out activity.

**Answers:** motorway (It isn't a natural feature.)

### Ending the lesson

**Review the lesson and reflect on learning.**
- Say **Today we've learnt how to talk about future plans using the present continuous tense.**
- Ask **Which was your favourite activity today? Which activity was easy / difficult?**

### Extra activity

**Reinforcement**
- The pupils make holiday plans for a trip to Brazil.

### Key Competences and Key Learning Outcomes

- Read a story with a cultural focus
- Use the Internet to investigate Brazil
- Listen for specific information
- Think about stories and the importance of sharing stories
- Learn about the legend of the Vitória Régia water lily

### Key language

- *climb, dive, reach, save, touch, turn into; deep, full moon, hill, legend, moon, reflection, river, stars, water lily*
- *She loved looking at the moon. Naia climbed up a tree. Why is it important that people share stories?*

### Materials

- Pupil's Book p95; Activity Book p92; Class CD4; Teacher's App on Navio

### Optional materials

- Teacher's Resource Bank: Trinity Exams Practice cards (selected from the Starter Unit and Units 1, 2, 3, 4, 5, 6, 7 and 8)

## At a Glance Lesson Plan

### Starting the lesson

- Use the Trinity Exams Practice cards (optional).
- Review flowers and plants.
- Set learning objectives.

### Activity 1: Before you read

- Read and discuss.

### Activity 2

- Listen and read.

▶ *CD4 Track 5 p294*

Go to the Activity Book.

### Values

- Read and discuss.

## Pupil's Book

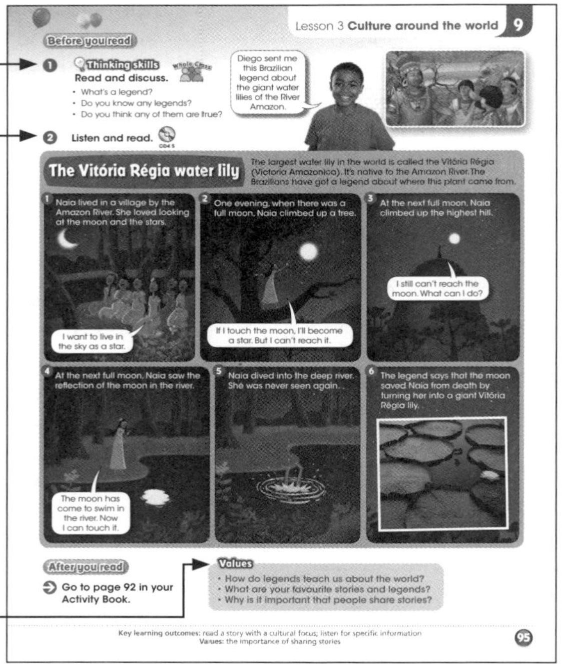


### Ending the lesson

- Review the lesson and reflect on learning.

### Extra activity

**Extension**

- Tell a simple legend from your country.

## Activity Book

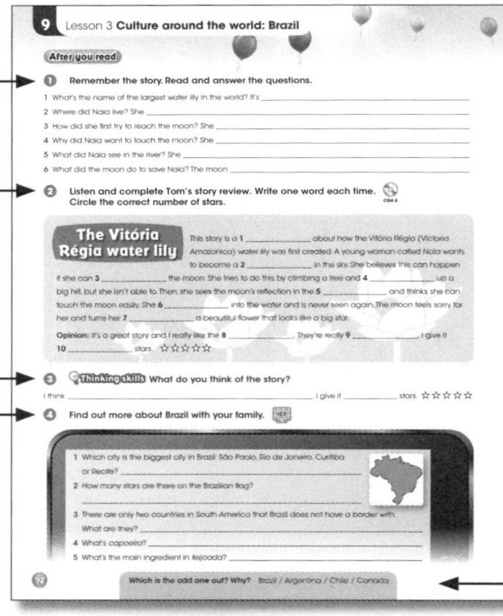


### Activity Book: After you read

**Activity 1**

- Remember the story. Read and answer the questions.

**Activity 2**

- Listen and complete Tom's story review.

▶ *CD4 Track 6 p294*

- Write one word each time. Circle the correct number of stars.

**Activity 3**

- What do you think of the story?

**Activity 4**

- Find out more about Brazil with your family.

**Odd one out activity**

- Which is the odd one out? Why?

### Digital resources

**Teacher's Digital:** You can also teach this lesson using the Teacher's App on Navio.

**Pupil's Digital:** Encourage your pupils to use the Pupil's App on Navio to practise the activities from this lesson.

Powered By NAVIO

**Starting the lesson**

**Use the Trinity Exams Practice cards (optional).**
- The pupils practise asking and answering questions.

**Review flowers and plants.**
- Ask the pupils if they know the words for any flowers in English. They may know *rose, tulip* or *sunflower.* Ask the class if they have grown any plants or if their family have.

**Set learning objectives.**
- Say **Today we're going to read a story from Brazil.**

**Pupil's Book Activity 1: Before you read**

**Read and discuss.**
- Read the first two questions as a class. Encourage the pupils to share any legends they know. Legends are old stories from the past.
- Ask **Do you think any of the legends you know are true?** Encourage the pupils to discuss their ideas between them.

**Pupil's Book Activity 2**

**Listen and read.**
▶ *CD4 Track 5 p294*
- Ask the pupils if they know any plants that float on the river. What do they look like? Explain what a water lily is. It has roots at the bottom of the river, but the leaves and flowers float on top of the water.
- Play the CD. The pupils follow in their books. Ask the pupils if they think this legend is true.
- Ask questions to check understanding.

**Suggested comprehension questions:**
- Frame 1: **Where did Naia live?** (*In a village by the Amazon River*).
- Frame 2: **Why did Naia climb the tree one evening?** (*She wanted to touch the moon.*)
- Frame 3: **What did she climb the next full moon?** (*The highest hill.*)
- Frame 4: **Why did she dive into the river?** (*She saw the moon's reflection in the river. She wanted to* touch *the moon.*)
- Frames 5 and 6: **What happened to her?** (*She was never seen again. The legend says that the moon turned her into a giant water lily.*)

**Activity Book: After you read**

**Activity 1**

**Remember the story. Read and answer the questions.**
- The pupils read and answer the questions.

**Answers:** **1** called Vitória Régia. **2** lived in a village by the Amazon River. **3** climbed up a tree. **4** wanted to be a star. **5** saw the reflection of the moon. **6** turned her into a Vitória Régia lily.

**Activity 2**

**Listen and complete Tom's story review. Write one word each time. Circle the correct number of stars.**
▶ *CD4 Track 6 p294*
- Read out the story review as a class. Ask the pupils to guess the missing words.
- Play the CD without pausing. The pupils listen and complete as much of the information as possible.
- Play the CD again, pausing after each piece of key information to check the information and spelling. The pupils circle the correct number of stars.

**Answers:** **1** legend **2** star **3** touch **4** walking **5** river **6** dives **7** into **8** pictures **9** colourful **10** four

**Activity 3**

**What do you think of the story?**
- The pupils write their opinion and give a rating.

**Activity 4**

**Find out more about Brazil with your family.** ICT
- Read out the questions about Brazil. Ask **Where can you find out this information?** (*Internet, library, asking friends and family.*) The pupils complete the activity at home.
- If you prefer to do this activity in the class, connect to a children's website which has information about Brazil such as: http://kids.nationalgeographic.com/kids/places/find/brazil/, www.sciencekids.co.nz/sciencefacts/countries/brazil.html or www.timeforkids.com/destination.
- Read out the questions. The pupils work as a class to find and write the answers.

**Answers:** **1** São Paolo **2** 27 **3** Ecuador, Chile **4** a Brazilian martial art **5** beans

**Odd one out activity**

**Which is the odd one out? Why?**
- The pupils complete the odd one out activity.

**Answers:** Canada (It isn't in Latin America.)

**Values**

**Read and discuss.**
- Read out each question and discuss it as a class.
- Encourage the pupils to think about how they feel when they read stories and what they learn from stories. Ask the pupils to think about how legends teach people about the world.

**Ending the lesson**

**Review the lesson and reflect on learning.**
- Say **Today we've read a story from Brazil.**
- Ask **Which was your favourite activity today? Which activity was easy / difficult?**

**Extra activity**

**Extension**
- Ask the class to think about some legends from their country.
- Organise the pupils into groups. Ask them to write a simple version of the story.

## Key Competences and Key Learning Outcomes

- Act out a short dialogue in pairs
- Learn and practise using the first conditional
- Identify and practise correct pronunciation of contracted forms in first conditional sentences

## Key language

- *close, late, search on the Internet, water lily*
- *If you search on the Internet, you'll find lots of great photos. If you play a lot of sport, you'll keep fit. If we're late, they won't let us in. If you don't wear a coat, you'll be cold.*

## Materials

- Pupil's Book p96; Activity Book p93; Class CD4; Teacher's App on Navio

## Optional materials

- Teacher's Resource Bank: Trinity Exams Practice cards (selected from the Starter Unit and Units 1, 2, 3, 4, 5, 6, 7 and 8)
- Natural places flashcards

# At a Glance Lesson Plan

## Pupil's Book

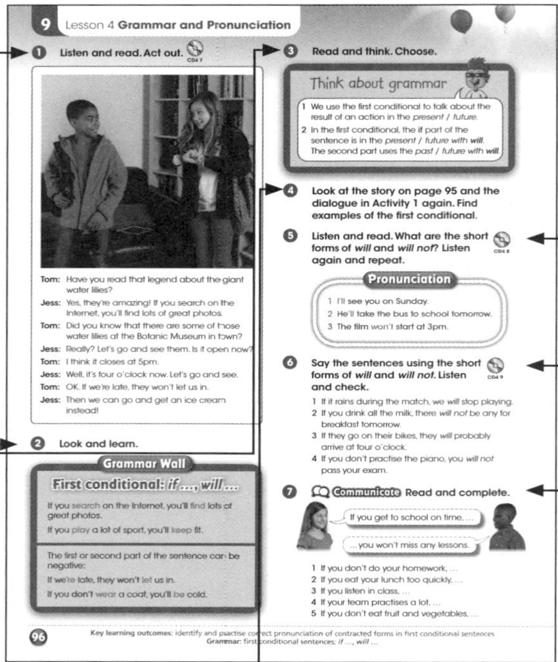

### Starting the lesson

- Use the Trinity Exams Practice cards (optional).
- Review the story in Lesson 3.
- Set learning objectives.

### Activity 1

- Listen and read.
- ▶ ***CD4 Track 7 p295***
- Act out.

### Activity 2

- Look and learn – Grammar wall

### Activity 3

- Read and think.
- Choose.

### Activity 4

- Look at the story on page 95 and the dialogue in Activity 1 again.
- Find examples of the first conditional.

### Activity 5

- Listen and read.
- ▶ ***CD4 Track 8 p295***
- What are the short forms of *will* and *will not?*
- Listen and again and repeat.

### Activity 6

- Say the sentences using the short forms of *will* and *will not.*
- Listen and check.
- ▶ ***CD4 Track 9 p295***

### Activity 7

- Read and complete.
- Go to the Activity Book.

### Ending the lesson

- Review the lesson and reflect on learning.

### Extra activity

**Reinforcement**

- Play a predicting game.

### Digital resources

**Teacher's Digital:** You can also teach this lesson using the Teacher's App on Navio.

**Pupil's Digital:** Encourage your pupils to use the Pupil's App on Navio to practise the activities from this lesson.

Powered By NAVIO

## Activity Book

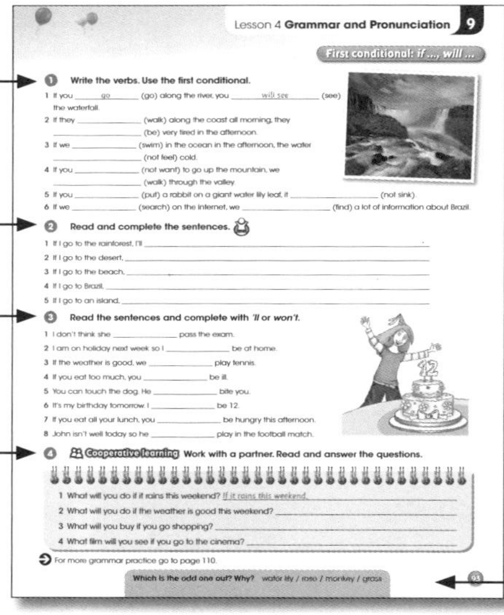

### Activity Book

**Activity 1**

- Write the verbs. Use the first conditional.

**Activity 2**

- Read and complete the sentences.

**Activity 3**

- Read the sentences and complete with *'ll* or *won't.*

**Activity 4**

- Work with a partner. Read and answer the questions.

**Odd one out activity**

- Which is the odd one out? Why?

# Detailed Lesson Plan

**Starting the lesson**

**Use the Trinity Exams Practice cards (optional).**
- The pupils practise asking and answering questions.

**Review the story in Lesson 3.**
- Ask the pupils to remember the story about Naia. Write *touch* on the board. Ask the pupils for as many verbs from the story as they can remember.

**Set learning objectives.**
- Say **Today we're going to learn how to use the first conditional tense.**

**Pupil's Book Activity 1**

**Listen and read. Act out.**

▶ ***CD4 Track 7 p295***
- The pupils look at the photo. Ask **What are Tom and Jess doing? What do you think they are talking about?**
- Play the CD. The pupils listen and read the dialogue. Check understanding. Ask **Has Jess read the legend? Where can they see real water lilies? What time does the museum close?**
- Play the CD again, pausing after each sentence for the pupils to repeat.
- The pupils practise the dialogue in pairs.

**Pupil's Book Activity 2**

**Look and learn – Grammar wall**
- Read the information on the Grammar wall as a class.
- Ask **What verbs can you see? What tense are they? Which part of the sentence is negative?**

**Pupil's Book Activity 3**

**Read and think. Choose.**
- The pupils complete the sentences in pairs.

**Answer:** **1** present **2** present, future

**Pupil's Book Activity 4**

**Look at the story on page 95 and the dialogue in Activity 1 again. Find examples of the first conditional.**
- The pupils find examples of the first conditional in the story and the dialogue.

**Pupil's Book Activity 5**

**Listen and read. What are the short forms of *will* and *will not*? Listen again and repeat.**

▶ ***CD4 Track 8 p295***
- Focus the pupils on the sentences. Play the CD. Ask them what the short forms of 'will' and 'will not' are. Confirm that they are ''ll' and 'won't'.
- Play the CD again. The pupils listen and repeat the sentences.

**Pupil's Book Activity 6**

**Say the sentences using the short forms of *will* and *will not*. Listen and check.**

▶ ***CD4 Track 9 p295***
- Invite the pupils to read the sentences aloud changing the 'will' each time to its contracted form. Ask other pupils to say if they think it was said correctly.
- Ask the pupils to practise in pairs.
- Play the CD. Ask the pupils to listen and repeat.

**Pupil's Book Activity 7**

**Read and complete.**
- In pairs, the pupils complete the sentences.

**Activity Book**

**Activity 1**

**Write the verbs. Use the first conditional.**
- The pupils complete the sentences with the correct form of the verbs.

**Answers:** **1** go, will see **2** walk, will be **3** swim, won't feel **4** don't want, will walk **5** put, won't sink **6** search, will find

**Activity 2**

**Read and complete the sentences.**
- The pupils complete the sentences with their own answers.

**Activity 3**

**Read the sentences and complete with *'ll* or *won't*.**
- The pupils complete the sentences with the correct contracted form.

**Answers:** **1** 'll **2** won't **3** 'll **4** 'll **5** won't **6** 'll **7** won't **8** won't

**Activity 4**

**Work with a partner. Read and answer the questions.**
- The pupils work in pairs to answer the questions.

**Odd one out activity**

**Which is the odd one out? Why?**
- The pupils complete the odd one out activity.

**Answers:** monkey (It isn't a plant.)

**Ending the lesson**

**Review the lesson and reflect on learning.**
- Say **Today we've learnt how to use the first conditional tense.**
- Ask **Which was your favourite activity today? Which activity was easy / difficult?**

**Extra activity**

**Reinforcement**
- Use the natural places flashcards to practise the first conditional. Show the coast flashcard. Say **If you go to the coast, what will you see?** The pupils should answer using *You'll see*. Repeat with another flashcard.

### Key Competences and Key Learning Outcomes

- Identify and say the names of items to take on a trip
- Listen for specific information
- Practise activity types found in the Cambridge Exams: A2 Key for Schools
- Do a communication task

### Key language

- *anorak, dictionary, money, passport, suitcase, ticket, towel, umbrella, wallet; binoculars, guidebook, MP3 player, pencils, sketchpad*
- *If we go on the trip to Legoland, when will we leave?*
- **Extension:** *puzzle book, sun hat, toothbrush, washbag*

### Materials

- Pupil's Book p97; Activity Book p94; Class CD4; Teacher's App on Navio; Teacher's Resource Bank: Unit 9
- Outdoor activities and equipment flashcards; Dictionaries

### Optional materials

- Teacher's Resource Bank: Trinity Exams Practice cards (selected from the Starter Unit and Units 1, 2, 3, 4, 5, 6, 7 and 8)

## At a Glance Lesson Plan

### Pupil's Book

#### Starting the lesson

- Use the Trinity Exams Practice cards (optional).
- Review outdoor activities and equipment.
- Set learning objectives.

#### Activity 1

- Where do you think this person is travelling to?
- Look and match.
- Listen, check and repeat.

▶ *CD4 Track 10 p295*

#### Activity 2

- Listen and say which bags belong to Kate and Jack.

▶ *CD4 Track 11 p295*

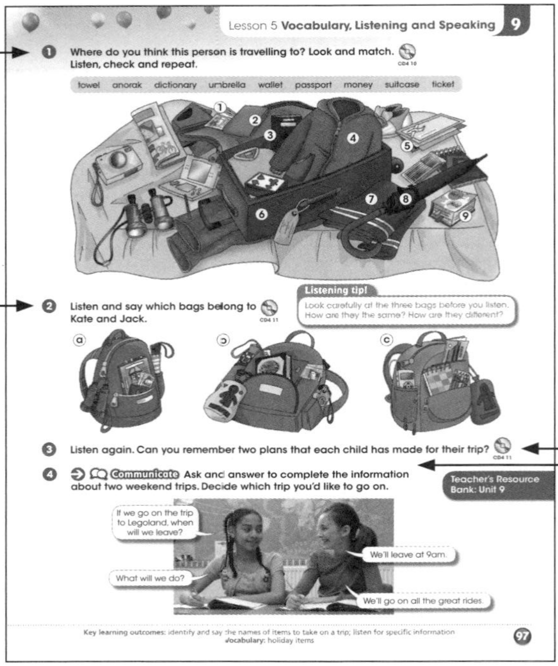


#### Activity 3

- Listen again.

▶ *CD4 Track 11 p295*

- Can you remember two plans that each child has made for their trip?

#### Activity 4

- Ask and answer to complete the information about two weekend trips.
- Decide which trip you'd like to go on (Teacher's Resource Bank: Unit 9).

Go to the Activity Book.

#### Ending the lesson

- Review the lesson and reflect on learning.

#### Extra activities

**Reinforcement**

- Find out more about places you'd like to visit.

**Vocabulary extension**

- Present four additional vocabulary items.

### Activity Book

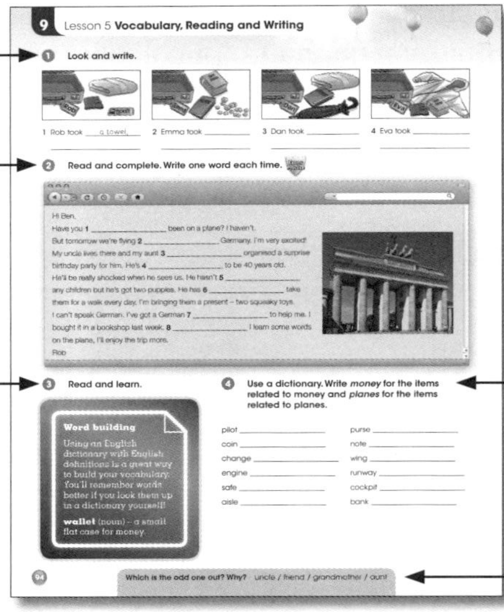


#### Activity Book

**Activity 1**

- Look and write.

**Activity 2**

- Read and complete. Write one word each time.

**Activity 3**

- Read and learn.

**Activity 4**

- Use a dictionary. Write *money* for the items related to money and *planes* for the items related to planes.

**Odd one out activity**

- Which is the odd one out? Why?

### Digital resources

**Teacher's Digital:** You can also teach this lesson using the Teacher's App on Navio.

**Pupil's Digital:** Encourage your pupils to use the Pupil's App on Navio to practise the activities from this lesson.

Powered By NAVIO

# Detailed Lesson Plan

**Starting the lesson**

**Use the Trinity Exams Practice cards (optional).**
- The pupils practise asking and answering questions.

**Review outdoor activities and equipment.**
- Ask the class if they can remember the words for outdoor activities and equipment that they learnt in Unit 2. Ask **What items would you take on a camping trip?**
- Hold the outdoor activities and equipment flashcards and put them on the board one by one as the pupils name them.

**Set learning objectives.**
- Say **Today we're going to learn some objects that people take on holiday with them.**

**Pupil's Book Activity 1**

**Where do you think this person is travelling to? Look and match. Listen, check and repeat.**

▶ ***CD4 Track 10 p295***
- Ask the pupils to describe what they can see in the scene and where this person is travelling to.
- The pupils match the words in the box to the pictures in the scene.
- Play the CD. The pupils listen and check.
- Play the CD again, pausing after each action for the pupils to repeat.

**Pupil's Book Activity 2**

**Listen and say which bags belong to Kate and Jack.**

▶ ***CD4 Track 11 p295***
- Ask the pupils to describe each of the bags and their contents. Ask **Where do you think each person is going to go?**
- Play the CD. The pupils listen and decide which is Kate's bag and which is Jack's bag.

**Answer:** **Kate:** c **Jack:** a

**Pupil's Book Activity 3**

**Listen again. Can you remember two plans that each child has made for their trip?**

▶ ***CD4 Track 11 p295***
- The pupils listen again. They try and remember two plans that each child has made.
- Play the CD.

**Pupil's Book Activity 4**

**Ask and answer to complete the information about two weekend trips. Decide which trip you'd like to go on (Teacher's Resource Bank: Unit 9).**
- Invite two pupils to read out the speech bubbles.
- Organise the class into pairs (A and B). Give Pupils A the first worksheet from Teacher's Resource Bank Unit 9 and give Pupils B the other worksheet.
- Ask a confident pair to demonstrate the activity. They ask and answer questions to complete the information about a trip to either Legoland or the Dorset coast. Then ask the rest of the class to do the same activity in pairs.

**Activity Book**

**Activity 1**

**Look and write.**
- The pupils look at the pictures and complete the sentences.

**Answers:** **1** a towel, a ticket, a wallet **2** money, a passport, a dictionary **3** a passport, a towel, an umbrella **4** an anorak, a wallet, a dictionary

**Activity 2**

**Read and complete. Write one word each time.**
- Focus the pupils on the picture. Ask them to describe what they can see and if they know where the monument is. (*In Berlin, Germany*.)
- The pupils identify the missing words.

**Answers:** **1** ever **2** to **3** has **4** going **5** got **6** to **7** dictionary **8** If

**Activity 3**

**Read and learn.**
- Read the information as a class.

**Activity 4**

**Use a dictionary. Write *planes* for the items related to money and *money* for the items related to planes.**
- Invite a pupil to read out the information. Hand out dictionaries to the pupils.
- Read out the words as a class. The pupils group the words.

**Answers:** **money:** coin, note, change, purse, safe, bank **plane:** pilot, wing, runway, engine, cockpit, aisle

**Odd one out activity**

**Which is the odd one out? Why?**
- The pupils complete the odd one out activity.

**Answers:** friend (He / She isn't a family member.)

**Ending the lesson**

**Review the lesson and reflect on learning.**
- Say **Today we've learnt the names of objects to take on holiday and we've played a communication game.**
- Ask **Which was your favourite activity today? Which activity was easy / difficult?**

**Extra activities**

**Reinforcement**
- Divide the class into pairs. Either in the class or at home, the pupils find out more information about a place they would like to visit.
- Ask the pupils to prepare a very short presentation for the class including at least five interesting facts about the place.

**Vocabulary extension**
- Present four additional outdoor equipment words: *puzzle book, sun hat, toothbrush, washbag.*
- Use the Vocabulary booster on NAVIO to practise these new words.

### Key Competences and Key Learning Outcomes

- Do pre-reading tasks to predict content and raise interest
- Read a website for general understanding
- Scan a travel itinerary for specific information

- Talk about places you would like to visit

- Read and understand a tourist website
- Give an opinion on the text

**Key language**
- *crab, crocodile, shark, squid, starfish; anorak, aquarium, borrow, cinema, goggles, high-speed boat trip, lifejacket, London, online, slow down, scared of heights, screen, tickets, view*
- *It takes (30 minutes) to go round. If you buy your tickets online, you'll pay less. Which place would you most like to visit?*

**Materials**
- Pupil's Book p98; Activity Book p95; Class CD4; Teacher's App on Navio

**Optional materials**
- Teacher's Resource Bank: Trinity Exams Practice cards (selected from the Starter Unit and Units 1, 2, 3, 4, 5, 6, 7 and 8)

## At a Glance Lesson Plan

### Pupil's Book

**Starting the lesson**
- Use the Trinity Exams Practice cards (optional).
- Review capital cities.
- Set learning objectives.

**Activity 1: Before you read**
- Read and discuss.

**Activity 2**
- What are the places in the photos?
- Read and find out.

**Activity 3: After you read**
- What do you think?
- Go to the Activity Book.

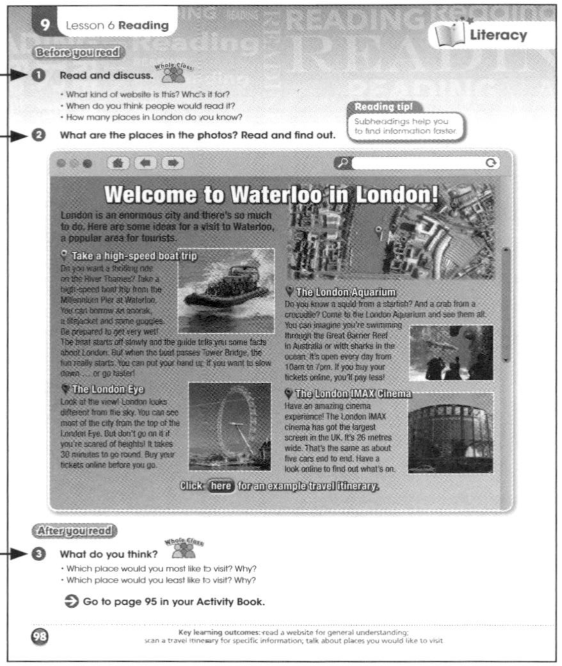


**Ending the lesson**
- Review the lesson and reflect on learning.

**Extra activity**

**Reinforcement**
- Write about four places for a tourist website.

### Activity Book

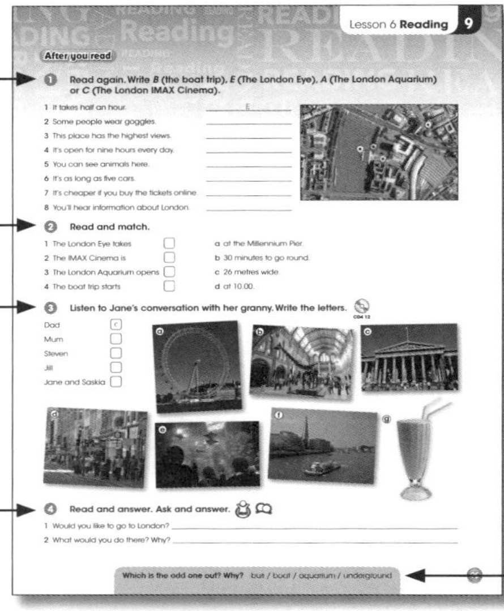


**Activity Book: After you read**

**Activity 1**
- Read again. Write *B* (the boat trip), *E* (The London Eye), *A* (The London Aquarium) or *C* (the London IMAX Cinema).

**Activity 2**
- Read and match.

**Activity 3**
- Listen to Jane's conversation with her granny.

▶ ***CD4 Track 12 p295***
- Write the letters.

**Activity 4**
- Read and answer. Ask and answer.

**Odd one out activity**
- Which is the odd one out? Why?

### Digital resources

**Teacher's Digital:** You can also teach this lesson using the Teacher's App on Navio.

**Pupil's Digital:** Encourage your pupils to use the Pupil's App on Navio to practise the activities from this lesson.

Powered By NAVIO

# Detailed Lesson Plan

**Starting the lesson**

**Use the Trinity Exams Practice cards (optional).**
- The pupils practise asking and answering questions.

**Review capital cities.**
- In preparation for the lesson, talk about cities. Ask **How many capital cities do you know?**
- Ask the pupils if they like living (or would like to live) in a big city. Ask **Would you like to visit a big city like London? What would you do there?**

**Set learning objectives.**
- Say **Today we're going to read about London in a text from a website.**

**Pupil's Book Activity 1: Before you read**

**Read and discuss.**
- Read the questions as a class. Prompt the pupils to answer in as much detail as possible. Ask if the pupils have looked at similar websites and why.

**Pupil's Book Activity 2**

**What are the places in the photos? Read and find out.**
- Ask the pupils to look at the photos without reading the text. Ask **What sort of places are they? Which place looks the most interesting and why?**
- Give the pupils one minute to skim the text to discover any more information about each place.
- (Books closed.) Ask the pupils to give you the information.
- (Books open.) Read the text as a class. Check understanding after each paragraph.

**Pupil's Book Activity 3: After you read**

**What do you think?**
- Read the questions as a class. Prompt the pupils to answer the questions for themselves in pairs.
- If you wish to do so, have a quick class vote to see which places are the most and least popular. Continue to ask the pupils to give reasons for their answers.

**Activity Book: After you read**

**Activity 1**

**Read again. Write *B* (the boat trip), *E* (The London Eye), *A* (The London Aquarium) or *C* (The London IMAX Cinema).**
- The pupils read each sentence and write the correct letter. The pupils refer back to the text in the Pupil's Book when necessary.

**Answers:** **1** E **2** B **3** E **4** A **5** A **6** C **7** A **8** B

**Activity 2**

**Read and match.**
- The pupils match the sentence halves.

**Answers:** **1** b **2** c **3** d **4** a

**Activity 3**

**Listen to Jane's conversation with her granny. Write the letters.**

▶ ***CD4 Track 12 p295***
- Read the names and look at the pictures as a class. Make it clear that there are some pictures that will not be matched with a person.
- Play the CD. The pupils listen and match.
- Play the CD again, pausing after each piece of key information if you wish.

**Answers:** **Jane and Saskia:** e **Steven:** g **Jill:** d **Mum:** a **Dad:** c

**Activity 4**

**Read and answer. Ask and answer.**
- The pupils answer the questions in pairs.

**Odd one out activity**

**Which is the odd one out? Why?**
- The pupils complete the odd one out activity.

**Answers:** aquarium (It isn't a form of transport.)

**Ending the lesson**

**Review the lesson and reflect on learning.**
- Say **Today we've read about London on a tourist website.**
- Ask **Which was your favourite activity today? Which activity was easy / difficult?**

**Extra activity**

**Reinforcement**
- Ask the pupils, in pairs, to think of a town or city that they know. The pupils think of four places that they would put on a tourist website for the place. They write one or two sentences about each place.

## Key Competences and Key Learning Outcomes

- Identify prepositions of time
- Learn the language and structure of a travel itinerary
- Identify the features of a travel itinerary
- Use criteria to check your writing
- Share your writing with another pupil
- Write a travel itinerary

**Key language**

- *arrive, have a picnic, milkshake, on the left, past, plenty of, take the Tube, through, towards, tour; at 9:00, for two hours, in the morning, on Saturday*
- *Arrive at Waterloo Station. Walk through Jubilee Gardens towards the River Thames. Go past the London Eye. He played tennis for two hours.*

**Materials**

- Pupil's Book p99; Activity Book p96; Teacher's App on Navio

**Optional materials**

- Teacher's Resource Bank: Trinity Exams Practice cards (selected from the Starter Unit and Units 1, 2, 3, 4, 5, 6, 7 and 8)

## At a Glance Lesson Plan

### Pupil's Book

**Starting the lesson**

- Use the Trinity Exams Practice cards (optional).
- Review places in London.
- Set learning objectives.

**Activity 1: Investigate a text**

- An itinerary tells us when and where we're going to do something.
- Which of these things do you think are important for an itinerary?

**Activity 2**

- Read the travel itinerary.
- What activities are planned before and after lunch?

**Activity 3: Discuss a text**

- Read the travel itinerary again.
- Answer the questions.

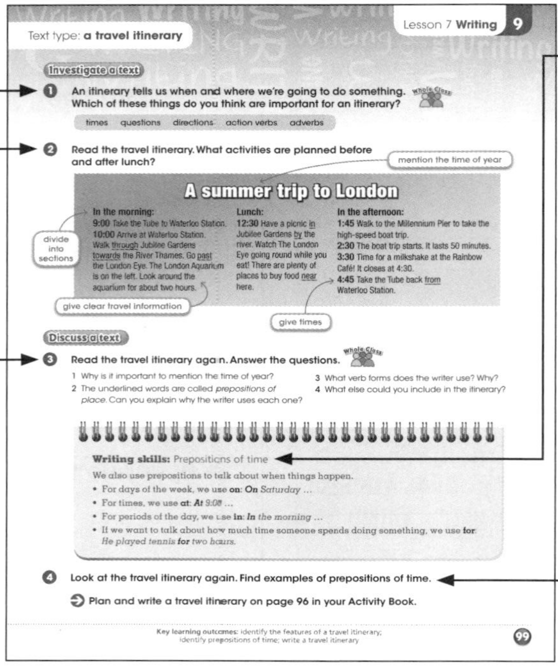

**Writing skills**

- Read about using prepositions of time.

**Activity 4**

- Look at the travel itinerary again.
- Find examples of prepositions of time.

Go to the Activity Book.

**Ending the lesson**

- Review the lesson and reflect on learning.

**Extra activity**

**Reinforcement**

- Write about your trip.

### Digital resources

**Teacher's Digital:** You can also teach this lesson using the Teacher's App on Navio.

**Pupil's Digital:** Encourage your pupils to use the Pupil's App on Navio to practise the activities from this lesson.

Powered By NAVIO

### Activity Book

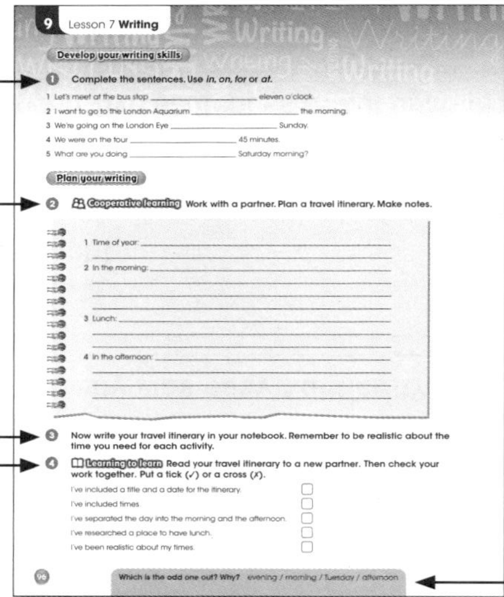

**Activity Book**

**Activity 1: Develop your writing skills**

- Complete the sentences. Use *in*, *on*, *for* or *at*.

**Activity 2: Plan your writing**

- Work with a partner. Plan your travel itinerary. Make notes.

**Activity 3**

- Now write your travel itinerary in your notebook. Remember to be realistic about the time you need for each activity.

**Activity 4**

- Read your travel itinerary to a new partner. Then check your work together. Put a tick (✓) or a cross (✗).

**Odd one out activity**

- Which is the odd one out? Why?

**Starting the lesson**

**Use the Trinity Exams Practice cards (optional).**
- The pupils practise asking and answering questions.

**Review places in London.**
- Ask the pupils to remember the tourist website about London in Lesson 6. Ask **Can you remember the four activities that the website suggested?** (*High-speed boat trip, London Eye, London Aquarium, London IMAX Cinema*.)

**Set learning objectives.**
- Say **Today we're going to write a travel itinerary.**

**Pupil's Book Activity 1: Investigate a text**

**An itinerary tells us when and where we're going to do something. Which of these things do you think are important for an itinerary?**
- The pupils look at the words in the box. Explain that an example of an itinerary is on the page. It shows someone when and where they are going to do things. We use them for planning trips, holidays or events.
- The pupils decide what is required for an itinerary.

**Answer:** times, directions, action verbs

**Pupil's Book Activity 2**

**Read the travel itinerary. What activities are planned before and after lunch?**
- Read the text as a class.
- Check understanding and answer the question. Ask **Does it look like a busy day or a relaxing day?**

**Pupil's Book Activity 3: Discuss a text**

**Read the travel itinerary again. Answer the questions.**
- Read and discuss the questions as a class.
- Ask the pupils to do the questions in pairs. Then discuss them as a class. Check understanding of the prepositions of place with the class.
- For question 3 highlight the use of imperative verbs. Explain that these are the same as the infinitive form of the verb.
- Then ask the final question. An itinerary could include prices. It could also include options for people to do different things at some times of the day.

**Writing skills**
- Read about using prepositions of time.

**Pupil's Book Activity 4**

**Look at the travel itinerary again. Find examples of prepositions of time.**
- The pupils find more examples of prepositions of time in the text.

**Activity Book**

**Activity 1: Develop your writing skills**

**Complete the sentences. Use *in*, *on*, *for* or *at*.**
- The pupils complete the sentences with the correct preposition of time.

**Answer:** **1** at **2** in **3** on **4** for **5** on

**Activity 2: Plan your writing**

**Work with a partner. Plan your travel itinerary. Make notes.**
- Read out the notes. Then elicit examples of how pupils can complete each section.
- Organise the class into Writing Partners. The pupils decide where to go in the morning and afternoon.

**Activity 3**

**Now write your travel itinerary in your notebook. Remember to be realistic about the time you need for each activity.**
- The pupils now write out their itinerary with a Writing Partner. They can refer to the Pupil's Book to help them organise it. Suggest they divide it into three sections: *In the morning*, *Lunch* and *In the afternoon*.

**Activity 4**

**Read your travel itinerary to a new partner. Then check your work together. Put a tick (✓) or a cross (✗).**
- Read through the statements as a class.
- Organise the class into new Writing Partners. One pupil reads aloud their text to their partner. The other pupil listens. The pupils work together to decide if the text fulfils the criteria and tick the corresponding boxes. The pupils can add, improve or correct the text at this stage.
- The pupils swap roles.

**Odd one out activity**

**Which is the odd one out? Why?**
- The pupils complete the odd one out activity.

**Answers:** Tuesday (It isn't a time of day.)

**Ending the lesson**

**Review the lesson and reflect on learning.**
- Say **Today we've written a travel itinerary.**
- Ask **Which was your favourite activity today? Which activity was easy / difficult?**

**Extra activity**

**Reinforcement**
- The pupils imagine they have been on their trip. They write a short chronological account of the trip. Remind them to use time connectives and write some of these on the board: *first, then, eventually, after that, finally*.

### Key Competences and Key Learning Outcomes

- Listen to and have a conversation about planning a trip
- Present your trip to the class

- Listen to a conversation for general understanding
- Listen to a conversation and identify key functional language
- Review learning and reflect on progress in the unit

- Sing a song

**Key language**
- *bridge, bus, bus stop, picnic, picnic place, river, sunny, waterfall*
- *What time shall we start?, Why don't we take the bus together at half past nine?, Good idea! That's a great idea. Perfect! Yes, brilliant!*

**Materials**
- Pupil's Book p100; Activity Book p97; Class CD4; Teacher's App on Navio
- Leaflets and maps of your local area

**Optional materials**
- Teacher's Resource Bank: Trinity Exams Practice cards (selected from the Starter Unit and Units 1, 2, 3, 4, 5, 6, 7 and 8)

## At a Glance Lesson Plan

### Pupil's Book

**Starting the lesson**
- Use the Trinity Exams Practice cards (optional).
- Review natural places.
- Set learning objectives.

**Activity 1**
- What can you see in the pictures?
- What do you think you are going to hear about?

**Activity 2**
- Listen to the conversation.
- ▶ ***CD4 Track 13 p295***
- Put the pictures in order.

**Activity 3**
- Listen again.
- ▶ ***CD4 Track 13 p295***
- Complete four questions that Alice asks.

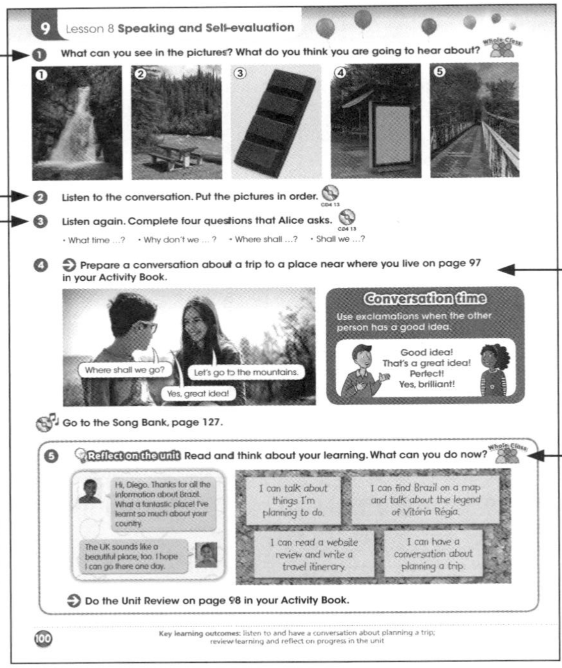


**Activity 4**
- Prepare a conversation about a trip to a place near where you live on page 97 in your Activity book.
- Go to page 97 in the Activity Book.

**Song**
- ▶ ***CD4 Track 28 p298***
- ▶ ***CD4 Track 29 p298 (optional karaoke version)***

**Activity 5**
- Read and think about your learning. What can you do now?
- Go to page 98 in the Activity Book.

**Ending the lesson**
- Review the lesson and reflect on learning.

**Extra activity**
- Describe your trip using past tenses.

### Activity Book

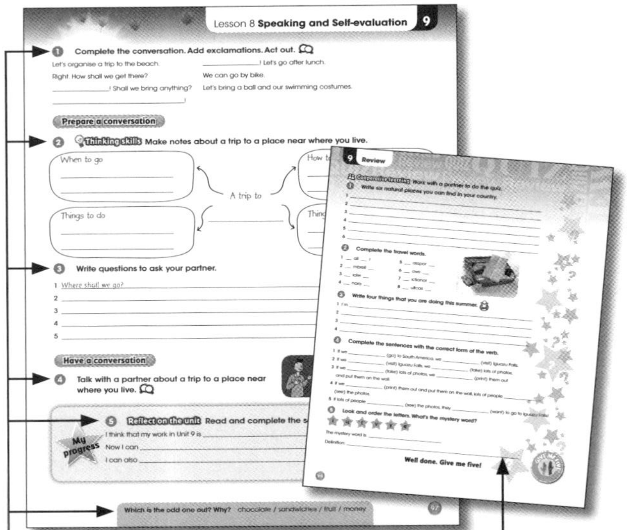


**Activity Book page 98: Review**
- Work with a partner to do the quiz.

**Activity Book**

**Activity 1**
- Complete the conversation.
- Add exclamations.
- Act out.

**Activity 2**
- Make notes about a trip to a place near where you live.

**Activity 3**
- Write questions to ask your partner.

**Activity 4**
- Talk with a partner about a trip to a place near where you live.

**Activity 5**
- Read and complete the sentences.

**Odd one out activity**
- Which is the odd one out? Why?

### Digital resources

**Teacher's Digital:** You can also teach this lesson using the Teacher's App on Navio.

Powered By NAVIO

# Detailed Lesson Plan

## Starting the lesson

**Use the Trinity Exams Practice cards (optional).**

- The pupils practise asking and answering questions.

**Review natural places.**

- Do a quiz to practise the natural places vocabulary. Ask questions like **What's the biggest ocean in the world?** (*the Pacific*) **In which continent is the Amazon Rainforest?** (*South America*) **What's the name of the big waterfall on the border of Canada and the USA?** (*Niagara Falls*)

**Set learning objectives and use the talk cards.**

- Say **Today we're going to prepare a conversation about our favourite item of clothing.**

## Pupil's Book Activity 1

**What can you see in the pictures? What do you think you are going to hear about?**

- Ask different pupils to describe the pictures. Ask them to think of a story that involves the pictures.

**Answers:** **1** a waterfall **2** a picnic place next to a river **3** some chocolate **4** a bus stop **5** a bridge

## Pupil's Book Activity 2

**Listen to the conversation. Put the pictures in order.**

▶ ***CD4 Track 13 p295***

- Play the CD. Ask pupils if what they heard is similar to their story in Activity 1.

**Answer:** 5, 4, 1, 3, 2

## Pupil's Book Activity 3

**Listen again. Complete four questions that Anna asks.**

▶ ***CD4 Track 13 p295***

- Direct pupils to the four question prompts. Ask if they can remember the questions.
- Play the CD. Pupils check in pairs. Then play again and check as a class.

**Answers:** What time shall we start?; Why don't we take the bus together at half past nine?; Where shall we go first?; Shall we have lunch there?

## Pupil's Book Activity 4

**Prepare a conversation about a trip to a place near where you live on page 97 in your Activity Book.**

- Read the speech bubbles with the pupils. Model the phrases in the Conversation Time box and get the class to repeat.

## Song

- Go to the Song Bank on page 127 to do the song activities (see p245).

***CD4 Track 28 p298***

***CD4 Track 29 p298 (optional karaoke version)***

## Pupil's Book Activity 5

**Read and think about your learning. What can you do now?**

- Read the speech bubbles and notes with the pupils. Then look back through the unit and prompt them to identify things that they have done/learnt.

## Activity Book page 98: Review

**Work with a partner to do the quiz.**

- Organise the class into pairs. Set a time limit for the pupils to do the quiz (10–15 minutes). Stress that the pupils are not competing with each other.
- Read out the five tasks that the pupils have to complete. Check understanding. Then say **Ready, steady ... Go!**
- The pupils work in their pairs to do the quiz.
- Correct the answers as a class.

**Answers:** **2** **1** wallet **2** umbrella **3** ticket **4** anorak **5** passport **6** towel **7** dictionary **8** suitcase **4** **1** go, will visit **2** visit, will take **3** take, will print **4** print, will see **5** see, will want **5** valley, a low land point usually between two mountains

## Activity Book

**Activity 1**

**Complete the conversation. Add exclamations. Act out.**

- Pupils add the exclamations. Then they perform the dialogue in pairs.

**Activity 2**

**Make notes about a trip to a place near where you live.**

- Tell pupils about a place near where you live. Ask pupils for more ideas of places in the countryside near where they live. Then pupils complete the boxes with their own information. Make sure pupils have a different place from their partner.

**Activity 3**

**Write questions to ask your partner.**

- Direct pupils to the five headings in Activity 2 and explain that they need to form questions about them. Then pupils complete the questions. Check as a class.

**Answers:** **1** Where shall we go? When shall we go? What shall we do there? How can we get there? What shall we bring?

**Activity 4**

**Talk with a partner about a trip to a place near where you live.**

- In pairs, pupils ask and answer the questions from Activity 3.
- Invite one or two pairs to perform their conversations for the class.

**Activity 5**

**Read and complete the sentences.**

- Pupils work alone to review their work in the unit.

**Odd one out activity**

**Which is the odd one out? Why?**

**Answer:** money (It isn't food.)

## Ending the lesson

**Review the lesson and reflect on learning.**

- Say **Today we've learnt how to have a conversation about a trip to a place near where we live.**

# Video and 21st Century Skills

## Key Competences and Key Learning Outcomes

- Watch and understand a video about different places where people live
- Show curiosity about the lives of people who live in different places
- Learn about daily life in Alaska, and its weather, animal life and geographical features

## Key language

- *climate, glacier, fishing, moose, otter, snow storm, state*
- *What is your home like? How do you get to school?*

## Materials

- Pupil's Book p101; Activity Book p99; Class CD4; Teacher's App on Navio
- Teacher's Resource Bank: Talk cards

## Optional materials

- Teacher's Resource Bank: Trinity Exams Practice cards (selected from the Starter Unit and Units 1–8)

## At a Glance Lesson Plan

### Pupil's Book

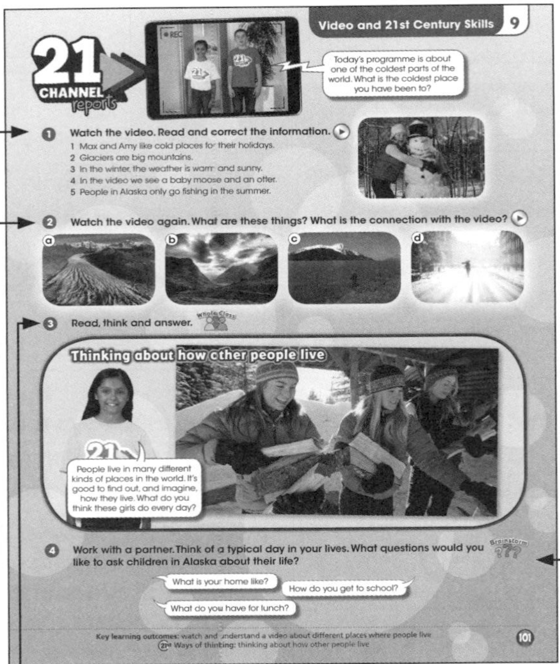


**Starting the lesson**

- Use the Trinity Exams Practice cards (optional).
- **Think-Pair-Share** Review natural places vocabulary.
- Set learning objectives and use the talk cards.

**Activity 1**

- Before you watch
- Watch the video.
  *Unit 9 video*
- Read and correct the information.

**Activity 2**

- Watch the video again.
  *Unit 9 video p304*
- What are these things?
- What is the connection with the video?

**Activity 3**

- Read, think and answer.

**Activity 4**

- Work with a partner.
- Think of a typical day in your lives.
- What questions would you like to ask children in Alaska about their lives?

Go to the Activity Book.

**Ending the lesson**

- Review the lesson and reflect on learning.

**Extra activity**

- A guessing game about life in different countries.

### Digital resources

**Teacher's Digital:** You can also teach this lesson using the Teacher's App on Navio.

**Pupil's Digital:** Encourage your pupils to use the Pupil's App on Navio to practise the activities from this lesson.

Powered By NAVIO

### Activity Book

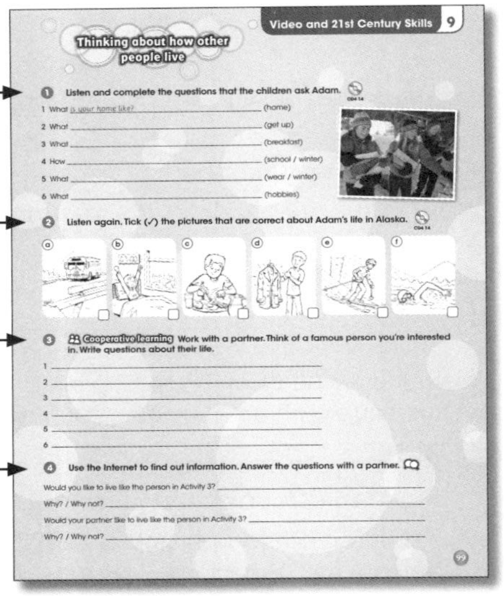


**Activity Book**

**Activity 1**

- Listen and complete the questions that the children ask Adam.

▶ *CD4 Track 14 p296*

**Activity 2**

- Listen again.
- Tick (✓) the pictures that are correct about Adam's life in Alaska.

▶ *CD4 Track 14 p296*

**Activity 3**

- Work with a partner.
- Think of a famous person you're interested in.
- Write questions about their life.

**Activity 4**

- Use the Internet to find out information.
- Answer the questions with a partner.

# Detailed Lesson Plan

## Starting the lesson

**Use the Trinity Exams Practice cards (optional).**

- The pupils practise asking and answering questions.

**Think-Pair-Share Review natural places vocabulary.**

- Ask **Can you remember the natural places vocabulary?** The class thinks silently for a minute.
- Then the pupils work with a Talk Partner to name the natural places.
- Invite different Talk Partners to say a different natural place. Hold up the corresponding flashcard and prompt the class to repeat the word.
- Finally, repeat the procedure, asking different pairs of Talk Partners each time, until all the natural places have been named.

**Set learning objectives and use the talk cards.**

- Say **Today we're going to watch a video and then ask and answer questions about life in Alaska**.
- Point to the talk cards to show the pupils the different ways they will be working in the lesson.

## Pupil's Book Activity 1

**Before you watch**

- Read the speech bubble to pupils. Ask **What is the coldest place you have been to?** Elicit responses from a number of pupils.

**Watch the video. Read and correct the information.**

*p304*

- Watch Part 1 of the video. Ask pupils **What are you going to see next?**
- Play Part 2 of the video. Pupils look at the first sentence in Activity 1. Ask **Is it correct?** Pupils correct the sentence if they can.
- Play the video again. Pupils correct the information. Check answers as a group.

**Answers:** **1** Amy likes hot places for her holidays. **2** Glaciers are big rivers of ice. **3** In the winter, it can be cold and foggy. **4** We see a moose and a baby otter. **5** People go fishing in the winter, too.

## Pupil's Book Activity 2

**Watch the video again. What are these things? What is the connection with the video?**

- Ask a pupil **What can you see in picture a?** Ask a different pupil **What is the connection with the video?**
- Play the video. Check the answers as a class.

**Answers:** **a** A glacier. There are many glaciers in Alaska. **b** A mountain. There are many mountains in Alaska. **c** A man fishing. Fishing is a popular activity in Alaska. **d** A snow storm. Snow storms happen in Alaska.

## Pupil's Book Activity 3

**Read, think and answer.**

- Read the speech bubble and ask pupils to look at the photo. Ask **What are the girls doing?** Teach the words *chop*, *logs*, and *firewood*. Ask **Why are they doing this? Do they do it every day?** Pupils offer ideas.

## Pupil's Book Activity 4

**Work with a partner. Think of a typical day in your lives. What questions would you like to ask the children in Alaska about their life?**

- Ask a pupil **Name something you do every day. When do you do it?** Repeat with different pupils.
- Pupils work in pairs to think of questions.

## Activity Book

**Activity 1**

**Listen and complete the questions that the children ask Adam.**

▶ *CD4 Track 14 p296*

- Pupils try to form the questions before they listen.

**Answers:** **1** What is your home like? **2** What time do you get up? **3** What do you have for breakfast? **4** How do you get to school in the winter? **5** What do you wear in the winter? **6** What hobbies have you got?

**Activity 2**

**Listen again. Tick (✓) the pictures that are correct about Adam's life in Alaska.**

▶ *CD4 Track 14 p296*

- Ask a pupil **What can you see in picture a?** Repeat with different pupils for the other photos. Ask **Are all the pictures correct about Adam's life?**

**Answers:** **a** correct **b** correct **c** incorrect (Adam usually has cereal and yoghurt for breakfast.) **d** incorrect (The most important clothes in winter are your shoes.) **e** correct **f** incorrect (Adam's other hobby is hiking.)

**Activity 3**

**Work with a partner. Think of a famous person you're interested in. Write questions about their life.**

- In pairs, pupils choose a famous person who they are both interested in.
- They write some questions that are connected to the famous person's profession or information they already know about them.

**Activity 4**

**Use the Internet to find out information. Answer the questions with a partner.**

- Pupils research the answers to their questions in Activity 3.
- Ask a pupil **Which famous person did you research? Would you like to live like him/her? Why? / Why not?** Ask pupils to discuss in pairs if they would like to live like the famous people that they researched. Finally, they complete the sentences about their own and their partners' opinions.

## Ending the lesson

**Review the lesson and reflect on learning.**

- Say **Today we've watched a video about Alaska. What have we learnt about how other people live?** Elicit ideas from the pupils.
- Ask **Which was your favourite activity today? Which activity was easy / difficult?**

# Project 3: An eco tourist attraction



### Key Competences and Key Learning Outcomes

- Share information about places and landscapes around the world
- Investigate different eco tourist attractions
- Listen for specific information and take notes
- Share the information with your group
- Learn about a famous tourist attraction in the UK

**Key language**

- *beach, cliff, hill, lake, marsh, mountain, plain, river, sand dune, stream, valley, waterfall; arctic, alpine, desert, rainforest; biologist; climate, landscape, landforms*
- *What's the (landscape) like in a tropical rainforest? Which natural environment shall we choose for our tourist attraction?*

**Materials**

- Pupil's Book pp102; Activity Book p100; Class CD4; Teacher's App on Navio

## At a Glance Lesson Plan

### Starting the lesson

- Set learning objectives.

### Activity 1: Share knowledge

- Read and discuss the questions for each landscape.

### Activity 2: Investigate

- Listen and complete the notes about the Eden Project on page 100 in your Activity Book.

▶ *CD4 Track 15 p296*

Go to the Activity Book.

### Activity 3: Investigate

- In pairs or groups, investigate a natural environment for your attraction. Make notes on page 100 in your Activity Book.

Go to the Activity Book.

## Pupil's Book

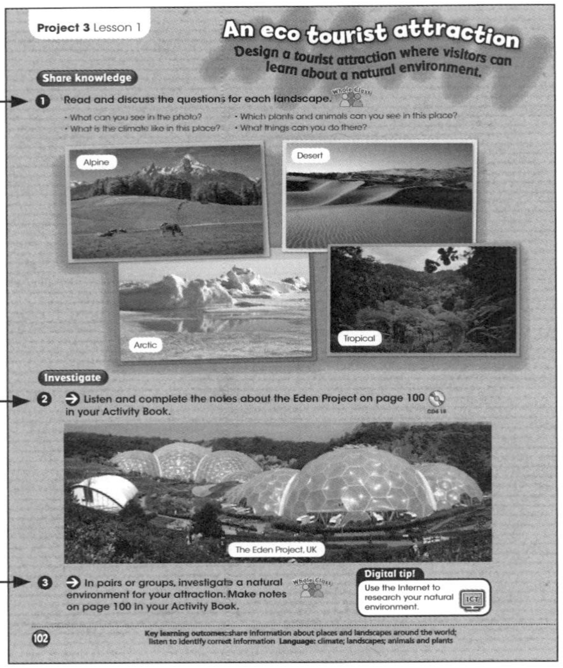


### Ending the lesson

- Review the lesson and reflect on learning.

**Extension activity**

- Do further research on the Eden project.

### Link to Science

- **Landscapes:** Review the three types of landscapes and landforms.

## Activity Book

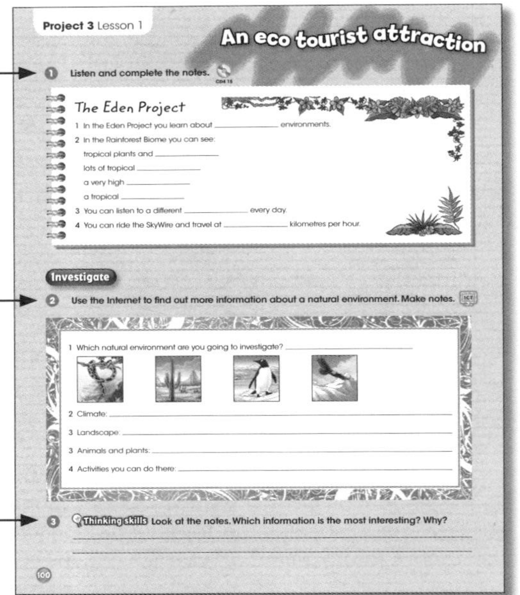


### Activity Book

**Activity 1**

- Listen and complete the notes.

▶ *CD4 Track 15 p296*

**Activity 2**

- Use the Internet to find out more information about a natural environment. Make notes.

**Activity 3**

- Look at the notes. Which information is the most interesting? Why?

### Digital resources

**Teacher's Digital:** You can also teach this lesson using the Teacher's App on Navio.

**Pupil's Digital:** Encourage your pupils to use the Pupil's App on Navio to practise the activities from this lesson.

Powered By NAVIO

# Detailed Lesson Plan

**Starting the lesson**

**Set learning objectives.**

- Say **Today we're going to begin another project.**
- Focus the group's attention on the Task box at the top of the page. Read the text as a class.

**Pupil's Book Activity 1: Share knowledge**

**Read and discuss the questions for each landscape.**

- Work as a class to read and discuss the questions.

**Pupil's Book Activity 2: Find out more information**

**Listen and complete the notes about the Eden Project on page 100 in your Activity Book.**

▶ *CD4 Track 15 p296*

- Read the instructions. Ask the pupils to open their Activity Books (page 100).

**Activity Book**

**Activity 1**

**Listen and complete the notes.**

▶ *CD4 Track 15 p296*

- Read the questions as a class and predict the answers.
- Play the CD. The pupils listen and follow the information in their books.
- Play the CD again, pausing after each piece of key information. The pupils say and write the answer each time.

**Answers:** **1** natural **2** trees; butterflies; waterfall; village **3** story **4** 80

**Pupil's Book Activity 3: Investigate**

**In pairs or groups, investigate a natural environment for your attraction. Make notes on page 100 in your Activity Book.**

- Organise the class into pairs or small groups. Invite a pupil to read the Digital tip.
- The pupils work in their groups to complete their section of notes in their Activity Books (page 100).

**Activity Book**

**Activity 2**

**Use the Internet to find out more information about a natural environment. Make notes.** ICT

- Ask the pupils to identify the four environments in the pictures and choose one. Make sure every environment has been chosen by eat least one pair or group.
- Pupils use computers or other available devices to research the information online.
- Suggested websites include:
  www.blueplanetbiomes.org/desert.htm
  www.blueplanetbiomes.org/alpine.htm
  www.blueplanetbiomes.org/rainforest.htm
  www.blueplanetbiomes.org/tundra.htm

**Activity 3**

**Look at the notes. Which information is the most interesting? Why?**

- Put each pair or group with another pair or group. The pupils compare their answers. They then decide which information is the most interesting.

**Ending the lesson**

**Review the lesson and reflect on learning.**

- Say **We've learnt about natural environments around the world.**
- Ask **Which was your favourite activity today? Which activity was easy / difficult?**

**Extension activity**

- Organise the class into groups of three. Ask them to use the Internet to investigate the Eden Project. The website is www.edenproject.com.

**Link to Science**

- If you are studying the Science topic of landscapes, you could take the opportunity to review the three principle types of landscapes (flat, mountain and coastal) and their common features. Write the three types at the top of the board and list the landforms you often see there.

# Project 3: An eco tourist attraction



### Key Competences and Key Learning Outcomes

- Present your poster to the rest of the class
- Investigate different eco tourist attractions
- Reflect on what you've learnt and how you've worked together
- Work in groups to plan an eco tourist attraction
- Design and draw a poster to advertise the eco tourist attraction

### Key language

- *activities, alpine, animals, cactuses, cave, hill, iceberg, ice skate, landforms, leaflet, penguin, plants, seal, snow*
- *Why don't we create (an alpine) environment? What about having (a river) in the attraction? We could grow (cactuses) there. Visitors could (ice skate) in the attraction. We need to have (toilets) for visitors.*

### Materials

- Pupil's Book pp103; Activity Book p101; Teacher's App on Navio
- Materials for poster (card, pencils, coloured pens, scissors, glue, etc.)

## At a Glance Lesson Plan

### Starting the lesson

- Set learning objectives.

### Activity 1: Plan and create your project

- In your pairs or groups, discuss the questions.
- Write the information on page 101 in your Activity Book.

Go to the Activity Book.

### Activity 2

- Design and draw a poster for your attraction.

### Activity 3: Present your project

- Present your poster to the class.
- Take turns to answer any questions.

## Pupil's Book

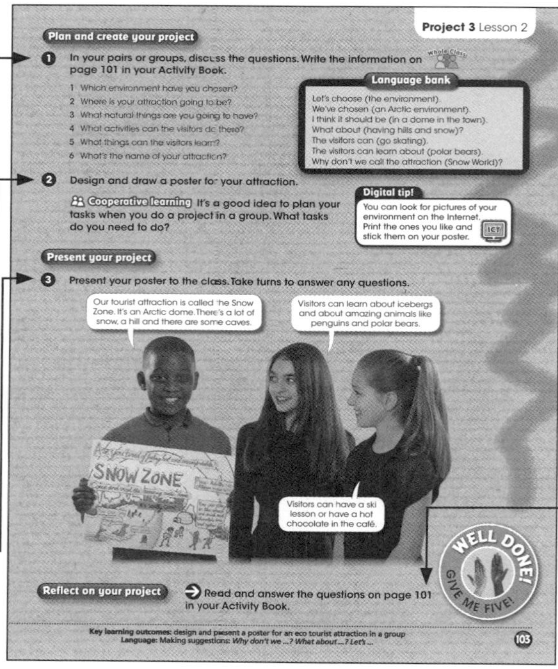


### Reflect on your project

- Read and answer the questions on page 101 in your Activity Book.

Go to the Activity Book.

### Ending the lesson

- Review the lesson and reflect on learning.

**Reinforcement activity**

- Display your work.

## Activity Book

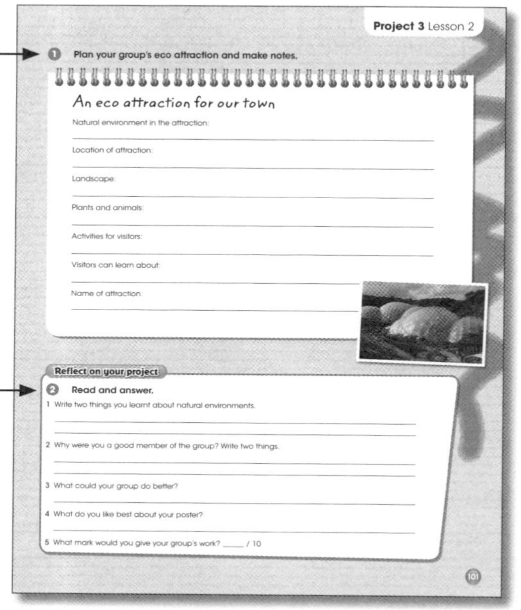


### Activity Book

**Activity 1**

- Plan your group's eco attraction and make notes.

**Activity 2: Reflect on your project**

- Read and answer.

### Digital resources

**Teacher's Digital:** You can also teach this lesson using the Teacher's App on Navio.

**Pupil's Digital:** Encourage your pupils to use the Pupil's App on Navio to practise the activities from this lesson.

Powered By NAVIO

# Detailed Lesson Plan

**Starting the lesson**

**Set learning objectives.**

- Say **Today we're going to continue the project.** Ask the pupils to tell you what they did in the last lesson.

**Pupil's Book Activity 1: Plan and create your project**

**In pairs or groups, discuss the questions. Write the information on page 101 in your Activity Book.**

- Focus the class on the activity. Invite a pupil to read out the questions. Check understanding and elicit possible answers each time. Use the structures in the Language bank to do this.
- The groups discuss the questions and record their decisions in their Activity Books. If they need more support, ask the groups to discuss one question at a time. First, ask the groups to write the natural environment in their Activity Books and choose their landforms. When all the groups have done this, move to the next question.
- Repeat the procedure with the remaining questions.

**Activity Book**

**Activity 1**

**Plan your group's eco attraction and make notes.**

- The pupils write the answers to the questions in the Pupil's Book Activity 1.

**Pupil's Book Activity 2**

**Design and draw a poster for your attraction.**

- The pupils draw a poster advertising their attraction. Explain to the class that each person in the group has got a job to do. The groups decide which task each member is going to do. Read the Cooperative learning tip and the Digital tip.
- Hand out a large piece of card or paper to each group. Ask them to take out their coloured pens and pencils. The pupils work as a group to design and draw their poster and a leaflet.

**Pupil's Book Activity 3: Present your project**

**Present your poster to the class. Take turns to answer any questions.**

- The pupils look at the photo and talk about what they can see. Ask **What is this group's natural environment?** Then ask three pupils to read out the speech bubbles.
- Invite different groups in turn to present their poster to the rest of the class. Ensure that each pupil in the group participates in the presentation. At the end of each presentation, ask the group a question and encourage the rest of the class to think of questions they'd like to ask. The group giving the presentation answers the questions.
- If you wish, have a class vote on the best tourist attraction.

**Reflect on your project**

**Read and answer the questions on page 101 in your Activity Book.**

- The pupils open their Activity Books and work in their groups to think about how they've worked, what they've learnt and what they've produced.
- Ask some groups to share their ideas with the class.

**Activity Book**

**Activity 2: Reflect on your project**

**Read and answer.**

- The pupils write the answers to the questions.

**Ending the lesson**

**Review the lesson and reflect on learning.**

- Say **Today we've done a project about natural environments.**
- Ask **Which was your favourite activity today? Which activity was easy / difficult?**

**Reinforcement activity**

- Make a display of the pupils' work so that other classes can enjoy and learn from the work.

# Happy New Year!



## Key Competences and Key Learning Outcomes

- Make and discuss your New Year's resolutions
- Listen to and perform a poem about New Year's resolutions
- Learn about New Year traditions in the UK
- Learn about New Year traditions around the world

## Key language

- *celebrate, count down, dawdle, envelope, feast, ink, New Year's Day, New Year's Eve, New Year's resolutions, strike midnight; curry, mangoes, noodles, pancakes, papaya*
- *I promise I will (watch less TV). I promise I won't (shout).*

## Materials

- Pupil's Book p104; Class CD4; Teacher's App on Navio

## Optional materials

- Teacher's Resource Bank: Trinity Exams Practice cards (selected from Starter Unit and Units 1, 2, 3, 4, 5, 6, 7, 8 and 9)

## At a Glance Lesson Plan

### Starting the lesson

- Use the Trinity Exams Practice cards (optional).
- Set learning objectives.

### Activity 1

- Look at the photo.
- What do you think is happening?
- Read and find out.
- Then read and discuss.

### Activity 2

- Read about New Year in two more countries.
- Answer the questions.

### Activity 3

- Listen and read.
- Say the poem.
- ▶ ***CD4 Track 16 p296***
- Find out about New Year in China.
- When is it?
- How do people celebrate it?

## Pupil's Book

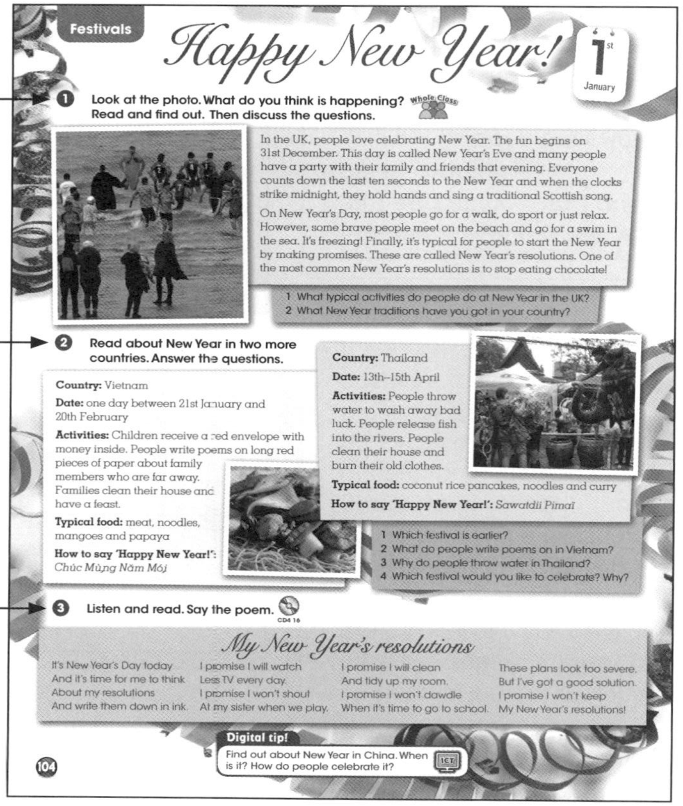
Festivals

Happy New Year! 1st January

1 Look at the photo. What do you think is happening? Read and find out. Then discuss the questions.

In the UK, people love celebrating New Year. The fun begins on 31st December. This day is called New Year's Eve and many people have a party with their family and friends that evening. Everyone counts down the last ten seconds to the New Year and when the clocks strike midnight, they hold hands and sing a traditional Scottish song.

On New Year's Day, most people go for a walk, do sport or just relax. However, some brave people meet on the beach and go for a swim in the sea. It's freezing! Finally, it's typical for people to start the New Year by making promises. These are called New Year's resolutions. One of the most common New Year's resolutions is to stop eating chocolate!

1 What typical activities do people do at New Year in the UK?
2 What New Year traditions have you got in your country?

2 Read about New Year in two more countries. Answer the questions.

Country: Vietnam
Date: one day between 21st January and 20th February
Activities: Children receive a red envelope with money inside. People write poems on long red pieces of paper about family members who are far away. Families clean their house and have a feast.
Typical food: meat, noodles, mangoes and papaya
How to say 'Happy New Year!': Chúc Mừng Năm Mới

Country: Thailand
Date: 13th–15th April
Activities: People throw water to wash away bad luck. People release fish into the rivers. People clean their house and burn their old clothes.
Typical food: coconut rice pancakes, noodles and curry
How to say 'Happy New Year!': Sawatdii Pimai

1 Which festival is earlier?
2 What do people write poems on in Vietnam?
3 Why do people throw water in Thailand?
4 Which festival would you like to celebrate? Why?

3 Listen and read. Say the poem. CD4 16

My New Year's resolutions

It's New Year's Day today
And it's time for me to think
About my resolutions
And write them down in ink.

I promise I will watch
Less TV every day.
I promise I won't shout
At my sister when we play.

I promise I will clean
And tidy up my room.
I promise I won't dawdle
When it's time to go to school.

These plans look too severe,
But I've got a good solution.
I promise I won't keep
My New Year's resolutions!

Digital tip! Find out about New Year in China. When is it? How do people celebrate it?

104

### Ending the lesson

- Review the lesson and reflect on learning.

### Extra activity

**Extension**

- Find out about how New Year is celebrated in another country.

## Digital resources

**Teacher's Digital:** You can also teach this lesson using the Teacher's App on Navio.

**Pupil's Digital:** Encourage your pupils to use the Pupil's App on Navio to practise the activities from this lesson.

# Detailed Lesson Plan

## Starting the lesson

**Use the Trinity Exams Practice cards (optional).**

- The pupils practise asking and answering questions.

**Set learning objectives.**

- Ask **Which day is the last day of the year? Which day is the first day of the New Year?** Then say **Today we're going to learn about how people celebrate New Year around the world.**

## Pupil's Book Activity 1

**Look at the photo. What do you think is happening? Read and find out. Then read and discuss.**

- Focus the pupils' attention on the photo. Prompt the pupils to make predictions about what is happening. Ask **Do you think it's summer? Do you think the people are enjoying themselves?**
- Say **Let's read and find out.** Read the text as a class. Confirm that the people are swimming in the sea on New Year's Day.
- Read the first question. The pupils identify the different activities that British people do at New Year.
- Read the second question. Prompt the pupils to describe what activities people do in their country at New Year.

## Pupil's Book Activity 2

**Read about New Year in two more countries. Answer the questions.**

- Explain to the class that they are going to find out how people celebrate New Year in two different countries: Vietnam and Thailand. If you have a world map in the classroom, show the pupils the two countries.
- Encourage the pupils to describe what they can see in the photos. The pupils then read the fact files.
- Check the pupils' understanding by asking questions. Ask **Where do children receive money at New Year?** (*Vietnam.*) **Where do people throw water?** (*Thailand.*) **Which country celebrates New Year in April?** (*Thailand.*) The pupils listen and name the country each time.

## Pupil's Book Activity 3

**Listen and read. Say the poem.**

▶ ***CD4 Track 16 p296***

- Ask the pupils if they can remember what the promises that people make at New Year are called. (*New Year's resolutions*). Ask **Do you ever make New Year's resolutions? Is it a good idea?**
- Say **Let's listen to a poem about New Year's resolutions.** Play the CD. The pupils listen and read. Check understanding.
- Read out each line of the poem. Ask the class to repeat. Then play the CD again. Ask the class to join in saying the poem.
- Finally, if the pupils are very confident, read out the poem as a class without the support of the CD.

**Find out about New Year in China. When is it? How do people celebrate it?** ICT

- Read the instructions at the bottom of the page. Challenge the pupils to find out the information on the Internet, in groups or as a homework activity.

**Answers:** Chinese New Year is celebrated at the end of January or at the beginning of February. The celebrations last for 15 days. People eat special food, clean their houses, exchange gifts and red packets with money and light fireworks.

## Ending the lesson

**Review the lesson and reflect on learning.**

- Say **Today we've learnt lots of things about New Year around the world. What do you remember?**
- Ask **Which was your favourite activity today? Which activity was easy / difficult?**

## Extra activity

**Extension**

- Ask the pupils to copy the fact file headings into their notebooks. They then choose a different country and research how New Year is celebrated there. They write the information in their file.

# World Environment Day



## Key Competences and Key Learning Outcomes

- Learn about carbon footprints
- Listen to and do a quiz to find out about your carbon footprint

- Discuss what you should and shouldn't do to reduce your carbon footprint

- Learn about World Environment Day

## Key language

- *absorb, burn, $CO_2$, carbon, carbon footprint, coal, energy, environment, gas, oxygen, standby, trap; less, more, the least, the most; always, every day, never, once or twice a (week), sometimes, usually; by (car), on foot*
- *How often do you leave the TV on standby? How much TV do you watch every day?*

## Materials

- Pupil's Book p105 ; Class CD4; Teacher's App on Navio

## Optional materials

- Teacher's Resource Bank: Trinity Exams Practice cards (selected from the Starter Unit and Units 1, 2, 3, 4, 5, 6, 7, 8 and 9)

## At a Glance Lesson Plan

### Starting the lesson

- Use the Trinity Exams Practice cards (optional).
- Set learning objectives.

### Activity 1

- What's a carbon footprint?
- Read and find out.

### Activity 2

- Read the text again.
- Answer the questions.

### Activity 3

- Listen and calculate Anna's carbon footprint.

▶ *CD4 Track 17 p296*

### Activity 4

- What should Anna do to reduce her carbon footprint?
- Find out about the next World Environment Day.
- Where will it be celebrated?
- What will the theme be?

## Pupil's Book

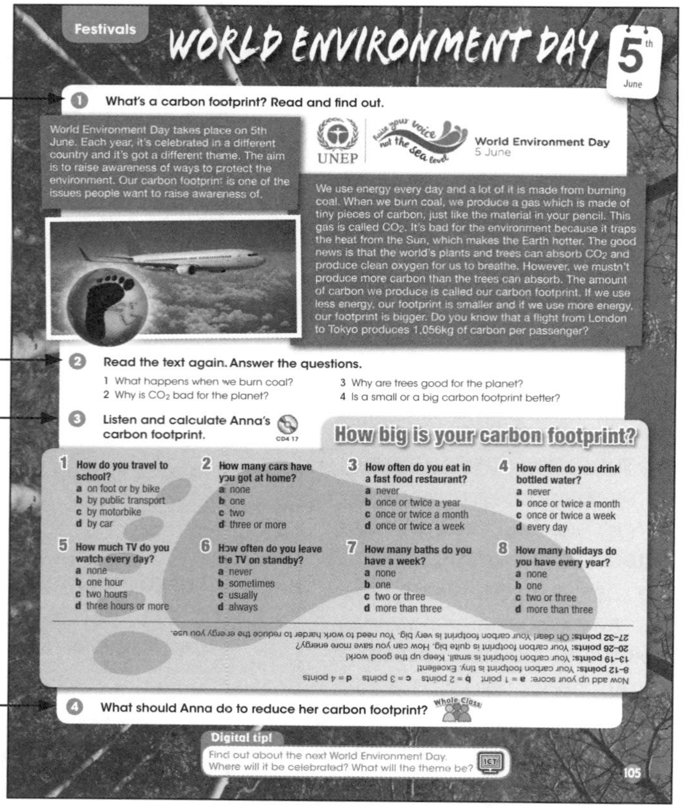
Festivals

WORLD ENVIRONMENT DAY 5th June

1 What's a carbon footprint? Read and find out.

World Environment Day takes place on 5th June. Each year, it's celebrated in a different country and it's got a different theme. The aim is to raise awareness of ways to protect the environment. Our carbon footprint is one of the issues people want to raise awareness of.

UNEP World Environment Day 5 June

We use energy every day and a lot of it is made from burning coal. When we burn coal, we produce a gas which is made of tiny pieces of carbon, just like the material in your pencil. This gas is called $CO_2$. It's bad for the environment because it traps the heat from the Sun, which makes the Earth hotter. The good news is that the world's plants and trees can absorb $CO_2$ and produce clean oxygen for us to breathe. However, we mustn't produce more carbon than the trees can absorb. The amount of carbon we produce is called our carbon footprint. If we use less energy, our footprint is smaller and if we use more energy, our footprint is bigger. Do you know that a flight from London to Tokyo produces 1,056kg of carbon per passenger?

2 Read the text again. Answer the questions.

1 What happens when we burn coal?
2 Why is $CO_2$ bad for the planet?
3 Why are trees good for the planet?
4 Is a small or a big carbon footprint better?

3 Listen and calculate Anna's carbon footprint.

How big is your carbon footprint?

1 How do you travel to school? a on foot or by bike b by public transport c by motorbike d by car

2 How many cars have you got at home? a none b one c two d three or more

3 How often do you eat in a fast food restaurant? a never b once or twice a year c once or twice a month d once or twice a week

4 How often do you drink bottled water? a never b once or twice a month c once or twice a week d every day

5 How much TV do you watch every day? a none b one hour c two hours d three hours or more

6 How often do you leave the TV on standby? a never b sometimes c usually d always

7 How many baths do you have a week? a none b one c two or three d more than three

8 How many holidays do you have every year? a none b one c two or three d more than three

4 What should Anna do to reduce her carbon footprint?

Digital tip! Find out about the next World Environment Day. Where will it be celebrated? What will the theme be?

105

### Ending the lesson

- Review the lesson and reflect on learning.

### Extra activity

**Extension**

- Use an online carbon footprint calculator to find out how much carbon you produce.

## Digital resources

**Teacher's Digital:** You can also teach this lesson using the Teacher's App on Navio.

**Pupil's Digital:** Encourage your pupils to use the Pupil's App on Navio to practise the activities from this lesson.

Powered By NAVIO

### Starting the lesson

**Use the Trinity Exams Practice cards (optional).**

- The pupils practise asking and answering questions.

**Set learning objectives.**

- Say **It's (almost) World Environment Day. On this day people all around the world think about how to protect the environment.**

### Pupil's Book Activity 1

**What's a carbon footprint? Read and find out.**

- Focus the pupils on the drawing. Ask them to explain or predict what a carbon footprint is. Ask **What are footprints?** (*The marks we leave behind us.*) **Where can we see footprints?** (*In the sand, mud, etc.*) **Is the footprint on the drawing clean or dirty?** (*Dirty.*)
- The pupils read the text as a class to discover what a carbon footprint is.

### Pupil's Book Activity 2

**Read the text again. Answer the questions.**

- The pupils work in pairs to answer the questions.

### Pupil's Book Activity 3

**Listen and calculate Anna's carbon footprint.**

▶ *CD4 Track 17 p296*

- Focus the pupils on the quiz. Ask them to scan the information quickly to answer the following questions: **What is the quiz about? How many questions are there? How many options are there for each question? Which question words can you see? Where are the scores?**
- Ask the pupils to write down the numbers 1–8 in their notebooks. Explain that they should record the letter for Anna's answer each time.
- Play the CD, pausing whenever necessary to allow the pupils to record Anna's answers.
- Ask the pupils to add up Anna's score and find out the size of her carbon footprint.

**Answers:** **1** d **2** b **3** d **4** d **5** b **6** d **7** a **8** b **Score:** 23 points. Her carbon footprint is quite big.

### Pupil's Book Activity 4

**What should Anna do to reduce her carbon footprint?**

- The pupils think about how Anna can reduce the energy she uses. They make sentences using 'should' and 'shouldn't'. (*Anna should drink more tap water. Anna should eat less fast food.*)

**Find out about the next World Environment Day. Where will it be celebrated? What will the theme be?** ICT

- Read the instructions at the bottom of the page. Challenge the pupils to find out the information on the Internet, in groups or as a homework activity.

### Ending the lesson

**Review the lesson and reflect on learning.**

- Say **Today we've learnt about carbon footprints. What information did you find out that surprised you?**
- Ask **Which was your favourite activity today? Which activity was easy / difficult?**

### Extra activity

**Extension**

- If you have access to the Internet in the classroom, use an online carbon footprint calculator. The pupils find out how much carbon they produce in kilograms. The pupils need to do this individually.

Date: ____________ Units: ________

1 **What did my pupils learn in these units?**

2 **How did my pupils work? (✓)**

individually ☐ in pairs ☐ in small groups ☐

in large groups ☐ as a class ☐

3 **Which key competences did my pupils develop? Give a score from 1 to 5 (5 being the highest).**

- Competence in linguistic communication ☐
- Competence in mathematics, science and technology ☐
- Digital competence ☐
- Learning to learn ☐
- Social and civic competences ☐
- Sense of initiative and entrepreneurship ☐
- Cultural awareness and expression ☐

4 **Which lessons / activities were the most successful and why?**

5 **Which lessons / activities did my pupils find the most difficult and why?**

6 **What did I try in the classroom for the first time? How did it go?**

7 **Which resources did I find most useful? (including webpages)**

8 **What could I do differently next time I teach these units?**

### Pupil's Book Song Bank Unit 1 (page 125)

**Activity 1**

**Read and discuss the questions.**

- Work as a class to answer the questions about shopping.

**Activity 2**

- **Listen and sing *Shopping is fun!***

▶ ***CD4 Track 18 p296***

▶ ***CD4 Track 19 p297 (optional karaoke version)***

- Explain to the pupils that they are going to listen to a song called *Shopping is fun!*
- Ask **Does the singer like shopping for clothes?**
- Play the CD. The pupils listen and read the song in their book. Confirm that the singer likes shopping for clothes, but not when he goes shopping with his mum.
- Play the CD again. The pupils sing along with the recording.
- When the pupils are familiar with the song, you can use the karaoke version to practise it.

### Pupil's Book Song Bank Unit 3 (page 125)

**Activity 1**

**Read and discuss the questions.**

- Work as a class to answer the questions about life in the city.

**Activity 2**

- **Listen and sing *Life in the city.***

▶ ***CD4 Track 20 p297***

▶ ***CD4 Track 21 p297 (optional karaoke version)***

- Explain to the pupils that they are going to listen to a song called *Life in the city.*
- Ask **What did the singer do in the city at the weekend?**
- Play the CD. The pupils listen and read the song. Confirm that the singer went shopping, went to the theatre and visited a museum.
- Play the CD again. The pupils sing along with the recording.
- When the pupils are familiar with the song, you can use the karaoke version to practise it.

# Detailed Lesson Plan

## Pupil's Book Song Bank Unit 4 (page 126)

**Activity 1**

**Read and discuss the questions.**

- Work as a class to answer the questions about computer games.

**Activity 2**

- **Listen and sing *Let's play!***

▶ ***CD4 Track 22 p297***

▶ ***CD4 Track 23 p297 (optional karaoke version)***

- Explain to the class that they are going to listen to a song called *Let's play!*
- Ask **What actions does the player do in the song?**
- Play the CD. The pupils listen and read the song. Confirm that the singer picks up the handset, presses A, tilts the handset, shakes the handset and uses the arrows.
- Play the CD again. The pupils sing along with the recording.
- When the pupils are familiar with the song, you can use the karaoke version to practise it.

## Pupil's Book Song Bank Unit 6 (page 126)

**Activity 1**

**Read and discuss the questions.**

- Work as a class to answer the questions about free-time activities.

**Activity 2**

- **Listen and sing *Are you creative?***

▶ ***CD4 Track 24 p297***

▶ ***CD4 Track 25 p297 (optional karaoke version)***

- Explain to the class that they are going to listen to a song called *Are you creative?*
- Ask **Which creative activities do the singers sing about?**
- Play the CD. The pupils listen and read the song. Confirm that the singers sing about circus skills (juggling and tightrope walking), performing (film making and acting) and music (playing the drums and singing).
- Play the CD again. The pupils sing along with the recording.
- When the pupils are familiar with the song, you can use the karaoke version to practise it.

## Pupil's Book Song Bank Unit 7 (page 127)

**Activity 1**

**Read and discuss the questions.**

- Work as a class to answer the questions about getting up.

**Activity 2**

**Listen and sing *Sleepy head.***

▶ ***CD4 Track 26 p297***

▶ ***CD4 Track 27 p297 (optional karaoke version)***

- As a class answer the questions about getting up.
- Explain to the class that they are going to listen to a song called *Sleepy head.*
- Ask **What actions has the singer already done in the song?**
- Play the CD. The pupils listen and read the song. Confirm that the singer has: had breakfast, brushed his / her teeth, done his / her homework, combed hair, packed his / her schoolbag and tidied his / her room.
- Play the CD again. The pupils sing along with the recording.
- When the pupils are familiar with the song, you can use the karaoke version to practise it.

## Pupil's Book Song Bank Unit 9 (page 127)

**Activity 1**

**Read and discuss the questions.**

- Work as a class to answer the questions about packing a bag or suitcase.

**Activity 2**

- **Listen and sing *My holiday suitcase.***

▶ ***CD4 Track 28 p298***

▶ ***CD4 Track 29 p298 (optional karaoke version)***

- Work as a class to answer the questions about packing a bag or suitcase.
- Explain to the class that they are going to listen to a song called *My holiday suitcase.*
- Ask ***What does the singer pack in the suitcase?***
- Play the CD. The pupils listen and read the song. Confirm that the singer packs lots of different things and elicit some examples.
- Ask ***What's the problem at the end of the song?*** (*The singer can't close the suitcase.*) ***Why not?*** (*There are too many things.*)
- Play the CD again. The pupils sing along with the recording.
- When the pupils are familiar with the song, you can use the karaoke version to practise it.

**Key Competences and Key Learning Outcomes**

- Review *too* and *not enough* and clothes vocabulary

LEARN
- Practise the following Key for Schools tasks: Reading and Writing Part 1, Listening Part 1 and Speaking Part 2
- Learn a strategy to help you if you don't understand a text

**Key language**
- *advertisement, half price, label, leather, raincoat, sale, shop sign, special offer, walking boots*

**Materials**
- Pupil's Book p115; Activity Book p120 & 129; Class CD4; Teacher's App on Navio
- Teacher's Resource Bank: Talk cards

**Optional materials**
- Teacher's Resource Bank: Trinity Exams Practice cards (selected from Unit 1)

## At a Glance Lesson Plan

### Starting the lesson
- Use the Trinity Exams Practice cards (optional).
- Review *too* and *not enough*.
- Set learning objectives and use the talk cards.

### Activity 1
**A2 Key for Schools: Reading and Writing Part 1**
- Read the sign.
- Then read and complete the sentences.
- Which words in the sign help you?

### Activity 2
**A2 Key for Schools: Reading and Writing Part 1**
- Read the texts.
- What type of texts are they?
- Then read and choose the correct answer for each text.

### Activity 3
**A2 Key for Schools Reading and Writing Part 1**
- Can you think of other types of short texts that people read and write?

Go to the Activity Book.

## Pupil's Book

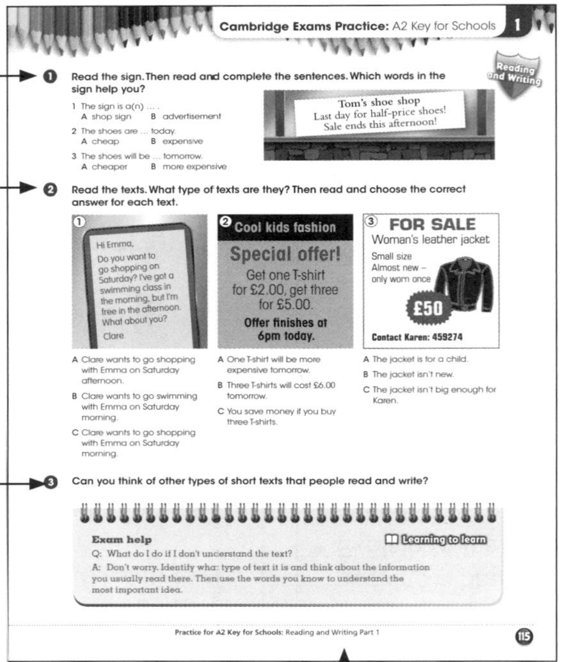


### Exam help
- Read the Exam help as a class.

### Ending the lesson
- Review the lesson and reflect on learning.

### Extra activity
**Reinforcement**
- Play an alphabet game to revise clothes.

### External Exams Video
**Additional Cambridge Exams Practice Video: A2 Key for Schools**
- Additional external exams preparation material, including videos, worksheets and practice tests, can be found in the Teacher's Resource Bank on Navio.

### Digital resources

**Teacher's Digital:** You can also teach this lesson using the Teacher's App on Navio.

**Pupil's Digital:** Encourage your pupils to use the Pupil's App on Navio to practise the activities from this lesson.

Powered By NAVIO

## Activity Book

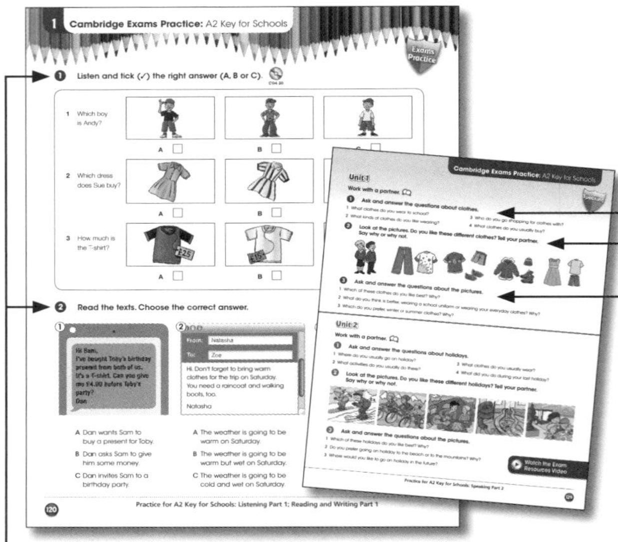


### Activity Book page 120
**A2 Key for Schools: Listening Part 1**
**Activity 1**
- Listen and tick (✓) the right answer (A, B or C).

▶ ***CD4 Track 30 p298***

**A2 Key for Schools: Reading and Writing Part 1**
**Activity 2**
- Read the texts. Choose the correct answer.

### Activity Book page 129
**A2 Key for Schools: Speaking Part 2**
**Activity 1**
- Ask and answer the questions about clothes.

**Activity 2**
- Look at the pictures.
- Do you like these different clothes?
- Tell your partner.
- Say why or why not.

**Activity 3**
- Ask and answer the questions about the pictures.

# Detailed Lesson Plan

## Starting the lesson

**Use the Trinity Exams Practice cards (optional).**

- The pupils practise asking and answering questions.

**Review *too* and *not enough*.**

- Say **I don't like this shirt. It's too tight. I don't like these trousers. They aren't long enough.** Throw a soft ball to a pupil and prompt him / her to say a similar pair of sentences. The pupil then throws the ball to another pupil who does the same. Repeat several times.

**Set learning objectives and use the talk cards.**

- Say **Today we're going to practise activities for an exam and remember what we've learnt in Unit 1**.
- Point to the talk cards to show the pupils the different ways they will be working in the lesson.

## Pupil's Book Activity 1

**A2 Key for Schools: Reading and Writing Part 1**

**Read the sign. Then read and complete the sentences. Which words in the sign help you?**

- Read the sign with the pupils. Check they understand *half-price* and *sale*.
- Pupils work in pairs to choose the correct answers.
- Check answers as a class. Then discuss which words helped them and why.

**Answers:** **1** B (half-price shoes, sale) **2** A (Last day for half-price shoes) **3** B (Sale ends this afternoon)

## Pupil's Book Activity 2

**A2 Key for Schools: Reading and Writing Part 1**

**Read the texts. What type of texts are they? Then read and choose the correct answer for each text.**

- Ask pupils what type the texts are, and how they know (*1 an email or text/instant message – it starts with Hi + name, and finishes with a name*; *2 an advertisement – it describes a special offer*; *3 an advertisement – it's selling a product*).
- Pupils work alone to choose the correct options. Tell them to use words in the texts to help them.
- Finally, check answers as a class.

**Answers:** **1** A **2** B **3** B

## Pupil's Book Activity 3

**A2 Key for Schools: Reading and Writing Part 1**

**Can you think of other types of short texts that people read and write?**

- Pupils make a list of short texts. Encourage them to think of texts that are both digital and written by hand.

## Exam help

- Read the Exam help as a class.

## External Exams Video

**Additional Cambridge Exams Practice Video: A2 Key for Schools**

- Additional external exams preparation material, including videos, worksheets and practice tests, can be found in the Teacher's Resource Bank on Navio.

## Activity Book page 120

**Activity 1**

**A2 Key for Schools: Listening Part 1**

**Listen and tick (✓) the right answer (A, B or C).**

▶ *CD4 Track 30 p298*

- Read the first question **Which boy is Andy?** Ask the pupils to describe what they can see in the first set of pictures.
- Play the CD, pausing after the first exchange. The pupils listen and tick the correct picture. Repeat the procedure with the other exchanges.

**Answers:** **1** C **2** A **3** C

**Activity 2**

**A2 Key for Schools: Reading and Writing Part 1**

**Read the texts. Choose the correct answer.**

- Ask the pupils **What type of texts can you see? How do you know?** (*1 an email or text/instant message – it starts and ends with a name*; *2 an email – there is a from/to boxes*; *3 an advertisement – it describes a product*)
- Pupils work on their own to choose the correct answers. They can check in pairs before checking as a class if you want.

**Answers:** **1** B **2** C **3** B

## Activity Book page 129

**A2 Key for Schools: Speaking Part 2**

This section helps pupils to practise Part 2 of the A2 Key for Schools Speaking exam. In the first phase of Part 2, candidates are presented with artwork on a particular topic. They discuss the artwork together. In the second phase, the interlocutor extends the conversation with further questions related to the topic.

**Activity 1**

**Ask and answer the questions about clothes.**

- Brainstorm vocabulary for clothes. Then pupils discuss the questions in pairs.

**Activity 2**

**Look at the pictures. Do you like these different clothes? Tell your partner. Say why or why not.**

- Ask different pupils to describe each picture. Then pupils give their opinions about the different holidays in pairs. Make sure they justify their opinions with *because*.

**Activity 3**

**Ask and answer the questions about the pictures.**

- Pupils discuss the questions. Round off the activity by asking different pairs to ask and answer each question in front of the class.

## Ending the lesson

**Review the lesson and reflect on learning.**

- Say **Today we've practised activities for an exam and remembered what we've learnt in Unit 1**.
- Ask **Which was your favourite activity today? Which activity was easy / difficult?**

## Extra activity

**Reinforcement**

- Play an alphabet game. In teams of 3 or 4, ask pupils to think of one word related to clothes beginning with each letter of the alphabet. After 5 minutes, the team with most words wins.

## Key Competences and Key Learning Outcomes

- Review past simple and holiday vocabulary

- Practise the following Key for Schools tasks: Reading and Writing Part 4, Listening Part 5 and Speaking Part 2
- Learn how to check that you have written the correct answer

**Key language**

- *at the back, at the front, campsite, canoe, caravan, go canoeing, hire, lonely, photography, rope bridge, sunshade, top*

**Materials**

- Pupil's Book p116; Activity Book p121 & 129; Class CD4; Teacher's App on Navio
- Teacher's Resource Bank: Talk cards

**Optional materials**

- Teacher's Resource Bank: Trinity Exams Practice cards (selected from Units 1 and 2)

## At a Glance Lesson Plan

### Pupil's Book

**Starting the lesson**

- Use the Trinity Exams Practice cards (optional).
- Review Past simple.
- Set learning objectives and use the talk cards.

**Activity 1**

**A2 Key for Schools: Reading and Writing Part 4**

- Look at the photo.
- What do you think the text is about?

**Activity 2**

**A2 Key for Schools: Reading and Writing Part 4**

- Read the text with the missing words.
- Can you answer the questions?

**Activity 3**

**A2 Key for Schools: Reading and Writing Part 4**

- Choose the correct words to complete the text in Activity 2.
- Try to explain why you chose each word.

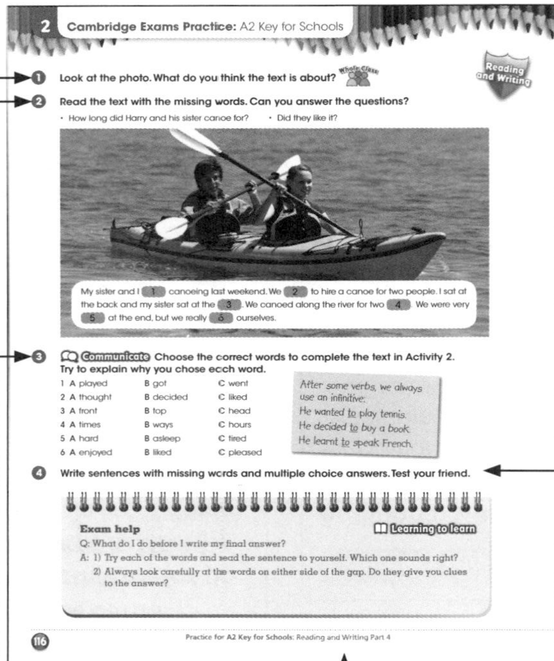


**Activity 4**

**A2 Key for Schools Reading and Writing Part 4**

- Write sentences with missing words and multiple choice answers.
- Test your friend.

Go to the Activity Book

**Exam help**

- Read the Exam help as a class.

**Ending the lesson**

- Review the lesson and reflect on learning.

**Extra activity**

**Reinforcement**

- Play a sentence building game to revise holiday activities.

**External Exams Video**

**Additional Cambridge Exams Practice Video: A2 Key for Schools**

- Additional external exams preparation material, including videos, worksheets and practice tests, can be found in the Teacher's Resource Bank on Navio.

### Activity Book

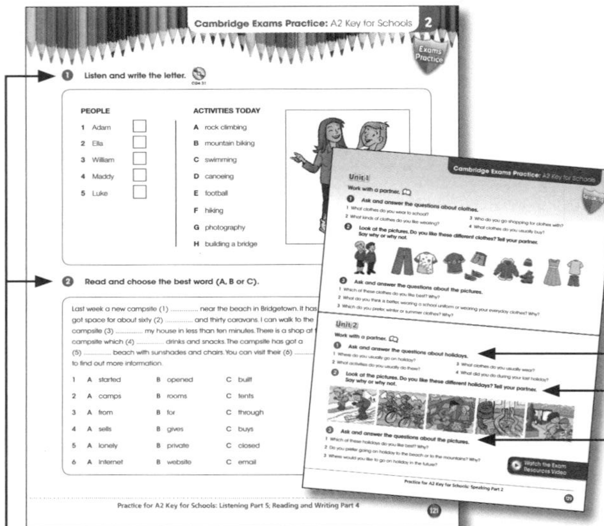


**Activity Book page 121**

**A2 Key for Schools: Listening Part 5**

**Activity 1**

- Listen and write the letter.

▶ ***CD4 Track 31 p298***

**A2 Key for Schools: Reading and Writing Part 4**

**Activity 2**

- Read and choose the best word (A, B or C).

**Activity Book page 129**

**A2 Key for Schools: Speaking Part 2**

**Activity 1**

- Ask and answer the questions about holidays.

**Activity 2**

- Look at the pictures.
- Do you like these different holidays?
- Tell your partner.
- Say why or why not.

**Activity 3**

- Ask and answer the questions about the pictures.

## Digital resources

**Teacher's Digital:** You can also teach this lesson using the Teacher's App on Navio.

**Pupil's Digital:** Encourage your pupils to use the Pupil's App on Navio to practise the activities from this lesson.

Powered By NAVIO

# Detailed Lesson Plan

## Starting the lesson

**Use the Trinity Exams Practice cards (optional).**

- The pupils practise asking and answering questions.

**Review past simple.**

- Ask three pupils **What did you do yesterday?** Then ask a fourth pupil **What did (name of one of the first three) do yesterday?** Continue asking pupils what they did, occasionally asking what one of their classmates did, to ensure that they all listen hard.

**Set learning objectives and use the talk cards.**

- Say **Today we're going to practise activities for an exam and remember what we've learnt in Unit 2.**
- Point to the talk cards to show the pupils the different ways they will be working in the lesson.

## Pupil's Book Activity 1

**A2 Key for Schools: Reading and Writing Part 4**

**Look at the photo. What do you think the text is about?**

- Ask pupils to cover the photo and describe the photo in as much detail as possible.
- Ask them to guess what type of text it might be. Don't confirm at this stage.

## Pupil's Book Activity 2

**A2 Key for Schools: Reading and Writing Part 4**

**Read the text with the missing words. Can you answer the questions?**

- Ask pupils to read the text and tell them not to worry about the missing words. Ask **What type of text is it?** (a story). Tell pupils to try and answer the two questions in pairs.

**Answers:** They canoed for two hours. Yes, they liked it.

## Pupil's Book Activity 3

**A2 Key for Schools: Reading and Writing Part 4**

**Choose the correct words to complete the text in Activity 2. Try to explain why you chose each word.**

- Pupils complete the gaps and then check answers as a class.

**Answers:** **1** C **2** B **3** A **4** C **5** C **6** A

## Pupil's Book Activity 4

**A2 Key for Schools: Reading and Writing Part 4**

**Write sentences with missing words and multiple choice answers. Test your friend.**

- Tell pupils to write sentences and choose words to gap.
- Pupils can write their sentences in pairs and then swap with another pair. Strong pupils can work alone.

## Exam help

- Read the Exam help as a class.

## External Exams Video

**Additional Cambridge Exams Practice Video: A2 Key for Schools**

- Additional external exams preparation material, including videos, worksheets and practice tests, can be found in the Teacher's Resource Bank on Navio.

## Activity Book page 121

**Activity 1**

**A2 Key for Schools: Listening Part 5**

**Listen and write the letter.**

▶ *CD4 Track 31 p298*

- Ask **How many people are there? How many activities are there?** Explain that pupils need to listen for the activities that each person did today.
- Play the CD. Pupils listen and write the letter. Then check as a class.

**Answers:** **1** mountain biking **2** football **3** building a bridge **4** photography **5** swimming

**Activity 2**

**A2 Key for Schools: Reading and Writing Part 4**

**Read and choose the best word (A, B or C)**

- Ask the pupils to describe the picture. Ask them what they think happened in the story.
- Pupils complete the gaps alone.
- Check answers as a class. Make sure pupils explain why they chose the words.

**Answers:** **1** B **2** C **3** A **4** A **5** B **6** B

## Activity Book page 129

**A2 Key for Schools: Speaking Part 2**

This section helps pupils to practise Part 2 of the A2 Key for Schools Speaking exam. In the first phase of Part 2, candidates are presented with artwork on a particular topic. They discuss the artwork together. In the second phase, the interlocutor extends the conversation with further questions related to the topic.

**Activity 1**

**Ask and answer the questions about holidays.**

- Brainstorm vocabulary for holiday places and activities. Then pupils discuss the questions in pairs.

**Activity 2**

**Look at the pictures. Do you like these different holidays? Tell your partner. Say why or why not.**

- Ask different pupils to describe each picture. Then pupils give their opinions about the different holidays in pairs. Make sure they justify their opinions with *because*.

**Activity 3**

**Ask and answer the questions about the pictures.**

- Pupils discuss the questions. Round off the activity by asking different pairs to ask and answer each question in front of the class.

## Ending the lesson

**Review the lesson and reflect on learning.**

- Say **Today we've practised activities for an exam and remembered what we've learnt in Unit 2.**
- Ask **Which was your favourite activity today? Which activity was easy / difficult?**

## Extra activity

**Reinforcement**

- Play a sentence building game. Say **Last week, I went on holiday. Last week, I went on holiday. I travelled by train. Last week, I went on holiday. I travelled by train. I stayed on a campsite.** Ask a strong pupil to repeat and add their own line. Continue build the story with different strong pupils for as long as the class are enjoying the activity.

### Key Competences and Key Learning Outcomes

- Review places in a city vocabulary

- Practise the following Key for Schools tasks: Reading and Writing Part 2, Listening Part 2 and Speaking Part 2
- Learn a strategy to help if you don't know the answer to question

- Learn about the cities of Liverpool, York and Edinburgh

### Key language

- *capital, collection, cruise, floor, railway, rock, sail, views*

### Materials

- Pupil's Book p117; Activity Book p122 & 130; Class CD4; Teacher's App on Navio
- Teacher's Resource Bank: Talk cards

### Optional materials

- Teacher's Resource Bank: cards (selected from Unit 1–3)

## At a Glance Lesson Plan

### Starting the lesson

- Review things to do in the city.
- Set learning objectives and use the talk cards.

### Activity 1

**A2 Key for Schools: Reading and Writing Part 2**

- Quickly read about the girls' three cities.
- Which one would you like to visit?

### Activity 2

**A2 Key for Schools: Reading and Writing Part 2**

- Read the questions and choose the correct answer.

### Activity 3

**A2 Key for Schools: Reading and Writing Part 2**

- Check your answers with a partner.
- Where did you find the answers in the texts?
- Which questions were the most difficult? Why?

Go to the Activity Book.

## Pupil's Book

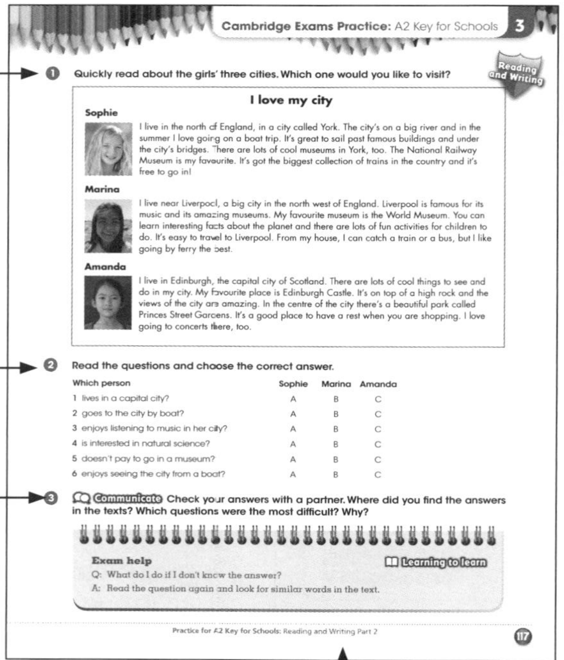


### Exam help

- Read the Exam help as a class.

### Ending the lesson

- Review the lesson and reflect on learning.

### Extra activity

**Reinforcement**

- Play a guessing game to revise places in a city.

### External Exams Video

**Additional Cambridge Exams Practice Video: A2 Key for Schools**

- Additional external exams preparation material, including videos, worksheets and practice tests, can be found in the Teacher's Resource Bank on Navio.

### Digital resources

**Teacher's Digital:** You can also teach this lesson using the Teacher's App on Navio.

**Pupil's Digital:** Encourage your pupils to use the Pupil's App on Navio to practise the activities from this lesson.

Powered By NAVIO

## Activity Book

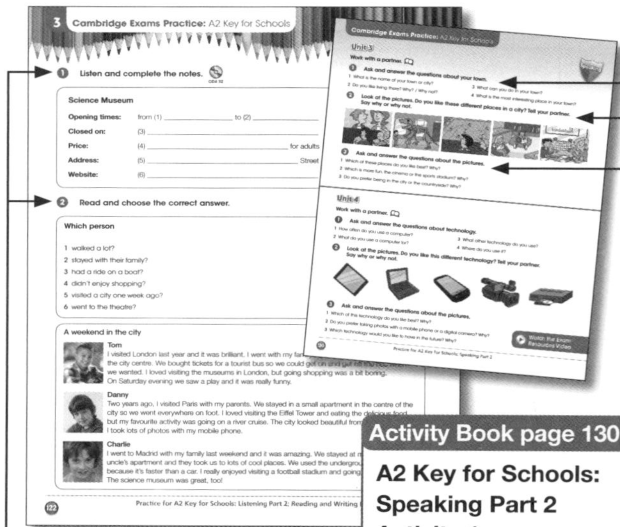


### Activity Book page 122

**A2 Key for Schools: Listening Part 2**

**Activity 1**

- Listen and complete the notes.

▶ *CD4 Track 32 p298*

**A2 Key for Schools: Reading and Writing Part 2**

**Activity 2**

- Read and choose the correct answer.

### Activity Book page 130

**A2 Key for Schools: Speaking Part 2**

**Activity 1**

- Ask and answer the questions about your town.

**Activity 2**

- Look at the pictures.
- Do you like these different places in a city?
- Tell your partner.
- Say why or why not.

**Activity 3**

- Ask and answer the questions about the pictures.

### Starting the lesson

**Use the Trinity Exams Practice cards (optional).**

- The pupils practise asking and answering questions.

**Review things to do in the city.**

- Mime an action from the things to do in the city vocabulary. Ask **What am I doing?** Pupils offer answers. Invite a pupil to the front of the lesson, and whisper an action for him/her to mime from the same vocabulary set. He/she asks **What am I doing?** Repeat with more pupils.

**Set learning objectives and use the talk cards.**

- Say **Today we're going to practise activities for an exam and remember what we've learnt in Unit 3**.
- Point to the talk cards to show the pupils the different ways they will be working in the lesson.

### Pupil's Book Activity 1

**A2 Key for Schools: Reading and Writing Part 2**

**Quickly read about the girls' three cities. Which one would you like to visit?**

- Pupils read the texts quickly. Ask two or three pupils which city they would like to visit and why.

### Pupil's Book Activity 2

**A2 Key for Schools: Reading and Writing Part 2**

**Read the questions and choose the correct answer.**

- Do the first question as a class. Ask pupils who answer correctly where they found the answer (*Amanda – I live in Edinburgh, the capital city of Scotland*). Then do the second question as a class. Ask which two girls mention boats (*Sophie and Marina*). Ask **Does Sophie travel to the city by boat?** (*No, she loves going on a boat trip*). **Does Marina travel to the city by boat?** (*Yes, she likes going by ferry*). Make sure pupils realise that they sometimes need to find similar words in the text, not exactly the same words. They should read carefully to make sure that the information matches.

**Answers:** **1** C **2** B **3** C **4** B **5** A **6** A

### Pupil's Book Activity 3

**A2 Key for Schools: Reading and Writing Part 2**

**Check your answers with a partner. Where did you find the answers in the text? Which questions were the most difficult? Why?**

- Pupils work in pairs and tell each other which words in the text were similar or the same as words in the sentences. (*music – concerts*; *natural science – the planet*; *doesn't pay – free*; *boat – boat trip*)
- As a class, discuss where they found the information and which questions were most difficult.

### Exam help

- Read the Exam help as a class.

### External Exams Video

**Additional Cambridge Exams Practice Video: A2 Key for Schools**

- Additional external exams preparation material, including videos, worksheets and practice tests, can be found in the Teacher's Resource Bank on Navio.

### Activity Book page 122

**Activity 1**

**A2 Key for Schools: Listening Part 2**

**Listen and complete the notes.**

▶ ***CD4 Track 32 p298***

- Tell pupils to look at the picture and the form. Ask **What place are you going to hear information about? What information do you need?**
- Play the CD. Pause after each answer.
- Play the CD again without pausing. Pupils check answers as a class.

**Answers:** **1** 9 o'clock (in the morning) **2** 6 o'clock (in the evening) **3** Mondays **4** Museum **5** goscience.com

**Activity 2**

**A2 Key for Schools: Reading and Writing Part 2**

**Read and choose the correct answers.**

- Pupils work alone to choose the correct answers. Then check as a class.

**Answers:** **1** B **2** C **3** B **4** A **5** C **6** A

### Activity Book page 130

**A2 Key for Schools: Speaking Part 2**

This section helps pupils to practise Part 2 of the A2 Key for Schools Speaking exam. In the first phase of Part 2, candidates are presented with artwork on a particular topic. They discuss the artwork together. In the second phase, the interlocutor extends the conversation with further questions related to the topic.

**Activity 1**

**Ask and answer the questions about your town.**

- Brainstorm vocabulary for places in a town. Then pupils discuss the questions in pairs.

**Activity 2**

**Look at the pictures. Do you like these different places in a city? Tell your partner. Say why or why not.**

- Ask different pupils to describe each picture. Then pupils give their opinions about the different places in pairs. Make sure they justify their opinions with *because*.

**Activity 3**

**Ask and answer the questions about the pictures.**

- Pupils discuss the questions. Round off the activity by asking different pairs to ask and answer each question in front of the class.

### Ending the lesson

**Review the lesson and reflect on learning.**

- Say **Today we've practised activities for an exam and remembered what we've learnt in Unit 3**.
- Ask **Which was your favourite activity today? Which activity was easy / difficult?**

### Extra activity

**Reinforcement**

- Play a guessing game. Invite a pupil to the front of a class and tell him/her to think of a place in a city. Ask yes/no questions about the place, for example **Is the place noisy? Can you spend money there? Have we got one in our town?** After 10 questions, invite pupils to guess the place.

### Key Competences and Key Learning Outcomes

- Review obligation and no obligation and technology vocabulary
- Practise the following Key for Schools tasks: Reading and Writing Part 3, Listening Part 4 and Speaking Part 2
- Learn about the order in which you should do the different parts of an exam task
- Read a text about a young computer games designer

**Key language**

- *championship, company, drawing, hockey, karaoke, luckily, machine, race, screen, thick*

**Materials**

- Pupil's Book p118; Activity Book p123 & 130; Class CD4; Teacher's App on Navio
- Teacher's Resource Bank: Talk cards
- Unit 4 flashcards

**Optional materials**

- Teacher's Resource Bank: Trinity Exams Practice cards (selected from Unit 1–4)

## At a Glance Lesson Plan

### Pupil's Book

**Starting the lesson**

- Use the Trinity Exams Practice cards (optional).
- Review obligation and no obligation.
- Set learning objectives and use the talk cards.

**Activity 1**

**A2 Key for Schools: Reading and Writing Part 3**

- Look at the picture.
- What do you think the text is about?

**Activity 2**

**A2 Key for Schools: Reading and Writing Part 3**

- Read the text.
- Then read the question and choose the correct answer.

**Activity 3**

**A2 Key for Schools: Reading and Writing Part 3**

- Compare and explain your answers from Activity 2.

**Activity 4**

**A2 Key for Schools: Reading and Writing Part 3**

- Read another text.
- Then read and choose the right answers.

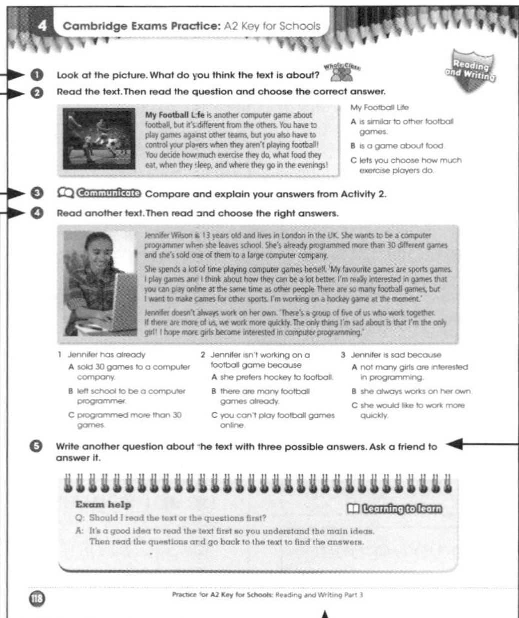

**Activity 5**

**A2 Key for Schools: Reading and Writing Part 3**

- Write another question about the text with three possible answers.
- Ask a friend to answer it.

Go to the Activity Book.

**Exam help**

- Read the Exam help as a class.

**Ending the lesson**

- Review the lesson and reflect on learning.

**Extra activity**

**Reinforcement**

- Play a 'look and listen' game to revise technology vocabulary.

**External Exams Video**

**Additional Cambridge Exams Practice Video: A2 Key for Schools**

- Additional external exams preparation material, including videos, worksheets and practice tests, can be found in the Teacher's Resource Bank on Navio.

### Digital resources

**Teacher's Digital:** You can also teach this lesson using the Teacher's App on Navio.

**Pupil's Digital:** Encourage your pupils to use the Pupil's App on Navio to practise the activities from this lesson.

Powered By NAVIO

### Activity Book

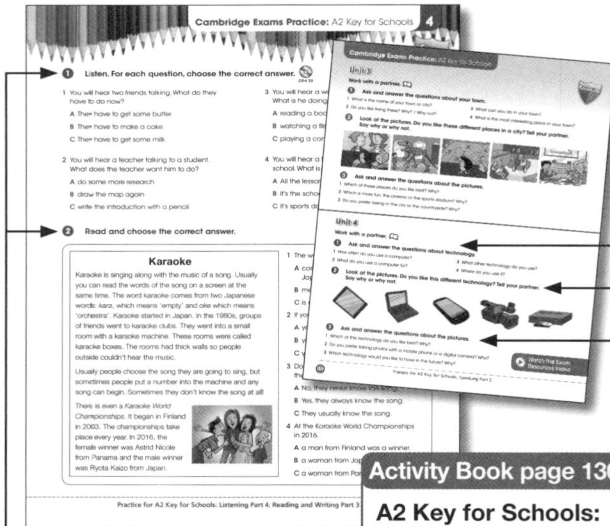

**Activity Book page 123**

**A2 Key for Schools: Listening Part 4**

**Activity 1**

- Listen.
- For each question, choose the correct answer.

▶ *CD4 Track 33 p298*

**A2 Key for Schools: Reading and Writing Part 3**

**Activity 2**

- Read and choose the correct answer.

**Activity Book page 130**

**A2 Key for Schools: Speaking Part 2**

**Activity 1**

- Ask and answer the questions about technology.

**Activity 2**

- Look at the pictures.
- Do you like this different technology?
- Tell your partner.
- Say why or why not.

**Activity 3**

- Ask and answer the questions about the pictures.

**Starting the lesson**

**Use the Trinity Exams Practice cards (optional).**

- The pupils practise asking and answering questions.

**Review obligation and no obligation.**

- Ask a pupil to come to the front of the class. Tell him/her to think of a sport. Ask questions about the sport such as **Do you have to play in a team? Do you have to score a goal? Do you have to hit a ball with a racket?** After four questions, summarise the information for the class, for example **You have to hit the ball with a racket. You don't have to score a goal.** Ask pupils to guess the sport. Pupils repeat the activity in pairs.

**Set learning objectives and use the talk cards.**

- Say **Today we're going to practise activities for an exam and remember what we've learnt in Unit 4**.
- Point to the talk cards to show the pupils the different ways they will be working in the lesson.

**Pupil's Book Activity 1**

**A2 Key for Schools: Reading and Writing Part 3**

**Look at the picture. What do you think the text is about?**

- Ask a pupil to describe the photo. Then ask **What is the text about?** Pupils offer ideas.

**Pupil's Book Activity 2**

**A2 Key for Schools: Reading and Writing Part 3**

**Read the text. Then read the question and choose the correct answer.**

- Pupils read the text and choose the correct answer.

**Answer:** C

**Pupil's Book Activity 3**

**A2 Key for Schools: Reading and Writing Part 3**

**Compare and explain your answers from Activity 2.**

- Tell pupils to compare their answers and explain to each other why the other two options are wrong.
- Ask the class if the text mentions food, and what it says about it (*Yes, you decide what food your players eat*). Ask them if Option B is correct. (*No*)

**Pupil's Book Activity 4**

**A2 Key for Schools: Reading and Writing Part 3**

**Read another text. Then read and choose the right answers.**

- Pupils read and choose the correct answers.
- Tell them to check in pairs and explain why the incorrect options are incorrect.

**Answers:** **1** C **2** B **3** A

**Pupil's Book Activity 5**

**A2 Key for Schools: Reading and Writing Part 3**

**Write another question about the text with three possible answers. Ask a friend to answer it.**

- Pupils write a sentence with three possible endings, two of which are incorrect. Tell them to make sure the incorrect options are definitely incorrect rather than not mentioned in the text.

**Exam help**

- Read the Exam help as a class.

**External Exams Video**

**Additional Cambridge Exams Practice Video: A2 Key for Schools**

- Additional external exams preparation material, including videos, worksheets and practice tests, can be found in the Teacher's Resource Bank on Navio.

**Activity Book page 123**

**Activity 1**

**A2 Key for Schools: Listening Part 3**

**Listen. For each question, choose the correct answer.**

▶ ***CD4 Track 33 p298***

- Play the CD. Pause after the first conversation and check the answer.
- Play the rest of the track.
- Play the CD again without pausing. Then check as a class.

**Answers:** **1** A **2** B **3** A **4** C

**Activity 2**

**A2 Key for Schools: Reading and Writing Part 3**

**Read and choose the correct answer.**

- Ask the pupils to read the text quickly. Ask general questions to check understanding.
- Pupils choose the correct answers. Ask them to explain why the incorrect options are incorrect. Finally check as a class.

**Answers:** **1** A **2** B **3** C **4** C

**Activity Book page 130**

**A2 Key for Schools: Speaking Part 2**

This section helps pupils to practise Part 2 of the A2 Key for Schools Speaking exam. In the first phase of Part 2, candidates are presented with artwork on a particular topic. They discuss the artwork together. In the second phase, the interlocutor extends the conversation with further questions related to the topic.

**Activity 1**

**Ask and answer the questions about technology.**

- Brainstorm vocabulary for technology. Then pupils discuss the questions in pairs.

**Activity 2**

**Look at the pictures. Do you like this different technology? Tell your partner. Say why or why not.**

- Ask different pupils to describe each picture. Then pupils give their opinions about the different places in pairs. Make sure they justify their opinions with *because*.

**Activity 3**

**Ask and answer the questions about the pictures.**

- Pupils discuss the questions. Round off the activity by asking different pairs to ask and answer each question in front of the class.

**Ending the lesson**

**Review the lesson and reflect on learning.**

- Say **Today we've practised activities for an exam and remembered what we've learnt in Unit 4**.

### Key Competences and Key Learning Outcomes

- Review verbs of the senses and animal vocabulary
- Practise the following Key for Schools tasks: Reading and Writing Part 4, Listening Part 5 and Speaking Part 2
- Learn a strategy to help if you aren't sure which word to choose in a multiple choice activity

### Key language

- *accident, cage, fruit bat, hunter, incredible, jump, lizard, ostrich, owl, protect, reptile, species*

### Materials

- Pupil's Book p119; Activity Book p124 & 131; Class CD4; Teacher's App on Navio
- Teacher's Resource Bank: Talk cards

### Optional materials

- Teacher's Resource Bank: Trinity Exams Practice cards (selected from Unit 1–5)

## At a Glance Lesson Plan

### Starting the lesson

- Use the Trinity Exams Practice cards (optional).
- Review verbs of the senses.
- Set learning objectives and use the talk cards.

### Activity 1

**A2 Key for Schools: Reading and Writing Part 4**

- Read, think and say.
- How are these words different?

### Activity 2

**A2 Key for Schools: Reading and Writing Part 4**

- Read and complete the sentence with a word from Activity 1.

### Activity 3

**A2 Key for Schools: Reading and Writing Part 4**

- Read the text with the missing words.
- Close your books.
- What shark facts can you remember?

### Activity 4

**A2 Key for Schools: Reading and Writing Part 4**

- Read the text again.
- Choose the correct answer for each gap.

## Pupil's Book

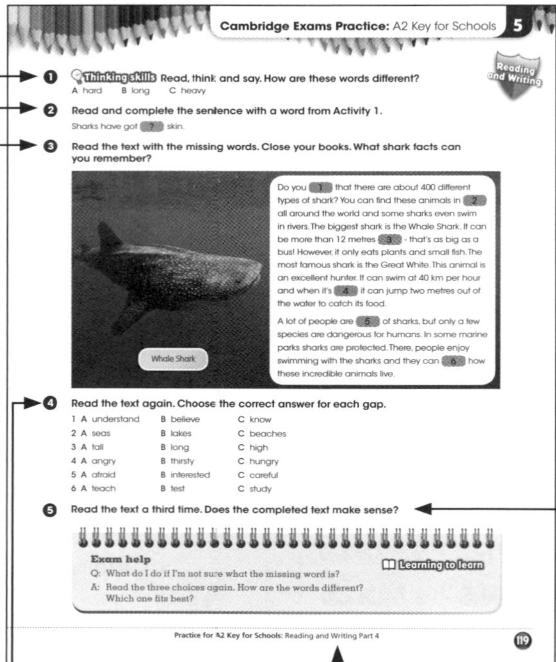
Cambridge Exams Practice: A2 Key for Schools 5

1 Thinking skills Read, think and say. How are these words different?
A hard B long C heavy

2 Read and complete the sentence with a word from Activity 1.
Sharks have got (7) skin.

3 Read the text with the missing words. Close your books. What shark facts can you remember?

Whale Shark

Do you (1) that there are about 400 different types of shark? You can find these animals in (2) all around the world and some sharks even swim in rivers. The biggest shark is the Whale Shark. It can be more than 12 metres (3) - that's as big as a bus! However, it only eats plants and small fish. The most famous shark is the Great White. This animal is an excellent hunter. It can swim at 40 km per hour and when it's (4) it can jump two metres out of the water to catch its food.
A lot of people are (5) of sharks, but only a few species are dangerous for humans. In some marine parks sharks are protected. There, people enjoy swimming with the sharks and they can (6) how these incredible animals live.

4 Read the text again. Choose the correct answer for each gap.

| | | |
|---|---|---|
| 1 A understand | B believe | C know |
| 2 A seas | B lakes | C beaches |
| 3 A tall | B long | C high |
| 4 A angry | B thirsty | C hungry |
| 5 A afraid | B interested | C careful |
| 6 A teach | B test | C study |

5 Read the text a third time. Does the completed text make sense?

Exam help
Q: What do I do if I'm not sure what the missing word is?
A: Read the three choices again. How are the words different? Which one fits best?
Learning to learn

Practice for A2 Key for Schools: Reading and Writing Part 4 119

### Activity 5

**A2 Key for Schools: Reading and Writing Part 4**

- Read text a third time.
- Does the completed text make sense?

Go to the Activity Book

### Exam help

- Read the Exam help as a class.

### Ending the lesson

- Review the lesson and reflect on learning.

### Extra activity

**Reinforcement**

- Play a categories game to revise animal vocabulary.

### External Exams Video

**Additional Cambridge Exams Practice Video: A2 Key for Schools**

- Additional external exams preparation material, including videos, worksheets and practice tests, can be found in the Teacher's Resource Bank on Navio.

### Digital resources

**Teacher's Digital:** You can also teach this lesson using the Teacher's App on Navio.

**Pupil's Digital:** Encourage your pupils to use the Pupil's App on Navio to practise the activities from this lesson.

Powered By NAVIO

## Activity Book

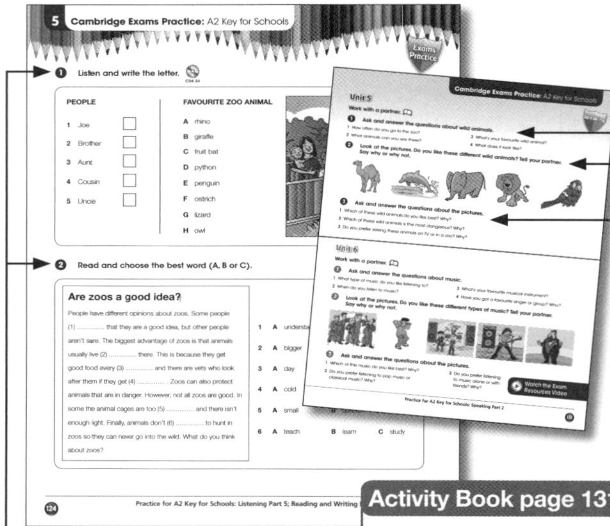
5 Cambridge Exams Practice: A2 Key for Schools

1 Listen and write the letter.

| PEOPLE | | FAVOURITE ZOO ANIMAL |
|---|---|---|
| 1 Joe | | A rhino |
| 2 Brother | | B giraffe |
| 3 Aunt | | C fruit bat |
| 4 Cousin | | D python |
| 5 Uncle | | E penguin |
| | | F ostrich |
| | | G lizard |
| | | H owl |

2 Read and choose the best word (A, B or C).

Are zoos a good idea?

Practice for A2 Key for Schools: Listening Part 5; Reading and Writing 124

Cambridge Exams Practice: A2 Key for Schools

Unit 5
Work with a partner.
1 Ask and answer the questions about wild animals.
2 Look at the pictures. Do you like these different wild animals? Tell your partner. Say why or why not.
3 Ask and answer the questions about the pictures.

Unit 6
Work with a partner.
1 Ask and answer the questions about music.
2 Look at the pictures. Do you like these different types of music? Tell your partner. Say why or why not.
3 Ask and answer the questions about the pictures.

Practice for A2 Key for Schools: Speaking Part 2

### Activity Book page 124

**A2 Key for Schools: Listening Part 4**

**Activity 1**

- Listen and write the letter.

▶ ***CD4 Track 34 p298***

**A2 Key for Schools: Reading and Writing Part 5**

**Activity 2**

- Read and choose the best word (A, B or C).

### Activity Book page 131

**A2 Key for Schools: Speaking Part 2**

**Activity 1**

- Ask and answer the questions about wild animals.

**Activity 2**

- Look at the pictures.
- Do you like these different wild animals?
- Tell your partner.
- Say why or why not.

**Activity 3**

- Ask and answer the questions about the pictures.

**Starting the lesson**

**Use the Trinity Exams Practice cards (optional).**
- The pupils practise asking and answering questions.

**Review verbs of the senses.**
- Close your eyes, hold out your hand, choose a sensible pupil and say **Put an object in my hand.** Describe how the object feels, smells and sounds (by knocking it gently on the desk), ie **It feels hard. It smells like wood.** Then guess what it is. Pupils tell you if you're right or not. Pupils repeat the activity in pairs.

**Set learning objectives and use the talk cards.**
- Say **Today we're going to practise activities for an exam and remember what we've learnt in Unit 5**.
- Point to the talk cards to show the pupils the different ways they will be working in the lesson.

**Pupil's Book Activity 1**

**A2 Key for Schools: Reading and Writing Part 4**

**Read, think and say. How are these words different?**
- Ask pupils in pairs to think of something hard, something long and something heavy. Elicit ideas.

**Pupil's Book Activity 2**

**A2 Key for Schools: Reading and Writing Part 4**

**Read and complete the sentence with a word from Activity 1.**
- Read the sentence with the pupils. Ask them to raise their hands if they think *hard* is the answer. Repeat with *long* and *heavy*.

**Answer:** A

**Pupil's Book Activity 3**

**A2 Key for Schools: Reading and Writing Part 4**

**Read the text with the missing words. Close your books. What shark facts can you remember?**
- Give pupils 3 minutes to read the text. Then they close their books. In pairs, students think of other information they remember. After a few minutes, they can open their books to check.

**Pupil's Book Activity 4**

**A2 Key for Schools: Reading and Writing Part 4**

**Read the text again. Choose the correct answer for each gap.**
- Pupils choose the answers. Then they check in pairs and explain why their answers are correct.

**Answers:** **1** C **2** A **3** B **4** C **5** A **6** C

**Pupil's Book Activity 5**

**A2 Key for Schools: Reading and Writing Part 4**

**Read the text a third time. Does the completed text make sense?**
- Tell pupils to check their answers by reading the text with the answers. Tell them they should always use clues in the text to confirm their answers.

**Exam help**
- Read the Exam help as a class.

**External Exams Video**

**Additional Cambridge Exams Practice Video: A2 Key for Schools**
- Additional external exams preparation material, including videos, worksheets and practice tests, can be found in the Teacher's Resource Bank on Navio.

**Activity Book page 124**

**Activity 1**

**A2 Key for Schools: Listening Part 5**

**Listen and write the letter.**

▶ *CD4 Track 34 p298*
- Ask **How many people are there? How many animals are there?** Explain that pupils need to listen for each person's favourite animal.
- Play the CD. Pause after you hear *… I think the giraffes were the best.* Ask **Which animals did you hear for Adam?** (*rhinos and giraffes*) **What is the answer?** (*giraffes*) **Why?** (*because he thinks they were the best*).
- Play the rest of the track. Then check as a class.

**Answers:** **1** A **2** D **3** E **4** C **5** G

**Activity 2**

**A2 Key for Schools: Reading and Writing Part 4**

**Read and choose the best word (A, B or C).**
- Ask the pupils to read the text quickly.
- Pupils choose the answers. Then check as a class.

**Answers:** **1** B **2** C **3** A **4** B **5** A **6** B

**Activity Book page 131**

**A2 Key for Schools: Speaking Part 2**

This section helps pupils to practise Part 2 of the A2 Key for Schools Speaking exam. In the first phase of Part 2, candidates are presented with artwork on a particular topic. They discuss the artwork together. In the second phase, the interlocutor extends the conversation with further questions related to the topic.

**Activity 1**

**Ask and answer the questions about wild animals.**
- Brainstorm vocabulary for wild animals. Then pupils discuss the questions in pairs.

**Activity 2**

**Look at the pictures. Do you like these different wild animals? Tell your partner. Say why or why not.**
- Ask different pupils to describe each picture. Then pupils give their opinions about the different places in pairs. Make sure they justify their opinions with *because*.

**Activity 3**

**Ask and answer the questions about the pictures.**
- Pupils discuss the questions. Round off the activity by asking different pairs to ask and answer each question in front of the class.

**Ending the lesson**

**Review the lesson and reflect on learning.**
- Say **Today we've practised activities for an exam and remembered what we've learnt in Unit 5**.
- Ask **Which was your favourite activity today? Which activity was easy / difficult?**

### Key Competences and Key Learning Outcomes

- Review vocabulary for making art and entertainment
- Practise the following Key for Schools tasks: Reading and Writing Part 7, Listening Part 1 and Speaking Part 2
- Learn about which tenses you need to use when writing a story

**Key language**
- *circus, clown, lion, lovely, tiger*

**Materials**
- Pupil's Book p120; Activity Book p125 & 131; Class CD4; Teacher's App on Navio
- Teacher's Resource Bank: Talk cards

**Optional materials**
- Teacher's Resource Bank: Trinity Exams Practice cards (selected from Unit 1–6)

## At a Glance Lesson Plan

### Starting the lesson
- Use the Trinity Exams Practice cards (optional).
- Review vocabulary for making art and entertainment.
- Set learning objectives and use the talk cards.

### Activity 1
**A2 Key for Schools: Reading and Writing Part 7**
- Work in pairs and look at the exam question.
- Write down five words that are important in the story.
- Compare your list with another pair.
- Are they the same?

### Activity 2
**A2 Key for Schools: Reading and Writing Part 7**
- Two pupils, David and Milly, have written stories from the pictures.
- Answer the questions.
- Which story do you think will get the best mark?

## Pupil's Book

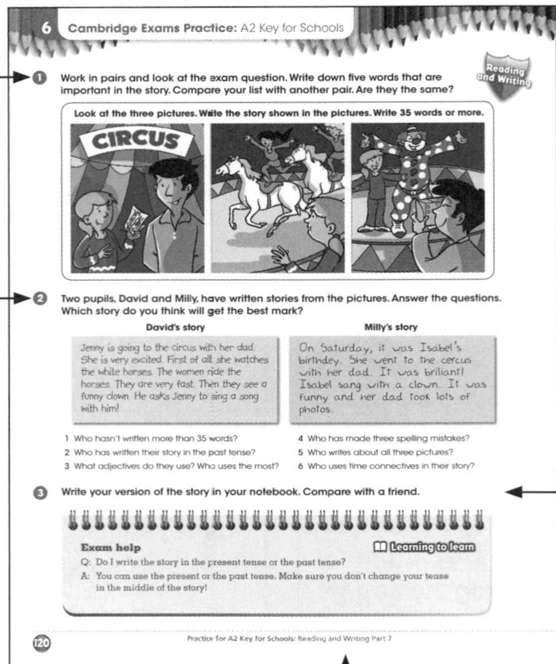
6 Cambridge Exams Practice: A2 Key for Schools

1 Work in pairs and look at the exam question. Write down five words that are important in the story. Compare your list with another pair. Are they the same?

Look at the three pictures. Write the story shown in the pictures. Write 35 words or more.

2 Two pupils, David and Milly, have written stories from the pictures. Answer the questions. Which story do you think will get the best mark?

David's story

Jenny is going to the circus with her dad. She is very excited. First of all she watches the white horses. The women ride the horses. They are very fast. Then they see a funny clown. He asks Jenny to sing a song with him!

Milly's story

On Saturday, it was Isabel's birthday. She went to the circus with her dad. It was brilliant! Isabel sang with a clown. It was funny and her dad took lots of photos.

1 Who hasn't written more than 35 words?
2 Who has written their story in the past tense?
3 What adjectives do they use? Who uses the most?
4 Who has made three spelling mistakes?
5 Who writes about all three pictures?
6 Who uses time connectives in their story?

3 Write your version of the story in your notebook. Compare with a friend.

Exam help
Q: Do I write the story in the present tense or the past tense?
A: You can use the present or the past tense. Make sure you don't change your tense in the middle of the story!

120 Practice for A2 Key for Schools: Reading and Writing Part 7

### Activity 3
**A2 Key for Schools: Reading and Writing Part 7**
- Write your version of the story in your notebook.
- Compare with a friend.
- Go to the Activity Book.

### Exam help
- Read the Exam help as a class.

### Ending the lesson
- Review the lesson and reflect on learning.

### Extra activity
**Reinforcement**
- Build a short story as a class.

### External Exams Video
**Additional Cambridge Exams Practice Video: A2 Key for Schools**
- Additional external exams preparation material, including videos, worksheets and practice tests, can be found in the Teacher's Resource Bank on Navio.

### Digital resources

**Teacher's Digital:** You can also teach this lesson using the Teacher's App on Navio.

**Pupil's Digital:** Encourage your pupils to use the Pupil's App on Navio to practise the activities from this lesson.

Powered By NAVIO

## Activity Book

### Activity Book page 125
**A2 Key for Schools: Listening Part 1**
**Activity 1**
- Listen and tick (✓) the right answer (A, B or C).

▶ ***CD4 Track 35 p299***

**A2 Key for Schools: Reading and Writing Part 7**
**Activity 2**
- Look at the three pictures.
- Write the story shown in the pictures. Write 35 words or more.

### Activity Book page 131
**A2 Key for Schools: Speaking Part 2**
**Activity 1**
- Ask and answer the questions about music.

**Activity 2**
- Look at the pictures.
- Do you like these different types music?
- Tell your partner.
- Say why or why not.

**Activity 3**
- Ask and answer the questions about the pictures.

# Detailed Lesson Plan

**Starting the lesson**

**Use the Trinity Exams Practice cards (optional).**

- The pupils practise asking and answering questions.

**Review making art and entertainment vocabulary.**

- Say **What am I doing?** Mime one of the marking art and entertainment vocabulary items. When students guess it correctly, invite a pupil to the front of the class and give him/her a new item to mime. Repeat for the remaining items.

**Set learning objectives and use the talk cards.**

- Say **Today we're going to practise activities for an exam and remember what we've learnt in Unit 6**.
- Point to the talk cards to show the pupils the different ways they will be working in the lesson.

**Pupil's Book Activity 1**

**A2 Key for Schools: Reading and Writing Part 7**

**Work in pairs and look at the exam question. Write down five words that are important in the story. Compare your list with another pair. Are they the same?**

- Pupils work in pairs and write words for the pictures. Finally make a class list of important words and agree on the five most important.

**Pupil's Book Activity 2**

**A2 Key for Schools: Reading and Writing Part 7**

**Two pupils, David and Milly, have written stories from the pictures. Answer the questions. Which story do you think will get the best mark?**

- Pupils read the stories and answer the questions.
- Check answers as a class. Then ask: **Is it important to write about all 3 pictures?** (yes) **Is it important to write 35 words or more?** (yes) **Is it important to use the past tense?** (no, you can use past tenses or present tenses) **Is it important to use adjectives and connectives?** (yes, because they make the story easier to read and more interesting) Ask pupils to say who will get a better mark.

**Answer:** **1** Milly **2** Milly **3** David: excited, white, fast, funny; Milly: brilliant, funny **4** Milly (birthday, circus, brilliant) **5** David **6** David
David's story will get the best mark.

**Pupil's Book Activity 3**

**A2 Key for Schools: Reading and Writing Part 7**

**Write your version of the story in your notebook. Compare with a friend.**

- Pupils write their own stories.
- Pupils swap their stories. They can use the questions in Activity 2 to decide if the stories will get a good mark.

**Exam help**

- Read the Exam help as a class.

**External Exams Video**

**Additional Cambridge Exams Practice Video: A2 Key for Schools**

- Additional external exams preparation material, including videos, worksheets and practice tests, can be found in the Teacher's Resource Bank on Navio.

**Activity Book page 125**

**Activity 1**

**A2 Key for Schools: Listening Part 1**

**Listen and tick (✓) the right answer (A, B or C).**

▸ ***CD4 Track 35 p299***

- Ask different pupils to describe the pictures in Question 1.
- Play the CD. Pupils tick the correct letter. Then check as a class.

**Answers:** **1** B **2** A **3** C **4** C

**Activity 2**

**A2 Key for Schools: Reading and Writing Part 7**

**Look at the three pictures. Write the story shown in the pictures. Write 35 words or more.**

- Ask pupils to briefly describe the pictures before they write their stories. Then they swap their stories with a partner and check them as if they are examiners.

**Suggested answer:** Rob arrived at his school concert with his guitar. He was feeling very nervous. Soon, the concert started. Rob's friend Josh was playing the drums. All their friends were watching. Rob wasn't feeling nervous now – he was feeling great!

**Activity Book page 131**

**A2 Key for Schools: Speaking Part 2**

This section helps pupils to practise Part 2 of the A2 Key for Schools Speaking exam. In the first phase of Part 2, candidates are presented with artwork on a particular topic. They discuss the artwork together. In the second phase, the interlocutor extends the conversation with further questions related to the topic.

**Activity 1**

**Ask and answer the questions about music.**

- Brainstorm vocabulary for types of music and musical instruments. Then pupils discuss the questions in pairs.

**Activity 2**

**Look at the pictures. Do you like these different types of music? Tell your partner. Say why or why not.**

- Ask different pupils to describe each picture. Then pupils give their opinions about the different places in pairs. Make sure they justify their opinions with *because*.

**Activity 3**

**Ask and answer the questions about the pictures.**

- Pupils discuss the questions. Round off the activity by asking different pairs to ask and answer each question in front of the class.

**Ending the lesson**

**Review the lesson and reflect on learning.**

- Say **Today we've practised activities for an exam and remembered what we've learnt in Unit 6**.
- Ask **Which was your favourite activity today? Which activity was easy / difficult?**

**Extra activity**

**Reinforcement**

- Build a short story as a class. Say the first line of a story, ie **Last week, Anna went to the beach.** Choose a pupil to say the next line of the story. Continue with more pupils until you feel the story has finished.

## Key Competences and Key Learning Outcomes

- Review accidents vocabulary and Present perfect with *just*
- Practise the following Key for Schools tasks: Reading and Writing Part 5, Listening Part 5 and Speaking Part 2
- Learn a strategy for when you don't know a missing word
- Think about the importance of visiting someone who has had an accident

## Key language

- *look forward, message, missing, plural, preposition, popcorn, score a goal, singular*

## Materials

- Pupil's Book p121; Activity Book p126 & 132; Class CD4; Teacher's App on Navio
- Teacher's Resource Bank: Talk cards

## Optional materials

- Teacher's Resource Bank: Trinity Exams Practice cards (selected from Unit 1–7)

# At a Glance Lesson Plan

### Starting the lesson

- Use the Trinity Exams Practice cards (optional).
- Review accidents vocabulary.
- Set learning objectives and use the talk cards.

### Activity 1

**A2 Key for Schools: Reading and Writing Part 5**

- Read the message with the missing words.
- Which photo is Ruby?

### Activity 2

**A2 Key for Schools: Reading and Writing Part 5**

- Read the text again.
- Read the clues and think of a word for each gap.

### Activity 3

**A2 Key for Schools: Reading and Writing Part 5**

- Compare your answers with a friend.
- Explain why you chose each word.

Go to the Activity Book.

## Pupil's Book

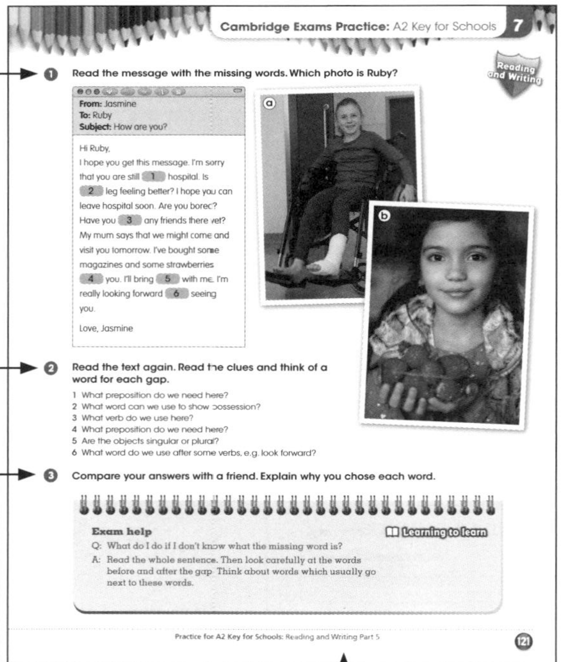


### Exam help

- Read the Exam help as a class.

### Ending the lesson

- Review the lesson and reflect on learning.

### Extra activity

**Reinforcement**

- Play a miming game to revise Present perfect with *just*.

### External Exams Video

**Additional Cambridge Exams Practice Video: A2 Key for Schools**

- Additional external exams preparation material, including videos, worksheets and practice tests, can be found in the Teacher's Resource Bank on Navio.

### Digital resources

**Teacher's Digital:** You can also teach this lesson using the Teacher's App on Navio.

**Pupil's Digital:** Encourage your pupils to use the Pupil's App on Navio to practise the activities from this lesson.

Powered By NAVIO

## Activity Book

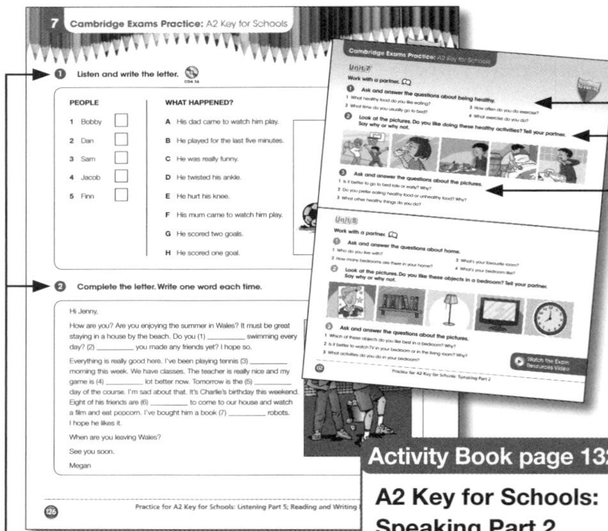


### Activity Book page 126

**A2 Key for Schools: Listening Part 5**

**Activity 1**

- Listen and write the letter.

▶ *CD4 Track 36 p299*

**A2 Key for Schools: Reading and Writing Part 5**

**Activity 2**

- Complete the letter. Write one word each time.

### Activity Book page 132

**A2 Key for Schools: Speaking Part 2**

**Activity 1**

- Ask and answer the questions about being healthy.

**Activity 2**

- Look at the pictures.
- Do you like doing these healthy activities?
- Tell your partner.
- Say why or why not.

**Activity 3**

- Ask and answer the questions about the pictures.

# Detailed Lesson Plan

### Starting the lesson

**Use the Trinity Exams Practice cards (optional).**

- The pupils practise asking and answering questions.

**Review accidents vocabulary.**

- Play a memory game with the accidents vocabulary flashcards. Show them to the pupils one by one, and place them facing down or facing away in different parts of the room. Remember what the items show! Then say sentences in the present perfect to describe the flashcards, ie **She's cut her finger.** Pupils try to remember where the card is and point to it. Reveal the correct card each time. After you have said all the items, point to a flashcard, tell pupils to remember what the item is and make a present perfect sentence.

**Set learning objectives and use the talk cards.**

- Say **Today we're going to practise activities for an exam and remember what we've learnt in Unit 7**.
- Point to the talk cards to show the pupils the different ways they will be working in the lesson.

### Pupil's Book Activity 1

**A2 Key for Schools: Reading and Writing Part 5**

**Read the message with the missing words. Which photo is Ruby?**

- Ask pupils to describe the photos. Ask **Have you ever had an accident and been to hospital? What happened?** Different pupils describe their experiences.
- Pupils read the email quickly and identify Ruby. Ask them how they know which girl is her.

**Answers:** a is Ruby

### Pupil's Book Activity 2

**A2 Key for Schools: Reading and Writing Part 5**

**Read the text again. Read the clues and think of a word for each gap.**

- Pupils read and answer the questions. Make sure they understand that the questions in Activity 2 relate to the gaps in Activity 1.

**Answers:** **1** in **2** your **3** made **4** for **5** them **6** to

### Pupil's Book Activity 3

**A2 Key for Schools: Reading and Writing Part 5**

**Compare your answers with a friend. Explain why you chose each word.**

- Pupils compare their answers in pairs. If they have any different answers, tell them to decide together which they think are correct. Then check as a class. Ask **Are the missing words usually long or short?** (short)

### Exam help

- Read the Exam help as a class.

### External Exams Video

**Additional Cambridge Exams Practice Video: A2 Key for Schools**

- Additional external exams preparation material, including videos, worksheets and practice tests, can be found in the Teacher's Resource Bank on Navio.

### Activity Book page 126

**Activity 1**

**A2 Key for Schools: Listening Part 5**

**Listen and write the letter.**

▸ *CD4 Track 36 p299*

- Ask **How many people are there? How many sentences are there?** Explain that pupils need to listen carefully to match the actions to the people – they will hear ideas from all the sentences but only five of them are correct.
- Play the CD. Then check answers as a class.

**Answers:** **1** G **2** E **3** H **4** F **5** B

**Activity 2**

**A2 Key for Schools: Reading and Writing Part 5**

**Complete the letter. Write one word each time.**

- Pupils work alone to complete the letter. Tell them to decide first what type of word they need – preposition, pronoun, verb, etc. If they don't know, tell them to guess – it's always better to put an answer, even if it's wrong. Then they check in pairs and explain why they chose those words. Then check as a class.

**Answers:** **1** go **2** Have **3** every / each **4** a **5** last **6** going **7** about / on

### Activity Book page 132

**A2 Key for Schools: Speaking Part 2**

This section helps pupils to practise Part 2 of the A2 Key for Schools Speaking exam. In the first phase of Part 2, candidates are presented with artwork on a particular topic. They discuss the artwork together. In the second phase, the interlocutor extends the conversation with further questions related to the topic.

**Activity 1**

**Ask and answer the questions about being healthy.**

- Brainstorm vocabulary for healthy food and activities. Then pupils discuss the questions in pairs.

**Activity 2**

**Look at the pictures. Do you like doing these healthy activities? Tell your partner. Say why or why not.**

- Ask different pupils to describe each picture. Then pupils give their opinions about the different places in pairs. Make sure they justify their opinions with *because*.

**Activity 3**

**Ask and answer the questions about the pictures.**

- Pupils discuss the questions. Round off the activity by asking different pairs to ask and answer each question in front of the class.

### Ending the lesson

**Review the lesson and reflect on learning.**

- Say **Today we've practised activities for an exam and remembered what we've learnt in Unit 7**.
- Ask **Which was your favourite activity today? Which activity was easy / difficult?**

### Extra activity

**Reinforcement**

- Mime waking up to the class and elicit the sentence *You've just woken up*. Invite pupils to the front of the class and give them more sentences beginning *You've just* to mime. Examples you could use: You've just twisted your ankle. You've just received some good news. You've just finished class. You've just eaten a big lunch.

### Key Competences and Key Learning Outcomes

- Review the passive

- Practise the following Key for Schools tasks: Reading and Writing Part 5, Listening Part 2 and Speaking Part 2
- Learn about what kinds of words are usually missing in this exam task

- Read a text about the importance of cleaning up your neighbourhood

### Key language

- *arts and crafts, barbecue, can, factory, hobby, rubbish, pick up, pond, secretary*

### Materials

- Pupil's Book p122; Activity Book p127 & 132; Class CD4; Teacher's App on Navio
- Teacher's Resource Bank: Talk cards

### Optional materials

- Teacher's Resource Bank: Trinity Exams Practice cards (selected from Unit 1–8)

## At a Glance Lesson Plan

### Pupil's Book

**Starting the lesson**

- Use the Trinity Exams Practice cards (optional).
- Review the topic of recycling.
- Set learning objectives and use the talk cards.

**Activity 1**

**A2 Key for Schools: Reading and Writing Part 5**

- Look at the subject of the email.
- What do you think the email is about?

**Activity 2**

**A2 Key for Schools: Reading and Writing Part 5**

- Read the email to find out if you are right.

**Activity 3**

**A2 Key for Schools: Reading and Writing Part 5**

- Read the text again.
- Read the clues and think of a word for each gap.

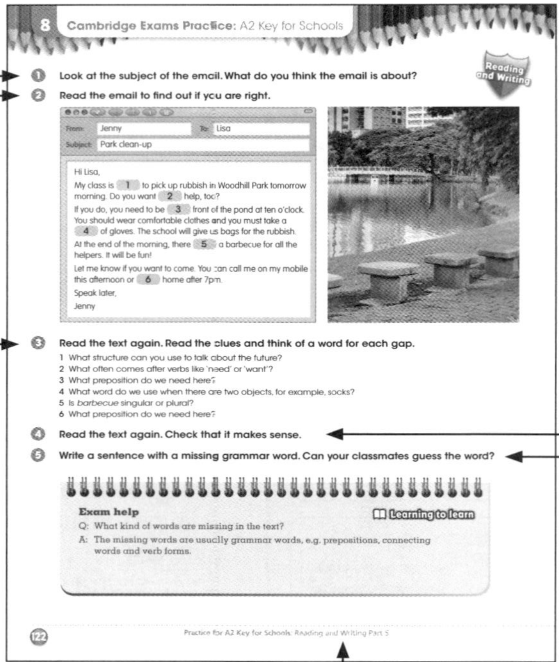
8 Cambridge Exams Practice: A2 Key for Schools

Reading and Writing

1 Look at the subject of the email. What do you think the email is about?

2 Read the email to find out if you are right.

From: Jenny To: Lisa
Subject: Park clean-up

Hi Lisa,
My class is (1) to pick up rubbish in Woodhill Park tomorrow morning. Do you want (2) help, too?
If you do, you need to be (3) front of the pond at ten o'clock. You should wear comfortable clothes and you must take a (4) of gloves. The school will give us bags for the rubbish.
At the end of the morning, there (5) a barbecue for all the helpers. It will be fun!
Let me know if you want to come. You can call me on my mobile this afternoon or (6) home after 7pm.
Speak later,
Jenny

3 Read the text again. Read the clues and think of a word for each gap.
1 What structure can you use to talk about the future?
2 What often comes after verbs like 'need' or 'want'?
3 What preposition do we need here?
4 What word do we use when there are two objects, for example, socks?
5 Is barbecue singular or plural?
6 What preposition do we need here?

4 Read the text again. Check that it makes sense.

5 Write a sentence with a missing grammar word. Can your classmates guess the word?

Exam help
Learning to learn
Q: What kind of words are missing in the text?
A: The missing words are usually grammar words, e.g. prepositions, connecting words and verb forms.

122

**Activity 4**

**A2 Key for Schools: Reading and Writing Part 5**

- Read the text again.
- Check that it makes sense.

**Activity 5**

**A2 Key for Schools: Reading and Writing Part 5**

- Write a sentence with a missing grammar word.
- Can your classmates guess the word?

Go to the Activity Book.

**Exam help**

- Read the Exam help as a class.

**Extra activity**

**Reinforcement**

- Do a true/false quiz to revise the passive.

**External Exams Video**

**Additional Cambridge Exams Practice Video: A2 Key for Schools**

- Additional external exams preparation material, including videos, worksheets and practice tests, can be found in the Teacher's Resource Bank on Navio.

### Digital resources

**Teacher's Digital:** You can also teach this lesson using the Teacher's App on Navio.

**Pupil's Digital:** Encourage your pupils to use the Pupil's App on Navio to practise the activities from this lesson.

Powered By NAVIO

### Activity Book

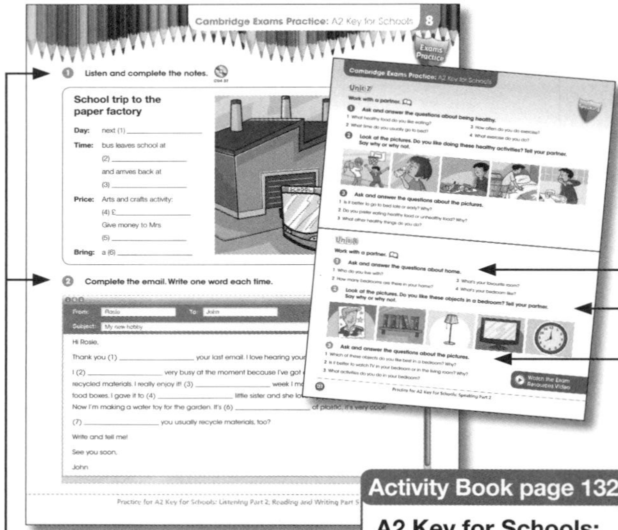
Cambridge Exams Practice: A2 Key for Schools 8

1 Listen and complete the notes.

School trip to the paper factory
Day: next (1)
Time: bus leaves school at (2)
and arrives back at (3)
Price: Arts and crafts activity: (4) £
Give money to Mrs (5)
Bring: a (6)

2 Complete the email. Write one word each time.

**Activity Book page 127**

**A2 Key for Schools: Listening Part 2**

**Activity 1**

- Listen and complete the notes.

▶ *CD4 Track 37 p299*

**A2 Key for Schools: Reading and Writing Part 5**

**Activity 2**

- Complete the email. Write one word each time.

**Activity Book page 132**

**A2 Key for Schools: Speaking Part 2**

**Activity 1**

- Ask and answer the questions about home.

**Activity 2**

- Look at the pictures.
- Do you like doing these objects in a bedroom?
- Tell your partner.
- Say why or why not.

**Activity 3**

- Ask and answer the questions about the pictures.

**Starting the lesson**

**Use the Trinity Exams Practice cards (optional).**

- The pupils practise asking and answering questions.

**Review the topic of recycling.**

- Ask pupils **What do you recycle? What recycled products can we buy? Why is recycling important?** Pupils discuss the questions in pairs.

**Set learning objectives and use the talk cards.**

- Say **Today we're going to practise activities for an exam and remember what we've learnt in Unit 8.**
- Point to the talk cards to show the pupils the different ways they will be working in the lesson.

**Pupil's Book Activity 1**

**A2 Key for Schools: Reading and Writing Part 5**

**Look at the subject of the email. What do you think the email is about?**

- Ask pupils to describe the photo. Ask **Does the park look clean?** Then they offer ideas about the email.

**Answer:** It's about a class trip to a park to pick up rubbish.

**Pupil's Book Activity 2**

**A2 Key for Schools: Reading and Writing Part 5**

**Read the email to find out if you are right.**

- Pupils read the email. Ask general questions to check understanding.
- Ask **Have you ever picked up rubbish in your town? Would you like to?** Pupils offer ideas.

**Pupil's Book Activity 3**

**A2 Key for Schools: Reading and Writing Part 5**

**Read the text again. Read the clues and think of a word for each gap.**

- Ask pupils **Are the missing words usually long or short?** (short) Then direct them to the gaps and the sentences.
- Pupils work alone to complete the letter. Tell them to decide first what type of word they need – preposition, pronoun, verb, etc. If they don't know, tell them to guess – it's always better to put an answer, even if it's wrong. Don't check answers yet.

**Pupil's Book Activity 4**

**A2 Key for Schools: Reading and Writing Part 5**

**Read the text again. Check that it makes sense.**

- Tell pupils to check their work. Then check as a class.

**Answers:** **1** going **2** to **3** in **4** pair **5** is **6** at

**Pupil's Book Activity 5**

**A2 Key for Schools: Reading and Writing Part 5**

**Write a sentence with a missing grammar word. Can your classmates guess the word?**

- Tell pupils to write sentences and choose words to gap. Choose sentences from several pairs or pupils and allow the whole class to try to find their missing words.

**Exam help**

- Read the Exam help as a class.

**External Exams Video**

**Additional Cambridge Exams Practice Video: A2 Key for Schools**

- Additional external exams preparation material, including videos, worksheets and practice tests, can be found in the Teacher's Resource Bank on Navio.

**Activity Book page 127**

**Activity 1**

**A2 Key for Schools: Listening Part 5**

**Listen and complete the notes.**

▶ ***CD4 Track 37 p299***

- Tell pupils to look at the picture. Ask **What place are you going to hear information about? What information do you need?** Explain that they need to write one word or number in each gap.
- Play the CD. Pause after each answer.
- Play the CD again without pausing. Then check answers as a class.

**Answers:** **1** Monday **2** 8.30 **3** 4 o'clock **4** 0 / free **5** Thomas **6** snack

**Activity 2**

**A2 Key for Schools: Reading and Writing Part 5**

**Complete the email. Write one word each time.**

- Pupils work alone to complete the email. Then they check in pairs and explain why they chose those words. Then check as a class.

**Answers:** **1** for **2** am **3** Last **4** my **5** it **6** made **7** Do

**Activity Book page 132**

**A2 Key for Schools: Speaking Part 2**

This section helps pupils to practise Part 2 of the A2 Key for Schools Speaking exam.

**Activity 1**

**Ask and answer the questions about home.**

- Brainstorm vocabulary for rooms and objects in a house. Then pupils discuss the questions in pairs.

**Activity 2**

**Look at the pictures. Do you like these objects in a bedroom? Tell your partner. Say why or why not.**

- Ask different pupils to describe each picture. Then pupils give their opinions about the different places in pairs. Make sure they justify their opinions with *because*.

**Activity 3**

**Ask and answer the questions about the pictures.**

- Pupils discuss the questions. Round off the activity by asking different pairs to ask and answer each question in front of the class.

**Ending the lesson**

**Review the lesson and reflect on learning.**

- Say **Today we've practised activities for an exam and remembered what we've learnt in Unit 8.**
- Ask **Which was your favourite activity today? Which activity was easy / difficult?**

## Key Competences and Key Learning Outcomes

- Review present continuous for future plans and natural places vocabulary
- Practise the following Key for Schools tasks: Reading and Writing Part 6, Listening Part 1 and Speaking Part 2
- Learn the most important thing to check when you finish writing

**Key language**
- *bell, milkshake, tour bus, tower, wide*

**Materials**
- Pupil's Book p123; Activity Book p128 & 133; Class CD4; Teacher's App on Navio
- Teacher's Resource Bank: Talk cards

**Optional materials**
- Teacher's Resource Bank: Trinity Exams Practice cards (selected from Unit 1–9)

# At a Glance Lesson Plan

## Pupil's Book

### Starting the lesson
- Use the Trinity Exams Practice cards (optional).
- Review present continuous for future plans.
- Set learning objectives and use the talk cards.

### Activity 1
**A2 Key for Schools: Reading and Writing Part 6**
- Look at the photo.
- What do you think the text messages are about?

### Activity 2
**A2 Key for Schools: Reading and Writing Part 6**
- Luke sent text messages to three different friends.
- Read their answers.
- Which three questions did Luke ask?

### Activity 3
**A2 Key for Schools: Reading and Writing Part 6**
- Read the exam question and the pupils' answers.
- Answer the questions.

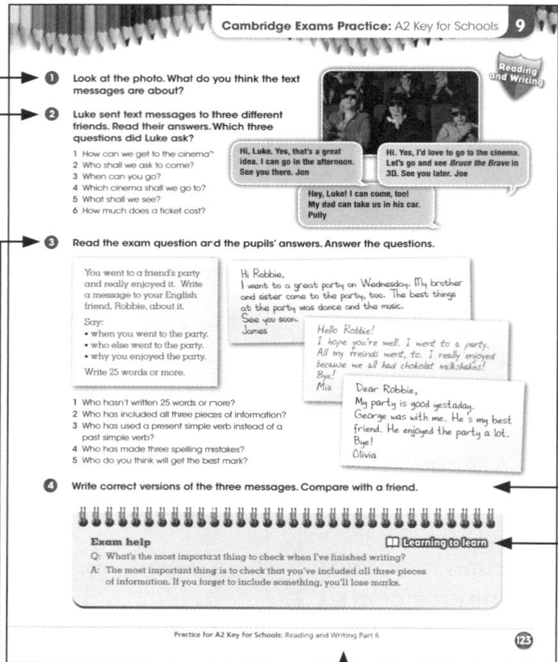
Cambridge Exams Practice: A2 Key for Schools 9

1 Look at the photo. What do you think the text messages are about?

2 Luke sent text messages to three different friends. Read their answers. Which three questions did Luke ask?
1 How can we get to the cinema?
2 Who shall we ask to come?
3 When can you go?
4 Which cinema shall we go to?
5 What shall we see?
6 How much does a ticket cost?

Hi, Luke. Yes, that's a great idea. I can go in the afternoon. See you there. Jon
Hi. Yes, I'd love to go to the cinema. Let's go and see *Bruce the Brave* in 3D. See you later. Joe
Hey, Luke! I can come, too! My dad can take us in his car. Polly

3 Read the exam question and the pupils' answers. Answer the questions.

You went to a friend's party and really enjoyed it. Write a message to your English friend, Robbie, about it.
Say:
- when you went to the party.
- who else went to the party.
- why you enjoyed the party.
Write 25 words or more.

Hi Robbie,
I went to a great party on Wednesday. My brother and sister come to the party, too. The best things at the party was dance and the music.
See you soon.
James

Hello Robbie!
I hope you're well. I went to a party. All my friends went, to. I really enjoyed because we all had chokolat milkshakes!
Bye!
Mia

Dear Robbie,
My party is good yestaday. George was with me. He's my best friend. He enjoyed the party a lot.
Bye!
Olivia

1 Who hasn't written 25 words or more?
2 Who has included all three pieces of information?
3 Who has used a present simple verb instead of a past simple verb?
4 Who has made three spelling mistakes?
5 Who do you think will get the best mark?

4 Write correct versions of the three messages. Compare with a friend.

Exam help
Learning to learn
Q: What's the most important thing to check when I've finished writing?
A: The most important thing is to check that you've included all three pieces of information. If you forget to include something, you'll lose marks.

Practice for A2 Key for Schools: Reading and Writing Part 6 123

### Activity 4
**A2 Key for Schools: Reading and Writing Part 6**
- Write correct versions of the three messages.
- Compare with a friend.

Go to the Activity Book.

### Exam help
- Read the Exam help as a class.

### Extra activity
**Reinforcement**
- Play a guessing game to revise natural places.

### External Exams Video
**Additional Cambridge Exams Practice Video: A2 Key for Schools**
- Additional external exams preparation material, including videos, worksheets and practice tests, can be found in the Teacher's Resource Bank on Navio.

## Activity Book

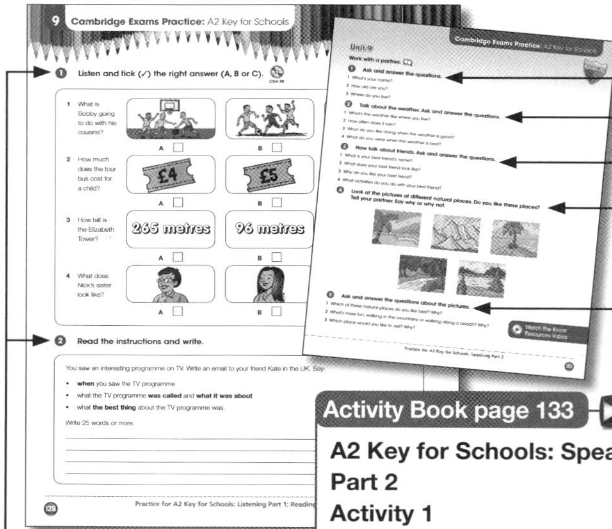
9 Cambridge Exams Practice: A2 Key for Schools

1 Listen and tick (✓) the right answer (A, B or C).
1 What is Scooby going to do with his cousins?
2 How much does the tour bus cost for a child?
£4 £5
3 How tall is the Elizabeth Tower?
265 metres 96 metres
4 What does Nick's sister look like?

2 Read the instructions and write.

Practice for A2 Key for Schools: Listening Part 1; Reading and Writing Part 1 128

Cambridge Exams Practice: A2 Key for Schools

Practice for A2 Key for Schools: Speaking Part 2 133

### Activity Book page 128
**A2 Key for Schools: Listening Part 1**
**Activity 1**
- Listen and tick (✓) the right answer (A, B or C).

▶ *CD4 Track 38 p299*

**A2 Key for Schools: Reading and Writing Part 1**
**Activity 2**
- Read the instructions and write.

### Activity Book page 133
**A2 Key for Schools: Speaking Part 2**
**Activity 1**
- Ask and answer the questions.

**Activity 2**
- Talk about the weather. Ask and answer the questions.

**Activity 3**
- Now talk about friends. Ask and answer the questions.

**Activity 4**
- Look at the pictures of different natural places.
- Do you like doing these places?
- Tell your partner.
- Say why or why not.

**Activity 5**
- Ask and answer the questions about the pictures.

## Digital resources

**Teacher's Digital:** You can also teach this lesson using the Teacher's App on Navio.

**Pupil's Digital:** Encourage your pupils to use the Pupil's App on Navio to practise the activities from this lesson.

Powered By NAVIO

**Starting the lesson**

**Use the Trinity Exams Practice cards (optional).**

- The pupils practise asking and answering questions.

**Review present continuous for future.**

- Say **Stand up if you're going to the cinema this weekend. Sit down if you're visiting your grandparents next week.** Continue with more instructions and present continuous sentences with a future time phrase.

**Set learning objectives and use the talk cards.**

- Say **Today we're going to practise activities for an exam and remember what we've learnt in Unit 9**.
- Point to the talk cards to show the pupils the different ways they will be working in the lesson.

**Pupil's Book Activity 1**

**A2 Key for Schools: Reading and Writing Part 6**

**Look at the photo. What do you think the text messages are about?**

- Ask pupils to describe the photo and say what they think the text messages are about as a class.

**Answer:** They're about a trip to the cinema.

**Pupil's Book Activity 2**

**A2 Key for Schools: Reading and Writing Part 6**

**Luke sent text messages to three different friends. Read their answers. Which three questions did Luke ask?**

- Read the text messages with the class.
- Pupils work in pairs to identify who answered the questions and what they said. Then check as a class.

**Answers:** 1, 3, 5

**Pupil's Book Activity 3**

**A2 Key for Schools: Reading and Writing Part 6**

**Read the exam question and the pupils' answers. Answer the questions.**

- Read the exam question with the class. Pupils read the stories and answer the questions.
- Check answers as a class. Then ask: **Is it important to write 25 words or more?** (yes). **Is it important to include all three pieces of information?** (yes) **Is it important to use the past tense?** (yes)

**Answers:** **1** Olivia **2** Robbie didn't say when the party was, Olivia didn't say why she enjoyed the party. **3** James **4** Robbie **5** James will get the best mark because he answered all the questions well.

**Pupil's Book Activity 4**

**A2 Key for Schools: Reading and Writing Part 6**

**Write correct versions of the three messages. Compare with a friend.**

- Pupils work alone to correct all the mistakes. Then they swap and check each other's work.

**Exam help**

- Read the Exam help as a class.

**External Exams Video**

**Additional Cambridge Exams Practice Video: A2 Key for Schools**

- Additional external exams preparation material, including videos, worksheets and practice tests, can be found in the Teacher's Resource Bank on Navio.

**Activity Book page 128**

**Activity 1**

**A2 Key for Schools: Listening Part 1**

**Listen and tick (✓) the right answer (A, B or C).**

▸ *CD4 Track 38 p299*

- Play the CD. Pupils listen and tick the right answer. Then check as a class.

**Answers:** **1** A **2** 4 **3** B **4** C

**Activity 2**

**A2 Key for Schools: Reading and Writing Part 6**

**Read the instructions and write.**

- Pupils write their emails. Then they swap and check each other's emails.

**Suggested answer:** Hi Kate
Last night, I saw a really interesting TV programme. It was called Blue Earth, and it was about animals. For me, the best thing was the tiger!
See you soon, Lucy

**Activity Book page 133**

**A2 Key for Schools: Speaking Part 2**

This section helps pupils to practise Part 2 of the A2 Key for Schools Speaking exam.

**Activity 1**

**Ask and answer the questions.**

- Pupils take turns to answer the questions.

**Activity 2**

**Talk about the weather. Ask and answer the questions.**

- Brainstorm vocabulary for the weather. Then pupils discuss the questions in pairs.

**Activity 3**

**Now talk about friends. Ask and answer the questions.**

- If you want, put pupils with a different partner.

**Activity 4**

**Look at the pictures of different natural places. Do you like these places? Tell your partner. Say why or why not.**

- Ask different pupils to describe each picture. Then pupils give their opinions about the different places in pairs. Make sure they justify their opinions with *because*.

**Activity 5**

**Ask and answer the questions about the pictures.**

- Pupils discuss the questions. Round off the activity by asking different pairs to ask and answer each question in front of the class.

**Ending the lesson**

**Review the lesson and reflect on learning.**

- Say **Today we've practised activities for an exam and remembered what we've learnt in Unit 9**.

# Grammar and Vocabulary Practice answers

## Unit 1

### AB page 102 Activity 1

**1** go **2** is playing **3** 'm doing **4** don't play **5** 's snowing **6** Does; wear

### AB page 102 Activity 2

**1** My brother rides his bike to school. **2** Are you wearing your helmet? **3** What time do you go to bed? **4** I play football every day. **5** She isn't wearing baggy trousers today.

### AB page 102 Activity 3

Pupils act out the dialogue in pairs when they finish.

**1** too **2** enough **3** too **4** enough

### AB page 102 Activity 4

Read the speech bubbles with the class. Then pupils think of new actions to act out in pairs.

### AB page 102 Activity 5

**1** leggings **2** waistcoat **3** tracksuit **4** jeans **5** cardigan **6** belt

### AB page 102 Activity 6

**1** flowery **2** short-sleeved **3** tight **4** baggy **5** plain; patterned

## Unit 2

### AB page 103 Activity 1

**1** Was **2** Were **3** were **4** was **5** was **6** were

### AB page 103 Activity 2

**1** I went **2** Did you enjoy **3** My brother bought **4** I didn't jump **5** They saw **6** Did he swim

### AB page 103 Activity 3

Pupils act out the dialogue in pairs when they finish.

**1** go **2** was **3** go **4** met **5** took **6** walked **7** did **8** didn't **9** see **10** did

### AB page 103 Activity 4

Read the speech bubbles with the class. Then pupils think of new verbs and repeat the dialogue.

### AB page 103 Activity 5

**1** torch **2** matches **3** sun cream **4** rucksack **5** compass **6** life jacket

### AB page 103 Activity 6

**1** white water rafting **2** hiking **3** rock climbing **4** camping **5** mountain biking

## Unit 3

### AB page 104 Activity 1

**1** Victoria was running in the playground.
**2** Noel was writing an email. **3** My friends were watching the football match. **4** I was swimming in the swimming pool. **4** It was raining. **5** I was reading a book about animals.

### AB page 104 Activity 2

**1** Were you eating breakfast at eight o'clock?
**2** What were you doing at six o'clock? **3** Was it raining at lunchtime? **4** Was Alex playing football at four o'clock?

### AB page 104 Activity 3

Pupils act out the dialogue in pairs when they finish.

**1** started **2** was playing **3** had **4** did you do **5** decided **6** were watching

### AB page 104 Activity 4

Read the speech bubbles with the class. Then pupils think of new times and repeat the dialogue.

### AB page 104 Activity 5

**1** square **2** fountain **3** castle **4** traffic lights **4** bridge **5** statue

### AB page 104 Activity 6

**1** sightseeing **2** crossroads **3** pavement **4** pedestrian crossing **5** meet friends

## Unit 4

### AB page 105 Activity 1

**1** has to **2** don't have to **3** have to **4** have to **5** have to **6** doesn't have to

### AB page 105 Activity 2

**1** Joe had to tidy his room today. **2** I didn't have to walk to school today. **3** My dad had to play rugby at school. **4** We didn't have to bring our homework to school today.

### AB page 105 Activity 3

**Suggested answers: 1** you feel tired the next day **2** it's nice to have a picnic **3** they burn **4** people usually stay at home **5** the cars go

### AB page 105 Activity 4

Read the speech bubbles with the class. Then pupils think of their own machines in pairs.

### AB page 105 Activity 5

**1** laptop **2** karaoke **3** website **4** pause **5** tablet **6** computer game

### AB page 105 Activity 6

**1** interactive whiteboard **2** video call **3** mobile phone **4** webcam **5** swipe the screen

## Unit 5

### AB page 106 Activity 1

**1** can't **2** must **3** could **4** can't **5** might **6** can't

### AB page 106 Activity 2

**Suggested answers: 1** it can't be a mouse
**2** it might be a parrot **3** it might be a penguin
**4** it can't be a bird **5** it must be an insect
**6** it could be a giraffe **7** it can't be a shark

### AB page 106 Activity 3

Pupils act out the dialogue in pairs when they finish.

**1** taste **2** sounds **3** looks **4** smells

### AB page 106 Activity 4

**Suggested answers: 1** loud **2** might be silk **3** can't be perfume **4** soft **5** might be a crocodile **6** must be a donkey **7** nice

### AB page 106 Activity 5

**1** whiskers **2** fangs **3** beak **4** spikes **5** wings; feathers **6** scales; fins

### AB page 106 Activity 6

**1** donkey **2** Grasshoppers **3** praying mantis **4** Moles **5** eagle **6** Swans **7** bull **8** Silkworms

## Unit 6

### AB page 107 Activity 1

**1** Have **2** haven't **3** hasn't **4** haven't **5** Has **6** has

### AB page 107 Activity 2

Pupils write answers that are true for them.

### AB page 107 Activity 3

Pupils act out the dialogue in pairs when they finish.

**1** played **2** have sung **3** was **4** sang **5** have **6** have played **7** played

# Grammar and Vocabulary Practice answers

### AB page 107 Activity 4

Read the speech bubbles with the class. Then pupils think of new verbs and repeat the dialogue.

### AB page 107 Activity 5

**1** art exhibition **2** sculpture **3** circus **4** poems **5** magazines **6** dance show

### AB page 107 Activity 6

**1** juggle **2** paint a portrait **3** sing in a choir **4** orchestra **5** compose music

## Unit 7

### AB page 108 Activity 1

**1** already **2** yet **3** yet **4** yet **5** yet **6** already **7** yet

### AB page 108 Activity 2

**1** I've just passed an English test. **2** I've just swept the floor. **3** She's just cut her finger. **4** They've just done a lot of exercise. **5** She's just met a film star. **6** She's just twisted her ankle.

### AB page 108 Activity 3

**1** yet **2** already **3** yet **4** just **5** already

### AB page 108 Activity 4

Pupils answer the questions for them.
**1** Have you had lunch? **2** Have you seen your friends? **3** Have you written in English? **4** Have you done your homework?

### AB page 108 Activity 5

**1** serve drinks **2** shopping **3** decorate **4** furniture **5** sell tickets **6** swept

### AB page 108 Activity 6

**1** twisted your ankle **2** burnt your hand **3** cut your finger **4** broken your arm **5** scratched your leg

## Unit 8

### AB page 109 Activity 1

**1** are grown **2** is grown **3** is produced **4** are produced **5** is grown **6** are grown

### AB page 109 Activity 2

Pupils ask and answer the questions in pairs.
**Suggested answers: 1** Where is coffee grown?; It's grown in Colombia. **2** Where is paper produced?; It's produced in a factory. **3** Where are oranges grown?; They're grown in Spain. **4** Where are apples grown?; They're grown in England. **5** Where are computers produced?; They're produced in China.

### AB page 109 Activity 3

Pupils act out the dialogue in pairs when they finish.
**1** is **2** is **3** removed **4** rolled **5** use

### AB page 109 Activity 4

Read the speech bubbles with the class. Then pupils think of new verbs and repeat the dialogue.

### AB page 109 Activity 5

**1** buttons **2** elastic band **3** carton **4** cardboard **5** straw **6** bottle tops

### AB page 109 Activity 6

**1** lolly sticks **2** fabric **3** string **4** collected **5** transported **6** used

## Unit 9

### AB page 110 Activity 1

**1** 'm playing tennis **2** Are; visiting **3** is going to the supermarket **4** 're watching a film **5** 're staying in England **6** 're visiting your grandmother

### AB page 110 Activity 2

**1** If it's cold tomorrow, I'll stay at home. **2** If it rains tomorrow, I won't go to the beach. **3** If I go to the coast, I'll see the beach. **4** If I fall in the lake, I'll get very cold and wet. **5** If I break the window, Dad will be very angry.

### AB page 110 Activity 3

Pupils act out the dialogue in pairs when they finish.
**1** doing **2** will walk **3** come **4** will

### AB page 110 Activity 4

**Suggested answers: 1** they'll have a great time **2** I'll be really happy **3** I won't forgive him **4** If I forget my homework **5** If I go to bed late **6** If our teacher doesn't give us any homework

### AB page 110 Activity 5

**1** rainforest **2** waterfall **3** desert **4** canyon **5** island **6** valley

### AB page 110 Activity 6

**1** umbrella **2** passport **3** money; wallet **4** suitcase **5** anorak **6** towel

### Key Competences and Key Learning Outcomes
- Learn how to improve your concentration in class

**Key language**
- *chat, comfortable, concentrate, correctly, distract, discussion, funny, outside, rucksack, sleepy*
- *Do you chat with your friends in class? Yes, sometimes. What about you?*

**Materials**
- Activity Book p111, Teacher's App on Navio

**Optional materials**
- Teacher's Resource Bank: Trinity Exams Practice cards (selected from Unit 1)

## Detailed Lesson Plan

**Use the Trinity Exams Practice cards (optional).**
- The pupils practise asking and answering questions.

**Set learning objectives.**
- Say **Today we're going to talk about concentrating in class.**

### Activity Book

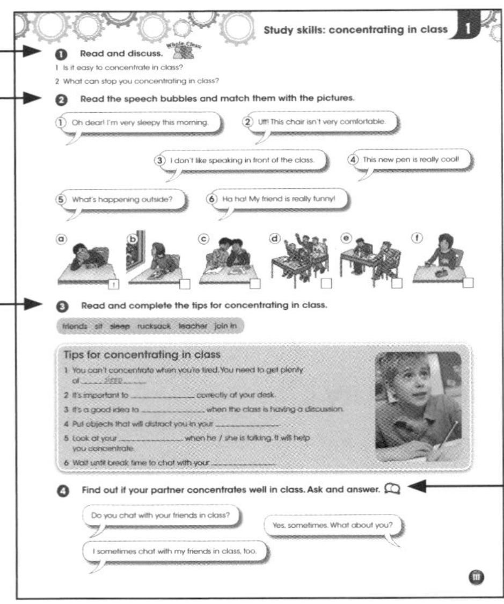


### Activity 1
**Read and discuss.**
- Ask a pupil to read the questions. Pupils discuss the questions in pairs. Then have a class discussion.

### Activity 2
**Read the speech bubbles and match them with the pictures.**
- Ask different pupils to describe the pictures. Then ask a pupil to read the first speech bubble and match it to a picture.
- Pupils work on their own to match the speech bubbles with the pictures.
- Check as a class by having different pupils read the speech bubbles. Ask pupils if they do any of these activities. Tell them it's OK to be honest!

**Answers: 1** a **2** e **3** d **4** f **5** b **6** c

### Activity 3
**Read and complete the tips for concentrating in class.**
- Direct pupils to the words in the box and check they understand the task.
- Pupils work alone to complete the tips. Then they can check in pairs.
- Ask if any of the tips are helpful for the situations in Activity 2.

**Answers: 1** sleep **2** sit **3** join in **4** rucksack **5** teacher **6** friends

### Activity 4
**Find out if your partner concentrates well in class. Ask and answer.**
- Read the speech bubbles with the pupils. Ask various confident pupils to give their answers to the first question.
- Direct pupils to the situations in Activity 2, and ask them to ask and answer more questions. If they find it difficult, elicit more questions from the class, ie *Do you sometimes look out of the window in class? Do you always put interesting objects in your rucksack?*

### Ending the lesson
**Review the lesson and reflect on learning.**
- Say **Today we've learnt how to concentrate in class.**
- Ask **Which was your favourite activity today? Which activity was easy / difficult?**

### Extra activity
**Reinforcement**
- Tell pupils to close their books and watch you. Pretend to be a pupil in class, but pretend to be bored and start looking out of the window or at something else. Then stop, and ask the pupils to describe what you were doing. Then elicit a tip to help you. Put pupils into groups, tell them to act out more examples of poor concentration, and suggest tips to each other.

**Key Competences and Key Learning Outcomes**

- Learn strategies for doing your homework more effectively

**Key language**

- *desk, switch off, task, text messages tidy, urgent*
- *Do you think it's a good idea to watch TV? Why not?*

**Materials**

- Activity Book p112, Teacher's App on Navio
- Coloured pens and paper

**Optional materials**

- Teacher's Resource Bank: Trinity Exams Practice cards (selected from Units 1 and 2)

## Detailed Lesson Plan

**Starting the lesson**

**Use the Trinity Exams Practice cards (optional).**

- The pupils practise asking and answering questions.

**Set learning objectives.**

- Say **Today we're going to talk about doing our homework.**

**Activity 1**

**Read and discuss.**

- Ask a pupil to read the questions. Pupils discuss the questions in pairs. Then have a class discussion.

**Activity 2**

**Is it a good or bad idea to do these things when you do your homework? Write.**

- Direct pupils to the diagram. Elicit the meaning of *It depends* (sometimes good, sometimes bad).
- Point out that *watch TV* is in the *bad idea* section. Ask pupils if they agree, and ask them to explain why.
- Pupils work alone to complete the diagram, then compare their answers in pairs.

### Activity Book

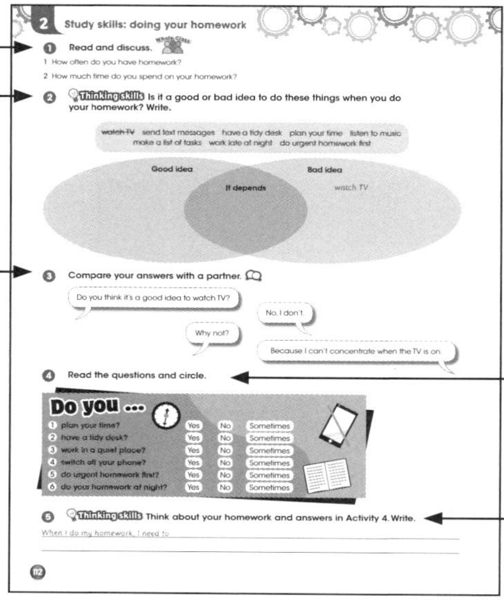


**Activity 3**

**Compare your answers with a partner.**

- Ask a pupil to read the speech bubbles. Then pupils compare their answers in pairs. Tell them to explain why they think each activity is a good or a bad idea.
- Have a class vote to find out where most pupils wrote each activity.

**Activity 4**

**Read the questions and circle.**

- Read the questions with the pupils and check they understand the activity.
- Pupils work alone to circle their answers. Then they compare in pairs. Ask various pupils to tell the class something about their partner's homework habits.

**Activity 5**

**Think about your homework and answer the questions in Activity 4. Write.**

- Pupils write the answers to the questions in Activity 4.

**Ending the lesson**

**Review the lesson and reflect on learning.**

- Say **Today we've learnt how to do our homework better.**
- Ask **Which was your favourite activity today? Which activity was easy / difficult?**

**Extra activity**

**Reinforcement**

- Pupils make a homework poster for their bedrooms to remind them of the tips from the lesson. They can include their own ideas too for doing their homework more effectively. Tell them to look at each other's posters and vote for the best one. Provide pens and paper for them.

**Key Competences and Key Learning Outcomes**

- Learn how to use the Internet to look for information
- Learn how to use search engines to find and check information

**Key language**

- *keywords, erupt, search engine, search results, webpage*

**Materials**

- Activity Book p113, Teacher's App on Navio

**Optional materials**

- Teacher's Resource Bank: Trinity Exams Practice cards (selected from Units 1, 2 and 3)

## Detailed Lesson Plan

### Starting the lesson

**Use the Trinity Exams Practice cards (optional).**

- The pupils practise asking and answering questions.

**Set learning objectives.**

- Say **Today we're going to talk about using the Internet to look for information.**

### Activity 1

**Read and discuss.**

- Ask a pupil to read the questions. Pupils discuss the questions in pairs. Then have a class discussion.

### Activity 2

**Read and order the instructions for using the Internet to look for information.**

- Ask a pupil to read the question (*When was the last time a volcano erupted in Italy*?) Pupils offer guesses.
- Read through each box. Elicit that the three words in the **search engine** are the **keywords.**
- Pupils work in pairs to order the rest of the stages.
- Check that they understand the words **webpage** and **results.**

**Answers: 1** Write keywords … **2** Look at the list of search results … **3** Read the webpage carefully … **4** Go back to the search results …

## Activity Book

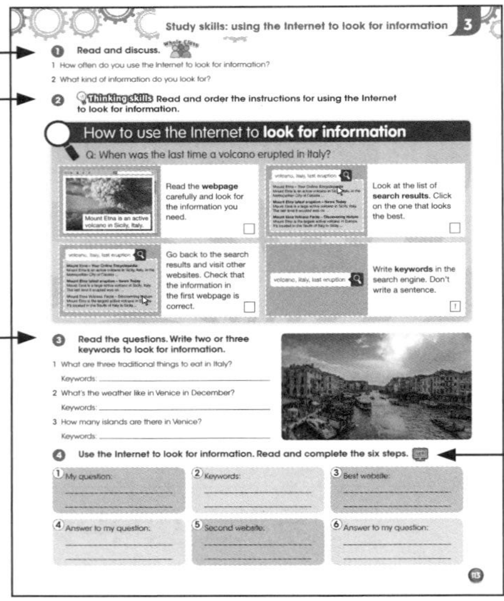

### Activity 3

**Read the questions. Write two or three keywords to look for information.**

- Ask a pupil to describe the photo and ask where it is (Venice).
- Read the first question with the class. Explain that the keywords are the words that contain important information. Elicit the keywords.
- Pupils work in pairs to complete the keywords for the other sentences.

**Answers: 1** traditional food, Italy **2** weather, Venice, December **3** number/how many, islands, Venice

### Activity 4

**Use the Internet to look for information. Read and complete the six steps.**

- Read the headings with pupils. Tell them to think of a question they want to answer. If they can't think of one, tell them to think of something or someone they're interested in and would like to know more about.
- Allow them to use computers or other devices to research the answers to their questions.
- Different pupils present their questions and information to the class.

### Ending the lesson

**Review the lesson and reflect on learning.**

- Say **Today we've learnt how use the Internet to look for information.**
- Ask **Which was your favourite activity today? Which activity was easy / difficult?**

### Extra activity

**Reinforcement**

- Pupils write an Internet quiz. In pairs, pupils write five quiz questions about anything they like – the answers should be available on the Internet. Put them with another pair, tell them to swap questions, and use the Internet to find the answers to each other's questions. The pupils who find the answers first are the winners in each group.

**Key Competences and Key Learning Outcomes**

- Learn how to use a dictionary

**Key language**

- *alphabetical order, folder, hardware, headword, headwords, technical, technician, translation, definition*

**Materials**

- Activity Book p114, Teacher's App on Navio
- Bilingual dictionaries (enough for one per pair or small group)

**Optional materials**

- Teacher's Resource Bank: Trinity Exams Practice cards (selected from Units 1, 2, 3 and 4)

## Detailed Lesson Plan

### Starting the lesson

**Use the Trinity Exams Practice cards (optional).**

- The pupils practise asking and answering questions.

**Set learning objectives.**

- Say **Today we're going to talk about using a dictionary.**

### Activity 1

**Read and discuss.**

- Ask a pupil to read the questions. Pupils discuss the questions in pairs. Then have a class discussion.

### Activity 2

**The words in a dictionary are in alphabetical order. Put these words in the alphabetical order. Write number 1–5.**

- Ask the class which pupil's name comes first in the dictionary, and which pupil's name comes last. Elicit the meaning of **alphabetical order**.
- Pupils work alone to order the words. Then they check in pairs.

**Answers:** a **1** camera **2** karaoke **3** laptop **4** tablet **5** website b **1** pause **2** tap **3** tilt **4** start **5** swipe c **1** tablet **2** tap **3** technical **4** technician **5** technology

## Activity Book

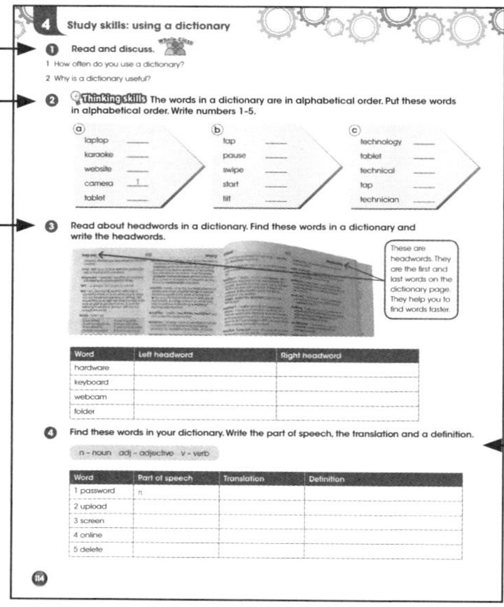

### Activity 3

**Read about headwords in a dictionary. Find these words in a dictionary and write the headwords.**

- Read the box with the class. Then give every pair or group a dictionary to do the activity. If the dictionaries are different, the headwords may be different.

### Activity 4

**Find these words in your dictionary. Write the part of speech, the translation and a definition.**

- Elicit what information a dictionary entry gives about a word. Ask pupils for an example of a noun, and adjective and a verb.
- As a class, work through the table for the first word (*password*).
- Pupils complete the table in pairs or groups, depending how many dictionaries you have. They can also use an online bilingual dictionary for this activity.

### Ending the lesson

**Review the lesson and reflect on learning.**

- Say **Today we've learnt how to use a dictionary.**
- Ask **Which was your favourite activity today? Which activity was easy / difficult?**

### Extra activity

**Reinforcement**

- Play a definitions game. Show pupils the word *skunk* and give them three definitions: 1 A small black and white mammal. 2 A type of food that is popular in the USA. 3 A large boat. In groups, pupils guess the correct definition, then check in a dictionary. Then pupils play the game in groups. They find a new word in the dictionary, write two incorrect and one correct definitions, and test each other.

**Key Competences and Key Learning Outcomes**

- Learn how to present your written work

**Key language**

- *corrections, cute, full stop, handwriting, nocturnal, powerful, sense of smell, Tasmanian devil*
- *Carl's homework has got correct spelling. Sam's homework has got some spelling mistakes.*

**Materials**

- Activity Book p115, Teacher's App on Navio

**Optional materials**

- Teacher's Resource Bank: Trinity Exams Practice cards (selected from Units 1, 2, 3, 4 and 5)

## Detailed Lesson Plan

**Starting the lesson**

**Use the Trinity Exams Practice cards (optional).**

- The pupils practise asking and answering questions.

**Set learning objectives.**

- Say **Today we're going to talk about presenting our written work.**

**Activity 1**

**Read and discuss.**

- Ask a pupil to read the questions. Pupils discuss the questions in pairs. Then have a class discussion.

**Activity 2**

**Look at the two pieces of written work. Circle six differences.**

- Focus on the two texts, and ask the class if they think Sam or Carl will get a better mark. Elicit ideas why.
- Elicit some differences between the texts that pupils can see. Tell them there are a lot of differences, but they only need to find six. Pupils work alone to circle six differences.

## Activity Book

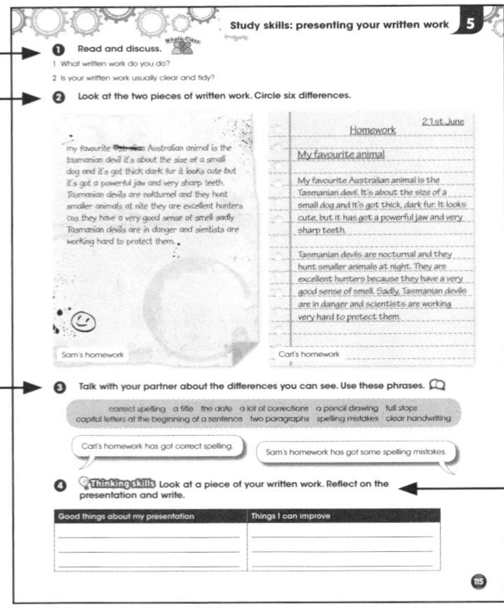


**Activity 3**

**Talk with your partner about the differences you can see. Use these phrases.**

- Ask a pupil to read the speech bubbles. Then pupils compare the differences that they found, using the phrases in the box.
- Ask a pupil to read the speech bubbles. Then pupils compare the differences that they found in pairs, using the phrases in the box. Check all the differences as a class.

**Activity 4**

**Look at a piece of your written work. Reflect on the presentation and write.**

- Ask pupils to choose a text from their notebook. It doesn't have to be in English. Tell them to think about the aspects in Activity 3 and complete the table.

**Ending the lesson**

**Review the lesson and reflect on learning.**

- Say **Today we've learnt how to present written work.**
- Ask **Which was your favourite activity today? Which activity was easy / difficult?**

**Extra activity**

**Reinforcement**

- Pupils write a text in their notebooks, called *About me*. Tell them they can write anything they like, but they only have 5 minutes. After 5 minutes, say **stop**. Pupils swap their texts with a partner, and check the aspects from Activity 3 in each other's texts. They tell each other what's good about the texts, and what they can improve.

**Key Competences and Key Learning Outcomes**

- Learn how to record vocabulary

**Key language**

- *body, drums, frets, neck, saxophone, string*

**Materials**

- Activity Book p116, Teacher's App on Navio

**Optional materials**

- Teacher's Resource Bank: Trinity Exams Practice cards (selected from Units 1, 2, 3, 4, 5 and 6)

## Detailed Lesson Plan

**Starting the lesson**

**Use the Trinity Exams Practice cards (optional).**

- The pupils practise asking and answering questions.

**Set learning objectives.**

- Say **Today we're going to talk about recording vocabulary.**

**Activity 1**

**Read and discuss.**

- Ask a pupil to read the questions. Pupils discuss the questions in pairs. Then have a class discussion.

**Activity 2**

**Look at the ways of recording vocabulary. How often do you do these things?**

- Direct pupils to the six methods of recording vocabulary. Ask different pupils to read or describe the six diagrams.
- Ask a strong pupil **How often do you use a translation when you record vocabulary?** In pairs, pupils tell each other how often they use these methods.

### Activity Book

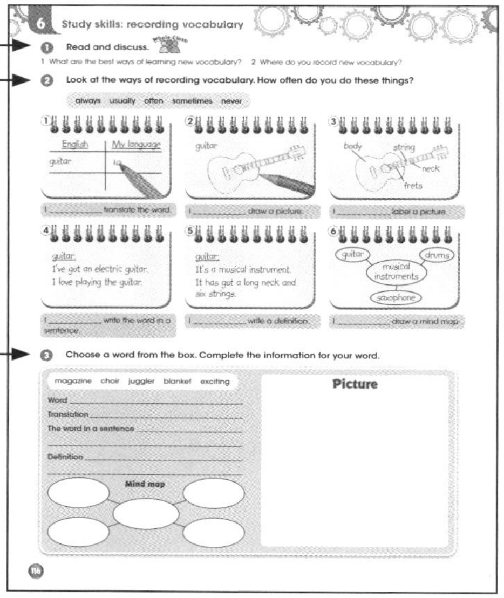


**Activity 3**

**Choose a word from the box. Complete the information for your word.**

- Work through the word *magazine* with the pupils, asking them to provide a translation, example sentence and definition. For the mind map, elicit what category a magazine belongs to (*things that you read*), and elicit more items from the category.
- Pupils choose a different word and work alone to complete the information and draw a picture.

**Ending the lesson**

**Review the lesson and reflect on learning.**

- Say **Today we've learnt how record vocabulary.**
- Ask **Which was your favourite activity today? Which activity was easy / difficult?**

**Extra activity**

**Reinforcement**

- Play a categories game. Give pupils various words from the level, and tell them to write down as many words belonging to the same category as possible. The pupil with the most correct words for each category wins.

**Key Competences and Key Learning Outcomes**
- Learn how to remember vocabulary

**Key language**
- *crossword, memory, notice board, puzzle*

**Materials**
- Activity Book p117, Teacher's App on Navio

**Optional materials**
- Teacher's Resource Bank: Trinity Exams Practice cards (selected from Units 1, 2, 3, 4, 5, 6 and 7)

## Detailed Lesson Plan

### Starting the lesson

**Use the Trinity Exams Practice cards (optional).**
- The pupils practise asking and answering questions.

**Set learning objectives.**
- Say **Today we're going to talk about remembering vocabulary.**

### Activity 1

**Read and discuss.**
- Ask a pupil to read the questions. Pupils discuss the questions in pairs. Then have a class discussion.

### Activity 2

**Read the ideas for remembering vocabulary and match them with the pictures. Can you think of other ideas?**
- Ask different pupils to describe the pictures. Then ask a pupil to read the first speech bubble and match it to one of the pictures.
- Pupils work in pairs to match the rest of the speech bubbles to the pictures. Feed back as a class and ask what other ideas pupils can think of.

## Activity Book

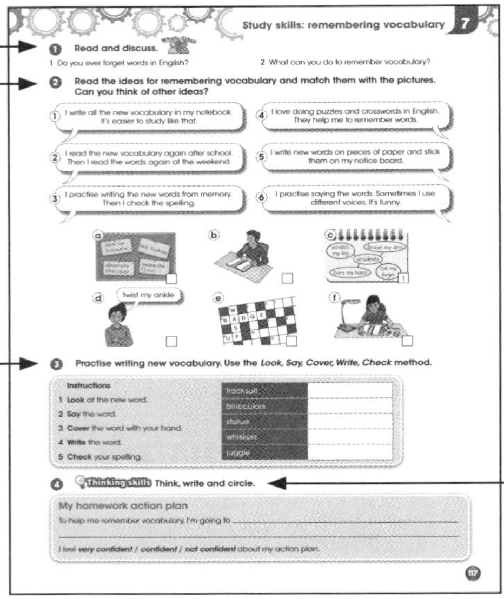

### Activity 3

**Practise writing new vocabulary. Use the *Look, Say, Cover, Write, Check* method.**
- Read through the five stages with the pupils. Then practise with the first word (*tracksuit*) as a class.
- Pupils work alone to practise the rest of the words. Ask different pupils if they managed to remember all the words and spell them correctly.

### Activity 4

**Think, write and circle.**
- Pupils complete the sentences with the ideas that they liked the most from Activities 2 and 3.

### Ending the lesson

**Review the lesson and reflect on learning.**
- Say **Today we've learnt how to remember vocabulary.**
- Ask **Which was your favourite activity today? Which activity was easy / difficult?**

### Extra activity

**Reinforcement**
- Pupils write a crossword for another pair to solve. In pairs, pupils choose a number of new words from the level, or from a previous level, work out how to fit them into a crossword, and draw the blank crossword. Then they think of clues for each word. Pupils swap their blank crosswords and clues with another pair and complete them.

**Key Competences and Key Learning Outcomes**

- Learn how to guess what new words mean

**Key language**

- *crossword, appliance, bad-tempered, cheeky, grumpy, iceberg, immense, Musk Ox, polite, spotless, wellies*

**Materials**

- Activity Book p118, Teacher's App on Navio
- Bilingual dictionaries (enough for one per pair or small group)

**Optional materials**

- Teacher's Resource Bank: Trinity Exams Practice cards (selected from Units 1, 2, 3, 4, 5, 6, 7 and 8)

## Detailed Lesson Plan

**Starting the lesson**

**Use the Trinity Exams Practice cards (optional).**

- The pupils practise asking and answering questions.

**Set learning objectives.**

- Say **Today we're going to talk about guessing what new words mean.**

**Activity 1**

**Read and discuss.**

- Ask a pupil to read the questions. Pupils discuss the questions in pairs. Then have a class discussion.

**Activity 2**

**Read and guess what the underlined words mean. Circle the meaning you think is correct.**

- Read the title and introduction with the class. Elicit the meaning of *detective* and *clue*. Then read through clue 1. Point out that the meaning of the second sentence is often similar to the first, so therefore *He wasn't polite* has a similar meaning to *He was cheeky*.
- Pupils work in pairs to read the rest of the clues and guess the meanings. Check as a class.

**Answers:** **1** b **2** c **3** a **4** c

## Activity Book

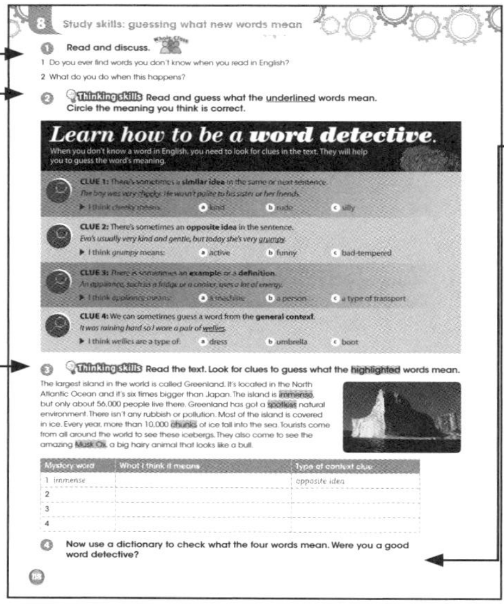
8 Study skills: guessing what new words mean

1 Read and discuss.

1 Do you ever find words you don't know when you read in English?

2 What do you do when this happens?

2 Thinking skills Read and guess what the underlined words mean. Circle the meaning you think is correct.

*Learn how to be a word detective.*

When you don't know a word in English, you need to look for clues in the text. They will help you to guess the word's meaning.

CLUE 1: There's sometimes a **similar idea** in the same or next sentence. *The boy was very cheeky. He wasn't polite to his sister or her friends.* I think cheeky means: a kind b rude c silly

CLUE 2: There's sometimes an **opposite idea** in the sentence. *Eva's usually very kind and gentle, but today she's very grumpy.* I think grumpy means: a active b funny c bad-tempered

CLUE 3: There is sometimes an **example** or a **definition**. *An appliance, such as a fridge or a cooker, uses a lot of energy.* I think appliance means: a a machine b a person c a type of transport

CLUE 4: We can sometimes guess a word from the **general context**. *It was raining hard so I wore a pair of wellies.* I think wellies are a type of: a dress b umbrella c boot

3 Thinking skills Read the text. Look for clues to guess what the highlighted words mean.

The largest island in the world is called Greenland. It's located in the North Atlantic Ocean and it's six times bigger than Japan. The island is immense, but only about 56,000 people live there. Greenland has got a spotless natural environment. There isn't any rubbish or pollution. Most of the island is covered in ice. Every year, more than 10,000 chunks of ice fall into the sea. Tourists come from all around the world to see these icebergs. They also come to see the amazing Musk Ox, a big hairy animal that looks like a bull.

| Mystery word | What I think it means | Type of context clue |
|---|---|---|
| 1 immense | | opposite idea |
| 2 | | |
| 3 | | |
| 4 | | |

4 Now use a dictionary to check what the four words mean. Were you a good word detective?

**Activity 3**

**Read the text. Look for clues to guess what the highlighted words mean.**

- Ask pupils if they know anything about Greenland.
- Read the start of the text as a class. Elicit what immense means. (*Opposite idea, because there is an idea starting with 'but'*).
- Pupils read the rest of the text and complete the table in pairs.

**Answers:** **1** immense; very big; opposite idea **2** spotless; very clean; similar idea **3** chunks; pieces; general context **4** Musk Ox; large animal; definition

**Activity 4**

**Now use a dictionary to check what the four words mean. Were you a good detective?**

- Allow pupils to check the words in a dictionary. Ask the class who guessed all four words correctly.

**Ending the lesson**

**Review the lesson and reflect on learning.**

- Say **Today we've learnt how to guess what new words mean.**
- Ask **Which was your favourite activity today? Which activity was easy / difficult?**

**Extra activity**

**Reinforcement**

- Pupils work in pairs to guess the meaning of the underlined words. Then they check in a dictionary.

1 I don't have any siblings, but my best friend has got one brother and two sisters.

2 Be careful – the street is slippery because of the ice.

3 I hate getting up early at the weekend. I prefer to have a lie-in.

**Key Competences and Key Learning Outcomes**

- Learn how to revise

**Key language**

- *revise, revision, tips*

**Materials**

- Activity Book p119, Teacher's App on Navio
- Card for making vocabulary cards

**Optional materials**

- Teacher's Resource Bank: Trinity Exams Practice cards (selected from Units 1, 2, 3, 4, 5, 6, 7, 8 and 9)

## Detailed Lesson Plan

### Starting the lesson

**Use the Trinity Exams Practice cards (optional).**

- The pupils practise asking and answering questions.

**Set learning objectives.**

- Say **Today we're going to talk about revising.**

### Activity 1

**Read and discuss.**

- Elicit the meaning of *revise* and *revision*, and ask pupils when this is important. Ask a pupil to read the questions. Pupils discuss the questions in pairs. Then have a class discussion.

### Activity 2

**Read the tips for revising. Give each tip a mark from 1 to 4.**

- Read through the tips as a class. Check if pupils remember the *Lok, Say, Cover, Write, Check* method and mind maps. Ask them what they think revision cards are and how they can use them.
- Pupils work alone to give each tip a mark.

## Activity Book

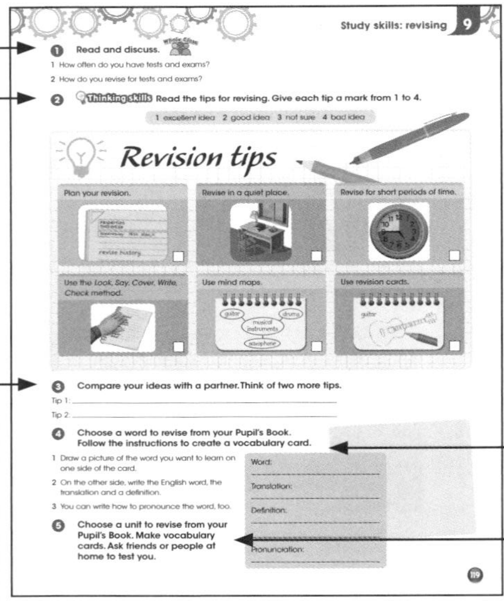

### Activity 3

**Compare your ideas with a partner. Think of two more tips.**

- Pupils work in pairs to compare their marks, and explain why they gave each tip the marks.
- Elicit another revision tip from the class. If they can't think of anything, give them some ideas, for example **Revise together with a friend. Revise in the morning when you aren't tired.** In pairs, pupils think of more ideas. Then make a class list of new tips.

### Activity 4

**Choose a word to revise from your Pupil's Book. Follow the instructions to create a vocabulary card.**

- Ask a pupil to choose a word from somewhere in their pupil's book. Work through the stages in the vocabulary card as a class. For pronunciation, you can use phonetic transcript if your pupils are familiar with it, or give another word that rhymes with the word.

### Activity 5

**Choose a unit to revise from your Pupil's Book. Make vocabulary cards. Ask friends or people at home to test you.**

- Pupils choose a unit. They use vocabulary cards to revise the words from that unit. Then they ask people ot test them on the words.

### Ending the lesson

**Review the lesson and reflect on learning.**

- Say **Today we've learnt how to revise.**
- Ask **Which was your favourite activity today? Which activity was easy / difficult?**

### Extra activity

**Reinforcement**

- Choose a vocabulary page from the Pupil's Book. Give pupils 10 minutes to revise the vocabulary and try and remember it. Then give them a mini-test. Afterwards, ask different pupils what method they used to try to revise the vocabulary.

## Starter Unit Lesson 1

Pupil's Book

### CD1 TRACK 01

**PB page 4 Activity 3**

1
**Boy:** How old is Callum?
**Girl:** He's 11 years old.
2
**Boy:** When's Jess's birthday?
**Girl:** It's on the third of February.
3
**Boy:** Has Tom got any brothers or sisters?
**Girl:** No. He hasn't got any brothers or sisters.
4
**Boy:** What's Jess's favourite school subject?
**Girl:** It's Maths.
5
**Boy:** What's Tom's favourite food?
**Girl:** He likes pizza and tomatoes.
6
**Boy:** What does Callum look like?
**Girl:** He's got short brown hair and brown eyes, and he's short.
7
**Boy:** What's Jess like?
**Girl:** She's friendly, active and a bit noisy!

## Starter Unit Lesson 2

Pupil's Book

### CD1 TRACK 02

**PB page 5 Activity 2**

1 It's the drink that is made of oranges.
2 They're the toys that have got soft fur.
3 It's the fruit that is yellow and begins with the letter 'b'.
4 He's the person who's buying a sandwich.
5 They're things which you drink from.

## Starter Unit Lesson 3

Pupil's Book

### CD1 TRACK 03

**PB page 6 Activity 1**

1
**Tom:** What are all these balloons for?
**Callum:** There's going to be a balloon race.
**Jess:** What's a balloon race?
**Callum:** People buy a balloon. They write a question and their email address on a label. Then we let go of all the balloons.
**Tom:** And then what?
**Callum:** The balloons float away. Some of them land near here, but some land in other countries.
2
**Tom:** They land in other countries? Really?
**Callum:** Yes. A few years ago, a balloon went from England to China.
**Tom:** What happens when a balloon lands?
**Callum:** Hopefully, someone reads the question on the label and sends a message. The balloon that travels the furthest is the winner.
**Jess:** What a great idea! Let's buy some balloons.

## Starter Unit Lesson 4

Pupil's Book

### CD1 TRACK 04

**PB page 7 Activity 1**

Balloon races

How does a balloon race work?

The balloons have got a gas called helium inside them. Helium is lighter than air. Each balloon usually rises about eight kilometres and then bursts, but some travel a long way and land in other countries.

What are the rules for balloon races?

The balloons must be made of latex and the labels must be made of paper.
Latex and paper are organic, so they will degrade naturally.
The balloons shouldn't have the string attached when they're released.
You musn't tie the balloons together.
You mustn't let go of more than 5,000 balloons at the same time.

FUN FACT In 2007, a four-year-old girl released a balloon in Manchester, England. A boy found the balloon six weeks later. The boy lived in China, 9,500 km away!

## Starter Unit Lesson 4

Activity Book

### CD1 TRACK 05

**AB page 5 Activity 1**

From Manchester to China

In July 2007, Alice Maines, who was four years old, went to a summer fair at her school in Manchester. There was a balloon race at the school and Alice's dad wrote a question and her address on the label of a balloon. Alice let go of the balloon. After six weeks, they received a letter from a 13-year-old boy in China! His name was Nathan. He found the label on the 25th of August, when he was playing basketball with his friends. This balloon travelled about 9,500 kilometres – much further than any of the other balloons. There was a prize for the person who found the balloon. The prize was a ticket to visit a zoo near Manchester. The boy couldn't travel to England, so the school sent him a box full of letters and pictures. No one knows how the balloon travelled to China. Some people think that the balloon got stuck to part of a plane!

## Unit 1 Lesson 1

Pupil's Book

### CD1 TRACK 06

**PB page 8 Activity 3**

**1** waistcoat
**2** tie
**3** cardigan
**4** leggings
**5** baseball boots
**6** tracksuit
**7** polo shirt
**8** jeans
**9** top
**10** tights
**11** belt
**12** sweatshirt

## Unit 1 Lesson 1

Pupil's Book

### CD1 TRACK 07

**PB page 8 Activity 4**

1
**Girl:** Men and boys usually wear this when they want to look smart. They wear it around their neck. It's long and thin.
**Boy:** tie
2
**Girl:** You wear these on your feet. They're light and comfortable. You can wear them to do sport, too.
**Boy:** baseball boots
3
**Girl:** You wear this around your waist. It's often made of leather. It's long and thin and it holds up your trousers.
**Boy:** belt
4
**Girl:** Girls wear these on their legs. They're usually made of cotton and they're very comfortable. They can be long or short and are a bit like trousers.
**Boy:** leggings
5
**Girl:** You wear this on your body. You wear it over a shirt or a T-shirt. It hasn't got any sleeves.
**Boy:** waistcoat
6
**Girl:** You wear this to do sport. It's got two parts, a jacket or a sweatshirt and a pair of trousers, and it's very comfortable.
**Boy:** tracksuit
7
**Girl:** You wear these on your legs. They're often blue and the material is very strong. Boys and girls wear them.
**Boy:** jeans
8
**Girl:** This is something that you wear above the waist. It can have short sleeves like a T-shirt or long sleeves like a shirt.
**Boy:** top
9
**Girl:** You wear this on the top part of your body. It's like a sweater, but it's got buttons at the front.
**Boy:** cardigan
10
**Girl:** You wear this on the top part of your body when it's cold and when you do sport. It's casual and it's very comfortable. It's made of cotton.
**Boy:** sweatshirt
11
**Girl:** This can be casual or sporty. You wear it on the top part of your body. It's made of cotton. It's got a collar and it's usually got short sleeves.
**Boy:** polo shirt
12
**Girl:** Girls wear these to cover their legs and feet in the winter. They wear them with a skirt or a dress. They can be different colours.
**Boy:** tights

# Audioscript

## Unit 1 Lesson 2

Pupil's Book

### CD1 TRACK 08

**PB page 10 Activity 1**

**Jess:** Hi, Nico. Did your friends like the T-shirts?
**Nico:** Yes, they did. Thanks for your help.
**Jess:** You're welcome. Do you usually wear T-shirts?
**Nico:** Yes, I do. But I'm not wearing one now. I'm wearing my ski clothes.
**Jess:** Your ski clothes? But it's autumn. You can't ski in the autumn.
**Nico:** You can in Switzerland. Some ski stations are open all year here.
**Jess:** That's incredible! Are you wearing a helmet?
**Nico:** Yes, I am. I always wear a helmet and I always wear goggles to protect my eyes. Look!
**Jess:** What a great photo! But how can you use your phone when you're wearing gloves?
**Nico:** It's easy. My gloves fasten with Velcro, so I can put them on and take them off really quickly. Velcro is a really cool material. I'll send you some information about it.

## Unit 1 Lesson 2

Activity Book

### CD1 TRACK 09

**AB page 7 Activity 3**

**Receptionist:** Upton sports centre. Can I help you?
**Dad:** I'm interested in some ice skating lessons for my daughter.
**Receptionist:** That's no problem. How old is your daughter?
**Dad:** She's ten.
**Receptionist:** Let me see … We've got ice skating lessons for children on Monday, Wednesday and Friday. Which day is best for you?
**Dad:** Erm … She's got a swimming lesson on Monday and she usually has homework on Wednesday, so I think Friday is best. What time is the lesson?
**Receptionist:** It's at five o'clock. No … wait a minute … I'm sorry, the lesson is at six o'clock for ten to twelve year olds.
**Dad:** And who's the teacher?
**Receptionist:** The teacher's name is Penny.
**Dad:** How do you spell that, please?
**Receptionist:** P-E-N-N-Y.
**Dad:** That sounds great. How much does the lesson cost?
**Receptionist:** Lessons are ten pounds an hour for adults and five pounds an hour for children.
**Dad:** Perfect. Does my daughter have to wear any special clothes for the lesson?
**Receptionist:** She needs to wear warm clothes, of course, and she must wear gloves to protect her hands.
**Dad:** We'll be there at six o'clock on Friday. Thank you very much.
**Receptionist:** You're welcome.
**Dad:** Goodbye.
**Receptionist:** Goodbye.

## Unit 1 Lesson 3

Pupil's Book

### CD1 TRACK 10

**PB page 11 Activity 2**

***A brilliant idea***
**Narrator:** This story begins in Switzerland in 1948. George de Mestral, an engineer, takes his dog for a walk. He's wearing woollen trousers and a woollen jacket.
**Frame 1**
**Narrator:** George walks through a forest with his dog. There are lots of wild plants and flowers.
**George:** Follow me. Good dog!
**Frame 2**
**Narrator:** After the walk, George notices that there are seeds on his woollen clothes and on the dog's fur.
**George:** Oh dear! These seeds are very difficult to take off.
**Frame 3**
**Narrator:** He's very curious about the seeds, so he looks at them under a microscope.
**George:** How interesting! They've got lots of tiny hooks.
**Frame 4**
**Narrator:** George invents a material that has got the same tiny hooks as the seeds. The material can stick together, but people think it's a silly idea.
**Woman:** This material is too heavy and it isn't pretty enough.
**Frame 5**
**Narrator:** George works on his invention for ten more years. He uses nylon, which is strong and light. He calls the new invention Velcro.
**Man:** What a brilliant idea!
**Frame 6**
**Narrator:** Now people all over the world use Velcro. You can find it on all kinds of clothes and shoes. Did you know that astronauts have got a piece of Velcro inside their helmets so they can scratch their noses?

## Unit 1 Lesson 3

Activity Book

### CD1 TRACK 11

**AB page 8 Activity 2**

**Jess:** You have to read this, Callum.
**Callum:** What is it?
**Jess:** It's a true story called 'A brilliant idea'.
**Callum:** That sounds good. What's the story about?
**Jess:** It's about a Swiss engineer called George de Mestral.
**Callum:** An engineer! Does he invent something?
**Jess:** Yes, he does. The story begins when he takes his dog for a walk through a forest. When he gets home he finds seeds all over his clothes.
**Callum:** Seeds!
**Jess:** That's right. Anyway, George looks at the seeds and finds out that they have got lots of hooks on them. So he starts thinking and invents a new material that has hooks, too.
**Callum:** That's clever. Do people like the material?
**Jess:** No, they don't. But George doesn't mind. He carries on working and decides to make the hooks with a new material called nylon.
**Callum:** Really?
**Jess:** Yes! And ten years later George creates Velcro.
**Callum:** Wow! So Velcro has got lots of hooks on it?
**Jess:** That's right. Now millions of people all over the world use Velcro on their clothes!
**Callum:** What's your favourite part of the story?
**Jess:** That's easy. It's the fact about astronauts. Do you know that astronauts have got Velcro in their helmet?
**Callum:** That's cool! So do you recommend the story?
**Jess:** Yes, I do. I think the story is really interesting and I give it five stars.
**Callum:** Five stars! I'm definitely going to read it now.

## Unit 1 Lesson 4

Pupil's Book

### CD1 TRACK 12

**PB page 12 Activity 1**

**Frame 1**
**Tom:** That story about Velcro was really interesting. Are you wearing any Velcro, Jess?
**Jess:** Yes, I am. I've got some on my watch strap.
**Tom:** But your strap is too big. Your watch will fall off.
**Jess:** Don't worry. I can make the strap smaller.
**Frame 2**
**Tom:** Be careful! The strap isn't big enough now.
**Jess:** Ow! You're right.
**Tom:** Can you change it again?
**Jess:** Yes, of course. It's perfect now.

## Unit 1 Lesson 4

Pupil's Book

### CD1 TRACK 13

**PB page 12 Activity 5**

trousers
sweatshirt
enough
cardigan
comfortable
fashionable
unfashionable
uncomfortable

## Unit 1 Lesson 4

Activity Book

### CD1 TRACK 14

**AB page 9 Activity 3**

**1** trousers, sandals, bracelet
**2** umbrella, pyjamas
**3** cardigan, fashionable, uniform
**4** uncomfortable, unfashionable

## Unit 1 Lesson 5

Pupil's Book

**CD1 TRACK 15**

**PB page 13 Activity 1**

**1** a short-sleeved T-shirt
**2** a long-sleeved T-shirt
**3** a striped dress
**4** a flowery dress
**5** tight trousers
**6** baggy trousers
**7** a patterned tie
**8** a plain tie

## Unit 1 Lesson 5

Pupil's Book

**CD1 TRACK 16**

**PB page 13 Activity 2**

**Boy:** Hi, Laura. Look at this picture of my friends.
**Girl:** That's nice. What are your friends' names?
**Boy:** Their names are Andy, Karen, Sue, Harry and Jack.
**Girl:** Which one's Andy?
**Boy:** He's the one who's wearing a shirt and a tie.
**Girl:** Oh yes. I can see him. He's wearing a patterned tie and a plain shirt.
**Boy:** That's right. Andy loves smart clothes.
**Girl:** And which one's Karen?
**Boy:** She's wearing casual clothes. She's wearing flowery leggings and a baggy sweater.
**Girl:** Oh yes. I can see her now. She's wearing baseball boots, too.
**Boy:** Yes. Karen's very fashionable.
**Girl:** So the girl who's wearing the striped T-shirt and a long skirt is Sue.
**Boy:** That's right.
**Girl:** What's the name of the boy who's wearing shorts?
**Boy:** The one wearing a T-shirt or the one wearing a sweatshirt?
**Girl:** The one wearing a sweatshirt, the plain sweatshirt.
**Boy:** That's Jack.
**Girl:** What's the other boy called?
**Boy:** He's called Harry.
**Girl:** I love his cap.
**Boy:** Yes, it's great. Harry often wears a baseball cap.
**Girl:** What a great picture. Thanks for showing it to me.
**Boy:** You're welcome.

## Unit 1 Lesson 6

Activity Book

**CD1 TRACK 17**

**AB page 11 Activity 3**

Be the first to buy an amazing hagfish T-shirt. It's available in six amazing colours: red, black, purple, white, blue and grey – and there are three sizes you can choose from. You can buy a small, medium or large size. The large size is perfect if you prefer wearing baggy clothes. The material is soft, light and very resistant, and it's easy to wash! Just put it in the washing machine with the rest of your clothes.
A hagfish T-shirt usually costs ten pounds, but today and today only, there's a special offer.
You can buy one T-shirt for ten pounds and two T-shirts for fifteen pounds. That's right! Two amazing hagfish T-shirts for fifteen pounds!
To order you need to phone this number: 685524.
Here's the telephone number again: 685524.
Don't wait! Phone now for your own amazing hagfish T-shirt!

## Unit 1 Lesson 8

Pupil's Book

**CD1 TRACK 18**

**PB page 16 Activity 2**

**Anna:** That's a nice T-shirt, Julia.
**Julia:** Oh? Thanks Anna. It's new.
**Anna:** Is it your favourite item of clothing?
**Julia:** No, my favourite is my hat.
**Anna:** A hat! Really? What's it like?
**Julia:** Well, it's grey and it's made of wool. But the best thing is the pattern. It's got a face on it.
**Anna:** A face! No way!
**Julia:** It's a bear's face and it's got pom-poms for ears.
**Anna:** Awww! When do you wear the hat? I've never seen it.
**Julia:** I usually wear it when I visit my grandparents. They live in the mountains and it gets really cold there.
**Anna:** Really? Where did you buy it?
**Julia:** I didn't buy it. It was a birthday present. I love it!
**Anna:** Why do you like it so much?
**Julia:** Well, it's soft and warm. And it looks great, too! Anyway, what about you? What's your favourite item of clothing?
**Anna:** Oh! I love my new baseball boots.

## Unit 1

### Video and 21st Century Skills

Activity Book

**CD1 TRACK 19**

**AB page 15 Activity 1**

**Amy:** Why don't we enter the design competition, Max?
**Max:** Good idea, Amy. What do we need to do?
**Amy:** We need to design a new sports kit for the basketball team.
I've got some sketches of my ideas. Look!
**Max:** They're great!
**Amy:** Thanks, but we need to develop them. Look at the T-shirts.
Do you prefer a plain T-shirt or a patterned T-shirt?
**Max:** I prefer a patterned T-shirt. What about you?
**Amy:** I prefer a patterned T-shirt, too. Do you like this striped T-shirt or the other one?
**Max:** I don't like the other one very much. It's too strange.
**Amy:** I agree with you. I think the striped one is better.
**Max:** But how can we make it special?
**Amy:** We can draw a star on the front. Look!
**Max:** That looks great!
**Amy:** Thanks. Here are my sketches of shorts. I like these plain white ones.
**Max:** Oh. I don't. They're too light. I think a dark colour is better.
**Amy:** Let's have the black shorts then.
**Max:** OK. Now we need to choose the socks.
**Amy:** I prefer short socks.
**Max:** I agree. Long socks are too uncomfortable.
**Amy:** There are plain black or plain white socks. Which ones do you prefer?
**Max:** I prefer the white socks.
**Amy:** Me too. That's it. We've designed a new basketball kit.
We've got a striped T-shirt with a star on the front, dark shorts and plain, short white socks.
**Max:** Excellent. I hope we win!

## Unit 2 Lesson 1

Pupil's Book

**CD1 TRACK 20**

**PB page 18 Activity 3**

**1** whitewater rafting
**2** helmet
**3** lifejacket
**4** camping
**5** wetsuit
**6** map
**7** compass
**8** torch
**9** hiking
**10** rucksack
**11** rock climbing
**12** mountain biking

## Unit 2 Lesson 1

Pupil's Book

**CD1 TRACK 21**

**PB page 18 Activity 4**

**1**
**Boy:** You wear this to keep warm in the water. It's made of rubber.
**Girl:** wetsuit
**2**
**Boy:** This is a hard object. You wear it to protect your head.
**Girl:** helmet
**3**
**Boy:** For this activity, you wear a helmet. You use your arms and your legs to move upwards slowly. This is a good activity if you like being high up.
**Girl:** rock climbing
**4**
**Boy:** This object shows you which direction to go in. It's usually small and round.
**Girl:** compass
**5**
**Boy:** This activity is a type of cycling. You do it on rough ground. You wear a helmet, too.
**Girl:** mountain biking
**6**
**Boy:** You usually hold this object in your hand. You use it to see in the dark.
**Girl:** torch

# Audioscript

7
**Boy:** You usually wear strong shoes or boots to do this activity. You walk through woods or up hills or mountains.
**Girl:** hiking
8
**Boy:** This object is a soft bag. You wear it on your back, especially when you're hiking or rock climbing.
**Girl:** rucksack
9
**Boy:** You usually wear this object if you're in a boat. It helps you float or swim in the water if you fall in.
**Girl:** lifejacket
10
**Boy:** This object helps you find your way around. It's usually made of paper, but you can also use one on a computer, a tablet or a smartphone.
**Girl:** map
11
**Boy:** You do this activity on a river. You sit in a boat with other people. You wear a helmet and a lifejacket. The river usually flows very fast.
**Girl:** whitewater rafting
12
**Boy:** This is an outdoor activity. People sleep in tents and usually make food and eat outside.
**Girl:** camping

## Unit 2 Lesson 2

Pupil's Book

### CD1 TRACK 22

#### PB page 20 Activity 1

**Callum:** Hi, Danielle. Thanks for the photos. Do you do any adventure activities?
**Danielle:** Yes, I went canyoning with my family last weekend.
**Callum:** Canyoning? What's that?
**Danielle:** You walk along narrow rivers between rocks. Wait – I'll send you a photo.
**Callum:** That looks fun … and a bit scary! Did you enjoy it?
**Danielle:** Oh yes. We jumped and climbed over rocks and swam a bit, too. The best thing was the sound of the water.
**Callum:** What do you mean?
**Danielle:** The water was really loud. We couldn't hear anything. It was really exciting! Then later, we went into some beautiful caves and it was really quiet.
**Callum:** Was it dark inside the caves?
**Danielle:** Yes, but we brought some waterproof torches with us. I know a great story about some caves near here. I'll send it to you.

## Unit 2 Lesson 2

Activity Book

### CD1 TRACK 23

#### AB page 17 Activity 3

**Girl:** Hi George, did you go mountain biking on Saturday?
**Boy:** No, we changed our minds. My Dad took us rock climbing.
**Girl:** Really? Where did you go?
**Boy:** There's a fantastic climbing wall in Oxford. We went there.
**Girl:** Did you go with your brother and sister?
**Boy:** No, it was just me and my Dad. My brother and sister didn't want to come.
**Girl:** Was it difficult?
**Boy:** There were three walls: yellow, green and red. Yellow was the easiest and red was the most difficult. It was my first time, so I started on the yellow wall. Then I tried the green wall.
**Girl:** Did you have to wear a helmet?
**Boy:** Yes, they gave me ropes and a helmet.
**Girl:** It sounds great! I'm going to ask my parents to take me. How much did it cost?
**Boy:** It was eight pounds for one hour.
**Girl:** That's not bad … Is it open all day?
**Boy:** It's open from nine o'clock until six o'clock on Saturdays.
**Girl:** That's great. Thanks!

## Unit 2 Lesson 3

Pupil's Book

### CD1 TRACK 24

#### PB page 21 Activity 2

***The fantastic discovery***
**Narrator:** For many years, people in the village of Montignac in the Dordogne told stories about the woods nearby. They said that there was treasure in caves under the woods.
Frame 1
**Narrator:** In 1940, four boys – Marcel, Georges, Simon and Jacques – and their dog, Robot, went to look for the treasure.
**Marcel:** Come on! Let's try to find this treasure.
**Frame 2**
**Narrator:** Robot ran ahead and found a hole by a tree.
**Marcel:** This is it! It's the entrance to the caves.
**Frame 3**
**Narrator:** The boys made the hole bigger. Then, one by one, they climbed into it.
**Jacques:** Is it safe, Marcel?
**Marcel:** Yes, I think so. Come on!
**Frame 4**
**Narrator:** All four boys were now safely inside a big dark cave. They used a lantern to look up at the walls and the ceiling.
**Marcel:** Wow! They look like bulls and deer. I think they're really old paintings.
Frame 5
**Narrator:** At first, they kept the cave a secret, but then they told some friends. Soon everyone wanted to see the cave.
**Jacques:** You can go in, but you have to wait your turn.
Frame 6
**Narrator:** They told their teacher, Mr Laval. He brought a friend who was an expert.
**Man 1:** Boys and their dog discover prehistoric cave paintings
**Man 2:** Mr Breuil (pictured here with Jacques Marsal, Marcel Ravidat and their teacher Mr Laval) told the boys that the paintings were 17,000 years old!

## Unit 2 Lesson 3

Activity Book

### CD1 TRACK 25

#### AB page 18 Activity 2

**Callum:** Read this story, Tom.
**Tom:** What is it?
**Callum:** It's called A fantastic discovery. It's a true story set in France in 1940.
**Tom:** OK … Who are the main characters?
**Callum:** Four French boys and their dog, Robot.
**Tom:** A dog?
**Callum:** Yes … and the dog plays an important part in the story. The boys wanted to find some treasure in the woods near the village.
**Tom:** There's some treasure in the woods?
**Callum:** For many years, people in the village said that treasure was hidden in those woods.
**Tom:** Wow!
**Callum:** Anyway, Robot found a hole and the boys climbed into it. They had a lantern with them.
**Tom:** What happened next?
**Callum:** They found a huge cave and on the walls they saw some amazing paintings of animals!
**Tom:** Did they tell anyone about the cave?
**Callum:** They kept it secret for a few days and then they showed it to some friends and their teacher. Then their teacher brought an expert to the cave. He told them that the paintings were over 17,000 years old!
**Tom:** Wow! That's really old! What's your favourite part of the story?
**Callum:** Erm … I think it's the moment they see the paintings for the first time.
**Tom:** Yes, what a surprise they had! Do you recommend the story?
**Callum:** I do! I think the story was really exciting and I give it … erm … four stars.
**Tom:** Sounds good. I think I'll read it now.

## Unit 2 Lesson 4

Pupil's Book

### CD1 TRACK 26

#### PB page 22 Activity 1

**Tom:** That story about the caves is a real adventure story! I like France. I went there three years ago.
**Callum:** Really? Why did you go to France?
**Tom:** I went on holiday. Look! Here are some photos of our trip.
**Callum:** Nice photos! Who did you go with?
**Tom:** I went with my parents and my cousins.
**Callum:** What did you do there?
**Tom:** We went camping near the beach. We explored the rocks and the woods. We didn't find any cave paintings though!

## Unit 2 Lesson 4

Pupil's Book

### CD1 TRACK 27

#### PB page 22 Activity 5

**1** When did you go there?
**2** Who did you go with?
**3** What did you do there?
**4** Did you go on Wednesday?
**5** Did you go with Max?
**6** Did you go canoeing?

## Unit 2 Lesson 4

Activity Book

**CD1 TRACK 28**

**AB page 19 Activity 3**

1 What did you do there?
2 Did you go rock climbing?
3 How long did you stay there?
4 Why did you go mountain biking?
5 Did you go by train?
6 Did your brother go with you?

## Unit 2 Lesson 5

Pupil's Book

**CD1 TRACK 29**

**PB page 23 Activity 1**

1 insect repellent
2 binoculars
3 saucepan
4 sun cream
5 rope
6 sleeping bag
7 walking boots
8 camping stove
9 matches
10 wildlife guidebooks

## Unit 2 Lesson 5

Pupil's Book

**CD1 TRACK 30**

**PB page 23 Activity 2**

**Boy 1:** Right. So which of these places do you want to go to?
**Girl:** Let's go to Lonely Island.
**Boy 1:** Really? Why? There isn't much there.
**Girl:** Exactly. It will be exciting – a real survival adventure.
**Boy 2:** Hmmm. It will be very hot. There isn't much shade there. What about Whispering Woods? There's protection from the sun.
**Girl:** But it's dark in the woods and there will be lots of insects. I hate insects.
**Boy 1:** The other choice is Mighty Mountain. That will be fun. We all like walking and there are lots of interesting walks in the area.
**Boy 2:** Yes, that's true. And there are some trees for protection from the sun. But there isn't a river.
**Girl:** Yes, I'd like to swim a bit.
**Boy 1:** Well, there's a river at Whispering Woods. We could bring some insect repellent with us to keep off the insects. Is that OK, Suzy?
**Girl:** I don't know. I still prefer Lonely Island. We can swim there, too.
**Boy 2:** I think David is right. There will be trees and a river at Whispering Woods.
**Girl:** Oh, OK then. But let's bring lots of insect repellent!

## Unit 2 Lesson 5

Pupil's Book

**CD1 TRACK 31**

**PB page 23 Activity 3**

**Boy 1:** OK, we've got a tent, sleeping bags, a rucksack and some food. What else do we need to bring?
**Girl:** Some insect repellent!
**Boy 1:** Ah yes. We won't forget that! I don't think we need wetsuits or life jackets.
**Boy 2:** No – the river isn't deep. A torch would be useful and a map of the woods.
**Boy 1:** We probably need a compass, too. Do you think we need sun cream?
**Girl:** Oh yes. We need protection because it'll be sunny.
**Boy 2:** And let's bring some binoculars. We can look for birds and other animals.
**Girl:** That's a good idea. So, we should bring the wildlife guidebook, too.
**Boy 1:** Excellent. That sounds perfect.

## Unit 2 Lesson 6

Activity Book

**CD1 TRACK 32**

**AB page 21 Activity 3**

There was excitement on the coast of Wales on Wednesday when a man was stuck halfway up a cliff. The man's name was Kevin Brown. He was 30 years old and from Liverpool. Kevin tried to climb up the rocks, but he couldn't get to the top – and then he couldn't get down … He phoned his brother, Gary, who then phoned the police. A rescue helicopter came and pulled him to safety. He was very lucky that he didn't fall down. This is what Mr Brown said afterwards:
"It wasn't a very clever thing to do … Oh! and a big thank you to the helicopter rescue team. They were fantastic."
Mr Brown also said he was going to stay on the beach tomorrow.

## Unit 2 Lesson 8

Pupil's Book

**CD1 TRACK 33**

**PB page 26 Activity 2**

**Hannah:** Hi, Mike. How are you?
**Mike:** I'm OK, Hannah. I'm looking at photos. Look. It's my favourite place to visit.
**Hannah:** Let's see. Wow. That looks beautiful. Where is it?
**Mike:** It's a place called Land's End in Cornwall, which is in the south west of England.
**Hannah:** That's a long way away. Where do you stay? In a hotel?
**Mike:** No. We stay in my grandad's caravan. It's on a big caravan park.
**Hannah:** Oh, I would love to sleep in a caravan. Is it near the beach?
**Mike:** Yes, it is. There is so much to do there. We go walking on the cliffs or go swimming and surfing in the sea.
**Hannah:** What can you eat there?
**Mike:** There's a great café in the village. The pizza, chocolate cakes and milkshakes are all delicious!
**Hannah:** When did you last go there?
**Mike:** I went there last summer with my parents and my grandparents. We all stayed in the caravan.
**Hannah:** What did you do there?
**Mike:** One day we went on a boat trip along the coast. We saw people on a fishing boat. It was so much fun!
**Hannah:** Well, that sounds great.
**Mike:** What about you? What's your favourite place to visit?
**Hannah:** I love visiting my cousins in London.
**Mike:** Really? When did you last go there?

## Unit 2
### Video and 21st Century Skills

Activity Book

**CD1 TRACK 34**

**AB page 25 Activity 1**

**Max:** So are you ready to do some research on Charles Blondin, Amy?
**Amy:** Yes, I am, Max. Here are my questions. Tell me what you think. Where was he from? What did he do? Where did he do it? When did he first do it? Did many people watch him? Did he ever fall?
**Max:** They're great questions! You can use the questions for your research on the Internet.
**Amy:** Yes. Then I'll present the answers to you!
**Max:** OK, great!
**Narrator:** Later.
**Amy:** Hey, Max. I've found out about Charles Blondin. It was really interesting. Why don't you ask me the research questions? I can answer them now.
**Max:** OK. Let's see … Where was Charles Blondin from?
**Amy:** Charles Blondin was born in France. He lived most of his life in the UK.
**Max:** What did he do?
**Amy:** He was famous for tightrope walking in dangerous places.
**Max:** Where did he do it?
**Amy:** He walked over the river in Niagara Falls in the US. He did it 17 times. Sometimes he carried another person! Sometimes he covered his eyes.
**Max:** When did he first do it?
**Amy:** He first did it in 1859.
**Max:** Did many people watch him?
**Amy:** Yes. Many people came to watch him and he was very famous.
**Max:** Did he ever fall?
**Amy:** No, he didn't.
**Max:** Wow!
**Amy:** Look! I can show you some pictures.

## Unit 3 Lesson 1

Pupil's Book

**CD1 TRACK 35**

**PB page 28 Activity 3**

1 square
2 fountain
3 bridge
4 castle
5 traffic lights
6 crossroads
7 pedestrian crossing

# Audioscript

**8** pavement
**9** tower
**10** town hall
**11** statue
**12** steps

## Unit 3 Lesson 1

**Pupil's Book**

**CD1 TRACK 36**

**PB page 28 Activity 4**

**1**
**Girl:** This building is tall and narrow. You need to go up some steps to get to the top. And you usually get a great view from the top!
**Boy:** tower
**2**
**Girl:** This is an old building. It's got high, thick walls. Kings and queens built these in the past to protect their towns and cities.
**Boy:** castle
**3**
**Girl:** You can find this next to a road. It's narrow and it's got a hard surface. People walk on it.
**Boy:** pavement
**4**
**Girl:** This building is usually in the centre of a town. It's where the people who look after the town work.
**Boy:** town hall
**5**
**Girl:** You can often see this in a square or garden. It shoots water into the air. People sometimes throw money into it.
**Boy:** fountain
**6**
**Girl:** This object is a machine that controls the traffic. It's got three lights on it. When the light is red, you must stop your car.
**Boy:** traffic lights
**7**
**Girl:** This structure is often used to decorate parks and important buildings. It can have the shape of a person or an animal. It's usually made of stone.
**Boy:** statue
**8**
**Girl:** You use this structure when you want to cross over a river. It's usually long and narrow.
**Boy:** bridge
**9**
**Girl:** You can use these when you want to walk up or down, indoors or outdoors. You have to climb lots of them to reach the top of a tall building!
**Boy:** steps
**10**
**Girl:** You usually see this place in the centre of a town or a city. It's often got four sides with buildings around it. There's sometimes a fountain in the middle, too.
**Boy:** square
**11**
**Girl:** This is the place where two streets cross. There are often traffic lights here.
**Boy:** crossroads
**12**
**Girl:** This is a place where you can cross the road safely. There are usually black and white stripes on the ground. But you need to check that the cars stop before you cross the road.
**Boy:** pedestrian crossing

## Unit 3 Lesson 2

**Pupil's Book**

**CD1 TRACK 37**

**PB page 30 Activity 1**

**Tom:** Hi, Paola. Did your cousin enjoy the tour?
**Paola:** Yes, she did. She loved it. The best part was the visit to the Colosseum. It's an incredible building. Look!
**Tom:** Wow! What did you do there?
**Paola:** We learnt about Roman gladiators, and guess what! We saw our favourite actor. He was making a film.
**Tom:** I don't believe it! Was he wearing a gladiator's costume?
**Paola:** Yes, he was. But he wasn't carrying a sword.
**Tom:** What was he doing?
**Paola:** He was riding a horse around the ring. He was great.
**Tom:** That sounds brilliant. I love Ancient History.
**Paola:** Do you? I know a great website about Ancient History. I'll send you the link.

## Unit 3 Lesson 2

**Activity Book**

**CD1 TRACK 38**

**AB page 27 Activity 3**

**Girl:** Hi, Sam. Did you have a good day yesterday?
**Boy:** Yes, I had a great day.
**Girl:** Really? What did you do?
**Boy:** Well, in the morning I went swimming with my friends. We went to the new sports centre.
**Girl:** Oh! What's it like?
**Boy:** It's great. There are really cool slides and there's a wave pool, too.
**Girl:** It sounds brilliant! Did you stay there long?
**Boy:** Yes, we did. We got there when it opened at ten o'clock and we stayed until one o'clock.
**Girl:** One o'clock!
**Boy:** That's right. We were there for three hours.
**Girl:** Wow! What did you do after that?
**Boy:** We had lunch in the café and then we went to the cinema. We saw the new science fiction film, *Alien Invasion*.
**Girl:** Was it any good?
**Boy:** Not bad, but it was a bit long.
**Girl:** How long was it?
**Boy:** Well, it started at a quarter to four and it finished at a quarter to seven.
**Girl:** Goodness … That's three hours! What did you do after that?
**Boy:** I went home. I was really tired so I went to bed at nine o'clock and at half past nine I was fast asleep!

## Unit 3 Lesson 3

**Pupil's Book**

**CD1 TRACK 39**

**PB page 31 Activity 2**

***The tragedy of Pompeii***
Narrator: In 79 AD, a volcano called Vesuvius erupted in the south of Italy. A 17-year-old poet called Pliny wrote some letters describing what happened. We can still read his letters today.
**Frame 1**
**Narrator:** Pliny was living with his mother at his uncle's house on the coast, near the city of Pompeii.
**Pliny's mum:** Look! There's a dark cloud above the volcano. I think it's erupting.
**Frame 2**
**Narrator:** Pliny's uncle went by boat to rescue some friends who lived near Pompeii. When he arrived, hot ash and rocks were falling from the sky.
**Pliny's uncle:** It's dangerous here, but we can't turn back now. We must help my friends.
**Frame 3**
**Narrator:** Many people were leaving and the ground was shaking. Pliny's uncle went to his friends' house.
**Man:** I think it will stop soon. Let's sleep in the garden tonight where it's safer.
**Frame 4**
**Narrator:** The next morning, Pliny's uncle returned to the boat with his friends.
**Man:** The sea is too dangerous to sail. It's better to wait.
**Frame 5**
**Narrator:** Vesuvius erupted again when Pliny's uncle was waiting to return. Some people escaped, but his uncle died.
**Pliny:** My uncle was a very brave man.
**Frame 6**
**Narrator:** Pompeii lay under volcanic ash until a Spanish engineer discovered the city again in 1748.
Archaeologists found this bread in Pompeii. It was baking in the oven when Vesuvius erupted.

## Unit 3 Lesson 3

**Activity Book**

**CD1 TRACK 40**

**AB page 28 Activity 2**

**Callum:** What are you reading, Tom?
**Tom:** It's a story called 'The tragedy of Pompeii'.
**Callum:** That sounds exciting. What's the story about?
**Tom:** It's a true story. It's about a volcano that erupted in Italy almost two thousand years ago.
**Callum:** Wow! What happened?
**Tom:** Well, a young poet called Pliny and his uncle were living near the city of Pompeii and saw the volcano erupt.
**Callum:** What happened after the volcano erupted?
**Tom:** Pliny's uncle decided to rescue some friends who lived near the volcano and he sailed there on his boat.
**Callum:** Did Pliny's uncle find his friends?
**Tom:** Yes, he found their house. But they had to sleep in the garden that night because it was too dangerous to be indoors.

**Callum:** What happened next?
**Tom:** The next day they went to the beach, but they couldn't leave because there were lots of big waves. Soon after, there was another eruption and Pliny's uncle died.
**Callum:** Oh! That's terrible.
**Tom:** Yes, it is. When Pliny heard what happened, he wrote letters to his family and friends to tell them the news. Do you know that we can still read the letters today?
**Callum:** That's amazing. Do you recommend the story?
**Tom:** I think the story's very interesting, but it's a bit sad, too. I give it four stars.

## Unit 3 Lesson 4

Pupil's Book

### CD1 TRACK 41

#### PB page 32 Activity 1

**Frame 1**
**Jess:** What an incredible story! Volcanoes are really scary.
**Tom:** Yes, but scientists know a lot more about volcanoes now.
**Jess:** You're right. And people know what to do in an emergency, like when there's a fire.
**Frame 2**
**Jess:** There was a fire alarm at our school last year.
**Tom:** Oh yes. I remember. What were you doing when the alarm rang?
**Jess:** I was studying Maths when it rang.
**Tom:** What did you do next?
**Jess:** I walked to the playground with my class.

## Unit 3 Lesson 4

Pupil's Book

### CD1 TRACK 42

#### PB page 32 Activity 5

**1** Was he sleeping?
**2** He was sleeping.
**3** Yes, he was.
**4** I was drinking.
**5** Yes, she was.
**6** Was he running?
**7** Was she cooking?
**8** Yes, I was.
**9** She was speaking.
**10** I was studying.

## Unit 3 Lesson 4

Activity Book

### CD1 TRACK 43

#### AB page 29 Activity 3

**1** Was he eating an apple?
**2** She was crossing the road.
**3** He was getting off the bus.
**4** Was he taking a photo?
**5** He was wearing a pair of jeans.

## Unit 3 Lesson 5

Pupil's Book

### CD1 TRACK 44

#### PB page 33 Activity 1

**1** meet a friend
**2** catch a taxi
**3** go sightseeing
**4** cross the road
**5** wait for a bus
**6** have a snack
**7** get on the bus
**8** get off the bus

## Unit 3 Lesson 5

Pupil's Book

### CD2 TRACK 01

#### PB page 33 Activity 2

**1**
**Girl:** Hi, John.
**Boy:** Hi, Sarah. Where are you going?
**Girl:** I'm going to the city centre.
**Boy:** I went to the city centre yesterday afternoon.
**Girl:** Really? Were you there when it was stormy?
**Boy:** Yes, I was.
**Girl:** What were you doing when it started to rain?
**Boy:** I was getting on the bus.
**Girl:** Pardon? What did you say?
**Boy:** I said that I was getting on the bus.
**Girl:** Oh. Did you get wet?
**Boy:** No, I didn't.
**Girl:** That was lucky.
**2**
**Boy:** Where were you yesterday afternoon, Sarah?
**Girl:** I was at a castle with my parents.
**Boy:** I'm sorry. Could you say that again, please?
**Girl:** Yes, of course. I was at a castle with my parents.
**Boy:** That sounds interesting. What were you doing when it started to rain?
**Girl:** I was taking a photo.
**Boy:** Oh dear. Did you get wet?
**Girl:** Not really. I was wearing a hat.
**Boy:** That was lucky.
**Girl:** Yes, it was.

## Unit 3 Lesson 6

Activity Book

### CD2 TRACK 02

#### AB page 31 Activity 3

**Jane:** Hi, Sam. Do you want to do this questionnaire about reading with me?
**Sam:** OK. Why don't you ask the questions and I answer them?
**Jane:** That's a good idea. Are you ready for the first question?
**Sam:** Yes, go on.
**Jane:** Question number one: How much do you like reading?
**Sam:** Hmm ... I'm not mad about reading like my brother, but I like it quite a lot.
**Jane:** Thanks. Here's question two: What types of fiction do you like reading?
**Sam:** Well, I love books with lots of action like spy stories and adventure stories. And I really enjoy mystery stories with clever detectives. But my favourite books are horror stories. I love scary stories!
**Jane:** Me too. Horror stories are great! Are you ready for the last question?
**Sam:** Yes, I am.
**Jane:** Question number three: Where do you like reading?
**Sam:** Hmmm ... I like reading in class, but I prefer reading at home. I often read in the living room, but my favourite place for reading is ... in bed!

## Unit 3 Lesson 8

Pupil's Book

### CD2 TRACK 03

#### PB page 36 Activity 2

**Lucy:** Where were you last Saturday, Sam?
**Sam:** I was at the Crown sports centre. Do you know it, Lucy?
**Lucy:** Not really. Where is it?
**Sam:** It's on the other side of town … near the park.
**Lucy:** Is it your favourite place in town?
**Sam:** Yes, I suppose it is.
**Lucy:** How often do you go there?
**Sam:** Once or twice a week. I always go on Saturdays. And I try to go in the middle of the week, too. It depends on my homework.
**Lucy:** What do you do there?
**Sam:** I usually go swimming. It's got an indoor pool and an outdoor pool.
**Lucy:** Really?
**Sam:** Yeah! They're brilliant.
**Lucy:** Who do you usually go with?
**Sam:** I go with my sister and my dad on Saturday mornings. What about you? What's your favourite place in town?
**Lucy:** It's the 3D cinema. Do you know it?
**Sam:** Yes, I do.
**Lucy:** What do you think of it?
**Sam:** I think it's great.

## Unit 3

## Video and 21st Century Skills

Activity Book

### CD2 TRACK 04

#### AB page 35 Activity 1

**Max:** What are you doing, Amy?
**Amy:** I'm doing my homework. I need to compare the countryside and the city and then decide which one is better.
**Max:** Why don't you use a Venn diagram to organise your ideas?
**Amy:** Good idea. I'll draw one now … Let's think about living in the city first.
**Max:** Well, there's a lot of entertainment in the city, like cinemas and theatres. There are universities, too.
**Amy:** You're right. But there's also a lot of traffic in the city and sometimes there's pollution.
**Max:** Let's write those ideas down: entertainment, universities, traffic and pollution … Now, what about living in the countryside?
**Amy:** Well, it's quiet and there's clean air. People are friendly in the countryside, too.
**Max:** Quiet, clean air and friendly… Is there anything that's the same in the city and the countryside?
**Amy:** Yes, there's good food in both places.
**Max:** So, which place is better, the city or the countryside?

# Audioscript

**Amy:** Hmm … the city is more exciting than the countryside. There are more opportunities to study, too.
**Max:** But what about the traffic and the pollution?
**Amy:** You're right. The countryside is cleaner and quieter than the city.
**Max:** Which do you prefer and why?
**Amy:** I think I prefer the city.
**Max:** Why?
**Amy:** Because there's more entertainment. I love going to the cinema and to museums.
**Max:** Great! Good luck with writing the assignment!
**Amy:** Thanks. And thanks for your help, Max.

## My project 1 Lesson 1

Pupil's Book

### CD2 TRACK 05

### PB page 38 Activity 2

**Teacher:** Hello, everyone. Today we've got a visitor in the classroom. His name is Mr Jones and he's a nurse. He's here to answer your questions about being healthy. I want you to listen carefully and make some notes.
**Nurse:** Hello, everyone.
**Children:** Hello, Mr Jones.
**Nurse:** Thank you for inviting me to your class. Who's got the first question for me?
**Girl 1:** I have. Why is our diet important?
**Nurse:** That's an excellent question. A good diet helps you to grow and it helps your body fight diseases. The important thing to remember is that you need to eat a variety of food every day. That means eating lots of different types of food.
**Girl 1:** What things should we eat every day?
**Nurse:** Well, you need to eat fruit and vegetables because they've got lots of vitamins which keep your body healthy. You should eat at least two types of fruit a day and two types of vegetables a day. You also need to eat dairy food like cheese and yoghurts as they're good for your bones and teeth. It's a good idea to eat these every day. Food like meat and eggs help you grow tall and strong. You should eat these two or three times a week, too. Finally, you need food to give you energy. Food like pasta and rice will help you be active all day.
**Girl 1:** Is there any food that's bad for you?
**Nurse:** Hmmm … You mustn't eat too much fat or sugar. Food like cakes and sweets have got a lot of fat and sugar, so you should only eat these a few times a week.
**Girl 1:** OK. Thank you.
**Nurse:** Has anyone else got a question?
**Boy:** Yes, I have. My question is: is it important to do exercise?
**Nurse:** Yes, it is, of course. It's important to do exercise at least three times a week. Exercise helps make our heart, our muscles and our bones stronger. It's also very important to be active every day. You can walk the dog or walk to school. It's very easy.
**Boy:** Thank you.
**Teacher:** We've got time for one more question. Anna, would you like to ask a question?
**Girl 2:** Yes, I would. What other things do we need to do to be healthy?
**Nurse:** It's important to be clean. You should wash your hands before you have a meal. You need to brush your teeth two or three times a day, too.
**Girl 2:** OK. Thank you.
**Teacher:** Well, that was very interesting. Thank you very much for coming to our school, Mr Jones.
**Nurse:** You're very welcome.

## Unit 4 Lesson 1

Pupil's Book

### CD2 TRACK 06

### PB page 40 Activity 3

**1** karaoke
**2** tablet
**3 CD player**
**4** MP3 player
**5** computer game
**6** mobile phone
**7** camera
**8** website
**9** webcam
**10** video call
**11** laptop
**12** interactive whiteboard

## Unit 4 Lesson 1

Pupil's Book

### CD2 TRACK 07

### PB page 40 Activity 4

**1**
**Boy:** This is a computer that you can carry around. To close it, you usually fold down the screen.
**Girl:** laptop
**2**
**Boy:** You hold this object in your hand. You can talk to friends or text them. You can often use this object to listen to music and play games, too.
**Girl:** mobile phone
**3**
**Boy:** This is a place on the Internet where people can find out information about a subject. The Internet consists of millions of these.
**Girl:** website
**4**
**Boy:** This is a large screen that is often used in classrooms. It's connected to a computer and teachers and students can control it by touching the screen.
**Girl:** interactive whiteboard
**5**
**Boy:** This is a phone call through a computer. You can see the other person as you speak.
**Girl:** video call
**6**
**Boy:** This is a small machine that you use to listen to music. You download songs onto it using your computer. You often use headphones with it.
**Girl:** MP3 player
**7**
**Boy:** This is a singing activity. You read the words on a screen and sing with the music.
**Girl:** karaoke
**8**
**Boy:** You can use this with your computer to see and speak to people in other places. It usually connects to the top of your computer.
**Girl:** webcam
**9**
**Boy:** This is a small flat computer. You can control it by touching the screen. You can use it to surf the Internet, read books, play games and do many other things.
**Girl:** tablet
**10**
**Boy:** You use this to play music. You put CDs into it and you can usually carry it from place to place.
**Girl:** CD player
**11**
**Boy:** This is a machine that you use to take photos. You can usually connect it to a computer to see and store the photos.
**Girl:** camera
**12**
**Boy:** This is something that you play on a computer. You can play it on a small electronic machine that you hold in your hands, or you can play it on a desktop or a laptop computer.
**Girl:** computer game

## Unit 4 Lesson 2

Pupil's Book

### CD2 TRACK 08

### PB page 42 Activity 1

**Jess:** Hi, Lena. Thanks for the photos. I love music, too. I've got an MP3 player. Have you?
**Lena:** Yes. I listen to it all the time! I prefer it to my CD player. Before, I had to carry CDs everywhere, but now I don't have to. And I've got a LOT of CDs. Look!
**Jess:** Wow! I can see why you prefer your MP3 player.
**Lena:** Sometimes our teacher plays music on the interactive whiteboard at school. We've got one in every classroom now.
**Jess:** Really? We have to go to another classroom to use the interactive whiteboard.
**Lena:** They're great, but you have to have a good internet connection. It wasn't working yesterday. We sometimes use the webcam for video calls, too.
**Jess:** That's great. Who do you speak to?
**Lena:** Last week, a famous author talked to us about writing books.
**Jess:** What a good idea!
**Lena:** There's an amazing story about a webcam. It happened near my town in Germany. I'll send it to you.
**Jess:** OK. Thanks.

## Unit 4 Lesson 2

Activity Book

### CD2 TRACK 09

### AB page 39 Activity 3

OK everyone, listen carefully. After lunch we are going to use the interactive whiteboard for a video call. We are going to talk to the author David Sandhurst. He lives in the UK, but he's in New York at the moment. He is going to talk to us about his book, *Computer World*. Do you remember it? It's a story about a group of children who find a green stone. It's a magic stone and it takes them to another world.
After, we can ask him some questions. But, there are some important instructions. We're using a webcam so he can see us clearly. If you want to ask a question, you have to put your hand up so the author can see you. You don't have to shout,

just speak normally and clearly. You have to be quiet when he is speaking. And remember to say thank you at the end! The video call will be about 20 minutes. Then we can talk about it together for about 15 minutes. Is that clear?

## Unit 4 Lesson 3

**Pupil's Book**

**CD2 TRACK 10**

### PB page 43 Activity 2

***Lost on the beach***
**Narrator:** The beaches in northern Germany are very long and wide. In the winter, ice covers the beaches and some of the sea. You have to be very careful when you walk there in the evening. It's easy to get lost.
**Frame 1**
**Narrator:** A few years ago, a tourist was walking on the beach on a very cold evening. He wanted to take photos of the sunset.
**Man:** Wow! This is beautiful.

**Frame 2**
**Narrator:** It started to get dark. The man was far from the shore and it was foggy.
**Man:** Oh no! I can't see the shore.

**Frame 3**
**Narrator:** In southern Germany, a woman was watching a live webcam of the sunset at the same beach.
**Frame 4**
**Narrator:** Suddenly, the man had an idea.
**Man:** If I take photos, the camera flashes. Maybe someone will see the flashes.
**Frame 5**
**Narrator:** The woman saw the flashes on her computer screen and she called the police.
**Woman 1:** I'm watching the webcam at Sankt Peter-Ording. There's a light flashing. I think someone is lost on the beach.

**Frame 6**
**Narrator:** At the beach, the police used their car lights to help the man. He was safe!
**Woman 2:** Man saved by webcam
Yesterday, a woman in Germany watched a live sunset on her computer and saved a life!
This morning, the man said, "I'm lucky someone was watching the webcam and I'm very grateful that she called the police."

## Unit 4 Lesson 3

**Activity Book**

**CD2 TRACK 11**

### AB page 40 Activity 2

**Jess:** This is an interesting story, Callum.
**Callum:** What's it about?
**Jess:** It's called 'Lost on the beach'. It's a true story. It happened in northern Germany in 2010. A man was walking on the beach. It was very icy, cold and dark and he got lost.
**Callum:** It's hard to get lost on the beach, isn't it?
**Jess:** Well, there was ice on the water and on the beach. And there were no lights on the shore.
**Callum:** Ah … so he didn't know where the shore was.
**Jess:** That's right. Well, he had an idea. He took photos. He wanted someone to see the flashes from the camera.
**Callum:** That's a good idea.
**Jess:** Yes, and he was very lucky. A woman in southern Germany was watching the beach on her computer.
**Callum:** Really? Why?
**Jess:** There is a webcam at the beach and she liked to watch the beautiful sunsets there. Anyway, she saw the flashes and phoned the police.
**Callum:** And what did the police do?
**Jess:** They used their car headlights to show the man where the shore was. They rescued him.
**Callum:** Hmmm … that's interesting!
**Jess:** I think it's an amazing story. It shows us how, using technology, people far away can help. I liked the end especially. I give this story five stars.

## Unit 4 Lesson 4

**Pupil's Book**

**CD2 TRACK 12**

### PB page 44 Activity 1

**Frame 1**
**Jess:** Well, that story shows that webcams are very useful. Is that your camera, Callum?
**Callum:** Yes. If I press the red button, it records a video. And if I press the green button, it takes a photo.
**Frame 2**
**Callum:** Hey, Tom!
**Tom:** Yes?
**Callum:** Say 'cheese' … Great picture, Tom!

## Unit 4 Lesson 4

**Pupil's Book**

**CD2 TRACK 13**

### PB page 44 Activity 5

When it rains, my dad takes me to school.

## Unit 4 Lesson 4

**Pupil's Book**

**CD2 TRACK 14**

### PB page 44 Activity 6

**1** If you walk in the rain, you get wet.
**2** When you don't eat, you get hungry.
**3** When babies are hungry, they cry.

## Unit 4 Lesson 4

**Activity Book**

**CD2 TRACK 15**

### AB page 41 Activity 2

**1** If you don't sleep, you get tired.
**2** When the sun shines, clothes dry more quickly.
**3** If you leave a pizza in a hot oven for an hour, it burns.
**4** When it rains, the grass gets wet.
**5** When the traffic lights turn red, the cars stop.

## Unit 4 Lesson 5

**Pupil's Book**

**CD2 TRACK 16**

### PB page 45 Activity 1

**1** start the game
**2** pause the game
**3** swipe the screen
**4** tap the screen
**5** tilt the screen
**6** move up
**7** move left
**8** move right
**9** move down

## Unit 4 Lesson 5

**Pupil's Book**

**CD2 TRACK 17**

### PB page 45 Activity 2

**Boy:** Hi, Sophie. Do you want to play a game with me on my tablet?
**Girl:** Yes. What games have you got?
**Boy:** This is good. It's called Fruity Fun.
**Girl:** OK. What do you have to do?
**Boy:** You have to cut all the fruit. It's very easy to play.
**Girl:** What are the controls?
**Boy:** You swipe the screen when you see a fruit. And that's it!
**Girl:** Hmmm. Have you got any driving games?
**Boy:** This is called Cool Cars. You have to win the race.
**Girl:** And what are the controls?
**Boy:** If you tilt the screen, you go left and right. And if you tap the screen you go more slowly.
**Girl:** That looks good. Let's play that.
**Boy:** Wait a moment. I like this one. It's called Run, Run, Run!
**Girl:** Oh right. What do you have to do?
**Boy:** You have to run very fast. Some monsters are trying to catch you.
**Girl:** And what are the controls?
**Boy:** In this game, you swipe the screen. If you swipe left, you go left and if you swipe right, you go right. And if you swipe up, you jump. And if you swipe down, you go through a tunnel.
**Girl:** Hmmm. That sounds good, but I really like cars. Can we play that one?
**Boy:** Yes, OK.

## Unit 4 Lesson 6

**Activity Book**

**CD2 TRACK 18**

### AB page 43 Activity 3

**Interviewer:** Hello. What's your name?
**Michael:** Michael.
**Interviewer:** And how old are you?
**Michael:** I'm 11.
**Interviewer:** What did you think of the Newsround website?
**Michael:** Well … I quite liked it, but I'm not very interested in the news. I liked the section about animals.

# Audioscript

**Interviewer:** What was the best thing you found?
**Michael:** Erm … There were some great photos of snakes.
**Interviewer:** And what about the Tate Kids website?
**Michael:** Oh! It's fantastic! I love art, so this was perfect for me.
**Interviewer:** And what was the best thing you found on that website?
**Michael:** I liked the art activities. I learnt lots of new things like how to make masks and hats. The best part was learning to make a sculpture with soap!
**Interviewer:** That sounds great. Thank you, Michael!
**Michael:** You're welcome.
**Interviewer:** Over to you now, Kelly. How old are you?
**Kelly:** I'm 10, but I'll be 11 next month.
**Interviewer:** And what did you think of the Newsround website?
**Kelly:** I liked it. I really love sport and science. I read a lot about Manchester United, my favourite football team!
**Interviewer:** So what was the best thing you found?
**Kelly:** I think the news quiz was the best bit. I got 7 out of 10!
**Interviewer:** Well done! And what did you think of the Tate Kids website?
**Kelly:** Well, actually I thought it was boring because I don't like art very much.
**Interviewer:** Did you like anything on the site?
**Kelly:** Well, the best thing was the stories about famous artists. I quite enjoyed that.
**Interviewer:** OK. Thanks a lot, Kelly.

## Unit 4 Lesson 8

**Pupil's Book**

### CD2 TRACK 19

### PB page 48 Activity 2

**Leah:** Beth, you love your new watch. You look at it all the time.
**Beth:** Yes, I like it, Leah. But I only look at it when I want to know the time!
**Leah:** Is it your favourite object? Or is there something you like more than your watch?
**Beth:** Actually, my favourite object is my MP3 player and headphones.
**Leah:** Why do you like it so much?
**Beth:** Well, I like listening to music and now I can listen to music anywhere. I can listen to music in bed, in the car or I can connect it to speakers so my friends can listen, too.
**Leah:** What does it look like? Is it one of those bright, silver ones?
**Beth:** In fact, it's pink. It's quite bright, too! The headphones are pink and white.
**Leah:** Where did you get it from?
**Beth:** Actually, I don't know. It was a present from my parents for my 10th birthday.
**Leah:** What music do you listen to? Pop music? I love pop music.
**Beth:** Well, I like dance music, but actually my favourite music is jazz music.
**Leah:** Really? I don't know any jazz music.
**Beth:** Well I can play you some! Come with me …

## Unit 4

## Video and 21st Century Skills

**Activity Book**

### CD2 TRACK 20

### AB page 47 Activity 1

**Max:** Hi, Amy. What are you doing?
**Amy:** I'm reading about these glasses.
**Max:** Glasses? You don't wear glasses.
**Amy:** I know. But these are called AR glasses. They are special glasses.
**Max:** AR? What does that mean?
**Amy:** AR means "augmented reality". It's different from virtual reality.
With virtual reality you see a completely different world. But with
augmented reality, you see things on top of what you see
normally.
**Max:** OK. Give me an example.
**Amy:** OK. imagine I am in the centre of London. I put on these AR
glasses. If I look at a building, I see information about it on my
glasses. What is the name of the building? How tall is it? Why is it
important? Any information I want to know!
**Max:** And then what?
**Amy:** If you are interested, you can ask more questions. What time is it
open? What other places can I go to?
**Max:** Wow! That sounds fun. But is it REALLY helpful for people?
**Amy:** Yes, I think so. People won't get lost. They can always see where they are. Also, it can help blind people and people who can't see very well.
**Max:** Ah yes, that's good. But there are negative things, too.
**Amy:** Really? What?
**Max:** People will stop being careful when they walk. They won't look carefully when they cross the road!
**Amy:** Maybe.
**Max:** And they are expensive, too.
**Amy:** Yes, that's true.
**Max:** I don't think they look very good! They are very big!
**Amy:** Well, they are a little bigger than normal glasses, that's true.

## Unit 5 Lesson 1

**Pupil's Book**

### CD2 TRACK 21

### PB page 50 Activity 3

**1** fur
**2** whiskers
**3** fangs
**4** scales
**5** spikes
**6** claws
**7** jaw
**8** fins
**9** tail
**10** wings
**11** feathers
**12** beak

## Unit 5 Lesson 1

**Pupil's Book**

### CD2 TRACK 22

### PB page 50 Activity 4

**1**
**Girl:** These are long, sharp teeth. They're used for biting and for catching other animals.
**Boy:** fangs
**2**
**Girl:** This is part of a bird's mouth. It's hard and it's curved. Birds use it for eating.
**Boy:** beak
**3**
**Girl:** You can find these on the feet of birds and other animals. They're hard and sharp. Birds and animals use them for holding things.
**Boy:** claws
**4**
**Girl:** You can find these on an insect or a bird. They move them up and down to fly.
**Boy:** wings
**5**
**Girl:** These are hard, flat pieces of skin that cover the body of some animals. You can find them on fish and snakes.
**Boy:** scales
**6**
**Girl:** These are long, strong hairs on an animal's face. Cats use them to navigate in the dark.
**Boy:** whiskers
**7**
**Girl:** This part of the body is on the face and it's got a top part and a bottom part. The bottom part moves up and down. It's used for biting, chewing and eating.
**Boy:** jaw
**8**
**Girl:** This is at the back of an animal's body. It can be long or short. It can be straight or curly, too.
**Boy:** tail
**9**
**Girl:** This is soft hair. It covers the body of animals like cats and dogs. It's nice to touch.
**Boy:** fur
**10**
**Girl:** These are soft and light. They can be different colours. They cover a bird's body.
**Boy:** feathers
**11**
**Girl:** These are small and hard, and they're often sharp at the top. Some animals have got them on their body for protection. Crocodiles have got them on their back.
**Boy:** spikes
**12**
**Girl:** You can find these on a fish. They're thin and flat, and they're usually shaped like a triangle. They use them to swim.
**Boy:** fins

## Unit 5 Lesson 2

**Pupil's Book**

**CD2 TRACK 23**

**PB page 52 Activity 1**

**Steve:** Hi, Callum. Can you guess what my favourite Australian animal is?
**Callum:** Give me a clue.
**Steve:** OK. It's got fur.
**Callum:** It must be a mammal then. Is it a koala?
**Steve:** No, it isn't. Here's your second clue: it lives in water.
**Callum:** Hmm ... it can't be a dolphin because they don't have fur. It could be a seal. They're mammals and they live in water.
**Steve:** Wrong again. Here's your final clue: it's got a beak and a poisonous spike.
**Callum:** A mammal with fur, a beak and a poisonous spike! What is it?
**Steve:** It's a platypus. Look! Here's a photo. The spike is on its back leg.
**Callum:** How amazing! Do you know any other strange Australian animals?
**Steve:** Yes, I do. Here's a link to an interesting web page. Can you guess what the animal is?

## Unit 5 Lesson 2

**Activity Book**

**CD2 TRACK 24**

**AB page 49 Activity 3**

**Radio presenter:** Good evening and welcome to 'Animal world'. Today we're going to talk to James White, a zoo keeper from Australia. Hello, James.
**Zoo keeper:** Hello!
**Radio presenter:** Which animal are you going to talk about today?
**Zoo keeper:** I'm going to talk about an Australian bird called the cassowary bird.
**Radio presenter:** That sounds interesting. What does a cassowary bird look like?
**Zoo keeper:** Well, it's one of the biggest birds in the world. It's between one and a half and two metres tall – that's the same as a human adult – and it weighs about 58 kilograms.
**Radio presenter:** That's VERY big. What else can you tell us about its appearance?
**Zoo keeper:** The male and female look very similar. They've both got shiny black feathers and a red crest on their head. They've also got bright blue necks and long legs.
**Radio presenter:** Can cassowary birds fly?
**Zoo keeper:** No, they can't. But they've got very strong legs for running. At the end of their legs they've got three toes and very, very sharp claws. Do you know that the middle claw is 12 centimetres long? That's almost as long as a pencil.
**Radio presenter:** Oh dear. That sounds dangerous! How fast can cassowary birds run?
**Zoo keeper:** Their legs are very powerful. They can run at about 50 kilometres per hour.
**Radio presenter:** That's amazing. Are they friendly birds?
**Zoo keeper:** Not at all. They're very dangerous so if you see a cassowary bird in the wild you should walk slowly and quietly away. Never try to feed a cassowary bird.
**Radio presenter:** Thank you very much, James. That was very interesting.
**Zoo keeper:** You're welcome. Goodbye.

## Unit 5 Lesson 3

**Pupil's Book**

**CD2 TRACK 25**

**PB page 53 Activity 2**

***The bunyip***
**Narrator:** The first European settlers arrived in Australia about 250 years ago. Life was hard because of the hot dry climate. There were lots of strange plants and animals, too.
**Frame 1**
**Narrator:** The settlers soon heard about a terrible beast called a bunyip. It lived in water holes called billabongs.
**Man 1:** Don't put your tent near the billabong and be very quiet when you collect water.
**Frame 2**
**Narrator:** At nighttime, the settlers often felt scared.
**Man 2:** What's that noise? It sounds like a lion.
**Man 3:** It's a bunyip. It hunts at night, so stay close to the fire.
**Frame 3**
**Narrator:** Several years later, Hamilton Hume, an explorer, found some bones near a lake.
**Hamilton:** This skeleton looks like a hippo, but hippos don't live in Australia. Could it be a bunyip?
**Frame 4**
**Narrator:** Over the years, many people reported seeing bunyips.
**Journalist:** What did it look like?
**Man 4:** It had a long tail, dark fur and terrible fangs.
**Frame 5**
**Narrator:** Nowadays, children in Australia enjoy scary stories about bunyips. You can even buy bunyip toys.
**Mum:** The red eyes burned through the night and a scream broke the silence.
**Frame 6**
**Narrator:** There are many theories about bunyips. What do you think?
**Child 1:** Bunyips could be big river seals.
**Child 2:** Bunyips may be prehistoric animals.
**Child 3:** Bunyips could be real monsters.
**Child 4:** Bunyips might be stories to scare people.

## Unit 5 Lesson 3

**Activity Book**

**CD2 TRACK 26**

**AB page 50 Activity 2**

**Tom:** What are you reading, Callum?
**Callum:** I'm reading a story called 'The bunyip'. It explains the myth of an Australian monster.
**Tom:** That sounds interesting. When did the myth begin?
**Callum:** It began about 250 years ago when the first settlers arrived in Australia. These settlers heard about a terrible monster.
**Tom:** And that was the bunyip?
**Callum:** That's right. The settlers believed that the bunyip lived in water holes and rivers and that it hunted at night.
**Tom:** How scary! Was there any evidence that the monster existed?
**Callum:** Well, an explorer found some strange bones near a lake and people thought that they were the bones of a bunyip.
**Tom:** Anything else?
**Callum:** Yes. People also reported seeing bunyips in the countryside at night and these descriptions appeared in newspapers.
**Tom:** Do people still believe in bunyips nowadays?
**Callum:** No, they don't. They think that people saw large mammals like river seals.
**Tom:** That's a possibility.
**Callum:** They also think that the myth was invented by native people to scare away the settlers.
**Tom:** That could be true, too. Do you recommend the story?
**Callum:** Yes, I do. It's interesting and a bit scary. I give it four stars.

## Unit 5 Lesson 4

**Pupil's Book**

**CD2 TRACK 27**

**PB page 54 Activity 1**

**Frame 1**
**Callum:** This information about bunyips is so cool. I want to see one!
**Jess:** What does a bunyip look like?
**Callum:** It looks like a big dog. It's got long hair and pointed ears.
**Frame 2**
**Jess:** Does it look scary?
**Callum:** Oh yes. It's got red eyes and sharp fangs.
**Jess:** What does it sound like?
**Callum:** It sounds like a lion ... ROAR!
**Jess:** Oh Callum! You scared me.

## Unit 5 Lesson 4

**Pupil's Book**

**CD2 TRACK 28**

**PB page 54 Activity 5**

**1** What does it look like?
**2** Does it look scary?
**3** What does it taste like?
**4** Does it feel soft?
**5** What does it smell like?
**6** Does it look good?

## Unit 5 Lesson 4

**Activity Book**

**CD2 TRACK 29**

**AB page 51 Activity 3**

**1** What do they taste like?
**2** What does it sound like?
**3** Does it feel soft?
**4** What do they look like?
**5** Does it sound too loud?
**6** Does it smell bad?
**7** What does it smell like?
**8** Does it feel hard?

# Audioscript

## Unit 5 Lesson 4

Activity Book

**CD2 TRACK 30**

**AB page 51 Activity 4**

**1** [sound of a guinea pig]
**2** [sound of an elephant]
**3** [sound of a whale]
**4** [sound of an owl]
**5** [sound of a wolf]
**6** [sound of a seal]
**7** [sound of a rattlesnake]
**8** [sound of a chicken]
**9** [sound of a mosquito]

## Unit 5 Lesson 5

Pupil's Book

**CD2 TRACK 31**

**PB page 55 Activity 1**

**1** bull
**2** donkey
**3** swan
**4** grasshopper
**5** silkworm
**6** praying mantis
**7** mole
**8** eagle

## Unit 5 Lesson 5

Pupil's Book

**CD2 TRACK 32**

**PB page 55 Activity 2**

**1**
**Girl:** Hi, Sam. Can you guess the animal I'm thinking about?
**Boy:** Let me see. Is the animal colourful?
**Girl:** Yes, it is.
**Boy:** Hmm. It could be the praying mantis or the spider. What does it look like?
**Girl:** It's got six legs and it's got two wings. It doesn't look dangerous.
**Boy:** Ah ha! It must be the [beep].
**Girl:** You're right!
**2**
**Boy:** Now it's my turn. Can you guess the animal I'm thinking about?
**Girl:** OK. Is it a domestic animal?
**Boy:** No, it isn't.
**Girl:** OK. So it can't be the budgie. It might be the eagle or it may be the swan. What does it look like?
**Boy:** It's got sharp claws and a curved beak. It looks fierce.
**Girl:** OK. It must be the [beep].
**Boy:** You're right!

## Unit 5 Lesson 6

Activity Book

**CD2 TRACK 33**

**AB page 53 Activity 3**

**Journalist:** Hello. I work for the *Daily News*. Can I ask you some questions, please?
**Girl:** Yes, of course. What do you want to know?
**Journalist:** First, what's your name and where are you from?
**Girl:** My name's Susie and I'm from Saltney. It's a town on the coast.
**Journalist:** Saltney? How do you spell that?
**Girl:** S-A-L-T-N-E-Y.
**Journalist:** Thank you and you're 11 years old, aren't you?
**Girl:** That's right.
**Journalist:** When did you visit Loch Ness?
**Girl:** I went there last week with my parents. It was really cool.
**Journalist:** And what happened when you were there?
**Girl:** Well, I was riding my bike next to the lake when I saw something in the water.
**Journalist:** Really? What did you see?
**Girl:** I'm not sure what it was. It was dark and very long and it was moving fast.
**Journalist:** How did you feel? Were you afraid?
**Girl:** Yes, a little bit.
**Journalist:** Did you take a photo?
**Girl:** No, I didn't. I was too scared. I cycled to the picnic area as fast as possible. My parents were there and I told them all about it.
**Journalist:** So, do you think you saw the Loch Ness Monster?
**Girl:** Yes, I do. I went back to the lake with my dad and we didn't see anything in the water, but I'm sure it was the Loch Ness Monster.
**Journalist:** That's very interesting. Thank you very much for all the information, Susie.
**Girl:** You're welcome.

## Unit 5 Lesson 8

Pupil's Book

**CD2 TRACK 34**

**PB page 58 Activity 2**

**Eva:** Hi, Ben. What are you doing?
**Ben:** I'm looking at some photos of pets, Eva.
**Eva:** Let me see … Aw! They're lovely.
**Ben:** Did you have a pet when you were small, Eva?
**Eva:** Yes, I did. I had some tropical fish when I was little.
**Ben:** What were they like?
**Eva:** Well, they looked amazing. They were different colours and, I remember, one was striped.
**Ben:** Would you like to have some more tropical fish?
**Eva:** Not really. They're a bit boring.
**Ben:** Oh? Which pet would you like in the future?
**Eva:** I'd like a puppy. I think dogs are the best pets. Do you agree?
**Ben:** I'm not sure. They're friendly and fun, but they're a lot of work, too.
**Eva:** Really? What do they need?
**Ben:** They need a lot of exercise. You need to take them for a walk every day. How do you feel about that?
**Eva:** Oh! I don't mind.

## Unit 5

### Video and 21st Century Skills

Activity Book

**CD2 TRACK 35**

**AB page 57 Activity 1**

**Max:** Are there any wild animals in danger in the UK, Amy?
**Amy:** I don't know. Why don't we look on the Internet? … It says here that bats are in danger.
**Max:** Bats?!
**Amy:** Yes, the number of bats in the UK has gone down a lot in the last few years.
**Max:** I've never seen a bat. Where do they live?
**Amy:** They like dark, quiet places so they often live in trees, caves and under bridges.
**Max:** And what do they eat?
**Amy:** They eat insects. Do you know that one bat can eat more than 3,000 insects in a night?
**Max:** Wow!
**Amy:** I wonder why they're in danger.
**Max:** It says that they're in danger because there are fewer trees now. There are fewer insects, too.
**Amy:** What a pity. Does it say what people can do to help?
**Max:** Yes, it does. One idea is to create a bat-friendly garden. You plant flowers to attract insects and you build boxes for bats to sleep in.
**Amy:** That's brilliant, but how can we tell people about it?
**Max:** What about making a poster?
**Amy:** That's a good idea. We can put the poster in the library. What else can we do?
**Max:** We could give a presentation to our class.
**Amy:** I like that idea, too. What shall we do first?
**Max:** Let's start with the poster. I can find out about flowers for the bat-friendly garden.
**Amy:** And I can find out how to make bat boxes.
**Max:** What a great plan!

## Unit 6 Lesson 1

Pupil's Book

**CD2 TRACK 36**

**PB page 60 Activity 3**

**1** pop concert
**2** magazines
**3** classical music concert
**4** play
**5** poems
**6** art exhibition
**7** sculpture
**8** 3D film
**9** circus
**10** dance show
**11** ballet
**12** comedy show

## Unit 6 Lesson 1

Pupil's Book

**CD2 TRACK 37**

**PB page 60 Activity 4**

**1**
**Boy:** This is a kind of dance that tells a story. It's usually a dance to classical music.
**Girl:** ballet

2
**Boy:** This is a piece of art, but it isn't a painting. It can be made of stone, wood, metal or many other materials.
**Girl:** sculpture
3
**Boy:** This usually happens inside a big tent. People do exciting, dangerous or funny things.
**Girl:** circus
4
**Boy:** This is a kind of entertainment that's funny. It can be one person, or more people, who are trying to make you laugh.
**Girl:** comedy show
5
**Boy:** This is a kind of entertainment with one person, or a group of people, moving together to music. The people can move slowly or with lots of energy.
**Girl:** dance show
6
**Boy:** You can buy these in a newsagents. They can be about sport, music, clothes or many other things.
**Girl:** magazines
7
**Boy:** You can see this at a cinema. You have to wear special glasses to watch it.
**Girl:** 3D film
8
**Boy:** This is music that a group of people perform on a stage to entertain others. It's usually modern music and includes people singing and people playing musical instruments, like guitars and drums.
**Girl:** pop concert
9
**Boy:** You can see this in a theatre. There are actors performing and it tells a story.
**Girl:** play
10
**Boy:** This is something that a group of people perform to entertain others. It's often with an orchestra. They play instruments like violins, flutes and trumpets.
**Girl:** classical music concert
11
**Boy:** This is a collection of paintings or sculptures that you can go and see. It's usually in a gallery.
**Girl:** art exhibition
12
**Boy:** You can find these in books. They've often got short lines of text with words that rhyme. People often read them aloud for other people to listen to.
**Girl:** poems

## Unit 6 Lesson 2

**Pupil's Book**

**CD2 TRACK 38**

**PB page 62 Activity 1**

**Tom:** Hi, Nancy. That arts festival looks fun. Did you enjoy it?
**Nancy:** Yes, I did. And I won first prize in the poetry competition!
**Tom:** Wow! That's great!
**Nancy:** Thanks! I'm really happy. I was so nervous, though. Have you ever been to a poetry competition?
**Tom:** No, I haven't. But I've been to a pop concert. I love singing. Do you?
**Nancy:** Yes, I sing in the school choir. Look! Here's a photo of our concert last week.
**Tom:** I've been to a big choir concert. It was amazing.
**Nancy:** Lucky you! Do you know about the African Children's Choir?
**Tom:** No. Are they good?
**Nancy:** Yes, they're brilliant! They started in Uganda. That's where I was born. I'll send you some information about them.
**Tom:** That sounds really interesting. Thanks!

## Unit 6 Lesson 2

**Activity Book**

**CD2 TRACK 39**

**AB page 59 Activity 3**

**Radio presenter:** Hello everyone and welcome to Arts World. Today we are at the Children's Arts Festival in London. I am with Polly and Charlie who are having fun here today. Hello!
**Polly and Charlie:** Hello!
**Radio presenter:** So, Polly, tell me. When did the festival start?
**Polly:** It started at ten this morning and it finishes at about nine in the evening.
**Radio presenter:** And what is happening at the festival?
**Polly:** There are so many things! There are lots of concerts: pop ...
**Radio presenter:** Are there any classical music concerts?
**Polly:** Yes, there are. An orchestra is playing at two o'clock. There's also a comedy show at two o'clock.
**Radio presenter:** Are there any classes you can take?
**Polly:** Yes, there are! There are circus classes, singing classes and dance classes.
**Radio presenter:** Have you been to any events or classes today, Charlie?
**Charlie:** Yes, I've been to a comedy show and a juggling class.
**Radio presenter:** Great! Can you juggle now?
**Charlie:** Well ... I can juggle better now!
**Radio presenter:** How about you, Polly?
**Charlie:** I've been to two pop concerts because I love pop music. And I've been to a singing class, too.
**Radio presenter:** Do you have to pay for the classes?
**Charlie:** No, they're all free. But you have to get there early because they are very popular.
**Radio presenter:** I'm quite hungry now ... Can you buy food here?
**Polly:** Oh yes! Look over there. There's Italian food, Spanish food, Mexican food and Chinese food, too.

## Unit 6 Lesson 3

**Pupil's Book**

**CD2 TRACK 40**

**PB page 63 Activity 2**

***A choir for Africa***
**Narrator:** This story begins in Uganda, a country in the centre of Africa. It was 1984 and there was a war in Uganda. The people were very poor.
**Frame 1**
**Narrator:** One day, Ray Barnett was listening to the radio at home in Canada.
**Radio presenter:** Thousands of children in Uganda haven't got enough food. Many of them are dying.
**Frame 2**
**Narrator:** Ray went to Uganda to help. One day, he drove a boy to his aunt's house. The boy sang for the whole journey.
**Ray:** That's beautiful!
**Frame 3**
**Narrator:** After hearing the boy sing, Ray decided to create a children's choir.
**Ray:** Wow! I want people in other countries to hear them.
**Frame 4**
**Narrator:** The choir sang at concerts in Canada. People loved their music.
**Woman:** I've seen the choir four times. I'm their biggest fan.
**Frame 5**
**Narrator:** Ray helped the people in Uganda to use the money for new homes and new schools.
**Man:** Thanks for helping us.
**Frame 6**
**Narrator:** There are now about 40 African Children's Choirs. They've won awards and they've sung in front of the Queen of England.

## Unit 6 Lesson 3

**Activity Book**

**CD3 TRACK 01**

**AB page 60 Activity 2**

**Jess:** What are you reading, Tom?
**Tom:** I'm reading a story called 'A choir for Africa'. It's about the African Children's Choir.
**Jess:** What's the story about exactly?
**Tom:** It's a great story about a man called Ray Barnett who wanted to help poor children in Uganda.
**Jess:** Oh, right. When was this?
**Tom:** It was in 1984. He heard on the radio that many children were dying in Uganda. He flew there to try to help.
**Jess:** And how did he help?
**Tom:** One day he heard a boy singing very beautifully and he decided to create a choir.
**Jess:** That sounds like fun ... but how did that help them?
**Tom:** Well, they were a very good choir! They travelled to Canada to sing. People paid money to see them. Ray used this money to build houses and schools in Uganda.
**Jess:** Wow! That's great.
**Tom:** And they've been to many different places! They've even been to England a few times, too!
**Jess:** Really?
**Tom:** Yes! And they met the Queen of England.
**Jess:** How exciting! You're right, Tom, that's a nice story.
**Tom:** Let's see ... I think it's an inspiring and happy story. I give it four stars.

## Unit 6 Lesson 4

**Pupil's Book**

**CD3 TRACK 02**

**PB page 64 Activity 1**

**Tom:** Have you listened to the African Children's Choir?

# Audioscript

**Jess:** No, I haven't. Let's listen …
They're excellent. Has Callum seen this clip?
**Tom:** Yes, he has. He loved it.
**Jess:** Why is Callum singing now?
**Tom:** He's practising for the school choir.
**Jess:** Has he ever sung in a choir?
**Tom:** No, he hasn't. He needs to practise more!

## Unit 6 Lesson 4

Pupil's Book

### CD3 TRACK 03

**PB page 64 Activity 5**

**1** Have you ever eaten Chinese food?
**2** Have you ever taken photos from a plane?
**3** Have you ever written an email in English?
**4** Have you ever given your teacher a present?
**5** Have you ever ridden a horse?
**6** Have you ever broken a promise?

## Unit 6 Lesson 4

Activity Book

### CD3 TRACK 04

**AB page 61 Activity 3**

**1** festival
**2** garden
**3** listen
**4** wetsuit
**5** taken
**6** help
**7** children
**8** leggings
**9** umbrella
**10** steps
**11** open
**12** tablet

## Unit 6 Lesson 5

Pupil's Book

### CD3 TRACK 05

**PB page 65 Activity 1**

**1** act in a play
**2** play in an orchestra
**3** juggle
**4** sing in a choir
**5** create a comic
**6** write a poem
**7** compose music
**8** make a sculpture
**9** paint a portrait
**10** make a film

## Unit 6 Lesson 5

Pupil's Book

### CD3 TRACK 06

**PB page 65 Activity 2**

**Robbie:** OK, Polly and Tim. Let's see who's done the most things. Have you ever juggled?
**Polly:** I have. Have you juggled, Tim?
**Tim:** Yes, I have, too.
**Robbie:** And I have – so that's all of us! Have you ever painted a portrait?
**Polly:** Hmmm … no, I haven't. Have you, Tim?
**Tim:** I have. I painted a portrait of my brother last week. He didn't like it much!
**Robbie:** I painted a portrait, too. I love painting. Right – the next question. Have you made a film or have you acted in a play?
**Polly:** I've made a film and I've acted in a play.
**Tim:** And I've made a film. Polly and I made a film together! But I haven't acted in a play. What about you, Robbie?
**Robbie:** I haven't made a film or acted in a play. Right – what about music? Have you ever composed music, Polly?
**Polly:** No, I haven't. That's really hard. I like singing, but I haven't composed music.
**Tim:** I haven't composed music. But you like music a lot, Robbie. Have you ever composed music?
**Robbie:** Yes, I have. We compose music in Piano Club. And the last question … Have you created a comic?
**Polly:** That's easy. We've all created a comic. We created a comic in school together last term!
**Robbie:** So who's done the most things?

## Unit 6 Lesson 5

Pupil's Book

### CD3 TRACK 07

**PB page 65 Activity 3**

**1** Have you ever acted in a play?
**2** Have you ever played in an orchestra?
**3** Have you ever juggled?
**4** Have you ever sung in a choir?
**5** Have you ever created a comic?
**6** Have you ever written a poem?
**7** Have you ever composed music?
**8** Have you ever made a sculpture?
**9** Have you ever painted a portrait?
**10** Have you ever made a film?

## Unit 6 Lesson 6

Pupil's Book

### CD3 TRACK 08

**PB page 66 Activity 3**

***An Orchestra of One***
by Helen Douglas

I like to play the French horn.
Its sound is deep and low.
I take the deepest breath I can
And then I blow and blow.

The violin is easy
When the music's nice and slow.
But when it's something faster,
It's hard work with the bow.

The cello is much bigger.
Double bass is bigger still.
I haven't learnt to play it yet,
But one day soon I will.

The flute is very pretty
And sounds sweet as can be.
The clarinet is deeper
And sounds quite sad to me.

I love to play the drums.
I bang them really loudly.
I crash the giant cymbals
And twirl the drumsticks proudly.

I could be an orchestra,
An orchestra of one.
I'd run from drum to violin.
Oh, wouldn't that be fun?

## Unit 6 Lesson 6

Activity Book

### CD3 TRACK 09

**AB page 63 Activity 3**

**Journalist:** Hello. Can I ask you some questions, please? It's for the music magazine, *Orchestra!*
**Neil:** Yes, of course.
**Journalist:** What's your name?
**Neil:** My name's Neil Adams.
**Journalist:** How old are you, Neil?
**Neil:** I'm 15 years old. It was my birthday yesterday.
**Journalist:** Oh, happy birthday!
**Neil:** Thank you.
**Journalist:** Do you play any musical instruments?
**Neil:** Yes, I do! I play the violin.
**Journalist:** When did you start learning the violin?
**Neil:** I started when I was eight years old. I had a lesson once a week. Then, I started playing in the school orchestra when I was ten.
**Journalist:** Do you play any other musical instruments?
**Neil:** Well, I play the piano and I can play the cello a bit, too. But I am much better at the violin.
**Journalist:** Do you have to practise a lot?
**Neil:** I practise alone every day for about 45 minutes. It's very hard work. I practise with the orchestra twice a week, too. That's more fun.
**Journalist:** What do you like about playing the violin?
**Neil:** I love the sound of the violin. It can sound sad and emotional, but also sound happy and fun. Playing with the orchestra is amazing. It's so loud and exciting!
**Journalist:** Have you played in any big concerts?
**Neil:** Well, we are going to play in front of 1000 people on Saturday at the City Concert Hall.
**Journalist:** Wow! Are you nervous?
**Neil:** Yes, a little bit. But I'm excited, too.
**Journalist:** I think I'll go and buy a ticket!
**Neil:** I'm sorry, but you can't. There aren't any tickets left. They have sold them all!
**Journalist:** Really? That's amazing. Oh well. I will see you at the next concert! Enjoy the concert and good luck!
**Neil:** Thanks very much.
**Journalist:** And thanks for finding the time to speak to me.
**Neil:** You're welcome.

## Unit 6 Lesson 8

Pupil's Book

### CD3 TRACK 10

**PB page 68 Activity 2**

**Martha:** Hello, Tyler.
**Tyler:** Hi, Martha.

**Martha:** What's your favourite kind of entertainment? Is it music, theatre, books …?
**Tyler:** I like films best. Do you?
**Martha:** Yes, I love films, too. So – what kind of films do you like?
**Tyler:** I like comedies, but most of all I like adventure films.
**Martha:** Ah – adventure films. And what's your favourite film?
**Tyler:** Erm – that's hard. I like lots of films. I really enjoyed *The Jungle Book* – that's my favourite film at the moment. Have you seen it, too?
**Martha:** Yes, I have. I loved it, too! Have you ever seen a 3D film?
**Tyler:** Oh yes – it's great for action films. I've seen about four or five 3D films.
**Martha:** Can you remember the first film you saw?
**Tyler:** The first film I saw was *Madagascar*. I was only four years old. I thought it was really scary – I don't know why!
**Martha:** Where do you usually go to watch films?
**Tyler:** Well. I watch some films at the cinema. But my favourite thing is to watch films at home with a group of my friends. We turn off the lights and eat popcorn! Do you like popcorn, too?
**Martha:** Yes, I love it! Have you ever made a film yourself?
**Tyler:** Actually, I am really interested in making films. I've made some short films with my friend. We used a video camera from school. They're not serious films, they're quite funny. They are animated films with model characters – and we love doing them. Maybe one day I'll be a famous film director!

# Unit 6
## Video and 21st Century Skills

Activity Book

**CD3 TRACK 11**

**AB page 67 Activity 1**

**Amy:** Hey, Max. Let's think of some food and drink to sell at the talent day, too.
**Max:** What about orange juice? And some biscuits?
**Amy:** Let's be different and original. What else can we think of?
**Max:** Hmm. You're right. Most people will sell biscuits and juice.
Let's think of something different.
**Amy:** What about some fruit? We can sell strawberries or melon. We could make fruit salad!
**Max:** The weather is very hot and the fruit will go brown. I don't think fruit is a good idea.
**Amy:** Maybe not … So, is it going to be hot? I've got an idea!
**Max:** OK.
**Amy:** I've got a cool box. You put ice blocks in it and it keeps food cold.
**Max:** OK, great. What can we put in it?
**Amy:** We can bring some ice cream.
**Max:** Great idea. Let's have chocolate ice cream. And strawberry ice cream, too.
**Amy:** Some people don't like chocolate or strawberry ice cream. How about vanilla ice cream?
**Max:** OK. But let's bring chocolate sauce and strawberry sauce to put on it.
**Amy:** Brilliant. I'll go and look for the cool box.
**Max:** I will buy the ice cream!
**Amy:** See you later, Max.
**Max:** Yes, bye Amy.

# My project 2 Lesson 1

Pupil's Book

**CD3 TRACK 12**

**PB page 70 Activity 2**

**Tour guide:** Welcome to the castle everyone. My name's Peter and I'm your guide today. As you know, this castle was built in the Middle Ages. This period of history began in 476 AD and it lasted for one thousand years. Has anybody got a question?
**Boy:** Yes, I have. What was life like in the Middle Ages?
**Tour guide:** It wasn't very nice. There was lots of fighting so people built strong castles for protection.
**Girl:** Who did the land belong to in the Middle Ages?
**Tour guide:** It belonged to the king. The king ruled the country and everything belonged to him. He travelled a lot so he needed palaces and castles all around the country.
**Boy:** What did the king do with all his land?
**Tour guide:** Well, he kept some of the land and he rented the rest to the nobles.
**Girl:** The nobles? Who were they?
**Tour guide:** The nobles were people who were loyal to the king. They lived in castles and had a lot of power, too.
**Boy:** What did the nobles have to do for the king?
**Tour guide:** They had to send knights to the king's army. These knights fought in terrible wars. They wore armour made of metal and were very strong and brave.
**Girl:** Where did the knights live?
**Tour guide:** They lived in the castle with the nobles and the king.
**Boy:** Were a lot of people rich in the Middle Ages?
**Tour guide:** Absolutely not. About 90% of people were peasants. The peasants worked on the land and they provided the food for the king, the nobles and the knights. They lived in very small wooden huts.
**Girl:** Was life hard for the peasants?
**Tour guide:** Yes, it was. They had to work a lot and they didn't have enough food.

# My project 2 Lesson 2

Pupil's Book

**CD3 TRACK 13**

**PB page 71 Activity 1**

**Narrator:** A poor peasant is walking to the town market. He's carrying a heavy sack on his back.
**Peasant:** I need to take this food to the market, but it's too heavy for me.
**Narrator:** We can hear the sound of a horse on the path.
**Peasant:** I can hear someone. Maybe this person will help me.
**Narrator:** A noble approaches on a horse. The peasant bows.
**Peasant:** Kind noble, will you help me? This sack is heavy and I must take it to the market. My wife is sick and my children are hungry.
**Noble:** Get out of my way, peasant! I'm too important to help you.
**Narrator:** The noble rides away and the peasant continues walking. Then he hears another horse.
**Peasant:** I can hear another horse. Maybe this person is kinder.
**Narrator:** The Queen approaches and stops her horse.
**Peasant:** It's the Queen!
**Narrator:** The peasant bows very low.
**Queen:** What's the matter, peasant? Why do you look so sad?
**Peasant:** This sack is very heavy. I must take it to the market. My wife and children are hungry.
**Queen:** I'll help you, but you must promise me one thing in return.
**Peasant:** Yes, yes. I promise.
**Queen:** Come closer. No one must hear …
**Narrator:** The Queen whispers secretly to the peasant.

# Unit 7 Lesson 1

Pupil's Book

**CD3 TRACK 14**

**PB page 72 Activity 3**

**1** blow up balloons
**2** decorate the room
**3** send invitations
**4** clean the furniture
**5** choose the music
**6** make posters
**7** sell tickets
**8** make a cake
**9** sweep the floor
**10** go shopping
**11** serve drinks
**12** put out the food

# Unit 7 Lesson 1

Pupil's Book

**CD3 TRACK 15**

**PB page 72 Activity 4**

**1**
**Girl:** You use your mouth to do this. When you've finished, you tie them up and you sometimes tie string on them, too.
**Boy:** blow up balloons
**2**
**Girl:** You do this to invite people to an event, like a party. You write them and then you post them.
**Boy:** send invitations
**3**
**Girl:** You need to use water and a cloth or a sponge for this job. You do this to make things in a room clean again.
**Boy:** clean the furniture
**4**
**Girl:** You do this when you have to buy something. You need some bags and some money. You can buy all kinds of things: food, clothes, books …

# Audioscript

**Boy:** go shopping
**5**
**Girl:** To do this, you need to pour something into a glass and give it to someone. You can also do this by carrying the glasses on a tray.
**Boy:** serve drinks
**6**
**Girl:** You usually use butter, eggs, flour and sugar to do this. You also use an oven to bake it.
**Boy:** make a cake
**7**
**Girl:** This is something you do before an event, like a fair or a show. You usually give people a piece of paper and they give you some money to pay for the event.
**Boy:** sell tickets
**8**
**Girl:** You need to do this to clean a part of a room when it's dirty. You use a broom or a brush to do this.
**Boy:** sweep the floor
**9**
**Girl:** You can look through your CDs or search on your MP3 player to do this. People usually enjoy listening to this when they're at a party.
**Boy:** choose the music
**10**
**Girl:** You can do this with pens and paper, or you can use a computer to decorate them, too. You usually do this to give people some information about an event.
**Boy:** make posters
**11**
**Girl:** You can use balloons, streamers or coloured paper to do this. You can use posters, too.
**Boy:** decorate the room
**12**
**Girl:** You need to use plates to do this. You put the items on a table so that it's easy for people to eat.
**Boy:** put out the food

## Unit 7 Lesson 2

Pupil's Book

**CD3 TRACK 16**

**PB page 74 Activity 1**

**Jess:** Hi, Jacob. The party sounds great. It's wonderful that your school is helping the hospital.
**Jacob:** Well, the hospital helps people every day, so it's nice to do something for them. And we can raise some money at the same time.
**Jess:** Have you done anything to help yet?
**Jacob:** Yes. I've already made some cupcakes. Here's a photo. What do you think?
**Jess:** Wow! They look amazing. How did you make them with your broken arm?
**Jacob:** My sister helped me. She held the bowl and I stirred the mixture with my good arm.
**Jess:** What else have you done?
**Jacob:** I've already sold some tickets, but I haven't sold all of them yet.
**Jess:** Well done! I'm sure you'll raise lots of money for the hospital.
**Jacob:** I hope so. Hospitals are so important. Did you know that there was an important medical discovery here in Toronto? I'll send you the link.
**Jess:** OK. Thanks!

## Unit 7 Lesson 2

Activity Book

**CD3 TRACK 17**

**AB page 71 Activity 3**

**Teacher:** Dylan! Dylan! Can you come here?
**Dylan:** Hi, Mrs Townsend!
**Teacher:** Right. Have you done everything for the concert?
**Dylan:** Not everything. I haven't cleaned the chairs yet.
**Teacher:** That's OK. You can do that now. Have you put out the food?
**Dylan:** No. I'm going to do that at the end.
**Teacher:** That is very sensible. What else? You've already decorated the room ... excellent. Have you blown up the balloons yet?
**Dylan:** Yes. They're over there, look! I am going to sweep the floor now. I haven't done that yet.
**Teacher:** OK. Well done, Dylan. Oh, and what about the windows? Have you closed all the windows?
**Dylan:** Yes. I've closed them all.
**Teacher:** Wonderful! I'll see you later. How exciting!
**Dylan:** Bye Mrs Townsend.

## Unit 7 Lesson 3

Pupil's Book

**CD3 TRACK 18**

**PB page 75 Activity 2**

***Finding a cure***
**Narrator:** This story begins in 1919. Elizabeth Hughes was living with her family in Washington DC, in the USA. Her father was a famous American politician.
Frame 1
**Narrator:** When Elizabeth was 11, she became ill. The doctor said she had diabetes.
**Doctor:** There's no cure. If she eats very little food, she can live longer.
**Frame 2**
**Narrator:** A scientist in Toronto, Dr Frederick Banting, was looking for a cure for diabetes.
**Dr Banting:** We need to identify the chemical in the pancreas that controls the amount of sugar in the blood.
**Frame 3**
**Narrator:** Elizabeth became thin and weak.
**Father:** She's just eaten, but she's still hungry.
**Mother:** But it's dangerous to give her more food.
**Frame 4**
**Narrator:** In 1922, Dr Banting discovered the chemical and called it insulin. Elizabeth's mother went to see him to ask for help.
**Dr Banting:** But we haven't finished testing it yet.
**Frame 5**
**Narrator:** Dr Banting agreed to try. He gave Elizabeth insulin twice a day.
**Mother:** Look! She's just walked around the garden on her own.
**Frame 6**
**Narrator:** Elizabeth took insulin every day and she lived a healthy life until she was more than 70 years old.
Dr Banting received the Nobel Prize for medicine in 1923.

## Unit 7 Lesson 3

Activity Book

**CD3 TRACK 19**

**AB page 72 Activity 2**

**Callum:** What are you reading, Jess?
**Jess:** Jacob sent me this story about the discovery of insulin. It happened in Toronto in Canada.
**Callum:** Insulin? That's the chemical that people with diabetes need to inject. Is that right?
**Jess:** Yes. And this is the story of one of the first people to take insulin. Her name was Elizabeth. She was 11 years old when a doctor told her she had diabetes ... and that there wasn't a cure.
**Callum:** Oh no. What did they do?
**Jess:** There wasn't much her parents could do. They could only give her a bit of food each day, so she got very thin.
**Callum:** Why is that?
**Jess:** Because people with diabetes can't control the amount of sugar in their blood. They can be very ill if they eat too much sugar.
**Callum:** So what happened next?
**Jess:** Well at the same time, a Canadian scientist was trying to discover the chemical that people with diabetes needed.
**Callum:** And did the scientist find it?
**Jess:** Yes, he did. Just in time he discovered it and called it insulin. He injected it into Elizabeth twice a day. She started to get better.
**Callum:** How long did she live for?
**Jess:** She lived a long life. She died when she was more than 70 years old.
**Callum:** And now many people take insulin every day, don't they?
**Jess:** Yes. Millions of people take insulin. It has saved many people's lives. I think it's a really important story and everyone should know about it. I give it five stars.

## Unit 7 Lesson 4

Pupil's Book

**CD3 TRACK 20**

**PB page 76 Activity 1**

**Jess:** Have you read the story about the discovery of insulin?
**Callum:** Yes, I've just read it. What an amazing story!
**Jess:** I've just met the new girl at school, Mary. She's got diabetes. She has to inject insulin twice a day.
**Callum:** Really? What else does Mary have to do?
**Jess:** She has to eat healthy food.
**Callum:** Well, we all have to do that.
**Jess:** That's true. Look! I've just eaten a healthy snack.

## Unit 7 Lesson 4

Pupil's Book

**CD3 TRACK 21**

**PB page 76 Activity 5**

**1** He's been to England twice.
**2** I've just finished my homework.
**3** I've already eaten my lunch.
**4** Have you bought the balloons yet?

## Unit 7 Lesson 4

**Activity Book**

**CD3 TRACK 22**

**AB page 73 Activity 3**

**1** I've just written a long email.
**2** Have you eaten your breakfast yet?
**3** I've already blown up twenty balloons.
**4** I've just put out the garden furniture.
**5** Jason's just seen a very scary film.
**6** Have you done your homework yet?

## Unit 7 Lesson 5

**Pupil's Book**

**CD3 TRACK 23**

**PB page 77 Activity 1**

**1** I've burnt my hand.
**2** I've bruised my arm.
**3** I've broken my arm.
**4** I've cut my finger.
**5** I've hurt my knee.
**6** I've twisted my ankle.
**7** I've scratched my leg.

## Unit 7 Lesson 5

**Pupil's Book**

**CD3 TRACK 24**

**PB page 77 Activity 2**

**1**
**Boy:** What's happened to you?
**Girl:** I've burnt my hand.
**Boy:** Oh no. What were you doing?
**Girl:** I was helping my dad with the cooking. I touched the pan by mistake.
**2**
**Girl:** Hello. What have you done?
**Boy:** I've bruised my arm.
**Girl:** What were you doing?
**Boy:** I was mountain biking and I fell off my bike …
**3**
**Boy:** So, what's happened to you?
**Girl:** I've broken my arm.
**Boy:** What were you doing?
**Girl:** I was playing tennis with my brother, and I fell over.
**4**
**Girl:** Hello. What have you done?
**Boy:** I've cut my finger.
**Girl:** Oh. What were you doing?
**Boy:** I was helping my mum with the cooking. I was cutting tomatoes.
**5**
**Boy:** Hello. What's happened to you?
**Girl:** I've hurt my knee.
**Boy:** OK. What were you doing?
**Girl:** I was rock climbing with my friends.
**6**
**Girl:** Oh dear – what have you done?
**Boy:** I've twisted my ankle.
**Girl:** What were you doing?
**Boy:** I was playing football with my friends.
**7**
**Boy:** Hello. What have you done?
**Girl:** I've scratched my leg.
**Boy:** OK. What were you doing?
**Girl:** I was hiking with my family in the woods.

## Unit 7 Lesson 6

**Activity Book**

**CD3 TRACK 25**

**AB page 75 Activity 3**

**TV presenter:** Welcome back to *Kids Keep Active* where we look at the different things that young people do. I have Freddie here with me. Hi Freddie.
**Freddie:** Hello.
**TV presenter:** Freddie, you do some volunteering. Is that right?
**Freddie:** Yes. Our family loves animals. All of us help out at the Animal Shelter.
**TV presenter:** And what do you do?
**Freddie:** I walk some of the dogs with my mum. We go there every Saturday at 11 o'clock. They walk all the dogs at the same time.
**TV presenter:** How many dogs do you walk?
**Freddie:** We usually take two or three dogs.
**TV presenter:** And where do you go?
**Freddie:** We go to the woods and they run around a lot.
**TV presenter:** How long do you go for?
**Freddie:** About 45 minutes. That is usually enough.
**TV presenter:** And do you take the same dogs each time?
**Freddie:** Sometimes … but usually they are different, I get to meet lots of different dogs!
**TV presenter:** And why do you like doing it?
**Freddie:** I love being outside and walking. The dogs are all really friendly and fun, too! It's great to help them.
**TV presenter:** Are they looking for more volunteers?
**Freddie:** Oh yes! If anyone is interested please go to the Animal Shelter website or ring 357682.
**TV presenter:** That's great! I'll repeat that: 357682. Thanks for all the information … Good luck with all the dog walking!

## Unit 7 Lesson 8

**Pupil's Book**

**CD3 TRACK 26**

**PB page 80 Activity 2**

**Philip:** Hi, Luke. We are going to raise money for our drama club. We need money for our costumes for the play.
**Luke:** Hi, Philip. Have you decided how to raise money yet?
**Philip:** Yes, we are going to have a talent show next week.
**Luke:** A talent show? How does that work?
**Philip:** It's a competition. We ask people to enter. They have to perform a song or a play. The winner will receive a prize.
**Luke:** A prize? What's the prize?
**Philip:** Four tickets to the cinema.
**Luke:** When is the competition?
**Philip:** It's on Friday at four o'clock. People have to buy tickets to come to the show. That's how we will raise the money!
**Luke:** How much do the tickets cost?
**Philip:** They cost four pounds for adults and two pounds for children.
**Luke:** That's great. I'll go!

## Unit 7

### Video and 21st Century Skills

**Activity Book**

**CD3 TRACK 27**

**AB page 79 Activity 1**

**Amy:** How can we help the younger people in the school? Has anyone had any ideas yet?
**Max:** Yes, I have, Amy. Let's help them to read books. We could start a book club for them.
**Amy:** That's a good idea, Max. Who is going to organise it?
**Max:** All four of us can help. I can lead the group, if you like.
**Amy:** OK. What shall we do first?
**Max:** Well, someone has to think of some good books to read. Does anyone want to volunteer to do that?
**Brian:** Yes, my little brother reads a lot. I've got some good ideas.
**Max:** OK. Thanks, Brian. That's brilliant.
**Amy:** What else shall we do?
**Max:** Someone has to design and draw some posters. Kelly, you're good at drawing. Are you happy to do that?
**Kelly:** OK, Max. But I don't know what to put on the posters.
**Max:** How about you draw a picture first, then we can decide what information to put on it.
**Kelly:** OK, Max.
**Amy:** What can I do, Max?
**Max:** What would you like to do, Amy?
**Amy:** I know the teachers of the younger children. Shall I tell them about the book club?
**Max:** What a good idea! I can look for a room for the club.
**Amy:** OK, Max. Let's go!
**Max:** Wait a second. Let's decide when we could have the club. I am free on Tuesdays at lunchtime. Is that OK for you Kelly and Brian?
**Kelly:** I'm sorry. I am only free on Wednesdays and Fridays.
**Brian:** Yes, I can do it on Wednesdays or Thursdays.
**Max:** OK. Let's say Wednesdays at lunchtime. Is everyone happy to do that?
**All:** Yes.
**Max:** Great. Let's meet again tomorrow at lunchtime.
**Kelly:** Good idea.
**Brian:** Yes, great. See you then.

## Unit 8 Lesson 1

**Pupil's Book**

**CD3 TRACK 28**

**PB page 82 Activity 3**

**1** cardboard box
**2** cardboard tube
**3** elastic band
**4** lolly stick
**5** bottle top
**6** straw
**7** carton
**8** can
**9** string

# Audioscript

**10** button
**11** fabric
**12** plastic bottle

## Unit 8 Lesson 1

Pupil's Book

**CD3 TRACK 29**

**PB page 82 Activity 4**

**1**
**Boy:** This is a container for drinks like lemonade and cola. It's made of metal.
**Girl:** can
**2**
**Boy:** This is a long thin tube. It's made of plastic. It's used for drinking.
**Girl:** straw
**3**
**Boy:** This is a piece of cloth. It's used for making things like clothes, curtains or toys.
**Girl:** fabric
**4**
**Boy:** This object is small and round. It's made of metal or plastic. It's used for covering the top of a bottle.
**Girl:** bottle top
**5**
**Boy:** This object has got the shape of a circle. It's made of rubber and it can stretch easily. It's used for holding things together.
**Girl:** elastic band
**6**
**Boy:** This is a long and thin object. It's small and it's made of wood. You hold it when you eat an ice lolly.
**Girl:** lolly stick
**7**
**Boy:** This object is made of cardboard. You can find it in the middle of a roll of toilet paper or kitchen paper.
**Girl:** cardboard tube
**8**
**Boy:** This is a container for liquids like milk, juice and soup. It's made of thick cardboard.
**Girl:** carton
**9**
**Boy:** This is a thin rope. It's made of cotton or nylon. You can tie things together with it.
**Girl:** string
**10**
**Boy:** This is a small round object. It can be made of metal or plastic. It's got holes in the middle. It's used for keeping clothes together.
**Girl:** button
**11**
**Boy:** This is a container for liquids like water or cola. You can see the liquid through it. It can be big or small.
**Girl:** plastic bottle
**12**
**Boy:** This container can be big or small. It's made of cardboard. Breakfast cereals usually come in it.
**Girl:** cardboard box

## Unit 8 Lesson 2

Pupil's Book

**CD3 TRACK 30**

**PB page 84 Activity 1**

**Callum:** Hi, Kana. Thanks for the photos. My favourite toy was the robot. I can't believe you made it from recycled objects.
**Kana:** Thanks. Do you know that real robots are produced in my country?
**Callum:** Really? Is there a lot of technology in Japan?
**Kana:** Yes, there is. Cameras, computers and printers are produced here, too.
**Callum:** What about food?
**Kana:** Well, rice is grown in the countryside. But some vegetables are grown in factories in the middle of the city. Look, here's a photo.
**Callum:** Wow! That's amazing. I love the plants on the outside of the building.
**Kana:** There's a lot more technology in my country. I'll send you some information.
**Callum:** That sounds great. Thanks.

## Unit 8 Lesson 2

Activity Book

**CD3 TRACK 31**

**AB page 81 Activity 3**

**Radio presenter:** Good evening and welcome to *Amazing Science* – the radio programme about science and technology. Today we're going to find out about a very special airplane – the Airbus A380. Sue Taylor is an engineer and she's here to tell us about it. Hello, Sue.
**Woman:** Hello, Tim.
**Radio presenter:** So, why is the Airbus A380 so special?
**Woman:** It's special because it's the biggest passenger plane in the world. It can carry 850 passengers.
**Radio presenter:** Eight hundred and fifty! That's amazing. And where is this super plane made?
**Woman:** That's another interesting thing. It isn't made in one country. It's made in four countries. Each country makes a different part of the plane.
**Radio presenter:** Really? Which countries are they?
**Woman:** They're the UK, France, Spain and Germany.
**Radio presenter:** What's made in the UK?
**Woman:** The wings are made in the UK. Then they're transported to France by boat.
**Radio presenter:** What about the other parts of the plane?
**Woman:** The tail is made in Spain and the body is made in Germany. They're transported to France by boat, too.
**Radio presenter:** What about the nose of the plane?
**Woman:** That's made in France.
**Radio presenter:** So, what happens when all the pieces arrive in France?
**Woman:** Then the plane is put together. There's a big factory in the south of France where they do this. Finally, pilots fly the plane to Germany and it's painted there.
**Radio presenter:** What a good example of countries working together. Have you even flown in the Airbus A380 plane, Sue?
**Woman:** Yes, I have ... and it's brilliant!

## Unit 8 Lesson 3

Pupil's Book

**CD3 TRACK 32**

**PB page 85 Activity 2**

***Fish-bots***
**Narrator:** Kyg-lab is a place in Japan where people go to learn about marine life. Its president is called Masamichi Hayashi.
**Frame 1**
**Narrator:** Hayashi is a marine biologist with an interest in technology.
**Hayashi:** I'm going to build some robotic fish to show people how fish move.
**Frame 2**
**Narrator:** He wanted to protect the oceans and teach people about recycling.
**Hayashi:** I wonder if I can recycle this rubbish to build my fish.
**Frame 3**
**Narrator:** He collected plastic bottles, food containers and even a raincoat.
**Hayashi:** These objects are produced in other countries, but they float to Japan.
**Frame 4**
**Narrator:** Hayashi has made over 100 robots from recycled rubbish. They move like real sea animals.
**Hayashi:** This fish can open and close its mouth. It can also eat artificial prey.
**Frame 5**
**Boy:** How are the robots operated?
**Hayashi:** They're operated by remote control.
**Hayashi:** This turtle can collect rubbish from the water.
**Frame 6**
**Narrator:** Children from all over Japan visit Kyg-lab to observe and touch the robotic fish.

## Unit 8 Lesson 3

Activity Book

**CD3 TRACK 33**

**AB page 82 Activity 2**

**Tom:** What are you reading, Callum?
**Callum:** I'm reading a story about fish-bots.
**Tom:** Fish-bots! What are they?
**Callum:** They're these amazing robots in Japan. They look like fish.
**Tom:** Wow! Does the story explain how the robots are made?
**Callum:** Not really. It begins by introducing Masamichi Hayashi. He's a marine biologist and he teaches people about the oceans and the animals that live there. He's also interested in technology and one day he decided to build some fish robots to show people how these animals move.
**Tom:** What a great idea!
**Callum:** Yes! And what's more amazing is that he decided to make the fish robots from rubbish. He collected lots of different rubbish from the beaches and he used objects like plastic bottles, fabric and food trays to make the fish.
**Tom:** I don't believe it.
**Callum:** It's true. Now he's made more than 100 robots. Some of them are incredible. They can open and close their mouths and do tricks.
**Tom:** Can visitors watch the fish?
**Callum:** Yes, they can. And they can touch some of the fish, too.
**Tom:** Do you recommend the story?
**Callum:** Absolutely. It was very interesting, but I wanted to read some more information about how the robots are made so I only give it four stars.

## Unit 8 Lesson 4

Pupil's Book

**CD3 TRACK 34**

**PB page 86 Activity 1**

**Callum:** Have you ever seen a robotic fish from Japan?
**Jess:** Yes, I have. It looks like a real fish. What's it made of?
**Callum:** It's made of recycled rubbish.
**Jess:** My T-shirt is made of recycled material, too.
**Callum:** Really? What's it made of?
**Jess:** It's made of plastic bottles.
**Callum:** That's amazing! Where are those T-shirts made?
**Jess:** I don't know. Let me look at the label … Ah! They're made in Japan, too!

## Unit 8 Lesson 4

Pupil's Book

**CD3 TRACK 35**

**PB page 86 Activity 5**

**1** Italy
**2** Japan
**3** Switzerland
**4** Canada
**5** Egypt
**6** Germany
**7** Brazil
**8** Argentina

## Unit 8 Lesson 4

Activity Book

**CD3 TRACK 36**

**AB page 83 Activity 3**

**1** Japan, Brazil
**2** Egypt, China
**3** Italy, Germany, Portugal, Mexico
**4** Australia, America, Romania

## Unit 8 Lesson 5

Pupil's Book

**CD3 TRACK 37**

**PB page 87 Activity 1**

**1** collect paper
**2** transport paper
**3** wash paper
**4** remove ink
**5** add water
**6** roll paper
**7** cut paper
**8** use paper

## Unit 8 Lesson 5

Pupil's Book

**CD3 TRACK 38**

**PB page 87 Activity 2**

**1**
**Dad:** Have you finished reading your magazine, Lily?
**Lily:** Yes, I have.
**Dad:** Don't forget to put it in the recycling bin then.
**Lily:** OK. How is paper recycled, Dad?
**Dad:** Well, first the paper is collected.
**Lily:** Oh yes. There's a blue container in front of the supermarket for paper.
**2**
**Dad:** Next, the paper is transported to a recycling plant.
**3**
**Lily:** What happens in the recycling plant?
**Dad:** The paper is washed.
**4**
**Lily:** What happens after that?
**Dad:** Well, the ink is then removed there.
**5**
**Lily:** What happens after that?
**Dad:** Next, water is added so the paper gets wet and soft.
**6**
**Dad:** And after that, this material is rolled to make long rolls of paper.
**7**
**Lily:** What happens to this paper?
**Dad:** The rolled paper is cut into pieces to make more books and magazines.
**8**
**Lily:** And these books and magazines are used again.
**Dad:** That's right. That means we cut down fewer trees.
**Lily:** Wow! Recycling is fantastic!

## Unit 8 Lesson 6

Activity Book

**CD3 TRACK 39**

**AB page 85 Activity 3**

**Teacher:** Good morning everybody.
**Children:** Good morning Miss Evans.
**Teacher:** I want to tell you all about our new school project. We're going to work together to make a school greenhouse. Has anybody got a greenhouse at home? Sally?
**Sally:** My grandad's got a greenhouse. He grows tomatoes and peppers in it.
**Teacher:** What's your grandad's greenhouse made of?
**Sally:** It's made of glass.
**Teacher:** Thank you. Well, the school greenhouse isn't going to be made of glass. It's going to be made of recycled plastic bottles.
**Children:** Wow! Oooh!
**Teacher:** Now listen carefully because I'm going to tell you what your class is going to do.
Class one: you're going to collect the bottles. We need lots and lots of plastic bottles so the other pupils will help. You need to check that the bottles are the same size.
Class three: you're going to wash the bottles and take off the labels. You need to wear rubber gloves to do this because the water is hot and soapy.
Next is class four: When the bottles are clean and dry, you're going to cut off the bottom of the bottles.
Class two: Your job is to make the walls of the greenhouse. You're going to put the plastic bottles onto canes. There are ten bottles on each cane.
Who's next? Ah yes, class five. You're going to work in the school garden. You need to dig some holes and make frames for the roof, the walls and the door of the greenhouse. Adults will help with this, too.
Class six: You're going to put the greenhouse together. You need to put the canes onto the frames then screw the frames to the posts.
Finally, when the greenhouse is ready each class can grow some plants.

## Unit 8 Lesson 8

Pupil's Book

**CD3 TRACK 40**

**PB page 90 Activity 2**

**Anthony:** Do you think it's important to protect the environment, Robin?
**Robin:** Absolutely, Anthony!
**Anthony:** Me too. What do you do to save energy?
**Robin:** Well, I always switch off the lights when I leave the room.
**Anthony:** That's good. Do you usually switch off the TV, too?
**Robin:** Not always …
**Anthony:** Oh? Well, you know you should do that. What about transport? How often do you go to school by car?
**Robin:** Not very often. I usually walk because I live quite near to school.
**Anthony:** That's great. It's better to walk. Have you ever recycled rubbish before?
**Robin:** Of course! I do it every week. What about you?
**Anthony:** Oh, I do it every week, too.
**Robin:** Do you ever forget?
**Anthony:** Absolutely not!

## Unit 8

### Video and 21st Century Skills

Activity Book

**CD3 TRACK 41**

**AB page 89 Activity 1**

**Max:** Hi, Uncle Pete.
**Uncle Pete:** Hi, Max. Hi, Amy. Oh, You don't look very happy. What's the matter?
**Max:** We're trying to create a digital poster, but it isn't very good. You're a graphic designer. Can you help us, please?
**Uncle Pete:** Yes, of course. The first thing you need to do is identify who the poster is for.
**Amy:** It's for our friends and other children at school. We want them to recycle more.
**Uncle Pete:** What a good idea! Well, when you create a poster, you need to use bright colours, like red and orange. You need to find interesting pictures too.
**Amy:** Anything else?
**Uncle Pete:** Yes. It's important to think of a slogan.

# Audioscript

**Max:** What's a slogan?
**Uncle Pete:** It's a short phrase that catches people's attention. For example, 'Stop, think, recycle!'
**Amy:** What about 'Go Green!'?
**Uncle Pete:** That's a great slogan, too. Well done! Another good idea is to use WOW words.
**Max:** WOW words?!
**Uncle Pete:** Yes. They're exciting words that make a text more interesting: like 'amazing' or 'brilliant'. Finally, you need to use an interesting font.
**Max:** What's a font?
**Uncle Pete:** It's the design of the letters and numbers. There are lots of different fonts to choose from on a computer.
**Max:** Thanks, Uncle Pete. That information was really useful.
**Amy:** Yes, we're going to make a great poster now.
**Uncle Pete:** Ha, ha. Good luck!

## Unit 9 Lesson 1

Pupil's Book

### CD4 TRACK 01

### PB page 92 Activity 3

**1** desert
**2** canyon
**3** ocean
**4** lake
**5** island
**6** reef
**7** volcano
**8** coast
**9** valley
**10** plain
**11** rainforest
**12** waterfall

## Unit 9 Lesson 1

Pupil's Book

### CD4 TRACK 02

### PB page 92 Activity 4

**1**
**Girl:** This is a very big sea. The three biggest are the Pacific, the Atlantic and the Indian.
**Boy:** ocean
**2**
**Girl:** This is the part of the land that's next to the sea. You can sometimes find rocks and beaches here.
**Boy:** coast
**3**
**Girl:** This is a long line of rock or coral under the sea. The top of it is just above the water or just below it.
**Boy:** reef
**4**
**Girl:** This is an area of low land. It's between mountains and hills. It's usually got a river going through it.
**Boy:** valley
**5**
**Girl:** This is a place where water goes over rocks or a cliff. It falls from a high place to a lower place.
**Boy:** waterfall
**6**
**Girl:** This is a big area of water. It's got land all around it.
**Boy:** lake
**7**
**Girl:** There are lots of trees and it usually rains a lot here. This is found in a hot, tropical part of the world. Many different kinds of animals live here.
**Boy:** rainforest
**8**
**Girl:** This is a long, deep valley. It's got high sides that are made of rock.
**Boy:** canyon
**9**
**Girl:** This is a big, flat area of land. You can find many of these in Africa or in the USA. Animals often live here.
**Boy:** plain
**10**
**Girl:** This is an area of land that's got water all around it.
**Boy:** island
**11**
**Girl:** This is a big area of land where the weather is always dry. There isn't much water and there are only a few plants. It's often made of sand or rocks.
**Boy:** desert
**12**
**Girl:** This is a kind of mountain. Hot gas and rock can come out of a hole at the top of it. It can be dangerous.
**Boy:** volcano

## Unit 9 Lesson 2

Pupil's Book

### CD4 TRACK 03

### PB page 94 Activity 1

**Tom:** Hi, Diego. Thanks for the photos and the fun facts. Brazil sounds like a great place! Where are you going for your summer holiday?
**Diego:** Summer? It's winter here! Brazil is south of the equator. Look!
**Tom:** Oh, of course! Are you going on a winter holiday?
**Diego:** Yes, we've got two weeks off school. This year, I'm staying with my grandmother for a week and then we're visiting the Amazon Rainforest.
**Tom:** Wow! Lucky you. That photo you sent was amazing. Are you going with your parents?
**Diego:** Yes. And my cousins are coming, too. We're doing a canoe trip and we're going camping in the rainforest.
**Tom:** I hope you have a good time.
**Diego:** Thanks! There are some interesting legends about the Amazon Rainforest. I'll send you one of my favourites.
**Tom:** OK. Great!

## Unit 9 Lesson 2

Activity Book

### CD4 TRACK 04

### AB page 91 Activity 3

OK everyone. Listen. I have to explain to everyone about tomorrow. As you know, we are going to the Science Museum tomorrow. Remember that you have to be here at the school at nine o'clock. We're meeting by the big tree in front of the school. The coach is leaving at 9.15. Don't be late! We're arriving at the museum at about 10.30. We'll be there for two hours. Then we're having lunch at one o'clock in the park. Remember to bring a packed lunch and a drink. Then we are driving back to the school. Tell your parents that the coach is arriving at the school at 3.30.
You all need to bring a rucksack with your notebook and pens and pencils. Oh! It might be cold, so please wear a coat. And you must all wear school uniform!
See you all tomorrow at nine o'clock!

## Unit 9 Lesson 3

Pupil's Book

### CD4 TRACK 05

### PB page 95 Activity 2

***The Vitória Régia water lily***
**Narrator:** The largest water lily in the world is called the Vitória Régia (Victoria Amazonica). It's native to the Amazon River. The Brazilians have got a legend about where this plant came from.
**Frame 1**
**Narrator:** Naia lived in a village by the Amazon River. She loved looking at the moon and the stars.
**Naia:** I want to live in the sky as a star.
**Frame 2**
**Narrator:** One evening, when there was a full moon, Naia climbed up a tree.
**Naia:** If I touch the moon, I'll become a star. But I can't reach it.
**Frame 3**
**Narrator:** At the next full moon, Naia climbed up the highest hill.
**Naia:** I still can't reach the moon. What can I do?
**Frame 4**
**Narrator:** At the next full moon, Naia saw the reflection of the moon in the river.
**Naia:** The moon has come to swim in the river. Now I can touch it.
**Frame 5**
**Narrator:** Naia dived into the deep river. She was never seen again.
**Frame 6**
**Narrator:** The legend says that the moon saved Naia from death by turning her into a giant Vitória Régia lily.

## Unit 9 Lesson 3

Activity Book

### CD4 TRACK 06

### AB page 92 Activity 2

**Callum:** What are you reading, Tom?
**Tom:** Diego sent me a story about these giant water lilies.
**Callum:** Is it a good story?
**Tom:** Yes! It's a legend, actually. It's a story about how the Vitória Régia water lily was first created.
**Callum:** How does the story go?

**Tom:** Well, it's about a young woman called Naia. She believes that if she can touch the moon she will become a beautiful star in the sky. She wants this more than anything.
**Callum:** So does she try to touch the moon?
**Tom:** Yes, she does. She climbs a tree and walks up a big hill, but of course she can't touch the moon.
**Callum:** What does she do next?
**Tom:** She walks by the river one evening and she sees the reflection of the moon in the river. She thinks the moon has come down to the river to have a swim.
**Callum:** Really? So she tries to touch the reflection ...
**Tom:** Yes, that's right. In fact, she dives into the water. And she's never seen again.
**Callum:** Oh dear! Is that the end of the story?
**Tom:** No ... The moon saw what happened and felt sorry for Naia. The moon turned her into a beautiful flower and gave her enormous leaves to catch the light of the moon. The flower looks like a big star in the water. So you see ... she got what she wanted ... she became a star.
**Callum:** That's a good story.
**Tom:** Yes, and I really like the pictures. They're really colourful! I give the story five stars.

## Unit 9 Lesson 4

Pupil's Book

### CD4 TRACK 07

#### PB page 96 Activity 1

**Tom:** Have you read that legend about the giant water lilies?
**Jess:** Yes, they're amazing! If you search on the Internet, you'll find lots of great photos.
**Tom:** Did you know that there are some of those water lilies at the Botanic Museum in town?
**Jess:** Really? Let's go and see them. Is it open now?
**Tom:** I think it closes at 5pm.
**Jess:** Well, it's four o'clock now. Let's go and see.
**Tom:** OK. If we're late, they won't let us in.
**Jess:** Then we can go and get an ice cream instead!

## Unit 9 Lesson 4

Pupil's Book

### CD4 TRACK 08

#### PB page 96 Activity 5

**1** I'll see you on Sunday.
**2** He'll take the bus to school tomorrow.
**3** The film won't start at 3pm.

## Unit 9 Lesson 4

Pupil's Book

### CD4 TRACK 09

#### PB page 96 Activity 6

**1** If it rains during the match, we'll stop playing.
**2** If you drink all the milk, there won't be any for breakfast tomorrow.
**3** If they go on their bikes, they'll probably arrive at four o'clock.
**4** If you don't practise the piano, you won't pass your exam.

## Unit 9 Lesson 5

Pupil's Book

### CD4 TRACK 10

#### PB page 97 Activity 1

**1** money
**2** wallet
**3** passport
**4** anorak
**5** ticket
**6** suitcase
**7** towel
**8** umbrella
**9** dictionary

## Unit 9 Lesson 5

Pupil's Book

### CD4 TRACK 11

#### PB page 97 Activity 2

**1**
**Harry:** Hi, Kate. Where are you going?
**Kate:** Hi, Harry. I'm going to The Lake District for the weekend.
**Harry:** I've never been there. What's it like?
**Kate:** I love it. The lakes and the hills are beautiful. I'm staying with my aunt in a small village.
**Harry:** Have you planned your trip?
**Kate:** Yes. We're going for a long walk on Saturday.
**Harry:** Are you taking an anorak? If it rains, you'll get really wet.
**Kate:** Yes, good idea. I'll take my anorak.
**Harry:** It's a long train journey, too. You should take a good book. If you don't take something to read, you'll get bored.
**Kate:** I've got my MP3 player. If I get bored, I'll listen to some music.
**Harry:** And what are you doing on Sunday?
**Kate:** I'm going to sit by the lake with my aunt.
**Harry:** Sit by the lake? And do what?
**Kate:** I'm taking my sketchpad and pencils. I'm going to draw some pictures.
**Harry:** Great. I look forward to seeing them.
**2**
**Harry:** Hi, Jack. Are you going somewhere, too?
**Jack:** Yes. I'm going to London. I'm going on the bus with my mum.
**Harry:** Oh right. What are you going to do there?
**Jack:** We're meeting my brother. He works in London.
**Harry:** Oh, I see.
**Jack:** He's taking us on a tour. I've got my guidebook, an umbrella and my binoculars, too.
**Harry:** Binoculars? Why do you need them?
**Jack:** We're going up some tall buildings. If I take my binoculars, I'll see the views across London.
**Harry:** Where else are you going?
**Jack:** We're going to a big market, so I'm taking lots of money to buy presents.
**Harry:** Oh – I hope you're going to buy something for me.
**Jack:** If I see something nice, I'll buy it for you!
**Harry:** Thanks!

## Unit 9 Lesson 6

Activity Book

### CD4 TRACK 12

#### AB page 95 Activity 3

**Granny:** Hello, Jane.
**Jane:** Hi, Granny.
**Granny:** Did you have a good time in London?
**Jane:** Yes, we did. We got to London in time for lunch. We had a delicious pizza at an Italian restaurant.
**Granny:** What did you do after lunch?
**Jane:** Well ... it wasn't very easy because we all wanted to do different things! Some of us wanted to go to museums, some on tours and others wanted to go shopping!
**Granny:** So what did you do in the end?
**Jane:** We couldn't agree, so we did different things! Dad wanted to go to the Natural History Museum to learn about dinosaurs, but it wasn't open so he went to the British Museum, where he saw some amazing Egyptian mummies.
**Granny:** Did Mum go with him?
**Jane:** No, she didn't. She doesn't like museums much. She went on the London Eye. She was going to go with Steven, but he's scared of heights.
**Granny:** So what did Steven do?
**Jane:** He had a milkshake in Jubilee Gardens and waited for Mum.
**Granny:** How about Jill?
**Jane:** She wanted to go shopping, of course, so she went to Oxford Street. There are a lot of shops there!
**Granny:** And didn't you want to do any of those things?
**Jane:** I was with my friend Saskia. We love animals so we walked along the river to the Aquarium.
**Granny:** Was it good?
**Jane:** It was fantastic! I think we all enjoyed our different activities!

## Unit 9 Lesson 8

Pupil's Book

### CD4 TRACK 13

#### PB page 100 Activity 2

**Alice:** Let's organise a trip to the river.
**Jack:** OK. Good idea! It's going to be sunny on Saturday. Let's go in the morning.
**Alice:** Right. What time shall we start?
**Jack:** Let's meet at the bridge at quarter past ten.
**Alice:** Why don't we take the bus together at half past nine?
**Jack:** OK. That's a great idea. Let's meet at the bus stop at half past nine. We can get off the bus at the bridge.
**Alice:** Where shall we go first?
**Jack:** Let's walk to the waterfall first. Then we can stop for some chocolate.
**Alice:** Perfect!
**Jack:** After that we can walk to the river. There is a picnic place by the river.

# Audioscript

**Alice:** Shall we have lunch there?
**Jack:** Yes. Then we can come home.
**Alice:** Yes, brilliant. That sounds like fun!

# Unit 9

## Video and 21st Century Skills

Activity Book

### CD4 TRACK 14

### AB page 99 Activity 1

**Amy:** Hey. Look at this website. This is Adam. He lives in a town in Alaska. We can ask him some questions about life in Alaska.
**Max:** Great. I wonder what he does every day.
**Amy:** First, let's think of some questions.
**Max:** OK. What is your home like? What time do you get up? What do you have for breakfast?
**Amy:** Wait a second! Let's write down the questions.
**Max:** Sorry!
**Amy:** OK … How do you get to school in the winter?
**Max:** Ah, yes, and … What do you wear in the winter?
**Amy:** What hobbies have you got?
**Max:** Yes, that's a good question.
**Amy:** OK. I think that's enough. Let's send them.

**Amy:** Look, Adam has replied!
**Max:** What has he said?
**Amy:** He's answered our questions. I'll read it.
"Hi. I live in Juneau, it's the capital of Alaska, but it is a small town. It is on the coast, but the mountains are very near.
I live in a house on a big island. Many people in Juneau live there. We have to go across the bridge to go to school. I go by bus in the summer and the winter, too. If there is a lot of snow we sometimes walk. I get up at seven o'clock and I usually have cereal and yoghurt for breakfast.
In the winter the most important clothes are your shoes! You need strong, warm boots to walk through the snow. And my hobbies? I love skiing and hiking. Everyone in Juneau is very active!
**Max:** That's great. I'd like to live like that. Would you?
**Amy:** I'm not sure!

# Project 3 Lesson 1

Pupil's Book

### CD4 TRACK 15

### PB page 102 Activity 2

**Radio presenter:** Good afternoon and welcome to Sunshine Radio. I'm Sally Harris and today I'm talking to Tom Strong. He's a biologist at the Eden Project. Hello, Tom.
**Tom:** Hello, Sally.
**Radio presenter:** First of all, what is the Eden Project?
**Tom:** Well, it's a very exciting attraction where you learn about natural environments around the world. In the centre of the attraction there are two enormous biomes. One is a Rainforest Biome and the other is a Mediterranean Biome.
**Radio presenter:** Can you tell us a little bit about the Rainforest Biome? What can you see there?
**Tom:** In the Rainforest Biome you can see lots of tropical plants and trees. It's home to more than a thousand species and you can see where food like chocolate, cola and chewing gum comes from.
**Radio presenter:** That sounds very interesting. Can you see any animals in the biome?
**Tom:** Yes, you can. There are lots of tropical butterflies. They fly around freely and they sometimes sit on visitors' bags or clothes.
**Radio presenter:** What about water? Is there a lake in the biome?
**Tom:** No, there isn't a lake. But you can see a very high waterfall. The waterfall helps to keep the air humid for the plants.
**Radio presenter:** So … tropical trees and plants, wild butterflies and a waterfall. Is there anything else to see?
**Tom:** Oh yes! If you explore the Rainforest Biome carefully you can find a tropical village. The village has got houses and gardens so you can see how tribes live in the rainforest.
**Radio presenter:** How interesting! Can visitors do any other activities while they are there?
**Tom:** They can listen to a story from another part of the world. There are different stories every day. And visitors who like exciting rides can ride on the SkyWire.
**Radio presenter:** The SkyWire? What's that?
**Tom:** It's a ride. You slide down a wire above the biomes at more than 80 kilometres per hour.
**Radio presenter:** So it's a ride for very brave visitors.
**Tom:** That's right.
**Radio presenter:** I'm afraid that's all we've got time for today. Thank you very much indeed for talking to us today, Tom.

# Festivals: Happy New Year!

Pupil's Book

### CD4 TRACK 16

### PB page 104 Activity 3

It's New Year's Day today
And it's time for me to think
About my resolutions
And write them down in ink.

I promise I will watch
Less TV every day.
I promise I won't shout
At my sister when we play.

I promise I will clean
And tidy up my room.
I promise I won't dawdle
When it's time to go to school.

These plans look too severe,
But I've got a good solution.
I promise I won't keep
My New Year's resolutions!

# Festivals: World Environment Day

Pupil's Book

### CD4 TRACK 17

### PB page 105 Activity 3

**Sam:** Hi, Anna. Do you want to do a quiz with me?
**Anna:** OK. What's it about?
**Sam:** It's about our carbon footprint.
**Anna:** What's that?
**Sam:** It's the quantity of energy we use. If we use a lot of energy, we leave a big carbon footprint and if we don't use much energy, our carbon footprint is small.
**Anna:** That sounds interesting. Do you want to ask or answer the questions?
**Sam:** I'll ask the questions. Here's the first one – How do you travel to school?
**Anna:** That's easy. I travel by car.
**Sam:** Thanks. Next question – How many cars have you got at home?
**Anna:** We've got one car. My mum drives it to work and my dad uses public transport.
**Sam:** OK. Number three – How often do you eat in a fast food restaurant?
**Anna:** I go to a fast food restaurant once a week.
**Sam:** Really? That's a lot!
**Anna:** I know. I love burgers and chips. I usually go with my dad on Friday evening.
**Sam:** Question number 4 is next. – How often do you drink bottled water?
**Anna:** Hmmm … We always have bottled water at home, so I drink it every day. But I drink tap water in the school playground.
**Sam:** Thanks. Number 5 – How much TV do you watch every day?
**Anna:** Not a lot. I suppose I watch about one hour.
**Sam:** And number 6 – How often do you leave the TV on standby when you aren't watching it?
**Anna:** Oh, I always leave it on standby. I hardly ever remember to switch the TV off.
**Sam:** There are just two questions left now. Number seven is – How many baths do you have a week?
**Anna:** I never have a bath. I prefer taking showers.
**Sam:** And number 8 – how many holidays do you have every year?
**Anna:** We have a holiday every summer. We go to my grandma's house in the mountains in August.
**Sam:** Thanks, Anna. That's the end of the quiz. I'll calculate your carbon footprint now. Let me see ... You've got [beep] points, which means that you've got a [beep] carbon footprint.

# Song Bank: Unit 1

Pupil's Book

### CD4 TRACK 18

### PB page 125 Activity 2

***Shopping is fun!* song**
*My clothes don't fit me anymore.*
*My T-shirt is too small.*
*My favourite jeans aren't long enough.*
*I need to buy some more.*

*Shopping for clothes is fun,*
*But I have to go with my mum.*
*Shopping for clothes is fun,*
*But not when I'm with my mum.*

*I want to buy some boots,*
*But she says they're too big.*
*And I want to buy a sweatshirt,*
*But she says it's too bright.*

*Shopping for clothes is fun,*
*But I have to go with my mum.*
*Shopping for clothes is fun,*
*But not when I'm with my mum.*

*The coat I like isn't warm enough*
*And the tracksuit is too plain.*
*So I have to go to another shop*
*And try on some clothes again.*

*Shopping for clothes is fun,*
*But I have to go with my mum.*
*Shopping for clothes is fun,*
*But not when I'm with my mum.*

## Song Bank: Unit 1

Pupil's Book

**CD4 TRACK 19**

**PB page 125 Activity 2**

**Karaoke version: *Shopping is fun!* song**

## Song Bank: Unit 3

Pupil's Book

**CD4 TRACK 20**

**PB page 125 Activity 2**

***Life in the city* song**
*I spent the weekend in the city.*
*City life is cool.*
*I spent the weekend in the city,*
*But now I'm back at school.*
*Life in the city,*
*Life in the city is cool.*

*On Saturday at twelve o'clock,*
*I was shopping in the centre.*
*I bought some baseball boots*
*And a baggy sweater.*
*Life in the city,*
*Life in the city is cool.*

*On Saturday at eight o'clock,*
*I was watching a cool play*
*With actors who were singing*
*And dancing on the stage.*
*Life in the city,*

*Life in the city is cool.*

*On Sunday at eleven o'clock,*
*I was looking at some bones*
*From a dinosaur that lived*
*A long long time ago.*
*Life in the city,*
*Life in the city is cool.*

*I spent the weekend in the city.*
*City life is cool.*
*I spent the weekend in the city,*
*But now I'm back at school.*
*Life in the city,*
*Life in the city is cool.*

## Song Bank: Unit 3

Pupil's Book

**CD4 TRACK 21**

**PB page 125 Activity 2**

**Karaoke version: *Life in the city* song**

## Song Bank: Unit 4

Pupil's Book

**CD4 TRACK 22**

**PB page 126 Activity 2**

***Let's play!* song**
*Strategic, racing, action games.*
*Computer games are cool to play.*
*Pick up the handset.*
*Now press A.*
*Your car is ready.*
*Let's play!*
*If you tilt the handset,*
*You start to race.*
*If you tilt it more,*
*You accelerate.*

*If you shake the handset,*
*You begin to jump*
*And do cool tricks.*
*Come on! It's fun.*
*Up, down, left, right.*
*Use the arrows,*
*That's right.*

*5, 4, 3, 2, 1.*
*The game is over.*
*You've won!*

*Strategic, racing, action games.*
*Computer games are cool to play.*

## Song Bank: Unit 4

Pupil's Book

**CD4 TRACK 23**

**PB page 126 Activity 2**

**Karaoke version: *Let's play!* song**

## Song Bank: Unit 6

Pupil's Book

**CD4 TRACK 24**

**PB page 126 Activity 2**

***Are you creative?* song**
*Are you creative?*
*Have you got imagination?*
*Are you creative?*
*Or do you need some inspiration?*

*Have you ever juggled balls?*
*Have you balanced on a rope?*
*Circus skills are great.*
*Come and have a go.*

*Are you creative?*
*Have you got imagination?*
*Are you creative?*
*Or do you need some inspiration?*

*Have you ever made a film?*
*Have you acted in a show?*
*Performing is great.*
*Come and have a go.*

*Are you creative?*
*Have you got imagination?*
*Are you creative?*
*Or do you need some inspiration?*

*Have you ever played the drums?*
*Have you sung on your own?*
*Music is great.*
*Come and have a go.*

*Are you creative?*
*Have you got imagination?*
*Are you creative?*
*Or do you need some inspiration?*

## Song Bank: Unit 6

Pupil's Book

**CD4 TRACK 25**

**PB page 126 Activity 2**

**Karaoke version: *Are you creative?* song**

## Song Bank: Unit 7

Pupil's Book

**CD4 TRACK 26**

**PB page 127 Activity 2**

***Sleepy head* song**
*Get up, get up.*
*Get out of bed.*
*Get up, get up,*
*Sleepy head.*

*I've already had my breakfast.*
*I've already brushed my teeth.*
*But you haven't got up yet.*
*You're still asleep.*

*Get up, get up.*
*Get out of bed.*
*Get up, get up,*
*Sleepy head.*

*I've already done my homework.*
*I've already combed my hair.*
*But you haven't got up yet.*
*You're still in bed.*

*Get up, get up.*
*Get out of bed.*
*Get up, get up,*
*Sleepy head.*

*I've already packed my schoolbag.*
*I've already tidied my room.*
*But you haven't got up yet.*
*Hurry up!*
*We're late for school!*

*Get up, get up.*
*Get out of bed.*
*Get up, get up,*
*Sleepy head.*

## Song Bank: Unit 7

Pupil's Book

**CD4 TRACK 27**

**PB page 127 Activity 2**

**Karaoke version: *Sleepy head* song**

# Audioscript

## Song Bank: Unit 9

Pupil's Book

**CD4 TRACK 28**

**PB page 127 Activity 2**

***My holiday suitcase* song**

*My suitcase is packed.*
*I'm ready for my trip.*
*I'd better look inside again*
*Before I close the zip.*

*There's a swimsuit and a towel.*
*I've packed a snorkel, too.*
*But if it starts to rain,*
*What will I do?*

*My suitcase is packed.*
*I'm ready for my trip.*
*I'd better look inside again*
*Before I close the zip.*

*There's a sweater and an umbrella.*
*I've packed an anorak, too.*
*But if I get too bored,*
*What will I do?*

*My suitcase is packed.*
*I'm ready for my trip.*
*I'd better look inside again*
*Before I close the zip.*

*There's a guidebook and a sketchpad.*
*I've packed some board games, too.*
*But if I need a snack,*
*What will I do?*

*My suitcase is packed.*
*I'm ready for my trip.*
*I'd better look inside again*
*Before I close the zip.*

*There's a sandwich and some biscuits.*
*I've packed some chocolate, too.*
*Now I can't close my suitcase.*
*What can I do?*

## Song Bank: Unit 9

Pupil's Book

**CD4 TRACK 29**

**PB page 127 Activity 2**

**Karaoke version: *My holiday suitcase* song**

## Unit 1 Cambridge Exams Practice

Activity Book

**CD4 TRACK 30**

**AB page 120 Activity 1**

**1** Which boy is Andy?
**Boy:** Where's Andy?
**Girl:** He's over there. Look! He's wearing a pair of shorts and a T-shirt.
**Boy:** Is he wearing a dark T-shirt?
**Girl:** No, that's Ben. Andy's wearing a white one.
**Boy:** Oh yes. I can see him now.
**2** Which dress does Sue buy?
**Girl 1:** Are you going to buy the striped dress, Sue?
**Girl 2:** No, it's too big for me.
**Girl 1:** That's a pity. What about the flowery dress?
**Girl 2:** It's nice, but I prefer the plain one. I'll buy that one.
**3** How much is the T-shirt?
**Boy:** Will you buy me this T-shirt, Mum?
**Mum:** How much is it? I don't want to spend more than 15 pounds.
**Boy:** Well, it says 20 pounds on the label, but there's a sale today and everything is half price.
**Mum:** OK. It's only ten pounds today. That's a good price.

## Unit 2 Cambridge Exams Practice

Activity Book

**CD4 TRACK 31**

**AB page 121 Activity 1**

**Girl 1:** Hi, Anna. What activity did you do today?
**Girl 2:** I wasn't feeling very well today, so I just stayed here and read my book.
**Girl 1:** Oh dear! I hope you are feeling better.
**Girl 2:** I am, thanks! I'm waiting for Adam. He really likes canoeing, but the river was too dangerous today, so he went mountain biking in the woods.
**Girl 1:** Oh, right. ... And what about your other friends? Did Ella go mountain biking, too?
**Girl 2:** She went mountain biking yesterday. Today she played football – her favourite sport!
**Girl 1:** What did William do today? He had a rope and some wood with him.
**Girl 2:** Ah! He helped a group of people build a new rope bridge over the river.
**Girl 1:** That sounds like fun. Maddy was there, too.
**Girl 2:** Yes, she was. She didn't help with the bridge. The group wanted someone to take photos and Maddy has got a good camera.
**Girl 1:** What about Luke. What did he do?
**Girl 2:** He wanted to go hiking, but he left his walking boots at home. So he went to the pool instead for a swim.

## Unit 3 Cambridge Exams Practice

Activity Book

**CD4 TRACK 32**

**AB page 122 Activity 1**

Do you want a day out that's fun for all the family? Then come to the Science Museum. There are three floors of amazing science activities and you can watch a film in the 3D cinema. The museum opens its doors at nine o'clock in the morning and it stays open until six o'clock in the evening. But the last time you can buy an entrance ticket is at five o'clock. The museum is open six days a week from Tuesday to Sunday – I'm sorry, we're closed on Mondays – and tickets are five pounds for adults. It's free for children under the age of 16. The museum is easy to find. It's in Museum Street, in front of the bus station. You can find out more information about visiting the museum on its website: goscience.com. That's g-o-s-c-i-e-n-c-e-dot – com. We hope to see you soon!

## Unit 4 Cambridge Exams Practice

Activity Book

**CD4 TRACK 33**

**AB page 123 Activity 1**

**1** You will hear two friends talking. What do they have to do now?
**Boy:** Let's have a look at the list. What else do we have to buy?
**Girl:** Eggs. We've got those. And flour. We've got that. Did you get some milk?
**Boy:** Yes, I did. But I didn't get the butter.
**Girl:** OK. We have to get that now. Then we'll have everything. This cake is going to be delicious.
**2** You will hear a teacher talking to a student. What does the teacher want him to do?
I think this is a great idea for a project, Simon. You did a lot of work last week. Your Internet research was excellent. The introduction is really exciting. I want to find out more! I think you can do the drawings a bit better. You should draw this map again. Remember to use a pencil first!
**3** You will hear a woman talking to her son. What is he doing at the moment?
**Mum:** Matt! Where are you? Can you come here, please?
**Matt:** I can't. I have to finish this. It's so exciting! It's about life in space.
**Mum:** You can finish it later. Can you help me make the lunch?
**Matt:** But there are only ten more pages and I have to talk about it at school tomorrow.
**Mum:** OK. You can have five minutes.
**4** You will hear a head teacher talking to the school. What is special about today?
Hello everyone! As you know, today is not a normal day. Luckily, it's warmer today, too. In the morning, the younger children have to go outside. They will run short races. In the afternoon, it's the turn of the older children. They will do many different sports. Remember to enjoy yourself – win OR lose!

## Unit 5 Cambridge Exams Practice

Activity Book

**CD4 TRACK 34**

**AB page 124 Activity 1**

**Girl:** Hi, Joe. Did you have a good time at the zoo yesterday?
**Boy:** Yes, I did. It was really interesting. I saw some amazing animals and I learnt lots of new information, too.
**Girl:** Really? Which was your favourite animal?
**Boy:** Hmmm … The rhinos were great, but I think the giraffes were the best.
**Girl:** What about your brother? Did he like the giraffes, too?
**Boy:** He quite liked them, but he loved the lizards and the snakes. His favourite animal was the python. It was more than five metres long.
**Girl:** That's amazing! Did your aunt like the snakes?

**Boy:** No, she didn't. She preferred the birds. There were owls, ostriches and penguins at the zoo.
**Girl:** Really? Which ones were her favourite?
**Boy:** That's easy. She loved the penguins. You could see them swimming under the water. They were really funny.
**Girl:** And what about your cousin? Does he still love lizards?
**Boy:** Yes, he does. But yesterday he liked the fruit bats the most. They were enormous.
**Girl:** Who else went to the zoo with you?
**Boy:** My uncle.
**Girl:** And which was his favourite animal?
**Boy:** He loved the reptiles, especially the lizards. Some of them were really colourful.

## Unit 6 Cambridge Exams Practice

**Activity Book**

**CD4 TRACK 35**

**AB page 125 Activity 1**

**1** Where is the girl going to go on Saturday?
**Girl:** Can we do something interesting on Saturday, Dad?
**Father:** I suppose so. What do you want to do? Shall we go to the cinema and see a 3D film? You enjoyed that last week.
**Girl:** No. I want to do something else this time. The school choir are going to sing in a concert in the park. Can we go and watch them?
**Father:** Yes, OK.
**2** How much is a ticket for the circus?
**Boy:** Mum, can we go to the circus next week?
**Mum:** I'm not sure. How much are the tickets? Last year they were £15 – that's quite expensive.
**Boy:** Normally they are £20, but look – they are half price. The tickets are £10 each. So can we go?
**Mum:** Erm … OK. Let's all go.
**Boy:** Great!
**3** Which is the pop group *Power*?
**Boy:** Do you know the pop group called *Power*?
**Girl:** I think so. There are two men and two women in the group.
**Boy:** No. *Power* are just three women. You are thinking of *Rhythm* – they are two men and two women.
**4** Which animals have they got at Brown's Circus?
**Boy:** Did you go to Brown's Circus last week?
**Girl:** Yes, we did. It was a lot of fun. The clowns were great.
**Boy:** Were there any lions or tigers?
**Girl:** No, there was a lovely white horse. But there weren't any lions, tigers or any other animals.

## Unit 7 Cambridge Exams Practice

**Activity Book**

**CD4 TRACK 36**

**AB page 126 Activity 1**

**Mum:** Hi, Finn. How was the football match? Did you enjoy it?
**Finn:** Yes, it was fun. I'm really tired now. We won the match 3-1.
**Mum:** Well done! Did Bobby play?
**Finn:** Yes, he did. He played really well. He scored two goals. Do you know his brother, Dan?
**Mum:** Yes, what about him?
**Finn:** Well, he wasn't very lucky. He hurt his knee after five minutes. He couldn't play after that.
**Mum:** Oh dear! I hope he's OK. Was Sam playing?
**Finn:** Yes. He was amazing as usual. But he hurt himself, too. He fell over and hurt his foot.
**Mum:** Has he twisted his ankle?
**Finn:** No, he hasn't. He's OK, I think. He played the whole game. He scored a goal, too … Oh, and something was really funny …
**Mum:** What was really funny?
**Finn:** Jacob's mum was watching the match. His dad was watching his sister's match, so he couldn't come. Anyway, Jacob's mum was shouting "Come on!" really loudly. It was so funny!
**Mum:** Hmmm … And what about you, Finn? Did you play the whole match?
**Finn:** I only played for the last five minutes ...
**Mum:** Why are you tired, then?
**Finn:** Well, I ran all the way home.
**Mum:** Oh, Finn …

## Unit 8 Cambridge Exams Practice

**Activity Book**

**CD4 TRACK 37**

**AB page 127 Activity 1**

Good morning everyone. As you know, we've got a trip to a paper factory next Monday. We're going to see how paper is recycled. Then, in the afternoon, we're going to do some arts and crafts with recycled paper. Remember – you need to be at school early on Monday because the bus leaves at half past eight. We'll be back at school at four o'clock. The trip to the factory is free, but you need to pay two pounds-fifty for the arts and crafts activity. Please can you give the money to the new school secretary tomorrow? Her name is Mrs Thomas. That's T-H-O-M-A-S. Finally, you don't need to bring any books on Monday, but you do need to bring a snack to eat in the morning. Is that clear? Great!

## Unit 9 Cambridge Exams Practice

**Activity Book**

**CD4 TRACK 38**

**AB page 128 Activity 1**

**1** What is Bobby going to do with his cousins?
**Girl:** What are you doing in the summer holidays, Bobby?
**Boy:** We're staying in England. My cousins are coming to stay with us.
**Girl:** What are you going to do with them?
**Boy:** They love playing football and basketball. I love basketball, too, so I think we'll play that a lot.
**2** How much does the tour bus cost for a child?
**Mum:** Hello. What time does the tour start?
**Bus driver:** It starts in about 15 minutes.
**Mum:** OK. Can I have four tickets please, two adults and two children?
**Bus driver:** Of course. That's 20 pounds, please.
**Mum:** Are the tickets five pounds each?
**Bus driver:** It's cheaper for children: four pounds. Adults are six pounds.
**3** How tall is the Elizabeth Tower?
… and to our left you can see the River Thames. Isn't it beautiful? The river is about 265 metres wide here. And there you can see the Elizabeth Tower. Some people call it Big Ben, but that is the name of the bell inside the tower. The tower is 96 metres tall. And can you see the clock? There are four clocks – one on each side of the tower. Each clock is seven metres wide.
**4** What does Nick's sister look like?
**Girl:** Where are we meeting your sister, Nick?
**Boy:** Here by this waterfall. She said to meet her at 11 o'clock.
**Girl:** Is that her?
**Boy:** No, that woman's got short hair. My sister's got long hair. She always wears a hat and she's got glasses, too.

# Videoscript

## Unit 1

### 21st Century Video

**PB page 17 Activities 1 and 2**

**Amy:** Hi everyone. My name's Amy.

**Max:** And my name's Max.

**Oli:** And I'm Oli, the cameraman.

**Max:** Welcome to our first programme on Channel 21.

**Amy:** In these programmes we show you videos about fun and interesting things.

**Max:** We interview people too!

**Amy:** Today's programme is about fashion! We've come to my aunt's café to ask people what they think about fashion.

**Amy:** Are you interested in fashion, aunt May?

**Barista 1:** Yes, I am. I usually wear fashionable clothes. But only if I like them.

**Amy:** What's your style?

**Barista 2:** That's easy! I always wear baggy clothes. They're comfortable and they look great, too.

**Amy:** Would you like to be a fashion designer?

**Customer 1:** Yes, I would. I think it's a creative job and I love clothes.

**Amy:** I decided to find out about the work of a fashion designer. Here's my video.

**Amy:** When you design clothes, you need to be creative. Fashion designers sketch their ideas on paper … or they use a tablet. Fashion designers do research too. They look at other people's work and ideas. Fashion designers talk about their ideas with other people. They listen to different opinions. When the design is ready. The fashion designers choose the material. They cut it to make the clothes. Then they sew the material to make the clothes. They use a sewing machine. This item of clothing is almost ready now. The fashion designer checks that it isn't too big or too small. Here are some finished designs. This girl's wearing a patterned shirt, a spotted skirt and a hat. These clothes are cool! These girls are wearing tracksuits and trainers. I don't like the flowery design. What about you? Look at this boy. He's wearing a short-sleeved, spotted shirt and a tie. This boy's wearing a patterned shirt and a waistcoat. He's wearing a bow tie! These clothes are smart. What do you think of these designs?

**Max:** That was a great video, Amy.

**Amy:** Thanks, Max.

**Max:** Why don't you design some clothes?

**Amy:** Remember! You need to develop your ideas. Here are some tips to help:

**Max:** It's important to talk about your ideas with other people.

**Amy:** You need to be practical too. How much time have you got? What materials have you got?

**Max:** Finally, it's a good idea to do some research. You can learn a lot from other people's work.

**Amy:** Good luck with your designs.

**Max:** See you next time. Bye.

## Unit 2

### 21st Century Video

**PB page 27 Activities 1 and 2**

**Max:** Hello. I'm Max.

**Amy:** And I'm Amy. Welcome back to Channel 21.

**Max:** Today's programme is about adventurous sports. Really adventurous sports.

**Amy:** Some of them are very scary.

**Max:** Do you think so? We are at my dad's office today. Let's ask people about their adventurous friends.

**Max:** Have you got any adventurous friends?

**Worker 1:** Let me think. My friend Rick ran a long race last week. It was 150 kilometres. He didn't sleep. He ran all day and all night!

**Max:** Wow!

**Max:** Have you got any adventurous friends?

**Worker 2:** My friend Liz goes mountain climbing. She climbs when snowing, raining, or icy.

**Max:** Do you do adventurous things?

**Max's dad:** Me? Errr … I went to the shops on my bike yesterday.

**Max:** Oh, Dad … !

**Max:** I wanted to find out more so I did some research online. Here's my video!

Some people do incredible things. In the water, in the mountains … and in the air. These people are white-water rafting. They're wearing helmets and life jackets. Be careful of those rocks!
Many people go skiing in the mountains but snowboarding is very popular too. These people are doing some incredible jumps! This sport is called paragliding. I'd love to do this! They are flying very low by the beach. But these people are high up! Look at the views! This man is in the air too! He is tightrope walking. He isn't wearing any shoes. He uses his arms for balance. Look at this man in Austria. He's sleeping on the tightrope! Now that is scary!

**Amy:** That was great. Who was the first person to do tightrope walking? Do you know?

**Max:** There was a famous tightrope walker called Charles Blondin. You should do some research. Then you can tell the class about him!

**Amy:** OK. Where do I begin?

**Max:** Well, before you start your research, think of some questions about him. Think of questions that you want to know the answer to.

**Amy:** OK. Good idea.

**Max:** Why don't you do some research about an adventurous sport?

**Amy:** See you soon! Bye.

# Unit 3

## 21st Century Video

### PB page 37 Activities 1 and 2

**Amy:** Hello everyone. Welcome back to Channel 21. I'm Amy.

**Max:** And I'm Max. Today's programme is about our favourite city. Can you guess which one it is?

**Amy:** Before we tell you, let's find out about other people's favourite cities.

**Max:** We've come to the library to interview people today.

**Amy:** Excuse me, what's your favourite city?

**Librarian 1:** That's easy. My favourite city is Paris. You can see lots of amazing monuments there, like the Eiffel Tower.

**Amy:** What's your favourite city?

**Adult 1:** I love Istanbul because it's so beautiful. Actually, I'm looking at a guide book about Istanbul now. I'm going there on holiday next week.

**Amy:** Have you got a favourite city?

**Librarian 2:** Yes, I have. It's Madrid. There's a lot to see and do there – it's an exciting city!

**Amy:** Our favourite city is exciting, beautiful and it's got lots of monuments. Welcome to Venice!

People call Venice the floating city. That's because it's got more than one hundred islands. There aren't any roads in the city centre, there are canals.

Many tourists have a trip on a gondola when they visit Venice. It's very relaxing, but you need to be careful with the bridges!

This is the biggest and busiest canal in Venice. There are always lots of water buses and water taxis here.

This canal isn't busy. It's in a quiet street. Do you like the colours of the houses?

The biggest and most important square in the city is St Mark's. Thousands of people visit the square and climb the tower every day.

Venice is famous for its beautiful masks. Tourists often buy a mask as a souvenir.

Look! These people are wearing traditional masks and traditional clothes from Venice. Oh dear! The dog doesn't look very happy.

Venice is also famous for its amazing ice cream. It's perfect to have an ice cream at the end of the day.

**Max:** That was a great video. It helps me with my school project too.

**Amy:** Really? Which project?

**Max:** I've got to compare two cities. I'm going to compare London and Venice.

**Amy:** Why don't you use a Venn diagram to organise your ideas? Look! You write things that are the same in the middle of the diagram: Venice and London have got lots of monuments. You write things that are different on the sides. Look – London is a capital city, but Venice isn't.

**Max:** That's really useful. Thanks.

**Amy:** Good luck with your project. Why don't you use a Venn diagram to compare things too?

**Max and Amy:**: See you next time. Bye!

# Unit 4

## 21st Century Video

### PB page 49 Activities 1 and 2

**Max:** Hi everyone. Welcome back to Channel 21. I'm Max.

**Amy:** And I'm Amy. Today's programme is about new technology. It's about one kind of technology. Can you guess what it is?

**Max:** Before we tell you, let's talk to my family about technology.

**Max:** Hi, Mum. What technology do you use the most?

**Max's mum:** Let me think. I use my e-reader a lot. I take it on the train and read books on it every day.

**Max:** Hi uncle Frank. What technology do you use the most?

**Uncle Frank:** Well, I use my phone all the time. I listen to music, I read the news and I check emails on it.

**Max:** Hi Dad. What technology do you use the most?

**Max's dad:** Well, I work on my laptop every day. We have video calls, too. I also play games on it!

**Max:** Here's my video. It's about a great new technology – virtual reality!

This is a virtual reality headset. You can use one at home or at school.

It's easy to experience virtual reality. You can use a mobile phone in a cardboard headset. There are many virtual reality apps for your phone.

When you put on the headset, you can see a virtual world all around you. If you move your head, the picture in the headset changes.

With some headsets, you can use your hands. You can swipe and click buttons in the air!

In some schools, children use the headsets to learn about different places. You can imagine you are in …
… the jungle, …
… in the mountains …
… or on the moon!

Virtual reality is important for many jobs too. People can learn and practise how to do things– like this scientist.

This man is using a virtual reality headset and controlling a robotic hand at the same time! How will people use virtual reality in the future?

**Amy:** Virtual reality is amazing. With a virtual reality headset, you can travel anywhere!

**Max:** Yes, it's fun. But we should think about it can help people, too.

**Amy:** What do you mean?

**Max:** People can use virtual reality to practise things.

**Amy:** Oh yes!

**Max:** Can *you* think of some more things?

**Amy:** See you next time. Bye!

# Videoscript

## Unit 5

### 21st Century Video

**PB page 59 Activities 1 and 2**

**Amy:** Hi everyone. Welcome back to Channel 21. I'm Amy.

**Max:** And I'm Max. Today's programme is about a serious topic – animals that are in danger.

**Amy:** When animals are in danger, it means that there aren't many of their species left on the planet.

**Max:** So we need to protect them.

**Amy:** Let's go to my aunt's café and ask people what they know about this topic.

**Amy:** Excuse me. Do you know any animals that are in danger?

**Barista 2:** Yes, I do. Blue whales.

**Amy:** Why are they in danger?

**Barista 2:** Because people hunt them.

**Amy:** Do you know any animals that are in danger?

**Customer 2:** Yes, mountain gorillas.

**Amy:** Why are they in danger?

**Customer 2:** Actually, I'm not sure.

**Amy:** Do you know any animals that are in danger, aunt May?

**Barista 1:** Yes, koalas.

**Amy:** Why are they in danger?

**Barista 1:** I think it's because there are fewer forests for them to live in.

**Amy:** I wanted to find out more about one of these animals. So, here's my video about … koalas!

Koalas live in the east of Australia. Some people think they're bears, but they're not. They're marsupials, like kangaroos. Koalas look like teddy bears. They've got grey fur on their back and cream fur on their front. They've got long claws too. Perfect for climbing! Koalas haven't got a lot of energy - they sleep about 18 hours every day. Baby koalas are called joeys. Look! The mother carries the joey on her back. Koalas eat leaves from the eucalyptus tree. They need to eat a lot! In the past there were lots of eucalyptus forests like this in Australia. But now they are disappearing.

Some forests are disappearing because humans cut down the trees to build roads.

The gas from power stations can harm eucalyptus trees too.

All animals need a clean and safe place to live. We need to protect the koala's habitat so that there are plenty of eucalyptus leaves for the koalas to eat.

**Max:** That was a great video, Amy.

**Amy:** Thanks, Max. I really want to help animals that are in danger.

**Max:** Me too. There are lots of things we can do. Why don't we make a list?

**Amy:** OK! And after that, we can make an action plan. What would *you* write on the list?

**Max:** Bye everyone. See you next time.

## Unit 6

### 21st Century Video

**PB page 69 Activities 1 and 2**

**Max:** Hi! Welcome back to Channel 21. I'm Max.

**Amy:** And I'm Amy. It's the school talent day next week. We haven't prepared anything. What are we going to do, Max?

**Max:** Hmm. Everyone is going to sing or dance. I'd like to do something different and fun.

**Amy:** OK. But what?

**Max:** Well, maybe we can get some ideas in today's programme. It's about art. We're here in my dad's office to ask people some questions about this topic.

**Max:** Are you interested in art?

**Worker 1:** Yes, a bit. I like drawing cartoons a lot. I always drew comics when I was young.

**Max:** Do you like art?

**Worker 3:** I'm not very good at art myself! But I love going to art galleries. I like sculptures.

**Max:** Have you ever painted a portrait, Dad?

**Max's dad:** Yes! You know that I love painting. I've even done a painting of you!

**Max:** Oh, Dad … !

**Max:** Here's my video about art. Amy, there might be some ideas here for the talent day.

**Amy:** I hope so!

**Max:** Amy and I love drawing people and we like cartoons too.
Look at this man. He's drawing a cartoon portrait of a girl. He's using a black pen. It's good, isn't it?
This man is drawing two sisters. He has coloured in one of the pictures.
Maybe we can draw cartoon portraits on the talent day.
Here's another idea. These are chalks.
The teachers say that we can draw on the playground. We could draw a big picture like this. Everyone could help us.
Or we could have a competition like this! Children can work in groups. They have one hour to finish their drawings. Let's hope that it doesn't rain!

I think these are great ideas for our talent day. What do you think, Amy?

**Amy:** I'd like to do cartoon portraits. It's a really original idea!

**Max:** OK. Let's do it! What would you do for a talent day? Try and be different and original.

**Max:** Think about what other people are going to do – then do something different!

**Amy:** Look for inspiration to help you. You can speak to people or use the Internet.

**Max:** Good luck with your ideas!

**Amy:** See you soon! Bye!

# Unit 7

## 21st Century Video

**PB page 81 Activities 1 and 2**

**Amy:** Hello again. I'm Amy.

**Max:** And I'm Max. Welcome back to Channel 21.

**Amy:** Today we want to find out about volunteering. Who does it? And what do they do?

**Max:** We're here at the library again.

**Amy:** Yes. I want to ask people about volunteering. Let's see what they say!

**Amy:** Hello. Do you do any volunteering?

**Librarian 1:** I love animals! One day, I would like to help at an animal care home. But I haven't volunteered yet.

**Amy:** Do you do any volunteering?

**Adult 2:** My son plays in the local rugby team. I played a lot of rugby when I was young, so I help the team every Saturday.

**Amy:** Do you do any volunteering?

**Librarian 2:** Yes, I volunteer here in the library. I tell stories to little children once a month.

**Amy:** That's great!

**Amy:** I want to find out more. Here's my video about … volunteering!

**Amy:** It's good to volunteer to help. You can do great things for the community. Look at this beach. There are many old bottles and pieces of plastic.

These children are thinking about how to clean up the beach. Lara is the leader. She listens to everyone's ideas and writes down a plan.
The group of volunteers meet at the beach. They've got big bags and special sticks to pick up the rubbish. They find an old tyre too. Soon they have finished and the beach is clean. Now it's safer for people to go swimming and sit on the beach.
The volunteers take the rubbish away. But they'll be back next week!

**Amy:** What a brilliant idea! It's good for the animals, too.

**Max:** How do you organise something like that? I'm not a very good leader.

**Amy:** Are you sure? Let's think about what you need to be a good leader. Are you fair?

**Max:** Yes, I think so.

**Amy:** You're organised too. And you listen to others.

How about *you*? Are you a good leader?

**Max:** Bye everyone. See you next time.

# Unit 8

## 21st Century Video

**PB page 91 Activities 1 and 2**

**Amy:** Hi everyone. Welcome back to Channel 21. I'm Amy.

**Max:** And I'm Max. Today's programme is about recycling.

**Amy:** Do you recycle?

**Max:** Let's find out what my family recycles.

**Max:** What are you recycling, dad?

**Max's dad:** I'm recycling this cardboard and these newspapers.

**Max:** What are you recycling, mum?

**Max's mum:** I'm taking these plastic bottles to the recycling containers.

**Max:** Do you recycle, uncle Frank?

**Max's dad:** Yes, of course. Look! I'm recycling this rubbish for my garden.

**Max:** I wanted to find out why it's important to recycle. Here's my video. I hope you like it!

**Max:** Every day, people put lots of rubbish in the bin. It's collected by a big lorry. But what happens to it?
Most rubbish is buried under the ground. But there isn't enough space for all our rubbish. We need to reduce our rubbish.

Plastic rubbish is a big problem because plastic lasts a long time. We can see it on the beach, in the mountains and in the countryside.

There's plastic rubbish in the sea too. Some sea animals think that the plastic is food and they eat it.

The good news is that we can recycle 75% of our rubbish. Look! This family is putting plastic bottles in a recycling container.

The plastic bottles are cut into small pieces. These pieces are melted to make small balls. Lots of things are made from recycled plastic. This pen is cool!
Recycling is important to make the world cleaner and safer for everyone.

**Amy:** What a fantastic video, Max.

**Max:** Thanks, Amy. Unfortunately, lots of people don't recycle.

**Amy:** We need to persuade people – tell them that recycling is a good idea. What about making a poster and putting it on the wall?

**Max:** It's OK, but I think a digital poster is better. We can send it to our friends and family by email.

**Amy:** We can put it on the school website too.

**Max:** Brilliant! Let's go and design a digital poster. What other things can we do to persuade people?

**Amy:** Bye everyone. See you next time!

# Videoscript

## Unit 9

### 21st Century Video

**PB page 101 Activities 1 and 2**

**Amy:** Hello again. I'm Amy.

**Max:** And I'm Max. Welcome to Channel 21 for the last time! We're at my dad's office again.

**Amy:** We're going on holiday next week. We're going to different places. Max likes cold places.

**Max:** Amy likes hot places.

**Amy:** Today we are thinking about different places where people live.

**Max:** Where would you like to live?

**Amy:** I asked some people here what they think.

**Amy:** Where would you like to live?

**Worker 1:** In the future, I'd like to live in a small village in Scotland. I like the mountains … and the rain.

**Amy:** Would you like to live somewhere hot?

**Worker 2:** Yes, I would. I'd like to live near the beach. Maybe in Australia because I like surfing too!

**Amy:** Where would you like to live?

**Max's dad:** I love living here in a big city. And the weather is perfect. It's not too hot or cold.

**Amy:** I wanted to find out more about a cold place. Just for Max! Here's my video. Would you like to live here?
Alaska is the biggest state in the USA. But it is very cold here. There are many mountains and glaciers there. Glaciers are big rivers of ice. Here is a glacier. And here is a waterfall near the glacier. People come to Alaska to go mountain climbing in the ice and snow. It can be cold and foggy in Alaska in the winter, but people live in towns here. Here, parents collect their children from school after a big snow storm! But after a snow storm you can make a big snowman! Many animals enjoy the cold climate here. This is a moose. It's eating leaves. And these are bears. And this baby otter is eating some fish. People eat fish too. Fishing is a popular activity in the summer and in the winter too.

**Amy:** What do you think, Max? Would you like to live there?

**Max:** Yes I think I would! But it's very different to where *we* live. I want to find out more about how people live there. What kind of houses do they live in?

**Amy:** Where do people go to school?

**Max:** What do people eat?

**Amy:** Can you think of more questions? See you next time!